# Lecture Notes in Computer Science    1676

Edited by G. Goos, J. Hartmanis and J. van Leeuwen

**Springer**

*Berlin*
*Heidelberg*
*New York*
*Barcelona*
*Hong Kong*
*London*
*Milan*
*Paris*
*Singapore*
*Tokyo*

Mukesh Mohania    A Min Tjoa (Eds.)

# Data Warehousing and Knowledge Discovery

First International Conference, DaWaK'99
Florence, Italy, August 30 – September 1, 1999
Proceedings

 Springer

Series Editors

Gerhard Goos, Karlsruhe University, Germany
Juris Hartmanis, Cornell University, NY, USA
Jan van Leeuwen, Utrecht University, The Netherlands

Volume Editors

Mukesh Mohania
School of Computer and Information Science
University of South Australia
The Levels, Adelaide, Australia 05
E-mail: cismkm@ares.Levels.UniSA.Edu.Au

A Min Tjoa
IFS, Technical University of Vienna
Resselgasse 3, A-1040 Vienna, Austria
E-mail: amin@ifs.tuwien.ac.at
        tjoa@garbo.ifs.tuwien.ac.at

Cataloging-in-Publication data applied for


Die Deutsche Bibliothek - CIP-Einheitsaufnahme


**Data warehousing and knowledge discovery** : first international conference ;
proceedings / DaWaK '99, Florence, Italy, August 30 - September 1, 1999.
Mohania Mukesh ; A Min Tjoa (ed.). - Berlin ; Heidelberg ; New York ; Barcelona
; Hong Kong ; London ; Milan ; Paris ; Singapore ; Tokyo : Springer, 1999
(Lecture notes in computer science ; Vol. 1676)
ISBN 3-540-66458-0




CR Subject Classification (1998): H.2, H.3, I.2, C.2.4, H.5

ISSN 0302-9743
ISBN 3-540-66458-0 Springer-Verlag Berlin Heidelberg New York

© Springer-Verlag Berlin Heidelberg 1999
Printed in Germany

Typesetting: Camera-ready by author
SPIN: 10704224    06/3142 – 5 4 3 2 1 0    Printed on acid-free paper

# Message from the Program Chairs

Data Warehousing and Knowledge Discovery technology is emerging as a key technology for enterprises that wish to improve their data analysis, decision support activities, and the automatic extraction of knowledge from data.

The first international Conference on Data Warehousing and Knowledge Discovery (DaWaK'99) sought to fill an important gap in both data warehousing and knowledge discovery. The conference focused on the logical and the physical design of data warehousing and knowledge discovery systems. The scope of the papers covers the most recent and relevant topics in the areas of data warehousing, multidimensional databases, OLAP, knowledge discovery and data & web mining, and time series databases.

These proceedings present the research and experience papers selected for presentation at DaWaK'99, held in Florence, Italy. We received more than 88 papers from over 22 countries and the program committee finally selected 31 long papers and 9 short papers. The conference program also included two invited talks, namely, "Dynamic Data Warehousing" by Dr. Umeshwar Dayal, HP Labs, U.S.A, and "On Tractable Queries and Constraints" by Prof. G. Gottlob, Technical University of Vienna, Austria.

We would like to thank the conference general chair (Prof. Yahiko Kambayashi), DEXA'99 workshop general chair (Prof. Roland Wagner) and the organising committee of the 10th International Conference on Database and Expert Systems Applications (DEXA'99) for their support and cooperation. Many many thanks are due to Ms Gabriela Wagner for providing a great deal of help and assistance. We are very indebted to all program committee members and the referees, who have reviewed the papers in a very careful and timely manner. We would also like to thank all the authors who submitted their papers to this conference.

Finally, our thanks go out to all of you who attended the conference here in Florence. We hope you to had a great week of fun, sight-seeing, and of course, excellent technical discussions.

Mukesh Mohania and A Min Tjoa
Programe Committee Chairs

June 1999

# Program Committee

**General Chair:**
Prof. Yahiko Kambayashi (Kyoto University Sakyo, Japan)

**Program Chairs:**
Mukesh Mohania (University of South Australia )
A Min Tjoa (Vienna University of Technology, Austria)

**Program Committee:**
Divyakant Agrawal (University of California at Santa Barbara, USA)
Paolo Atzeni (Università di Roma Tre, Italy)
Elena Baralis (Politecnico di Torino, Italy)
Stefan Berchtold (AT&T Labs Research, USA)
Bharat Bhargava (Purdue University, USA)
Jamie Callan (UMass Amherst, USA)
Stefano Ceri (Politecnico di Milano, Italy)
Peter Chamoni (University of Duisburg, Germany)
Qiming Chen (HP labs, USA)
Arbee L.P. Chen, (National Tsing-Hua University, Taiwan)
S. Choenni (National Aerospace Laboratory, The Netherlands)
Anindya Datta (Georgia Institute of Technology, USA)
J. S. Deogun (University of Nebraska-Lincoln, USA)
Usama Fayyad (Microsoft, USA)
Ronen Feldman (Bar-Ilan University, Israel)
S. K. Gupta (I.I.T., Delhi, India)
Marc Gyssens (University of Limburg, Belgium)
Jiawei Han (Simon Fraser University, Canada)
John Harrison (University of Queensland, Australia)
Kamal Karlapalem (HKUST, China)
Samuel Kaski (Helsinki University of Technology, Finland)
Hiroyuki Kawano (Kyoto University, Japan)
Masaru Kitsuregawa (University of Tokyo, Japan)
Willi Kloesgen (GMD, Germany)
Laks V.S. Lakshmanan (Concordia University, Canada)
Wolfgang Lehner (University of Erlangen, Germany)
Leonid Libkin (Bell Labs, USA)
Qing Li (City University of Hong Kong, China)
Tok Wang Ling (NUS, Singapore)
E.-P. Lim (NTU, Singapore)
Sanjay Madria (NTU, Singapore)
Heikki Mannila (Microsoft Research, USA)
Stefano Paraboschi (Politecnico di Milano, Italy)
Calton Pu (Oregon Graduate Institute of Science and Technology, USA)
Vijay Raghavan (University of Southern Louisiana, USA)
John Roddick (University of South Australia, Australia)
E. A. Rundensteiner (Worcester Polytechnic Institute, USA)
N.L.Sarda (I.I.T. Mumbai, India)
Michael Schrefl (University of South Australia, Australia)
Il-Yeol Song (Drexel University, USA)
Ernest Teniente (Univarsitat Politecnica de Catalunya, Spain)
Hannu Toivonen (Rolf Nevanlinna Institute, Finland)

Millist Vincent (University of South Australia, Australia)
Beat Wuthrich (Hong Kong University of Science and Technology, China)
Yanchun Zhang (University of Southern Queensland, Australia)
Jan Zytkow (Wichita State University, USA)

# List of External Referees

Geert Jan Bex
Sourva Bhowmick
J. Buzydlowski
Chua Eng Huang Cecil
Li Chen
Yong-Chuang Chen
L. Feng
Hakan Ferhatosmanoglu
Bart Goethals
Vivek Gopalkrishnan
Stefan Gyles
Jia-Lien Hsu
Christopher Jermaine
Ng Wee Keong
Andreas Koeller
Krista Lagus
H.V. Leong
Chia-Yen Liu
Jixue Liu
Ye Liu
Dimitris Meretakis
Tadashi Ohmori
Iko Pramudiono
J. Pun
ShiGuang Qiu
I. Stanoi
Kian-Lee Tan
Y. Wu
Xin Zhang
Edward Yeh

# Table of Contents

## Invited Talk

## Multidimensional Databases

## Knowledge Discovery

## Association Rules

## Indexing and Object Similarities

## Generalised Association Rules and Data & Web Mining

## Time Series Databases

## Data Mining Applications and Data Analysis

# Dynamic Data Warehouse Design *

Dimitri Theodoratos        Timos Sellis

Department of Electrical and Computer Engineering
Computer Science Division
National Technical University of Athens
Zographou 157 73, Athens, Greece
{dth,timos}@dblab.ece.ntua.gr

**Abstract.** A data warehouse (DW) can be seen as a set of materialized views defined over remote base relations. When a query is posed, it is evaluated locally, using the materialized views, without accessing the original information sources. The DWs are dynamic entities that evolve continuously over time. As time passes, new queries need to be answered by them. Some of these queries can be answered using exclusively the materialized views. In general though new views need to be added to the DW.

In this paper we investigate the problem of incrementally designing a DW when new queries need to be answered and extra space is allocated for view materialization. Based on an AND/OR dag representation of multiple queries, we model the problem as a state space search problem. We design incremental algorithms for selecting a set of new views to additionally materialize in the DW that fits in the extra space, allows a complete rewriting of the new queries over the materialized views and minimizes the combined new query evaluation and new view maintenance cost.

## 1   Introduction

Data warehouses store large volumes of data which are frequently used by companies for On-Line Analytical Processing (OLAP) and Decision Support System (DSS) applications. Data warehousing is also an approach for integrating data from multiple, possibly very large, distributed, heterogeneous databases and other information sources.

A Data Warehouse (DW) can be abstractly seen as a set of materialized views defined over a set of (remote) base relations. OLAP and DSS applications make heavy use of complex grouping/aggregation queries. In order to ensure high query performance, the queries are evaluated locally at the DW, using exclusively the materialized views, without accessing the original base relations.

When the base relations change, the materialized at the DW views need to be updated. Different maintenance policies (deferred or immediate) and maintenance strategies (incremental or rematerialization) can be applied.

* Research supported by the European Commission under the ESPRIT Program LTR project "DWQ: Foundations of Data Warehouse Quality"

## 1.1 The problem: Dynamic Data Warehouse Design

DWs are dynamic entities that evolve continuously over time. As time passes, new queries need to be answered by them. Some of the new queries can be answered by the views already materialized in the DW. Other new queries, in order to be answered by the DW, necessitate the materialization of new views. In any case, in order for a query to be answerable by the DW, there must exist a complete rewriting [5] of it over the (old and new) materialized views. Such a rewriting can be exclusively over the old views, or exclusively over the new views, or partially over the new and partially over the old views. If new views need to be materialized, extra space need to be allocated for materialization.

One way for dealing with this issue is to re-implement the DW from scratch for the old and the new queries. This is the *static* approach to the DW design problem. Re-implementing the DW from scratch though, has the following disadvantages:

(a) Selecting the appropriate set of views for materialization that satisfies the conditions mentioned above is a long and complicated procedure [9, 10, 8].

(b) During the materialization of the views in the DW, some old view materializations are removed from the DW while new ones are added to it. Therefore, the DW is no more fully operational. Given the sizes of actual DWs and the complexity of views that need to be computed, the load window required to make the DW operational may become unacceptably long.

In this paper we address the *Dynamic DW Design Problem*: given a DW (a set of materialized views), a set of new queries to be answered by it and possibly some extra space allocated for materialization to the DW, select a set of new views to additionally materialize in the DW such that:

1. The new materialized views fit in the extra allocated space.
2. All the new queries can be answered using exclusively the materialized views (the old and the new).
3. The combination of the cost of evaluating the new queries over the materialized views and the cost of maintaining the new views is minimal.

## 1.2 Contribution and outline

The main contributions of this paper are the following:

- We set up a theoretical basis for incrementally designing a DW by formulating the dynamic DW design problem. The approach is applicable to a broad class of queries, including queries involving grouping and aggregation operations.
- Using an AND/OR dag representation of multiple queries (multiquery AND/OR dags) we model the dynamic DW design problem as a state space search problem. States are multiquery AND/OR dags representing old and new materialized views and complete rewritings of all the new queries over the materialized views. Transitions are defined through state transformation rules.
- We prove that the transformation rules are sound, and complete. In this sense a goal state (an optimal solution) can be obtained by applying transformation rules to an initial state.

- We design algorithms for solving the problem that incrementally compute the cost and the size of a state when moving from one state to another.
- The approach can also be applied for statically designing a DW, by considering that the set of views already materialized in the DW is empty.

This paper is organized as follows. Next section contains related work. In Section 3, we provide basic definitions and state formally the DW design problem. In Section 4 the dynamic DW design problem is modeled as a state space search problem. Incremental algorithms are presented in Section 5. The final section contains concluding remarks. A more detailed presentation can be found in [11].

## 2 Related work

We are not aware of any research work addressing the incremental design of a DW. Static design problems using views usually follow the following pattern: select a set of views to materialize in order to optimize the query evaluation cost, or the view maintenance cost or both, possibly in the presence of some constraints.

Work reported in [2, 3] aims at optimizing the query evaluation cost: in [2] greedy algorithms are provided for queries represented as AND/OR graphs under a space constraint. A variation of this paper aims at minimizing the total query response time under the constraint of total view maintenance cost [3].

[6] and [4] aim at optimizing the view maintenance cost: In [6], given a materialized SQL view, an exhaustive approach is presented as well as heuristics for selecting additional views that optimize the total view maintenance cost. [4] considers the same problem for select-join views and indexes together.

The works [7, 12] aim at optimizing the combined query evaluation and view maintenance cost: [7] provides an A* algorithm in the case where views are seen as sets of pointer arrays under a space constraint. [12] considers the problem for materialized views but without space constraints.

None of the previous approaches requires the queries to be answerable exclusively from the materialized views in a non-trivial manner. This requirement is taken into account in [9] where the problem of configuring a DW without space restrictions is addressed for a class of select-join queries. This work is extended in [10] in order to take into account space restrictions, multiquery optimization over the maintenance queries, and auxiliary views, and in [8] in order to deal with PSJ queries under space restrictions.

## 3 Formal statement of the problem

In this section we formally state the dynamic DW design problem after providing initial definitions.

**Definitions.** We consider relational algebra queries and views extended with additional operations as for instance grouping/aggregation operations. Let $\mathbf{R}$ be a set of base relations. The DW initially contains a set $\mathbf{V_0}$ of materialized views defined over $\mathbf{R}$, called *old views*. A set $\mathbf{Q}$ of new queries defined over $\mathbf{R}$ needs to be answered by the DW. It can be the case that these queries can be answered using exclusively the old views. In general though, in order to satisfy this requirement, a set $\mathbf{V}$ of new materialized views needs to be added to the DW. Since the queries in $\mathbf{Q}$ can be answered by the new state of the DW, there must exist a complete rewriting of every query in $\mathbf{Q}$ over the views in $\mathbf{V}_0 \cup \mathbf{V}$. Let $Q \in \mathbf{Q}$. By $Q^V$, we denote a complete rewriting of $Q$ over $\mathbf{V}_0 \cup \mathbf{V}$. This notation is extended to sets of queries. Thus, we write $\mathbf{Q}^V$, for a set containing the queries in $\mathbf{Q}$, rewritten over $\mathbf{V}_0 \cup \mathbf{V}$.

**Generic cost model.** The *evaluation cost of* $\mathbf{Q}^V$, denoted $E(\mathbf{Q}^V)$, is the weighted sum of the cost of evaluating every query rewriting in $\mathbf{Q}^V$.

In defining the maintenance cost of $\mathbf{V}$ one should take into consideration that the maintenance cost of a view, after a change to the base relations, may vary with the presence of other materialized views in the DW [6]. As in [6], we model the changes to different base relations by a set of transaction types. A transaction type specifies the base relations that change, and the type and size of every change. The cost of propagating a transaction type is the cost incurred by maintaining all the views in $\mathbf{V}$ that are affected by the changes specified by the transaction type, in the presence of the views in $\mathbf{V} \cup \mathbf{V}_0$. The *maintenance cost of* $\mathbf{V}$, denoted $M(\mathbf{V})$, is the weighted sum of the cost of propagating all the transaction types to the materilaized views in $\mathbf{V}$.

The *operational cost of the new queries and views* is $T(\mathbf{Q}^V, \mathbf{V}) = E(\mathbf{Q}^V) + cM(\mathbf{V})$. The parameter $c, c \geq 0$, is set by the DW designer and indicates the relative importance of the query evaluation vs. the view maintenance cost.

The *storage space needed for materializing the views in* $\mathbf{V}$ is denoted $S(\mathbf{V})$.

**Problem statement.** We state now the *dynamic DW design problem* as follows.

*Input*

A set $\mathbf{V}_0$ of old views over a set $\mathbf{R}$ of base relations.

A set $\mathbf{Q}$ of new queries over $\mathbf{R}$.

Functions, $E$ for the query evaluation cost, $M$ for the view maintenance cost and $S$ for the materialized views space.

A constant $t$ indicating the extra space allocated for materialization.

A constant $c$.

*Output*

A set of new views $\mathbf{V}$ over $\mathbf{R}$ such that:

(a) $S(\mathbf{V}) \leq t$.

(b) There is a set $\mathbf{Q}^V$ of complete rewritings of the queries in $\mathbf{Q}$ over $\mathbf{V}_0 \cup \mathbf{V}$.

(c) $T(\mathbf{Q}^V, \mathbf{V})$ is minimal.

# 4 The dynamic DW design as a state space search problem

We model, in this section, the dynamic DW design problem as a state space search problem.

## 4.1 Multiquery AND/OR dags

A *query dag* for a query is a rooted directed acyclic graph that represents the query's relational algebra expression. Query dags do not represent alternative equivalent relational algebra rewritings of the query definition over the base relations (that is alternative ways of evaluating the query). Alternative rewritings can be represented compactly by using AND/OR dags [7]. A convenient representation of query evaluations using AND/OR dags [6] is adopted in rule-based optimizers [1]. This representation, distinguishes between AND nodes and OR nodes: *a query AND/OR dag* for a query is a rooted bipartite AND/OR dag $\mathcal{G}_Q$. The nodes are partitioned into AND nodes and OR nodes. AND nodes are called *operation nodes* and are labeled by a relational algebra operator while OR nodes are called *equivalence nodes* and are labeled by a relational algebra expression (a view). The root node and the sink nodes of $\mathcal{G}_Q$ are equivalence nodes labeled by the query $Q$ and the base relations respectively. In the following we may identify equivalence nodes with their labels.

An AND/OR dag $\mathcal{G}'_Q$ is a *subdag* of an AND/OR dag $\mathcal{G}_Q$ if dag $\mathcal{G}'_Q$ is a subdag of dag $\mathcal{G}_Q$, and for every AND (operation) node in $\mathcal{G}'_Q$, all its incoming and outgoing edges in $\mathcal{G}_Q$ are also present in $\mathcal{G}'_Q$. An AND/OR dag is an *AND dag* if no OR (equivalence) node has more than one outgoing edges.

Multiple queries and alternative ways of evaluation can be represented by multiquery AND/OR dags. A *multiquery AND/OR dag* for a set of queries is a bipartite AND/OR dag, similar to a query AND/OR dag, except that it does not necessarily have a single root. Every query in the query set is represented by an equivalence node in the multiquery AND/OR dag. Equivalence nodes representing queries are called *query nodes* and their labeling expressions are preceded in the multiquery dag by a *. All the root nodes (and possibly some other equivalence nodes) are query nodes.

*Example 1.* Consider the relations `Department(DeptID, DeptName)` (D for short) and `Employee(EmpID, EmpName, Salary, DeptID)` (E for short). An underlined attribute denotes the primary key of the relation. Figure 1 shows a multiquery AND/OR dag $\mathcal{G}$ for the queries $Q_1 = \sigma_{\texttt{Salary}>1000}(E \bowtie D)$ and
$Q_2 = <\texttt{DeptID}, \texttt{DeptName}> \mathcal{F} < \texttt{AVG(Salary)} > (\sigma_{\texttt{Salary}>1000}(E \bowtie D))$. Some attribute names are abbreviated in the figure in a self-explanatory way. Notice

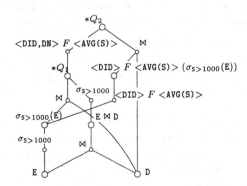

**Fig. 1.** A multiquery AND/OR dag for the queries $Q_1$ and $Q_2$

also that the query node labeled by $*Q_1$ is not a root node. Three alternative rewritings over the base relations for query $Q_2$ are represented in $\mathcal{G}$.    □

## 4.2 States

A multiquery AND/OR $\mathcal{G}$ determines, in our context, the views and the rewritings of the queries in $\mathbf{Q}$ over views that can be under consideration for solving the dynamic DW problem.

**Definition 1.** Given $\mathcal{G}$ and $\mathbf{V}_0$, a *state* $s$ is an AND/OR subdag of $\mathcal{G}$, where some equivalence nodes may be *marked*, such that:

(a) All the query nodes of $\mathcal{G}$ are present in $s$,

(b) All the equivalence nodes of $\mathcal{G}$ that are in $\mathbf{V}_0$ are present in $s$ and these are the only marked nodes in $s$,

(c) Only query nodes or marked nodes can be root nodes. □

Intuitively, sink nodes represent views materialized in the DW. Marked nodes represent the old views (already materialized in the initial DW) that can be used in the rewriting of a new query. Sink nodes that are not marked represent new materialized views. A *query dag for a query $Q$ in $s$* is a connected AND subdag of $s$ rooted at query node $Q$ in $s$ whose sink nodes are among the sink nodes of s. It represents a complete rewriting of $Q$ over the materialized views (sink nodes) of $s$. Since all the query nodes of $\mathcal{G}$ are present in $s$, there is at least one query dag for a query $Q$ in $s$, for every query $Q$ in $\mathbf{Q}$. Therefore, *a state provides information for both:*

*(a) new views to materialize in the DW, and*

*(b) complete rewritings of each new query over the old and the new materialized views.*

*Example 2.* Figures 2-3 show different states for the multiquery graph of Figure 1 when $\mathbf{V}_0 = \{\mathtt{D}\}$. The labels of the operation nodes are written symbolically in the figures. Marked nodes are depicted by filled black circles. For instance, in Figure 3(a), the nodes E, D and $V_1$, where $V_1 = \sigma_{\mathtt{Salary}>1000}(\mathtt{E})$, are materialized views. Node D is an old view and E and $V_1$ are new views. Two alternative rewritings for the query $Q_1$ are represented: the query definition $Q_1 = \sigma_{\mathtt{Salary}>1000}(\mathtt{E} \bowtie \mathtt{D})$ and a rewriting of $Q_1$ using the materialized view $V_1$, $Q_1 = V_1 \bowtie \mathtt{D}$. For the query $Q_2$ the rewriting $Q_2 = <\mathtt{DeptID}> \mathcal{F} < \mathtt{AVG(Salary)}> (V_1) \bowtie \mathtt{D}$ is represented.

In the state of Figure 3(c) the only new materialized view is query $Q_1$. The following rewriting is represented: $Q_2 = <\mathtt{DeptID}, \mathtt{DeptName}> \mathcal{F} < \mathtt{AVG(Salary)}> (Q_1)$. Note that this state is not a connected graph. □

With every state $s$, a cost and a size is associated through the functions *cost* and *size* respectively: $cost(s) = T(\mathbf{Q}^V, \mathbf{V})$, while $size(s) = S(\mathbf{V})$.

## 4.3 Transitions

In order to define transitions between states we introduce two state transformation rules. The state transformations may modify the set of sink nodes of a state, and remove some edges from it. Therefore, they modify, in general, the set of new views to materialize in the DW and the rewritings of the new queries over the materialized views.

**State transformation rules.** Consider a state $s$. A path from a query node $Q$ to a node $V$ is called *query free* if there is no node in it other than $Q$ and $V$ that is a query node.

*R1* Let $Q$ be a query node and $V$ be a non-sink equivalence node in $s$. Nodes $Q$ and $V$ need not necessarily be distinct, but if they are distinct, $V$ should not be a query node. If

(a) there is a query free path from $Q$ to $V$, or nodes $Q$ and $V$ coincide, and

(b) there is no path from $V$ to a non-marked sink node that is not a base relation,

then:

(a) Remove from $s$ all the edges and the non-marked or non-query nodes (except $V$) that are on a path from $V$, unless they are on a path from a query node that does not contain $V$. (Thus, node $V$ becomes a sink node.)

(b) Remove from the resulting state all the edges and the non-marked or non-query nodes that are on a path from $Q$, unless they are on a query dag for $Q$ in $s$ that contains a query free path from $Q$ to $V$, or they are on a path from a query node that does not contain $Q$.

*R2* Let $Q$ be a query node and $V$ be a distinct equivalence node in $s$, that is a sink or a query node and is not a base relation. ($V$ can be a marked node). If

(a) there is a query free path from $Q$ to $V$, and

(b) there is a query dag for $Q$ in $s$ that does not contain a query free path from $Q$ to $V$,

then:

Remove all the edges and the non-marked or non-query nodes that are on a path from $Q$, unless they are on a query dag for $Q$ in $s$ that contains a query free path from $Q$ to $V$, or they are on a path from a query node that does not contain $Q$.

*Example 3.* Consider the state $s$ of Figure 2(a). We apply in sequence state transformation rules to $s$. Figure 2(b) shows the state resulting by the application

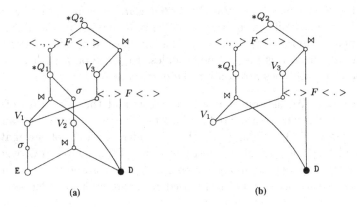

**Fig. 2.** States

of $R1$ to query node $Q_1$ and to equivalence node $V_1$ of $s$. By applying $R1$ to nodes $Q_2$ and $V_1$ of $s$, we obtain the state of Figure 3(a). The state of Figure 3(b) results

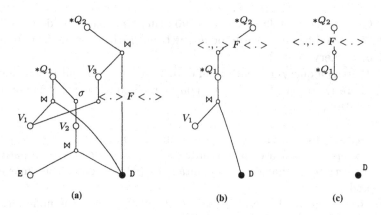

**Fig. 3.** States resulting by the application of the state transformation rules

from the application of $R2$ to query nodes $Q_2$ and $Q_1$ of the state of Figure 2(b). Figure 3(c) shows the state resulting by the application of $R1$ to nodes $Q_2$ and $Q_1$ of state $s$ (Figure 2(a)). Query node $Q_1$ represents now a materialized view. □

The state transformation rules are sound in the sense that the application of a state transformation rule to a state results in a state. Note that the soundness of the state transformation rule entails that *a transformation of a state preserves the existence of a complete rewriting of all the new queries over the materialized views.*

We say that there is a *transition* $T(s, s')$ from state $s$ to state $s'$ if and only if $s'$ can be obtained by applying a state transformation rule to $s$.

### 4.4 The search space

We define in this subsection the search space. We first provide initial definitions and show that the state transformation rules are complete.

**Definition 2.** Given $\mathcal{G}$ and $\mathbf{V}_0$, the *initial state* $s_0$ is a state constructed as follows. First, mark all the equivalence nodes of $\mathcal{G}$ that are in $\mathbf{V}_0$. Then, for each marked node, remove all the edges and the non-marked or non-query nodes that are on a path from this marked node, unless they are on a path from a query node and this path does not contain the marked node. □

**Assumptions.** We assume that all the views and the rewritings of the new queries over the views considered are among those that can be obtained from the multiquery AND/OR dag $\mathcal{G}$. Further, consider a set of $\mathbf{V}$ of new materialized views and let $\mathbf{Q}^V$ be a set of cheapest rewritings of the queries in $\mathbf{Q}$ over $\mathbf{V}_0 \cup \mathbf{V}$. In computing the view maintenance cost of $\mathbf{V}$, we assume that a materialized view that does not occur in $\mathbf{Q}^V$ is not used in the maintenance process of another view in $\mathbf{V}$.

**Definition 3.** Given $\mathcal{G}$ and $\mathbf{V}_0$, a goal state $s_g$ is a state such that there exists a solution $\mathbf{V}$ satisfying the conditions:
(a) The non-marked sink nodes of $s_g$ are exactly the views in $\mathbf{V}$, and
(b) The cheapest rewritings of the queries in $\mathbf{Q}$ over $\mathbf{V}_0 \cup \mathbf{V}$ are represented in $s_g$.

The following theorem is a completeness statement for the state transformation rules.

**Theorem 1.** *Let $\mathcal{G}$ be a multiquery AND/OR dag for a set of new queries $\mathbf{Q}$, and $\mathbf{V}_0$ be a set of old views. If there is a solution to the DW design problem, a goal state for $\mathcal{G}$ and $\mathbf{V}_0$ can be obtained by finitely applying in sequence the state transformation rules to the initial state for $\mathcal{G}$ and $\mathbf{V}_0$.* □

**Search space definition.** Viewing the states as nodes and the transitions between them as directed edges of a graph, the *search space* is determined by the initial state and the states we can reach from it following transitions in all possible ways. Clearly, the search space is, in the general case, a finite rooted directed acyclic graph which is not merely a tree. As a consequence of Theorem 1, there is a path in the search space from the initial state $s_0$ to a goal state $s_g$.

## 5 Algorithms

In this section we present incremental algorithms for the dynamic DW design problem. Heuristics that prune the search space are provided in [11].

The cost and the size of a new state $s'$ can be computed incrementally along a transition $T(s, s')$ from a state $s$ to $s'$ [11]. The basic idea is that instead of recomputing the cost and the size of $s'$ from scratch, we only compute the changes incurred to the query evaluation and view maintenance cost, and to the storage space of $s$, by the transformation corresponding to $T(s, s')$.

Any graph search algorithm can be used on the search space to exhaustively examine the states (by incrementally computing their cost and size), and return a goal state (if such a state exists). We outline below, a variation of the exhaustive algorithm guaranteeing a solution that fits in the allocated space, and a second one that emphasizes speed at the expense of effectiveness.

**A two phase algorithm.** This algorithm proceeds in two phases. In the first phase, it proceeds as the exhaustive algorithm until a state satisfying the space constraint is found. In the second phase, it proceeds in a similar way but excludes from consideration the states that do not satisfy the space constraint. A two phase algorithm is guaranteed to return a solution that fits in the allocated space, if a goal state exists in the search space. In the worst case though, it exhaustively examines all the states in the search space.

**An r-greedy algorithm.** Exhaustive algorithms can be very expensive for a large number of complex queries. The r-greedy algorithm proceeds as follows: for a state considered (starting with the initial state) all the states that can be reached following at most $r$ transitions are systematically generated and their cost and size are incrementally computed. Then, the state having minimal cost among those that satisfy the space constraint, if such a state exists, or a state having minimal size, in the opposite case, is chosen for consideration among them. The algorithm keeps the state $s_f$ satisfying the space constraint and having the lowest cost among those examined. It stops when no states can be generated from the state under consideration and returns $s_f$. This algorithm is not guaranteed to return a solution to the problem that fits in the allocated space, even if a goal state exists.

# 6 Conclusion

In this paper we have dealt with the issue of incrementally designing a DW by stating and studying the dynamic DW design problem: given a set of old views materialized in the DW, a set of new queries to be answered by the DW, and extra space allocated for materialization, select a set of new views to materialize in the DW that fits in the extra space, allows a complete rewriting of the new queries over the materialized views and minimizes the combined evaluation cost of the new queries and the maintenance cost of the new views. A dynamic DW design process allows the DW to evolve smoothly in time, without interrupting its operation due to materialized view removal. We have modeled the dynamic DW design problem as a state space search problem, using a multiquery AND/OR dag representation of the new queries. Transitions between states are defined through state transformation rules which are proved to be sound and complete. We have designed generic incremental algorithms and heuristics to reduce the search space. Also shown is that this approach can be used for statically designing a DW.

# References

[1] G. Graefe and W. J. McKenna. The Volcano Optimizer Generator: Extensibility and Efficient Search. In *Proc. of the 9th Intl. Conf. on Data Engineering*, 1993.

[2] H. Gupta. Selection of Views to Materialize in a Data Warehouse. In *Proc. of the 6th Intl. Conf. on Database Theory*, pages 98–112, 1997.

[3] H. Gupta and I. S. Mumick. Selection of Views to Materialize Under a Maintenance Cost Constraint. In *Proc. of the 7th Intl. Conf. on Database Theory*, 1999.

[4] W. Labio, D. Quass, and B. Adelberg. Physical Database Design for Data Warehousing. In *Proc. of the 13th Intl. Conf. on Data Engineering*, 1997.

[5] A. Levy, A. O. Mendelson, Y. Sagiv, and D. Srivastava. Answering Queries using Views. In *Proc. of the ACM Symp. on Principles of Database Systems*, 1995.

[6] K. A. Ross, D. Srivastava, and S. Sudarshan. Materialized View Maintenance and Integrity Constraint Checking: Trading Space for Time. In *Proc. of the ACM SIGMOD Intl. Conf. on Management of Data*, pages 447–458, 1996.

[7] N. Roussopoulos. View Indexing in Relational Databases. *ACM Transactions on Database Systems*, 7(2):258–290, 1982.

[8] D. Theodoratos, S. Ligoudistianos, and T. Sellis. Designing the Global Data Warehouse with SPJ Views. To appear in *Proc. of the 11th Intl. Conf. on Advanced Information Systems Engineering*, 1999.

[9] D. Theodoratos and T. Sellis. Data Warehouse Configuration. In *Proc. of the 23rd Intl. Conf. on Very Large Data Bases*, pages 126–135, 1997.

[10] D. Theodoratos and T. Sellis. Data Warehouse Schema and Instance Design. In *Proc. of the 17th Intl. Conf. on Conceptual Modeling*, pages 363–376, 1998.

[11] D. Theodoratos and T. Sellis. Dynamic Data Warehouse Design. *Technical Report, Knowledge and data Base Systems Laboratory, Electrical and Computer Engineering Dept., National Technical University of Athens*, pages 1–25, 1998.

[12] J. Yang, K. Karlapalem, and Q. Li. Algorithms for Materialized View Design in Data Warehousing Environment. In *Proc. of the 23rd Intl. Conf. on Very Large Data Bases*, pages 136–145, 1997.

# Star/Snow-Flake Schema Driven Object-Relational Data Warehouse Design and Query Processing Strategies *

Vivekanand Gopalkrishnan[1]     Qing Li[1]     Kamalakar Karlapalem[2]

[1] Department of Computer Science, City University of Hong Kong, Kowloon, Hong Kong, PRC
{vivek, csqli}@cityu.edu.hk
[2] Department of Computer Science, University of Science and Technology, Clear Water Bay, Hong Kong, PRC
kamal@cs.ust.hk

**Abstract.** The conventional star schema model of Data Warehouse (DW) has its limitations due to the nature of the relational data model. Firstly, this model cannot represent the semantics and operations of multi-dimensional data adequately. Due to the hidden semantics, it is difficult to efficiently address the problems of view design. Secondly, as we move up to higher levels of summary data (multiple complex aggregations), SQL queries do not portray the intuition needed to facilitate building and supporting efficient execution of complex queries on complex data. In light of these issues, we propose the Object-Relational View (ORV) design for DWs. Using Object-Oriented (O-O) methodology, we can explicitly represent the semantics and reuse view (class) definitions based on the ISA hierarchy and the class composition hierarchies, thereby resulting in a more efficient view mechanism. Part of the design involves providing a translation mechanism from the star/snowflake schema to an O-O representation. This is done by flattening the fact-dimension schema and converting it to a class-composition hierarchy in an O-O framework. Vertically partitioning this O-O schema further increases the efficiency of query execution by reducing disk access. We then build a Structural Join Index Hierarchy (SJIH) on this partitioned schema to facilitate complex object retrieval and avoid using a sequence of expensive pointer chasing (or join) operations.

## 1   Introduction

In order to support complex *OLAP* queries and data visualization, data warehouses primarily contain historical, consolidated data. This multi dimensional data is represented in popular relational systems by a *star / snowflake schema* [RBS97] [Mic95]. This framework also supports summary views on pre-aggregated data. Querying efficiency can be enhanced by materializing these views [GM95] and by building indexes on them.

---

* This work is supported, in part, by The UGC Research Grants Council of HKSAR under grant CityU 733/96E.

In [VLK98], we examined issues involved in developing the *Object-Relational View (ORV)* mechanism for the data warehouse. Here, *OR* means an *object-oriented* front-end or views to underlying *relational* data sources. So, the architecture and examples we provide follow our interpretation of OR. It must be noted though, that the merits of this proposal can be applied to views in *Object-Relational Databases (ORDBs)* [CMN97] also. The layered architecture of the ORV is as shown in figure 1.

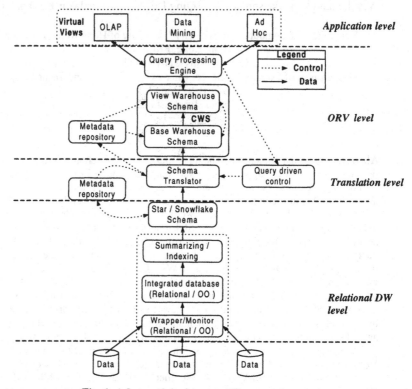

**Fig. 1.** A Layered Architectural Framework

In this framework, two models are captured; both have a multi layer architecture, consisting of wrapper/monitors, integrator and summarizing units. In the first model, *relational - OO* translation is done after database integration, hence the warehouse data is built on the underlying integrated framework. In the second model, we perform translation into the *O-O* model at the wrapper level, so that the *canonical* model for the integrated schema is the *O-O* model, offering more flexibility in dealing with diverse semantics of the underlying data [NS96].

The Complete Warehouse Schema (CWS) in both models contains *Base classes (BWS)* which include some directly mappable classes and some derived *View* classes *(VWS)* based on summarizing queries. Further more, views *(Virtual classes)* can be inherited from this *CWS*. These views may be partially or completely materialized.

Primary issues include translating the relational data structures into a class hierarchy, defining class structures for the summary views, supporting object ids for object instances of the views (classes) generated, handling those classes with respect to maintenance and providing links to other classes in the hierarchy, and accessing and querying these view classes.

## 1.1 Paper Contribution and Organization

Based on the issues discussed in [VLK98], this paper puts forward an *object-relational (OR) view* approach to address the issues in data warehousing. More specifically, we devise a translation mechanism from the *star/snowflake schema* to an object oriented (O-O) representation. We also identify some query processing strategies utilizing vertical partitioning and SJIH techniques for complex queries on complex objects.

The rest of the paper discusses how the above mentioned issues can be tackled and our proposal to solve them. In section 2, we present an overview of our ORV approach. In section 3, we provide algorithms to translate a *star/snowflake schema* to an *O-O* model. In section 4, we refine the *schema* using some query processing strategies, and apply the *SJIH* in a data warehousing environment. Finally, we conclude in section 5 and highlight subsequent work.

# 2 Overview of the ORV Approach

We detail in this section the *object - relational view (ORV)* approach to data warehousing. As *O-O* data models are semantically richer, the *ORV* mechanism can explicitly state multi-dimensional data semantics. Also as we shall see in the following sections, the *ORV* approach leads to better view design and easier maintainability. The *ORV's* support for query-centric indexing facilities also provides an improvement in query performance. Note that in this paper, we deal only with the part of the data warehouse that is translated from relational to the OO model.

## 2.1 Motivating Example

In a relational DW, the fundamental *star schema* consists of a single *fact table*, and a single denormalized *dimension* table for each dimension of the multidimensional data model. To support attribute hierarchies the *dimension* tables can be normalized to create *snowflake schemas*, resulting in smaller *dimension* tables that lead to lesser join cost and hence help in improving query performance and in view maintenance. We adapt an example from [CD97] to demonstrate the need for the ORV approach.

Figure 2 shows a *snowflake schema* for a *Sales* DW with one fact table and *dimension* tables representing *Time, Product, Customer,* and *Address* hierarchies. OLAP queries could be posed on various predicates along a single hierarchy, as well as on predicates along multiple hierarchies. Summary tables could be defined along a predicate or set of predicates by separate *fact* tables and corresponding *dimension* table(s). These summary tables could be materialized depending on various materialization selection algorithms to improve querying cost. As seen in the figure,

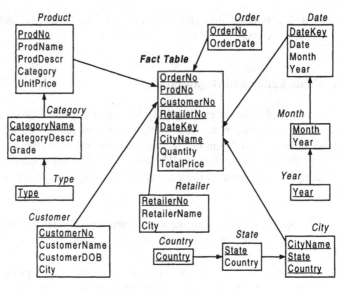

**Fig. 2.** A Sample Snowflake Schema

the dimension tables in the *snowflake schema* (along with schema for summary tables) are in a *composition hierarchy*. Hence they can be naturally represented as an Object-Oriented schema. Therefore, querying costs (*join*) on complex predicates along this *snowflake schema* should be analogous to querying costs by *pointer chasing* mechanism in an O-O framework.

From [FKL98], we see that the *Structural Join Index Hierarchy (SJIH)* mechanism is far superior to *pointer chasing* operations for Complex Object retrieval, especially in queries involving predicates from multiple paths. Experimental results [Won98] conform with the analytical results of this cost model.

## 2.2    Methodology for ORV Design

Our view design methodology depends partly on the type and pattern of queries that access the DW frequently. By incorporating these access patterns, we can form an efficient framework for retrieving popular queries. Note though that as the queries change, the *O-O schema* may require changes in terms of partitioning and indexing, but the underlying schema is fairly static because of embedded semantics. This implicit support of semantics also enables efficient retrieval of multiple query paths along the same dimension hierarchy. For example in the *Time* dimension, multiple paths could be along the Week, Month & Season compositions. These are supported by the Class Composition Hierarchy *(CCH)* framework as shown in figure 3.

As shown in figure 4, we illustrate our methodology in three phases, Phase-2 & Phase-3 are repeated until the OO schema and SJIH are optimized. These phases are explained in detail in the following sections.

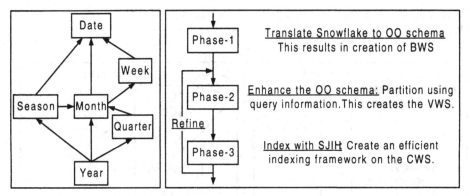

**Fig. 3.** The Time Hierarchy          **Fig. 4.** The ORV Design methodology

# 3 Translating from Snowflake to O-O Schema

The fundamental star schema model consists of a single Fact Table (FT) and multiple Dimension Tables (DTs). This can be further subclassed as *snowflake* (normalizing along DTs) and *multi-star* (normalizing along FTs) and combinations of *multi-star & snowflake schema* models. We illustrate our translation mechanism here on the single *star / snowflake schema* model. Note that a generic extension to include *multi-star schema* models can be easily derived due to advantages of the O-O model as stated in section 2.

### 3.1    Star / Snowflake Schema

A snowflake schema consists of a single Fact Table (FT) and multiple Dimension Tables (DT). Each tuple of the FT consists of a (foreign) key pointing to each of the DTs that provide its multidimensional coordinates. It also stores numerical values (non-dimensional attributes, and results of statistical functions) for those coordinates. The DTs consist of columns that correspond to attributes of the dimension. DTs in a *star* schema are denormalized, while those in *snowflake* schema are normalized giving a Dimension Hierarchy. A generalized view of the snowflake schema is presented in figure 5.

**Preliminaries**

Every tuple in the FT consists of the *fact* or *subject* of interest, and the dimensions that provide that *fact*. So each tuple in the FT corresponds to one and only one tuple in each DT. Whereas one tuple in a DT may correspond to more than one tuple in the FT. So we have a 1:N relationship between FT : DTs.

Let the *snowflake schema* be denoted as *SS*.
No. of FT $= 1$; No. of DT $= x$.

We denote the relations between the FT and DTs as:

$Rel (FT, DT_i) = R_i$

$1 \leq i \leq x$ ; where x is the no. of DTs

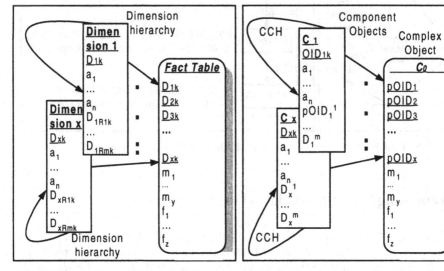

**Fig. 5.** Generalized view of a snowflake schema    **Fig. 6.** Corresponding initial O-O schema

Let the Relations between DTs in a dimension hierarchy be denoted as:

$Rel (DT_i^r, DT_i^{r+1}) = R_i^r$

$0 \leq r \leq m$ ; where m is the no. of relations in the hierarchy under $DT_i$.

and $DT_i^0 = DT_i$

**Table 1.** Elements of the Fact Table (FT)

| | |
|---|---|
| $\{D_{ik}\}$ | set of Dimension keys, each corresponding to a Dimension Table (DT). $1 \leq i \leq x$ ; where x is the no. of DTs |
| $\{m_i\}$ | set of member attributes. $0 \leq j \leq y$ ; where y is the no. of attributes |
| $\{f_s\}$ | set of results of statistical functions. $1 \leq s \leq z$ ; where z is the no. of function results. |

**Table 2.** Elements of the Dimension Table ($DT_i$)

| | |
|---|---|
| $D_{ik}$ | Index of the DT |
| $\{a_i\}$ | Set of member attributes. $0 \leq j \leq n$ ; where n is the no. of attributes. |
| $\{R_{irk}\}$ | set of keys of relations which forms its Dimension Hierarchy. $0 \leq r \leq m$ ; where m is the no. of relations in the hierarchy under DTi |

## 3.2 Query-driven Methodology for OO Schema Refinement

Our methodology intends to capture the *hidden* semantics behind a DW schema design, by incorporating the *star / snowflake schema* information with the *query type* and *pattern* information. Frequent Data warehousing queries can be thought of being decomposed and categorized into the following form :

$$Q \rightarrow \{ Q_1 \cup Q_2 \}$$

where $Q_1$ is the set of queries that would lead to *vertically partitioning* the schema, and $Q_2$ is the set of queries that would induce *horizontally partitioning* of the schema.

Based on this classification, we can refine the resultant schema in two complementary ways. Refinement-1, which involves $Q_1$ is covered immediately below, while Refinement-2, which involves $Q_2$ is covered under section 4.

## Refinement 1 - vertical partitioning

In an OODB environment, vertical partitioning can be regarded as a technique for refining the OODB schema through utilizing the query semantics to generate a finer class composition hierarchy of any class. The refinement can be accomplished in a step-by-step manner, as shown below.

We note that in terms of predicates accessed in the DTs, queries of type $Q_1$ can be defined as

$$Q_1 \rightarrow ( DT_i^r . \{ a_j \} ) \qquad \text{where } \{a_j\} \text{ is a set of attributes of } DT_i^r.$$

*Step V1.* For the Fact Table FT in the snowflake schema, create a class $C_0$ in the O-O schema.

$$\text{Create } C_0$$

*Step V2.* For each Dimension Table $DT_i$ in the snowflake schema, create a class $C_i$ in the O-O schema.

$$\forall \ DT_i \ \text{Create } C_i$$

*Step V3.* For each relation $R_i$ in the snowflake schema, create a pointer to OID, $pOID_i$ in class $C_0$ in the O-O schema.

$$\forall \ R_i \quad \text{Create } C_0 \ . \ pOID_i \ = \ OID(C_i)$$

*Step V4.* For each member attribute $m_j$ in FT in the snowflake schema, create an attribute $m_j$ in class $C_0$ in the O-O schema.

$$\forall \ m_j \ \text{in FT Create } C_0 \ . \ m_j$$

*Step V5.* For each result-value attribute $f_s$ in FT in the snowflake schema, create an attribute $f_s$ in class $C_0$ in the O-O schema.

$$\forall \ f_s \ \text{in FT Create } C_0 \ . \ f_s$$

*Step V6.* For each relation $R_i^r$ in the snowflake schema, create a class $C_i^r$ in the O-O schema.

$$\forall \ R_i^r \ \text{Create } C_i^r$$

*Step V7.* For each member attribute $a_j$ in $DT_i^r$ in the snowflake schema, create an attribute $a_j$ in class $C_i$ in the O-O schema.

$$\forall \ i(\forall r \ DT_i^r . \ a_j \ \text{Create } C_i . \ a_j \ )$$

*Step V8.* For each relation $R_i^r$ in the snowflake schema, create a pointer to OID, $pOID_i^r$ in class $C_i$ in the O-O schema.

This is a recursive step, as it navigates through the dimension hierarchy. The relations between the various nodes of the DT are explicitly captured, so steps 6-7 can be repeated in the hierarchy loop.

$$\forall\ R_{irk}\ \texttt{Create}\ C_{ir}\ .\ pOID_i^r\ =\ OID(C_i^r)$$

*Step V9.* For each Query $Q_i$ in $Q_1$, which accesses a set of $\{a_j\}$ belonging to a DT in $D_i$, vertically partition the corresponding class $C_i$ in the O-O schema.

$$\forall\ Q_i\ (\forall d\ DT_n.\ \{a_j\}\ \texttt{Create}\ C_{nj}\ \leftarrow\ C_n)$$

### 3.3 Corresponding O-O Representation

As seen in figure 6, the generalized view of the O-O schema is similar to that of the snowflake schema. The class corresponding to FT is $C_0$.

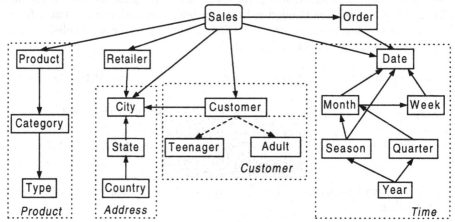

**Fig. 7.** The OO Schema.
The figure shows the class composition hierarchy for the *Time* dimension after refinement 1,
and the is-a hierarchy (shaded area) for the *Customer* dimension after refinement 2.

Figure 7 (without the shaded area) shows the translated *O-O schema* for the *Sales* example taken in previous sections, which is generated by tracing the steps of the above algorithm step-by-step: Note that this hierarchy is not a mere mapping of FTs and DTs from the *snowflake schema*. The classes mapping to the DTs are further vertically partitioned according to the queries acting on them. For an example of multiple paths within a single dimension hierarchy, let us consider the *Time (Date)* hierarchy. If the queries access *Date* by multiple paths like *Day_of_Week*, or *Day_of_Month* or *Week_of_Quarter*, they must be supported within the same path, instead of having to access disjoint *entities (classes)*.

## 4. Query Processing Strategies

In this section, we enhance the *O-O schema* by further horizontally partitioning it in Refinement-2. We complement this partitioned schema with the *Structural Join Index*

*Hierarchy (SJIH)* to facilitate complex object retrieval and avoid using a sequence of expensive *pointer chasing (or join)* operations.

## 4.1 Refinement 2 - horizontal partitioning

In terms of values of predicates accessed in the DTs, queries of type $\mathbf{Q_2}$, can be defined as

$Q_2 \rightarrow$ ( $DT_{ir}. a_j$ . $\{v_k\}$ ) where $v_k$ is a set of values of attribute $a_j$ of $DT_i^r$.
*Step H1.* For each Query $Q_i$ in $\mathbf{Q_2}$, which accesses a record containing a set of values $\{v_k\}$ for attribute $a_j$ belonging to a DT in $D_i$, horizontally partition the corresponding class $C_i$ in the O-O schema.

$\forall Q_i (\forall d\ DT_d. a_j\ . \{v_k\}\ \text{Create}\ C_{djk}\ ::\ C_d)$

This forms the *is-a hierarchy* of the *O-O* schema. Here, the classes mapping to the DTs are further horizontally partitioned according to the queries acting on them. This *subclassing* ensures that *specialized classes* are available while maintaining a high degree of *reusability*.

**Corresponding O-O representation**: The class analogous to FT is $C_0$ (Sales) as noted in sec. 3, and the algorithm can be extended for *multi-star schema* by partitioning $C_0$ to obtain the CCH and is-a hierarchies. As seen in fig. 7, the resultant O-O schema after Refinement-2 contains *specializations* for the *Customer* class (the shaded area). This schema is the *CWS*, over which summary views may be built.

## 4.2 Indexing – SJIH

The *Structural Join Index Hierarchy (SJIH)* [FKL98] is a comprehensive framework for efficient complex object retrieval in both forward and reverse directions. It is a sequence of OIDs which provides direct access to component objects of a complex object, possibly through different paths. We use the SJIH on our *ORV schema*, and extend its applicability from *class composition hierarchies* to also include *is-a hierarchies*, thereby encompassing the *Complete Warehouse Schema (CWS)* in ORV.

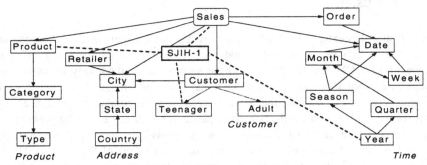

**Fig. 8.** Sample SJIH on the OO Schema.

The total cost of the SJIH framework can be broadly categorized as storage cost, index retrieval cost and index maintenance cost. In this paper we also incorporate *query-centric* information including *selectivity* to determine the selection of forward and backward paths (> 2 paths) during creation (storage) and retrieval of SJIH.

As shown in figure 8, the SJIH is built on objects from first level classes Sales, Product, Customer, and Date (Year) in the class composition hierarchy. As class Customer is subclassed as Teenager, the SJIH now involves the is-a along with the CC hierarchies. The implicit link provided by the *O-O* system between classes and their subclasses provides the link from the complex object (Sales) to the specializations (Teenager) of its component objects (Customer). This SJIH can utilize the is-a link along with the CCH links already exploited by previous works.

The storage and retrieval cost involve determination of an optimum traversal path between the objects. In such a case, $n$ paths will have to be traversed of which one path would be in the forward direction and the other $(n-1)$ would be in the reverse directions. The cost is proportional to the cardinality of the Join Index.

According to the cost model as shown in [Fun98], the Cardinality of a SJI, rooted by a class $C_i$, is given as : $n = \|C_i\| \times \text{MF}(C_i)$ where MF is the Multiplying Factor.

In general, MF is given as: $\text{MF}(C_i) = K_i \times \text{OP}_i(f_{C_i - C_j} \times \text{MF}(C_j))$

where $C_j$ is a child class of $C_i$; $K_i$ is a constant depending on the degree of sharing/forward fan-out between the root and its shared sub-classes; and $\text{OP}_i$ is either the *max* or the *product* of the forward fan-out values, depending on whether the pair-up between classes is constrained or unconstrained.

A sample query, query parameters and proposed indexes are illustrated in the Appendix. By following the heuristic hill-climbing algorithm provided in [Fun98], we find that the optimal SJIH for the given query would be the second one which involves the classes Sales (S), Teenager (T), Product (P), and Year (Y), which incurs the least total number of page accesses (cf. Table B of Appendix).

## 5. Conclusion

The *O-O* model is extremely flexible and provides in all stages for OLAP operations on a Data Warehouse. The *ORV* model can provide an intuitive and efficient framework of a DW. In this paper we have shown our methodology to achieve an efficient transformation between the relational DW and an *OO* DW, and devised efficient query retrieval using the SJIH. Currently we're conducting analytical and experimental studies to show the benefit of partitioning for retrieval. The preliminary results are quite encouraging. Subsequent work involves a study on other indexing aspects like storage cost and maintenance cost. The support of the *O-O* model for dynamic schema changes will help in maintaining the DW during updates and also during the occasional structural changes. Metadata handling and indexing with dynamic reclassification of objects and OID manipulation is also an interesting field of investigation. To support our model, a classification of DW benchmarking queries is also being investigated, with effects on view design. A prototype system is currently being developed to address many of these challenging issues and to demonstrate the effectiveness of the ORV approach to data warehousing.

# References

[CMN97] Michael J. Carey, Nelson Mendonça Mattos, Anil Nori, "Object-Relational Database Systems: Principles, Products, and Challenges (Tutorial)", SIGMOD Conference 1997.

[CD97] Surajit Chaudhuri and Umeshwar Dayal, "An Overview of Data Warehousing and OLAP Technology", SIGMOD Record 26 (1) 1997, pp. 65-74.

[FR97] Gustav Fahl, Tore Risch, "Query Processing Over Object Views of Relational Data", VLDB Journal 6(4) 1997, pp. 261-281.

[Fun98] Chi-wai Fung, "Vertical Class Partitioning and Complex Object Retrieval in Object Oriented Databases", PhD. Thesis, Department of Computer Science, HKUST, Dec 1998.

[FKL98] Chi-wai Fung, Kamalakar Karlapalem, Qing Li, "Structural Join Index Hierarchy: A Mechanism for Efficient Complex Object Retrieval", proc. FODO Conference 1998, pp. 127-136.

[GB+97] Giovanna Guerrini, Elisa Bertino, Barbara Catania, Jesus Garcia-Molina, "A Formal View of Object-Oriented Database Systems", TAPOS 3(3) 1997, pp. 157-183.

[GM95] Ashish Gupta, Inderpal Singh Mumick, "Maintenance of Materialized Views: Problems, Techniques, and Applications", Data Engineering Bulletin 18 (2) 1995, pp. 3-18.

[KL95] Kamalakar Karlapalem, Qing Li, "Partitioning Schemes for Object Oriented Databases", RIDE-DOM 1995, pp. 42-49.

[KK95] Won Kim, William Kelley, "On View Support in Object-Oriented Database Systems", in Won Kim (ed.), Modern Database Systems (The Object Model, Interoperability, and Beyond), pp. 108-129, Addison-Wesley, 1995.

[Mic95] Microstrategy, Inc., "The Case for Relational OLAP", White paper 1995.

[NS96] Shamkant Navathe, Ashoka Savasere, "A Schema Integration facility Using Object-Oriented Data Model", in Omran A. Bukhres, Ahmed K. Elmagarmid (eds.), Object-Oriented Multidatabase Systems: A solution for Advanced Applications, pp. 105-128, Prentice Hall, 1996.

[RBS97] Red Brick Systems Inc., "Star Schema Processing for Complex Queries", White paper 1997.

[SLT91] Marc H. Scholl, Christian Laasch, Markus Tresch, "Updatable Views in Object-Oriented Databases", DOOD 1991, pp. 189-207.

[VLK98] Vivekanand Gopalkrishnan, Qing Li, Kamalakar Karlapalem, "Issues of Object-Relational View Design in Data Warehousing Environment", IEEE SMC Conference 1998, pp. 2732-2737.

[Won98] Wong Hing Kee, "Empirical Evaluation of Vertical Class Partitioning & Complex Object Retrieval in Object Oriented Databases", M.Phil. thesis, HKUST, 1998.

# Appendix

*Sample query Q: Total Sales of Products in {P_SET}, to Teenagers, group by Product, by Year.*

Assumptions
- {P_SET} contains 50% of all Products.
- 80% of Sales to Teenagers consist of Products in {P_SET}.
- 20% of Customers are Teenagers.

**Table A.** Query Parameters

| Reference (i→j) | $f_o$ | R | $\|C_i\|$ | $\|C_j\|$ |
|---|---|---|---|---|
| Sales→Product | 1 | 100 | 50M | .5M |
| Sales→Customer | 1 | 50 | 50M | 1M |
| Sales→Teenager | 1 | 250 | 50M | 2M |
| Sales→Date | 1 | 500 | 50M | 36.5K |
| Prod→Category | 1 | 10 | .5M | 1K |
| Product→Retailer | 50 | 100 | .5M | 50K |
| Category→Type | 100 | 5 | 1000 | 10 |
| Retailer→City | 1 | 4 | 50,K | 12.5K |
| Customer→City | 1 | 80 | 1M | 12.5K |
| Year→Mon | 12 | 1 | 10 | 120 |
| Mon→Date | 30 | 1 | 120 | 3.6K |
| Year→Date | 365 | 1 | 10 | 3.6K |
| Country→State | 25 | 1 | 10 | 250 |
| State→City | 5 | 1 | 250 | 1.2K |
| Country→City | 125 | 1 | 10 | 1.2K |

**Table B.** Disk I/ O cost for Q

| No | Type of Index | No. of Page access |
|---|---|---|
| 1 | SJIH-1 (S, C, P, Y) | 19532 |
| 2 | SJIH-2 (S, T, P, Y) | 3907 |
| 3 | SJIH-3 (S1, S2); S1(S, T, P); S2(S, Y) | 12113 |
| 4 | SJIH-4 (S3, S4, S5); S3(T, P); S4(S, T); S5(S, Y) | 12892 |

Notes:
- The Sales class is the root and contains the 'value' desired in most queries, viz. '$ sales' or 'units'.
- Since each Sales object can appear in only one object path; i.e. there no Sales object is shared by any two objects in the same class, the maximum cardinality of any SJI involving Sales is equal to the cardinality of the Sales class. So MF calculations using degree of sharing is not required.
- Duplicate factor in SJI is ignored here, as we're not concerned with managing object deletions.
- Only one Product is sold in a Sale.

# The Design and Implementation of Modularized Wrappers/Monitors in a Data Warehouse

Jorng-Tzong Horng[1], Jye Lu[1], Baw-Jhiune Liu[1], and Ren-Dar Yang[2]

[1] Department of Computer Science and Information Engineering
National Central University, Jungli, Taiwan
[2] Software Engineering Lab.
Institute for Information Industry, Taipei, Taiwan

**Abstract.** To simplify the task of constructing wrapper/monitor for the information sources in data warehouse systems, we provide a modularized design method to reuse the code. By substituting some parts of wrapper modules, we can reuse the wrapper on a different information source. For each information source, we also develop a toolkit to generate a corresponding monitor. By the method, we can reduce much effort to code the monitor component. We also develop a method to map the object-relational schema into relational one. The mapping method helps us make an uniform interface between a wrapper and an integrator.

## 1 Introduction

In contradiction to on-demand approach (extract data only when processing queries) of traditional databases, data warehouse systems provide a in-advanced approach (interested data are retrieved from information sources in advance). Because processed information has been stored in data warehouse, there exists inconsistency between data warehouse and underlying information sources. According to the WHIPS (WareHouse Information Project at Stanford) architecture [HGMW+95], we can use Monitor/Wrapper components to detect modification in information sources and to maintain the consistency between information sources and data warehouse system.

Monitor/Wrapper is germane to underlying information sources, so we code different Monitors/Wrappers for different information sources. It wastes much cost to re-write the Monitor/Wrapper for each information source. We can divide the wrapper into several modules. When new protocols applied or new information sources occupied, we can substitute some modules and reuse others to construct Wrapper/Monitor rapidly.

This paper focuses on how the modularized design is applied on a wrapper, and discusses how to solve the mismatch between the query processor and the information source.

The remainder of the paper is organized as follows. In section 2, we overview the related work. In section 3, we propose the architecture and modules for designing a wrapper/monitor. We show some examples in section 4 and conclude in section 5.

## 2 Related Work

The goal of WHIPS [HGMW+95] is to develop algorithms and tools for the efficient collection and integration of information from heterogeneous and autonomous sources, including legacy sources. There are three main components in WHIPS architecture: data warehouse, integrator, and monitor/wrapper.

**Data warehouse** stores integrated information available for applications. **Integrator** receives update notification sent by monitor. If this update affects integrated information in the data warehouse, integrator must take appropriate actions, including retrieving more information from information sources. **Monitor** component detects the modification applied to the information source. These modifications will be passed to integrator module. **Wrapper** component translates queries propounded by query processor from internal representation used by data warehouse system to native query language used by information sources.

The goal of the TSIMMIS [CGMH+94] project is to develop tools that facilitate the rapid integration of heterogeneous information sources. TSIMMIS project uses a common information model (*Object Exchange Model*, OEM [PGMW95]) to represent the underlying data. Translator in TSIMMIS convert the query language in OEM into the native query language, and convert the results into OEM.

University of Maryland has proposed an architecture of an *Interoperability Module* (IM) to process queries on heterogeneous databases [Chang94,CRD94]. The IM resolves the conflicts among different databases by two kinds of parameterized canonical representations (CR). [Chang94] proposes two kinds of parameterized canonical form to resolve two kinds of heterogeneity, query language and different schema respectively.

## 3 System Design and Implementation

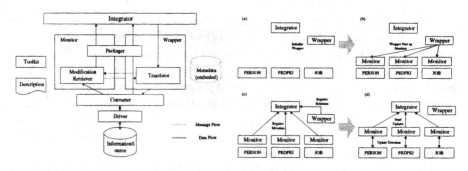

**Fig. 1.** System Architecture          **Fig. 2.** System Initialization

## 3.1 System Architecture

*(A) Functions of Each Module*
We first briefly describe functions of each module in our system architecture shown in Figure 1. *Driver* is responsible for retrieving data requested by other modules. *Converter* resolves the representation conflicts among the information source and wrapper/monitor. *Modification Retriever* detects the changes in information source and propagates the messages to notify integrator. *Packager* transforms data from internal form into the form recognizable by integrator. *Translator* resolves the schema conflicts between the information sources and the integrator.

*(B) The Interaction between Monitor/Wrapper and Integrator*
**System Initialization** We initialize each wrapper of information sources when the integrator is started (Figure 2(a)). Wrapper will start up the monitors which belong to the information source (Figure 2(b)). The wrapper notifies the integrator what relations it handles, and monitors send the corresponding relation schema to the integrator. All schema information will be registered at integrator (Figure 2(c)). Finally, monitor module checks the update message. If monitor finds any update, it will notify the integrator (Figure 2(d)).

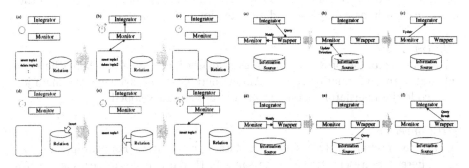

**Fig. 3.** Periodically Update Detection in Oracle     **Fig. 4.** Query Arrived at Wrapper

**Periodically Update Detection** Every update will be stored in a table before it is sent (Figure 3(a)). At the predetermined time, monitor sends the updates to the integrator (Figure 3(b)) and cleans the table (Figure 3(c)).

Then, when another update applied on the relation (Figure 3(d)), the update will be recorded in the table (Figure 3(e)). The update will be sent to the integrator at next predetermined time (Figure 3(f)).

**Query Arrived at Wrapper** When a query arrived at the wrapper component, the wrapper first notifies the monitor to detect the updates (Figure 4(a)). The monitor detects the modifications from the information source (Figure 4(b)) and sends the updates to the integrator (Figure 4(c)). Wrapper does not send the query to the information source until the update detection completes.

When monitor completes its detection, it will notify the wrapper to continue the query (Figure 4(d)). Then, wrapper sends the query to information source and gets the results (Figure 4(e)). Finally, the results will be sent to the integrator (Figure 4(f)).

## 3.2   The Design of Each Module

In this subsection, we introduce a design of each module in system architecture.

### (A) Packager
Internal data type in wrapper and monitor is defined for efficiency or simplicity, but the type may differ from the type used between the integrator and packager. Packager module is responsible for transforming internal data type into one that integrator can recognize.

### (B) Modification Retriever
Modification retriever module can retrieve data from converter, filter the interested data, then ask the packager to propagate these data to integrator. When the module works with an non-cooperative information source, it can use other detecting methods to achieve update detection.

### (C) Translator
Translator module provides mappings of query language and schema between integrator and information source. Among heterogeneous systems, the main job is to code the translator module when a wrapper is developed.

### (D) Converter
Converter module resolves conflicts in data representation. For example, we may use different representations of the same DATE data in databases, e.g., '1975-03-19', so the module takes responsibility of transforming into the same style that integrator has, e.g., '19-MAR-75'. Converter serves not only Wrapper but Monitor, because detection information also needs to be transformed to the style belonging to integrator.

### (E) Driver
Driver module processes the query forwarded by the converter module. Driver module should be provided by information source vendor, or be coded by programmer in the worse case. The interface of a database driver tends to be unified or to use multi-tier architecture. This makes it easier to develop a Converter module quickly.

*(F) Miscellaneous Modules*

The Toolkit uses a description file, which describes the schema of the information source, to generate the corresponding monitor. We can rapidly develop a monitor by using the toolkit. For different information sources, we should develop corresponding toolkits to match the demands.

Metadata provides the processing information about the information source to execute query, transform data and retrieve data. It may be embedded in the code of each module.

## 3.3 Implemetation Tool and Environment

The whole system is implemented by Java Language. We distribute the Java-to Java applications by *Remote Method Invocation* (RMI). In the WHIPS, they use CORBA (ILU) to hide the low-level communication. *Java Database Connectivity* (JDBC) is an access interface of relational databases. It provides an uniform way to access different relational databases by Java.

In this paper, we use two database systems, PostgreSQL and Oracle, as the information sources when we implement our system. In the early implementation, we use PostgreSQL 6.2 and Oracle7 on Solaris. We use PostgreSQL 6.3 on FreeBSD and Oracle8 on Solaris later in our implementation.

## 3.4 Detailed Implementation of Each Module

*(A) Driver Module*

We use the JDBC driver provided by DBMS vendors as the driver module.

*(B) Converter Module*

The main job of converter module in our approach is to resolve the conflicts in data representation. When a query arrived at converter module, we use a parser to find the conflicts and between different data formats and convert them to one that information source has. Then the translated query will be sent to driver module. We provide the same interface as Translator module, so integrator can directly communicate with convert.

*(C) Packager Module*

The packager module in our approach is responsible for translating the internal data into strings. The reason to use string as a data type is simple because integrator component can directly form a query by using these string and transform them into another type.

Besides, each object has `toString()` method in Java, so the transformation can be directly applied on every object. We can also define our class type, which overrides the method, to support new data types.

### (D) Modification Retriever Module

For cooperative information sources, such as Oracle, we use triggers to record the modification information in another table, and periodically retrieve data from this table to notify integrator. For non-cooperative information sources, such as PostgreSQL, we use snapshot algorithm to retrieve the modification. In our approach, the source code of this module is generated by toolkit module.

### (E) Toolkit Module

If there are a lot of tables in one database, it will be very helpful to use toolkit to generate modification retriever module. This module takes the description file and generates corresponding source code of the modification retriever module.

When the information source changes, we can modify the description file and generate modification retriever quickly. In different information sources, we must develop corresponding toolkits to meet the different demands.

### (F) Translator Module

In our approach, we provide a relational schema to the integrator component. Therefore, we should map the schema between the underlying information source and the integrator.

Oracle8 is an object-relational database system. When we use Oracle8 as one of the information source, we must provide some mappings. In the following, we introduce these mappings. The direction of the mapping is from translator to integrator.

### OID

*We map an OID into a primary key.* We need to identify the primary key to satisfy the demand of Strobe algorithm. Oracle8 can offer an oid for each object, so we can directly use oid as the primary key.

### CLASS

*We map the class into a relation.* When integrator retrieves data from the relation, we map it to retrieve data from a class. REF is an oid referencing to another object. REFs will be mapped into foreign keys that reference to primary keys, i.e. OIDs.

### Set

*We map the set into another table.* When queries are applied on the mapped relation, we can translate them into the native form.

### Relationship

#### Association

*We map references into foreign keys.* As discussed above, the REF will be mapped into join between two relations.

**Nested Attribute**

*We map the nested attributes into another relation.* We map the nested attribute into a foreign key which references to an instance of the additional relation. Querying on the additional relation will result in translating the query.

# 4 Examples

In our PDM example database [Chang96], we briefly show how much effort we saved in Table 1. The description file can be created by our toolkit interface, then our toolkit will process the file and generate the monitor component. As we see in Table 1, there are total 1942 lines in 6 monitors on the PostgreSQL while 1322 lines in 15 monitors on the Oracle. In the example, we can save about 80% effort to code our monitors (1322 lines) by the toolkit (200 lines) on Oracle. We can also save about 65% effort to code our monitors (1942 lines) by the toolkit (629 lines) on PostgreSQL. The main reason to save the effort is the vast amount tables, and the average monitor size is shorter than the toolkit module. Once there are only few tables in the database, the cost is even higher when we develop a toolkit. Coding a monitor on a non-cooperative information source (PostgreSQL) is more complex than on a cooperative one (Oracle). By our toolkit, all the details of a monitor can be ignored when we develop our monitor. The more tables on a information source, the more benefit we can acquire. The toolkit is also adequate to the situation when the schema may be changed.

|  | Oracle | PostgreSQL |
|---|---|---|
| Toolkit File | 200 lines | 629 lines |
| Tables | 15 | 6 |
| Generated Files | 1322 lines | 1942 lines |
| Description Files | 107 lines | 41 lines |

**Table 1.** Generating Monitors with a Toolkit

## 4.1 Query on the Object-Relational DBMS

In this subsection, we show how translator module processes the SQL over an Object-Relational database, Oracle8. As we see in Section 3, there are conflicts between the integrator and the database. Integrator sends the pure relational query to the translator module, but the Oracle8 may use additional features which the query cannot handle.

Therefore, we provide pseudo tables for integrator so that the semantic of the SQL applied on these tables can be easily retrieved.

## (A) The Schema

The database contains four types: employee, department, location and phone type (Figure 5).

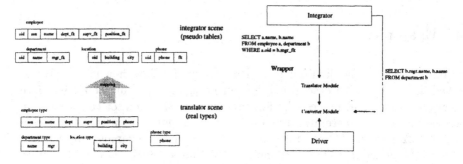

**Fig. 5.** Mapping Schema      **Fig. 6.** Communicate with Converter Module

### employee type
dept refers to the department object, which employee works in; supv refers to the supervisor object of employee type; position is a nested attribute, contains building and city attributes; phone is a set of phone type.

### department type
mgr refers to the manager object of employee type.

### location type
This type can hold office-information for employees.

### phone type
The phone attribute is the phone number of an employee.

## (B) Queries Sent by Integrator

Because the integrator uses relational schema, we map the object-relational schema into relational one (Figure 5). Queries based on relational model will be translated into what can be processd by the information source, which uses an object-relational model. By mapping the schema and translating the query, we provide pseudo tables and ability to use the SQL language which acts on these tables.

## (C) Directly Communicate with Converter Module

If integrator and information source use the same data model, the integrator can directly communicate with converter module. For example, if the integrator can handle the additional features of Oracle8, query can be delivered to converter module directly. We use another example to show how to achieve it.

Consider the following query based on the relational model, and the query will be sent to translator module.

```
SELECT a.name, b.name
FROM employee a, department b
WHERE a.oid = b.mgr_fk
```

The equivalent query of an information source based on object-relational model is as follows.

```
SELECT b.mgr.name, b.name
FROM department b
```

The query is then sent to converter directly. That is, integrator can directly communicate with the converter module and skip the translator module if integrator and information source use the same version of database, e.g., Oracle8 (Figure 6). We use the JDBC Drvier for Oracle7 now, so only a subset of the new features in Oracle8 can be provided via the converter module.

## 5  Conclusions

In this paper, we first describe a modularized design for wrapper/monitor in relational databases. We also show the architecture and fuctions of each module. We demonstrate how a monitor component works on a non-cooperative information source as correctly as cooperative one. Besides the snapshot algorithm [LGM96], there are still other solutions to solve this problem. We create monitors and a wrapper for each site; every monitor is generated by corresponding toolkit, which reduces a lot of onerous jobs. Next, we use several examples to show the flows of message passing when system is initialized, update occured and query arrived. Because we use database as the information sources, we can use transactions to maintain the order among updates and queries. The sequence number will be sent to the integrator component, so integrator can determine whether an event is ealier than the others. Finally, we demonstrate how a translator module works with integrator. Integrator can also communicate with converter module directly, because both module use the same interface.

## References

[AK97] Naveen Ashish, Craig A. Knoblock: "Wrapper Generation for Semi-structured Internet Sources." *SIGMOD Record 26(4)*: 8-15, 1997

[Chang94] Yahui Chang: "Interoperable Query Processing among Heterogeneous Databases." *University of Maryland technical report* 94-67, 1994.

[Chang96] Chih-Chung Chang, Amy J.C. Trappey: "A Framework of Product Data Management System - Procedures and Data Model." *Master's thesis, Department of Industrial Engineering*, National Tsing Hua University, Hsinchu, Taiwan, R.O.C., June 1996.

[CGMH+94] Sudarshan S. Chawathe, Hector Garcia-Molina, Joachim Hammer, Kelly Ireland, Yannis Papakonstantinou, Jeffrey D. Ullman, Jennifer Widom: "The TSIMMIS Project: Integration of Heterogeneous Information Sources." *In the Proceedings of IPSJ Conference* 1994, 7-18.

[CRD94] Yahui Chang, Louiqa Raschid, Bonnie J. Dorr: "Transforming Queries from a Relational Schema to an Equivalent Object Schema: A Prototype Based on F-logic." *In the Proceedings of the International Symposium on Methodologies in Information Systems* 1994: 154-163

[GRVB98] Jean-Robert Gruser, Louiqa Raschid, Maria Esther Vidal, Laura Bright: "Wrapper Generation for Web Accessible Data Sources." *In the Third IFCIS Conference on Cooperative Information Systems (CoopIS'98)* 1998.
Also see *ftp://ftp.umiacs.umd.edu/pub/louiqa/BAA9709 /PUB98/CoopIS98.ps*

[HBGM+97] Joachim Hammer, Hector Garcia-Molina, Svetlozar Nestorov, Ramana Yerneni, Markus M. Breunig, Vasilis Vassalos: "Template-Based Wrappers in the TSIMMIS System." *In the Proceedings of the Twenty-Sixth SIGMOD International Conference on Management of Data* 1997: 532-535

[HGMW+95] Joachim Hammer, Hector Garcia-Molina, Jennifer Widom, Wilburt Labio, Yue Zhuge: "The Stanford Data Warehousing Project." *In the IEEE Data Engineering Bulletin 18(2)*: 41-48 (1995)

[LGM96] Wilburt Labio, Hector Garcia-Molina: "Efficient Snapshot Differential Algorithms for Data Warehousing." *Proceedings of VLDB Conference* 1996: 63-74

[LPTB+98] Ling Liu, Calton Pu, Wei Tang, Dave Buttler, John Biggs, Paul Benninghoff, Wei Han, Fenghua Yu: "CQ: A Personalized Update Monitoring Toolkit". *In the Proceedings of the ACM SIGMOD*, May, 1998.
Also see *http://www.cse.ogi.edu/DISC/CQ/papers /sigmod-demo.ps*

[PGGM+95] Yannis Papakonstantinou, Ashish Gupta, Hector Garcia-Molina, Jeffrey D. Ullman: "A Query Translation Scheme for Rapid Implementation of Wrappers." *In the International Conference on Deductive and Object-Oriented Databases* 1995: 161-186

[PGMU96] Yannis Papakonstantinou, Hector Garcia-Molina, Jeffrey D. Ullman: "MedMaker: A Mediation System Based on Declarative Specifications." *In the IEEE International Conference on Data Engineering* 1996: 132-141

[PGMW95] Yannis Papakonstantinou, Hector Garcia-Molina, Jennifer Widom: "Object Exchange Across Heterogeneous Information Sources." *In the IEEE International Conference on Data Engineering* 1995: 251-260

[Wid95] Jennifer Widom: "Research Problems in Data Warehousing." *In the Proceedings of the 4th Int'l Conference on Information and Knowledge Management (CIKM)* 1995: 25-30

[WGLZ+96] Janet L. Wiener, Himanshu Gupta, Wilburt Labio, Yue Zhuge, Hector Garcia-Molina, Jennifer Widom: "A System Prototype for Warehouse View Maintenance." *In the Proceedings of the ACM Workshop on Materialized Views: Techniques and Applications* 1996: 26-33

[ZGMH+95] Yue Zhuge, Hector Garcia-Molina, Joachim Hammer, Jennifer Widom: "View Maintenance in a Warehousing Environment." *In the Proceedings of the ACM SIGMOD Conference* 1995: 316-327

[ZGMW96] Yue Zhuge, Hector Garcia-Molina, Janet L. Wiener: "The Strobe Algorithms for Multi-Source Warehouse Consistency." *In the Proceedings of the Conference on Parallel and Distributed Information Systems* 1996.
Also see *http://www-db.stanford.edu/pub/papers /strobe.ps*

# Managing Meta Objects
# for Design of Warehouse Data

Takao MIURA[1], Wataru MATSUMOTO[1] and Isamu SHIOYA[2]

[1] Dept.of Electrical and Electronic Engineering, Hosei University
Kajinocho 3-7-2, Koganei, Tokyo, Japan
[2] SANNO College, Kamikasuya 1563, Isehara, Kanagawa, Japan

**Abstract.** In this work, we discuss issues about designing data in warehouses and make clear why meta objects are really important during designing data warehouse process. Our key ideas are *deification* and *queries as objects*. We harmonize objects and meta objects seamlessly in the design process by these ideas. We discuss an experimental prototype system called *Harmonized Objects and Meta objects Environments* (HOME).

## 1 Motivation

Recently much attention has been paid on data warehousing and online analytical processing (OLAP). This is a subject-oriented, non-volatile, time-varying and integrated system for decision support in better and faster ways[1]. Relevant information are collected into repositories. *Objects* are data which describe some information of interests in the repositories. By *meta-objects* we mean knowledge of data in the repository, and sometimes called *data about data*.

In database worlds, such kind of information called a *scheme* have been discussed for a long time to obtain rules of classification standards to data and design methodologies. Note that data warehousing requires *both* traditional database processing and environments for database design processing. That is, all the processes are executed in trials and errors manner, there happen many changes of database schemes and heavy queries to database schemes to obtain design guidelines. Moreover we might need some techniques for scheme discovery[3]. In this work, we put an emphasis on manipulation of meta-objects to establish seamless operations between objects (instances) and meta-objects.

Traditionally we have manipulated scheme contents by means of *special* mechanisms while *data manipulation* have been done by means of expression over meta-objects. Thus users were forced to separate meta-objects from objects and to utilize them at different stages with different languages. More important is that it is hard to obtain *seamless* manipulation of objects and meta-objects such as querying meta-objects under given conditions over objects. The lack of the seamless manipulation causes severe problems because in data warehousing we always manipulate objects and meta-objects equivalently. Especially in conceptual modeling of data warehousing we want to obtain *views* in terms of meta-objects by looking at the objects.

In this investigation, we propose two basic ideas called *reification* and *deification* by which we can manipulate objects and meta-objects seamlessly, which have been developed originally for logic programming[9]. Then we discuss some algebraic language extended for both meta-objects and query evaluation.

In the next section, we discuss the basic ideas and the feasibility about the primitive features of our approach. Section 3 contains key consideration about our proposed language putting stress on scheme management, evaluation of meta-objects and *queries as values*. Section 4 contains related works and we conclude our investigation in section 5.

## 2 MetaObjects and Scenario

In this investigation we assume an object model for data modelling where every object $e$ carries a finite set $\tau(e)$ of types as its own intentional information. For *tuples* (also called associations, that means relationship among objects) we define some classification rules called *relation schemes* $R$ (or predicates) over some set $A_1..A_w$ of types[3] . We assume that every tuple $< a_1, .., a_w >$ carries a finite set $\tau(e)$ of relation schemes as its own intentional information, and that every tuple is consistent with the definition of relation schemes, i.e., every $a_i$ has the type $A_i$. By *instance* we mean one of these primitives.

Our basic ideas of this investigation come from some framework of scheme definitions and and interaction among objects. First, we assume a *core set* of meta-objects to keep scheme information and also to describe themselves. By giving a scheme structure in advance, we could describe the exact meaning of meta-objects and their manipulation.

Second, we introduce *queries as values*. This is because meta-objects play special roles when we *evaluate* them, that is, we can relate them to instances in warehouses by means of evaluation mechanism to meta-objects. Similarly queries correspond to sets of instances by the same mechanism though they are not primitive symbols in schemes, then queries can give the meaning of instances as if they were meta-objects.

Third, we discuss the heart of this investigation, *reification* and *deification*[9]. *Deification* mean an embodiment of meta-objects, that is, *evaluation*. By this technique we relate a meta-object $m$ to a set of instances $\mathcal{M}$, denoted by $\$m = \mathcal{M}$. For example, given a relation scheme $R=R(A_1, .., A_w)$, $\$R$ means a relation (a set of tuples) $r$ over $A_1 \times ... \times A_w$. For an attribute $A_1$ in $R$, $\$\Pi_{A_1}(R)$ means the evaluated result of $\Pi_{A_1}(R)$ while $\$\Pi_{\$A_1}(R)$ means the set of tuples in $R$ of which values on $A_1$ are evaluated again. For example, $\Pi_{RelName}(RelationCatalog)$ becomes all the relation names while $\Pi_{\$RelName}(RelationCatalog)$ generates all the relations defined in the database.

When we have a query $Q$, $\$Q$ means the result of the evaluation. For a tuple $R(a_1...a_w)$, $\$R(a_1..a_w)$ is defined as $TRUE$ if $< a_1..a_w >$ is in $\$R$ and $FALSE$ otherwise. For an object $e$, $\$e$ means $NULL$ if it is terminal symbol. Finally, given (meta)objects $m_1, .., m_k$, we define $\${m_1, .., m_k} = {\$m_1, ..., \$m_k}$.

*Reification* is a technique of abstraction to instances, just the opposite operator of deification. For an object $e$, we define $\hat{}e$ as its intensional information, i.e., $\tau(e)$. Thus we might say $\hat{}R$ is RelName:name, $\hat{}R.A_1$ is AttrName:name, $\hat{}name$ is DomName:name and $\hat{}$RelName is AttrName:name. In the case of tuples $R(a_1, .., a_w)$, $\hat{}R(a_1, .., a_w)$ is defined to be $R$ while $\hat{}< a_1, .., a_w >$ is $\tau(< a_1, .., a_w >)$. For query expression $Q$, $\hat{}Q$ contains a set of query domains whose value types are QUERY in $\tau(Q)$. Then we define $\hat{}{m_1, .., m_k} = { \hat{}m_1, ..., \hat{}m_k }$. Here we don't discuss reification of sets of instances[4] .

---

[3] They are also called *attributes*, denoted by $A_i : D_i$ where $A_i$ means a role in $R$ on which we put an emphasis and $D_i$ means some type.

[4] Readers might say how we can think about a set of instances obtained by evaluating

After these discussion, we introduce our algebraic language where we assume core part of the scheme structure within the language, i.e., it knows the scheme structure as common knowledge. Then operations over meta-objects could be defined by special (meta) semantics. We make algebraic expressions extended with $ and ^ notations. Thus we can specify queries over meta-objects as well as objects and the interaction by means of reification and deification.

# 3 Managing MetaObjects

In this section we describe the total architecture of our approach to harmonize objects and meta-objects. First we show how we can manage meta-objects in our scheme structure. Next we talk about *queries as values* : how we describe and evaluate them. Then we introduce some devices for reification and deification and we define extended relational algebra. Also we show the feasibility of this language.

## 3.1 Core Set of Scheme Structure

We describe our scheme structure to make clear the meaning of *exact semantics* of the scheme. Our primary purpose of this assumption is, in fact, we want to define our scheme within our own scheme structure. This means, if we define the treatment about our special scheme (by some softwares), we can define *every* scheme structure in terms of *our* scheme structure. To do that, it is enough to show some materialization of the scheme structure which is consistent with our assumption. And this is called *core set* of the scheme structure.

Remember we have 3 relations in our scheme; `RelationCalalog`, `AttrbuteCatalog` and `DomainCatalog`. Thus we expect that `RelationCatalog` relation should contain 3 tuples which correspond to these 3 relation schemes. We assume `name` domain has values of 32 byte long and `numeric count` and `type` domains have 4 byte integer. Then, for example, `RelationCatalog` has 40 byte tuples because of 1 `name` domain and two `count` domains. In a similar manner, we have the specific `DomName` relation as below:

| RelName | Arity | Width |
|---|---|---|
| RelationCatalog | 3 | 40 |
| AttributeCatalog | 5 | 104 |
| DomainCatalog | 3 | 40 |

| DomName | ValueType | ValueSize |
|---|---|---|
| name | CHARACTER | 32 |
| count | INTEGER | 4 |
| type | TYPE | 4 |

`AttributeCatalog` relation should contain 11 tuples for the 11 attributes of the 3 relation schemes:

| RelName | AttrName | DomName | Offset | Position |
|---|---|---|---|---|
| RelationCatalog | RelName | name | 0 | 1 |
| RelationCatalog | Arity | count | 32 | 2 |
| RelationCatalog | Width | count | 36 | 3 |
| AttributeCatalog | RelName | name | 0 | 1 |
| AttributeCatalog | AttrName | name | 32 | 2 |
| AttributeCatalog | DomName | name | 64 | 3 |
| AttributeCatalog | Offset | count | 96 | 4 |
| AttributeCatalog | Position | count | 100 | 5 |
| DomainCatalog | DomName | name | 0 | 1 |
| DomainCatalog | ValueType | type | 32 | 2 |
| DomainCatalog | ValueSize | count | 36 | 3 |

a meta-object $m$ or a query $Q$. Generally the set doesn't carry all the semantics within but we might *mine* them by means of knowledge discovery techniques such as *intentional queries*. We don't discuss this problem any more in this investigation but is open[3].

Note the type values CHARACTER, INTEGER, TYPE are 1,2,3 respectively describing what kind of values on this domain are held. In our prototype system, they are represented as string, integer and integer respectively.

## 3.2 Queries as Values

Queries can be seen as a kind of values, but we can *evaluate* them. Since we assume (extended) relational algebra, reader might imagine the algebraic expressions like "project [A,B] select [$\Gamma$] R(ABC)" as attribute values. It is worth noting that readers have to define *scheme* of these queries, that is, all the queries on an attribute must have *compatible* attributes (i.e., the same set of domains) in their output. For example, all the queries must be compatible with "A,B" on this query attribute in the above case. From the viewpoint of users' definition, the attribute seems to have *table values* over the common set of domains.

Let us discuss what kinds of relationship this feature have to meta-objects. We have a query $Q$ with a name $V$ and assume they are registered as a tuple $< V, Q >$ in *View* relation scheme over $ViewName \times ViewQuery$ that is meta-object in a database scheme. Then we can consider the evaluation of $Q$ as if the one of $V$. $V$ is not really a relation scheme because there is no materialization in the database but through *view relation*.

Now we assume query values on some attribute but not materialized. If we don't evaluate the queries, then readers can see the queries but not table values. If we evaluate queries, readers see the table values but not the queries. Both cases might happen since, in database design, we need a lot of view definitions and their results. Note we do *not* talk about nested relations that are materialized, but we calculate them dynamically through stored queries. That means some changes cause the modification of the table values immediately. The difference comes from *when* we evaluate the queries. This is the reason why we introduce *deification*.

**EXAMPLE 1** We assume a relation Student(Name, Address, Friend(Identifier,Home)) where Friend is a query attribute over name and address domains. Also we assume two other relations TV(FirstName, FamilyName, Address, Age, Female) for TV idols and and Sports(FamilyName, NickName, Job) for sports champions.

| Name | Address |
|------|---------|
| Friend(Identifier,Home) | |
| MIURA | Kawasaki |
| "project [FirstName,Address] select [Sex="female",Age=20] (TV)" | |
| MATSUMOTO | Tokyo |
| "project [FamilyName,Address] select [Job="Sumo"] (Sports)" | |

Note that, in the relation, there are two table values but they have compatible structure. That is, Identifier over name is compatible with FamilyName and FirstName. Similarly Home is compatible with Address.

After evaluating the relation above, we will get the (virtual) table below :

| Name | Address | Friend(Identifier,Home) | |
|------|---------|------|------|
| MIURA | Kawasaki | HIROSUE | Tokyo |
| | | HINAGATA | Yokohama |
| MATSUMOTO | Tokyo | HISAMOTO | Tokyo |
| | | HANAKO | Osaka |

□

Since we don't want to distinguish objects from meta-objects, we make up any queries consisting of the two types of symbols in query expressions. As we have pointed out, here we need some mechanisms to evaluate meta-objects and queries. We do that by means of deification, denoted by $ symbol. Relation schemes with $ mean sets of tuples while attributes with $ correspond to the set of tuples of which the values on the attributes are evaluated individually.

**EXAMPLE 2** In our previous example of Student(Name, Address, Friend(Identifier,Home)), we will obtain the relation containing query values if we evaluate Student, i.e., $Student(Name, Address, Friend).

When we want to obtain the one containing the tables values in Friend attribute, we evaluate the attribute first and then Student. that is, $Student(Name, Address, $Friend). □

To define such domains, we introduce QUERY as one of TypeValue and we should define s domain whose TypeValue is QUERY. In our prototype system described in the next section, the value is described in a form of *tagged* structure like MIME (Multi-purpose Internet Mail Extension) thus it has the fixed size in its length that is implementation-dependent. (Our implementation uses 128). More important is that we have to extend scheme structures: how can we describe schemes of query values ? Note the *core set* remain unchanged since no query value appears there.

Given query attributes such as Friend, we must have some expression in our scheme structure. First of all, an attribute Friend is defined over a special domain askfriend in ArrtibuteCatalog. This mean, in turn, domain values can be obtained by evaluating the queries of which definition described as a (virtual) relation. In the above example, we have Student.Friend entry in RelationCatalog and the relevant attributes in AttributeCatalog. This is nice and enough for our purpose since query domain may contain query domain inside.

**EXAMPLE 3** Let us describe Friend attribute in our scheme structure. We assume every address value has 32 byte long. First of all we must have the definitions of Student information. In RelationCatalog and AttributeCatalog, we have

| RelName | Arity | Width |
|---------|-------|-------|
| ... | ... | ... |
| Student | 3 | 128 |
| ... | ... | ... |

| RelName | AttrName | DomName | Offset | Position |
|---------|----------|---------|--------|----------|
| ... | ... | ... | ... | ... |
| Student | Name | name | 0 | 1 |
| Student | Address | address | 32 | 2 |
| Student | Friend | askfriend | 64 | 3 |
| ... | ... | ... | ... | ... |

Since Friend has an askfriend domain of QUERY values, RelationCatalog must contain Student.Friend entry. In a similar manner, AttributeCatalog relation should contain Identifier and Home attributes for Student.Friend *relation*. Thus we have:

| RelName | Arity | Width |
|---------|-------|-------|
| ... | ... | ... |
| Student | 3 | n+64 |
| Student.Friend | 2 | 64 |
| ... | ... | ... |

| RelName | AttrName | DomName | Offset | Position |
|---------|----------|---------|--------|----------|
| ... | ... | ... | ... | ... |
| Student | Name | name | 0 | 1 |
| Student | Address | address | 32 | 2 |
| Student | Friend | askfriend | 64 | 3 |
| Student.Friend | Identifier | name | 0 | 1 |
| Student.Friend | Home | address | 32 | 2 |
| ... | ... | ... | ... | ... |

DomainCatalog now contains askfriend entry and address in DomName entry where the ValueType are QUERY and CHARACTER respectively. □

## 3.3   Queries as Domains

To go one step further, we introduce a *query as domain*. That is, we will define *domain by query*. This is really useful because very often identical or very similar queries appear on query attributes. In this case we give the definition on the query attribute but not store them as values. The idea comes from the fact that some value can be obtained by other attributes or relations, and we define *view domain* of which domain is defined by a query but does not appear as materialized values in tuples.

**EXAMPLE 4** Assume we have a relation scheme StudentScore(Name, Address, Summary(Course,Score) and another relation Enroll(Name, Course, Score). And we want to classify StudentScore relation by each student.

| Name | Address |
|------|---------|
| Summary(Cource,Score) | |
| MIURA | Kawasaki |
| "project [Course,Score] select [Name="MIURA"] (Enroll)" | |
| MATSUMOTO | Tokyo |
| "project [Course,Score] select [Name="MATSUMOTO"] (Enroll)" | |

Looking at the query values, readers see the difference is just the Name condition. We define Summary attribute by a query "project [Course,Score] select [Name="%1"] (Enroll)" where %1 means the value in the first position of this scheme.

| Name | Address |
|------|---------|
| Summary:"project [Course,Score] select [Name="%1"] (Enroll)" | |
| MIURA | Kawasaki |
| MATSUMOTO | Tokyo |

By means of deification, we obtain StudentScore relation by $StudentScore that contain query values. But $StudentScore(Name, Address, $Summary) now contains query results in a Summary attribute. □

The parameters should be one of the values in each tuple (described as %1,..) of the relation scheme that defines the query domain or the tuple itself (described as %0), but self reference is not allowed. We note this query-domain supports GROUP-BY feature in SQL that is known really important in data warehousing[1], and in our case, no special syntax in introduced but a query domain.

To define such domains, we introduce QUERYDOMAIN as TypeValue and temporary domains query*nnn* (*nnn* = 000,001,...) as DomainCatalog entries. Given query domains such as Summary, an attribute Summary is defined over a special domain query*nnn* in ArrtibuteCatalog just same as the case of *queries as values*. But this time the domain name is query*nnn* by which we can obtain the pointer to the definition of query through QueryDefinition : QueryDefinition[*nnn*] = pointer to the definition

Note that our scheme structure is closed by *reification* and *deification* operators. That means no other meta-objects except the *core scheme* are required. Thus we can define our *scheme semantics* within our framework.

## 3.4   Extending Relational Algebra

Let us define extended relational algebra for the purpose of reification and deification. Here we discuss "select [cond] expr" (which means the execusion $\sigma_{cond}(expr)$), "project [attrs] expr" ($\Pi_{attrs}(expr)$), "join [cond] expr1 expr2" ($expr_1 \bowtie_{cond} expr_2$), "union expr1 expr2" ($expr_1 \cup expr_2$), "intersect expr1 expr2" ($expr_1 \cap expr_2$) and "difference expr1 expr2" ($expr_1 - expr_2$) over relation schemes $R$ (or

$R(A_1...A_w)$). In this work, in `cond` part of `select` operator, we discuss only boolean combination of primitive conditions of the form of $Attr_1 = Attr_2$ and $Attr = "const"$.

We extend these operators to input expressions. For example, $\sigma_{cond}(\{R_1, ..., R_n\})$ means $\{\sigma_{cond}(R_1), ..., \sigma_{cond}(R_n)\}$, $\{E_1, .., E_n\} \cap \{F_1, .., F_m\}$ means $\{E_i \cap F_j \mid i = 1, .., n, j = 1, .., m\}$, $\${E_1, .., E_n\}$ means $\{\$E_1, .., \$E_n\}$ and so on.

We define $\$Q$ for a query $Q$ as the evaluated results (sets of tuples) by $Q$. That is, for a relation scheme $R$, $\$R$ means the set $r$ of tuples of $R$, denoted by $[R]$. And, for instance, $\$(\text{select } [\text{cond}] \text{ expr})$ means the result by $\$$ to the result of $\sigma_{cond}(\text{expr})$. Note $\$\$Q$ is legal if the reult consists of the relation names.

In the case of `project` $\$$ plays special role: "`project [A,$B,$C] expr`" means, for each tuple $t$ in `$expr`, we replace $t$ by $< t[A], \$t[B], \$t[C] >$. That is, we evaluate $B$ and $C$ values of each tuple from `expr`. For brevity, we will denote "`project [A,$B,$C] R`" by $R(A, \$B, \$C)$. Similarly, in `cond` part of `select`, we have special forms of "`$A = $B`" and "`A IN $B`". This means, for every tuple from `expr` of `select` operation, we examine the evaluation results and compare the equality or the membership. Note there are some more select conditions such as set equality (`=`), membership (`IN`) and set inclusion (`CONTAIN`). Also note that the results are a collection of relations that might be sent to other queries. Also we define reification syntax to our algebra.

**EXAMPLE 5** Here are some example queries of our extended algebra.

1. `join [Student.Friend = Student.Friend] select [Address="Tokyo] Student select [Address="Yokohama"] Student`
   This query explores all the pairs of Tokyo Students and Yokohama Students who have identical queries on Friend.
2. `join [$(Student.Friend) = $(Student.Friend)] select [Address="Tokyo] Student select [Address="Yokohama"] Student`
   This query explores all the pairs of Tokyo Students and Yokohama Students who have identical set of friends.
3. `select ["MIURA" IN ($Friend).Identifier] Student(Name,Address,$Friend)`
   This query explores all the tuples who have "MIURA" as a friend.
4. `project [Name] $(project [RelName] select [AttrName="Name"] AttributeCatalog)`
   We obtain all the Name values that appear in *any* relations.

□

# 4   Related Works

Meta-knowledge refers to knowledge about its context. For instance, some notion could be described by formal logic where logical consequences and formal proofs are expressed by some meta-languages. But its is well known that the provability of *the* meta languages are undecidable, thus we have to abandon the solid foundation of logic by means of formal logic. But still we assume the usefulness of meta-knowledge from the viewpoint of various applications.

The aim of meta-knowledge is to make easier the interaction between users and the knowledge processing. Such meta-knowledge have been investigated to drive the process of knowledge acquisition, automated deduction, problem solving, programming and so on (see [6] for the variety of the investigation). Among others, in databases and data warehousing these knowledge play integral part of their activities where meta-knowledge means database schemes, all the common meaning of database instances.

*Database design* is nothing but the construction of meta-knowledge[2]. In data warehouses, meta-objects give *bridge* between users and data in the repositories by relating meaning to the contents[4, 5]. Concept learning from databases is one of the major research topics at the intersection of both databases and knowledge processing. This topic becomes hot day by day and much attention is paid from the viewpoint of *Data Mining Methods* (see [3] for more detail). When analyzing the description extensively, we might generate new schemes by utilizing meta-knowlegde. Such knowledge discovery process is called *scheme discovery in databases*.

Our series of works show how to obtain new database schemes that are suitable for current database instances. We have developed the theories from this point of view[7, 8].

## 5 Conclusion

In this work, we have discussed how to manage *data* and *data about data* (or *meta-objects*) seamlessly by means of *reification* and *deification*. This could result in suitable treatment of repository management and meta-data management which improve design and maintenance for data warehousing and general database processing. To do that, we developed *queries as values* and queries as domains and then we have proposed an extended algebra language. We have developed an experimental prototype system named *HOME* (Harmonized Objects and Meta-objects Environment). *HOME* consists of the kernel database system and user interfaces, and we have some application testbeds as well as data warehousing. Currently we discuss strategy control issues and optimization problems in the framework of *HOME*.

**Acknowledgement**
The authors thank Prof.M.Mohania (Univ.of South Australia) for the discussion about data warehouse processing.

## References

1. Chaudhuri, S. and Dayal, U.: An Overview of Data Warehousing and OLAP Technology, SIGMOD Record 26-1 (1997), pp.65-74
2. Elmasri, R. and Navathe, S.B.: Fundamentals of Database Systems, *Benjamin* (1989)
3. Fayyad, U.M., Piatetsky-Shapiro, G., Smyth, P. and Uthurusamy, R. (Eds): Advances in Knowledge Discovery and Data Mining, *MIT Press* (1996)
4. Inmon, W.H.: Building the Data Warehouse, John Wiley (1992)
5. Kimball, R.: The Data Warehouse Toolkit, John Wiley (1996)
6. Maes, P. and Nardi, D. (ed): Meta-Level Architectures and Reflection. North-Holland (1988)
7. Miura, T. and Shioya, I.: Learning Concepts from Databases, *Conference and Workshop of DEXA* (1998)
8. Shioya, I. and Miura, T.: Clustering Concepts from Databases, proc. *IEEE Tools with Artificial Intelligence* (ICTAI) (1998)
9. Shioya, I. and Miura, T.: Coordination Languages for Flexible Databases, proc.*KDEX* (1998)

# Dealing with Complex Reports in OLAP Applications

Thomas Ruf, GfK Marketing Services[1], Nuremberg, Germany
Juergen Goerlich, GfK Marketing Services[1], Nuremberg, Germany
Ingo Reinfels, University of Erlangen-Nuremberg[2], Germany

**Abstract.**

Slice&dice and drilling operations are key concepts for ad-hoc data analysis in state-of-the-art data warehouse and OLAP (On-Line Analytical Processing) systems. While most data analysis operations can be executed on that basis from a functional point of view, the representation requirements of applications in the SSDB (Scientific&Statistical DataBase) area by far exceed the means typically provided by OLAP systems. In the first part of the paper, we contrast the data analysis and representation approaches in the OLAP and SSDB field and develop a generalized model for the representation of complex reports in data warehouse environments. The second part of the paper describes the implementation of this model from a report definition, management and execution perspective. The research and implementation work was executed in the data warehouse project at GfK Marketing Services, a top-ranked international market research company. Various examples from the market research application domain will demonstrate the benefits of the work over other approaches in the data warehouse and OLAP domain.

## 1  Introduction

Data warehousing and OLAP (On-Line Analytical Processing) are two closely related key technologies to support the development of computer-aided management information systems. The aim of developing such systems dates back to the 60's; since then, a variety of approaches has appeared over time under different terms like Management Information Systems (MIS; [1]), Executive Information Systems (EIS; [5]), and Decision Support Systems (DSS; [7]). Data warehousing and OLAP are considered to be the key to overcome the two major drawbacks of earlier approaches towards of computer-aided management information systems:

- lack of access to integrated and consolidated data and

- lack of adequate, intuitive data analysis methods and user interfaces.

The first issue is addressed in data warehousing, where providing „subject-oriented, integrated, time-varying, non-volatile" data for further analysis ([6]) is the target. The

---

[1] Fuerther Strasse 27, D-90429 Nuremberg, Germany; [Thomas.Ruf, Juergen.Goerlich]@gfk.de
[2] Martensstrasse 3, D-91058 Erlangen, Germany; Ingo.Reinfels@stud.wiso.uni-erlangen.de

second issue is the focus of modern OLAP systems, where operations like slicing, dicing, and drilling are offered to the user in a table-oriented user interface metaphor ([3]).

The common logical grounds of data warehouse and OLAP systems is a distinction between quantifying and qualifying data. The former represent empirical data collected in the field (e.g. sales figures of products in certain shops over a given period of time), while the latter are descriptive data necessary to assign a meaning to the quantifying data. In the example above, qualifying data would describe the products, shops and time periods in a way that enables various segmentations of the base data according to application-oriented criteria (e.g. sum of sales of a product category in a distribution channel). To allow for such segmentations, qualifying data are organized in so-called dimensions with classification hierarchies defined upon them. For example, in the product dimension, single articles may be classified into product groups, product groups into categories, and those into sectors. Figure 1 shows an example of some instances of the article, product group, and category classification in the product dimension. Note that secondary classification attributes (e.g. Brand, VideoSystem, AudioSystem) are assigned to specific instances of the primary classification (e.g. Video); also note that different instances of the primary classification scheme have different secondary classification schemes assigned. We will come back to this important observation later; more details on this topic can be found in [8].

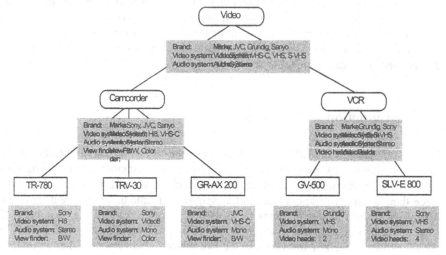

**Fig. 1.** Example of a product dimension classification

With one or more classification hierarchies defined upon every dimension, data warehouse and OLAP data can now be visualized as a multi-dimensional data cube, where the cells hold the quantifying data (often called facts), while the qualifying data describe the axes of the cube and can be used for addressing individual cells or groups of cells (Figure 2).

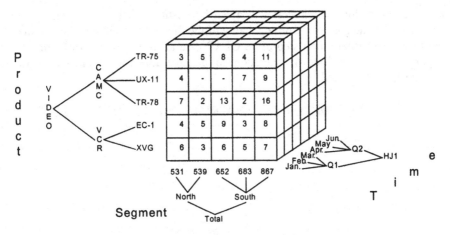

**Fig. 2.** Multi-dimensional data cube

With these basic data modeling concepts introduced, we can now switch to a reporting-oriented view.

## 2   Multi-dimensional data analysis

Whilst data warehousing is primarily targeted at providing consolidated data for further analysis, OLAP provides the means to analyze those data in an application-oriented manner. According to the underlying multi-dimensional data view with classification hierarchies defined upon the dimensions, OLAP systems provide specialized data analysis methods. The basic OLAP operations are:

- slicing (reducing the data cube by one or more dimensions),
- dicing (sub-selecting a smaller data cube and analyzing it from different perspectives) and
- drilling (moving up and down along classification hierarchies).

In the latter case, different instances of drilling operations may be distinguished:

- drill-down:   switching from an aggregated to a more detailed level within the same classification hierarchy;
- drill-up:   switching from a detailed to an aggregated level within the same classification hierarchy;
- drill-within:   switching from one classification to different one within the same dimension;
- drill-across:   switching from a classification in one dimension to different classification in a different dimension.

The results of these operations are typically visualized in cross-tabular form, i.e. mapped to a grid-oriented, two-dimensional layout structure. Higher-dimensional data are mapped to this two-dimensional layout by nesting different dimensions, which conflicts with the concept of orthogonality of the dimensions, but may be tolerated in the final data visualization step of an OLAP data analysis session. In Figure 3, the application of a drill-down operation to a three-dimensional cross-tab grid is graphically exemplified.

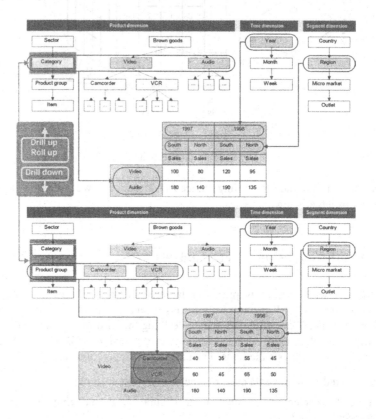

**Fig. 3.** Drill-down operation in a cross-tabular layout structure for three-dimensional data

For many years, cross-tabular report structures have proven to be an adequate means for batch-oriented reporting, particularly in the SSDB (Scientific&Statistical Data Base) area. In those systems, the process of „constructing" the final report structure was of minor interest. In OLAP systems, however, user support for interactive data analysis, i.e. navigation through the data cube by applying the OLAP operators described above, is of vital interest. Of the 12 OLAP rules defined by E.F. Codd ([4]), some directly relate to that area:

Rule 1: multi-dimensional conceptual views

Rule 10: intuitive data manipulation

Rule 11: flexible report generation

Additional requirements for interactive data analysis systems are found in the literature on design rules for information systems ([10]). They include:

- Information should be associated with their underlying definitions.
- Summary and detail information should be visibly separated from one another.

Together, these rules and requirements lead to four basic criteria which allow to assess the quality of the GUI design and the underlying user interaction principles in OLAP systems:

- user interface and user interaction concept for data navigation and analysis via slice&dice techniques;
- user interface and user interaction concept for data navigation and analysis via drill techniques;
- visualization concept for user-defined drill reports;
- visualization concept for heterogeneous report structures.

In the next section, these criteria will be used to identify strengths and weaknesses of state-of-the-art data warehouse and OLAP systems.

# 3 Report functionalities in state-of-the-art data warehouse and OLAP systems

Data warehouse and OLAP are nowadays offered in a great variety in the marketplace. All major database system providers have specific offers in their product portfolio. In addition, there exist numerous independent software houses specialized in this domain. Thus, it does not make sense to evaluate the different systems individually; instead, the evaluation criteria mentioned in the previous section will be discussed in a generalized manner.

The slice&dice functionality in current OLAP systems is mostly implemented using separate drag&drop and selection dialogues. This conflicts with Rule 10 of Codd's OLAP rules, as the user is forced to use different contexts (e.g. report window, selection window) in order to complete the task of report specification. A better concept would be to manipulate directly the visual representation of the report object by drag&drop operations. The attributes used to specify the slice&dice functions would be ideally presented in a tree-like selection list, as they are typically organized hierarchically.

Drill operations are offered to the users in the majority of current systems by selecting the drill anchor cell in the report object first and then by specifying the desired drill function from a context-sensitive menu. This approach is judged as quite straight-forward to use by most OLAP users. A functionally equivalent alternative would be to use the same concept as the one for slice&dice functions, i.e. selecting the target attribute for the drill operation from the tree-like attribute selection list and then dragging&dropping it onto the drill anchor cell.

User-defined drill reports are visualized in OLAP systems either within the original report object or in a separate report object. The first alternative is clearly to be favored, as only then the user can relate the drill data directly to the original drill anchor data. As a side remark, it should be noted that many systems, particularly those based on the MOLAP (Multi-dimensional OLAP) concept, only offer to traverse a pre-specified drill sequence, as aggregated data for drill operations are computed at session start. ROLAP (Relational OLAP) systems, on the other hand, typically allow for an ad-hoc specification of drill attributes, as aggregated data are computed dynamically during a session.

A joint visual representation of structurally heterogeneous report objects is a widely-used concept in the SSDB application domain. This approach guarantees that user reports have a compact layout, thus maximizing the amount of information presentable in one visible portion, e.g. a computer screen. Handling heterogeneous report components in separate report objects is facilitated by concepts like tab folders known from spreadsheet programs in modern GUI environments, but many users still prefer to „see everything immediately on one screen". This is particularly true for typical MIS / EIS / DSS users mentioned in the introductory section. In Figure 4, an example of a heterogeneous report with multiple drill instances is shown. Its different components will be explained in more detail in the following section.

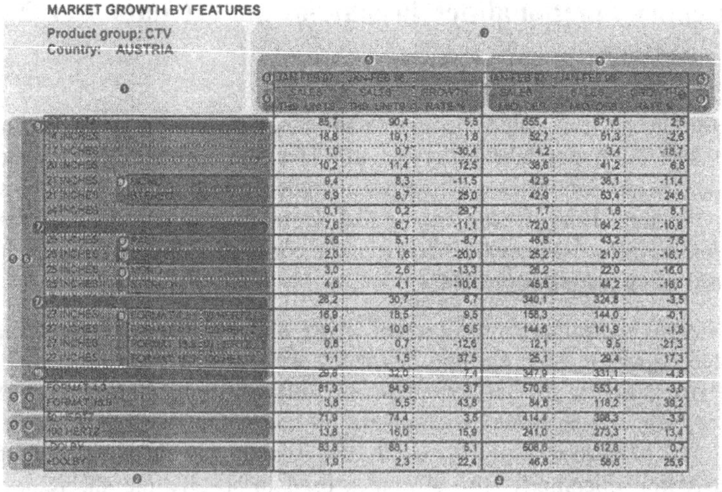
MARKET GROWTH BY FEATURES
Product group: CTV
Country: AUSTRIA
❶ Global filter
❷ Side heading group
❸ Top heading group
❹ Fact values
❺ Single headings
❻ Heading levels
❼ Drill anchors
❽ Drill groups
❾ Totals
❿ „Others" instances

**Fig. 4.** Heterogeneous report with multiple drill instances

In summary, the user interaction concept of most state-of-the-art data warehouse and OLAP systems is primarily geared at computer-literate users who are familiar with using context menus, multi-window systems, tab folders, and the like. For many other typical users of such systems, a more WYSIWYG(What You See Is What You Get)-like work style, where every operation is directly performed with the final report object, would be more intuitive. Finally, the requirements of many users for extremely compact, yet highly customizable information content within a report, is not sufficiently supported in most current systems, whereas Statistical Databases offer the required functionality since a long time ([14]).

# 4 Object model for complex reports

The report shown in Figure 4 is a real example from GfK, one of the largest market research companies in the world. The sample report contains a number of modeling challenges for any kind of reporting system:

- drillings with (e.g. case "27 INCHES") and without (e.g. case "21 INCHES") replacement of the drill anchor

- multiple drillings for the same drill anchor (e.g. case "25 INCHES")

- cascading drillings for a drill anchor (e.g. case "27 INCHES")

- „OTHERS" as the computed aggregate of all elements not explicitly selected

- multiple report anchors at the top report level

Reports of this kind cannot be generated in a joint layout structure with current data warehouse and OLAP systems. The current solution at GfK holds individual descriptions for every single report line, specified in a code scripting language relating to VSAM file positions and code values. This approach is highly error-prone due the lack of semantic links between the individually defined report line specifications. The number of report line specifications adds up to several ten thousands, which makes maintenance a high-cost effort.

As the system used at GfK has clearly reached its limits, a decision was made to implement a new report management system based upon data warehouse and OLAP technologies. During modeling sessions with a number of tool providers, it turned out that no current system covers all of the requirements mentioned above. Therefore, it was decided to develop a report object model on top of an existing data warehouse platform, which is then mapped to lower-level report objects provided with the selected data warehouse platform (in this particular case the DSS Suite from MicroStrategy). The report object model will be described in this section; some remarks on the implementation will be given in Section 6.

In Figure 5, the report object model developed at GfK is shown in an UML notation (for details on UML, see [2] and [13]). The model adopts the structure of a statistical table and distinguishes on a high level between headings and a global filter. The global filter describes which data are included in the analysis of the specified report. The top and side headings are first decomposed individually into their independent components (case (6) in the above example) and those, in turn, level by level according to the drill structures of the component. The heading level information class instances describe the facts or attributes used in the different report components. If the

48

instance describes an attribute, a sub-selection of data elements may be specified in an attribute filter class instance.

It should be noted that in the report object model cascading drillings are not specified recursively in the heading level information business class, but mapped to a sequential description within a heading level information business class instance (1). This allows for a compact description of complete drill splits, i.e. if a drill is applied to all instances of an attribute, the drills do not have to be specified instance by instance. For the same reason, multiple drill anchors are specified not as separate instances of the attribute business class, but are propagated to the attribute filter business class and jointly modeled there. Also note that facts (original or derived quantifying data) cannot be specified within a drilling. In other words, the fact structure of the report is determined globally in the heading level information class, which may also be interpreted as an inheritance of the anchor instance fact description to the drilling children. This guarantees for compatible fact structures across different drilling levels. Finally, it should be mentioned that the computation of Totals and Others is also specified individually for the different heading level and drills within the report object model.

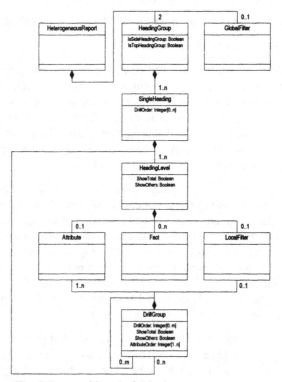

**Fig. 5.** Report object model for heterogeneous reports

In Figure 6, some core parts of the report object model describing the heterogeneous report shown in Figure 4 are depicted. The global filter is set to Productgroup="CTV" and Country="Austria". The top heading is decomposed into two separate heading components, of which the first one is specified down to the leaf nodes. For the side heading, only the first report component containing different drills is shown in some detail. Note that the modeling of the double drill to format and frequency for the 27" drill anchor must be executed as a cross-product operation on an implementation level.

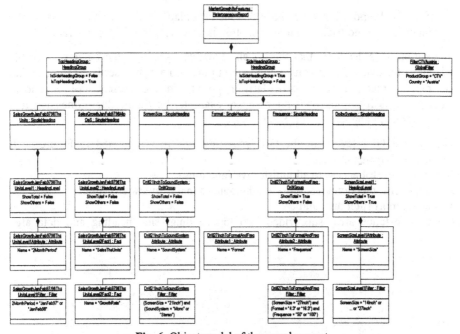

**Fig. 6.** Object model of the sample report

The report object model introduced in this section is complete in the sense that it covers all the situations relevant in real-world complex report applications. The only restriction the model imposes is that some compatibility between fact structures must be guaranteed across a report. The model strictly separates structural, attribute and instance information. On this basis, the model can be mapped to report object models found in state-of-the-art data warehouse and OLAP platforms, thus limiting the amount of implementation work to the minimally needed amount. Before describing a concrete implementation of the model on top of MicroStrategy's DSS Objects system, the basic concepts of the Graphical User Interface design will be described in the next section.

## GUI Design Principles for Complex Reporting Applications

Finding an adequate internal representation of the complex report structures needed for real-world data warehouse and OLAP application is only one side of the coin. Equally important is to find the right usage metaphor that allows a user to easily understand the system and thus to exploit its full potential.

It was described earlier in this paper that a WYSIWYG-like usage concept is considered as the best choice for a complex reporting application. The advantages of such an approach are two-fold:

- during the report design phase, the user is guided step by step by immediately seeing the results of this operations;

- for the final report, it is guaranteed that the information shown on the report is self-containing, i.e. no background information is necessary to interpret the report.

In addition, it is desirable that the system dynamically adopts the range of possible selections for every report construction step to the context the user is creating within the report object. This is particularly important in the presence of dependent secondary classifications, as is the case, for example, for the product dimension in a market research application (cf. Section 1).

The general GUI layout of the GfK reporting system is depicted in Figure 7. It consists of four major areas:
1. toolbar area for access to administrative functions,
2. component selection area, representing objects in a treeview structure,
3. global report filter area and
4. report instance area, subdivided into top heading, side heading and data area

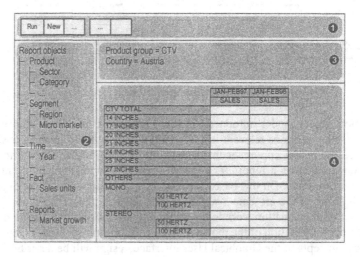

**Fig. 7.** Screen layout of the GfK reporting system

The usage paradigm of the system is that the user constructs the report by successively dragging and dropping attributes from the component selection area into the global report filter and report instance area. The work style with the system is exemplified for a drill operation in Figure 8.

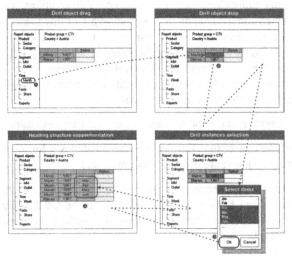

**Fig. 8.** Specification of a drill operation

In the first step, the Month attribute is selected from the components list and dragged into the report instance area. When the element is dropped onto the 1997 instance of the previously included Year attribute, a selection list open which allows for a sub-selection of instances to be shown in the report, and for the specification of a particular sort order in the final report. After closing the selection list, the report object is updated to reflect the changes the operation implies to the report design.

## Implementation

The complex object model described in this paper forms the core of the new GfK reporting system. This system is implemented on top of MicroStrategy's DSS Suite, in particular the DSS Objects system ([11]). DSS Objects offers an API (Application Programming Interface) to access the various functions needed to implement a ROLAP system. Application code is written in VisualBasic, as computing-intensive part of the application are run on the underlying Oracle database system.

The report model of MicroStrategy's DSS Suite consists of three basic concepts:

- templates, which describe the layout structure of a report as a combination of dimensional attributes, along with information on the facts to be shown,

- filters, which describe the data that go into a report as a collection of attribute values from the different dimensions, and

- reports, which are combinations of a template and a filter object.

The strict distinction between attribute and attribute value references in DSS's template and filter structures, respectively, enables a high degree of re-use for those components, as templates and filters may combined in an arbitrary manner. However, this concept is only applicable when the dimensional descriptions are the same for all elements of a dimension. In Section 1, it was shown that this assumption is not valid for many real-world applications. In our market research example, the feature attributes are valid only within a specific context, e.g. a product group. In those situations, combining a template containing references to attributes like „AudioSystem" and „VideoSystem" with a filter selecting the dishwasher product group, for example, would result in an empty report.

To overcome the problems mentioned above, two steps are necessary:

- during report design, ensure that only those attributes who are valid within the already specified context are offered to the user, and

- for report execution, decompose the complex report structure defined on application level into basic report objects that can be handled by the underlying data warehouse / OLAP tool, and re-combine the partial results into a single report object at user level.

We will only elaborate on the latter issue here; the former issue is a modeling issue discussed elsewhere in more detail ([12]).

In Figure 8, the interaction between an application-level complex report object and diverse tool-level basic reports is exemplified for a very simple case. The transformation of the complex report object is technically performed by decomposing the internal object representation of the complex report into a semantically equivalent set of DSS reports, which are executed in the DSS Objects environments. To do that, DSS Objects transforms the API call for a report execution in an SQL statement, which is then transmitted to the underlying database server and executed there. The results are handed back to the VisualBasic application as a two-dimensional array structure with heading information for every data cell. From the different data arrays containing the results of the different DSS Objects calls, the application picks the data needed cell after cell.

It should be intuitively clear that for real report objects needed in application like market research, the number of tool-level reports needed to generate a single application-level report may become enormous. However, the tool-level reports are then usually quite small, i.e. they touch only a relatively small number of instances. Together with an intelligent data aggregation mechanism, the needed system performance is still achievable ([9]).

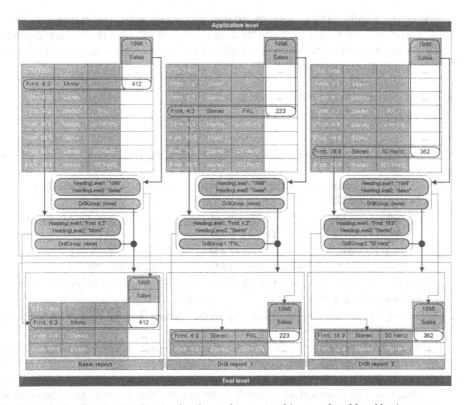

**Fig. 9.** Interaction between application level complex report objects and tool level basic reports

## Conclusion

Complex reports needed in real-world reporting applications are not sufficiently supported by state-of-the-art data warehouse and OLAP platforms. The usage principles found in those systems are too computer-centric and do not meet the requirements of many of the typical users of the such systems, in particular, the user demand for compact information presentation. In this paper, we have shown how existing tools can be extended by a complex report management layer built on top of the platform API.

The current implementation of the ideas presented in this paper within the GfK data warehouse project is close to completion. Test users appreciate the easy-to-use user interface of the system, in particular the context-driven user guidance through the feature-extended multi-dimensional data cubes. On the performance side, we did not go to the full limits of the application so far. However, should we experience serious performance problems, there are a number of performance tuning opportunities intrinsic to our approach besides the usual, system-oriented measures like partitioning and indexing. As complex reports are decomposed into relatively small and structurally simple reports, chances are high that those low-level reports may be re-used over and over again for different application-level reports. We are currently integrating into our architecture the results of some research towards a self-adapting aggregation management system.

# References

[1] Ackoff, R. L.: Management Misinformation Systems, in: *Management Science (1967) 4*, pp. 147-156

[2] Booch, G.; Rumbaugh, J.; Jacobson, I.,: *Unified Modeling Language User Guide*, Reading, Massachusetts, 1997

[3] Chaudhuri, S.; Dayal, U.: An Overview of Data Warehousing and OLAP Technology, *SIGMOD Record 26 (1997) 1*, pp. 65-74

[4] Codd, E.F.; Codd, S.B.; Salley, C.T.: *Providing OLAP (On-line Analytical Processing) to User Analysts: An IT Mandate*, White Paper, Arbor Software Corporation, 1993

[5] Gorry, G. A.; Scott Morton, M. S.: A Framework for Management Information Systems, in: *Sloan Management Review 13 (1971) 1*, pp. 55-70

[6] Inmon, W. H.: *Building the Data Warehouse*, Second Edition, New York e.a.: John Wiley&Sons, Inc., 1996

[7] Keen, P. G. W.; Scott Morton, M. S.: *Decision Support Systems: An Organizational Perspective*, Reading, Massachusetts, 1978

[8] Lehner, W.; Ruf, T.; Teschke, M.: CROSS-DB: A Feature-Extended Multidimensional Data Model for Statistical and Scientific Databases, in: *Proceedings of the 5$^{th}$ International Conference on Information and Knowledge Management* (CIKM' 96), Rockville, MD, Nov. 12-16), 1996, pp. 253-260

[9] Lehner, W.; Ruf, T.; Teschke, M.: Improving Query Response Time in Scientific Databases using Data Aggregation - A Case Study, in: *Proceedings of the 5$^{th}$ International Workshop on Database and Expert Systems Applications* (DEXA' 96, Zurich, Switzerland, Sept. 9-13), 1996, S. 201-206

[10] Mertens, P.; Griese, J.: Integrierte Informationsverarbeitung 2 - Planungs- und Kontrollsysteme in der Industrie, 7$^{th}$ Edition, Wiesbaden: Gabler, 1993

[11] MicroStrategy, Inc.: http://www.microstrategy.com/products/index.htm

[12] Ruf, T.; Baumann, G.; Albrecht, J.; Lehner, W.: *Revealing Real Problems in Real Data Warehouse Applications*, submitted for publication

[13] Rumbaugh, J., Jacobson, I., Booch, G.: *Unified Modeling Language Reference Manual*, Reading, Massachusetts 1997

[14] Shoshani, A.: OLAP and Statistical Databases: Similarities and Differences, in: *Proceedings of the 16$^{th}$ ACM SIGACT-SIGMOD-SIGART Symposium on Principles of Database Systems* (PODS' 97, Tucson, AZ), 1997, pp. 185-196

# OLAP-based Scalable Profiling of Customer Behavior

Qiming Chen, Umesh Dayal, Meichun Hsu

HP Labs, Hewlett-Packard, 1501 Page Mill Road, MS 1U4, Palo Alto, CA 94303, USA
{qchen,dayal,mhsu}@hpl.hp.com

**Abstract.** Profiling customers' behavior has become increasingly important for many applications such as fraud detection, targeted marketing and promotion. Customer behavior profiles are created from very large collections of transaction data. This has motivated us to develop a data-warehouse and OLAP based, scalable and flexible profiling engine. We define profiles by probability distributions, and compute them using OLAP operations on multidimensional and multilevel data cubes. Our experience has revealed the simplicity and power of OLAP-based solutions to scalable profiling and pattern analysis.

## 1 Introduction

Profiling customers' behavior aims at extracting patterns of their activities from transactional data, and using these patterns to provide guidelines for service provisioning, trend analysis, abnormal behavior discovery, etc. It has become increasingly important in a variety of application domains, such as fraud detection, personalized marketing and commercial promotion. It has also given rise to the need for a scalable infrastructure to support filtering, mining and analyzing massive transaction data continuously [1],[2],[4]. We have developed such an infrastructure with data-warehousing and OLAP technology.

In this paper we will focus on the construction and application of customer behavior profiles from telephone call data for the purpose of fraud detection. Typically, a customer's calling behavior is represented by the composition and periodic appearance of his call destination, time-window and duration. One way of doing fraud detection is to discover abnormal calling behavior, which may be further classified into the following two categories.

**Threshold based fraud detection.** For example

☐ a call is suspicious if its duration > 24 hours,

☐ a call is suspicious if its duration > 4 hours and it is made in the evening.

**Pattern based fraud detection.** For example,

☐ a caller (identified by phone number) is suspicious if his calling pattern is similar to a previously known fraudulent one.

Profiling callers' behavior is significant for both kinds of fraud detection. In threshold based fraud detection, without information about personalized calling behavior, only generalized thresholds may be set, such as to consider a call to be suspicious if it lasts over 24 hours. With the availability of a customer's calling behavior profile, *personalized*, rather than generalized thresholds can be set, so that

□ calls by John for 4 hours are considered usual, but

□ calls by Jane for 2 hours are considered unusual.

Thus, personalized or group-based thresholds can be used to provide more precise fraud detection than generalized thresholds. Similarly, pattern based fraud detection is based on profiles to do pattern matching. Each new customer's calling behavior is profiled and compared against known fraudulent profiles. Customer profiles are also useful for other summary information oriented applications.

To create and update customer behavior profiles, hundreds of millions of call records must be processed everyday. This has motivated us to develop a scalable and maintainable framework to support such profiling. The profiling engine is built on top of an Oracle-8 based telecommunication data-warehouse and Oracle Express, a multi-dimensional OLAP server. Profiles and calling patterns are represented as multidimensional cubes and based on the *probability distribution* of call volumes. The profiling engine is capable of building and updating customer calling behavior profiles *incrementally* by mining call records that flow into the data-warehouse daily, deriving *calling patterns* from profiles, analyzing and comparing the *similarity* of calling patterns. We have demonstrated the practical value of using an OLAP server as a scalable computation engine to support profile computation, maintenance and utilization.

We share the same view as described in [1] and [5], in taking advantage of OLAP technology for analyzing data maintained in data-warehouses. Particularly, we are in-line with the efforts described in [5] to use OLAP tools to support large-scale data mining. However, to our knowledge, there is no prior work reported on OLAP based customer behavior profiling and pattern analysis.

Section 2 introduces the concept of behavior profiling with probability distributions. Section 3 describes the architecture of our profiling engine. Section 4 illustrates how to compute profile cubes, and analyze and compare calling pattern cubes. Finally in section 5 some conclusions are given.

## 2 Probability Distribution based Profiling with OLAP

For customer behavior profiling, we first have to decide which features (dimensions) are relevant. For our calling behavior profiling application, the features of interest are the phone-numbers, volume (the number of calls), duration, time of day, and day of week for a customer's outgoing and incoming calls. Next, we have to select the granularity of each feature. Thus, the time of day feature may be represented by the time-bins 'morning', 'afternoon', 'evening' or 'night'; the duration feature may be represented by 'short' (shorter than 20 minutes), 'medium' (20 to 60 minutes), or 'long' (longer than 60 minutes). Finally, we have to decide the profiling interval (e.g. 3 months) over which the customer profiles will be constructed, and the periodicity of the profiles (e.g. weekly). Thus, in our application, a customer's profile is a weekly summarization of his calling behavior during the profiling interval.

Based on the profiled information, *calling patterns* of individual customers may be derived. Conceptually we can consider the following three kinds of calling patterns.

A *fixed-value based calling pattern* represents a customer's calling behavior with fixed values showing his "average" behavior. For example, a calling pattern from number A to number B says that on the average calls are short in afternoons and long in evenings.

A *volume based calling pattern* summarizes a customer's calling behavior by counting the number of calls of different duration in different time-bins. For example, a calling pattern from number A to number B says that there were 350 short calls in the mornings of the profiling period, etc.

A *probability distribution based calling pattern* represents a customer's calling behavior with probability distributions. For example, a calling pattern from number A to number B says that 10% of the calls in the morning were long, 20% were medium, 70% were short.

Probability distribution based calling patterns provide more fine-grained representation of dynamic behavior than fixed value based ones. They also allow calling patterns corresponding to different lengths of profiling interval to be compared.

We represent profiles and calling patterns as *cubes*. A cube has a set of underlying *dimensions*, and each cell of the cube is identified by one value from each of these dimensions. The set of values of a dimension *D*, called the *domain* of *D*, may be limited (by the OLAP *limit* operation) to a subset. A sub-cube (slice or dice) can be derived from a cube *C* by dimensioning *C* by a subset of its dimensions, and/or by limiting the value sets of these dimensions.

As mentioned above, the profile of a customer is a *weekly* summarization of his activities in the *profiling period*. For efficiency in our prototype system we group the information for profiling multiple customers' calling behavior into a single *profile cube* with dimensions *<duration, time, dow, callee, caller>*, where *dow* stands for day_of_week (e.g. Monday,..., Sunday), *callee* and *caller* are calling and called phone numbers. The value of a cell in a profiling cube measures the volume, i.e. number of calls, made in the corresponding duration-bin, time-bin in a day, and day of week, during the profiling period. In this way a profile cube records multiple customers' outgoing and incoming calls week by week. From such a multi-customer profile cube, *calling pattern cubes* of individual customers may be derived. They have similar dimensions as the profile cubes except that a calling pattern cube for outgoing calls is not dimensioned by *caller*, and a calling pattern cube for incoming calls is not dimensioned by *callee*, because they pertain to a single customer.

Multiple calling pattern cubes may be generated to represent a customer's calling behavior from different aspects. In our design, several calling pattern cubes representing *probability-based information* are actually derived from intermediate calling pattern cubes representing *volume-based information*.

Let us consider a volume-based cube *V* for a single customer derived from the above profile cube by totaling outgoing calls over days of week. *V* holds the counts of calls during the profiling period dimensioned by *<time, duration, callee>*, where dimension *time* has values 'morning', 'evening', etc; *duration* has values 'short', 'long', etc; dimension callee contains the called phone numbers. A cell in the cube is identified by one value from each of these dimensions. From cube $V$ the following different probability cubes (and others) may be generated:

☐ $C_{pri}$ for the prior probability of time-bin of calls wrt each callee, that is dimensioned by *<time, callee>*, and indicates the percentage of calls made in 'morning', 'afternoon', 'evening' and 'night' respectively.

☐ $C_p$ for the conditional probability of call duration-bin given time-bin of calls wrt each callee, that is dimensioned by *<time, duration, callee>*, indicates the percentage of calls that are 'long', 'medium' and 'short' respectively, given the time-bin.

☐ $C_{con}$ for the probabilistic consequence of the above, i.e. the probability of calls in every cell crossing dimensioned by *<time, duration, callee>* over the total calls.

All the above probability cubes, $C_{pri}$, $C_p$, and $C_{con}$, can be derived from cube V using OLAP operations. In the Oracle Express OLAP language, these are expressed as

☐ $C_{pri} = total(V, time, callee) / total(V, callee)$

☐ $C_p = (V / C_{pri}) / total(V, callee)$

☐ $C_{con} = V / total(V, callee)$

In the above expressions, total is a typical OLAP operation on cubes with numerical cell values. While *total(V)* returns the total of the cell values of $V$, *total(V, callee)* returns such a total dimensioned by callee, *total(V, time, callee)* returns such a total dimensioned by time and callee. In fact a dimensioned total represents a cube. The arithmetic operations on cubes, such as '/' used above, are computed cell-wise.

With the above mechanism it is only necessary to make volume cubes persistent data-warehouse objects. In the other worlds, only the volume based information need to be profiled; calling patterns, either based on volume or probability, can be derived.

## 3 Architecture of the Profiling Engine

The profiling engine provides the following major functions.

☐ Building and *incrementally* updating customer calling behavior profiles by mining call records flowing into the data-warehouse daily, using an OLAP server.

☐ Maintaining profiles by *staging data* between the data-warehouse and the OLAP multidimensional database.

☐ Deriving multilevel and multidimensional customer *calling patterns* from profiles for analysis.

☐ Comparing the similarity of customer calling patterns from volume and probability distribution points of view, and generating multilevel and multidimensional similarity measures, to be used in such applications as fraud detection.

The profiling engine is built on top of an Oracle-8 based data-warehouse and Oracle Express, an OLAP server (Figure 1). Call data records, customer behavior profiles and other reference data are stored in the warehouse. Call data records are fed in daily and dumped to archive after use [3]. The OLAP server is used as a computation engine for creating and updating profiles, deriving calling patterns from profiles, as well as analyzing and comparing calling patterns. The following process is repeated periodically (e.g. daily).

☐ Call data records are loaded into call data tables in the data-warehouse, and then loaded to the OLAP server to generate a *profile-snapshot cube* that is multi-customer oriented.

☐ In parallel with the above step, a *profile cube* covering the same set of customers is retrieved from the data-warehouse.

☐ The profile cube is updated by merging it with the profile-snapshot cube.

☐ The updated profile cube is stored back to profile tables in the data-warehouse. The frequency of data exchange between the data-warehouse and the OLAP server is controlled by certain data staging policies.

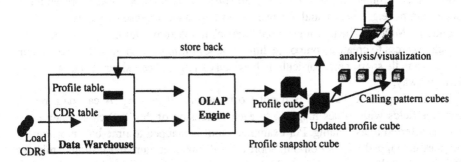

**Fig. 1.** Data warehouse and OLAP server based profiling engine architecture.

In order to reduce data redundancy and query cost, we chose to maintain minimal data in the profile tables in the data-warehouse. We include multiple customers' calling information in a single profile table or profile cube, without separating information on outgoing calls and incoming calls. We make the relational schema of the profile table directly correspond to the base level of the profile cube. Derivable values at higher levels are not maintained in the data-warehouse.

The OLAP engine actually serves as a *scalable* computation engine for generating *profile cubes*, deriving *calling pattern cubes*, analyzing individual calling patterns in multiple dimensions and at multiple levels, and comparing pattern similarity. From a performance point of view, it supports indexed caching, reduces database access dramatically and extends main memory based reasoning. From a functionality point of view, it allows us to deliver powerful solutions for profiling, pattern generation, analysis and comparison, in a simple and flexible way.

## 4 Profile Cubes and Calling Pattern Cubes

We deal with two general kinds of cubes: multi-customer based profile cubes and single customer based calling pattern cubes.

## 4.1 Profile Cubes

A profile cube, say PC, and a profile-snapshot cube, say PCS, have the same underlying dimensions, and contain profiling information of multiple customers in direct correspondence with the relational tables in the data-warehouse. In the Oracle Express language they are defined as

*define PC variable int <sparse <duration time dow callee caller>> inplace*

*define PCS variable int <sparse <duration time dow callee caller>> inplace*

where callee and caller are called and calling numbers; dimension *time* has values 'morning', 'evening', etc, for time-bins; dimension duration has values representing duration-bins (e.g. 'short'); and dimension *dow* has values representing days of week(e.g. 'MON'). The use of keyword "sparse" in the above definitions instructs Oracle Express to create a composite dimension *<duration time dow callee caller>*, in order to handle sparseness, particularly between calling and called numbers, in an efficient way.

Profile-snapshot cube PCS is populated by means of *binning*. A call data record contains fields with values mapping to each dimension of the PCS cube. Such mapping is referred to as binning. For example, '8am' is mapped to time-bin 'morning', 5 minutes is mapped to duration-bin 'short'. A call made at 8am and lasting 5 minutes falls into the cell corresponding to *time* = 'morning' and *duration* = 'short'.

Profile cube PC is retrieved from the database and updated by merging PCS, and then stored back to database. In Oracle Express, the merge of PC and PCS is simply expressed as

$$PC = PC + PCS$$

In this way customer profiles are updated incrementally as each new batch of call data records flow into the data-warehouse.

## 4.2 Hierarchical Dimensions for Multilevel Pattern Representation

Calling pattern cubes are derived from profile cubes and used to represent *the calling behavior* of *individual customers*. In order to represent such calling behavior at multiple levels, Dimensions *dow, time* and *duration* are defined as hierarchical dimensions, along which the calling pattern cubes can be rolled up.

A hierarchical dimension $D$ contains values at different levels of abstraction. Associated with $D$ there are a dimension $DL$ describing the levels of $D$, a relation $DL\_D$ mapping each value of $D$ to the appropriate level, and a relation $D\_D$ mapping each value of $D$ to its parent value (the value at the immediate upper level). Let $D$ be an underlying dimension of a numerical cube $C$ such as a volume-based calling pattern cube. $D$, together with $DL$, $DL\_D$ and $D\_D$, fully specify a dimension hierarchy. They provide sufficient information to rollup cube $C$ along dimension $D$, that is, to calculate the total of cube data at the upper levels using the corresponding lower-level data. A cube may be rolled up along multiple underlying dimensions. For example, the dow hierarchy is made of the following objects.

☐ *dow*(day of week): dimension with values 'MON', ... 'SUN' at the lowest level (dd level), 'wkday', 'wkend' at a higher level (ww level), and 'week' at the top level ('week' level).

☐ *dowLevel*: dimension with values 'dd', 'ww', 'week'

☐ *dow_dow*: relation (dow, dow) for mapping each value to its parent value, e.g.

> *dow_dow(dow 'MON') = 'wkday'*
>
> ...
>
> *dow_dow(dow 'SAT') = 'wkend'*
> *dow_dow(dow 'wkday') = 'week'*
> *dow_dow(dow 'wkend') = 'week'*
> *dow_dow(dow 'week') = NA*

☐ dowLevel_dow: relation (dow, dowLevel) for mapping each value to its level, e.g.

> *dowLevel_dow(dow 'MON') = 'dd'*
>
> ...
>
> *dowLevel_dow(dow 'wkday') = 'ww'*
> *dowLevel_dow(dow 'wkend') = 'ww'*
> *dowLevel_dow(dow 'week') = 'week'*

Analogously, the *time hierarchy* is made up of dimension *time*; dimension *timeLevel* with values 'day', 'month', 'year' and 'top'; parent relation *time_time* and level relation *timeLevel_time*. The *duration hierarchy* is made up of dimension *duration*; dimension *durLevel* with values 'dur_bin' and 'dur_all'; parent relation *dur_dur* and level relation *durLevel_dur*.

For profile storage, combination and updating, only the bottom levels are involved, therefore rolling up profile cubes such as PC is unnecessary. Rolling up is only applicable to calling pattern cubes for analysis purposes.

## 4.3 Calling Pattern Cubes

A calling pattern cube is associated with a *single customer*. As the calling behavior of a customer may be viewed from different aspects, different kinds of calling pattern cubes may be defined. These cubes are commonly dimensioned by *time, duration* and *dow* (day of week), and in addition, for those related to outgoing calls, dimensioned by *callee*, and for those related to incoming calls, dimensioned by *caller*. Their cell values represent the number of calls, the probability distributions, etc. Calling pattern cubes are derived from profile cubes, say, PC, and then may be rolled up.

**Volume based calling patterns.** Cube CB.o represents the outgoing calling behavior of a customer. In Oracle Express that is defined by

> *define CB.o variable int <sparse <duration time dow callee>> inplace*

Similarly, cube CB.d representing incoming calling behavior is defined by

> *define CB.d variable int <sparse <duration time dow caller>> inplace*

The cell values of these cubes are the number of calls falling into the given 'slot' of time, duration, day of week, etc. When generated, CB.o and CB.d are rolled up along dimensions *duration, time* and *dow*. Therefore,

*CB.o(duration 'short', time 'morning', dow 'MON')*
measures the number of short-duration calls this customer made to each callee (dimensioned by callee) on Monday mornings during the profiling interval. Similarly,

*CB.o(duration 'all', time 'allday', dow 'week')*
measures the number of calls this customer made to each callee (total calls dimensioned by callee) during the profiling interval.

Cubes representing probability distribution based calling patterns are derived from volume-based pattern cubes. Depending on the application requirements various cubes may be derived. We list below two kinds of calling pattern cubes for outgoing calls. Calling pattern cubes for incoming calls can be defined similarly.

**Probability distribution on all calls.** Cube P_CB.o for a customer represents the dimensioned probability distribution of outgoing calls over *all* the outgoing calls made by this customer, and is derived from CB.o in the following way

*define P_CB.o formula decimal <duration time dow callee>*
*EQ (CB.o/total(CB.o(duration 'all', 'allday', dow 'week')))*
where *total(CB.o(duration 'all', 'allday', dow 'week'))* is the total number of calls this customer made to all callees (remember that CB.o has already been rolled up, hence we can use its top-level value). The value of a cell is the above probability corresponding to the underlying dimension values.

**Probability distribution on calls to each callee.** Cube P1_CB.o is dimensioned by duration, ... and callee, and represents the probability distribution of a customer's outgoing calls over his total calls to the corresponding callee, and is also derived from CB.o as specified in the following

*define P1_CB.o formula decimal <duration time dow callee>*
*EQ (CB.o/total(CB.o(duration 'all', 'allday', dow 'week'), callee))*
where *total(CB.o(duration 'all', 'allday', dow 'week'), callee)* is the total number of calls this customer made to each callee (dimensioned by callee). The value of a cell is the above probability corresponding to the underlying dimension values.

## 4.4 Calling Pattern Similarity Comparison

Calling pattern comparison is important for such applications as fraud detection. Since the similarity of customer behavior can be represented from different angles, we compare calling patterns derived from customer calling behavior profiles, rather than comparing profiles directly. For example, some calling patterns might be similar in the volume of calls to the same set of callees, others might be similar in the time of these calls such as late nights. Our objective, therefore, is to enable the comparison of calling patterns along multiple dimensions and at multiple levels of the dimension hierarchies.

Given two input calling pattern cubes, say $C_1$ and $C_2$, the output of the comparison is a *similarity cube*, say $C_s$, rather than a single value. The similarity cube $C_s$ can be dimensioned differently from cubes $C_1$ and $C_2$ being compared. Each cell of $C_s$ represents the similarity of a pair of corresponding sub-cubes (slices or dices) of $C_1$ and $C_2$.

To support such cube similarity comparison, the following should be provided.

☐ The mapping from a cell of $C_s$ to a pair of corresponding sub-cubes of $C_1$ and $C_2$.

☐ The algebraic structure for summarizing cell-wise comparison results of a pair of sub-cubes to a single similarity measure to be stored in one cell of $C_s$.

For the latter, we have introduced the following two approaches. One treats a sub-cube as a bag, and summarizes cell-wise comparison results based on *bag overlap*. The other treats a sub-cube as a vector, and summarizes cell-wise comparison results based on *vector distance*.

Bag-overlap based approach is primarily used for comparing volume-based cubes, while vector-distance based approach can be used for comparing both volume-based and probability-based cubes. The similarity of volume-based calling patterns is meaningful only when they cover the same time-span. This limitation can be eliminated in measuring the similarity of probability-based calling patterns. This is especially useful in comparing a preset calling pattern with an ongoing one in real-time. For example, the following cube measures the similarity of probability-based outgoing calling patterns

*define P1SIM.o variable decimal <durLevel, timeLevel, dowLevel> inplace*

An instance of P1SIM.o is illustrated in Figure 2.

```
DOWLEVEL: week
                   -------P1SIM.O-------
                   ------DURLEVEL-------
TIMELEVEL           dur_all    dur_bin
---------------    ----------  ----------
time_all             1.00        0.71
time_bin             0.94        0.70


DOWLEVEL: ww
                   -------P1SIM.O-------
                   ------DURLEVEL-------
TIMELEVEL           dur_all    dur_bin
---------------    ----------  ----------
time_all             0.95        0.72
time_bin             0.92        0.71


DOWLEVEL: dd
                   -------P1SIM.O-------
                   ------DURLEVEL-------
TIMELEVEL           dur_all    dur_bin
---------------    ----------  ----------
time_all             0.77        0.63
time_bin             0.73        0.61
```

**Fig. 2.** P1SIM.o: Multilevel and multidimensional similarity cube

P1SIM.o is calculated by comparing two probability-based calling pattern cubes based on *vector-distance* using *a cell-to-subcube mapping*. It takes two calling pattern cubes, P1_CB.o and P1_CB2.o (defined in the same way as P1_CB.o) as input (since P1_CB.o and P1_CB2.o are "views" of CB.o and CB2.o, the latter can also be considered input cubes).

Let us look at the following two cells that are based on the same dimension values as the cells shown in the above P1SIM.o examples.

☐ Cell *P1SIM.o(durLevel 'dur_bin', timeLevel 'time_bin', dowLevel 'dd')* says that there is 61% similarity between a corresponding pair of probability-based sub-cubes of P1_CB.o and P1_CB2.o. These sub-cubes are based on low-level values of dimension *duration, time, dow* and all values of dimension *callee*. The value of the above cell is the vector-based summarization of cell-wise comparison of the above pair of sub-cubes.

☐ Cell *P1SIM.o(durLevel 'dur_all', timeLevel 'time_all', dowLevel 'week')* says that there is 100% similarity of a pair of sub-cubes of P1_CB.o and P1_CB2.o that are based on high-level values of dimension *duration, time* and *dow*, and all values of dimension *callee*.

For details of multidimensional calling pattern similarity comparison, see [6].

## 5  Conclusions

The problem of customer behavior profiling occurs in many applications such as telecommunications and electronic commerce. In this paper we have developed a data-warehouse and OLAP based framework for customer behavior profiling, and illustrated its use in a telecommunication application. A prototype has been implemented at HP Labs. Our work demonstrates the practical value of using OLAP server as a scalable computation engine for creating and updating profiles, deriving calling patterns from profiles, as well as analyzing and comparing calling patterns. We plan to introduce parallel data warehousing and OLAP architecture to further scale the profiling engine.

## References

1. S. Agarwal, R. Agrawal, P. Deshpande, A. Gupta, J.F. Naughton, R. Ramakrishnan, S. Sarawagi: On the Computation of Multidimensional Aggregates, Proc. VLDB'96 (1996)
2. Q. Chen, U. Dayal, Meichun Hsu: A Distributed OLAP Infrastructure for E-Commerce, International Conference on Cooperative Information Systems (CoopIs99), UK (1999)
3. H. Garcia-Molina, W. Labio, J.Yang: Expiring Data in a Warehouse, Proc.VLDB'98 (1998)
4. S. Geffner, A. El Abbadi, D. Agrawal, T. Smith: Relative Prefix Sums: An Efficient Approach for Querying Dynamic OLAP Data Cubes, Proc. ICDE'99 (1999)
5. J. Han: OLAP Mining: An Integration of OLAP with Data Mining, Proc. IFIP Conference on Data Semantics (DS-7), Switzerland (1997)
6. Q. Chen, U. Dayal, Meichun Hsu: Multidimensional and Multilevel Calling Pattern Similarity Comparison, Tech Rep. HP Labs, 1999.

# Compressed Datacubes for Fast OLAP Applications

Francesco Buccafurri[1], Domenico Rosaci[1], Domenico Saccá[2]

[1] DIMET,
Universitá di Reggio Calabria,
Loc. Feo di Vito, I-89100, Reggio Calabria, Italy,
bucca,rosaci@ns.ing.unirc.it
[2] DEIS,
Universitá della Calabria,
Arcavacata di Rende (Cs), I-87030, Rende (Cs), Italy,
sacca@unical.it

**Abstract.** A number of techniques have been proposed in the literature to optimize the querying of datacubes (i.e., matrix representations of multidimensional relations) in OLAP applications. In this paper we are concerned with the problem of providing very fast executions of range queries on datacubes by possibly returning 'approximate' answers. To this end, given a large datacube with non-negative values for the measure attribute, we propose to divide the datacube into blocks of possibly different sizes and to store a number of aggregate data for each of them (number of tuples occurring in the block, the sum of all measure values, minimum and maximum values). Then, when a range query (in particular, *count* and *sum*) is issued, we compute the answer on the aggregate data rather than on the actual tuples, thus returning 'approximated' results. We introduce a number of techniques to perform an estimation (with expected value and variance) of range query answers and compare the accuracies of their estimations. We finally present a comparative analysis with other recently proposed techniques; the results confirm the effectiveness of our approach.

## 1 Introduction

On-Line Analytical Processing (OLAP) is a recent querying paradigm which deals with aggregate databases [5, 16, 4, 2]. An important data model for OLAP is the multidimensional relation that consists of a number of *functional attributes* (also called *dimensions*) and one or more *measure attributes* [1, 13]. The dimension attributes are a key for the relation so that there are no two tuples with the same dimension value. Therefore a multidatabase relation can be seen as a multidimensional matrix of the measure values, called *datacube* [7]. Some elements of the matrix are null as their dimension values do not occur in the relation.

A range query on a datacube is an aggregation query over a given dimension range (a *cube*). Typical queries are *count*, *sum*, *max*, *min*, and *average*. Since the size of datacubes may be very large, most work in the literature is devoted to improve the performances of such range queries [1, 9, 11, 18].

In this paper we aim at providing very high performances in answering range queries (in particular, count and sum queries) by possibly paying the price of introducing some approximation in the results. To this end we propose to run a range query over a compressed representation of the datacube, that is, a partition of the datacube into blocks of possibly different sizes storing a number of aggregate data for each block. This approach is very useful when the user wants to have fast answers without being forced to wait a long time to get a precision which often is not necessary. In any case, approximated results will come with a detailed analysis of the possible error so that, if the user is not satisfied with the obtained precision, s/he may eventually decide to submit the query on the actual datacube. In this case, it is not necessary to run the query over all tuples but only on those portions of the range that do not fit the blocks.

Our approach is probabilistic in the sense that, given a range query (say, a *count* or a *sum* query) over a datacube $M$, we issue a query over a random datacube variable (say, $\tilde{M}^c$ for the count query and $\tilde{M}^s$ for the sum query) ranging over the population of all datacubes having the same compressed representation as $M$. The query answers are then random variables; so they will be described by an expected value and a variance. To achieve better estimations, we need to restrict the range for the random datacube variable by a suitable usage of the following aggregate data: the number of tuples (i.e., non-null elements), the total sum of the measure values, the minimum and the maximum values. We shall present 4 different techniques (called cases) which make a different usage of aggregate data:

1. $\tilde{M}^c$ (resp., $\tilde{M}^s$) ranges over the set of all datacubes having the same count (resp., sum) aggregate data as $M$ — thus the two queries are solved separately using the minimum amount of the available aggregate information;

2. $\tilde{M}^c$ and $\tilde{M}^s$ range over the same set of datacubes: the ones which have the same count and sum aggregate data as $M$ — therefore, as they use the same information, the two queries are solved together;

3. both $\tilde{M}^c$ and $\tilde{M}^s$ range over the set of all datacubes which have all the same aggregate data as $M$ (i.e., count, sum, min and max) — , as for the case 2, the two queries are solved together;

4. the two queries are solved separately as in the Case 1 but while the range of $\tilde{M}^c$ does not change at all, the range of $\tilde{M}^s$ is restricted to those databases which also have the same max aggregate data as $M$ — note that the information about min cannot be used as null values are not treated explicitly and, then, they must be assimilated to zero.

Our amalysis shows that the 4 cases give the same estimation for the answers (corresponding to a simple interpolation on the basis of the size of the query range w.r.t. the size of a block) for both queries and even the same error for the count query. On the other hand, they return different errors for the sum query. A theoretical analysis to determine which case returns the smallest error is not an easy task so we performed some experiments. As expected, Case 3 worked better than Case 2 but, surprisingly, Case 1 introduced smaller errors than Case 2 and Case 4 behaved better than Case 3. Thus Case 4 seems to be the best estimator. We can therefore draw two conclusions: (i) for the count query, any additional information is useless for it does not change the estimation and (ii) for the sum query, the aggregate count information is even 'dangerous' for it enlarges the estimation errors.

The paper is organized as follows. In Section 2 we discuss related work and in Section 3 we introduce the compressed representation of a datacube. In Section 4 we fix the probabilistic framework for estimating *count* and *sum* range queries on a datacube $M$ by means of aggregate data and then we provide query estimations for the above four cases. The experiments for determining the case with the smallest error are reported in Section 5. In Section 5.2 we compare our estimations for the sum query with the ones obtained by the recent, promising technique presented in [3]. Our experiments show that both approaches work equally fine in general but our results are definitely better when the values in the datacubes have same distorsions like the presence of null elements and different distributions of data for rows or columns.

## 2 Related Work

The idea of using aggregate data to improve performances in answering range queries was first proposed in [11]. To get very fast answers (e.g., running in constant time), a large amount of auxiliary information (e.g., as large as the size of the datacube) is required. When a reduced size of additional information is stored, the performances very much reduce as it is now necessary to access part of the datacube to reconstruct the entire answer: the smaller is the size, the higher is the number of original tuples which must be consulted. The tradeoff with our approach can be stated as follows. Both approaches aim to get fast answers: [11] invests in large space resources while we reduce our level of ambition about the quality (in terms of precision) of the answers.

The possibility of returning approximate answers has been exploited also in [10] but, in that case, the approximation is temporary since results are output on the fly while the tuples are being scanned and, at the end, after all tuples will be consulted, the user will eventually get the correct answer. In our case, the correct answer will never received but, on the other hand, the actual datacube will not accessed either so that we may eventually get higher performances.

The problem of estimating detail data from summarized ones has been studied in [6] and interesting results have been obtained by requiring the optimization of some criterion like the smoothness of the distribution of values. Our approach differs because of the particular criterion adopted (enforcing constraints on various aggregate data), of the fact that no regular data distribution is assumed and of our emphasis on the error estimation.

Histograms have been used since long time to summarize the contents of a database relation mainly to support query optimization [15]. A histogram stores the number of occurrences for groups of values of a given domain: from the aggregate data of a group, one has to estimate the number of occurrences of a given single value or subset of the group. A deal of renewed interest has been recently put on this topic, mainly to discover the best way of dividing the range of values into groups [12, 17, 14]. Such techniques could be applied in the design of the blocks in our approach although histograms are typically monodimensional and straightforward extentions to the multidimensional case do no seem to be feasible.

A recent interesting proposal of providing a succint description of a datacube and estimating the actual data with a certain level of accuracy is reported in [3]. Data compression is based on storing suitable coefficients of interpolation lines rather than aggregate data as for our approach. In Section 2 we shall compare the proposal of [3] with ours.

## 3 Compressed Representations of Datacubes

Let $\mathbf{i} = <i_1, \ldots, i_r>$ and $\mathbf{j} = <j_1, \ldots, j_r>$ be two $r$-tuples of cardinals, with $r > 0$. We extend common operators for cardinals to tuples in the natural way: $\mathbf{i} \leq \mathbf{j}$ means that $i_1 \leq j_1, \ldots i_r \leq j_r$; $\mathbf{i} + \mathbf{j}$ denotes the tuple $<i_1 + j_1, \ldots, i_r + j_r>$ and so on. Given a cardinal $p$ and $r > 0$, $\mathbf{p}^r$ (or simply $\mathbf{p}$, if $r$ is understood) denotes the $r$-tuple of all $p$. Finally, $[\mathbf{i}..\mathbf{j}]$ denotes the range of all tuples $\mathbf{q}$ for which $\mathbf{i} \leq \mathbf{q} \leq \mathbf{j}$.

A *multidimensional relation* $R$ is a relation whose scheme consists of $r > 0$ *functional attributes* (i.e., $r$ *dimensions*) and $s > 0$ *measure attributes*. The functional attributes are a key for the relation so that there are no two tuples with the same dimension value. For the sake of presentation but without loss of generality, we assume that (i) $s = 1$ and the domain of the unique measure attribute is the range $[0..w] =$, where $w > 0$, and (ii) $r \geq 1$ and the domain of each functional attribute $q$, $1 \leq q \leq r$, is the range $[1..n_q]$, where $n_q > 2$, i.e., the projection of $R$ on the functional attributes is in the range $[\mathbf{1}..\mathbf{n}]$, where $\mathbf{n} = <n_1, \ldots, n_r>$.

We consider the following *range queries* on $R$: given any range $[\mathbf{i}..\mathbf{j}]$ with $\mathbf{1} \leq \mathbf{i} \leq \mathbf{j} \leq \mathbf{n}$, (i) *count query*: $count^{[\mathbf{i}..\mathbf{j}]}(R)$ denotes the number of tuples of $R$ whose dimension values are in $[\mathbf{i}..\mathbf{j}]$, and (ii) *sum query*: $sum^{[\mathbf{i}..\mathbf{j}]}(R)$ denotes the sum of all measure values for those tuples of $R$ whose dimension values are in $[\mathbf{i}..\mathbf{j}]$.

Since the dimension attributes are a key, the relation $R$ can be naturally viewed as a $[\mathbf{1}..\mathbf{n}]$ matrix (i.e., a *datacube*) $M$ of elements with values in $[0..w]$ $\cup \{\epsilon\}$ such that for each $\mathbf{i}$, $\mathbf{1} \leq \mathbf{i} \leq \mathbf{n}$, $M[\mathbf{i}] = v \in [0..w]$ if the tuple $<\mathbf{i}, v>$ is in $R$ or otherwise $M[\mathbf{i}] = \epsilon$ — so, as in the latter case no tuple with dimension value $\mathbf{i}$ is present in $R$, $\epsilon$ stands for *null element*. The above range queries can be then reformulated in terms of array operations as follows: (i) $count(M[\mathbf{i}..\mathbf{j}]) = |\{\mathbf{q} : \mathbf{i} \leq \mathbf{q} \leq \mathbf{j} \text{ and } M[\mathbf{q}] \neq \epsilon\}|$; (ii) $sum(M[\mathbf{i}..\mathbf{j}]) = \sum_{\mathbf{q}=\mathbf{i}}^{\mathbf{j}} M[\mathbf{q}]$, where $\epsilon$ yields the value 0 in the summation.

We now introduce a *compressed representation* of the relation $R$ by dividing the datacube $M$ into a number of blocks and by storing a number of aggregate data for each of them. To this end, given $\mathbf{m} = <m_1, \ldots, m_r>$ for which $\mathbf{1} < \mathbf{m} < \mathbf{n}$, an $\mathbf{m}$-*compression factor* for $M$ is a set $F = \{f_1, \ldots, f_r\}$, such that for each $q$, $0 \leq q \leq r$, $f_q$ is a $[1 : m_q]$ array for which $0 = f_q[0] < f_q[1] < \cdots < f_q[m_q] = n_q$. $F$ determines the following $m_1 \times \cdots \times m_r$ blocks: for each tuple $\mathbf{k}$ in $[\mathbf{1} : \mathbf{m}]$, the *block with index* **k** is the submatrix of $M$ ranging from $F(\mathbf{k}-1)+1$ to $F(\mathbf{k})$, where $F(\mathbf{k})$ denotes the tuple $<f_1[k_1],\ldots,f_r[k_r]>$. The size (i.e., the number of elements) of a block **k** is $(f_1[k_1]-f_1[k_1-1])\times\cdots\times(f_r[k_r]-f_r[k_r-1])$.

For instance, consider the $[<1,1>..<10,6>]$ matrix $M$ in Figure 1.(a), which is divided into 6 blocks as indicated by the double lines. We have that $\mathbf{m}=<3,2>$, $f_1[0]=0$, $f_1[1]=3$, $f_1[2]=7$, $f_1[3]=10$, and $f_2[0]=0$, $f_2[1]=4$, $f_2[2]=6$. The block $<1,1>$ has size $3\times2$ and range $[<1,1>..<3,4>]$; the block $<1,2>$ has size $3\times2$ and range $[<1,5>..<3,6>]$, and so on.

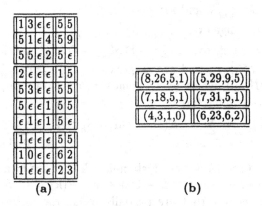

**Fig. 1.** A bidimensional datacube and its compressed representation

A *compressed representation* of the datacube $M$ consists of selecting an m-compression factor $F$ and storing the following aggregate data on the $F$-blocks of $M$: (i) the $[1..\mathbf{m}]$ datacubes $M_{count,F}$ and $M_{sum,F}$ such that for each $\mathbf{k}\in[1..\mathbf{m}]$, $M_{cs,F}[\mathbf{k}]=cs(M[F[\mathbf{k}-1]+1..F[\mathbf{k}]])$, where $cs$ stands for *count* or *sum*; (ii) the $[1..\mathbf{m}]$ datacubes $M_{max,F}$ and $M_{min,F}$ such that for each $\mathbf{k}\in[1..\mathbf{m}]$, $M_{mm,F}[\mathbf{k}]=0$ if all elements in the block $\mathbf{k}$ are null, or otherwise $M_{mm,F}[\mathbf{k}]=mm_{(F[\mathbf{k}-1]+1\leq\mathbf{q}\leq F[\mathbf{k}])\wedge M[\mathbf{q}]\neq\epsilon}(M[\mathbf{q}])$, where $mm$ stands for *max* or *min*.

The compressed representation of the datacube $M$ in Figure 1.(a) is represented in Figure 1.(b) by a matrix of 4-tuples, one for each block, Every 4-tuple indicates respectively the number of non-null elements, the sum of the elements, the max and the min in the block. For instance, the block $<1,1>$ has 8 non-null elements with sum 26, max 5 and min 1; the block $<1,2>$ has 5 non-null elements with sum 29, max 9, min 5 and so on.

# 4 Estimation of Range Queries over Compressed Datacubes

## 4.1 The Probabilistic Framework

We next introduce a probabilistic framework for estimating the answers of range queries (*sum* and *count*) by consulting aggregate data rather than the actual datacube. For such estimations we make the queries random by replacing the datacube $M$ with a random datacube variable ranging over the population of all datacubes which have the same aggregate data as $M$. We have the following datacube populations: for each $agg = count, sum, max, min$, $M^{-1}_{agg,F}$ is the set of all $[1..n]$ matrix $M'$ of elements in $[0..w] \cup \{\epsilon\}$ for which $M'_{agg,F} = M_{agg,F}$.

Let the queries $count(M[i..j])$ and $sum(M[i..j])$ be given. We shall estimate the two queries by the expected value $E$ and the variance $\sigma$ of $count(\tilde{M}^c[i..j])$ and $sum(\tilde{M}^s[i..j])$, respectively, where $\tilde{M}^c$ and $\tilde{M}^s$ are random datacube variables. We shall consider various ranges for the two random variables; in particular, we shall analyze the following 4 different cases:

1. $\tilde{M}^c$ ranges over $M^{-1}_{count,F}$ and $\tilde{M}^s$ over $M^{-1}_{sum,F}$;
2. both $\tilde{M}^c$ and $\tilde{M}^s$ range over $M^{-1}_{count,F} \cap M^{-1}_{sum,F}$;
3. both $\tilde{M}^c$ and $\tilde{M}^s$ range over $M^{-1}_{max,F} \cap M^{-1}_{min,F} \cap M^{-1}_{sum,F} \cap M^{-1}_{count,F}$;
4. $\tilde{M}^c$ ranges over $M^{-1}_{count,F}$ and $\tilde{M}^s$ ranges over $M^{-1}_{max,F} \cap M^{-1}_{sum,F}$.

Given $query(M[i..j])$, where $query$ stands for $count$ or $sum$, due to the linearity of the expected value (operator $E$) we have:

$$E(query(\tilde{M}[i..j])) = \sum_{k \in PB_F(i,j)} E(query(\tilde{M}[i_k..j_k])) + \sum_{q \in TB_F(i,j)} M_{query,F}[q]$$

where $TB_F(i,j)$ returns the set of block indices $k$ that are totally contained in the range $[i : j]$, (i.e., both $i \le F(k-1)+1$ and $F(k) \le j$), $PB_F(i,j)$ returns the set of block indices $k$ that are partially inside the range, and $i^k$ and $j^k$ are the boundaries of the portion of a block $k \in PB_F(i,j)$ which overlaps the range $[i : j]$. For example, for the datacube in Figure 1.(a), given $i = <4,3>$ and $j = <8,6>$, the block $<2,2>$ is totally contained in the range, the blocks $<2,1>$, $<3,1>$, $<3,2>$ are partially contained in the range (with boundaries $[<4,3>..<7,4>]$, $[<8,3>..<8,4>]$ and $[<8,5>..<8,6>]$, respectively), and the blocks $<1,1>$, $<1,2>$ are outside the range.

Concerning the variance, we assume statistical independence between the values of different blocks so that its value is determined by just summing the variances of all partially overlapped blocks without having to introduce any covariance, that is $\sigma^2(query(\tilde{M}[i..j])) = \sum_{k \in PB_F(i,j)} \sigma^2(query(\tilde{M}[i_k..j_k]))$. It turns out that we only need to study the estimation of a query ranging on one partial block as all other cases can be easily recomposed from this basic case.

From now on, we assume that the query range $[i..j]$ is strictly inside one single block, say the block $k$, i.e., $F[k-1]+1 \le i \le j \le F[k]$. Let $b$ be the size of the block $k$, $d$ $(0 < d \le b)$ be the size of elements in the range $[i..j]$, $t = M_{count,F}[k]$ be the number of non-null elements in the block $k$, $c = M_{sum,F}[k]$ be the sum of the elements in the block, $l = M_{min,F}[k]$ and $u = M_{max,F}[k]$ be the min and the max measure values in the block.

## 4.2 Estimating the count and sum query separately— Case 1

In the first case we estimate separately the two range query $count(M[i..j])$ and $sum(M[i..j])$ using their corresponding aggregate data.

**Theorem 1.** [3] *Given the random datacube variable $\tilde{M}^c$ over $M^{-1}_{count,F}$ and the random datacube variable $\tilde{M}^s$ over $M^{-1}_{sum,F}$, (1) the probability that the number of non-null elements of $\tilde{M}^c$ in the range [i..j] be h (for each h, $0 \le h \le t$) and (2) the probability that the sum of the elements of $\tilde{M}^s$ in the range [i..j] be s (for each s, $0 \le s \le c$) are equal to, respectively:*

$$P_1(h) = \frac{\binom{d}{h} \cdot \binom{b-d}{t-h}}{\binom{b}{t}} \quad \text{and} \quad P_1(s) = \frac{\binom{d+s-1}{s} \cdot \binom{b-d+c-s-1}{c-s}}{\binom{b+c-1}{c}}$$

We next compute the expected values and variances of the two random queries:

**Proposition 2.** *Let $\tilde{M}^c$ range over $M^{-1}_{count,F}$ and $\tilde{M}^s$ range over $M^{-1}_{sum,F}$. Then:*
$E(count(\tilde{M}^c[i..j])) = (d/b) \cdot t$, $\sigma^2(count(\tilde{M}^c[i..j])) = t \cdot (b-t) \cdot d \cdot \frac{b-d}{b^2 \cdot (b-1)}$, *and*
$E(sum(\tilde{M}^s[i..j])) = (d/b) \cdot c$, $\sigma^2(sum(\tilde{M}^s[i..j])) = \sum_{s=0}^{c}(((d/b) \cdot c - s)^2 \cdot P_1(s))$.

## 4.3 Estimating count and sum queries together — Case 2

The case 2 estimates both range queries, $count(M[i..j])$ and $sum(M[i..j])$, at one time, using the information about count and sum aggregate data.

**Theorem 3.** *Given the random datacube variable $\tilde{M}$ over $M^{-1}_{count,F} \cap M^{-1}_{sum,F}$, for each s, $0 \le s \le c$, and for each h, $0 \le h \le t$, the probability that both the sum and the number of all non-null elements in the range [i..j] be s and h, respectively, is:*

$$P_2(h,s) = \frac{Q(d,h,s) \cdot Q(b-d,t-h,c-s)}{Q(b,t,c)} \quad \text{where} \quad Q(x,y,z) = \begin{cases} 0 & \text{if } x < y \text{ or} \\ \binom{x}{y} \cdot \binom{y+z-1}{z} \end{cases}$$

**Proposition 4.** *Let $\tilde{M}$ range over $M^{-1}_{count,F} \cap M^{-1}_{sum,F}$. Then*
$E(sum(\tilde{M}[i..j])) = (d/b) \cdot c$, $\sigma^2(sum(\tilde{M}[i..j])) = \sum_{s=0}^{c}(((d/b) \cdot c-s)^2 \cdot \sum_{h=0}^{t} P_2(h,s))$,
$E(count(\tilde{M}[i..j])) = (d/b) \cdot t$, $\sigma^2(count(\tilde{M}[i..j])) = t \cdot (b-t) \cdot d \cdot \frac{b-d}{b^2 \cdot (b-1)}$.

The above proposition says that the count query does not need the additional information on the sum of the elements in a block to perform a good estimation. A different, surprising observation holds for the sum query: as discussed later in the paper, the knowledge of the number of non-null elements seems to reduce the accuracy of the estimation.

---

[3] For space reasons the proofs of theorems and propositions are omitted.

## 4.4 Estimating count and sum queries together using min and max — Case 3

We now exploit the information about the minimum and the maximum value for each block, stored in the two $[1..m]$ matrices $M_{min,F}$ and $M_{max,F}$. As in the case 2, we estimate both range queries, $count(M[i..j])$ and $sum(M[i..j])$ at one time using the same datacube range.

**Theorem 5.** *Given the random datacube variable $\tilde{M}$ ranging over $M_{max,F}^{-1} \cap M_{min,F}^{-1} \cap M_{sum,F}^{-1} \cap M_{count,F}^{-1}$, for each $s$, $0 \leq s \leq c$, and for each $h$, $0 \leq h \leq t$, the probability that both the sum and the number of all non-null elements in the range $[i..j]$ be $s$ and $h$, respectively, is: $P_3(h,s) = \frac{N(d,h,s) \cdot N(b-d,t-h,c-s)}{N(b,t,c)}$, where $N(x,y,z)$ is equal to:*

$$\begin{cases} 0 & \text{if } y \cdot u < z \text{ or } x < y, \text{ or otherwise} \\ \binom{x}{y} \cdot \sum_{\gamma=0}^{min(y, \lfloor \frac{z-y \cdot l}{u'+1} \rfloor)} (-1)^\gamma \cdot \frac{y!}{(y-\gamma)! \cdot max(1,\gamma)} \cdot \binom{y+z-y \cdot l - \gamma \cdot (u'+1)-1}{y-1} \end{cases}$$

*and $u' = u - l$.*

**Proposition 6.** *Let $\tilde{M}$ range over $M_{max,F}^{-1} \cap M_{min,F}^{-1} \cap M_{sum,F}^{-1} \cap M_{count,F}^{-1}$. Then:*
$E(sum(\tilde{M}[i..j])) = (d/b) \cdot c$, $\sigma^2(sum(\tilde{M}[i..j])) = \sum_{s=0}^{c}(((d/b) \cdot c - s)^2 \cdot \sum_{h=0}^{t} P_3(h,s))$,
$E(count(\tilde{M}[i..j])) = (d/b) \cdot t$, $\sigma^2(count(\tilde{M}[i..j])) = t \cdot (b-t) \cdot d \cdot \frac{b-d}{b^2 \cdot (b-1)}$.

## 4.5 Estimating sum queries without using count — Case 4

In this case we do not take into account the knowledge about the null elements that will be considered as elements with value 0. We shall use the sum and the max: the min will be used only when there ara no null elements in the block otherwise the min value becomes 0.

**Theorem 7.** *Given the random datacube variable $\tilde{M}$ ranging over $M_{max,F}^{-1} \cap M_{min,F}^{-1} \cap M_{sum,F}^{-1}$ if $t = 0$ or over $M_{max,F}^{-1} \cap M_{sum,F}^{-1}$ otherwise, for each $s$, $0 \leq s \leq c$, and for each $h$, $0 \leq h \leq t$, the probability that the sum of all elements in the range $[i..j]$ be $s$, is: $P_4(s) = \frac{L(d,s) \cdot L(b-d,c-s)}{L(b,c)}$, where $L(x,z)$ is equal to:*

$$\begin{cases} 0 & \text{if } y \cdot u < z, \text{ or otherwise} \\ \binom{x}{y} \cdot \sum_{\gamma=0}^{min(x, \lfloor \frac{z-x \cdot l'}{u'+1} \rfloor)} (-1)^\gamma \cdot \frac{y!}{(y-\gamma)! \cdot max(1,\gamma)} \cdot \binom{x+z-y \cdot l' - \gamma \cdot (u'+1)-1}{x-1} \end{cases}$$

*$l' = l$ if $t = 0$ or $0$ otherwise, and $u' = u - l'$.*

**Proposition 8.** *Let $\tilde{M}$ range over $M_{max,F}^{-1} \cap M_{min,F}^{-1} \cap M_{sum,F}^{-1}$ if $t = 0$ or over $M_{max,F}^{-1} \cap M_{sum,F}^{-1}$ otherwise. Then:*
$E(sum(\tilde{M}[i..j])) = (d/b) \cdot c$, $\sigma^2(sum(\tilde{M}[i..j])) = \sum_{s=0}^{c}(((d/b) \cdot c - s)^2 \cdot P_4(s))$.

# 5 Comparative Analysis

## 5.1 Comparison of the 4 Cases

Let us first consider the count query. We have that the 4 cases give the same results, meaning that for this query the only useful information is the number of non-null elements for each block. Although we cannot compare the 4 cases, we can make some general remarks on the estimation, particularly because we have a closed formula also for the error. Our first observation regards the density of the block, defined as $\delta = t/b$. Considering constants $b$ and $d$, the error gets the maximum value for $\delta = \frac{1}{2}$. It monotonically and symmetrically [4] decreases down to 0 by moving the value of $\delta$ from $\frac{1}{2}$ to 1 and from $\frac{1}{2}$ to 0, respectively. This can be intuitively explained by the fact that, the estimation of the count query corresponds to guessing the number of 1s in $t$ extractions of a binary variable in a sample set composed of $b$ bits, with probability of finding 1 equal to $d/b$. Clearly, $\delta = \frac{1}{2}$ represents the highest degree of uncertainty; on the contrary, for $\delta$ close to 1 (or to 0), the number of different configurations producing this density is small. Similar results can be obtained by considering the size $d$ of the range as the only variable. In this case, the maximum error occurs for $d = \frac{b}{2}$ while the error is 0 for $d = 0$ and $d = b$. Also this result is quite intuitive. Note that, in case the block is sufficiently dense (or sufficiently sparse), the error takes very small values. To give an idea, consider the case of $b = 10000$, $t = 5000$ and $d = \frac{b}{2}$: the error is 25. For a more dense block, for instance with $t = 7500$, a count query with size $d = 7500$ leads an error of $11, 25$. We got very small errors also in the experimental results reported later in this section.

Another intuitive observation regards the size $b$ of the block. It is easy to see, that the error is monotonically increasing with $b$, for a fixed density $\delta$ and a fixed $d > 1$. As expected, larger blocks in general imply higher loss of information.

Let us compare the 4 cases w.r.t. the sum query. They give the same estimation of the sum but different values for the error. The best method is then the one with computes the smallest error. The formulas are not easy to read and, therefore, we cannot characterize the behavior of the 4 cases on the basis of theoretical observations. We need to carry out a number of experiments. So we have taken a datacube block of 100 elements and we have randomly generated the values (including the null elements) for 10 block instances. Then for each instance we have computed a number of sum queries using different range sizes and we have compared the actual error (w.r.t. the estimated answer) and the errors computed by the 4 cases. The results confirm that all 4 cases provide a good estimation as the actual answer $S$ is always inside the interval $S^* \pm 2 \cdot E_S^i$. Surprisingly (at least for us), Case 1 computes smaller errors than Case 2 and Case 4 does the same w.r.t. Case 3. For example, given one of datacubes utilized in experiments and a range query with bounds [1..20] with actual value for the sum of 266 and actual value for count of 19, the estimated sum was 248.6 and the estimated count was 17: so, their respective actual errors were 17.4 and 2.

---

[4] The error evaluated for a density $\delta$ coincides with that evaluated for the density $1 - \delta$

| $R$ | $S$ | $S^*$ | $C$ | $C^*$ | $E_S$ | $E_C$ | $E_S^{1*}$ | $E_S^{2*}$ | $E_S^{3*}$ | $E_S^{4*}$ | $E_C^*$ |
|---|---|---|---|---|---|---|---|---|---|---|---|
| [ 11 : 20 ] | 116 | 124.3 | 9 | 8 | 8.3 | 1 | 39 | 46 | 25 | 18 | 1 |
| [ 41 : 50 ] | 109 | 124.3 | 7 | 8 | 15.3 | 1 | 39 | 46 | 25 | 18 | 1 |
| [ 61 : 70 ] | 98 | 124.3 | 7 | 8 | 26.3 | 1 | 39 | 46 | 25 | 18 | 1 |
| [ 81 : 90 ] | 119 | 124.3 | 8 | 8 | 5.3 | 0 | 39 | 46 | 25 | 18 | 1 |
| [ 1 : 30 ] | 372 | 372.9 | 25 | 25 | 0.9 | 0 | 59 | 70 | 47 | 31 | 2 |
| [ 11 : 40 ] | 337 | 372.9 | 23 | 25 | 35.9 | 2 | 59 | 70 | 47 | 31 | 2 |
| [ 31 : 60 ] | 349 | 372.9 | 25 | 25 | 23.9 | 0 | 59 | 70 | 47 | 31 | 2 |
| [ 51 : 80 ] | 371 | 372.9 | 25 | 25 | 1.9 | 0 | 59 | 70 | 47 | 31 | 2 |
| [ 61 : 90 ] | 365 | 372.9 | 23 | 33 | 7.9 | 10 | 59 | 70 | 47 | 31 | 2 |
| [ 1 : 20 ] | 266 | 248.6 | 19 | 17 | 17.4 | 2 | 52 | 61 | 40 | 27 | 2 |
| [ 21 : 60 ] | 455 | 497.2 | 31 | 33 | 42.2 | 2 | 63 | 74 | 50 | 34 | 2 |
| [ 41 : 80 ] | 480 | 497.2 | 32 | 33 | 17.2 | 1 | 63 | 74 | 50 | 34 | 2 |

**Table 1.** Experimental results: comparison of the 4 cases

The estimated errors were: 52 for Case 1, 61 for Case 2, 40 for Case 3 and 27 for Case 4. The estimated error for the count query coincided with the actual one (2). We obtained a similar behavior for the estimated errors also for the other range queries (some of these results are reported in Table 1). On the basis of the results of our experiments, we argue that the usage of count aggregate data is 'dangerous' as it increases the estimated error. On the other hand, the knowledge about max and min is useful since both Cases 3 and 4 compute smaller errors than Cases 1 and 2. Case 4 seems to be the best method but additional experiments are probably necessary before definitely assigning this title to it. In case one decides to use Case 4, then it is possible to save same space as follows. Since the min value is used in Case 4 only when there are no null elements, it is possible to use the same word for both min and count aggregate data: a 1-bit flag will then state which information is being stored in the word.

## 5.2 Comparison with Barbara&Sullivan's method

Barbara&Sullivan have proposed in [3] a particolar method (called quasi-cubes) to compress a bidimensional ($n \times m$) datacube by storing the sum of values for each row $i$ (suitably converted into probabilities $r_i$) and by constructing a regression line for each column $j$ of the form $p_{ij} = A_j \cdot r_i + B_j$ so that the element $(i, j)$ is estimated by the value $p_{ij} + s_{ij} \cdot \delta_j$, where $\delta_j$ is the average error of the regression and $s_{ij}$ values $\pm 1$ according to the position of the actual element $(i, j)$ w.r.t. the regression line. In sum, the quasi-cubes require the following data: $n$ values $r_i$ for the rows, $m$ tuples $(A_j, B_j, \delta_j)$ for the columns, $n \times m$ bit for the sign $s_{ij}$ and the total sum of all elements. It is also proposed to retain some actual values to improve the estimation but this will obviously increase the size of the compression. To compare the Barbara&Sullivan's method with our

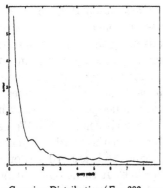

(a) : Gaussian Distribution ($E = 200$, $\sigma = 50$)

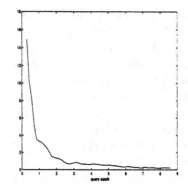

(b) : Gaussian Distribution ($E = 200$, $\sigma = 50$) with 25% of null values

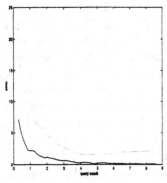

(c) : Different Gaussian Distribution sfor rows ($i$)
$E(i) = 50 + 1.5 \cdot i$; $\sigma(i) = 10 + 0.5 \cdot i$

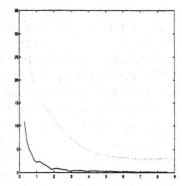

(d): Different Gaussian Distributions for rows ($i$)
$E(i) = 50 + 3 \cdot i$; $\sigma(i) = 10 + i$

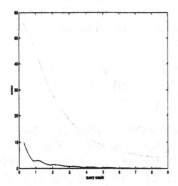

(e) : Different Gaussian Distributions for rows ($i$)
$E(i) = 50 + 6 \cdot i$; $\sigma(i) = 10 + 2 \cdot i$

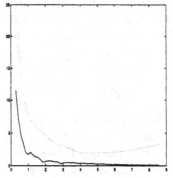

(f) :Different Gaussian Distributions for columns ($j$)
$E(j) = 50 + 1.5 \cdot i$; $\sigma(j) = 10 + 0.5 \cdot i$

Fig. 2. Experimental Results

approach, we have considered several datacubes of size $100 \times 100$, we have run several queries on each datacube and we have evaluated the correct answers and computed the ones determined by the two methods using the same compression factor of 15 (this means blocks of around 50 elements for our method). Since the Barbara&Sullivan's method does not provide any estimation error, the comparison has been made only w.r.t. the estimated values. Figure 2.(a) describes the actual errors of the two methods for datacubes with values generated according to a gaussian distribution with average $E = 200$ and deviation $\sigma = 50$. We have used dotted lines for the results of Barbara&Sullivan's method and full lines for our results. The reported errors refer to various queries that are ordered on the X axis according the ratio "size of the query range/50". It turns out that both methods yield very good results but our method behaves better in general except when the query range is very small. The fact that Barbara&Sullivan's method works better for small ranges is not surprising as the original goal of that method was to estimate single elements. We have obtained similar results by changing the variance of the distribution to the following values: 25, 75 and 100. Indeed our method works a bit better with larger variances. In particular, while average errors of two methods was the same (0.14) with variance 25, the avarage error of Quasi Cubes was 0.84 compared to 0.58 of our method. In the experiments reported in Figure 2.(b), we have modified the datacube generated with the above gaussian distribution (average 200 and variance 50) by inserting around 25% of null elements in a random way. The estimations of Barbara&Sullivan's method become much worse than ours: the distorsion of the nulls is partially absorbed by our block structure. The avarage error of our estimation is 1.93, while that of Quasi Cubes is 16.03. In this cases Barbara&Sullivan's method suggests to retain the positions of the nulls; but, then, the compression factor changes and the comparison becomes more difficult. Subsequent experiments have confirmed that our method works much better when some distorsions are added to a gaussian value distribution. Indeed in the experiments represented in Figures 2.(c) 2.(d) and 2.(e). we have used a different gaussian distribution for each row $i$ according to the following laws:

$$E(i) = 50 + 1.5 \cdot i; \ \sigma(i) = 10 + 0.5 \cdot i \quad \text{(Fig. 2.(c))}$$
$$E(i) = 50 + 3 \cdot i; \ \sigma(i) = 10 + i \quad \text{(Fig. 2.(d))}$$
$$E(i) = 50 + 6 \cdot i; \ \sigma(i) = 10 + 2 \cdot i \quad \text{(Fig. 2.(e))}$$

Similar results, shown in Figure 2.(f), were obtained by making the gaussian distribution vary for each column $i$ according to the same law of Figure 2.(c). In these cases the gap between avarage errors of two estimations was sensible. For instance, for experiments reported in Figure 2.(e) the avarage error of the Barbara&Sullivan's method was 18.8 while that of our method was 1.38.

# References

1. Agarwal, S., Agrawal, R., Deshpande, P., Gupta, A., Naughton, J.F., Ramakrishnan, R., Sarawagi, S., On the Computation of Multidimensional Aggregates, *Proc. of VLDB 1996*, pp. 506-521

2. Byard, J., Schneider, D., The Ins and Outs (and everything in between) of Data Warehousing, *ACM SIGMOD'96 Tutorial Notes*

3. Barbara, D., Sullivan, M., Quasi-Cubes: Exploiting approximations in multidimensional databases, *ACM SIGMOD Record*, 1996

4. Chaudhuri, S., Dayal, U., An Overview of Data Warehousing and OLAP Technology, *ACM SIGMOD Record 26(1)*, March 1997.

5. Codd, E.F., Codd, S.B., Salley, C.T., Providing OLAP (On-Line Analytical Processing) to User-Analysts, *An IT Mandate E.F. Codd and Associates, 1993*, Available from http: //www.arborsoft.com/papers/intro.html

6. Faloutsos, C., Jagadish, H.V., Sidiripoulos, N.D., Recovering Information from Summary Data, *Proc. VLDB'97*, Athens, 1997

7. Gray, J., Bosworth, A., Layman, A., Pirahesh, H., Data Cube: A Relational Aggregation Operator Generalizing Group-By, Cross-Tab, and Sub-Total, *Proc. of the ICDE 1996*, pp. 152-159

8. Haas, P.J., Naughton, J.F., Seshadri, S., Stokes, L., Sampling Based Estimation of the Number of Distinct Values of an Attribute, *Proc. of the VLDB 1995*, pp. 311-322

9. Harinarayan, V., Rajaraman, A., Ullman, J. D., Implementing Data Cubes Efficiently, *Proc. of the ACM SIGMOD 1996*, pp. 205-216

10. Hellerstein, J.M., Haas, P.J., Wang, H.J., Online Aggregation, Proc. of ACM SIGMOD'97, pp. 171-182.

11. Ho, C.T., Agrawal, R., Megiddo, N., Srikant, R., Range Queries in OLAP Data Cubes, *Proc. of the ACM SIGMOD Conference 1997*, pp. 73-88

12. Ioannidis, Y., Poosala, V., Balancing histogram optimality and practicality for query result size estimation, *Proc. of the ACM SIGMOD Conf. 1995*, pp. 233-244

13. Kenan Technologies, An Introduction to Multidimensional Database Technology, Available from http: //www.kenan.com/

14. Jagadish, H.V., Koudas, N., Muthukrishnan, S., Poosala, V., Sevcik, K., Suel, T., Optimal histograms for quality guarantees, *Proc. of the ACM SIGMOD Conference 1998*, pp. 275-286

15. Mannino, M.V., Chu, P., Sager, T., Statistical profile estimation in database systems, *ACM Computing Survey 20*, 3, pp. 192-221.

16. MicroStrategy Inc., The Case for Relational OLAP. A white paper available from http: //www.strategy.com/

17. Poosala, V., Ioannidis, Y.E., Haas, P.J., Shekita, E.J., Improved histograms for selectivity estimation of range predicates, *Proc. of the ACM SIGMOD Conference 1996*, pp. 294-305

18. Shukla, A., Deshpande, P.M., Naughton, J.F., Ramasamy, K., Storage estimation for multidimensional aggregates in the presence of hierarchies, *Proc. of VLDB 1996*, pp. 522-531.

# Compact Representation: An Approach to Efficient Implementation for the Data Warehouse Architecture

Nikolaos Kotsis    Douglas R. McGregor

Department of Computer Science University of Strathclyde, 26 Richmond street,
Glasgow G11XH, UK
nick,douglas@cs.strath.ac.uk

**Abstract.** Data Warehousing requires effective methods for processing and storing large amounts of data. OLAP applications form an additional tier in the data warehouse architecture and in order to interact acceptably with the user, typically data pre-computation is required. In such a case compressed representations have the potential to improve storage and processing efficiency. This paper proposes a compressed database system which aims to provide an effective storage model. We show that in several other stages of the Data Warehouse architecture compression can also be employed. Novel systems engineering is adopted to ensure that compression/decompression overheads are limited, and that data reorganisations are of controlled complexity and can be carried out incrementally. The basic architecture is described and experimental results on the TPC-D and other datasets show the performance of our system.

## 1 Introduction

The Relational Model [1] proved a sound base for database systems and has become the dominant standard approach to operational databases or On Line Transaction Processing (OLTP). The requirements of the On Line Analytical Processing (OLAP) are distinctly different from those of OLTP [2], [3]. Data Warehouses are integrated databases providing collected information from various heterogeneous information sources [4], while OLAP applications requiring aggregation in several dimensions. Multidimensional aggregation is a complex process and to provide access in real-time, *materialized views* are employed. These are pre-computed and stored sets of aggregated values and may take up large volumes of storage [27],[5]. Several researchers have proposed techniques for selection only subsets for materialization [6],[7],[8],[28]. However, in the existence of hierarchies in dimensions, the storage requirement is even higher than for a single level domain. Thus materialized views provide at best a partial solution in the Data Warehouse environment [9]. There is thus a need for a new generation of a DBMS able to achieve orders of magnitude improvements in performance.

Compression has been used to a limited extend on OLTP databases [13],[14],[15]. In the OLAP environment applications are less mature but compression through bit indexing has been applied in some of the systems [38], [16]. The advantages of data compression apply widely in database architecture, permitting more rapid processing more effective I/O and better communications performance [17]. In main memory databases for high performance applications a typical approach to data representation is to characterize domain values as a sequence of strings. Tuples are represented as a set of fixed length pointers or tokens referring to the corresponding domain values [18]. This approach provides significant compression but leaves each domain value represented by a fixed length pointer/token, typically a machine word in length. An alternative strategy is to store a fixed length reference number for each domain value instead of a pointer to the value [18],[19]. An optimal strategy for generating lexical tokens is described by Wang and Lavington [20]. Despite the considerable research into memory resident databases [10],[11],[12],[21],[39] most current DBMS are built around disk resident data. The balance is between the greater compactness of storage, with the greater efficiency of some storage operations, versus the greater software complexity and processing overheads of de-tokenizing, particularly if the symbol table is backing-store resident. The Peterlee Relational Test Vehicle PRTV - an early relational database prototype [22] applied two-dimensional compression by sorting similar records into adjacent locations and storing only a flag bit per field, with the differences. However such methods result in variable length tuples, destroying the simple addressability of fixed-length tuples. Compression/decompression may then become the dominant element in processing. Common compression techniques like Huffman [23], or LZW coding [24], are unsuitable for processing in databases because we require relational operations to work on the compressed data as well as random access to the rows of the table. The method of representing the relations in a compressed format must be such that the system is efficient in each of its modes of processing (e.g. loading, update retrieval).

# 2 Applying Compression in Data Warehousing

The Data Warehouse concept can be found in [25], [4], [3]. There are four stages, in the DW configuration, where compression can be applied:

- **Information Source to the Data Warehouse transfer:** This is an *in-advance* approach, and the encode/decode process is not time critical. Compressed data use less bandwidth and can thus be sent faster across communications networks. Compression thus facilitates loading and update of the Data Warehouse.
- **The Data Warehouse query stage:** Compression can result on average in $X8$ reduction in data volume in practice [26] while [17] observed processing $X6$ faster than with uncompressed data. For disk-based data a compressed representation reduces the I/O traffic, while more information can be retained in cache or main memory. For main memory databases, the benefit is retaining the faster RAM performance while reducing the cost of the necessary RAM storage. In Hibase, [26] where the compressed factor is at least eight, the cost of RAM is a relatively insignificant factor.
- **Distributed database systems (Data Marts) :** These systems are used as departmental subsets focused on selected subjects of users' interests [CD97]. Our system can potentially be used for caching. Data Marts are usually much smaller in size than the DW database.
- **Back-up storage and Recovery :** When the addressabilty of the individual tuples need not be preserved a further reduction in data volume can be achieved by

applying a secondary lossless compression algorithm prior to archiving and transmitting.

- **Client-server environment** : Potentially the compressed representation could be utilized in a client-server architecture. The dictionary could be distributed to every client and the compressed representation would be used for data transfer and querying. The volume cost of the dictionary is not significant considering the volume of the views when they are fully materialized. Table 1 shows the volume of the dictionary compared to the raw data and the materialized views for the TPC-D benchmark dataset [36], table Lineitem (scale factor 0.001).

|  | Data Volume |
|---|---|
| Dictionary | 1 MB |
| Raw data | 3.97 MB |
| Materialized views | 3.7 GB |

**Table 1.** Compression overhead compare to the Materialized views volume (Bytes)

## 3 Compressed relations

Table 2 has a single relation that describes the characteristics of a number of chips. If this is stored as a file of records, we have to make each field of these records big enough to hold the largest value that any of the records stores in that field. Since, is not likely to know exactly how large the individual values may be, the tendency will be to err on the side of caution and make the fields longer than is strictly necessary. In Hibase [26], *First Order Compression* reduces each field to an integer containing just sufficient bits to encode all the values that occur within the domain of that field in the database. In Table 2 since there are seven distinct part names, the parts column of the relation could be represented as a list of 3 *bit* numbers. Similarly, since there are only 3 distinct values for the number of pins, these could be represented as *2 bit* numbers. Once similar compression has been applied to the other fields, the resulting tuples are found to be only *7 bits* long (Table 2). Now the relation occupies only *49 bits*. Our compression mechanism converts the values in each column of a relational table into short integers, using a dictionary that is unique to the domain of each column. The compressed code for a field value is given by its position (i.e. subscript) in the corresponding dictionary which is used for fields containing text. Numeric fields are coded directly as variable length binary numbers and do not require the dictionary mechanism.

| | | | | | | | |
|---|---|---|---|---|---|---|---|
| ep900 | 40 | CMOS | Yes | 000 | 00 | 0 | 0 |
| ep310 | 20 | CMOS | Yes | 001 | 01 | 0 | 0 |
| DMPAL16L8 | 20 | TTL | Yes | 010 | 01 | 1 | 0 |
| DMPAL10L8 | 20 | TTL | Yes | 011 | 01 | 1 | 0 |
| MPM5032 | 28 | CMOS | No | 100 | 10 | 0 | 1 |
| CY2901 | 40 | CMOS | No | 101 | 00 | 0 | 1 |
| CY2909 | 28 | CMOS | No | 110 | 10 | 0 | 1 |

**Table 2.** The CHIPSEC database contents and its compressed representation

## 3.1 Data Structure for Relations

In the conventional horizontal data organization, the tuples of a relation are stored as records with fields adjacent o one another. In disk resident database systems the horizontal organization is more popular. It has the advantage that a single disk access fetches all fields of a tuple. Even for non-compressed RAM databases, the implementational simplicity of this approach commends it. It is equally valid however, to think of the relation as a sequence of columns, and implement these columns as vectors so that corresponding fields in successive tuples are stored adjacently-vertical data organization as shown in Figure1. A compressed data representation imposes constraints, which favour a vertical organization.

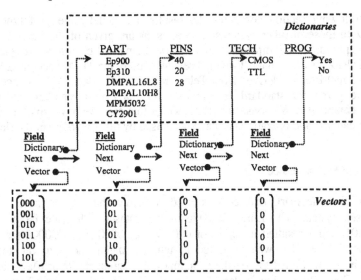

**Fig. 1.** A relation represented in a columnar format

Unlike a conventional database system, the field widths are not known when the schema is created. This is particularly the case when the data of the relation is being extended by tuple at a time insertion or update. The number of bits required to represent the domain of a field is proportional to the logarithm of the domain's current cardinality. As data is loaded the cardinality grows, and with it the number of bits required to represent a token. It is necessary for the data structures, which represent the relation, to be able to dynamically alter to accommodate varying tuple widths and in particular to do so incrementally with known overheads of limited and predictable extend. For example, suppose we have a field (e.g. the Chipname Field in our examples) that requires *3 bits* to encode its domain. If the number of unique strings used in the domain rises above *8*, we will need *4 bits* to represent them in encoded form. An extended version of the Hibase's description can be found [26].

### 3.2 Querying a Compressed Database

An essential feature of our approach is that operations are applied directly to datasets in their compressed format. Before a query is posed, is translated into the compressed domain, thus the amount of data that has to be moved into the CPU and processed is significantly reduced. The final answer has to be converted to the uncompressed representation. The computational cost of this decompression will be borne only by the tuples that are returned in the result, and normally a small fraction of those processed. The relational representation also includes compressed indexes to facilitate rapid access to required records. Dictionary and Indexing techniques will not be described in this paper but are used in the Hibase prototype and are partly responsible for its good performance.

# 4. Experimental results

The following section compares the results obtained by the prototype Hibase system with those of other systems. Comparisons are given of the volumes of data storage required. Data compression depends on the natural occurrence frequencies of different elements of the data. Two data sets were used, the TPC-D benchmark dataset [37] and a real-life one derived from Telecommunications data. Performance comparisons are given for standard benchmark operations on a standard international database dataset (the Wisconsin benchmark). In this case we have given timings for the same datasets and operations as have been used by other workers in the field.

## 4.1 Storage Performance

The TPC-D benchmark dataset was used to show the storage savings of the compressed system. The Lineitem table of the dataset with scale factors 0.0001, 0.001, 0.01, and 1 resulted in tuples of 600, 6000, 60000 and 6000000 respectively was chosen. The table was restricted to ten dimensions prior to the tests. The dimensions were: Orderkey, Partkey, Suppkey, Linenumber, Returnflag Linestatus, Shipdate, Commitdate, Receiptdate, Shipinstuct. Figure 2 shows the effectiveness of the compression. Table 3 gives a comparison of the volumes required for the four different relations derived from a Telecom data set. The datasets have mixed textual and numeric fields., each consisting of a single large relational table associating European Internet host and domain names with their IP addresses. The tables had eleven columns; one for the host name, four for the components of the domain names and six for the fields of the IP address. For each dataset, a primary index was constructed on the hostname along with a secondary composite index on the fields of the IP address. The overall compression factor is approximately 0.5. The Hibase prototype requires only approximately one eighth of the storage required by each conventional counterpart [24]. When the addressabilty of the individual tuples need not be preserved, a further reduction in data volume can be achieved by applying a secondary lossless compression algorithm prior to archiving and transmitting (Table 3). These results give an indication that the upper limit of compression is likely to be approximately twice that of the current prototype system.

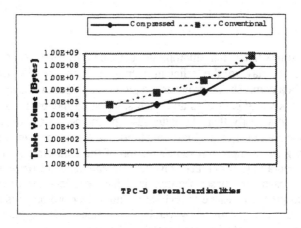

**Fig. 2.** Comparison in storage between Hibase and ASCII for the TPC-D dataset (scale factor 0.001)

| Flat File    (MB) | HIBASE Compression (KB) | HIBASE + LZW  Compression (KB) |
|---|---|---|
| 15 | 7775 | 3686 |
| 10 | 5305 | 2178 |
| 5 | 2420 | 1049 |
| 1 | 527 | 227 |

**Table 3.** First order compression (Hibase) and Second  order compression (LZW).

|  | No of Processors | 10% selection (ms) | 1% selection (ms) |
|---|---|---|---|
| Hibase | 1x 66 MHz  486 DX2 | 178 | 14 |
| Starburst | 1x25 MHz RS6000 | 169 | - |
| Monet | 4x150 MHz  MIPS | 900 | 287 |
| Prisma | 5x 68020 | - | 248 |

**Table 4.** 10K Wisconsin Benchmark: 13  numeric and 3 string attributes.

### 4.2 Processing  Performance comparison

A number of groups have published performance results using the Wisconsin benchmarks [30]. These include work on parallel database architectures, and also approaches using conventional disk based systems in conjunction with high performance memory [31], [32], [33], [34], [35], [36], [21]. Table 4 shows the Hibase performance figures relative to the others approaches for a 10K tuple Wisconsin Database, comprising 30 numerical and 3 string attributes.

# Conclusion

This paper demonstrates that appropriate data compression techniques have an important role to play in the efficient storage models for the Data warehouse architecture. Data compression provides a region of high performance, inaccessible to conventional disk-based databases and main-store-based databases, being faster than the former and less costly than the latter. The prototype system demonstrates good performance over a range of database functions. As many operations as possible are conducted using the compressed representation of the data directly, making processing and I/O operations faster than on the corresponding uncompressed data. The compressed representation described here is in fact beneficial throughout the storage hierarchy, from processor cache to archive medium. Our prototype is not a complete database management system. However it is a demonstration of the validity of the design concept at the level of the basic relational operations.

# References

1. Codd, E.F. A relational model for large shared databanks. In *Comm.of ACM* 13 (6):377-387, 1970
2. Codd, E.F., Codd, S.B. , Salley. C.T. Providing OLAP (On Line Analytical Processing) to User Analyst: An IT Mandate. Available at http://www.arborsoft.com/OLAP.html.
3. Chaudhuri, S., Dayal, U."An Overview of Data Warehousing and OLAP Technology *"Technical Report MSR- TR-97-14.,*Microsoft Research Advanced Technology.
4. Widom. J. Research Problems in Data Warehousing. In *Proc. 4th Intl. CIKM Conf.*, 1995.
5. Shukla, A., Deshpande, M.P., Naughton, J.F., Ramasamy, K. Storage Estimation for Multi-dimensional Aggregates in the Presence of Hierarchies. In. *Proc. 22nd VLDB*, pages 522-531,Mumbay, Sept. 1996.
6. Agarwal, S., Agrawal, R., Deshpande, M.P., Gupta, A., Naughton, J.F., Ramakrishnan, R., Sarawagi, S. On the Computation of Multidimensional Aggregates. *Proc. 22$^{nd}$ VLDB*, page 602, Mumbay, Sept. 1996.
7. Harinarayan, V., A.Rajaraman, J.D. Ullman. Implementing Data Cubes Efficiently. In *Proc. ACM SIGMOD '96*, Montreal, June 1996.
8. Gupta, V., Harinarayan, V., Rajaraman, A., Ullman, J. Index Selection for Olap *In Proc. 13th ICDE*, Manchester, UK April 1997.
9. Gupta, A.What is the Warehouse Problem? Are materialized views the answer? In Proc. *VLDB*, Mumbay, Sept. 1996.
10. Rosenberg, J., Keedy, J.K., Abramson, D. Addressing mechanisms for large Virtual memories. *Technical report, St.Andrews University, 1990*. CS/90/2.
11. Garcia-Molina, H. Salem, K. Main memory database systems: an overview. *IEEE Transactions on Knowledge and Data Engineering 4:6, 1992*, pp 509-516.
12. Mathews, R.Spintronics In *New Scientist*, February 98. Pages 24-28
13. Roth, M.A., Van Horn, S.J.Database Compression. In *SIG MOD RECORD*, Vol 22, No.3, September 1993
14. Iyer, B.R., Wilhite, D. Data Compression Support in Databases. In *Proc.of the 20nd VLDB*, page 695, Chile, 1994.
15. Cormack. G.V. Data Compression on a Database System. In *Communications of the ACM*, Volume 28, Number 12, 1985.
16. Ramakrishnan, R. *Database Management Systems*. WCB/ McGraw-Hill. 1998.

17. Graefe, G., Shapiro, L.D. Data Compression and Data Performance. *In Proc. of ACM/IEEE Computer Science Symp. on Applied Computing*, Kansas City, Apr.1991.

18. Pucheral, P., Thevenin, J., and Valduriez P., Efficient main memory data management using DBGraph storage model *Proc. of the 16th VLDB Conference, Brisbane 1990*, pp 683-695.

19. Goldstein, R.,and Strnad A.The MacAIMS data management system. *Proc. of the ACM SCIFIDET Workshop* on Data Description and Access, 1970.

20. Wang C., Lavington S.,The lexical token converter. high performance associative Dictionary for large knowledge bases. Department of Computer Science, University of Essex Internal Report CSM-133.

21. Lehman, T.J., Shekita, E.J.,Cabrera L. An Evaluation of Starburst's Memory Resident Storage Component. *IEEE Transactions Knowledge and Data Engineering*.Vol 4.No6,Dec 1992.

22. Todd, S.J.P., Hall, P.A., Hall, V., Hitchcock, P. An Algebra for Machine Computation" *IBM Publication UKSC 0066 1975*.

23. Huffman, D.A. A Method for the Construction of Minimum-Redundancy Codes", *Proc. of the IRE*, 40: 1098-1101 September 1952.

24. Welch, T.A. A technique for high Performance Data Compression , *IEEE Computer 17 June 1984), 8-19*.

25. Kimball, R. *"The Data Warehouse" Toolkit*. John Wiley, 1996.

26. Cockshott, W.P., McGregor, D.R., Kotsis, N., Wilson J. Data Compression in Database Systems in *IDEAS'98, Cardiff, July 1998*.

27. Labio, W.J., Quass, D., Adelberg, B."Physical Database Design for Data Warehouses." *TR-CS University of Stanford*.

28. Baralis,.E., Paraboschi,S., Teniente E. Materialized View Selection in a Multidimensional Databases. In *Proc. 23nd VLDB*, page 156, Athens, Sept. 1997.

29. Cockshott, W.P., Cowie, A.J., Rusell, G.W., McGregor, D. Memory Resident Databases: Reliability, Compression and Performance. *Research Report ARCH 11-93,Computer Science*, University of Strathclyde.

30. Bitton, D., DeWitt, D.J., Turbyfill, C. Benchmarking Database Systems–a systematic approach, in *Proc. VLDB 1983*.

31. Boncz, P.A., Kersten, M.L Monet: An Impressionist sketch of an advanced database . system. *Proceedings IEEE BIWIT workshop*. July1990. San Sebastian, Spain.

32. De Witt, D.J., Ghandeharizadeh, D., Schneider, D., Bricker, A., Hsiao, H., Rasmussen,R. The GAMMA database machine project. *IEEE Transactions on Knowledge and Data Engineering*, 2 ,44-62 (1990).

33. De Witt, D.J., Ghandeharizadeh, D., Schneider, D., Jauhari, R., Muralikrishna, M. Sharma, A. 1987. A single user evaluation of the GAMMA database machine. In *Proceedings of the 5th International Workshop on Database Machines*, October, Tokyo, Japan.

34. Leland, M.D.P., Roome, W.D., 1987.The Silicon Database Machine: Rational Design and Results.In *Proc.of the 5th International Workshop on Database Machines*. October, Tokyo, Japan.

35. Wischut, A.N., Flokstra, J., Apers, PMG., 1992. Parallelism in a Main Memory DBMS : The performance of PRISMA/DB, In *Proc. of the 18th International Conference of Very Large Databases*, August, Vancouver, Canada.

36. Eich, M.H.,1987. MARS: The design of a main memory database machine", In *Proc. of the 5th International Workshop on Database Machines*, October, Tokyo, Japan.

37. Raab, R. editor. TPC Benchmark™ D Standard Specification Revision 1.3.1 Transaction Processing Council 1998.

38. Wu, M.C., Buchmann, A.P. Encoded Bitmap Indexing for Data Warehouses. *In SIGMOD Conference* 1999.

39. DeWitt, D.J., Katz, R.H., Olken, F., Shapiro L.D., Stonebraker M.R., Wood, D. 1984 Implementation techniques for main memory database systems. *In Proceedings of ACM SIGMOD Conference*, New York, 1.

# On the Independence of Data Warehouse from Databases in Maintaining Join Views

Wookey Lee

SungKyul University, Anyang 8 Dong, Kyungki Do, Korea, 430-742
wook@hana.sungkyul.ac.kr

**Abstract.** In maintaining data warehouse views without interfering current databases, a *Join Differential File* (*JDF*) scheme is introduced. The scheme uses differential files from relevant logs of databases and join differential files by capturing the referential integrity signal between the base relations. Cost functions are formulated, that are analyzed the performance of the *JDF*, the base method, and the pseudo differential method in various conditions. The algorithm is shown to be much better than the other two methods with the high communication speed, more screening situation, and small *join differential files*.

## 1 Introduction

Data warehouse is a repository of the integrated information, available for querying and analyzing (i.e., DSS and data mining) [2], [10], [11]. The warehouse information, mainly derived from the base relations, can be stored as materialized views and can be aggregated or manipulated as multi-dimensional summaries. If some portions of the base relations are changed, the change should be applied to the views in order to guarantee the correctness of the data. Studies have been undertaken extensively on what is known as the *view maintenance problem* or the *materialized view* [1], [3], [7], [15], [17].

The *materialized view maintenance* with *join* operation is known to be *complex* [13]. Because the join is one of the most time-consuming and data intensive operations in relational database systems. In the data warehouse environment, join operations are very important to support multi-dimensional databases and an efficient join algorithm is essential [2], [3]

Three ways can be classified to support the join materialized views such as the base table method (*base*), the pseudo differential method (*pseudo*), and fully differential method (*differential* or possibly called *DJF*). The *base* method is the simplest way. It is to re-execute the view definition, but it may cause unacceptable costs each time [4]. Similarly joining after full replication or that of versioning may be an alternative for the data warehouse environment. Several approaches such as [9], [11], and [15] are suggested, but they are a kind of modified base table methods and usually are used to lock the current databases. In some cases, additional efforts are needed to make those replications (or versions) consistent.

Another efficient approach such as *Incremental Access Method* [14], *coherency indexes* [6], and *relevant logging* [3] is addressed. It maintains only the tuple identifiers (*TIDs*) and defers the updates to the base table as well as to the (join) views. It, however, turns out to be a *base table method* at the point of updating the base tables and the relevant (join) views. So we can appropriately call it a *pseudo differential* method.

In this paper we propose a join view update algorithm with *differential mode*. In suggesting a join view update scheme, a basic principle is kept in mind; In order to make the data warehouse system more efficient, interferences on the current database should be minimized.

The rest of the paper is organized as follows. Section 2 introduces the architecture of data warehouse views including a motivating example. Section 3 addresses the Join view-updating scheme. The cost functions with parameters and the performance analyses are suggested in Section 4 and 4 respectively. Section 6 concludes the paper.

## 2 The Architecture for the Data Warehouse Views

$R_i(TID_i, A_i, A_{FK})$ and $R_j(TID_j, A_j)$ are base relations, where the $TID's$ are tuple identifiers of the base relations, $A_r$ (for all $r = i, j$) is a set of attributes, and the $A_{FK}$ is a foreign key of the $R_i$ that is relevant to $TID_j$ of $R_j$. The data warehouse view is materialized and defined as $V(VID_v, A_v, C_v)$ where $VID_v$ is a view identifier, $C_v$ is a conditional predicate, and $A_v$ means a set of attributes of the view (for all $v \square i, j$). Let us suppose that we have a materialized view ($V$) defined as follows.

*Example 1* Employee information is collected in *EMP* table, and *DEPT* table has the department-name; *EMP*(e#, *salary, dno, time*) and *DEPT*(d#, *dname, time*). The view is defined as follows:

CREATE MATERIALIZED VIEW V (no, salary, dno, department, time)

AS SELECT E.e#, E.salary, D.dno, D.dname, T.time

FROM EMP E, DEPT D, TIME T WHERE E.e# = D.d# and T.time=E.time;

Suppose that the contents of table *EMP, DEPT, TIME* and the view *V* (fact_table) are represented with an ER Diagram as follows.

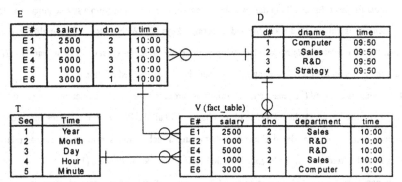

The base relations are changed by transactions. In this paper we want to suggest the changed portion as a *differential file (DF)*. The file can be derived from the active log of the base relation. We use the differential file schema and its algorithm as [17]. The *DF* of base relation ($R_i$) is defined as $dR_i(TID_i, A_i,$ *operation-type, $TS^d$*). The *operation-type* indicates the type of operations applied to the changed tuple. It has one of the two codes: *'insert'* or *'delete'*. A modification, of course, assumed to be a delete and an insert in series with the same time-stamp. The $TS^d$ is a time-stamp that the tuple of $DF$ is appended. (The $d$ represents the $DF$.) Without loss of generality, the time-stamp is assumed to be the same, so $TS^d = TS$. Then each record of changes is appended in the $DF$s (say, $dR_i$ and $dR_j$) respectively.

**Example   2** We suggest some changes in the example   1 as follows. In $dE$, the first tuple represents that a new employee `e7` is entered into the company at time 10:20. We can know that the salary of employee 'e2' is raised from 1000 to 1500 and his/her department is moved at time 10:25. Then employee 'e1' is deleted and 'e8' is newly inserted. In table $dD$, we can also find that the name of the 'Sales' department is changed to customer-service (CS).

dE

| e# | Salary | dno | operation-type | TS |
|----|--------|-----|----------------|-------|
| e7 | 4500 | 2 | insert | 10:20 |
| e2 | 1000 | 3 | delete | 10:25 |
| e2 | 1500 | 2 | insert | 10:25 |
| e1 | 2500 | 2 | delete | 10:30 |
| e8 | 3000 | 4 | insert | 10:40 |

dD

| d# | dname | operation-type | TS |
|----|-------|----------------|-------|
| 2 | Sales | Delete | 10:35 |
| 2 | CS | Insert | 10:35 |

## 3. The Updating Join View Scheme

### 3.1 The Differential Join File

In maintaining the *join materialized views*, we assume that joins are established within a *referential integrity (RI)* constraint. Of course there are so many non-foreign key joins, but joining by the foreign key[1] is the most frequent. Especially in data warehouse environment, the join with a star-schema or with a snowflake schema is almost always established in foreign keys [2]. Without loss of generality, we can assume that the base relation ($R_i$) has a relationship with another relation(s) (say, $R_j$) such that $A_{FK}$  $TID_j$. In this case the $R_i$ is said to be a referencing relation, and the $R_j$ a referenced relation.

When a tuple is changed (i.e., inserted, deleted, or updated) in a base table, a referential integrity (RI) constraint can be fired to check the relevance of the change. Not all the RI operations, but the insertions in the referencing relation are considered. Since the other changes such as an insert in the referenced relation and deletes in both referencing and referenced relation can be recorded in the $DF$s [11].

In this paper in order to update join materialized views without locking base relations, a new file called a *join differential file (JDF)* is introduced. The JDF is derived from the tuples of the referenced relation that the RI constraint indicates. The schema of the JDF of table $R_j$ is defined as $jR_j(TID_j, A_j, TS^j)$.

---

[1]) In establishing the *referential integrity (RI)* constraints, we assume that '*the safeness condition*' [12] is satisfied regardless of the firing order of integrity constraints [8].

The $TS^j$ is the time-stamp that the tuple of *JDF* is appended. The superscript $j$ represents the *JDF*. Without loss of generality the time-stamp is assumed to be $TS^j = TS$.

In maintaining the *JDF*, the duplicated tuples should be eliminated. For screening duplicated tuples, various methods are suggested such as [1], [3], and [17]. In this paper, we adopt [17]. The *Algorithm AppendJDF* represents how the *JDF* is appended. The tuple in the referenced relation indicated by the *RI* (due to an insert in the referencing relation) is appended in the *JDF*. The algorithm *DeleteJDF* represents the duplicate elimination procedure. Basically the algorithm prevents the *JDF* from being increased unceasingly.

| Algorithm AppendJDF | Algorithm DeleteJDF |
|---|---|
| Input: $jR_j$, the RI trigger in $dR_i$ | Input: $jR_j$, $dR_i$, $dR_j$, and an input to $jR_j$ |
| Output: Consistent $jR_j$ | Output: Consistent $jR_j$ |
| Method: | Method: |
| [1] If there is an RI trigger in $dR_i$, do | [1] If there is an input in $dR_j$ or in $jR_j$, else [6] |
| [2] If the trigger is an insert, else [5] | [2] If there is the same TID in $jR_j$ with the input of $jR_j$, else [4] |
| [3] Append the tuple that the trigger indicates in the $jR_j$. | [3] Then substitute the tuple in $jR_j$ by the input value |
| [4] Do the *DeleteJDF* | [4] If there is the same TID in $jR_j$ with the input of $dR_j$, else [6] |
| [5] End | [5] Then delete the tuple in $jR_j$ |
| | [6] End |

*Example  3* In the example  2, in order to insert a tuple (say, *e7*) in *EMP*, the *RI* checking for the relevance is required. In this case, the check gets confirmation, for the foreign key *dno*=2 exists in *DEPT*. Then we can get the tuple *dno* = 2 from the base table *DEPT* and append it to the *JDF* (say, *jD*). By the second operation (*e2*), *dno* = 2 is substituted the same tuple with the time-stamp 10:25 in *jD*. But at time 10:35 the duplicate elimination activated by a modification in *dD*, thus the *dno* = 2 is deleted in *jD*. Then by the last operation in *dE*, *dno* = 4 is appended. Therefore the *jD* is as follows; *jD* = {4, *strategy, 10:40*}.

## 3.2 Maintaining Join Materialized Views

Using the two files *DF* and *JDF* introduced above, the data warehouse can maintain the join-materialized views independent of the current database relations. In updating the views, it is necessary to determine which tuple needs to refer other relations. For the deleted tuples, it is sufficient to send the *TID* (with its *TS*) to the view. For inserted cases, all the changed contents (i.e., $dR_i$, $dR_j$, and $jR_j$) should be sent to the view. With these files, the view can be updated. It means that in maintaining the join-materialized view by the *JDF*, there is no need to lock the base tables.

*Example  4* With the *DFs* (*dE* and *dD*) and the *JDF* (*jD*), the join view in the example  1 can be refreshed. The deleted tuple {*e1, 2500, 2, delete, 10:30*} need not to refer the base table *D*. The other tuples of *dE* and *dD* in example  2 can be joined with the tuples of *jD* in example  3. Then the join data warehouse view (*V*) can be updated without locking the base tables at time 11:00 as follows.

| no | Salary | Dno | department | Time |
|----|--------|-----|------------|-------|
| e2 | 1000 | 2 | CS | 11:00 |
| e4 | 5000 | 3 | R&D | 11:00 |
| e5 | 2500 | 2 | CS | 11:00 |
| e6 | 3000 | 1 | computer | 11:00 |
| e7 | 4500 | 2 | CS | 11:00 |
| e8 | 3000 | 4 | Strategy | 11:00 |

## 3.3 The Base Table Algorithms

In comparing the algorithms, we consider *Semi-join* as a base table method (*Algorithm Base*) and a pseudo-differential method (*Algorithm Pseudo*). The *algorithm Pseudo* is assumed to utilize a set of tuple identifiers and adopts *Semi-join* in joining a view. The distribution of *operation type* among tuples is a random variable; it is assumed that the *operation type* distribution is the same as that of the differential tuples. The algorithms are addressed as follows.

## 4 Parameters and Cost Functions

| *Algorithm Base* | *Algorithm Pseudo* |
|------------------|--------------------|
| Input: join view $v$, $R_i$, $R_j$ | Input: join view $v$, $dR_i$, $R_i$, $dR_j$, $R_j$ |
| Output: Consistent view $v$ | Output: Consistent view $v$ |
| Method: | Method: |
| [1] For $R_i$ $\overline{Null}$ Do | [1] For $dR_i$ or $dR_j$ $\overline{Null}$ Do |
| [2] Read all tuples in the $R_I$ | [2] Read all tuples in the base table $dR_i$ and $dR_j$ |
| [3] Read the tuples of $R_j$ that matches with the attributes of $R_i$ | [3] Update $R_i$ and $R_j$ |
| [4] Join those tuples to the view $v$ | [4] Do Semi-join with $R_i$ and $R_j$ |
| [5] Update the view $v$ | [5] Join those tuples and send it to the view $v$ |
|  | [6] Update the view $v$ |

## 4.1 Parameters

$R_r$, $dR_r$, $jR_r$     Base table, *DF*, and *JDF* of $R_r$ respectively for $r = i, j$.

$dR_{i,D}$, $dR_{i,I}$     A set of deleted and inserted tuples in *DF* of $R_i$ respectively.

$B$     Page size (bytes).

$C_{I/O}$, $C_{com}$     I/O cost (ms/block) and transmission cost (bits/s).

$\Phi[k, n, m]$     Cost that accesses $k$ records in a file of $n$ records stored in $m$ pages [5].

$N(dR_i)$, $N(jR_i)$     Number of tuples of $dR_i$ per page ($=B/W_{Ri}$) and the number of *JDF* respectively.

$\zeta_s$, $SF$     Screen factor and the *Semi-join* factor respectively.

$W_B$, $H_B$     Width and the height of the B$^+$ tree respectively, where $H_B = \log_{B/W} \zeta_s * N(R)$.

$W_I$, $W_D$     Width (bytes) of each tuple with the *operation-type* = *insert* and *delete* respectively.

$W_{dRi}$, $W_v$     Width of $dR_i$ and width of view $v$ respectively.

## 4.2 The Cost Function of *JDF*

I/O cost functions and communication cost functions are denoted by *NIO*'s and *NCOM*'s respectively. In this paper we divide the inserted tuple and the deleted tuple. For the size of the deleted tuple is apparently smaller than that of inserted tuple. It is sufficient for the deleted tuple to send the identifier and its time-stamp (instead of *all* the tuple contents) in maintaining join (data warehouse) views. Cost functions and their explanations are denoted as follows:

$NIO1$ = Cost of reading $dR_i$ and maintaining it = $C_{I/O}[N(dR_{i,D})W_D + N(dR_{i,I})W_I]/B + 2*C_{I/O}[(H_{dRi}-1)+\Phi[SF*N(dR_i), SF*N(dR_i)W_{dRi}/B, a_s* SF*N(dR_i)W_{dRi}/B]]$.

$NIO2$ = Cost of reading $dR_j$ and maintaining it

$= C_{I/O}[N(dR_{j,D})W_D + N(dR_{j,I})W_I]/B + 2*C_{I/O}[(H_{dRj}-1)+\Phi[N(dR_j), N(dR_j)W_{dRj}/B, a_s*N(dR_j)W_{dRj}/B]]$.

$NIO3$ = Cost of reading $jR_j$ and maintaining the *JDF*

$= C_{I/O}*N(jR_j)*W_R/B + 2*C_{I/O}[(H_{jRj}-1)+\Phi[N(jR_j), N(jR_j)W_B/B, a_s*N(jR_j)W_B/B]]$.

$NIO4$ = Cost of accessing the $B^+$ tree of the view index and reading the view table

$= 2*C_{I/O}[(H_V-1)+\Phi[N(V), N(V)W_V/B, a_s*N(V)W_V/B]]$.

$NCOM1$ = Cost of transmitting tuples $(dR_i)$ to the view $\delta$ $8* SF*N(dR_i)*W_{dRi}/C_{com}$.

$NCOM2$ = Cost of sending joined tuple to the view = $8*N(dR_j)*W_{dRj}/C_{com}$

$NCOM3$ = Cost of sending the $jR_j$ to the view $\delta$ $8*N(jR_j)*W_{jRj}/C_{com}$.

Then the total cost of the algorithm *JDF* is $NIO1 + NIO2+ NIO3 + NIO4+ NCOM1 + NCOM2 + NCOM3$.

# 5 Performance Analysis

The following values are assigned to the parameters for the analysis. The block size is generally assumed to be $B$ = 4000 bytes, and the I/O cost $C_{I/O}$ = 25 ms/block. The size of the base table is assumed to be the same as $W_{Ri} = W_{Rj} = W_{dRi} = W_{dRj}$ = 200 bytes. The cardinality of the base table is assumed to be 1,000,000 and 500,000, and the size of differential file 10% of each base tables respectively in the experiment. The size of the inserted tuple is assumed to be the same as the base table, i.e., $W_I$ = 200 bytes. In the deleted case, the identifier (*TID*) will only be sent, so $W_D$ =8 bytes. The communication speed is varied from very low case and high-speed case, that is $C_{com}$ = 100Kbps ~ 10Mbps. Tuples are filtered from no screening case ($a_s$ = 1.0) and highly screened case ($a_s$ = 0.01). Three methods are analyzed such as (1) the base table method (*Base*), (2) the pseudo-differential method (*Pseudo*), and (3) the differential method (*JDF*).

Total six figures are suggested with respect to various criteria. Fig. 1 through Fig. 3 show that the total costs are all strongly dependent both on the screen factor and on the communication speed. Fig. 1 is different from the others, which represents that the size of the file is the most critical factor. If the tuples are filtered highly (up to about 0.01), the base table method is less advantageous than the *JDF* or the *Pseudo* method. Fig. 3 represents that if tuples are screened little (so, the screen factor is up to about 1.0), the *JDF* is less advantageous than the *Pseudo* or even in some cases than the *Base* method. It means that the differential method is not always preferable. But in reality the size of the *DF* is liable to be smaller than that of the base table, for the *DF* means a changed part of base table.

Fig. 4 and 5 represent the traverses of each cost due to the screen factors. The *Base* method is relatively stable as the screen factor increasing, but the *Pseudo* method increased rapidly and the *JDF* in the middle. As increasing the communication speed, the *JDF* gradually close up to the *Pseudo* method. Which means that the two methods are highly dependent upon the communication speed. Fig. 5 represents that in a low communication speed (100Kbps) the *JDF* is apparently lower than the other two methods. Fig. 4 and 5 represent two facts as follows: (1) If a base table is updated frequently, then the view maintenance by the *JDF* or by the *Pseudo* method is not said to be significantly advantageous (regardless of the communication speed). (2) If the communication speed is low (under 1Mbps), the *JDF* is apparently advantageous.

Fig. 6 represents that the costs of the three methods are depicted with respect to the size of the *DF*. The *Base* method is unwavering according to the changes of *DF*s, for it does not use the *DF*. It shows that the *JDF* scheme is preferable to the *Base* method, if the size of *DF* is less than that of the base table.

## 6 Conclusion

In this paper the *JDF* scheme with related algorithms is addressed for a data warehouse environment. Utilizing *differential file*s and a *join differential file*, the scheme is shown to be appropriate in maintaining the (data warehouse) join views without accessing the current database relations. Three methods such as (1) *Base* method, (2) pseudo-differential method (*Pseudo*), and (3) a differential method (*JDF*) are analyzed. Cost functions and trial runs showed that the *JDF* is useful in maintaining data warehouse join views. In the experiment, if the tuple is much screened and the communication speed is under 1Mbps, then the *JDF* is apparently advantageous. If a base table is updated frequently and less screened in ultra high communication speed, then the view maintenance by the *JDF* or by the *Pseudo* method is not significantly efficient. If the communication speed is low (under 1Mbps), the *JDF* is apparently advantageous.

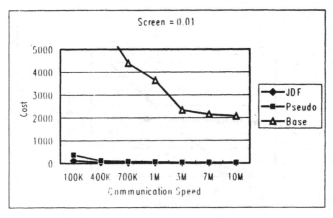

**Fig. 1. Cost traverse of JDF, Pseudo, and Base method with screening=0.01**

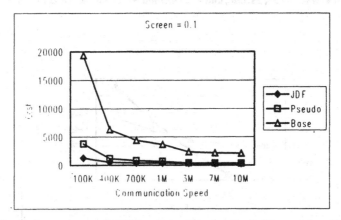

**Fig. 2. Cost traverse of JDF, Pseudo, and Base method with screening=0.1**

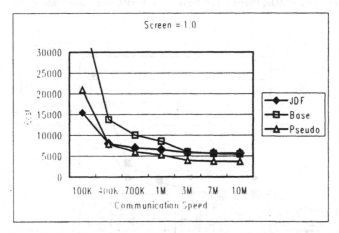

**Fig. 3. Cost traverse of JDF, Pseudo, and Base method with screening=1 .0**

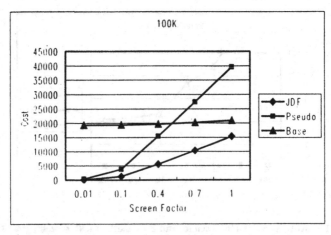

**Fig. 4. Cost traverse of JDF, Pseudo, and Base method with communication speed = 100kbps**

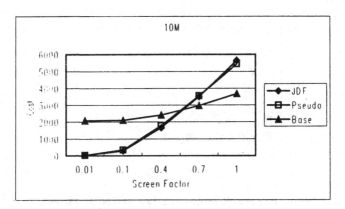

**Fig. 5. Cost traverse of JDF, Pseudo, and Base method with communication speed = 10Mbps**

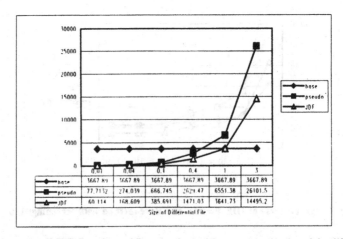

**Fig. 6. Cost traverse of JDF, Pseudo, and Base method with respect to the size of the differential file**

# References

1. Blakeley, J., Larson, P., Tompa, F.: Efficiently updating materialized views, ACM SIGMOD, Washington D.C., May (1986)
2. Buretta, M.: Data Replication, Wiley Computer Publishing (1997) 63-84
3. Chao, D., Diehr, G., Saharia, A.: Maintaining Remote Join Materialized Views, Working Paper, San Francisco State University (1996)
4. Colby, L., Kawaguchi, A., Lieuwen, D., Mumick, I. Ross, L.,: Supporting Multiple View Maintenance Polices, ACM SIGMOD (1997) 405-416
5. Diehr, G., Saharia, A.: Estimating Block Accesses in Database Organizations, IEEE TKDE, Vol. 6, No. 3, June (1994) 497-499
6. Gallersdorfer, R., Nicola, M.: Improving Performance of Replicated Databases through Relaxed Coherency, VLDB, Bombay, India (1996)
7. Goldring, R.: A Discussion of Relational Database Replication Technology, InfoDB, Spring (1994)
8. Horowitz, B.: A Run-Time Execution Model for Referential Integrity Maintenance, IEEE TKDE, (1992) 548-556
9. Labio, W., Garcia-Molina, H.: Efficient Snapshot Differential Algorithm for Data Warehousing, VLDB, Bombay, India (1996) 63-74
10. Lee, W., Park, J., Kang, S.: A Distributed Join Data Replicator, Journal of Computer Information Systems, Vol. 38, No. 4 (1998) 108-116
11. Lee, W., Park, J., Kang, S.: An Asynchronous Differential Join in Distributed Data Replications, Journal of Database Management, Vol. 10, No. 3, Idea-Group Publishing (1999) 3-12.
12. Lu, J., Moerkotte, G., Schue, J., Subrahmanian, V.: Efficient Maintenance of Materialized Mediated Views, ACM SIGMOD, San Jose (1996) 340-351
13. Markowitz, V.: Safe Referential Integrity Structures in Relational Databases, VLDB, Barcelona, Sept. (1991) 123-132
14. Mishra, P., Eich, M.: Join Processing in Relational Databases, ACM Computing Surveys, Vol. 24, No. 1, March (1992) 63-113
15. Roussopoulos, N.: An Incremental Access Method for ViewCashe: Concepts, Algorithms, and Cost Analysis, ACM TODS, Vol. 16, No. 3, Sept. (1991)
16. Staudt, M., Jarke, M.: Incremental Maintenance of Externally Materialized Views, VLDB, Bombay, India (1996) 75-86
17. Segev, A., Park, J.: Updating Distributed Materialized Views, IEEE TKDE, Vol. 1, No. 2, June (1989) 173-184

# Heuristic Algorithms for Designing a Data Warehouse with SPJ Views [*]

Spyros Ligoudistianos   Timos Sellis   Dimitri Theodoratos   Yannis Vassiliou

Department of Electrical and Computer Engineering
Computer Science Division
National Technical University of Athens
Zographou 157 73, Athens, Greece
{spyros,timos,dth,yv}@dblab.ece.ntua.gr

**Abstract.** A Data Warehouse (DW) can be abstractly seen as a set of materialized views defined over relations that are stored in distributed heterogeneous databases. The selection of views for materialization in a DW is thus an important decision problem. The objective is the minimization of the combination of the query evaluation and view maintenance costs. In this paper we expand on our previous work by proposing new heuristic algorithms for the DW design problem. These algorithms are described in terms of a state space search problem, and are guaranteed to deliver an optimal solution by expanding only a small fraction of the states produced by the (original) exhaustive algorithm.

## 1   Introduction

A Data Warehouse (DW) can be seen as a set of materialized views defined over distributed heterogeneous databases. All the queries posed to the DW are evaluated locally using exclusively the data that are stored in the views. The materialized views have also to be refreshed when changes occur to the data of the sources. The operational cost of a Data Warehouse depends on the cost of these two basic operations: query answering and refreshing. The careful selection of the views to be maintained in the DW may reduce this cost dramatically. For a given set of different source databases and a given set of queries that the DW has to service, there is a number of alternative sets of materialized views that the administrator can choose to maintain. Each of these sets has different refreshment and query answering cost while some of them may require more disk space than the available in the DW. The Data Warehouse design problem is the selection of the set of materialized views with the minimum overall cost that fits into the available space.

Earlier work [8] studies the DW design and provides methods that generate the view selections from the input queries. It models the problem as a state space search problem, and designs algorithms for solving the problem in the case of SPJ relational queries and views.

---

[*] Research supported by the European Commission under the ESPRIT Program LTR project "DWQ: Foundations of Data Warehouse Quality"

## 1.1 Related Work

Many authors in different contexts have addressed the view selection problem. H. Gupta and I.S. Mumick in [2] use an A* algorithm to select the set of views that minimizes the total query-response time and also keeps the total maintenance time less than a certain value. A greedy heuristic is also presented in this work. Both algorithms are based on the theoretical framework developed in [1] using AND/OR view directed acyclic graphs. In [3] a similar problem is considered for selection-join views with indexes. An A* algorithm is also provided as well as rules of thumb, under a number of simplifying assumptions. In [10], Yang, Karlapalem and Li propose heuristic approaches that provide a feasible solution based on merging individual optimal query plans. In a context where views are sets of pointer arrays, Roussopoulos also provides in [7] an A* algorithm that optimizes the query evaluation and view maintenance cost.

## 1.2 Contribution and Paper Outline

In this paper we study heuristic algorithms for the DW design problem. Based on the model introduced in [8, 9] we introduce a new A* algorithm that delivers the optimal design. This algorithm prunes the state space and provides the optimal solution by expanding only a small fraction of the whole state space. We also present two variations of the heuristic function used in A*, a 'static' and a 'dynamic' heuristic function. The dynamic heuristic function is able to do further pruning of the state space. To demonstrate the superiority of the A* algorithm, we compare it analytically and experimentally with the algorithms introduced in [8].

The rest of the paper is organized as follows. In Section 2 we formally define the DW design problem as a state space search problem providing also the cost formulas. In Section 3 we propose a new A* algorithm that delivers an optimal solution for the DW design problem. Improvements to the A* algorithm are proposed in Section 4. Section 5 presents experimental results. We summarize in Section 6.

## 2 The DW design problem

We consider a nonempty set of queries $\mathbf{Q}$, defined over a set of source relations $\mathbf{R}$. The DW contains a set of materialized views $\mathbf{V}$ over $\mathbf{R}$ such that every query in $\mathbf{Q}$ can be rewritten completely over $\mathbf{V}$ [4]. Thus, all the queries in $\mathbf{Q}$ can be answered locally at the DW, without accessing the source relations in $\mathbf{R}$. By $Q^V$, we denote a complete rewriting of the query $Q$ in $\mathbf{Q}$ over $\mathbf{V}$.

Consider a *DW configuration* $\mathbf{C} = <\mathbf{V}, \mathbf{Q}^V>$ [8, 9]. We define:

$E(\mathbf{Q}^V)$ : The sum of the evaluation cost of each query rewriting $Q_i^V$ in $\mathbf{Q}^V$ multiplied by the frequency of the assosiate input query $Q_i$,

$M(\mathbf{V})$ : The sum of the view maintenance cost of each view in $\mathbf{V}$,

$S(\mathbf{V})$ : The sum of the space needed for all views in $\mathbf{V}$,

$T(\mathbf{C})$ : The operational cost of $\mathbf{C}$ where:

$$T(\mathbf{C}) = cE(\mathbf{Q}^V) + M(\mathbf{V})$$

The parameter $c$ indicates the relative importance of the query evaluation cost and view maintenance cost.

The DW design problem can then be stated as follows [8]:

*Input:* A set of source relations $\mathbf{R}$. A set of queries $\mathbf{Q}$ over $\mathbf{R}$. The cost functions $E$, $M$, $T$. The space $t$ available in the DW for storing the views. A parameter $c$.

*Output:* A DW configuration $\mathbf{C} =< \mathbf{V}, \mathbf{Q}^V >$ such that $S(\mathbf{V}) \leq t$ and $T(\mathbf{C})$ is minimal.

In this paper we investigate the DW design problem in the case of selection-projection-join conjunctive queries without self-joins. The relation attributes take their values from domains of integer values. Atomic formulas are of the form $x \; op \; y + c$ or $x \; op \; c$, where $x$, $y$ are attribute variables, $c$ is a constant, and $op$ is one of the comparison operators $=, <, >, \leq, \geq$ but not $\neq$. A formula $F$ implies a formula $F'$ if both involve the same attributes and $F$ is more restrictive. ( For example $A = B$ implies $A \leq B + 10$). Atoms involving attributes from only one relation are called *selection atoms*, while those involving attributes from two relations are called *join atoms*.

## 2.1 Multiquery graphs

A set of views $\mathbf{V}$ can be represented by a *multiquery graph*. A multiquery graph allows the compact representation of multiple views. For a set of views $\mathbf{V}$, the corresponding multiquery graph, $\mathbf{G}^V$, is a node and edge labeled multigraph. The nodes of the graph correspond to the base relations of the views. The label of a node $R_i$ in $\mathbf{G}^V$ is the set containing the attributes of the corresponding relation that are projected in each view of $\mathbf{V}$. For every selection atom $p$ of the definition of a view $V$, involving attributes of $R_i$ there is a loop on $R_i$ in $\mathbf{G}^V$ labeled as $V : p$. For every join atom $p$ of the definition of a view $V$, involving attributes of $R_i$ and $R_j$ there is an edge between $R_i$ and $R_j$ in $\mathbf{G}^V$ labeled as $V : p$. The complete definition of the multiple query graph appears in [8].

## 2.2 Transformation Rules

In [8] we defined the following five transformation rules that can be applied to a DW configuration.

*Edge Removal:* A new configuration is produced by eliminating an edge labeled by the atom $p$ from the query graph of view $V$, and the addition of an associated condition to the queries that are defined over $V$.

*Attribute Removal:* If there are atoms of the form $A = B$ and $A$, $B$ are attributes of a view $V$, we eliminate $A$ from the projected attributes of $V$.

*View break:* Let $V$ be a view and $N_1$, $N_2$ two sets of nodes labeled by $V$ in $\mathbf{G}^V$ such that: (a) $N_1 \not\subseteq N2, N2 \not\subseteq N1$, (b)$N1 \cup N2$ is the set of all the nodes labeled by $V$ in $\mathbf{G}^V$ and (c) there is no edge labeled by $V$ between the nodes in $N_1 - N_2$ and $N_2 - N_1$. In this case this rule replaces $V$ by two views, $V_1$ defined over $N_1$ and $V_2$ defined over $N_2$. All the queries defined over $V$ are modified to be defined over $V_1 \times V_2$.

*View Merging:* A merging of two views $V_1$ and $V_2$ can take place if every condition of $V_1$ ($V_2$) implies or is implied by a condition of $V_2$ ($V_1$). In the new configuration, $V_1$ and $V_2$ are replaced by a view $V$ which is defined over the same source relations and comprises all the implied predicates. All the queries defined over $V_1$ or $V_2$ are modified appropriately in order to be defined over $V$.

*Attribute Transfer:* Suppose there are atoms of the form $A = c$, where $A$ is an attribute of a view $V$, we eliminate $A$ from the projected attributes $V$. All the queries defined over $V$ are modified appropriately.

## 2.3 The DW design problem as a state-space search problem

The DW design problem is formulated as a state space search problem. A *state s* is a DW configuration $\mathbf{C} = < \mathbf{V}, \mathbf{Q}^V >$. In particular, the state $\mathbf{C} = < \mathbf{G}^Q, \mathbf{Q}^Q >$ that represents the complete materialization of the input queries, is called the *initial state $s_0$*. There is a transition $T(s, s')$ from state $s$ to state $s'$, iff $s'$ can be obtained by applying any of the five transformation rules to $s$. It can be shown that by the application of the above transformation rules we can get all possible DW configurations [8]. With every state $s$ we associate, through the function $T(\mathbf{C})$, the operational cost of $\mathbf{C}$. Also, the space needed for materializing the views in $\mathbf{V}$ is given by $S(\mathbf{V})$. We can solve the DW design problem by examining all the states that are produced iteratively from $s_0$ and report the one with the minimum value for the function $T(\mathbf{C})$ that satisfies the constraint $S(\mathbf{V}) \leq t$.

It was evident that the number of all produced states of the state space is too large. An algorithm that solves the DW design problem by searching the state space within an acceptable time has to prune the state space and examine only a limited fraction of the states. Given a transition $T(s, s')$, the operational cost $T(\mathbf{C}')$ and the space $S(\mathbf{V}')$ of $s'$ are greater, equal or less than the corresponding $T(\mathbf{C})$ and $S(\mathbf{V})$ of $s$. Hence any algorithm that wishes to guarantee the optimality of the solution it delivers, it needs to examine every feasible state of the state-space.

In order to provide an algorithm that will be able to deliver an optimal solution for the DW design problem but at the same time will prune down the size of the state-space, we proceed as follows to alter the way states are created.

Consider the states $s_1 = < \mathbf{G}^{Q_1}, \mathbf{Q}_1^{Q_1} >, \ldots, s_n = < \mathbf{G}^{Q_n}, \mathbf{Q}_n^{Q_n} >$, where $\mathbf{Q}_1 = \{Q_1\}, \ldots, \mathbf{Q}_n = \{Q_n\}$. Let $S_i = \{s_i^1, \ldots, s_i^{k_i}\}$ denote the set of all the feasible states created from state $s_i$, $i = 1, \ldots, n$, by applying to $< \mathbf{G}^{Q_i}, \mathbf{Q}_i^{Q_i} >$ the transformation rules: edge removal, attribute removal, view break and attribute transfer. It is not hard to see that view merging cannot be applied to $< \mathbf{G}^{Q_i}, \mathbf{Q}_i^{Q_i} >$ or any of the other state produced from $S_i$.

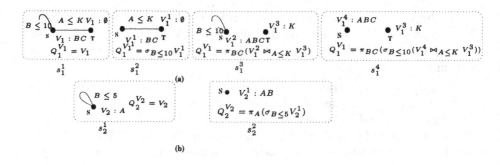

**Fig. 1.** The states of the set $S_1$ (a) and $S_2$ (b)

*Example 1.* Consider the queries $Q_1 = \pi_{BC}(\sigma_{B \leq 10}(S) \bowtie_{A \leq K} T)$, and $Q_2 = \pi_A(\sigma_{B \leq 5}(S))$. Figure 1(a) shows the elements of the set $S_1$ that we can get from $Q_1$ while Figure 1(b) shows the elements of $S_2$ that we can get from $Q_2$.

Consider now two configurations $< \mathbf{V}_1, \mathbf{Q}_1^{V_1} >$ and $< \mathbf{V}_2, \mathbf{Q}_2^{V_2} >$. By combining these configurations we can create a new configuration $< \mathbf{V}, \mathbf{Q}^V >$ as follows: $\mathbf{V} = \mathbf{V}_1 \cup \mathbf{V}_2$, $\mathbf{Q}^V = \mathbf{Q}_1^{V_1} \cup \mathbf{Q}_2^{V_2}$. The nodes of the multiquery graph of the new configuration are the nodes of the union of the original configurations. For each edge of the two original multiquery graphs, an identical edge is added to the multiquery graph of the new configuration. The same happens for each node label. The new multiquery graph expresses collectively all the views and the query rewritings of the two original configurations.

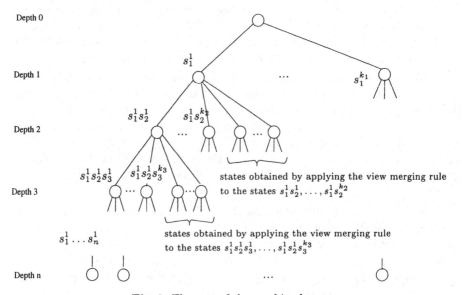

**Fig. 2.** The tree of the combined states

Combinations between states are defined similarly to combinations between configurations. By performing the combination between states we can create the

tree of combined states of the Figure 2. This tree is defined as follows: The
nodes of the tree are states and combined states. The root node is a state with
no views or query rewritings ($< \emptyset, \emptyset >$). The children of the root node are the
states $s_1^1, \ldots, s_1^{k_1}$. These nodes are at *depth* 1. The children of a node $s$ which
are expanded at *depth* $d$, $d > 1$, are the combined states resulting by combining
$s$ with each one of the states $s_d^1, \ldots, s_d^{k_d}$ plus all the states resulting by applying
the *view merging* transformation rule to these combined states (not necessarily
once). The leaves of the tree (nodes at *depth* $n$) are the states of the state space of
the DW design problem as this was formulated earlier. The tree of the combined
states of the example 1 is shown in Figure 3.

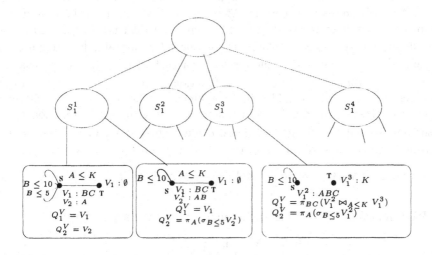

**Fig. 3.** The tree of the combined states for the sets $S_1$, $S_2$ of the Example 1

The operational cost function $T$ and the space function $S$ can be defined at
each node of the tree of combined states. At each node, $T$ and $S$ express the
operational cost and the space of the corresponding configuration. By induction
we can prove that given a node $n_1$ at *depth* $d_1$ and a node $n_2$ at *depth* $d_2$ where
$d_1 < d_2$ and $n_1$ is an ancestor of $n_2$ then $T(n_1) \leq T(n_2)$ and $S(n_1) \leq S(n_2)$.
This is true under the assumption that we consider no multi query optimization
and every view is maintained separately without using auxiliary views [9]. The
fact that the cost and the space function monotonically increase while we visit
the nodes of the tree from the root to the leaves, allows the design of algorithms
that find the optimal DW configuration by exploring only a small fraction of the
state space. The following Branch and Bound algorithm is such an algorithm.

**Branch and Bound algorithm:** The algorithm generates and examines the
tree in a depth-first manner. Initially it sets $c = \infty$. When it finds a leaf node
state $s$ that satisfies the space constraint and has cost $T(s) \leq c$ it keeps $s$ as $s_{opt}$
ans sets $c = T(s)$. The generation of the tree is discontinued below a node if this
node does not satisfy the space constraint or its cost exceeds $c$. When no more
nodes can be generated it returns the $s_{opt}$ as the optimal DW configuration.

# 3 A* Algorithm

We present an A* algorithm [6] that searches for the optimal solution in the tree of the combined states. The new algorithm prunes down the expanded tree more effectively than the Branch and Bound algorithm because at each step it uses also an estimation of the cost of the remaining nodes. The A* algorithm introduces two functions, $g(s)$ and $h(s)$ on states. The value of $g(s)$ expresses the cost of the state $s$ and is defined as the total operational cost of the associated configuration $\mathbf{C}$ $(g(s) = T(C))$. The value of $h(s)$ expresses an estimation of the additional cost that will be incurred in getting from $s$ to a final state. $h(s)$ is *admissible* if it always returns a value lower than the actual cost to a final state. If $h(s)$ is admissible then the A* algorithm that searches the tree of the combined states is guaranteed to find a final state (leaf node) $s_{opt}$ such that the operational cost of $s_{opt}$ is minimal among all final states [6]. In order to define $h(s)$, we introduce the function $l(s_i^j)$ for each $s_i^j \in S_i$, the set of feasible states created from $< \mathbf{G}^{Q_i}, \mathbf{Q}_i^{Q_i} >$. This function expresses a lower bound of the estimated cost that will be added to a combined state $s'$, in case $s'$ is produced by the combination of $s_i^j$ with a third state $s$. The value of the function $l(s_i^j)$ is the operational cost of the associated configuration $< \mathbf{V}_j, \mathbf{Q}_i^{V_j} >$ minus the view maintenance cost of the views that may contribute to a view merging.

$$l(s_i^j) = T(< \mathbf{V}_j, \mathbf{Q}_i^{V_j} >) - \sum_k M(V_j^k), \; V_j^k \, contributes \; to \; a \; view \; merging$$

We can also define $L(S_i)$ as the minimum $l(s_i^j)$ for each $s_i^j \in S_i$:

$$L(S_i) = \min_j [l(s_i^j)], \; s_i^j \in S_i$$

For a state $s$ at depth $i$ the heuristic function $h(s)$ is defined as:

$$h(s) = \sum_{j=i+1}^n L(S_j)$$

**Proposition 1.** *For every leaf node $s_l$ which is successor of the node $s$, $T(s_l) \geq g(s) + h(s)$ holds.*

The proof of the Proposition 1 is presented in [5].

**A* Algorithm:** The A* algorithm proceeds as follows: First it initializes $c = \infty$, constructs $S_1, \ldots, S_n$ and begins the tree traversal from the root node. When the algorithm visits a node it expands all its children. It computes the function $g(s) + h(s)$ for each one of the generated nodes and also the space function $S(s)$. Then, it continues to generate the tree starting from the state which has the lowest cost $g(s) + h(s)$. The generation of the tree is discontinued below a node if this node does not satisfy the space constraint or when $g(s) + h(s)$ exceeds $c$. When the algorithm finds a leaf node state $s_l$ that satisfies the space constraint and has cost $T(s) < c$, it keeps $s_l$ as $s_{opt}$ and sets $c = T(s)$. When no more nodes can be generated, the algorithm returns the $s_{opt}$ as the optimal DW configuration.

# 4 Improvements to the basic A* Algorithm

Consider two admissible heuristic functions $h_1$ and $h_2$. $h_1$ is said to be more *informed* than $h_2$ if for every non-final state $s$, $h_1(s) \geq h_2(s)$. When an A* algorithm is run using $h_2$, it is guaranteed to expand at least as many nodes as it does with $h_1$ [6] The definition of $h$ uses functions $L(S_i)$, $l(s_i^j)$ to pre-compute the additional cost from a state $s$ to a final state. $l(s_i^j)$, at each step, excludes from the estimation the maintenance cost of each view that may participate to a view merging, without considering the maintenance cost of the new view that will replace the merged views. Another point is the fact that in some cases the maintenance cost of a view is eliminated even if the merging of this view will generate no successor node. In order to get a more informed heuristic function, we define a new "dynamic" heuristic function $h'$. The new heuristic function uses the functions $L'$ and $l'$ which are "dynamic" versions of functions the $L$ and $l$. The functions $L'$, $l'$ are called "dynamic" because they are recomputed at each algorithm iteration. The main advantage of these functions is that they are able to exploit information from the states already expanded, making the new heuristic function $h'$ more informed than $h$. For each state $s$ at depth $d$ and for each $s_i^j \in S_i$ where $i > d$ the function $l'(s_i^j, s)$ is defined as follows:

$$l'(s_i^j, s) = T(< \mathbf{V}_j, \mathbf{Q}_i^{V_j} >) - \sum_k M(V_j^k) + \sum_k W(V_j^k, s)$$

$$W(V_j^k, s) = \begin{cases} 0 & : \text{ if } \exists V \in s, V \text{ can be merged with } V_j^k \\ \frac{M(V_j^k)}{n_j^k + 1} & : \text{ otherwise} \end{cases}$$

where $V_j^k$ may be contributing to a view merging and $n_j^k$ is the number of views that can be merged with $V_j^k$ and these views are in any of $S_{d+1}, \ldots, S_n$.

The function $L'(S_i, s)$, similarly as the function $L(S_i)$, is defined as the minimum $l'(s_i^j, s)$ for each $s_i^j \in S_i$. The heuristic function $h'$ for a state $s$ at depth $i$ is defined also as the sum of the function $L'(S_j, s)$ for each $j \in [i + 1, \ldots, n]$.

In [5] we prove that the heuristic function $h'$ is admissible. Obviously $h'(s) \geq h(s)$ for every state $s$ of the tree of the combined states, so $h'$ is more informed than $h$. That means that when the A* algorithm uses $h'$, less nodes are expanded compared to the case where $h$ is used.

# 5 Experimental Results

We have performed a sequence of experiments to compare the performance of the Branch and Bound algorithm and the A* algorithm, the latter using the two heuristic functions presented in the previous sections. The algorithms are compared in terms of the following factors: (a) the complexity of the input query set and (b) physical factors. The complexity of the query set is expressed by three parameters: the number of input queries, the number of selection and join edges of all the input queries, and the overlapping of the queries in the input

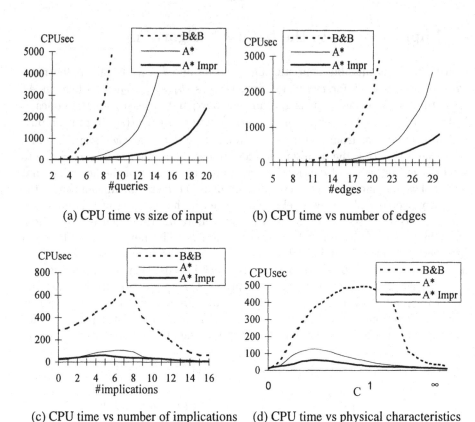

(a) CPU time vs size of input    (b) CPU time vs number of edges

(c) CPU time vs number of implications    (d) CPU time vs physical characteristics

**Fig. 4.** Experimental Results

query set. The query overlapping is expressed by the total number of implications between the selection or join atoms of different input queries. Finally the physical factors are expressed by the relative importance of the query evaluation and view maintenance cost (factor $c$ in Section 2).

**Experiment 1: The number of queries varies.** We study the performance of the algorithms when the number of the input queries varies. Figure 4.(a) shows the CPU time needed by each algorithm. The performance of the A* algorithm using the dynamic heuristic function $h'$ is denoted by *A* Impr*. Actually it is this algorithm that is significantly better than the other two.

**Experiment 2: The number of edges varies.** We study the performance of the algorithms as the number of selection and join edges of the input queries varies. Figure 4.(b) shows the CPU time needed by the Branch and Bound algorithm and the two variations of A* take. In this experiment too the improved A* algorithm is the winner.

**Experiment 3: The number of implications varies.** We study the performance of the algorithms while varying the number of implications between atoms of different queries. Figure 4.(c) shows the CPU time taken by the algorithms. As the number of implications grows and before it exceeds a certain limit, both

the Branch and Bound and the A\* algorithm execution time increases. When the number of implications exceeds this limit, the algorithms become fasters.
**Experiment 4: parameter c varies.** We run the algorithms while varying the parameter $c$. Figure 4.(d) reports the CPU time needed by the algorithms. When $c$ is close to 0 or much greater than 1 (the view maintenance cost or the query evaluation cost is important), then all the algorithms perform very efficiently. In the middle interval the algorithms are slower.

## 6  Summary

In this paper we have studied heuristic algorithms that solve the DW design problem, by extending the work presented in [8]. We have studied the DW design problem as a state space search problem and proposed a new A\* algorithm that guarantees to deliver an optimal solution by expanding only a small fraction of the states produced by the (original) exhaustive algorithm and the Branch and Bound algorithm proposed in [8]. We have also studied analytically the behaviour of the A\* algorithm and proposed a new improved heuristic function. Finally we implemented all the algorithms and investigated their perfomance with respect to the time required to find a solution.

Interesting extensions of the present work include the following: (a) The use of auxiliary views in the maintenance process of the other views, and (b) The enlargement of the class of queries to include aggregate queries.

## References

[1] H. Gupta. Selection of Views to Materialize in a Data Warehouse. In *Proc. of the 6th ICDT Conf.*, pages 98–112, 1997.

[2] H. Gupta and I. S. Mumick. Selection of Views to Materialize Under a Maintenance Cost Constraint. In *Proc. of the 7th ICDT Conf.*, pages 453–470, 1999.

[3] W. Labio, D. Quass, and B. Adelberg. Physical Database Design for Data Warehousing. In *Proc. of the 13th Intl. Conf. on Data Engineering*, 1997.

[4] A. Levy, A. O. Mendelson, Y. Sagiv, and D. Srivastava. Answering Queries using Views. In *Proc. of the ACM Symp. on Principles of Database Systems*, pages 95–104, 1995.

[5] S. Ligoudistianos. *Design and Operational Issues of Data Warehouse Systems.* PhD thesis, NTUA, 1999.

[6] N. J. Nilsson. *Principles of Artificial Intelligence.* Morgan Kaufmann Publ, 1980.

[7] N. Roussopoulos. View Indexing in Relational Databases. *ACM Transactions on Database Systems*, 7(2):258–290, 1982.

[8] D. Theodoratos, S. Ligoudistianos, and T. Sellis. Designing the Global DW with SPJ Queries. *Proc. of the 11th (CAiSE) Conference*, June 1999.

[9] D. Theodoratos and T. Sellis. Data Warehouse Configuration. In *Proc. of the 23rd Intl. Conf. on Very Large Data Bases*, pages 126–135, 1997.

[10] J. Yang, K. Karlapalem, and Q. Li. Algorithms for Materialized View Design in Data Warehousing Environment. In *Proc. of the 23rd Intl. Conf. on Very Large Data Bases*, pages 136–145, 1997.

# Posse: A Framework for Optimizing Incremental View Maintenance at Data Warehouses*

Kevin O'Gorman, Divyakant Agrawal, and Amr El Abbadi

Department of Computer Science
University of California
Santa Barbara, CA 93106
{kogorman,agrawal,amr}@cs.ucsb.edu

**Abstract.** We propose the Posse[1] framework for optimizing incremental view maintenance at data warehouses. To this end, we show how for a particular method of consistent probing it is possible to have the power of SQL view queries with multiset semantics, and at the same time have available a spectrum of concurrency from none at all as in previously proposed solutions to the maximum concurrency obtained by issuing all probes in parallel. We then show how optimization of the probing process can be used to select various degrees of concurrency for the desired tradeoffs of concurrency against processing cost and message size.

## Keywords:

View Maintenance, Data Warehouse, Distributed Query Optimization.

## 1    Introduction

Data warehousing is increasingly used to collect information from diverse and possibly heterogeneous data sources and to provide a platform for quick response to queries. For efficient query processing, the views are commonly materialized at the data warehouse, giving rise to the need to keep the views up-to-date with respect the data sources. This can either be performed by complete re-computation of the views or by *incremental maintenance* techniques [1–3].

We consider the case of a warehouse with multiple data sources, which may be separate physical sites or independent relations within a site. The data warehouse stores materialized views which are expressed as SQL queries over data sources. Each data source locally responds to user queries and updates. Updates at the data sources are propagated as update messages to the warehouse and must be integrated into the materialized view in order to keep it up-to-date, but this poses several problems.

---

* This work is partially supported by the NSF under grant numbers CCR-9712108 and EIA-9818320
[1] In the USA at least, a *posse* is a group of citizens temporarily deputized into the police force, for a (more or less loosely coordinated) search.

First, the update message contains information only about changes at the data source where the update occurred, but the corresponding change to the view may depend on information at other data sources. Accordingly, the data warehouse must *probe* (i.e. query) the other data sources where the additional information resides, and must delay installation of the change to the materialized view until all the necessary information arrives. This is in effect a distributed query, which gives rise to several optimization issues regarding the sequence in which to send the probes, and the data to be requested in each probe.

Second, because of the delays introduced in probing the data sources, it can happen that updates occur concurrently at the data sources being probed, and consequently the replies to the probes may reflect updates that occur in some sense "after" the update which is being processed. Without some sort of compensation, the effects of these *interfering* updates could result in the materialized view becoming inconsistent with respect to the data sources.

Existing algorithms for incremental maintenance of materialized views in a data warehouse [4–6] have focused primarily on this problem of compensation for interfering updates. The ECA, STROBE and SWEEP algorithms limit themselves to select-project-join (SPJ) view queries and relational (i.e. duplicate-free) semantics, whereas warehouse views typically use aggregation and group-by queries to reduce query processing times, and multiset (bag) semantics. The PSWEEP algorithm [9] extends SWEEP by introducing parallel evaluation of updates, but retains SWEEP's focus on linear joins and relational semantics. We develop the Posse framework which can express all these prior algorithms and adds concurrency within each update, multiset semantics, aggregates and group-by queries, and optimizations of the query plans.

The rest of this paper is organized as follows: Sect. 2 presents the definitions and assumptions for the rest of the paper. Section 3 introduces a motivational example that will be used in the rest of the paper. Section 4 describes the theoretical and conceptual environment for addressing issues of consistency and correctness. Section 5 presents the main result of this paper, the framework in which optimizations and consistency can coexist. Section 6 concludes the paper.

## 2 Definitions and Assumptions

The data sources report to the data warehouse all updates to their local relations, and the data sources are capable of processing and responding to SQL queries relating to their contents. The data warehouse defines one or more materialized views expressible in SQL, including **GROUP BY** and **HAVING** clauses, and aggregate functions. Queries from the data warehouse take the form of SQL queries. We refer to such a query as a *probe*. We refer to a probe and its reply as *belonging to* the update or to the update message that gave rise to the probe. Where it is not ambiguous, we use a name of a relation as found in the view query to label a data source and updates originating from that source.

Communication is via reliable point-to-point FIFO channels. Data sources are independent in that they do not synchronize or communicate with each other, and updates to the data sources are mutually independent. Data sources process updates and queries atomically, queries are processed in the order of their arrival, and messages relating to these events are transmitted in the same order as the processing of the events.

An update message takes the form of a *delta table* which is a relation augmented with a signed integer cardinality. The cardinality is not an attribute of the schema, but encodes both the number of duplicates of a tuple for multiset semantics and the insertion (positive) or deletion (negative) sense of an update message or probe reply. We use the terms multiset and relation interchangeably in this paper, and regard a multiset as having the form of a delta table with only positive cardinalities, although we omit the cardinality from multiset examples when the cardinalities are all +1. We extend the operations of relational algebra to apply to delta tables in the natural way, consistent with their interpretation as multisets.

## 3  Motivation

We use an example to demonstrate the operation of a data warehouse. This example comprises a data warehouse with a single view defined over the three data sources of Fig. 1, which are (part of) an entity-relationship schema describing university enrollment and teaching assistant appointments. The data warehouse materializes a single view over these relations:

```
CREATE VIEW DoubleStatus(Prof,Conflicts)
  AS SELECT T1.Prof,COUNT(E.Student)
    FROM Assists A, Enrollment E, Teaches T1, Teaches T2
    WHERE T1.Prof = T2.Prof AND T1.Course = A.Course
      AND T2.Course = E.Course AND E.Student = A.Student
    GROUP BY T1.Prof
```

**Enrollment**

| Student | Course |
|---------|--------|
| Kevin   | CS201  |
| Mary    | CS103  |
| Mike    | CS101  |
| Sharon  | CS102  |

**Teaches**

| Course | Prof  |
|--------|-------|
| CS101  | Jones |
| CS102  | Smith |
| CS103  | Smith |
| CS201  | Jones |

**Assists**

| Student | Course |
|---------|--------|
| Kevin   | CS101  |
| Mary    | CS102  |

**Fig. 1.** The Example Base Relations

The ECA algorithm [4] cannot be used for our example view because ECA contemplates only a single data source. The STROBE algorithms [5] cannot handle the view because they require the view to contain a key for each base relation. The SWEEP algorithms [6] cannot support the view because of their limitation to select-project-join view queries.

The corresponding state of the view would be DoubleStatus in Fig. 2A, reflecting the fact that Jones and Smith each have one student (resp. Kevin and Mary) who is simultaneously an assistant and a student. The DoubleStatus view is an interesting example of a query that can be used to expose multiple relationships which may potentially represent e.g. conflict-of-interest relationships.

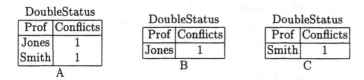

DoubleStatus

| Prof | Conflicts |
|------|-----------|
| Jones | 1 |
| Smith | 1 |

A

DoubleStatus

| Prof | Conflicts |
|------|-----------|
| Jones | 1 |

B

DoubleStatus

| Prof | Conflicts |
|------|-----------|
| Smith | 1 |

C

**Fig. 2.** The States of the View

Now suppose that an update occurs at the Enrollment relation, replacing the tuple (Mary, CS103) with the tuple (Mary, CS201) and Enrollment sends the update message *update E* of Fig. 3, and also suppose that there is an update to the Teaches relation replacing the tuple (CS201, Jones) with the tuple (CS201, Smith) resulting in the update message *update T* of Fig. 3. Let us also suppose that these update messages arrive at the data warehouse in the order given, before processing begins on either message.

*update E* (from Enrollment)

| Student | Course | Cardinality |
|---------|--------|-------------|
| Mary | CS201 | +1 |
| Mary | CS103 | −1 |

*update T* (from Teaches)

| Course | Prof | Cardinality |
|--------|------|-------------|
| CS201 | Smith | +1 |
| CS201 | Jones | −1 |

*reply(E, T)* (from Teaches, for *update E*)

| Course | Prof | Student | Cardinality |
|--------|------|---------|-------------|
| CS103 | Smith | Mary | −1 |
| CS201 | Smith | Mary | +1 |

**Fig. 3.** The Messages

The first update (*update E*) should change the contents of the DoubleStatus view so that Mary no longer has double status with regards to Smith. The state of the view after this update should be DoubleStatus in Fig. 2B. However, in order to arrive at this result, the update messages have to be joined with information from other base relations. The view contains none of the attributes that appear in *update E*, so that it becomes necessary to obtain information from, for example, the Teaches relation. But since *update T* has already arrived from that relation and is reflected in the contents of the Teaches relation, the current state of Teaches would be incorrect for computing the effect of *update E* by itself to produce Fig. 2B. Some sort of compensation for the effects of the concurrent *update T* must be applied.

## 4 The Environment

In this section we present the computational and conceptual environment for our framework for view maintenance. The correctness model is the conceptual standard for our definitions of consistency. The computational model comprises the machinery available to our algorithms.

### 4.1 The Correctness Model

Consider a system architecture in which, in addition to the materialized view, the data warehouse materializes copies or *mirrors* of all of the base relations. Updates to the base relations at the data sources are sent as update messages to the data warehouse. The processing of an update message at the data warehouse is a single atomic action which includes updating the materialized copy of the base relation, reevaluation of the view query, and installation of a new materialized view. We regard it as axiomatic that the operation of a system of this architecture is correct, and use it as the standard for comparison from the points of view of correctness and consistency.

### 4.2 The Computational Model

The framework we propose uses the computational model illustrated in Fig. 4. In this execution environment, the data warehouse does not contain mirrors of the base relations. As a result, it is necessary for the data warehouse to send probes to the data sources to obtain the information to complete processing of each update message.

The incoming messages at the data warehouse, both update messages and replies to probes, are kept in a *Message List*, and each message remains in the list until it has been completely processed. In the case of a probe reply, this completion may be more or less immediate, but it is helpful for such replies to reside in the Message List in order to keep track of their sequence of arrival with respect to other messages, because the message sequence then identifies the updates that are conflicting. In the case of update messages, completion occurs after all needed probes have been sent and replies have been processed, and when subsequently the update message is at the head of the Message List. At that time the computation of the appropriate change to the materialized view is complete, and the change is installed. The imposed sequence of installation of changes is thus the same sequence in which the update messages arrived, and can easily be seen to be the same order in which the same changes would be installed in the correctness model. The proof of correctness is omitted here, but follows directly from the order of installation of the updates and the correctness of the message compensation, developed in [6].

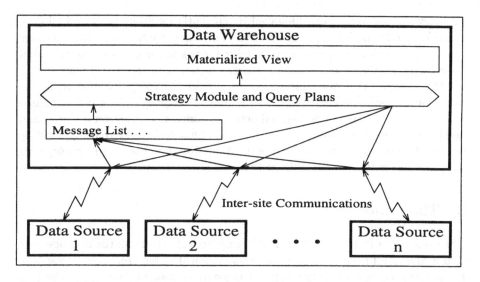

**Fig. 4.** The Computational Model

All messages at the data warehouse are handled by the *Strategy*, according to the warehouse and source schemas. In our implementation, the Strategy comprises schemas and query plans contained in a JavaBean whose superclasses provide the computational infrastructure which defines whether we are executing STROBE[5], SWEEP[6], or an Optimized Posse algorithm as discussed in Sect. 5.3.

For example, when implementing SWEEP or related algorithms, this infrastructure closely follows the local compensation method of [6]. This method recognizes that updates comprise insertions and deletions, and that these are commutative operations. It therefore turns out that by retaining update messages in the Message List, the data warehouse has preserved sufficient information to reconstruct replies to queries "as if" the queries had been issued and answered atomically at the same point in the message stream where the update arrived. Accordingly the data warehouse reconstructs the replies to queries that would have been received in the Correctness Model of Sect. 4.1. Since the probe replies must be capable of compensation for interfering updates, we refer to them as *locally compensatable*. This is related to the property that qualifies a view as being self-maintainable, but the domain of applicability is different. The full version of this paper [7] discusses some of the complexities of mapping the space of such queries, as well as the details of how aggregate functions and HAVING clauses may be implemented in our framework.

The computational model as presented here can achieve both complete consistency and the maximum possible concurrency. We call this approach the Concurrent Posse. The concurrency is achieved by installing a Strategy that, in service of each update, simply queries all data sources for their entire content, applying the view query to the compensated replies to compute a new materialized view. These queries can be issued concurrently for all updates and all data sources, as each update message arrives. The compensation algorithm assures consistency while the restriction of installing views in the order of the arrival of their corresponding updates assures the completeness of the consistency.

The Concurrent Posse algorithm operates in the computational model to define an extreme of concurrency at the cost of large message sizes, so that a spectrum of solutions can be realized between Concurrent Posse on the one hand and the existing algorithms [4–6] on the other. That such an extreme approach is feasible demonstrates the flexibility of the framework proposed here, and suggests the possibilities that lie between extremes.

# 5 The Framework

The Concurrent Posse algorithm may be impractical because of the message sizes that would result from asking for the transmission of all base relations in response to each update. On the other hand, if the data warehouse is going to send all queries immediately on receiving the update message, there may be insufficient information at hand to refine the query at that moment. This presents us with an opportunity to trade off two contributors to overall efficiency: concurrency and message size.

The Posse framework and the Optimized Posse algorithm that we present in this section, operating in the computational model we have already presented, provides a framework in which such tradeoffs can be conveniently exploited. We impose a conceptual structure on the schema and update processing, using rooted directed graphs to represent the organization of the algorithms we use.

## 5.1 Schema and Rooted DAG

At the data warehouse the Strategy associates a *query plan* with each data source, to be used for each update message received from that data source. Each query plan represents a schedule for issuing probes in response to an update message from a particular data source. We present each such query plan as a rooted directed acyclic graph (rooted DAG), with one vertex for each occurrence of a relation in a FROM clause in the view query.

Each non-root vertex is associated with a query to be used to probe the corresponding data source for the data relevant to the use of that instance of the relation in the processing of the query. Each vertex is labeled; the same name is used for any update message, probe or data associated with that vertex. Edges represent a dependency that can be expressed as "is completed before composing the probe of," and indicate that the probe for the destination vertex is delayed until the data from the source of that edge is available.

In general there is also a final query over the original update message and the probe responses, which produces the set of changes to be installed in the materialized view. We assume that this query is executed at the data warehouse after all probe replies have been received and corrected for interfering updates.

For Concurrent Posse the DAG is star-shaped: it contains an edge from the root to each leaf; this is our usual starting point for developing the final DAG.

We concern ourselves in this section with optimizations that correspond to adding or deleting one or more edges to the star-shaped graph for a query plan and choosing an appropriate query to associate with the destination vertex. Edges are deleted when the probe at the destination node has been combined with a probe at another node for the same data source. Added edges reduce the concurrency in the query plan by delaying the probe at the destination vertex until completion of the probe at the source vertex. The advantage in doing this derives from the possibility of greatly reducing message size, local processing cost or both. Properly chosen, these optimizations can improve query performance at the data source and message size in the response at the expense of loss of concurrency in processing.

## 5.2 Optimized Update Processing

In planning the maintenance of the DoubleStatus view one can apply various transformations to the query plan, as might be done by a query optimizer. We start with a "star-shaped" graph with edges from the root directly to each of the leaves and consider transformations that can be represented using the graph and associated probes.

These transformations are used in the graphs of Fig. 5, which corresponds to the example introduces in Sect. 3. First, each edge in the graph can be associated with a join involving information from the source node of the edge, and any previous nodes. Compared to simply requesting the entire content of the relation, this probe can (vastly) reduce message size.

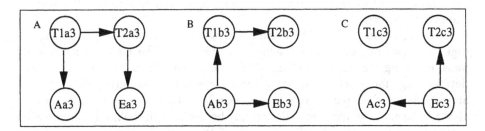

**Fig. 5.** Directed graphs for optimized query plans for the DoubleStatus view. Graph A is used for updates from the Teaches relation, Graph B for updates from Assists, and Graph C for updates from Enrollment.

Second, a probe can be delayed as seen in Fig. 5A at node Ea3; this probe of the Enrollment relation is delayed until the reply to the previous probe is available at the warehouse, providing information that can be used in the join.

Third, in a few cases multiple probes of a single relation can be combined, as seen in Fig. 5C at node T1c3 and T2c3. Node T1c3 has actually been bypassed because appropriate manipulation of the reply to the probe T2c3 can reconstruct the reply that would be received for T1c3. This optimization applies because the join between the two nodes is an equijoin with corresponding attributes.

Fourth, there is no query plan rooted at T2 because we have applied another optimization. In the general case without this optimization, we would "echo" updates from Teaches to that there would appear to be two data sources T1 and T2 whose updates "just happen" always to be identical and adjacent in the Message List.

The transformations chosen in these examples may or may not be the best in a given case. The combination of T1c3 and T2c3 may trade message complexity for computational complexity. Moreover, it may be better to use one of the variants of semijoin [8] for the other joins, and it may be better to choose different or additional dependency edges to add to the graph. Our purpose here is not the optimal choice of transformations but the description of a framework in which transformations can be applied to the algorithm for view maintenance. In any event, the goal of optimization is often achieved by the avoidance of very bad solutions, and it appears that this goal is achieved in these examples, and that a high degree of concurrency is maintained.

## 5.3 The Optimized Posse Algorithm

The Posse framework allows query plans that schedule concurrent probes to perform incremental view maintenance. We presume that the query plans are the output of an optimizer process which runs when the view query is defined. The Posse framework and its DAGs formalize the notion that the probes are initiated in a particular order rather than all at once as in Concurrent Posse. The opportunity for optimization lies in the fact that having information from prior probes and using in a join or semi-join operation may reduce the size of subsequent replies.

This algorithm operates by creating a thread of control for each update message, and creating and deleting additional threads as the DAG branches and joins, following the structure of the DAG associated with the source of the update message for which the delta to the view is being computed. As subpaths are completed, their partial results are assembled until the correct delta to the view has been computed. These deltas may be installed in the materialized view in order according to the delivery order of their update messages to achieve complete consistency [4] with the Correctness Model. Batching of updates can be used, in which case strong consistency is maintained. Variant commit orders may also be used where convergence is acceptable behavior.

## 6  Conclusion

We have presented a correctness model for evaluating the consistency and correctness of algorithms for the transport of base relation information for the incremental maintenance of a materialized view in a data warehouse. We have shown that a completely concurrent algorithm (Concurrent Posse) obtains complete concurrency of the probing process, albeit at the cost of increased message sizes. We have presented in the Posse framework in which distributed query optimizations can be applied to the Concurrent Posse approach in order to obtain reasonable performance of the incremental maintenance process, and have indicated areas in which further improvements might be obtained. Throughout, we have maintained the criterion of complete consistency with a correctness model that honors the order of arrival of update messages from the data sources. Our present approach uses fixed query plans determined in advance. In the future we plan to investigate dynamically determining the query plan and to explore alternate optimization criteria for choosing the query plans, and to fully characterize locally compensatable probes.

# References

1. A. Gupta, I. S. Mumick, V. S. Subramanian. Maintaining Views Incrementally. In *Proceedings of the ACM SIGMOD International Conference on Management of Data*, pages 157-166, May 1993.
2. T. Griffin and L. Libkin. Incremental Maintenance of Views with Duplicates. In *Proceedings of the ACM SIGMOD 1995 International Conference on Management of Data*, pages 328-339, May 1995.
3. Richard Hull, Gang Zhou. A Framework for Supporting Data Integration Using the Materialized and Virtual Approaches. In *Proceedings of the ACM SIGMOD International Conference on Management of Data*, pages 481-492, June 1996.
4. Yue Zhuge, Hector Garcia-Molina, Joachim Hammer, Jennifer Widom. View Maintenance in a Warehousing Environment. In *Proceedings of the ACM SIGMOD International Conference on Management of Data*, pages 316-327, May 1995.
5. Yue Zhuge, Hector Garcia-Molina, Janet L. Wiener. The Strobe Algorithms for Multi-Source Warehouse Consistency. In *Proceedings of the International Conference on Parallel and Distributed Information Systems*, December 1996.
6. D. Agrawal, A. El Abbadi, A. Singh, T. Yurek. Efficient View Maintenance in Data Warehouses. In *Proceedings of the 1997 ACM International Conference on Management of Data*, pages 417-427, May 1997.
7. Kevin O'Gorman, Divyakant Agrawal, Amr El Abbadi. Posse: A Framework for Optimizing Incremental View Maintenance at Data Warehouses. Technical Report TRCS99-18, University of California at Santa Barbara, Department of Computer Science, UCSB, Santa Barbara, CA, 93106, June, 1999.
8. Y. Kambayashi and M. Yoshikawa and S. Yajima. Query Processing for Distributed Databases using Generalized Semi-Joins. In *Proceedings of the ACM SIGMOD 1982 International Conference on Management of Data*, pages 151-160, May 1992.
9. Xin Zhang and Elke A. Rundensteiner. PSWEEP: Parallel View Maintenance Under Concurrent Data Updates of Distributed Sources. Technical Report WPI-CS-TR-99-14, Worcester Polytechnic Institute, Computer Science Department, Worcester, MA, 01609, March 1999.

# Genetic Algorithm for Materialized View Selection in Data Warehouse Environments

Chuan Zhang[1] and Jian Yang[2]

[1] School of Computer Science, University College, UNSW
ADFA, Canberra ACT 2600, Australia
czhang@cs.adfa.edu.au,
[2] Spatial Information Systems, CMIS, CSIRO
GPO Box 664, Canberra ACT 2601, Australia
Jian.Yang@cmis.CSIRO.AU

**Abstract.** Data Warehouse applications use a large number of materialized views to assist a Data Warehouse to perform well. But how to select views to be materialized is challenging. Several heuristic algorithms have been proposed in the past to tackle with this problem. In this paper, we propose a completely different approach, Genetic Algorithm, to choose materialized views and demonstrate that it is practical and effective compared with heuristic approaches.

## 1 Introduction

Data Warehousing is an in-advance approach to the integration of data from multiple, possibly very large, distributed, heterogeneous databases and other information sources. A Data Warehouse (DW) can be viewed as a repository of materialized views of integrated information available for querying and analysis.

The problem of selecting materialized views to efficiently support data warehouse application is proven to be a NP-complete [4]. Most of the work [9], [1], [6], [7], [3], [10], done in this area use heuristics to select materialized views in order to obtain a near optimal solution — the minimum sum of query response time and view maintenance time under some constraint. The "Greedy Algorithm" was usually exploited to select the materialized views in [5], [3], [4].

The algorithm used in optimization can be classified into four types [8], [2]: Deterministic algorithm, Randomized algorithm, Genetic algorithm (GA), Hybrid algorithm. GAs are different from many normal optimization and search procedures in three ways: working with a coding of the parameter set, searching for a solution from a population of points, using probabilistic transition rules to search the problem space. There are two issues we should consider. One is the representation transformation. GAs work on bit strings. However, the materialized view selection problem of interest here is usually represented as a directed acyclic graph (DAG) to which the GA cannot be directly applied. Another issue occurs because small change to the string in GA can produce large change to the DAG in our problem, sometimes these changes may produce invalid result.

The rest of the paper is organized as follows: Section 2 gives an example to illustrate briefly the problem for the selection of materialized views. In Section

3, we present the GA for the selection of materialized views. Section 4 presents the experimental results using our evolutionary approach. in Section 5 concludes by analyzing and summarizing our experiments results

## 2 Materialized View Selection Problem

### 2.1 Motivating Example

In this section, we first present an example to motivate the discussion of selection of materialized views in DW. The discussion is presented in terms of the relational data model with select, join, and aggregate operations. Our examples are taken from a DW application which analyzes trends in sales and supply, and which were used in [10]. The relations and the attributes of the schema for this application are:

```
Item(I_id, I_name, I_price)
Part(P_id, P_name, I_id)
Supplier(S_id, S_name,P_id, City, Cost, Preference)
Sales(I_id, Month, Year, Amount)
```

There are five queries, as follows:

```
Q1: Select  P_id, min(Cost), max(Cost)
    From Part, Supplier
    Where  Part.P_id=Supplier.P_id
           And  P_name in {"spark_plug", "gas_kit" }
           Group by P_id

Q2: Select  I_id, sum(amount*number*min_cost)
    From Item, Sales, Part
    Where  I_name in {"MAZDA","NISSAN","TOYOTA" }
           And year=1996
           And   Item.I_id=Sales.I_id
           And   Item.I_id=Part.I_id
           And   Part.P_id=
                           (Select P_id, min(Cost) as min_cost
                            From Supplier
                            Group by  P_id)
           Group by  I_id

Q3:Select  P_id, month sum(amount)
   From Item, Sales, Part
   Where  I_name in {"MAZDA", "NISSAN", "TOYOTA" }
          And year=1996
          And   Item.I_id=Sales.I_id
          And   Part.I_id=Item.I_id
          Group by   P_id , month

Q4: Select  I_id, Sum(amount *I_price)
    From Item, Sales
    Where  I_name in  {"MAZDA", "NISSAN", "TOYOTA"}
```

```
        And year=1996
        And  Item.I_id=Sales.I_id
        Group by   I_id
Q5: Select  I_id, avg(amount*I_price)
    From Item, Sales
    Where  I_name in {"MAZDA", "NISSAN", "TOYOTA"}
        and year=1996
        and Item.I_id=Sales.I_id
      Group by I_id.
```

Figure 1 represents a possible global query access plan for the five queries. The local access plans for the individual queries are merged based on the shared operations on common data sets. This is called a **Multiple View Processing Plan (MVPP)** in [10].

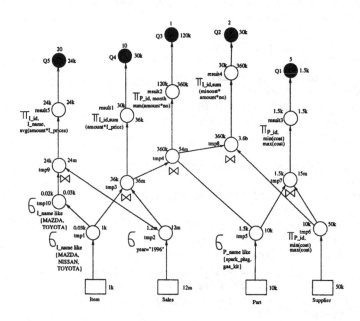

**Fig. 1.** A motivating example

Now the problem we are dealing with is how to select the views to be materialized so that the cost of query processing and view maintenance for the whole set of nodes in the MVPP is minimal.

An obvious approach is to apply the exhaustive algorithm for materialized view selection on the set of queries. However this approach is very expensive if the search space is big. Many researchers have therefore applied heuristics to trim the search space in order to get the results quickly. However only a near-optimal solution can be achieved. In order to avoid exhaustive searching the whole solution space, and to obtain a better solution than that obtained by heuristic, we exploit the GA to deal with this problem.

In the next section, we will present a brief specification of the cost model, then we will explain what the GA is and how to apply it to our problem.

## 2.2 Specification of Cost Model

An access plan is a labeled $DAG(V, A, C_a^q(v), C_m^r(v), f_q, f_u)$ where V is a set of vertices, A is a set of arcs over V. $C_a^q(v)$, $C_m^r(v)$ are costs, and $f_q$, $f_u$ are frequencies. The cost model is constructed as follows:

1. For every relational algebra operation in a query tree, for every base relation, and for every distinct query, create a vertex;
2. For $v \in V$, T(v) is the relation generated by corresponding vertex v. T(v) can be a base relation, intermediate result while processing a query, or the final result for a query;
3. For any leaf vertex v (that is one which has no edges coming into the vertex), T(v) corresponds to a base relation. Let L be a set of leaf nodes.
4. For any root vertex v (that is one which has no edges going out of the vertex), T(v) corresponds to a global query. Let R be a set of root nodes.
5. If the base relation or intermediate result relation T(u) corresponding to vertex u is needed for further processing at a node v, introduce an arc $u \longrightarrow v$;
6. For every vertex v, let S(v) denote the source nodes which have edges pointed to v; For any $v \in L$, $S(v) = \emptyset$. Let $S^*\{v\}$ be the set of descendants of v;
7. For every vertex v let D(v) denote the destination nodes to which v is pointed; For any $v \in R$, $D(v) = \emptyset$;
8. For $v \in V$, $C_a^q(v)$ is the cost of query q accessing T(v); $C_m^r(v)$ is the cost of maintaining T(v) based on changes to the base relation $S^*(v) \bigcap R$, if T(v) is materialized.
9. $f_q, f_u$ denote query frequency and base relation maintenance frequency respectively.

# 3 Genetic Algorithm for Materialized View Selection

Since GA simulates the biological process, most of the terminology is borrowed from biology. A detailed illustration of GA terminology can be found in [2]. One of the differences between GA and other commonly used techniques is that GA operates on *population* of *strings*, not a single string. Every *population* is called a *generation*. A single solution is called a *Phenotype* and is represented by a single string. Solutions are represented as *strings (chromosomes)*, that are composed of *characters (genes)* that can take one of several different *values (allels)*. GA creates an initial generation, G(0), and for each generation, G(t), generates a new one, G(t+1). An abstract view of the algorithm is shown in figure 2.

Each problem should have its own solutions represented as character strings by an appropriate encoding. *Selection, crossover* and *mutation* are three operators applied to successive string *populations* to create new populations. In other

---

```
begin
    Generate initial population, G(0);
    Evaluate G(0);
    t:=0;
    repeat
            t:=t+1;
            generate G(t) using G(t-1);
            alter G(t);
            evaluate G(t);
    until solution is found;
end;
```

---

**Fig. 2.** An abstract view of Genetic Algorithm

words these three operators are applied on G(t-1) to generate G(t) as shown in
Figure 2. Choosing a *fitness* function is important. *Fitness* is used in evaluating
individual G(t). In GA, the *average fitness* and the *fitness* of the best solution
increases with every new generation. In order to get the best solution, a lot of
generations should be evolved. Several stopping criteria exist for the algorithm.
For example, the algorithm may be halted when all solutions in a generation are
identical.

In this paper, we devise our GA based on the principle of Simple GA described in [2]. With some modification on the policy of selection and fitness, we
propose the following version of GA which is suitable for our problem.

### 3.1 The String Representation of Our Solution

Based on the principle of minimal alphabets of GA coding, the *string* is essentially a binary string of ones and zeroes.

The representation of our problem is a MVPP, which is a DAG rather than
a binary string. If we can map the representation from DAG to a binary string,
we can apply GA to our problem.

The mapping strategy is shown in figure 3.

For example, search through the DAG in figure 1 using width-first, we obtain
the mapping array as follows { [Q5,0], [Q4,0], [Q3,0], [Q2,0], [Q1,0], [result5,0],
[result1,0], [result2,0], [result4,0], [result3,0], [tmp9,0], [tmp3,0], [tmp4,0], [tmp8,0],
[tmp7,0], [tmp10,0], [tmp1,0], [tmp2,0], [tmp5,0], [tmp6,0]}, its length is 20 excluding the 4 source tables { Item, Sales, Part, Supplier}.

Suppose the result of GA is {0,1,0,0,1,1,0,0,0,0,0,0,0,0,0,0,0,1,1,1}. That means
that the nodes{Q4, Q1, result5, tmp2, tmp5, tmp6} should be materialized.

### 3.2 Mapping Cost Function in Our Problem to Fitness Function in Genetic Algorithm

The objective in our cost model is stated as the minimization of the sum of
query cost and maintenance cost, while the objective or fitness function of GA is
naturally stated as maximization. Therefore, there should be a transformation
from our cost function to the fitness function in GA. For example,

---

begin

1. Input a MVPP represented by a DAG;
2. Use a certain graph search strategy such as breadth-first, width-first or problem-oriented searching method to search through all of the nodes in the DAG and produce an ordered sequence of these nodes
3. Based on this sequence of nodes, create a two dimensional array to store the sequence of nodes and strings of 0s and 1s. One dimension is for the sequence of nodes, another dimension is for strings of 0s and 1s. Of the strings of 0s and 1s, 0 denotes that the corresponding node in the array, indexed by the same subscript, is unmaterialized. 1 representes the corresponding node in mapping array is materialized.

   This array is called the mapping array.

end;

---

**Fig. 3.** A mapping strategy

The commonly used transformation in GA is as follows:

$$f(x) = \begin{cases} C_{max} \text{ - c(x)} & \text{when } c(x) < C_{max} \\ 0 & \text{otherwise} \end{cases}$$

$c(x)$ denotes the cost function. There are a lot of ways to choose the coefficient $C_{max}$. $C_{max}$ may be taken as an input coefficient, as the largest $c(x)$ value observed so far. , as the largest $c(x)$ value in the current population, or the largest of the last $k$ generations.

### 3.3 Crossover

The crossover operator is a way of random number generation, string copies and swapping partially good solutions in order to get a better result.

For example, there are two strings from our example:

$L_1 = 1100100|0100100001111 \qquad L_2 = 0100110|1011000100111$

$L_1$ means that nodes {Q5, Q4, Q1, result4, tmp3, tmp1, tmp2, tmp5, tmp6} are materialized. $L_2$ means that nodes {Q4, Q1, result5, result2, result3, tmp9, tmp7, tmp2, tmp5, tmp6} are materialized. Suppose $k$ is chosen from 1 to 20 randomly. We obtain a $k$=7 (The symbol | represents the position of crossover applied). The results of the crossover are two new strings:

$L_1' = 1100100|1011000100111 \qquad L_2' = 0100110|0100100001111$

The two new individuals, $L_1'$ means that nodes {Q5, Q4, Q1, result2, result3, tmp9, tmp7, tmp2, tmp5, tmp6} are materialized and $L_2'$ means that nodes {Q4, Q1, result5, result4, tmp3, tmp1, tmp2, tmp5, tmp6} are materialized.

### 3.4 Mutation

The mutation operator is a means of the occasional random alteration of the value of a *string* position. It introduces new features that maybe not present in any member of the population. The mutation is performed on a bit by bit basis. For example, assume that the 16th gene from the individual $L_1$ =11

001000100100001111 is selected for a mutation. Since the 16th bit in this string is 0, it would be flipped into 1 with a probability equal to the mutation rate. So the individual $L_1$ after this mutation would be
$$L_1' = 11001000100100011111$$

## 3.5 Selection

The mechanics of a simple GA involve nothing more complex than copying *strings* and swapping *substrings*. The selection operator is a process in which *strings* are copied according to their fitness function. The string with higher fitness value has a higher chance to survive. It is used to select the good solutions in the population.

## 3.6 Modifying the Selection Policy

As mentioned before, GA can be applied to search the solution space. However because of the random characteristic of crossover and mutation, after crossover and mutation, some strings in the next generation might be "invalid", i.e. some nodes which cannot be materialized because some relevant nodes have been materialized.

In the following, we identify one rule to prevent some nodes being selected to be materialized.

**Rule 1:** v1 is a parent of v2 and v2 has the same ancestors(excluding v1) as v1 . We can prove that after v1 was materialized, there is no need to materialize v2.

**Proof:** To illustrate this, see figure ??. Let that $C_{q_i}(M)$ be the cost to compute $q_i$ from the set of materialized views M.

If v1 and v2 are materialized, then the total cost is:
$$C_1 = \sum_{q \in O_{v_1}} f_q(q)*C_q(v_1) + \sum_{q \in O_{v_2}} f_q(q)*C_q(v_2) + \sum_{r \in I_{v_1}} f_u(r)*C_m^r(v_1) + \sum_{r \in I_{v_2}} f_u(r)*C_m^r(v_2) \quad ....(1)$$

As v1 and v2 have the same parents, then (1) can be changed to:
$$C_1 = \sum_{q \in O_{v_1}} f_q(q)*(C_q(v_1)+C_q(v_2)) + \sum_{r \in I_{v_1}} f_u(r)*C_m^r(v_1) + \sum_{r \in I_{v_2}} f_u(r)* C_m^r(v_2)$$

Since v1 is materialized before v2, v2 cannot be reached by any queries, $C_q(v_2) = 0$, then (1) becomes:
$$C_1 = \sum_{q \in O_{v_1}} f_q(q) * C_a^q(v_1) + \sum_{r \in I_{v_1}} f_u(r) * C_m^r(v_1) + \sum_{r \in I_{v_2}} f_u(r) * C_m^r(v_2) \quad ....(2)$$

On the other hand, if we only materialize v1, the total cost is:
$$C_2 = \sum_{q \in O_{v_1}} f_q(q) * C_a^q(v_1) + \sum_{r \in I_{v_1}} f_u(r) * C_m^r(v_1)$$

Since v1, v2 are materialized, we can conclude that the benefit of materializing v1 and v2 is greater than the benefit of materializing v1, in other words, $C_2 > C_1$.

From $C_2 > C_1$, we obtain $\sum_{r \in I_{v_2}} f_u(r) * C_m^r(v_2) < 0$. This is impossible. Therefore in the presence of materialized view v1, we cannot materialize v2 under the condition mentioned above.

For example, with respect to the MVPP in Figure 1, after crossover and mutation, we get string {00000000001100101100}, this string means that {tmp3, tmp2, tmp7, tmp1} should be materialized. However since {tmp3, tmp9} are the parents of {tmp1, tmp2}, they have the same parents, then this string is "invalid". This means that the cost for this string {00000000001100101100} is greater than that for string {00000000001100100000} in which {tmp1,tmp2} are unmaterialized.

How to solve this problem? There are many approaches. One solution is to add a constraint on crossover and mutation operators. This approach gets rid of the "invalid" strings completely while results in the fast convergence to a local minimum.

An alternative approach is to relax the definition of validation, and include a penalty in the cost function to ensure that "invalid" solutions are expensive. But the design of the penalty function is somehow dependent on the experienced values.

We propose the algorithm shown in figure 4 which is based on the combination of the selection principle of GA and rule 1 to do postprocessing.

---

begin
  1. Obtain the initial solutions by GA;
  2. By rule 1, Repeat for each solution within these initial solutions,
    if there are parent and child nodes as follows:
      1) they have the same parents.
      2) they are materialized.
    then change the child nodes to be unmaterialized, to re-calculate the total cost.
      if this new total cost is less than the initial one
        then replace the initial solution with this new solution.
    until every initial solution is checked.
end;

---

**Fig. 4.** A revised algorithm

## 4  Experiment

Our experiment is built on the basis of the Simple Genetic Algorithm. Based on the Simple Genetic Algorithm program [?] which is a C-language translation and extension of the original Pascal SGA code presented in [2], we developed our implementation on SUN-OS V5. General experience shows that the probability of mutation should be much less than that of crossover. In our experiment, the probability of crossover is 0.9, for mutation is from 0.005 to 0.1. The maximum number of generations should be at least double of the population size. Figure 5 shows the comparison between the heuristic algorithm and Genetic Algorithm. The costs are normalized using heuristic algorithm as the reference. The heuristic algorithm used in [10] is a heuristic which is analogous to the Greedy Algorithm. To produce the results shown in figure 5, randomly produced 50 queries. The number of source relations involved in each query varies from 3 to 8. The nodes of the DAG varies from 24 to 200.

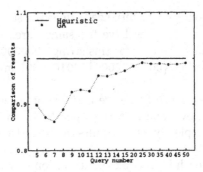

**Fig. 5.** Experimental results

From the results shown in figure 5, we can conclude that with respect to small number of the queries, GA works significantly better than the heuristic approach. When query number increases, the GA approaches closely to the heuristic. However since the total cost increases hugely, a little difference in the comparison of the results will result in a large amount of total cost saving.

With respect to performance, the heuristic needs a few seconds while the GA usually finishes within several minutes.

## 5 Conclusion

In this paper, we proposed a GA to deal with the selection of materialized views in DW. Due to the nature of the problem, we have shown that a GA is particularly suitable. We have also shown the representation of our problem in GA and three basic operators used: *selection, crossover, mutation.* Based on the principle of a Simple GA, we defined the fitness and cost function transformation and developed a modified policy of selection. Finally we modified the GA to cater for the "invalid" solutions. We have demonstrated that a GA is a feasible approach towards solving materialized view selection problem.

In this paper, we only considered a given MVPP. For a set of queries, normally there are lots of possible MVPPs. We have applied GA to this problem. In the future we will explore the possibility of using Genetic Programming to select the best MVPP from all the possible MVPPs and materialized views. We will also apply this method on a large number of nodes to test different scenarios.

## References

1. Elen Baralis, Stefano Paraboschi, and Ernest Teniente. Materialized view selection in a multidimensional database. *Proceedings of the 23rd VLDB Conference, Athens, Greece*, pages 156–165, 1997.
2. D.E. Goldberg. Genetic algorithms in search, optimization and machine learning. *Addison Wesley*, Reading(MA), 1989.
3. Himanshu Gupta. Selection of views to materialize in a data warehouse. *Proceedings of the International Conference on Data Engineering, Burmingham, U.K.*, pages 98–112, April, 1997.

4. Himanshu Gupta and Inderpal Singh Mumick. Selection of views to materialize under a maintenance cost constraint. *Proceedings of the International Conference on Data Engineering*, 1998.

5. Venky Harinarayan, Anand Rajaraman, and Jeffrey D. Ullman. Implementing data cubes efficiently. *ACM SIGMOD International Conference on Management of Data*, pages 205–227, 1996.

6. Wilburt Juan Labio, Dallan Quass, and Brad Adelberg. Physical database design for data warehouses. *Proceedings of the International Conference on Data Engineering*, pages 277–288, 1997.

7. K.A. Ross, Divesh Srivastava, and S. Sudarshan. Materialized view maintenance and integrity constraint checking: Trading space for time. *Proceedings of the ACM SIGMOD*, pages 447–458, 1996.

8. Michael Steinbrunn, Guido Moerkotte, and Alfons Kemper. Heuristic and randomized optimization for the join ordering problem. *VLDB*, 6(3):191–208, 1997.

9. Dimitri Theodoratos and Timos Sellis. Data warehouse configuration. *Proceedings of the 23rd VLDB Conference Athens, Greece, 1997*, pages 126–135, 1997.

10. Jian Yang, Kamalakar Karlapalem, and Qing Li. Algorithm for materialized view design in data warehousing environment. *VLDB'97*, pages 20–40, 1997.

# Optimization of Sequences of Relational Queries in Decision-Support Environments

Antonio Badia and Matthew Niehues

Computer Science and Computer Engineering department
University of Arkansas
Fayetteville AR 72701
E-mail: abadia@godel.uark.edu

## 1 Introduction

In this paper, we analyze collections of SQL queries which together answer a user's question for which no single SQL query can compute the solution. These collections usually define a series of views or temporary tables that constitute *partial solutions* to the question, and finally use an SQL query on those views/tables to get the final answer. We argue that this situation poses problems for traditional approaches to optimization. We show that many of these collections of queries follow some *patterns* and argue that the class of queries covered by such patterns is relevant for practical purposes. We show a way to implement these collections in an efficient manner. We have carried out experiments with the TPC-D benchmark in order to test our approach.

## 2 The Problem and Related Work

Some common business questions cannot be expressed with a single query in SQL ([1]). In this case, one can define a series of views or temporary tables that constitute *partial solutions* to the question, and finally use an SQL query on those views/tables to get the final answer. Thus the final result is constructed in a step-wise fashion.

*Example 1. In our examples we will assume a relation* R *with attributes* A, B, C, D. *The question "Give the smallest maximum value of* C *associated with a given* B*" can be answered by first creating a view as follows:*
CREATE VIEW V(B, MYMAX) AS SELECT B, max(C) FROM R GROUP BY B
*and then querying the view:*
SELECT * FROM V WHERE MYMAX = (SELECT min(MYMAX) FROM V)

By looking at the whole sequence, it is clear that the extra work involved in computing view V separately is not necessary. The problem is that SQL does not allow for *composition of aggregate functions*, as each aggregate is related to a GROUP BY clause (as max in the example) or to a subquery (as min in the example). There are other reasons why SQL may be unable to compute a solution with one single query, like having the aggregate computation depend on some condition.

There is a long body of research in query optimization, as the problem has tremendous practical importance. However, optimization of groups of SQL queries is not a topic that has been explored as much as single query optimization. The recent interest in data warehousing and decision support has motivated work on the use of views to solve complex queries in a step-by-step fashion, decomposing the problem into simpler ones ([2], [4]). Most of this work is focused on view maintenance and does not address the specific problem we present, which is the inability of the language to express some queries as one-step computations. Some work ([6], [8]) concerns optimization of multiple queries. [6] develops the idea (already present in past research) of discovering common subexpressions among groups of queries, executing the subexpressions once and storing the results for reuse. This approach takes as input the query plan for each query, not the query itself. The query plan produced may be optimal for the query, but suboptimal from the point of view of optimizing the whole sequence(in particular, some common subexpressions may be gone). To overcome this, it is proposed to consider several query plans per query. The approach of [8] allows queries to be broken down into subqueries for more flexibility in finding common subexpressions. A heuristic approach is proposed when considering all plans, since the search state may become very large. Both the work of [6] and [8] is limited to Select-Project-Join queries, without subqueries or aggregation. We note an important difference in coverages and goals between these approaches and ours: [6] and [8] try to optimize arbitrary groups of queries to improve system's throughput, while we look at particular *sequences* of queries: each subquery represents a different step (partial solution) towards the ultimate goal.

The work of Ross and Chatziantoniou in [7] has many similarities with the research developed here. [7] observes that the constraints of SQL do not allow the language to express many aggregate-based queries in a single query. An extension to SQL which would allow said queries to be expressed as a single query is proposed. An operator for the relational algebra is given that translates the SQL extension, and an algorithm to evaluate the new operator provided. Thus [7] is basically attacking the same problem that we deal with here. The algorithm proposed also seems to coincide with the for-loop programs that we provide as solutions to the examples, in that relations are first grouped and then aggregations are calculated in one pass, possibly over different groups. Thus, even though the solutions proposed here and in [7] are of a different nature, the end result seems very similar. An important difference is that the work reported here takes as input the original SQL and therefore requires nothing from the user, while [7] requires the user to rewrite the SQL query.

## 3 For-Loop Optimization

We represent SQL queries in an *schematic form*. With the keywords SELECT ... FROM ... WHERE we will use $L, L_1, L_2, \ldots$ as variables over a list of attributes;

$T, T_1, T_2, \ldots$ as variables over a list of relations, $F, F_1, F_2, \ldots$ as variables over aggregate functions and $\Delta, \Delta_1, \Delta_2, \ldots$ as variables over lists of conditions. Attributes will be represented by $attr, attr_1, attr_2, \ldots$. We will say that a pattern matches an SQL query when there is a correspondence $g$ between the variables in the pattern and the elements of the query.

*Example 2. The pattern*
SELECT L FROM T WHERE $\Delta_1$
    AND $attr_1$ = (SELECT F($attr_2$) FROM T WHERE $\Delta_2$)
*would match queries with embedded subqueries that contain an aggregate function (and nothing else) in the* SELECT *clause. Recall relation* R(A,B,C,D) *and let* S(E,F,G) *be another relation with* E *a foreign key referring to* A. *The SQL query*
SELECT * FROM R,S WHERE R.A = S.E and R.B = 'c' and S.F = 'd'
    and C = (SELECT max(C) FROM R,S
        WHERE R.A = S.E and R.B = 'c' and R.D = 'e')
*matches the pattern above with the correspondence* $g(\Delta_1) = \{R.A = S.E, R.B =' c', S.F =' d'\}$, $g(\Delta_2) = \{R.A = S.E, R.B =' c', R.D =' e'\}$, $g(T) = \{R, S\}$, $g(F) = \max$ *and* $g(attr_1) = g(attr_2) = C$.

We use these patterns to create for-loop programs. A *for-loop program* is an expression of the form
for (t in R) GROUP(t.attr,Body1) [Body2] Body3 \Body4\
where t is a tuple variable (called the *driving tuple*), R is a relational algebra expression called the *basic relation*, and each one of Body1...Body4 is called a *loop body*. A loop body is a sequence of statements, where each statement is either a variable assignment or a conditional statement. We write the assignments as v := e;, where v is a variable and e an expression. Both variables and expressions are either of integer, tuple or relation type. Expressions are made up of variables, constants, arithmetic operators (for integer variables) and the $\cup$ operator (for relation variables). If $e_1, \ldots, e_n$ are either integer expressions or attribute names, then $(e_1, \ldots, e_n)$ is a tuple expression. If u is a tuple expression, then {u} is a relation expression. Conditional statements are written as: if (cond) p1; or: if (cond) p1 else p2;, with both p1 and p2 being sequences of statements. The condition cond is made up of the usual comparison operators (=, <, > and so on) relating constants and/or variables. Parenthesis ({, }) are used for clarity. Also, for-loop programs obey the following constraints: first, the basic relation is built using only the join, project and select relational operators applied to base relations from the database. Second, the only tuple variable in the loop body is the driving tuple and the only relational variable is an special variable called result. The semantics of a for-loop program are defined in an intuitive way. Let attr be the name of an attribute in R, and let $t_1, \ldots, t_n$ be an ordering of the tuples of R such that for any $i, j \in \{1, \ldots, n\}$, if $t_i.\text{attr} = t_j.\text{attr}$, then $i = j + 1$ or $j = i + 1$ (in other words, the ordering provides a grouping of R by attribute attr). Then the program Body1 is done once for each tuple, and all variables in Body1 are reset for different values of attr (that is, Body1 is computed independently for each group), while program Body2 will be

executed *once* for every value of `attr` (i.e. once for every group) after `Body1` is executed. `Body3` is simply done once for each tuple in `R` and `Body4` is executed *once*, after the iteration is completed. The semantics of executing a program are intuitive.

*Example 3. The SQL query*
```
select B, avg(C) from R where A = 'a₁' group by B
```
*can be computed by the program*
```
count := 0; sum := 0; avg := 0; result := ∅;
for (t in π_{B,C}(σ_{A='a'₁}(R)))
    GROUP(t.B, {sum := sum + t.C; count := count + 1})
    [avg := sum/count; result := result ∪ {(t.B, avg)};]
```
*This example has neither a Body3 nor a Body4 fragment. Observe that it is assumed that variables* sum *and* count *get reset to their initial values for each group, while* avg *and* result *are global variables, and the instructions that contain them are executed only once for each group (once* sum *and* count *have been computed).*

In order to build a for-loop program we need to provide a basic relation and code for `Body`. This is derived from the pattern that the SQL query matches. The following example gives an intuitive view of the process.

*Example 4. Assume the pattern and the query of example 2. We then proceed as follows: the basic relation is built using $g(\Delta_1) \cap g(\Delta_2)$ (in this case, {R.A = S.E, R.B = 'c'}) applied to $g(T)$ (in this example, {R, S}). Thus the basic relation is $\sigma_{R.B='c'}(R \bowtie S)$ (after some basic relational optimization). For the body of the loop, we define a piece of code associated with the pattern. In this case, the code is*
```
max := -∞; result := ∅;
    if g(Δ₂) - g(Δ₁) update aggregate (max) and update result;
    if g(Δ₁) - g(Δ₂) compute result;
```

*where* result *and* max *are global variables. The concrete code depends on the linking operator and the linking function ("=" and* max *in example 2), since* compute aggregate, compute result *and* update result *are macros that must be further developed. The concrete code explains how to compute the condition in an iterative fashion. Once the particular code for "=" and* max *is added, the pattern for the query of example 2 expands into the following program:*
```
max := -∞; result := ∅;
for(t in σ_{R.B='c'}(R ⋈ S))
        if (t.D = 'e')
            if (t.C > max) { max := t.C; result := ∅; }
        if (t.F = 'd') {
            if (t.C = max) result := result ∪ {t};
        };
```

Given a question expressed as a set of queries, optimization as a group is only possible if the set of queries is presented to the optimizer as a *package*, so that the optimizer can examine them together as a unit. In that situation, it is possible to detect the relationship among views (tables) by looking at the FROM clauses. In some cases it may be possible to collapse several steps into a single one.

*Example 5. The query of example 1 has two parts. The first one is a view creation query which fits the pattern of example 3. The second one is a query which follows the pattern of example 2. The relation is established by the use of name V (the view created in the first part) in the FROM clause of the second part. Both patterns can be combined as follows: create a new pattern following example 3, and insert, inside the [] part of the body, the code introduced by example 2. The final program for the query of example 1 is:*

```
result:= ∅; curr-max := −∞; curr-min := +∞;
for(t in π_{B,C}(R))
    GROUP(t.B,
        if (t.C > curr-max) { result:= {(t.B, t.C)}; curr-max := t.C;}
        if (t.C = curr-max) { result:= result ∪ {(t.B,t.C)};)
    [if (t.C < curr-min) { result:= {t}; curr-min := t.C;}
        if (t.C = curr-min) { result:= result ∪ {t}; }]
```

*Recall that the code between [ and ] is done once for every group, after the code in the GROUP construct. Note, in particular, that curr-max is reset after every group computation, while curr-min is a global variable.*

## 4 Experimental Analysis

To test our approach we ran experiments using queries 11, 12, 14 and 15 of the TPC-D benchmark ([3]). Said queries fit in some of our patterns. We first ran the queries in two commercial relational database systems. Then the queries were manually transformed into for-loop programs and implemented in SQL with cursors[1]. The running times were compared; all queries showed improvements of about 50% (i.e. ran in about half the time). It is important to point out that the for-loop approach was implemented using the same systems and setup as the SQL queries; therefore both benefited from the same indices, buffer space, etc. In particular, the basic relation is computed as if it were a regular SQL query. Therefore, it is reasonable to assume that the improvement is due to the fact that the for-loop avoids duplication of efforts by reducing the number of intermediate results needed.

---

[1] The intuitive idea is to extract the basic relation from the tables in the database first (using SQL), and store it as a temporary result. The loop program can then be implemented in main memory using cursors, as one pass over the basic relation is all that is needed.

# 5    Conclusion and Further Research

We have introduced a new mechanism to implement a class of sequences of SQL queries. This class is not processed as efficiently as possible by relational processors. We presented the approach intuitively and discussed some experimental results.

There are several issues that may influence practical usage of the approach. One is whether the approach is useful in a sufficiently wide range of circumstances; another whether the approach can be integrated into existing query processors. The first issue cannot be answered simply, as it has some empirical aspects. We argue that, because of the SQL syntax, which forces groupings dependent on different attributes or selections to go on different queries, the class of queries covered here is significant[2]. With respect to the second, we note that the for-loop approach can be very easily expressed as in *iterator* and therefore could be incorporated into an extendible query processor like the VOLCANO system ([5]). Indeed, the for-loop takes a relation as input and produces a relation as output, and therefore could be embedded in an iterator module (note that the rest of the computation, the basic relation, is a standard SQL query).

This paper reports work in progress. The approach should be completely automatized and extended to deal with more cases; for instance, cases in which a mix of base tables and views are used in a FROM clause. The exact relationship between the present approach and that of [7] should be studied.

# References

1. R. Kimball, *What is wrong with decision support and how to fix it*, SIGMOD Record, vol. 24, n. 3, September 1994.
2. Gupta, A., Harinayaran, V. and Quass, D. *Aggregate-Query Processing in Data Warehousing Environments*, in Proceedings of the 21st VLDB Conference, Zurich 1995.
3. TPC-D Benchmark, TPC Council, http://www.tpc.org/home.page.html.
4. Levy, A., Mendelzon, A., Srivasta, D., and Sagiv, Y. *Answering Queries Using Views*, in Proceedings of PODS 1995.
5. Graefe, G. *Volcano -An Extendible and Parallel Query Evaluation System*, IEEE Transactions on Knowledge and Data Engineering, vol. 6, n. 1, 1994.
6. Park, J. and Segev, A. *Using common subexpressions to optimize multiple queries*, in Proceedings of the 1988 IEEE CS ICDE.
7. Ross, K. and Chatziantoniou, D., *Querying Multiple Features of Groups in Relational Databases*, Proceedings of the 22nd VLDB Conference, 1996.
8. Sellis, T. *Multiple-Query Optimization*, in ACM Transactions on Database Systems, vol. 13, n. 1, 1988.

---

[2] The fact that 4 queries out of 17 in the TPC-D benchmark are covered by the approach supports this assertion, especially since the benchmark was created to be representative of a wide range of decision-support queries.

# Dynamic Data Warehousing

Umeshwar Dayal, Qiming Chen, Meichun Hsu

HP Labs, Hewlett-Packard, 1501 Page Mill Road, MS 1U4, Palo Alto, CA 94303, USA
{dayal, qchen, mhsu}@hpl.hp.com

**Abstract.** Data warehouses and on-line analytical processing (OLAP) tools have become essential elements of decision support systems. Traditionally, data warehouses are refreshed periodically (for example, nightly) by extracting, transforming, cleaning and consolidating data from several operational data sources. The data in the warehouse is then used to periodically generate reports, or to rebuild multidimensional (data cube) views of the data for on-line querying and analysis. Increasingly, however, we are seeing business intelligence applications in telecommunications, electronic commerce, and other industries, that are characterized by very high data volumes and data flow rates, and that require continuous analysis and mining of the data. For such applications, rather different data warehousing and on-line analysis architectures are required. In this paper, we first motivate the need for a new architecture by summarizing the requirements of these applications. Then, we describe a few approaches that are being developed, including virtual data warehouses or enterprise portals that support access through views or links directly to the operational data sources. We discuss the relative merits of these approaches. We then focus on a *dynamic data warehousing* and OLAP architecture that we have developed and prototyped at HP Labs. In this architecture, data flows continuously into a data warehouse, and is staged into one or more OLAP tools that are used as computation engines to continuously and incrementally build summary data cubes, which might then be stored back in the data warehouse. Analysis and data mining functions are performed continuously and incrementally over these summary cubes. Retirement policies define when to discard data from the warehouse (i.e., move data from the warehouse into off-line archival storage). Data at different levels of aggregation may have different life spans depending on how they are to be used for downstream analysis and data mining. The key features of the architecture are the following: incremental data reduction using OLAP engines to generate summaries and enable data mining; staging large volumes and flow rates of data with different life spans at different levels of aggregation; and scheduling operations on data depending on the type of processing to be performed and the age of the data.

# Set-Derivability of Multidimensional Aggregates

J. Albrecht, H. Günzel, W. Lehner[1]

Department of Database Systems, University of Erlangen-Nuremberg
Martensstr. 3, 91058 Erlangen, Germany
{jalbrecht, guenzel, lehner}@informatik.uni-erlangen.de

**Abstract.** A common optimization technique in data warehouse environments is the use of materialized aggregates. Aggregate processing becomes complex, if partitions of aggregates or queries are materialized and reused later. Most problematic are the implication problems regarding the restriction predicates. We show that in the presence of hierarchies in a multidimensional environment an efficient algorithm can be given to construct - or to derive - an aggregate from one or more overlapping materialized aggregate partitions (*set-derivability*).

## 1 Introduction

In the last few years data warehousing has emerged from a mere buzzword to a fundamental database technology. Today, almost every major company is deploying an integrated, historic database, the data warehouse, as a basis for multidimensional decision support queries. The purpose is to provide business analysts and managers with online analytical processing (OLAP). Besides the use of big parallel database servers, a common optimization technique is to precompute aggregates, i.e. to use summary tables or materialized views (e.g. [3], [8], [9], [15]). Most of the presented algorithms base on the assumption that during the data warehousing loading process a pre-determined set of aggregates is materialized and used during the analysis phase. But there is also a great performance potential in the dynamic reutilization of cached query results ([1], [5]).

However, today the transparent reuse of aggregates is based on limited cases of query containment, i.e. the query must be contained in *one* certain aggregate. Since the implication problem for query restrictions containing the six comparison operators as well as disjunctions and conjunctions is solvable NP-hard [13], algorithms like [9] as well as commercial products (e.g. [3]) are based on aggregate views defined without restrictions to circumvent this problem. Using this approach, the definition and reuse of *aggregate partitions* for hot spots, like the current month or the most important product group, and the reuse of queries are impossible.

In many cases this is too restrictive. Consider the query *"Give me the total sales for the video product families by region in Germany"* and the tabular result illustrated in figure 1. The materialized query represents a partition of

| Sum(Sales) | Camcorder | HomeVCR |
|------------|-----------|---------|
| G-East     | 12        | 37      |
| G-West     | 22        | 32      |

**Fig. 1.** A partition of an aggregated data cube.

---

[1]  Current address: IBM Almaden Research Center, 650 Harry Road, San Jose, CA 95120, U.S.A.

an aggregated data cube. If there were two redundant aggregates in the database, one containing the sales for camcorders and the other one containing the sales for home VCRs, then the query could be computed by the union of these aggregates. The goal of this article is to provide a constructive solution for this problem.

In the presence of a set of materialized aggregate partitions, a multidimensional query optimizer has to determine under which circumstances and *how* a query can be computed from these aggregates (figure 2). The basis of our approach are multidimensional objects which were initially presented in [10]. Multidimensional objects provide the information to a multidimensional query optimizer for the transparent reuse of materialized aggregate partitions. Their definition includes semantic information about it genesis, i.e. the applied aggregation and the selection predicates. Thus, a certain class of aggregation queries can be directly translated into multidimensional objects. Queries involving composite aggregations can at least utilize multidimensional objects based on the component aggregates.

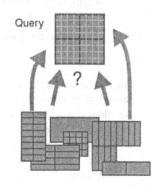

**Fig. 2.** Derivability problem: Can the query be computed from the set of multidimensional objects?

**Structure of the Paper.** The next section covers related work. Basis for the determination of derivability are the dimensional data structures presented in section 3. Section 4 introduces multidimensional objects and some basic operators. The derivability of multidimensional objects with a focus on the solution to implication problems in the presence of hierarchies is covered in section 5. The article closes with a short summary.

## 2 Related Work

The general idea of precomputing summary data appeared already in [4]. In the last few years it became very popular with the emergence of data warehousing and OLAP and the resulting need for an efficient and mostly read-only access to aggregates in a multidimensional context. Several articles deal with the selection and use of materialized views (e.g. [5], [8],[9]; see overview in [15]). In contrast to our approach, these articles are not able to construct a new query from a set of materialized queries but are limited to certain cases of query containment.

Summarizability and derivability are terms describing under which circumstances summary data can be derived from other summary data. [4] investigates conditions under which already aggregated cells might be further aggregated. Aggregation functions are classified as additive and computed. These notions correlate to the distinction of distributive and algebraic functions in [7]. The question under which circumstance a query is derivable from one or more other queries has been studied for a long time ([6], [13]). For summary data, disjointness and completeness are fundamental [4]. Another semantic condition, type compatibility, was identified by [11].

# 3 Dimensional Data Structures

The notion of a dimension provides a lot of semantic information especially about the hierarchical relationships between its elements like product groups or geographic regions. This information is heavily used for both aggregate queries and selections, and it provides the basis for the definition of multidimensional objects.

*Definition 1:* A *dimensional schema* is a partially ordered set of dimensional attributes $(\mathcal{D}\cup\{Total_D\};\rightarrow)$ where $\mathcal{D}=\{D_1,...,D_n\}$. $Total_{\mathcal{D}}$ is a generic element which is maximal with respect to "$\rightarrow$", i.e. $D_i\rightarrow Total_{\mathcal{D}}$ for each $D_i\in\mathcal{D}$.
An attribute $D_j$ is called a *direct parent* of $D_i$, denoted as $D_i\overset{\cdot}{\rightarrow}D_j$, if $D_i\rightarrow D_j$ and there is no $D_k$ with $D_i\rightarrow D_k\rightarrow D_j$.

Figure 3 shows examples for dimensional schemas illustrated as directed acyclic graphs according to the partial order "$\rightarrow$" which denotes a functional dependency, i.e. a 1:n relationship. $Total_{\mathcal{D}}$ is generic in the sense that it is not modeled explicitly.

*Definition 2:* The instances $c\in dom(D_i)$ of some dimensional attribute $D_i\in\mathcal{D}$ are called *classification objects* or *classes* of $D_i$. $D_i$ is called the level of c.
Moreover, $dom(Total_{\mathcal{D}}) := \{'ALL'\}$.
An *instance of a dimension* $\mathcal{D}$ is the set of all classes $c \in \cup_i dom(D_i)$.

A hierarchy can be specified by a *categorization*, i.e. a path to Total in a dimension. By defining $dom(Total):=\{'ALL'\}$ it is guaranteed that all classification hierarchies are trees having "ALL" as the single root node. A sample classification hierarchy for the categorization Article$\rightarrow$Family$\rightarrow$Group$\rightarrow$Area$\rightarrow$Total is shown in figure 4. The edges in such a tree can also be seen as a mapping from the descendents to the ancestors.

*Definition 3:* Let $D_i, D_j\in\mathcal{D}$ such that $D_i\rightarrow D_j$. A class $a\in dom(D_j)$ is called *ancestor* of class $b\in dom(D_i)$, denoted as ancestor(a,b), if and only if a maps to b according to the functional dependency $D_i\rightarrow D_j$. In this case b is called a *descendant* of a, i.e. descendant(b,a)$\Leftrightarrow$ancestor(a,b).
The domain of a class a with respect to the dimensional attribute $D_i$ is defined as the set of it descendents, i.e. $dom(a \mid D_i) = \{b\in dom(D_i): descendant(b,a)\}$.

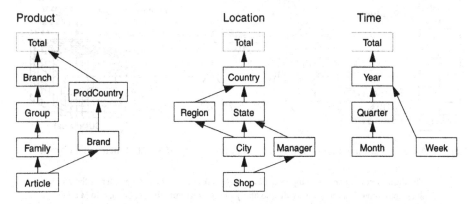

**Fig. 3.** Illustration the of dimensional schemas for the product, location and time dimension as directed acyclic graphs.

# 4 Multidimensional Data Structures

The following definition of multidimensional objects is an extension of the work presented in [10]. In contrast to other multidimensional data structures (see [12]), multidimensional objects contain additional information besides the measures and aggregation level (granularity) which is necessary to check the derivability. One thing is that instead of treating measures as simple attributes the information about the aggregation operation which was applied to the measure is made part of their definition.

*Definition 4:* Let $\Omega$ be a set of additive aggregation functions. A *measure* is tuple M = (N, O), where N is a *name* for the corresponding fact and O $\in$ $\Omega \cup$ {NONE, COMPOSITE} is the *operation type* applied to that specific fact.

We assume that a measure M has a numerical domain dom(M)$\in$ { $\mathbf{R}$, $\mathbf{N}$,$\mathbb{Q}$, $\mathbf{Z}$} and $\Omega$ = {SUM, COUNT, MIN, MAX}. Only additive operations (in the sense of [4]) are explicitly represented. Other operations are subsumed by the operation type COMPOSITE, i.e. those measures can not be used for the automatic derivation of higher aggregates. However, for many composite operations, like AVG, one can extend our concept by implicitly storing SUM and COUNT. The value NONE states that a measure is not aggregated.

*Definition 5:* A multidimensional object over the dimensions $\mathcal{D}_1,...,\mathcal{D}_d$ is a triple $\mathcal{M}$ = [M, G, S] where
- M = $(M_1,...,M_m)$ = ( $(N_1,O_1)$, ..., $(N_m,O_m)$ ) is a set of measures[2]
- G = $(G_1,...,G_n)$ is the granularity specification consisting of a set of dimensional attributes, i.e. $G_i \in \mathcal{D}_1 \cup ... \cup \mathcal{D}_d$ such that for each $G_i$, $G_j$: $G_i \not\rightarrow G_j$
- S is logical predicate denoting the scope.

The scope is a restriction predicate describing *which* data cells have been aggregated in this particular (sub-) cube. It may include any propositional logic expression involving the granularity attributes of $\mathcal{M}$ and any dimensional attribute that is functionally dependent on some $G_i \in$ G. For example, the multidimensional object in figure 4 is[3]

[ (Sales, SUM),(P.Family, L.City, T.Month),(P.Area='Brown Goods'^L.Country='Germany') ]

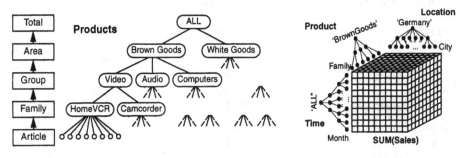

**Fig. 4.** A classification hierarchy for the product dimension and a multidimensional object.

---

[2] The definition of M and G as tuples is only for the sake of simplicity; the order of the elements does not matter. Therefore, we will also apply the set operators like $\in$, $\cup$, $\cap$, = to M and G.

[3] In the following examples we will abbreviate the dimension names Product, Location and Time with P, L and T, respectively.

In the literature on multidimensional data models several operators were defined on multidimensional data cubes [12]. Most important are selections and aggregations. The goal of this section is to define the influence of these operators on multidimensional objects, especially on the measures and the scope. Since the definition of operators is not the topic of this article, we will only shortly mention some operators.

Fundamental are the *metric projection* of the attributes $M'=(M_1',...,M_k')\subseteq M$, written as $\pi_{M'}(\mathcal{M}) = [M', G, S]$, and the *restriction* by a predicate P, defined as $\sigma_P(\mathcal{M}) = [M, G, S \wedge P]$. On set-compatible multidimensional objects $\mathcal{M}$ and $\mathcal{M}'$ (i.e. $M=M'$ and $G=G'$) one can define the common *set-operations* $\mathcal{M} \cup \mathcal{M}' = [M, G, S \vee S']$, $\mathcal{M} \cap \mathcal{M}' = [M, G, S \wedge S']$, and $\mathcal{M} \setminus \mathcal{M}' = [M, G, S \wedge \neg S']$. However, the most important operations on multidimensional objects are aggregations, which are defined first on the measures alone and then on multidimensional objects.

*Definition 6:* The application of an aggregation function F to a measure M = (N,O) results in a measure F(M)=(N,O') where
- O' = F if O=NONE or if F=O and O∈ {SUM,MIN,MAX},
- O' = COUNT if O=COUNT and F=SUM
- O' = COMPOSITE otherwise.

A granularity specification $G=(G_1,...,G_n)$ is *finer than or equal to* a granularity specification $G'=(G_1',...,G_k')$, denoted as $G \leq G'$, if and only if for each $G_j' \in G'$ there is a $G_i \in G$ such that $G_i \rightarrow G_j'$. For example (P.Article, L.City)≤(P.Group, L.Region)≤(P.Area).

*Definition 7:* The *aggregation* of a multidimensional object $\mathcal{M}$ by a family of aggregate functions $\Phi=(F_1,...,F_m)$ to the granularity $G' \geq G$ is defined as:
$$\Phi(G', \mathcal{M}) = [ (F_1(M_1),...,F_m(M_m)), G', S ]$$

For example, if $\mathcal{M} = [ (Sales, SUM),(P.Family),(P.Group = 'Video') ]$ then
(SUM) ( (P.Group), $\mathcal{M}$ ) = [ (Sales, SUM),(P.Group),(P.Group = 'Video') ] and
(AVG) ( (), $\mathcal{M}$ ) =[ (Sales, COMPOSITE),(P.Group),(P.Group = 'Video') ].

# 5 Derivability in the Presence of Hierarchies

Based on the definitions of the last section, we will now define under which conditions and how a multidimensional object can be computed from a set of materialized MOs. A necessary prerequisite to derive a multidimensional object is that the aggregation level of the original MOs is finer than the granularity of the derived MO. This condition directly corresponds to the relationship of the aggregates in an aggregation lattice [9]. Two further conditions, measure compatibility and reconstructibility, are necessary to define the derivability of multidimensional objects.

*Definition 8:* A multidimensional object $\mathcal{M} = (M, G, S)$ is *derivable* from a multidimensional object $\mathcal{M}' = (M',G',S')$ if and only if
- for each measure $M_i \in M$ there is $M_j' \in M'$ such that $N_i = N_j'$ and $O = O'$ or $O' = NONE$
- the granularity specification of $\mathcal{M}'$ is finer than $\mathcal{M}$, i.e. $G' \leq G$
- S is contained in S', i.e. $S \subseteq S'$ (or $S \rightarrow S'$) and S is reconstructible from S'.

Measure compatibility simply means that for example total sales are derivable from total sales. Most problematic is the third condition, one is that S is contained by S' (considering S and S' as sets of dimensional elements). How to check this condition and the notion of reconstructibility is explained in the next section.

### 5.1 Scope Normalization

In [13] it is shown that the problem to determine that some predicate S is implied by another predicate S' is NP-complete if the predicates may contain disjunctions and inequalities besides simple comparison operators. In this section we will give an efficient polynomial time algorithm, which solves implication problems in the presence of hierarchies on finite domains even for negations and disjunctions. The algorithm is based on compact scopes for which the determination of scope containment is very simple.

*Definition 9:* A scope S is *compact* if S is a conjunction of positive terms and there are no two different terms $\mathcal{D}_i.D_j=c$ and $\mathcal{D}_i.D_k=c'$ with ancestor(c, c').

Thus, the scope ((P.Family='Camcorder'∨P.Family='HomeVCR')∧L.Country='Germany') is not compact, but (P.Group='Video'∧L.Country='Germany') is.

A compact scope S is *contained* in a scope S' (denoted as S→S' or S⊆S') if and only if for each term $\mathcal{D}_i.D_k=c'$ in S' there exists a term $\mathcal{D}_i.D_j=c$ in S such that ancestor(c', c). For example, (P.Family='HomeVCR')⊄(P.Group='Video'∧L.Country='Germany') but (P.Family='HomeVCR' ∧L.Country='Germany')⊆(P.Group='Video').

Not only scope containment, but also all problems of finding the intersections or differences of two compact scopes can be solved simply by determining ancestor/descendant relationships of classes appearing in the conjunctive clauses. Both operations are based on the one-dimensional intersection and the difference of two classes. For the intersection of two classes c∈ dom(D$_i$) and c'∈ dom(D$_j$) holds c∩c'=c if ancestor(c',c) and c∩c'=∅ otherwise. For example in figure 5 M∩B=B and M∩E=∅. Intersections of classes in parallel hierarchies like P.Family='HomeVCR'∧P.Brand='Sony' are not resolved but treated as if it were separate dimensions. The difference of two classes can be computed by the algorithm ClassDifference as illustrated in figure 5 (see [2] for the complete algorithm).

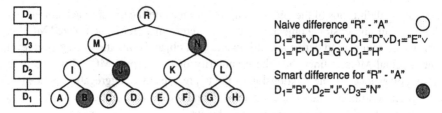

**Fig. 5.** Illustration of the algorithm ClassDifference.

Each scope can be transformed into a "minimal" disjunction of mutually disjoint compact scopes, the disjunctive scope normal form (DSNF). Based on the DSNF and the scope difference the scope implication problems for non-compact scopes can be solved in a constructive way. To explain the construction of the DSNF consider the following multidimensional object:

[(Sales, SUM),
 (P.Group, L.Region),
 (P.Group = 'Video' ∧ L.Region = 'G-East') ∨
 ((L.Region = 'G-West' ∨ L.Region = 'G-East') ∧
 P.Group = 'Video' ∧ P.Family ≠ 'Camcorder')]

| Sum(Sales) | Camcorder | HomeVCR |
|------------|-----------|---------|
| G-East | 12 | 37 |
| G-West | | 32 |

Intuitively, the scope definition is not minimal, because the terms L.Region='G-East' ∨ L.Region='G-West' can be reduced to L.Country='Germany'. In order to find all such terms, it is necessary to translate the predicate into conjunctive normal form where such terms appear in a single disjunctive clause and can be discovered easily. This kind of reduction together with the replacement of negative terms is realized by algorithm 1 (see [2] for details), which constructs the conjunctive scope normal form (CSNF), i.e. a minimal expression of the scope in CNF. The resulting scope for the example above is

(P.Group = 'Video' ∨ L.Country = 'Germany') ∧ (P.Group = 'Video') ∧
(L.Country = 'Germany') ∧ (L.Region = 'G-East' ∨ P.Family = 'HomeVCR')

The translation from CSNF into DSNF is analogous to translating CNF into DNF. This implies that all positive terms remain positive. The example yields the following DNF:

(P.Group = 'Video' ∧ L.Country = 'Germany' ∧ L.Region = 'G-East') ∨
(P.Group = 'Video' ∧ P.Family = 'HomeVCR' ∧ L.Country = 'Germany')

To make the clauses compact, for each class it must now be checked if an ancestor is also in the same clause. If so, the ancestor is removed. This leads to

(P.Group = 'Video' ∧ L.Region = 'G-East') ∨ (P.Family = 'HomeVCR' ∧ L.Country = 'Germany')

**Algorithm: ConjunctiveScopeNormalization**

```
Input:    Scope of a MO over dimensions 𝒟₁,...,𝒟ₙ
          in conjunctive normal form S = S₁^...^Sₖ
Output:   Scope S in conjunctive scope normal form
1  Begin
2     Foreach Sᵢ
3        replace all negative terms 𝒟ⱼ.Dₖ≠c by
4           ClassDifference(𝒟ⱼ.Total="ALL", 𝒟ⱼ.Dₖ≠c);
5
6        Foreach term 𝒟ⱼ.Dₖ=c
7           If (c' with Ancestor(c', c) is also contained)
8              remove 𝒟ⱼ.Dₖ≠c
9
10       Foreach term 𝒟ⱼ.Dₖ=c
11          let Dₚ represent a direct parent level,
12          i.e. 𝒟ⱼ.Dₖ ⇀ Dₚ;
13          p = GetAncestor(child | Dₚ);
14          If (all elements of dom(p | Dₖ) c are in Sᵢ)
15             replace c and all siblings by p;
16
17    End Foreach
18
19    Return S = S₁^ ... ^Sₙ;
20 End
```

**Algorithm: PatchWork**

```
Input:    A compact scope SC and
          a scope in DSNF S = SC₁∪...∪SCₙ
Output:   TRUE if S→SC, FALSE otherwise
1  Begin
2     remainder = {SC};
3     solution = ∅;
4
5     While remainder ≠ ∅ Do
6        Foreach R ∈ remainder
7           found = false;
8           For i = 1 To n
9              // check if this part of the remainder is
10             // intersected by a compact scope in S
11             If Intersection(R, SCᵢ)≠∅ Then
12                remainder = remainder \ {R} ∪
13                   ScopeDifference(R, SCᵢ);
14                solution = solution∪Intersection(R,SCᵢ);
15                found = TRUE;
16                Break;
17             End If
18          End For
19          If (Not found)
20             Return ∅;
21       End Foreach
22    End While
23    Return solution;
24 End
```

**Algorithm 1:** ConjunctiveScopeNormalization transforms a scope from conjunctive normal form to conjunctive scope normal form.

**Algorithm 2:** PatchWork constructs a solution in DSNF how to compute the compact scope SC from $SC_1,...,SC_n$.

By using the ScopeDifference it is now possible to make the clauses mutually disjoint. Therefore, a DSNF representation of the scope is

(P.Group = 'Video' ∧ L.Region = 'G-East') ∨ (P.Family = 'HomeVCR' ∧ L.Region = 'G-West')

Based on the DSNF, the problem if a scope $S_1=SC_{11}\vee...\vee SC_{1n}$ is contained in a scope $S_2=SC_{21}\vee...\vee SC_{2m}$ can be solved constructively by algorithm 2. For each conjunctive term $SC_{1i}$ the following steps are executed. The remainder is a set of "patches", i.e. "compact" fragments which still must be covered. For each remaining patch R it must be checked if $R\cap SC_{2i}\neq\varnothing$ for some i (line 11). If so, the intersection is removed from the remainder and added to the solution (lines 12-14). If for some remaining patch no intersecting clause from $S_2$ is found, then $S_1\not\subseteq S_2$. Thus, the solution itself is a set of mutually disjoint compact scopes (patches) and can be seen as an instruction *how* to compute $SC_{11}$ from $SC_2$.

However, this construction does not work in all cases because a multidimensional object still may not be *reconstructible* from the other one. Consider the query: *"Give me the total sales of all video and audio products per region"* expressed by the multidimensional object

$\mathcal{M}$ = [(Sales, SUM), (L.Region), (P.Group='Video'∨P.Group='Audio')].

If there was an aggregate with no restrictions (equivalent to Total="ALL" in all dimensions)

$\mathcal{M}'$ = [(Sales, SUM), (P.Area, L.Region), ()],

then question is, if $\mathcal{M}$ is derivable from $\mathcal{M}'$. It turns out that, although G≤G' and S⊆S', $\mathcal{M}'$ is not reconstructible from $\mathcal{M}$ because the two patches with P.Group='Video' and P.Group='Audio' can not be addressed in $\mathcal{M}$. The reason is that $\mathcal{M}'$ has already a higher granularity (P.Area) than the attributes in the patch clauses (P.Group). This must also be checked (see definition 8). However, in case S=S' it would work anyway.

## 5.2  Set-Derivability

A set of multidimensional objects { [M, G, $SC_1$],...,[M, G, $SC_n$] } can also be seen as a MO $\mathcal{M}$=[M, G, $SC_1\vee...\vee SC_n$] and the other way around. Since it is easy to aggregate MOs at a finer granularity G'≤G (definitions and 8) to G, one can easily extend algorithm 2 to construct one multidimensional object $\mathcal{M}_Q$ from a set of multidimensional objects $\mathcal{M}_1,...,\mathcal{M}_n$ at granularities G'≤G (figure 6). Thus, $\mathcal{M}_Q$ is *set-derivable* from $\mathcal{M}_1,...,\mathcal{M}_n$ if algorithm 3 yields a non-empty solution. Set-derivability in conjunction with a cost-based selection can serve as a basis to compute one query from a set of previously materialized queries. For an illustration consider the following multidimensional objects in DSNF:

$\mathcal{M}_1$ = [ (Sales, SUM), (P.Family, L.Region), (P.Group = 'Video' ∧ L.Country='Germany') ]

$\mathcal{M}_2$ = [ (Sales, SUM), (P.Group, L.City), ((P.Area = 'Brown Goods' ∧ L.Region='G-West') ]

$\mathcal{M}_3$ = [ (Sales, SUM), (P.Article, L.City), ((P.Group = 'Audio' ∧ L.Country = 'Germany') ∨
(P.Group = 'Video' ∧ L.Region='G-West') ]

The use of algorithm 2 in the context of set-derivability can be used to derive the query

$\mathcal{M}_Q$ = [ (Sales, SUM), (P.Goup, L.Region), ((P.Area = 'Brown Goods' ∧ L.Country='Germany') ]

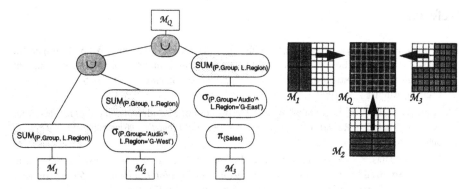

**Fig. 6.** Patch-working. The requested MO $\mathcal{M}_Q$ can be constructed from $\mathcal{M}_1$, $\mathcal{M}_2$ and $\mathcal{M}_3$.

from $\mathcal{M}_1$, $\mathcal{M}_2$ and $\mathcal{M}_3$ by the query execution plan depicted in figure 6. Such an approach overcomes the limitations of query containment for the reuse of cached aggregates and bears a high performance potential [1].

## 6 Summary and Future Work

The determination of the derivability of multidimensional aggregates is an essential task for a multidimensional query optimizer. In this article we presented multidimensional objects as an enriched data structure which helps to accomplish this task. We have shown that the inclusion of the semantics of aggregations on the measures in an extended multidimensional algebra allows much more flexibility for the selection of aggregates by the query optimizer than is possible today. For the derivability of multidimensional objects three conditions have to be checked: measure and granularity compatibility as well as scope containment. An efficient algorithm was given which solves the scope implication problem in the presence of hierarchies in a constructive way. The potential of the approach has already been proved for a certain class of multidimensional objects. Experimental results are given in [1].

Future research aims at an extension of the presented concept on a more complete multidimensional algebra, including other aggregation functions and also binary operations. Another idea is to include comparisons on the aggregated measure attributes in the scope restriction, a problem that has already been investigated in [14]. Our strategic goal is to supply the query optimizer with sufficient knowledge to solve problems of the following kind: *"Given a formula* Turnover=Sales*Price *and an aggregated sales data cube, under which circumstances is it possible to use this aggregated sales cube to derive an aggregated turnover cube?"* There are many possibilities under which the information about computed measures can be used to utilize materialized multidimensional objects for the actual computation. In several relevant cases binary operations do not change the operation type of the resulting measure, for example, (Stock,SUM)=(StockReceipt,SUM)-(Sales, SUM). In such cases the total Stock can be computed from the total StockReceipt minus the total Sales.

# References

1. Albrecht, J.; Bauer, A.; Deyerling, O.; Günzel, H.; Hümmer, W.; Lehner, W.; Schlesinger, L.: Management of multidimensional Aggregates for efficient Online Analytical Processing, in: *International Database Engineering and Applications Symposium* (IDEAS'99, Montreal, Canada, August 1-3), 1999

2. Albrecht, J.; Günzel, H.; Lehner, W.: Set-Derivability of Multidimensional Aggregates (long version), Technical Report, University of Erlangen, 1999 (http://www6.informatik.un-erlangen.de/publications)

3. Bello, R.; Dias, K.; Downing, A.;Feenan, J.; Norcott, W.; Sun, H.; Witkowski, A.;Ziauddin, M.: Materialized Views in Oracle, in: *Proceedings of 24th International Conference on Very Large Data Bases* (VLDB'98, New York, USA, August 24-27), 1998,

4. Chen, M. C.; McNamee, L.; Melkanoff, M.: A Model of Summary Data and its Applications in Statistical Databases, in: *Proceedings of the 4th International Working Conference on Statistical and Scientific Database Management* (4SSDBM, Rome, Italy, June 21-23), 1988

5. Deshpande, P.M.; Ramasamy, K.; Shukla, A.; Naughton, J.F.: Caching Multidimensional Queries Using Chunks, in: *Proceedings of the 27th International Conference on Management of Data* (SIGMOD'98, Seattle (WA), USA, June 2-4), 1998

6. Finkelstein, S.: Common Subexpression Analysis in Database Applications, in: *Proceedings of the 11th International Conference on Management of Data* (SIGMOD'82, Orlando (FL), June 2-4), 1982

7. Gray, J.; Bosworth, A.; Layman, A.; Pirahesh, H.: Data Cube: A Relational Aggregation Operator Generalizing Group-By, Cross-Tab, and Sub-Total, in: *Proceedings of the 12th International Conference on Data Engineering* (ICDE'96, New Orleans (LA), USA, Feb. 26-March 1), 1996

8. Gupta, A.; Harinarayan, V.; Quass, D.: Aggregate-Query Processing in Data Warehousing Environments, in: *Proceedings of the 21th International Conference on Very Large Data Bases* (VLDB'95, Zurich, Schwitzerland, Sept. 11-15), 1995, pp. 358-369

9. Harinarayan, V.; Rajaraman, A.; Ullman, J.D.: Implementing Data Cubes Efficiently, in: *Proceedings of the 25th International Conference on Management of Data*, (SIGMOD'96, Montreal, Quebec, Canada, June 4-6), 1996

10. Lehner, W.: Modeling Large Scale OLAP Scenarios, in: *6th International Conference on Extending Database Technology* (EDBT'98, Valencia, Spain, March 23-27), 1998

11. Lenz, H; Shoshani, A.: Summarizability in OLAP and Statistical Databases, in: *9th International Conferenc on Statistical and Scientfic Databases*, (SSDB'97, Olympia, Washington, Aug. 11-13), 1997

12. Sapia, C.; Blaschka, M.; Höfling, G.; Dinter, B.: Finding Your Way through Multidimensional Data Models, in: *9th International Workshop on Database and Expert Systems Applications* (DEXA'98 Workshop, Vienna, Austria, August 24-28), 1998

13. Sun, X.-H.; Kamel, N.; Ni, L.M.: Solving Implication Problems in Database Applications, in: *Proceedings of the 18th International Conference on Management of Data* (SIGMOD'89, Portland (OR), USA, May 31-June 2), 1989

14. Ross, K.; Srivastava, D.; Stuckey, P.; Sudarshan, S.: Foundations of Aggregation Constraints, in: *Theoretical Computer Science*, Volume 193, Numbers 1-2, Feb. 28, 1998

15. Theodoratos, D.; Sellis, T.: Data Warehouse Configuration, in: *Proceedings of the 23rd International Conference on Very Large Data Bases* (VLDB'97, Athens, Greece, Aug. 25-29), 1997

# Using the Real Dimension of the Data

Christian Zirkelbach

University Gh Kassel, Heinrich-Plett-Str. 40, D-34109 Kassel, Germany,
czi@db.informatik.uni-kassel.de,
WWW home page: http://www.db.informatik.uni-kassel.de/~czi/

**Abstract** This paper presents a method for extracting the real dimension of a large data set in a high-dimensional data cube and indicates its use for visual data mining. A similarity measure structures a data set in a general, but weak sense. If the elements are part of a high-dimensional host space (primary space), for instance a data warehouse cube, the resulting structure doesn't necessarily reflect the real dimension of the embedded (secondary) space. Mapping the set into the secondary space of lower dimension will not result in loss of information with regard to the semantics defined by the measure. However, it helps to reduce storage and computing efforts. Additionally, the secondary space itself reveals much about the set's structure and can facilitate data mining. We make a proposal for adding the property of a dimension to a metric and show how to determine the real (in general fractal) dimension of the underlying data set.

## 1   Introduction

Nick Roussopoulos [16] recently pointed out the multi-faced form of views: "What is a relational view? Is is a program? Is it data? Is it an index? Is it an OLAP aggregate?" Here we propose to add another faced to the list: Clustering a data set by means of a metric results in a (materialized) view for representing the structure of the set with respect to the given metric.

Initial suggestions reach back to the design of algorithms for geometric data-structures and an early attempt was the *Bisector Tree* of Kalantary and Mc-Donald [9]. Those were generalized by a hierarchical data-structure, so called *Metric Trees*, where each node represents a data cluster and is described by a representative (existing or artificial) element (called the *center of the cluster*) and a *cluster radius* defined by the maximum distance between the center and a cluster element. Whenever the current cluster is too coarse (i.e. has a too large radius) it is recursively refined into sub-clusters, represented by sub-trees. Thus, the cluster-radii decrease on a path from the root down to a leaf. In doing so, the metric itself is used as a black-box. This mechanism was published first in [13] and independently in [18]. Within this data structure, navigation over data spaces with aggregation is supported, as it is known from $NF^2$-tables [21]. In the context of data warehousing and multimedia, those ideas resurfaced [6], [5], [2], [22], [3].

Intensive theoretical and experimental studies were undertaken to establish a proper choice of cluster-centers in different metric spaces [14] of different application areas (for instance convex distance functions in $R^d$, Waterman distance measure in sequence spaces, Mahalanobis-distance, Canberra-metric, distance measures of Sokal&Sneath and Czekanowski&Dice in non-discrete spaces, and the measures of Maron, Kulczynski, and Kendall in discrete spaces), in order to minimize distance computing by means of a chain estimation based on the triangulation inequality [20], and to develop a dynamic paging concept [19]. However, the later papers that appeared in the context of data warehouses did not draw much from these experiences.

Here, we focus on experimental results on a special type of Metric Trees, called *Monotonic Bisector Tree*, which revealed that the developement of the cluster-radii corresponds directly to the real dimension of the data set [19]. For instance, the cluster radii of points distributed on a one-dimensional curve in $R^d$ decreased by a smaller factor $q$ than those scattered arbitrarily in a 2-dimensional manifold. At the same time $q$ is typical for sets of same dimension under same $L_p$-metric and is independent of the dimension $d$ of the host space. The main intension of this paper is to add theory to this observation and to prove that the decrease of the cluster radii is an indicator for the natural (in general fractal) dimension of a data set, which is independent of the dimension of the host-space. Thus, roughly speaking, a special type of Metric Tree can reveal the fractal dimension of a large data set in a warehouse cube of high dimension.

The remainder of this paper is organized as follows. After giving some formal definitions and properties in Chapter 2, we develop the basic idea in Chapter 3 and review briefly Monotonic Bisector Trees. Chapter 4 proves the strong relationship between the fractal dimension of a data set and its Monotonic Bisector Tree. Chapter 5 makes a proposal for applying the theory in visual data mining and Chapter 6 closes with a summary and an outlook on future activities. The paper is without proofs. Please note that the proofs can be found in the full version of this paper (http://www.db.informatik.uni-kassel.de/~czi/paper.ps).

## 2 Metric Spaces and Fractal Dimension

Let a *quasi-metric space* $(M, d)$ be composed of a non-empty data set $M$ and a similarity measure $d: M \times M \longrightarrow R_{\geq 0}$ enhanced with the following properties:

1. $\exists_{C_1 \geq 1} \forall_{a,b \in M} \ d(a, b) \leq C_1 \, d(b, a)$ (Quasi-Symmetry)
2. $\exists_{C_2 \geq 1} \forall_{a,b,c \in M} \ d(a, c) \leq C_2 \, [d(a, b) + d(b, c)]$
   (Quasi-Triangulation Inequality)
3. $\exists_{l \in I\!N} \forall_{a \in M} \forall_{r \geq 0} \exists_{\{a_1, \ldots, a_l\} \subset M} \ K_r(a) \subset \bigcup_{1 \leq i \leq l} K_{\frac{r}{2}}(a_i)$ (Covering)

Thereby, for $z \in M$ and $r \geq 0$ let $K_r(z) := \{x \in M \mid d(z, x) \leq r\}$ denote the *ball* with radius $r$, centered at $z$. In order to estimate the runtime of our algorithms, we additionally demand

4. $\forall_{a,b \in M} \ d(a, b)$ can be computed in constant time (efficiently computable)

Using $C_1 = C_2 = 1$ provides a real metric. The quasi-properties in 1 and 2 are only for technical reason and will be used to quantify the robustness of our algorithms with respect to skewed data or a distortion of the distance measure. For this reason we define:

$$\varepsilon := \frac{1}{C_2 (C_1 + 1)}$$

In the metric case, $\varepsilon = \frac{1}{2}$ holds. We assume $C_1, C_2$ to be close to 1. Please note that $d(a, a) = 0$ is not explicitly demanded since a quasi-non-negativity

$$\forall_{a,b \in M} \ d(a, a) \leq C_2 (d(a, b) + d(b, a)) \leq C_2 (d(a, b) + C_1 d(a, b)) = \varepsilon^{-1} d(a, b)$$

is implied by 1 and 2, depending on the density of the underlying data set.

The coverage property reveals a fractal Dimension ( $d = \log_2 l$ according to Mandelbrot's theory [12]) of the metric space. Intuitively we are familiar with this idea since a hypercube in $\mathbf{R}^d$ (i.e. a circle under $L_\infty$-metric) with edge-length $s$ can be covered with $2^d$ sub-cubes of edge-length $s/2$. Besides this approach, space-filling (fractal) curves have been already used for the refined stretching of the $\mathbf{R}^d$ [11], [1].

**Lemma 1.** *The four properties are independent.*

**Definition 1.** *Let $S \subset M$ be finite. For each $p \in S$ the set*

$$V_S(p) := \{x \in M \mid d(p, x) = 0 \vee \forall_{s \in S \setminus \{p\}} \ d(p, x) < d(s, x)\}$$

$$\bar{V}_S(p) := \{x \in M \mid \forall_{s \in S} \ d(p, x) \leq d(p, s)\}$$

*is called the open (closed) Voronoi-region of $p$ with respect to $S$. For $a, b \in M$ the set*

$$H(a, b) := \{x \in M \mid d(a, x) \leq d(b, x)\} = \bar{V}_{\{a,b\}}(a)$$

$$H^\circ(a, b) := \{x \in M \mid d(a, x) = 0 \vee \ d(a, x) < d(b, x)\} = V_{\{a,b\}}(a)$$

*is called the open (closed) Half-space of $a$ with respect to $\{a, b\}$. For $a, b \in M$ the bisector of $a$ and $b$ is defined:*

$$B(a, b) := H(a, b) \cap H(b, a)$$

*A bisector $B(a, b)$ separates two sets $A, B \subset M$ iff $A \subset H(a, b)$ and $B \subset H(b, a)$.*

*The set of all closed Voronoi-regions*

$$VD(S) := \{\bar{V}_S(p) \mid p \in S\}$$

*is called the Voronoi-diagram of $S$. Figure 1 gives an example.*

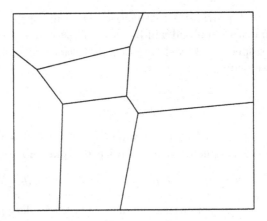

**Figure1.** Voronoi-diagram of 6 points in the Euclidean plane

**Lemma 2.** *Voronoi-regions are invariant with respect to a strictly monotonic transformation (i.e. a transformation of d to $d_\Phi := \Phi \circ d$, using a a strict monotonic mapping $\Phi : R_{\geq 0} \longrightarrow R_{\geq 0}$, $\Phi(0) = 0$) of the distance measure d.*

Lemma 2 proofs the Voronoi-partitioning of a set to be invariant under a class of distance measures. Additionally, we have to examine the impact of a monotonic transformation on the topological constants ($C_1$, $C_2$ on page 2).

**Lemma 3.** *Applying a strictly monotonic increasing transformation $d_\Phi := \Phi \circ d$ on d will not worsen (heighten) $C_1, C_2$ if*

$$\frac{\Phi}{id} : R_{>0} \longrightarrow R_{>0}, x \longmapsto \frac{\Phi(x)}{x}$$

*is monotonically decreasing, whereby l can not improve (lessen). Conversely, l will not worsen and $C_1, C_2$ will not improve if $\frac{\Phi}{id}$ is monotonically increasing.*

Besides proving a robustness with respect to skewed data, the last two lemmata demonstrate, how a carefully chosen, neighborhood-respecting distortion of the distance measure (for instance an acceleration) can be used to improve the properties of the measure. This might be of interest while experimenting with different distance functions.

**Definition 2.** *Let a Cluster be a tuple $(S, z)$, defined by the cluster center $z \in M$ and the finite base set $S \subset M$. For each $(S, z)$ let*

$$r(S, z) := \max\{d(z, s) \mid s \in S\}$$

*denote the radius.*

With respect to the distance measure $d$, a center acts as a representative of a cluster and the radius quantifies this relationship.

# 3   An Index Based on a Hierarchical Clustering Method

At first, we point to a simple observation: Let the distance measure $d$ be any $L_p$-metric. Imagine a finite set $S$ of points scattered in the one-dimensional interval $[-1,1]$ and let $0,1 \in S$. Taking the $0$ for the cluster center we gain a cluster $(S,0)$ with radius $r(S,0) = 1$. Next, we partition $S$ by means of the bisector of $0$ and $1$, yielding two sub-clusters $(S_0,0)$ and $(S_1,1)$ with radii $r_0 = 1$ and $r_1 = 0.5$ where $S_1 = \{s \in S \,|\, d(0,s) \leq d(1,s)\}$ and $S_2 = \{s \in S \,|\, d(0,s) > d(1,s)\}$. In the consecutive step $S_0$ is split by the bisector of its farthest point in $S_0$ which results in radii $r_{00}, r_{01} \leq 0.5$. Applying this simple partitioning method recursively in a depth-first-search manner, provides a reduction of the actual cluster-radius by factor $0.5$ after at most two consecutive separation steps. After mapping $[0,1]$ into the plane (for instance by $x \longmapsto (x, \sin x)$) this method results in the same reduction rate. But, after scattering the points of $S$ arbitrarily in the plane (making full use of the two dimensions), there are about $8$ consecutive steps necessary (depending on the used $p$) to halve the radii. Mapping the points into a fractal of dimension $1 < d < 2$ (for instance by $x \longmapsto (x, \sin 1/x)$) results in a value between both thresholds. In order to examine this observation, we reintroduce a data structure which is directly implied by the mechanism mentioned above.

**Definition 3.** *Let $(S, s_0)$ be a cluster where $S \subset M$ and $s_0 \in S$.*
*Let $a \colon \mathcal{P}(S) \times S \longrightarrow \{0,1\}$ be a so called* truncation function, *equipped with the following properties:*

$$\forall_{s \in S} \forall_{S' \subset S} \; |S'| \leq 2 \implies a(S', s) = 1 \quad and$$

$$\forall_{s \in S} \forall_{S'' \subset S' \subset S} \; a(S', s) = 1 \implies a(S'', s) = 1.$$

*A Monotonic-Bisector-Tree $MBT(S, s_0)$ is a rooted binary tree having the following features:*

1. *If $a(S, s_0) = 1$, then $MBT(S, s_0)$ consists of a single node containing the elements of $S$.*
2. *If $a(S, s_0) = 0$, then $MBT(S, s_0)$ is a binary tree with root $w$. $w$ contains $s_0$ and $s_1 \in S \backslash \{s_0\}$. The sons of $w$ are the sub-roots $w_0$ and $w_1$, corresponding to the two subtrees $MBT(S_0, s_0)$ and $MBT(S_1, s_1)$, where for $i \in \{0,1\}$ holds:*

$$S_i \cap S_{1-i} = \emptyset \quad \wedge \quad S \cap H^\circ(s_i, s_{1-i}) \subset S_i \subset S \cap H(s_i, s_{1-i})$$

*In this context, the radius of a $MBT(S, s)$ denotes the radius of the corresponding cluster $(S, s)$. The radius of a node denotes the radius of the corresponding subtree. The clusters given by the leaf-nodes of the tree (buckets) are called terminal clusters.*

The truncation function $a$ determines the fineness of the decomposition of $(S, s_0)$ based on $|S|$ and $r(S, s)$. We assume in the following that $a(S, s)$ can be computed in $\mathcal{O}(|S|)$ time and storage. We call a Monotonic Bisector Tree *completely developed*, iff $a(S, s) = 1 \implies |S| \leq 2$ holds.

Obviously, this binary tree structure stores $n + 1$ different points in $n$ nodes. Thus, the storage needed is linear in $|S|$. Figure 2 gives an example. Please note, that the redundancy implied by the inheritance of cluster-centers is just of logical nature and can be physically avoided by storing only the new center in a node and using a simple stack operation to retrieve the cluster center of an ancestor node.

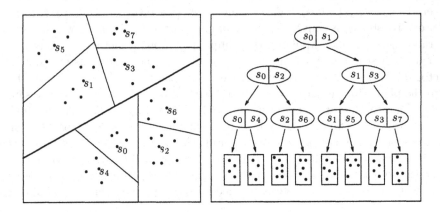

**Figure2.** Monotonic Bisector Tree in the Euclidean plane

**Lemma 4.** *MBTs do not have eccentric sons. The radii of the elements stored in nodes which appear on a path from the root to a leaf generate a monotonously decreasing sequence (justifying the term: monotonic tree).*

Up to now, the initial cluster center of a *MBT* was taken for granted. This is not the general case. The trivial determination of the best (with smallest radius) center results in $\mathcal{O}(|S|^2)$ distance computations. This might be unbearable in practice. The Computational Geometry community has brought forth faster algorithms which work in special spaces [15], [7]. On the other hand, however, the deviation caused by a randomly chosen initial center is bounded, since the triangulation inequality holds:

$$d(x,y) \leq C_2 \left( d(x, z_{opt}) + d(z_{opt}, y) \right) \leq C_2 \left( C_1 \, d(z_{opt}, x) + d(z_{opt}, y) \right) \leq \frac{r_{opt}}{\varepsilon}$$

where $x, y \in S$ and $z_{opt}$ denotes the best initial center with radius $r_{opt}$.

The index built-up algorithm, is straightforward to the motivation of this chapter:

1. Start with a cluster.
2. Use this cluster-element for the alternative cluster-center which defines the current cluster radius.

3. Split the current cluster by means of the bisector of the two centers and assign the resulting sub-clusters to two subtrees.
4. Recursively apply the partitioning-method to the subtrees, until the threshold value of the truncation-function is satisfied.

If we are faced with the problem, that the number of cluster centers that can be computed is bounded ($c$-means-clustering [4]), we vary the build-up algorithm and store the current cluster not in a stack, but in a max-heap. Thus, the partitioning step selects recursively the leaf-cluster with biggest radius (maximum error method).

## 4   Discovering the Fractal Dimension

**Theorem 1** *For each $0 < q < 1$ there is a $l := l(q) \in \mathbb{N}$, such that the build-up algorithm creates on every cluster $(S, s)$ with $S \subset M$ and center $s \in S$ a MBT with the following feature:*

*For every node $v$ of height $h$ it holds:* $r(v) \leq q^{\frac{h}{l}} r(S, s)$ .

*Thereby the required storage is $\mathcal{O}(|S|)$.*

In summary we can say that the simple build-up algorithm forces the cluster-radii of a MBT which appear on a path from the root down to a leaf to generate a geometrically decreasing sequence. Due to the fact that this holds for any host space, the decreasing rate is depending of the covering feature of the host space with lowest dimension, the natural dimension of the data set itself. This is in general a fractal dimension. Now, after observing the reduction rate $l(\varepsilon^2 q)$, we can compute this dimension:

$$\boxed{d = \log_{1/\varepsilon^2 q} \left( l(\varepsilon^2 q) + 1 \right)}$$

Now, the existence of hidden rules is proofed, if there is a discrepancy between the dimension of the host-space (data-cube) and the calculated dimension. Although this statement is the basic intension of the paper, we additionally state some features which ease the handling of a MBT. The next theorem examines the resolution of a MBT.

**Theorem 2** *Let $(S, s)$ be the initial cluster. If the truncation function $a: \mathcal{P}(S) \times S \longrightarrow \{0, 1\}$ satisfies*

$$\frac{r(S, s)}{r(S', s')} \geq C \geq 1 \quad \Longrightarrow \quad a(S', s') = 1 \quad (TerminalCluster)$$

*the height of the resulting tree can be estimated $h \in \mathcal{O}(\log C)$.*

The next theorem proofs the asymptotic optimal performance of the built-up algorithms of a MBT with respect to its height:

**Theorem 3** *The build-up algorithms need* $\mathcal{O}((1+h)\,|S|)$ *time to create a MBT on a cluster* $(S,s)$ *with height* $h$ .

Because the height of a MBT is bounded by its cardinality $|S|$, we derive from theorem 3 and theorem 2:

**Theorem 4** *Let* $C \geq 1$ *be given. The build-up algorithms need* $\mathcal{O}(\min\{\log C + 1, |S|\}\,|S|)$ *time for the creation of a MBT on* $(S,s)$ *such that* $\frac{r(S,s)}{r(b)} \geq C$ *holds for any leaf* $b$.

In order to ease the experimental handling of different distance measure we state the last theorem which is directly implied by lemma 2.

**Theorem 5** *MBTs created by the build-up algorithms are invariant with respect to a monotonic transformation of the distance measure.*

## 5   User Interface for Visual Data Mining

Based on the concept of coarsen and refinement, we suggest the visualization of a MBT for interactive visual data mining. Visualization is based on the development of a MBT with the help of the build-up algorithm until a threshold value for the number of leaf nodes is reached. This can be controlled by a suitable truncation function $a$, which the user can adjust.

Next, the resulting tree is mapped onto the screen: The cluster center of the root is associated with the middle of the window, the origin. The sub-clusters are arranged as discs in circular order around the origin. There are three degrees of freedom to be assigned: The size of a disc, its distance from the origin and the position of a disc in circular ordering around the origin. We suggest to associate the volume (fatness) of a disc to its significance (for instance the cardinality of the corresponding cluster) and to order the discs around the origin with respect to the corresponding cluster radius. The distance of a discs from the origin may reflect its distance from the center of the root. In this context, the distance of two cluster may be defined by the distance of the centers or the min/max-distance of the corresponding sets. Of course, the assignment of quantitative tree features to the three degrees of freedom is within the user.

The interaction is carried out by a generalization of the finger concept [21] as it is known from the navigation in $NF^2$-tables. For meaningful illustrations of $NF^2$-tables, compare [8] and [10]. A finger is a cursor for navigating in complex (structured) objects. Instead of a linear cursor, it offers three dimensions for incremental positioning: zoom in/out, next/last item of a list, next/last attribute within a record. Here, however, the hierarchy is of quantitative nature instead of a $NF^2$-tables qualitative nature. Mouse clicks and double-clicks on the discs can be used to roll-up/drill-down or zoom/unzoom the corresponding cluster. The circular order of the discs and the fatness of the discs can be orthogonally used to activate a "successing" cluster by pressing an arrow-key.

# 6 Summary and Outlook

In order to structure a high-dimensional data set, we have decided to index our space by means of a metric. Each individual view on the data must be expressed in terms of a metric. For each metric an index is created which materializes the metric view on the data set. We have shown that this index can be used to discover the real dimension of a large data set with respect to the chosen metric. We have proved, that the mechanism is fault tolerant with respect to the metric and to the data. We made a proposal to apply the finger technique on this index in order to support visual data mining. We demonstrated, that this approach is an alternative to plane projections, because the navigator can make full use of the real dimension of a data set and, by using polar coordinates, can choose a third degree of freedom. The main advantage is that the navigation works sensitive with respect to the given metric.

We have already implemented the finger concept on $NF^2$-tables by using Tcl/Tk [17]. Now, we plan to expand this user interface to handle metric navigation as described in the last section.

# References

1. T. Asano, D. Ranjan, T. Roos, and E. Welzl. Space filling curves and their use in the design of geometric data structures. *Lecture Notes in Computer Science*, 911, 1995.
2. Tolga Bozkaya and Meral Ozsoyoglu. Distance-based indexing for high-dimensional metric spaces. *SIGMOD Record (ACM Special Interest Group on Management of Data)*, 26(2), may 1997.
3. S. Brin. Near neighbor search in large metric spaces. In Umeshwar Dayal, Peter M. D. Gray, and Shojiro Nishio, editors, *VLDB '95: proceedings of the 21st International Conference on Very Large Data Bases, Zurich, Switzerland, Sept. 11-15, 1995*, pages 574–584, Los Altos, CA 94022, USA, 1995. Morgan Kaufmann Publishers.
4. Robert L. Cannon, Jitendra V. Dave, and James C. Bezdek. Efficient implementation of the fuzzy C-means clustering algorithms. *IEEE Trans. on Pattern Analysis and Machine Intelligence*, PAMI-8(2):248–255, March 1986.
5. P. Ciaccia, M. Patella, and P. Zezula. Processing complex similarity queries with distance-based access methods. *Lecture Notes in Computer Science*, 1377, 1998.
6. Paolo Ciaccia, Marco Patella, and Pavel Zezula. M-tree: An efficient access method for similarity search in metric spaces. In *VLDB'97, Proceedings of 23rd International Conference on Very Large Data Bases*, pages 426–435, 1997.
7. H. Edelsbrunner. *Algorithms in Combinatorial Geometry*. Springer, Berlin, 1987.
8. A. Heuer and G. Saake. *Datenbanken: Konzepte und Sprachen*. Thomson Publishing, Bonn, 1995.
9. G. McDonald I. Kalantari. A data structure and an algorithm for the nearest point problem. *IEEE Transactions on Software Engineering*, 9(5), 1983.
10. G. Lausen and G. Vossen. *Objektorientierte Datenbanken: Modelle und Sprachen*. Oldenbourg, München, 1996.

11. K.-J. Li and R. Laurini. The spatial locality and a spatial indexing method by dynamic clustering in hypermap systems. In Oliver Guenther and Hans-Joerg Schek, editors, *Proceedings of Advances in Spatial Databases (SSD '91)*, volume 525 of *LNCS*, pages 207–224, Berlin, Germany, August 1991. Springer.
12. Benuoit B. Mandelbrot. *The Fractal Geometry of Nature*. W. H. Freeman and Company, New York, 1983.
13. H. Noltemeier, T. Roos, and C. Zirkelbach. Partitioning of complex scenes of geometric objects. In P. Kall, editor, *Proceedings of the 15th IFIP Conference on System Modelling and Optimization*, volume 180 of *LNCIS*, Berlin, Germany, September 1991. Springer.
14. H. Noltemeier, K. Verbarg, and C. Zirkelbach. Monotonous bisector trees : A tool for efficient partitioning of complex scenes of geometric objects. In Burkhard Monien and Thomas Ottmann, editors, *Proceedings of Data Structures and Efficient Algorithms*, volume 594 of *LNCS*, pages 186–203, Berlin, Germany, September 1992. Springer.
15. F. P. Preparata and M. I. Shamos. *Computational Geometry : An Introduction*. Springer-Verlag, 1985.
16. N. Roussopoulos. Materialized views and data warehouses. *SIGMOD Record*, 27(1):21–26, March 1998.
17. Jens Thamm and Lutz Wegner. What you see is what you store: Database-driven interfaces. In *Proceedings of the 4th IFIP Working Conference on Visual Database Systems, L'Aquila, Italy May 27–29, 1998*, 1998. To appear.
18. Uhlmann. Satisfying general proximity / similarity queries with metric trees. *IPL: Information Processing Letters*, 40, 1991.
19. K. Verbarg. Räumliche indizes - celltrees. Master's thesis, University Würzburg, 1992.
20. T. L. Wang and D. Shasha. Query processing with distance metrics. In *Proc. Int'l. Conf. on Very Large Data Bases*, page 602, Brisbane, Australia, August 1990.
21. L. M. Wegner. Let the fingers do the walking: Object manipulation in an NF² database editor. In Hermann Maurer, editor, *Proceedings of New Results and New Trends in Computer Science*, volume 555 of *LNCS*, pages 337–358, Berlin, Germany, June 1991. Springer.
22. Pavel Zezula, Paolo Ciaccia, and Fausto Rabitti. M-tree: A dynamic index for similarity queries in multimedia databases. Technical Report TR96-0002, Progetto Mediterraneo, CNR-Pisa, 1996.

# On Schema Evolution in Multidimensional Databases[1]

Markus Blaschka, Carsten Sapia, Gabriele Höfling

FORWISS (Bavarian Research Center for Knowledge-Based Systems)
Orleansstr. 34, D-81667 Munich, Germany
Email: {blaschka, sapia, hoefling}@forwiss.tu-muenchen.de

**Abstract.** Database systems offering a multidimensional schema on a logical level (e.g. OLAP systems) are often used in data warehouse environments. The user requirements in these dynamic application areas are subject to frequent changes. This implies frequent structural changes of the database schema. In this paper, we present a formal framework to describe evolutions of multidimensional schemas and their effects on the schema and on the instances. The framework is based on a formal conceptual description of a multidimensional schema and a corresponding schema evolution algebra. Thus, the approach is independent of the actual implementation (e.g. MOLAP or ROLAP). We also describe how the algebra enables a tool supported environment for schema evolution.

## 1    Introduction

The main idea of a data warehouse architecture is the replication of large amounts of data gathered from different heterogeneous sources throughout an enterprise. This data is used by knowledge workers to drive their daily decisions. Consequently, easy-to-use interactive analysis facilities on top of the data warehouse are necessary. Most often multidimensional databases (specifically OLAP systems) are used for this purpose. These multidimensional information systems (MDIS) provide the user with a multidimensional view on the data and offer interactive multidimensional operations (e.g. slicing).

The user of an MDIS interactively formulates queries based on the structure of the multidimensional space (the MD schema of the database). This means that the schema of the MD database determines what types of queries the user can ask. Thus, the design of the schema in such an environment is a very important task. This has been recognized by the research community as several publications in the field of multidimensional schema design show (e.g. [7], [12]). Nevertheless, a complete methodology for designing and maintaining an MDIS must also take schema evolution into account which has so far received almost no attention. This paper provides a framework to formally approach the evolution issue for MDIS and shows how this formal frame-

---

[1] An extended version of this paper can be downloaded at
   http://www.forwiss.tu-muenchen.de/~system42/publications/

work can be used to implement a tool supported evolution process. In such an environment, the designer can specify the required schema evolution on a conceptual level and the corresponding implementation is adapted automatically.

To understand why schema evolution plays an important role especially in decision support environments (where data warehouse and OLAP applications are mostly found), let us first take a look at the typical design and maintenance process of such a system. Interactive data analysis applications are normally developed using an iterative approach. The main two reasons for this very dynamic behavior are:

- the interactive multidimensional analysis technology is new to the knowledge worker. This means that it is impossible for him to state his requirements in advance.
- the business processes in which the analyst is involved are subject to frequent changes. These changes in business processes are reflected in the analysis requirements [15]. New types of queries that require different data become necessary. Because the schema of an MDIS restricts the possible analysis capabilities, the new query requirements lead to changes in the MD database schema.

A single iteration of the design and maintenance cycle [17] consists of the phases **'Requirement Analysis'** (where the requirements of the users concerning data scope, granularity, structure and quality are collected), the **'Conceptual Design'** (where the required views of the users are consolidated into a single conceptual model and – during further iterations of the development cycle – the schema is adopted according to the changed requirements), the **'Physical (Technical) Design'** (where implementation decisions are taken), **'Implementation'** (rather mechanic realization of the specifications developed during the technical design phase), and the **'Operation'** phase (where new data is loaded to the database on a regular basis and the users analyze data). Typically, when a system is in operation, new requirements for different or differently structured data arise. If a certain amount of new requirements is reached, a new iteration is started.

The conceptual multidimensional data model is the central part of the design and maintenance cycle as it already contains a consolidation of all user requirements but does not yet contain implementation details. All data models that occur later in the design process are refinements of the conceptual model.

Thus, the starting point for our research of schema evolution operations and their effects is the conceptual level. The goal of our approach is to automatically propagate changes of the conceptual model to the other models along the design cycle. A prerequisite for this is a formal framework to describe the evolution operations and their effects, which we present in this paper.

The rest of the paper is structured as follows: In section 2 we discuss related work from the areas of data warehousing and object-oriented databases. Section 3 summarizes the objectives and benefits of our framework for multidimensional schema evolution. Section 4 develops a formal notion of multidimensional schemas and instances which serves as a basis for the description of schema evolution operations and their effects that is described in section 5. Section 6 sketches how the formal framework can be used to implement an interactive tool-supported schema evolution process. We conclude with directions for future work in section 7.

# 2 Related Work

A first approach to changing user requirements and their effects on the multidimensional schema is [11]. Kimball introduces the concept of "slowly changing dimensions" which encompasses so called structural changes, i.e. value changes of dimension attributes, like changing the address of a customer. Since data in an OLAP system is always time related, the change history has to be reflected. If a customer moves, both the old and the new address have to be stored. Solutions for this case (data evolution) are rather straightforward. The slowly changing dimensions approach is not complete and provides a rather informal basis for data and schema changes. Further, there are no clear decision criteria for the proposed implementation alternatives.

Golfarelli et al. [7], [8] proposed a methodological framework for data warehouse design based on a conceptual model called dimensional fact (DF) scheme. They introduce a graphical notation and a methodology to derive a DF model from E/R models of the data sources. Although the modeling technique supports semantically rich concepts it is not based on a formal data model. Furthermore, the framework does not concentrate on evolution issues which we believe is an important feature for the design and maintenance cycle.

Schema evolution has been thoroughly investigated in the area of object-oriented database systems (OODBMS) because - similar to the multidimensional case – there are conceptual relationships representing semantical information: the *isa* relationships representing inheritance between classes. Schema evolution in object-oriented database systems has been broadly discussed both in research prototypes and commercial products (e.g. [1], [20], [10]). We take these approaches as a foundation for our work and investigate how techniques and approaches from object-oriented schema evolution can be adopted to the case of multidimensional information systems.

Most research work in the area of OLAP and data warehousing concentrates on view management issues. These approaches see the warehouse database as a materialized view over the operational sources. The arising problems are how these views can be maintained efficiently (*view maintenance problem*, see e.g.[6]), which aggregations on which level improve performance with given space limitations (*view selection problem*, see e.g. [3]), and how the views can be adopted when changes in the view definition or view extent arise (*view adaptation and synchronization problem*, see e.g. [14], [16]). Our work supplements these approaches because we develop the warehouse schema from the user requirements and not from the schemas of the operational sources.

A recent approach to schema evolution is [9]. From the related work mentioned above this approach is the most closely related to our work. However, it differs in the following aspects. First, it only addresses changes in the dimensions. We provide a set of evolution operations covering also facts and attributes. Next, insertions of levels are limited to certain positions in a dimension. Our framework allows random insertions of dimension levels at any place of a given MD schema. Further, our approach is based on a conceptual level, thus not assuming any specific implementation details (e.g. a ROLAP implementation).

# 3 An Overview of the Schema Evolution Framework for MDIS

The objective of the work described in this paper is to propose a methodology that supports an automatic adaptation of the multidimensional schema and the instances, independent of a given implementation. We provide a conceptual multidimensional schema design methodology including a schema evolution algebra. Our vision of the warehouse design and maintenance cycle is that the whole system is specified and designed on a conceptual level. Changes that arise when the system is already in production would only be specified on the conceptual level. Our design and evolution environment cares for the necessary changes in the specific target system (i.e. database and query/management tools).

To this end, our general framework comprises
1. a data model (i.e. a formal description of multidimensional schemas and instances),
2. a set of formal evolution operations,
3. the descriptions of effects (extending to schema and instances) of the operations,
4. an execution model for evolution operations, and finally
5. a methodology how to use our framework.

This paper addresses points one, two and three. It further contains ideas for the methodology (point five). The main objectives of our framework for multidimensional schema design and evolution (see [2] for the complete list ) are

- automatic adaptation of instances: existing instances should be adapted to the new schema automatically. Further, the adaptation of instances should be possible separately from the adaptation of the schema (in case there are no instances yet), physical and/or logical adaptation should be possible.

- support for atomic and complex operations: our methodology defines atomic evolution operations as well as complex operations.

- clear definition of semantics of evolution operations: the semantics of a given schema evolution operation may offer more alternatives and are not always clear. Our methodology fixes an alternative for execution.

- providing a mechanism for change notification (forward compatibility): we provide a change notification mechanism and guarantee that existing applications do not have to be adapted to the new schema. Further, there is no need for immediate adaptations of the tool configurations.

- concurrent operation and atomicity of evolution operations: the framework should allow concurrency of schema changes and regular queries. Further, schema evolution transactions shall be atomic.

- different strategies for the scheduling of effects: the framework should offer lazy strategies for the execution of effects of a schema change. Based on a cost model, the system may schedule the execution of effects for a later point in time. If the adapted instances are needed immediately, the system notifies the user about possible arising performance problems.

- support of the design and maintenance cycle: the framework supports all phases of the design and maintenance cycle. Thus, we cover not only the initial design (where the OLAP system is not populated with instances yet), but allow also adaptations of a populated system.

Summing up, our approach shall be used as a basis for tool-supported warehouse schema changes. The framework provides an easy-to-use tool allowing to perform schema modifications without detailed knowledge about the specific implementation and tools. The schema designer does not have to adapt different configurations of a tool and a database schema which must be consistent for a given implementation, but the tool is responsible for performing the necessary steps in a consistent and semantically correct way providing a single point of control accessible via a graphical formalism.

The contributions and scope of this paper are a formal model for MD schemas and instances together with a set of evolution operations. We describe the effects of these evolution operations on the MD schema and the instances, thus providing a formal algebra for MD schema evolution.

## 4 Multidimensional Schema and Instances

Several interpretations of the multidimensional paradigm can be found both in the literature (e.g. [4], [5], [13], [21]) and in product implementations. A comparison of the formal approaches shows that most of them do not formally distinguish between schema and instances ([19]) as their main goal is a formal treatment of queries using algebras and calculi. For our research work, we need a formalism that can serve as a basis for defining the schema evolution operations and their effects (see section 5). Therefore, this section contains a formal definition of a multidimensional schema and its instances (which was inspired by the formal multidimensional models mentioned above, esp. [4], [5], [21]).

The schema (or MD model) of an MDIS contains the structure of the facts (with their attributes) and their dimension levels (with their attributes) including different classification pathes [19]. We assume a finite alphabet Z and denote the set of all finite sequences over Z as Z*.

**Definition 4.1 (MD model, MD schema):** An MD model $\mathcal{M}$ is a 6–tuple <F, L, A, *gran, class, attr*> where

- $F \subset Z^*$ is a finite set of fact names $\{f_1,...,f_m\}$ where $f_i \in Z^*$ for $1 \leq i \leq m$
- $L \subset Z^*$ is a finite set of dimension level names $\{l_1,...,l_k\}$ where $l_i \in Z^*$ for $1 \leq i \leq k$.
- $A \subset Z^*$ is a finite set of attribute names $\{a_1,...,a_p\}$ where $a_i \in Z^*$ for $1 \leq i \leq p$. Each attribute name $a_i$ has a domain $dom(a_i)$ attached.
- The names of facts, levels and attributes are all different, i.e. $L \cap F \cap A = \varnothing$
- *gran*: $F \rightarrow 2^L$ is a function that associates a fact with a set of dimension level names. These dimension levels *gran*(f) are called the base levels of fact f.
- *class* $\subseteq L \times L$ is a relation defined on the level name. The transitive, reflexive closure *class** of class must fulfill the following property: $(l_1,l_2) \in$ *class** $\Rightarrow (l_2,l_1) \notin$ *class**. That means that *class** defines a partial order on L. $(l_1,l_2) \in$ *class** reads "$l_1$ can be classified according to $l_2$."
- *attr*: $A \rightarrow F \cup L \cup \{\perp\}$ is a function mapping an attribute either to a fact (in this case the attribute is called a measure), to a dimension level (in this case it is called

dimension level attribute) or to the special ⊥-symbol which means that this attribute is not connected at all.

The MD model formalizes the schema of a multidimensional database. We use this formalism in section 5 to define a set of schema evolution operations. As we also want to analyze the effects of schema evolution operations on the instances of the schema, the remainder of this section presents a formal model for instances.

**Definition 4.2 (Domain of a Dimension Level):** The domain of a dimension level $l \in$ L is a finite set $dom(l) = \{m_1, \ldots, m_q\}$ of dimension member names.

**Definition 4.3 (Domain and Co-domain of a fact):** For a fact f the domain $dom(f)$ and co-domain $codom(f)$ are defined as follows:

$$dom(f) := \underset{l \in gran(f)}{X} dom(l)$$

$$codom(f) := \underset{\{a|attr(a)=f\}}{X} dom(a)$$

**Definition 4.4 (Instance of MD model):** The instance of an MD model $\mathcal{M}$ = <F, L, A, *gran, class, attr*> is a triple $\mathfrak{I}_\mathcal{M}$ = <R-UP, C, AV> where

- R-UP = $\{ r - up_{lev1}^{lev2} \}$ is a finite set of functions with

  $r - up_{lev1}^{lev2} : dom(lev1) \rightarrow dom(lev2)$ for all $(lev1, lev2) \in class$

- $C = \{c_{f_1}, \ldots, c_{f_m}\}$; $f_i \in$ F $\forall 1 \le i \le m$ is a finite set of functions

  $c_i$: $dom(f) \rightarrow codom(f)$; $f \in$ F. C maps coordinates of the cube to measures, thus defining the contents of the data cube.

- AV = $\{ av_1, \ldots, av_r \}$ is a finite set of functions which contains a function $av_a$ for each attribute a that is a dimension level attribute, i.e. $attr(a) \in$ L. The function $av_a$: $dom(attr(a)) \rightarrow dom(a)$ assigns an attribute value (for attribute a) to each member of the corresponding level.

## 5  Evolution Operations

After having formally defined the notion of a multidimensional schema and its instances, we present a set of formal evolution operations for MD models. For each operation, we introduce the operation with its parameters and describe the effect on the MD schema. Since the operations usually do not work on an database without instances, the modification of existing instances is also given.

Together with the exact definition of an MD model and an instance of such an MD model (in chapter 4), the evolution operations listed here provide a formal schema evolution algebra. A formal property of this schema evolution algebra is its closure, i.e. an algebra or language is closed if the result of any allowable operation is a legal construct in the language. The closure of our schema evolution algebra can be formally proved because the algebra recognizes only one underlying construct, an MD model. Every operation is defined to take an MD model as input argument and produces as output a new MD model. Therefore, by definition, the algebra is closed.

We provide a minimal set of atomic operations. Atomic refers to the property that every operation only 'tackles' (i.e. changes) exactly one set or function of the given MD model. Of course, for notational convenience, complex operations can be defined. These complex operations consist then of a sequence of atomic operations. A formal proof of the minimality and completeness of this set of operations is ongoing work.

Formally, a schema evolution operation *op* transforms an MD model $m$ =<F, L, A gran, class, attr> to an MD model $m'$. Some operations also require an adaptation of the instances $\Im_m$ to $\Im'_{m'}$. We always denote elements *before* the evolution with the regular letter (e.g. L), whereas a letter with an apostrophe (e.g. L') denotes the corresponding element *after* the evolution. For a function f:*dom*→*codom* let $f\big|_{dom'}$ denote the restriction of f to *dom'* $\subseteq$ *dom*

1. **insert level**: this operation extends an existing MD model by a new dimension level. The operation extends the set of levels without changing the classification relationships, thus creating an isolated element. Classifications Relationships have to be defined separately.

   Parameter: new level name $l_{new} \notin L$.

   $m'$=<F, L' := L ∪ { $l_{new}$ }, A gran', class', attr'>

   gran': F → $2^{L'}$; gran'(f) := gran(f)

   class' $\subseteq$ L' × L'; $(l_1, l_2) \in$ class' :⇔ $(l_1, l_2) \in$ class ∀$l_1, l_2 \in$ L'

   attr': A → F ∪ L' ∪ {⊥}; attr'(a) := attr(a)

   No effects on instances because informally the operation introduces a new and therefore empty dimension level. $\Im'_{m'}$ = <R-UP, C, AV>

2. **delete level**: deletes a dimension level $l_{del}$ from an MD model. The level must not be connected to a fact ($l_{del} \notin$ gran(f) ∀f∈ F) or via classification relationships (($l_{del}$, l) $\notin$ class ∧(l, $l_{del}$) $\notin$ class ∀l∈ L'). Further, the level must not have any attributes attached (attr(a) ≠ $l_{del}$ ∀a∈ A). Instances are deleted automatically together with the dimension level. Parameter: level name $l_{del} \in$ L.

   $m'$=<F, L' := L \ { $l_{del}$ }, A gran', class', attr'>.

   gran': F →$2^{L'}$; gran'(f) := gran(f)

   class' $\subseteq$ L' × L'; $(l_1, l_2) \in$ class' :⇔ $(l_1, l_2) \in$ class ∀$l_1, l_2 \in$ L'

   attr': A → F ∪ L' ∪ {⊥}; attr'(a) := attr(a)

   Instances: no effect because dimension members are deleted automatically. $\Im'_{m'}$ = <R-UP, C, AV>

3. **insert attribute**: creates a new attribute without attaching it to a dimension level or fact. Assigning an existing attribute to a dimension level or fact is a separate operation (connect attribute). Parameter: attribute name $a_{new} \notin$ A with dom($a_{new}$).

$m' = <F, L, A' := A \cup \{ a_{new} \}, gran, class, attr'>$

$attr': A' \to F \cup L' \cup \{\bot\}; attr'(a) := attr(a)$

Instances: no effect, $\mathfrak{I}'_{m'} = <$R-UP, C, AV$>$

4. **delete attribute**: deletes an existing, but disconnected attribute (i.e. the attribute is not attached to a dimension level or fact).

   Parameter: attribute name $a_{del} \in A$

   $m' = <F, L, A' = A - \{ a_{del} \}, gran, class, attr'>$

   $attr': A' \to F \cup L' \cup \{\bot\}; attr'(a) := attr(a)$

   Instances: no effect, $\mathfrak{I}'_{m'} = <$R-UP, C, AV$>$

5. **connect attribute to dimension level**: connects an existing attribute $a_{new}$ to a dimension level $l \in L$. Parameters: attribute name $a_{new} \in A$; dimension level $l \in L$, a function g for computing $a_{new}$. This function can also assign a default value.

   $m' = <F, L, A, gran, class, attr'>$

   $$attr' : A \to F \cup L \cup \{\bot\} \qquad attr'(a) := \begin{cases} l & if\ a = a_{new} \\ attr(a) & else \end{cases}$$

   Instances: $\mathfrak{I}'_{m'} = <$R-UP, C, AV$>$, R-UP not changed, C not changed.

   AV': define $av_{anew}$: dom (l) $\to$ dom($a_{new}$), AV' := AV $\cup \{av_{anew}\}$

   $$\forall m \in dom(l) : av_{a new}(m) := g(m)$$

6. **disconnect attribute from dimension level**: disconnects an attribute $a_{del}$ from a dimension level $l \in L$. Parameters: attribute name $a_{del} \in A$; dimension level $l \in L$.

   $m' = <F, L, A, gran, class, attr'>$

   $$attr' : A \to F \cup L \cup \{\bot\} \qquad attr'(a) := \begin{cases} \bot & if\ a = a_{del} \\ attr(a) & else \end{cases}$$

   Instances: $\mathfrak{I}'_{m'} = <$R-UP, C, AV$>$, R-UP not changed, C not changed.

   AV': let $av_{adel}$ be the corresponding attribute value function for $a_{del}$, AV' := AV - $\{ av_{del} \}$.

7. **connect attribute to fact:** connects an existing attribute $a_{new}$ to a fact $f \in F$. Parameters: attribute name $a_{new} \in A$; fact $f \in F$, a function g for computing $a_{new}$.

   $m' = <F, L, A, gran, class, attr'>$

   $$attr' : A \to F \cup L \cup \{\bot\} \qquad attr'(a) := \begin{cases} f & if\ a = a_{new} \\ attr(a) & else \end{cases}$$

   Instances: $\mathfrak{I}'_{m'} = <$R-UP, C', AV$>$, R-UP not changed, AV not changed.

   C := C - $\{c_t\} \cup \{c_t'\}$; $c_t'$: dom(f) $\to$ codom(f) with

   $$c'_f (x) := (z_1, ..., z_n, z_{n+1})\ with\ (z_1, ..., z_n) = c_f(x)\ and\ z_{n+1} = g(x)$$

8. **disconnect attribute from fact:** disconnects an existing attribute $a_{dis}$ from a fact $f \in F$. Parameters: attribute name $a_{dis} \in A$; fact $f \in F$.

$m' = <F, L, A\ gran, class, attr'>$

$$attr' : A \to F \cup L \cup \{\bot\} \qquad attr'(a) := \begin{cases} \bot & if\ a = a_{is} \\ attr(a) & else \end{cases}$$

Instances: $\mathfrak{I}'_{m'} = <R\text{-}UP, C', AV>$, R-UP not changed, AV not changed.
$C := C - \{c_f\} \cup \{c_f'\}$; $c_f'$: dom(f) $\to$ codom(f) with

$$c'_f(x) := (z_1, \ldots, z_{n-1})\ with\ (z_1, \ldots, z_{n-1}, z_n) = c_f(x)$$

9. **insert classification relationship**: this operations defines a classification relationship between two existing dimension levels. Parameters: levels $l_1, l_2 \in L$
   $m' = <F, L, A\ gran, class', attr>$
   $class' = class \cup \{(l_1, l_2)\}$
   Instances: $\mathfrak{I}'_{m'} = <R\text{-}UP', C, AV>$, C not changed, AV not changed.
   $R\text{-}UP' := R\text{-}UP \cup \{r - up_{l1}^{l2}\}$, $\forall$ m $\in$ dom($l_1$): $r - up_{l1}^{l2}$ (m):= k, k$\in$ dom($l_2$).

   Additionally, $r - up_{l1}^{l2}$ (dom($l_1$))$\subseteq$ dom($l_2$), i.e. $r - up_{l1}^{l2}$ is well-defined
   $\forall$ m $\in$ dom($l_1$).

10. **delete classification relationship**: removes a classification relationship without deleting the corresponding dimension levels. Parameter $(l_1, l_2) \in$ *class*
    $m' = <F, L, A\ gran, class', attr>$
    $class' = class - \{(l_1, l_2)\}$
    Instances: $\mathfrak{I}'_{m'} = <R\text{-}UP', C, AV>$, C not changed, AV not changed.
    $R\text{-}UP' := R\text{-}UP - \{r - up_{l1}^{l2}\}$

11. **insert fact:** this operation extends the MD model by a new fact. The operation extends the set of facts without attaching dimension levels to this fact. Dimensions for this fact have to be defined separately. Parameter: new fact $f_{new} \notin F$
    $m' = <F' := F \cup \{f_{new}\}, L, A\ gran', class, attr'>$

    $$gran'(f) : F' \to 2^{L'} \qquad gran'(f) := \begin{cases} \varnothing & if\ f = f_{new} \\ gran(f) & else \end{cases}$$

    $attr' : A \to F' \cup L \cup \{\bot\}$; $attr'(a) := attr(a)$
    Instances: $\mathfrak{I}'_{m'} = <R\text{-}UP, C', AV>$, R-UP not changed, AV not changed.
    $C'$: $C \cup \{c_{f_{new}}\}$, $c_{f_{new}}$: dom ($f_{new}$) $\to$ codom($f_{new}$), define c(x):= $\bot$
    $\forall$ x$\in$ dom($f_{new}$)

12. **delete fact:** removes a fact $f_{del}$ from an MD model. The fact must not be connected to a dimension (gran($f_{del}$)=$\varnothing$) and must also not contain any attributes $(attr(a) \neq f_{del}\ \forall$ a$\in$ A). Parameter: name of fact to be deleted $f_{del} \in F$
    $m' = <F' := F - \{f_{del}\}, L, A\ gran|_{F'}, class, attr'>$

    $attr' : A \to F' \cup L \cup \{\bot\}$ $attr'(a) = attr(a)$
    Instances: $\mathfrak{I}'_{m'} = <R\text{-}UP, C', AV>$, R-UP not changed, AV not changed.
    $C'$: $C - \{c_{f_{del}}\}$

**13. insert dimension into fact**: inserts a dimension at a given dimension level into an existing fact, thus increasing the number of dimensions by one. Parameters: level name $l \in L$ and fact name $f_{ins} \in F$. Additionally, a function *nv* is provided defining how to compute the new values for the fact based upon the now extended set of dimensions and the old value of the fact. Each cell of the old cube now becomes a set of cells, exactly reflecting the new dimension. This means that each old value of the fact is now related to all elements of the new dimension. For instance, assume we have daily repair cases of cars stored without the brand (i.e. we have no distinction between the brand of cars). Now we want to include the brand meaning that we insert a dimension at the level brand (cf. figure 1).

We have to provide a function that computes the new fact (repair cases by brand) based on the old dimensions (without brand) and the (old) number of repair cases. The old number of repair cases could be repair cases for a specific brand (alternative 1 in figure 1), a summarization over all brands (alternative 2), or other. The idea how the new values can be computed is stored in nv. For example, if we only had BMW cars before, then we would use the old fact value for BMW and $\perp$ for all other cars (because the values cannot be computed, alternative 1). If the old value was a sum over all brands, we could only take this value as a sum, whereas values for the single brands are unknown (corresponding to "?" in figure 1).

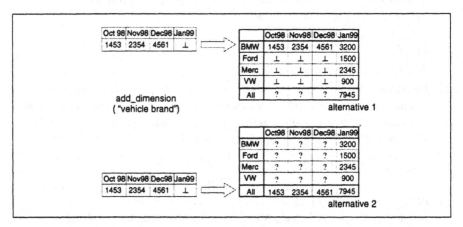

**figure 1: different alternatives for the instance adaptation**

More formally, the situation before is that $c(x_1,...,x_n)=z$. Now, after insertion of the new dimension we have $c(x_1,...,x_n,x_{n+1}) = y \; \forall \; x_{n+1} \in dom(l)$ and thus

$$nv : codom(f) \; x \; dom(l) \rightarrow codom(f), \quad nv(z, x_{n+1}) = y \quad \forall x_{n+1} \in dom(l)$$

Schema: $\mathcal{M}' = < F, L, A, gran', class, attr>$

$$gran'(f) : F \rightarrow 2^L \qquad gran'(f) := \begin{cases} gran(f) \\ gran(f) \cup \{l\} \end{cases} \quad for \quad \begin{matrix} f \neq f_{ins} \\ f = f_{ins} \end{matrix}$$

Instances: $\mathcal{J}'_{\mathcal{M}'} = <$R-UP, C', AV$>$, R-UP not changed, AV not changed.

$$c_{f_{ins}}' : dom\ (f_{ins}) \to codom\ (f_{ins}),$$

$$c_{f_{ins}}'(x_1,...,x_n,x_{n+1}) = nv(c_{f_{ins}}(x_1,...,x_n),x_{n+1}) \quad with\ x_{n+1} \in dom(l)$$

14. **delete dimension**: deletes a dimension (connected to the fact at level l) from a fact. Parameters: level name $l \in L$ and fact name $f_{del} \in F$. Additionally, an aggregation function $agg_z$ has to be provided which defines how the fact values have to be aggregated over the deleted dimension (e.g. summation).

$$\mathfrak{M}' = < F, L, A\ gran',\ class,\ attr>$$

$$gran'(f): F \to 2^L \qquad gran'(f) := \begin{cases} gran(f) & f \neq f_{dl} \\ gran(f) - \{l\} \end{cases} \quad for \quad \begin{matrix} f \neq f_{dl} \\ f = f_{dl} \end{matrix}$$

Instances: $\mathfrak{I}'_{\mathfrak{M}'} = $ <R-UP, C', AV>, R-UP not changed, AV not changed.

$$c_{f_{del}}' : dom\ (f_{del}) \to codom\ (f_{del}),$$

$$c_{f_{del}}'(x_1,...,x_{n-1}) = agg_{x_n}(c_{f_{del}}(x_1,...,x_n)) \quad with\ x_n \in dom(l)$$

# 6    Tool Support for the Evolution Process

When a considerable amount of requirements change for an MDIS that is operational, a new iteration of the development process is initiated (see section 1). First, the new and changed requirements are compiled and documented. The schema evolution process begins when these changed requirements are to be incorporated into the conceptual data model. Our vision is that the warehouse modeller works with the conceptual schema in a design tool based on a graphical representation (e.g. using the ME/R notation [18]). The tool enables the warehouse modeller to successively apply evolution operations $\varphi_1,... \varphi_n$ to the schema. When the designer is satisfied with the results, he commits his changes. At this time, the system checks the integrity of the resulting model and propagates the changes of the schema and instances to the implementation level, e.g. by transforming the evolution operations to a sequence of SQL commands. Thus, the warehouse modeller does not need to have knowledge about the specific implementation because the tool-supported environment allows him to work purely on the conceptual level.

# 7    Conclusions and Future Work

We suggested a framework for multidimensional schema evolution that enables the design of a tool supported schema evolution environment on a conceptual level. In this paper, we presented the core of this framework: a schema evolution algebra based on a formal description of multidimensional schema and instances. This algebra offers 14 atomic evolution operations that can be used to build more complex evolution operations. Furthermore, we described how this formalism can be embedded into the iterative tool-based design and maintenance process of multidimensional information systems. The future research work of our group will investigate the automatic propagation of effects to different implementations (e.g. multidimensional, relational) taking into account effects on predefined aggregates, indexing schemes and predefined reports.

# References

[1] J. Banerjee, W. Kim, H.-J. Kim, H.F. Korth: *Semantics and Implementation of Schema Evolution in Object-Oriented Databases*, Proc. SIGMOD Conference, 1987.

[2] M. Blaschka: *FIESTA : A Framework for Schema Evolution in Multidimensional Information Systems*, Proc. of 6th CAiSE Doctoral Consortium, 1999, Heidelberg, Germany

[3] E. Baralis, S. Paraboschi, E. Teniente: *Materialized view selection in a multidimensional database*, Proceedings Conference on Very Large Databases, Athens, Greece, 1997.

[4] L. Cabibbo, R. Torlone: *A Logical Approach to Multidimensional Databases*. Proc. EDBT 1998.

[5] A. Datta ,H. Thomas: *A Conceptual Model and an algebra for On-Line Analytical Processing in Data Warehouses*, Proc. WITS 1997

[6] A. Gupta, I. S. Mumick: *Maintenance of Materialized Views: Problems, Techniques, and Applications*, Data Engineering Bulletin, June 1995.

[7] M. Golfarelli, D. Maio, S. Rizzi, *Conceptual design of data warehouses from E/R schemes*, Proc. 31st Hawaii Intl. Conf. on System Sciences, 1998.

[8] M. Golfarelli, S. Rizzi, *A Methodological Framework for Data Warehouse Design*, ACM DOLAP Workshop, Washington 1998

[9] C.A. Hurtado, A.O. Mendelzon, A.A. Vaisman: *Maintaining Data Cubes under Dimension Updates*, Proceedings of the ICDE' 99, Sydney Australia

[10] G. Höfling, *Schema Evolution in Object-oriented Databases,*. PhD Thesis, Technische Universität München, 1996 (In German)

[11] R. Kimball: *Slowly Changing Dimensions*, Data Warehouse Architect, DBMS Magazine, April 1996, URL: http://www.dbmsmag.com

[12] W. Lehner, *Multidimensional Normal Forms*, Proceedings of SSDBM'98, Capri, Italy

[13] W. Lehner: *Modeling Large Scale OLAP Scenarios*. Proc. of the EDBT 98, Valencia Spain http://www6.informatik.uni-erlangen.de/dept/staff/lehner-publications.html

[14] M. Mohania: *Avoiding Re-computation: View Adaptation in Data Warehouses*. Proc. 8th International Database Workshop, Hong-Kong, Springer LNCS, 1997

[15] C. Quix: *Repository Support for Data Warehouse Evolution*. Proc. CAiSE99 Workshop on Design and Management of Data Warehouses (DMDW99), 1999.

[16] E.A. Rundensteiner, A.J. Lee, A. Nica: *On Preserving Views in Evolving Environments*. Proc. of the 4th KRDB Workshop, Athens, Greece, August 1997

[17] C. Sapia: *On Modelling and Predicting Query Behavior in OLAP Systems*. Proc. CAiSE99 Workshop on Design and Management of Data Warehouses (DMDW99), 1999.

[18] C. Sapia, M. Blaschka, G. Höfling, B. Dinter, *Extending the E/R Model for the Multidimensional Paradigm*, Proc. DWDM Workshop (ER98 Conference), Singapore.

[19] C. Sapia, M. Blaschka, G. Höfling, *An Overview of Multidimensional Data Models*, FORWISS Technical Report FR- 1999-001

[20] M. Tresch, *Evolution in Object Databases*, Teubner, Stuttgart, 1995 (In German)

[21] Panos Vassiliadis: *Modeling Multidimensional Databases, Cubes and Cube Operations*. Conference on Statistical and Scientific Databases (SSDBM) 1998

# Lazy Aggregates for Real-Time OLAP

Jukka Kiviniemi, Antoni Wolski, Antti Pesonen[+], Johannes Arminen

Technical Research Centre of Finland (VTT)
VTT Information Technology
P.O. Box 1201, 02044 VTT, Finland

{Jukka.Kiviniemi, Antoni.Wolski, Antti.Pesonen, Johannes.Arminen}@vtt.fi
http://www.vtt.fi/tte/projects/iolap

**Abstract.** In OLAP models, or data cubes, aggregates have to be recalculated when the underlying base data changes. This may cause performance problems in real-time OLAP systems, which continuously accommodate huge amounts of measurement data. To optimize the aggregate computations, a new consistency criterion called the tolerance invariant is proposed. Lazy aggregates are aggregates that are recalculated only when the tolerance invariant is violated, i.e., the error of the previously calculated aggregate exceeds the given tolerance. An industrial case study is presented. The prototype implementation is described, together with the performance results.

## 1 Introduction

Traditional OLAP (on-line analytical processing) [3] technology is developed mainly for commercial analysis needs. Data from various sources is compiled into multiattribute fact data tuples. They are used to compute multidimensional aggregates that make up the essence of OLAP.

An industrial process is often a subject of extensive analysis, too. However, the traditional OLAP technology is insufficient for such analysis. It lacks support for real-time operation and efficient time series analysis. Usually, the industrial analysis model, comprising of measurement data and derived data, must be up-to date instantly when the contents of the underlying data sources change. We claim that a certain level of temporal consistency [8] must be maintained, in an industrial analysis model.

In this paper, we present the requirements for Industrial OLAP (IOLAP) for industrial process analysis. We analyze problems encountered in a case study, having to do with handling time series data and maintaining consistency of the analysis structure in real-time. We introduce a method to decrease the amount of computation required to update the analysis model, by allowing the model to have some value-inaccuracy. We call this the lazy aggregation method. We present an example of a typical industrial application and summarize experimental results of applying the method.

---

[+]Currently on leave, at National Inst. of Standards and Technology, Gaithersburg, MD, U.S.A.

A theoretical abstraction of multidimensional analysis model, the data cube, was refined in [4]. The basic computation models for data cube were reviewed in [1]. A model for decomposition of data cube into a lattice was presented in [5]. Data cube maintenance and refreshing issues were addressed in [7]. We already introduced a time series database platform supporting active ECA rules [11].

The paper is organized as follows. In Section 2, we discuss IOLAP requirements. In Section 3, we introduce the concept of accuracy-based consistency enforcement and propose the lazy aggregate method. In Section 4, we focus on a case study and the prototype implementation. We conclude in Section 5.

## 2 IOLAP Model

Similarly to traditional OLAP models, the IOLAP data model involves base data and aggregate data. The base data reflects the current and past state of a process and is usually stored in a process database. An example of a process database management system implementation is given in [11].

Calculable data cubes may be represented as nodes in a combined aggregate lattice [5]. The lattice has $n+1$ levels where $n$ is the maximum number of dimensions. An example of a 4-level aggregate lattice is given in Figure 1.

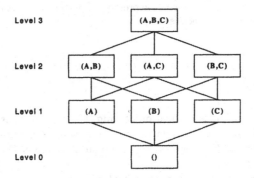

**Figure 1.** The aggregate lattice

The top level-3 ($l = n = 3$) aggregates are directly calculated from base data. They may be expressed as a tuple $< dim_A,\ dim_B,\ dim_C,\ fact>$ where *fact* is a value of an aggregate function over dimensions A, B, and C at a point $(dim_A,\ dim_B,\ dim_C)$ of a 3-dimensional space. We chose to represent both the base and aggregate data using the relational model. For example, if the base data is stored in a relational table having the schema (id, dimA, dimB, dimC, value), the level 3 node for the AVG function is produced with the SQL query:

```
SELECT dimA, dimB, dimC, AVG(value)
FROM base_table
GROUP BY dimA, dimB, dimC;
```

The lower level aggregates can be calculated from precalculated upper-level aggregates. We say that the aggregates at level *l* are calculated from the source data at level

$l+1(l = 0, ..., n-1)$ and the level $n$ is aggregated from the base (fact) data. The zero-level node is a single value aggregated over the whole base data set. The lattice can be also called an *N-cube* meaning a collection of $N$ cubes where $N = 2^n$.

The lattice may be materialized to a various extent. In two extreme cases, the aggregate data may be totally calculated at query time or they may be totally materialized in advance. There has been some research effort aimed at maintaining lattice consistency in a most efficient way, once the lattice is being refreshed [5, 7].

We take a different approach in this work. In IOLAP, the goal is to be able to perform real-time analysis using the latest process data. The temporal consistency of the analysis data is expected to be within sub-second range. We thus assume the lattice is fully materialized at all times, and we strive to avoid "insignificant" recalculations, i.e. such aggregate recalculations that would not be required from the accuracy point of view.

We propose a new consistency criterion that is based on numerical accuracy and leads to the concept of lazy aggregation. A user sets an allowable tolerance for an aggregate calculation error. Consequently, an aggregate value need not be recalculated if the existing value represents the current process within the given tolerance.

## 3 Lazy Aggregates

### 3.1 Definitions

**Definition 1: Error band.** Error band $\phi_v$ of variable $v$ is defined as a maximum deviation of the measured value $v_i$ from a specific reference norm.

$$\phi_v = \max_i ( abs( \varepsilon(v_i) ) ), \tag{1}$$

where $i$ spans all measured occurrences of $v$, and $\varepsilon(v_i)$ is an actual measurement error of $v_i$. Error band is typically expressed as an absolute percentage of full scale, e.g. 10%, and it is normally associated with a measurement equipment.

**Definition 2: Tolerance.** Tolerance $\alpha_v$ of a variable $v$ is an acceptable degree of variation of $v$. It is also usually expressed as an absolute percentage of full scale.

The above two concepts seem to be similar but there is a semantic difference between them: the error band stems from the physical characteristics of the measuring equipment, and the tolerance is an externally given requirement. Note, that we expect the measurement system to maintain, at any time the relation

$$\phi_v \leq \alpha_v \text{ for every variable } v. \tag{2}$$

Sometimes the error band values are not known, and the tolerance values are used instead. For simplicity of notation, we also assume that $\phi_v = \alpha_v$, for base data. For the purpose of evaluation of the error band of the aggregate values, we introduce the concept of the *base aggregate error band*.

**Definition 3: Base aggregate error band (BEB).** Base aggregate error band $BEB_a$ of an aggregate $a$ is a maximum deviation of the aggregate value from a real exact value. It is expressed as an absolute percentage of full scale. It is defined as a function:

$$BEB_a = f(S, A), \tag{3}$$

where $S = \{s_j \mid j = 1, ..., m\}$ is the set of available source values, $A = \{\alpha_j \mid j = 1, ..., m\}$ is the set of the corresponding tolerance values, and $m$ is the size of the source value set. There is a binary (correspondence) relation $< s_j, \alpha_j> \subset R$.

As we deal with the effect of propagating errors from function arguments to the function result, various approaches to error propagation may be used in order to establish an appropriate BEB function for each aggregate. For example, if we treat measurement values as value intervals, the interval arithmetic [6] may be applied.

BEB functions for some aggregates are trivial. For example, for the Maximum aggregate:

$$BEB_{MAX} = \alpha_j \text{ such as } MAX(S) = v_j. \tag{4}$$

In the case of the Average aggregate, the following approximation may be sufficient:

$$BEB_{AVG} = AVG(A). \tag{5}$$

We use BEB to characterize each lattice node element in terms of its maximum accuracy, i.e. the accuracy achieved when the node element value (aggregate value) is recalculated form the source data having some tolerance. We now proceed to characterize the error induced by *not* recalculating the aggregate.

We introduce the concept of an *actual error band* to reflect the instantaneous error band of an aggregate. It is recalculated each time there is a change to source data.

**Definition 4: Actual aggregate error band (AEB).** Actual aggregate error band AEB of a node element is defined as

$$AEB_a = BEB_a + abs(\sum_i \delta_i) \tag{6}$$

where $\delta_i$ is the error delta calculated for each i-th change (transaction) affecting a source data variable:

$$\delta_i = f_a(v_i, v\text{-}old_i, P_v) \tag{7}$$

where $v_i$ and $v\text{-}old_i$ are the new and old values of the source data and $P_v$ is the power (cardinality) of the set of $v_i$ values being aggregated. The function is aggregate-specific. The value of $i$ is set to zero each time the aggregate value is recalculated. Evaluation of AEB is triggered by any replacement of $v\text{-}old_i$ with $v_i$.

As a consistency criterion, we propose to maintain, in a lattice of aggregates, the following invariant:

**Definition 5: Tolerance invariant** (consistency criterion). For each $j$-$th$ element at the $p$-$th$ lattice node, the following holds:

$$\underset{p,j}{\forall}\ AEB_j^p \le \alpha_p \tag{8}$$

where $\alpha_p$ is a tolerance value associated with the aggregate at the node $p$.

## 3.2 Computational Model

The idea of the lazy aggregates is to delay the aggregate recalculation until the actual error band of the aggregate value exceeds the given tolerance. We propose to maintain tolerance invariant by way of a standard ECA rule (trigger) mechanism [9]. An ECA rule is associated with each aggregate at levels 1, ..., n. The aggregate recalculation at any level takes place in the following steps.

1. Event detection: a change of data source at level $l$ is detected.
2. Condition evaluation: the tolerance invariant at level $l-1$ is checked
3. Action execution (conditional): the aggregate at level $l-1$ is recalculated

As a result, the change in the base data is propagated downward the lattice in an optimized way. A possible scenario of aggregate recalculation is shown in Figure 2.

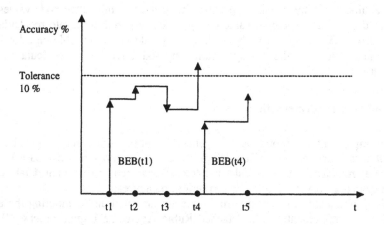

**Figure 2.** An example of lazy aggregate computation

In the example, at time $t1$, the aggregated power consumption is calculated and the base error band (BEB) is evaluated. At $t2$ and $t3$, the new measurement values are arrived and the evaluation of the tolerance invariant is fired. The corresponding error deltas are calculated but no aggregate recalculation is triggered as the resulting actual error band (AEB) is still within the tolerance. At $t4$, the accumulated AEB exceeds the tolerance value, which leads to aggregate recalculation and re-evaluation of BEB. At $t5$, again, the tolerance invariant holds, and no aggregate recalculation is needed.

# 4 Implementation and Results

## 4.1 Case Study

ABB Industry Oy is a leading manufacturer of electric drive systems for heavy industry. A typical product is a paper machine drive system [2]. It consists of few tens of high-power electric motors (drives), together with the associated frequency converters, and a control and supervision system. In the case study, the requirement is to be able to survey the overall drive operation in real-time. Drives are combined into drive sections which, in turn, are grouped according to machine parts such as wire, press and dryer. Several paper machines may be surveyed at a factory or at different locations, at the same time. Possible dimensions to be used in motor behavior analysis are thus: *section, machine part, machine, location, power range, type* and *manufacturing year*. Some of the dimensions may be considered different granularities of a single dimension. For example, machine part, machine and location may be granularities of the geographical dimension.

The variables measured at each motor are, typically, temperature, power and torque. The measured values constitute the base data of the case study IOLAP model. The data is collected at typical rate of one measurement record (a tuple of all measurement values) per second per motor. For a 100-motor installation, the update rate of 100/s is attained, for any variable type. If we required that the lattice node values are recalculated each time a source value changes, the required aggregate recalculation rate would be $(100 \cdot 2^n)/s = 1600/s$. Such a rate would not be feasible on a low-cost PC equipment. We apply the lazy aggregation method to reduce the recalculation rate significantly.

## 4.2 Prototype Implementation

We have implemented a prototype of a general-purpose N-cube server called Rubic [10]. Rubic is based on the existing RapidBase active time series database system [12]. The aggregates in the data cube lattice are organized as relational database tables. Triggers are associated with all time series and aggregates.

All the functionality of checking the tolerance invariant and computing the error band values is implemented in a detached Rubic Aggregate Engine process. When any value in time series or an aggregate node is changed, an appropriate trigger is fired and the aggregate engine handles the action. The action execution starts with the tolerance invariant checking and, depending on the result, either the actual error band is updated or the lattice node value is recalculated.

The analysis data is generated with a process data generator, which feeds new measurements values for each motor periodically. The aggregated results are analyzed using some general-purpose reporting tool connected to RapidBase via the ODBC driver.

## 4.3 Performance Results

The test scenario consists of 100 motors and the power of each motor is measured. The measurements are assumed to have a random walk behavior and each motor is handled independently.

The motors are analyzed on the basis of four dimensions (*type, power range, year of manufacturing,* and *machine part*). Thus, the used aggregate lattice contains $2^4=16$ tables, which are all materialized. The experiment is performed separately for two aggregate functions, AVG(power) and SUM(power). These functions were selected to represent distributive and algebraic aggregate function groups [4], respectively. We do not address holistic aggregate functions in our experiment. The arrival rate of the measurement values for each motor is 1/s. The tolerance values are varied within a range of 2% to 20%.

During the test run, the number of lattice recalculations is measured. The lattice recalculation is performed, when an updated error band exceeds the given tolerance. The result is expressed as a lattice recalculation percentage that is calculated with the following formula (for a given period of time):

$$RECALC\% = \frac{no._-of_-lattice_-element_-recalculations}{2^{no._-of_-dim.} * no._-of_-input_-transactions} \qquad (9)$$

The test was run under Windows NT 4 in a 333 MHz Pentium Pro PC with main memory of 128Mb. The experimental results are presented in Figure 3.

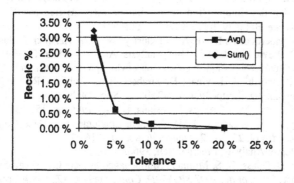

**Figure 3.** Experimental results

The experimental results begin with a tolerance value of 2%. The lower values were not attainable due to performance limitations. It can be clearly seen that, by using affordable tolerance level, say 5%, it is possible to reduce the number of lattice recalculations drastically. Furthermore, regardless of the aggregate function type, the performance is alike. However, neither function is demanding in terms of complexity nor are their BEB and AEG functions. More complex algebraic aggregate function may cause indeterminate performance degradation when using the lazy aggregate method.

# 5 Conclusions

We discussed the requirements for using OLAP in industrial analysis, and we found the OLAP concept useful for the purpose. However, the traditional OLAP approach must be enhanced to fulfill industrial analysis needs. Typical industrial data is time-based and it has a fast arrival rate. The accuracy of the data at various levels of the OLAP structure (data cube) varies in time as the underlying base data changes. We took the advantage of this phenomenon to utilize the accuracy of computations in the performance optimization scheme called lazy aggregates. Lazy aggregates are the aggregates that are calculated only if the accuracy of the previously calculated values is not within given tolerance. We defined the concepts of error band and the consistency criterion in the form of the tolerance invariant. We propose, how the lazy aggregate method can be implemented using an active main memory database. We provide a case study based on a paper industry application. We also provide a prototype implementation of a general-purpose N-cube server called Rubic. We analyze our lazy aggregate approach using Rubic and we find that, by using the lazy aggregate concept, it is possible to perform complex industrial analysis on a standard PC platform in the presence of fast data acquisition.

# References

1.  S. Agarwal, R. Agrawal, P. M. Deshpandre, A. Gupta, J. F. Naughton, R. Ramakrishnan, S. Sarawagi. On the Computation of Multidimensional Aggregates. *Proc. of the 22nd VLDB Conference*, Bombay, India, 1996, pp. 506-521.
2.  PPS 200: The papermaker's Drive. ABB Industry Oy, 1998, Helsinki, Finland.
3.  F. Codd, et al. Providing OLAP to User-Analysts: An IT Mandate. TR, E.F. Codd & Associates, 1993 (http://www.arborsoft.com/essbase/wht_ppr/ coddTOC.html)
4.  J. Gray, A. Bosworth, A. Layman, H. Pirahesh. Data Cube: A Relational Aggregation Operator Generalizing Group-By, Cross-Tab, and Sub-Totals. *Proc. of 12th Internat. Conf. on Data Engineering*, New Orleans, Louisiana, U.S.A., 1996, pp. 152-159.
5.  V. Harinarayan, A. Rajaman, J. D. Ullman. Implementing Data Cubes Efficiently. *SIGMOD Record*, Vol. 25, No. 2, June 1996, pp. 205-216.
6.  R. Moore. Interval Analysis, Prentice Hall, 1966.
7.  I. S. Mumick, D. Quass, B. S. Mumick. Maintenance of Data Cubes and Summary Tables in a Warehouse. *Proc. of the 1997 SIGMOD. Conf.*, Tucson. AZ, U.S.A., pp. 100-111.
8.  K. Ramamritham. Real-Time Databases. *Distributed and Parallel Databases*, 1(2), April 1993, pp. 199-226.
9.  J. Widom, S. Ceri (eds.). Active Database Systems: Triggers and Rules for Advanced Database Processing. Morgan Kaufmann, 1996.
10. A. Wolski, J. Arminen, J. Kiviniemi, A. Pesonen. Design of Rubic, Version 1.0. Research Report TTE1-1-99, VTT Information Technology, January 1999. (http://www.vtt.fi/-tte/projects/industrialdb/publs/rubic-design.pdf)
11. A. Wolski, J. Karvonen, A. Puolakka. The RAPID Case Study: Requirements for and the Design of a Fast-response Database System. *Proceedings of the First Workshop on real-Time Databases* (RTDB'96), Newport Beach, CA, USA, 1996, pp. 32-39 (http://www.vtt.fi/tte/projects/industrialdb/publs/case.pdf)
12. RapidBase Home Page, VTT Information Technology, 1999. (http://www.vtt.fi/tte/projects/rapid/)

# Incremental Refinement of Mining Queries

Elena Baralis          Giuseppe Psaila

Politecnico di Torino          Politecnico di Milano
Dip. Automatica e Informatica          Dip. Elettronica e Informazione
C.so Duca degli Abruzzi 24          P.za Leonardo da Vinci 32
10129 Torino (Italy)          20133 Milano (Italy)

baralis@polito.it          psaila@elet.polimi.it

**Abstract.** A first attempt to extract association rules from a database frequently yields a significant number of rules, which may be rather difficult for the user to browse in searching interesting information. However, powerful languages allow the user to specify complex mining queries to reduce the amount of extracted information. Hence, a suitable rule set may be obtained by means of a progressive refinement of the initial query. To assist the user in the refinement process, we identify several types of containment relationships between mining queries that may lead the process. Since the repeated extraction of a large rule set is computationally expensive, we propose an algorithm to perform an incremental recomputation of the output rule set. This algorithm is based on the detection of containment relationships between mining queries.

## 1 Introduction

Association rules allow the detection of the most common links among data items in a large amount of collected data. The number of extracted association rules may be huge, and not all the discovered associations may be meaningful for a given user. Several high level languages have been proposed [3, 5] to allow the user to specify accurate extraction criteria, following which the association rules are searched in the source data. These languages provide to the user a powerful instrument for both the specification and the refinement of mining queries, in order to better capture the user needs.

The design of an association rule mining query is a complex task in which we can distinguish two phases:

- *Identification and definition:* given a data source and user requirements, the correct class(es) of extraction criteria for the problem are identified. Next, the appropriate mining query is defined. We do not expect the initial output rule set to satisfy completely the user requirements.

- *Refinement:* the initial query is iteratively refined in order to better meet (possibly changing) user needs.

The identification and definition phase is extensively discussed in [2], where a correspondence between classes of extraction criteria and the corresponding mining queries is presented. In this paper we analyze the refinement phase. Given a mining query, we study the effect of modifications performed in order to better capture the user needs, either because the previous formulation did not completely match, or because they evolved in time.

We first identify a containment relationship between mining queries, called *dominance*. This relationship aims to identify a containment relationship between the output rule sets extracted by the compared queries. Next, we identify classes of refinement criteria and we characterize the relationship between progressively more complex queries inside each class by means of the above properties. When the query refinement satisfies the identified relationship, the actual rule extraction process may be significantly simplified. In this case, a rule set $\mathcal{R}_2$ extracted by a query $M_2$, which refines a query $M_1$ that produced rule set $\mathcal{R}_1$, can be incrementally obtained starting from rules in $\mathcal{R}_1$.

In related work, when the extracted rule set is too large, the most commonly proposed technique to help the user in finding relevant rules is a powerful rule browsing tool [3, 4]. This solution allows the user to specify only the simplest of the refinement criteria we discuss in this paper. In [4] the problem of selecting interesting association rules from a large set of discovered rules is addressed in a twofold way. Firstly, rule templates describing the structure of the rules the user is interested in allow the selection of a subset of the formerly discovered rules. Secondly, a graphical tool is proposed, which shows rules in a clever way, in order to highlight common parts. In [3], the notion of exploratory mining is introduced. Exploratory mining allows the user to extract all possible rules on all possible attributes, in order to help the user find interesting rules. However, only a purely practical approach to the problem is presented. An evolution of the concept of exploratory mining is provided in [6]: a language to specify constrained association rule queries is defined, in such a way it allows pruning optimizations performed during the actual extraction of association rules.

The paper is organized as follows. Section 1.1 describes the association rule mining operator MINE RULE [5], on which our discussion is based. Section 2 defines the comparison relationships among mining queries. In Section 3 the most relevant cases of query refinement are discussed, while in Section 4 an algorithm for the incremental computation of refined queries is presented. Finally, Section 5 discusses conclusions and future work.

## 1.1 Mining Queries

Mining queries for extracting association rules from relational data can be expressed by means of a SQL-like operator, named MINE RULE, defined in [5]. This section introduces the operator by showing its application to a running example, i.e. the Purchase table depicted in Figure 1, containing data about purchases in a store. Each purchase transaction is characterized by a unique identifier, a customer code and a date. For each bought item, the price and the purchased quantity are specified.

Consider customers that bought less than 10 items. Suppose the user is interested in extracting rules that associate a set of items (the *body*) with a single

| tr. | customer | item | date | price | q.ty |
|---|---|---|---|---|---|
| 1 | cust$_1$ | col_shirts | 12/17/96 | 85 | 1 |
| 1 | cust$_1$ | hiking_boots | 12/17/96 | 180 | 1 |
| 1 | cust$_1$ | jackets | 12/17/96 | 102 | 1 |
| 2 | cust$_3$ | brown_boots | 12/18/96 | 150 | 1 |
| 2 | cust$_3$ | col_shirts | 12/18/96 | 25 | 3 |
| 3 | cust$_2$ | col_shirts | 12/19/96 | 99 | 2 |
| 3 | cust$_2$ | brown_boots | 12/19/96 | 150 | 3 |
| 4 | cust$_3$ | jackets | 12/20/96 | 50 | 3 |
| 5 | cust$_2$ | col_shirts | 12/21/96 | 99 | 1 |

**Fig. 1.** The Purchase table for a big-store.

item (the *head*) bought by a single customer in the same date. In particular, the user wants items with price greater than or equal to \$100 in the body, and items having price less than \$100 in the head. Rules are interesting only if their support (the frequency of a rule among customers) is at least 0.2 (i.e., at least 20% of customers support the rule) and their confidence (the conditional probability that a customer buying items in the body buys also items in the head) is at least 0.3 (i.e., at least 30% of customers supporting the rule body also support the whole rule). The following query corresponds to the above problem.

```
MINE RULE FilteredSameDate AS
SELECT DISTINCT 1..n item AS BODY, 1..1 item AS HEAD, SUPPORT, CONFIDENCE
    WHERE BODY.price >= 100 AND HEAD.price < 100
FROM Purchase
GROUP BY customer HAVING COUNT(*) < 10
CLUSTER BY date HAVING BODY.date = HEAD.date
EXTRACTING RULES WITH SUPPORT: 0.2, CONFIDENCE: 0.3
```

The association rules are extracted by performing the following steps.

**Group computation.** The source data, contained in the Purchase table (FROM clause), is logically partitioned into groups (GROUP BY clause) such that all tuples in a group have the same value of attribute customer (in general, several

| cust | date | item | tr. | price | q.ty |
|---|---|---|---|---|---|
| cust$_1$ | 12/17/96 | col_shirts | 1 | 85 | 1 |
| | | hiking_boots | 1 | 180 | 1 |
| | | jackets | 1 | 102 | 1 |
| cust$_2$ | 12/19/96 | brown_boots | 3 | 150 | 3 |
| | | col_shirts | 3 | 99 | 2 |
| | 12/21/96 | col_shirts | 5 | 99 | 1 |
| cust$_3$ | 12/18/96 | col_shirts | 2 | 25 | 3 |
| | | brown_boots | 2 | 150 | 1 |
| | 12/20/96 | jackets | 4 | 50 | 3 |

**Fig. 2.** The Purchase table grouped by customer and clustered by date.

attributes are allowed in this clause; they are called grouping attributes). The total number of groups in the source data is computed in this step; we denote it as $G$ (used to compute rule support).

**Group filtering.** Only groups with less than 10 tuples must be considered for rule extraction; this is expressed by the group filtering condition in the HAVING clause associated to the GROUP BY clause.

**Cluster identification.** Each group is further partitioned into sub-groups called *clusters* (see Figure 2), such that tuples in a cluster have the same value for attribute date (attributes specified in this clause are called clustering attributes). The body (resp. head) of a rule is extracted from clusters, thus elements in the body (resp. head) share the same value of the clustering attribute; in absence of clusters (the CLUSTER BY clause is optional), rules are extracted from the trivial cluster, i.e. the entire group.

**Cluster coupling.** In order to compose rules, every pair of clusters (one for the body and one for the head) inside the same group is considered. Furthermore, the cluster filtering condition in the HAVING clause of the CLUSTER BY clause selects the cluster pairs that should be considered for extracting rules. In this case, a pair of clusters is considered only if the date of the left hand cluster (called *body cluster*) is the same as the date of the right hand cluster (called *head cluster*). In absence of cluster coupling (optional), all pairs of clusters are valid.

**Mining Condition.** Before rule extraction is performed, the tuple predicate in the SELECT ... WHERE clause is evaluated: given a pair of clusters and all tuples in the clusters, a rule is extracted only if tuples considered for body and head satisfy the predicate. Since this predicate is evaluated during the actual rule extraction phase, it is called *mining condition*. In our example, the mining condition selects only items with price greater than or equal to $100 for the bodies, and only items with price less than $100 for the heads. This clause is optional, and in its absence every tuple combination is valid.

**Rule extraction.** From each group, all possible associations of an unlimited set of items (clause 1..n item AS BODY), which is called the premise or body of the rule, with a single item (clause 1..1 item AS HEAD), which is called the consequent or head of the rule are extracted. An example of rule generated by the query is $\{brown\_boots, jackets\} \Rightarrow \{col\_shirts\}$, where elements in the body and in the head are items.

The number of groups that contain a rule $r$, denoted as $G_r$ (used to compute support and confidence of rules), and the number of groups that contain the body of $r$, denoted as $G_b$ (used to compute confidence of rules), are computed during this step.

Observe that, for a rule $r$, $G_r$ denotes the total number of groups, after the application of the group filtering condition, which contain a pair of clusters from which the rule is extracted, while $G_b$ gives the same information for the body.

**Support and confidence evaluation** The *support* of a rule is its frequency among groups $s = G_r/G$; the *confidence* is the conditional probability that the rule is found in a group which contains the body $c = G_r/G_b$. Support and confidence are then a measure of relevance of a rule. If they are lower than their respective minimum thresholds (0.2 for support and 0.3 for confidence, in our sample query), the rule is discarded.

The resulting rule set is the following.

$$\{\text{hiking\_boots}\} \Rightarrow \{\text{col\_shirts}\}, \qquad s = 0.33, c = 1$$
$$\{\text{jackets}\} \Rightarrow \{\text{col\_shirts}\}, \qquad s = 0.33, c = 0.5$$
$$\{\text{hiking\_boots,jackets}\} \Rightarrow \{\text{col\_shirts}\}, \quad s = 0.33, c = 1$$
$$\{\text{brown\_boots}\} \Rightarrow \{\text{col\_shirts}\}, \qquad s = 0.66, c = 1$$

We finally observe that, in absence of clusters, if body and head are not disjoint, rules are tautological (e.g., rule $\{brown\_boots, col\_shirts\} \Rightarrow \{col\_shirts\}$ is tautological). Since the association is obvious, tautological rules are not extracted. When instead clusters are specified, a rule such that body and head are not disjoint is tautological only if body and head are extracted from the same cluster, since the association is obvious only if body and head refer to the same value of the clustering attributes. Thus, for a rule $r$ potentially tautological, $G_r$ indicates the number of groups, after applying the group filtering condition, which contain at least a pair of distinct clusters from which $r$ is extracted.

## 2 Properties of Mining Queries

Mining queries that extract association rules from a database can be compiled into a set of rather complex queries that extract the relevant information from the database. In this setting, it is rather difficult to apply known techniques to detect interesting relationships (e.g., query containment) between queries.

Owing to the complex structure of mining queries, it is possible to define several different relationships between mining query pairs. In particular, in addition to the classical notion of equivalence, an inclusion relationship has been identified, which differ in the way support and confidence values for the rules are considered.

The above relationships are formally defined in Section 2.1, as well as their properties are described in Section 2.1. These relationships can be used to drive the refinement of the rule extraction process (see Section 3).

### 2.1 Relationships between Rule Sets

Consider two MINE RULE queries $M_1$ and $M_2$, which extract rule sets $\mathcal{R}_1$ and $\mathcal{R}_2$ respectively. To define the relationship between $M_1$ and $M_2$, we must consider both the sets of rules output by $M_1$ and $M_2$ and their support and confidence.

Intuitively, two mining queries $M_1$ and $M_2$ are equivalent if their output rule sets $\mathcal{R}_1$ and $\mathcal{R}_2$ always contain the same rules and each rule has the same value for support and confidence both in $\mathcal{R}_1$ and $\mathcal{R}_2$.

**Definition 1 (Equivalence):** Let $M_1$ and $M_2$ be two mining queries, extracting from the same source data rule sets $\mathcal{R}_1$ and $\mathcal{R}_2$ resp.. $M_1$ and $M_2$ are equivalent ($M_1 \equiv M_2$) if, for all instances of the source data, each rule $r$ in $\mathcal{R}_1$ is also in $\mathcal{R}_2$ and vice versa, with the same support and confidence. □

A mining query $M_1$ includes query $M_2$ when its output rule set $\mathcal{R}_1$ includes $\mathcal{R}_2$, output by $M_2$ and each common rule has the same value of support and confidence in both sets. Hence, the relevance of common rules w.r.t. the source data is the same.

**Definition 2 (Inclusion):** Let $M_1$ and $M_2$ be two mining queries, that extract from the same source data rule sets $\mathcal{R}_1$ and $\mathcal{R}_2$ respectively. Query $M_1$ includes $M_2$ (written as $M_1 \supseteq M_2$) if, for all instances of the source data, each rule $r$ in $\mathcal{R}_2$ is also in $\mathcal{R}_1$, with the same value of support and confidence. $\square$

Dominance is a weaker kind of inclusion, in which support and confidence of each rule $r$ in $\mathcal{R}_2$ may be lower than the values for the corresponding rule in $\mathcal{R}_1$.

**Definition 3 (Dominance):** Let $M_1$ and $M_2$ be two mining queries, that extract from the same source data rule sets $\mathcal{R}_1$ and $\mathcal{R}_2$ respectively, and $s_1, c_1$ (respectively $s_2, c_2$) support and confidence of a rule $r$ in $\mathcal{R}_1$ ($\mathcal{R}_2$). Query $M_1$ dominates $M_2$ (written as $M_1 \triangleright M_2$) if, for all instances of the source data, each rule $r$ in $\mathcal{R}_2$ is also in $\mathcal{R}_1$ and is characterized by $s_2 \leq s_1$ and $c_2 \leq c_1$. $\square$

**Theorem 1:** Equivalence is a particular case of inclusion; inclusion is a particular case of dominance. $\square$

Equivalence, inclusion, and dominance meet the *transitivity* property.

For the sake of brevity, proofs of theorems in this section, as well as theorems in the rest of the paper, are not reported here; they are extensively reported in [7].

## 3 Refinement of Mining Queries

The first attempt to extract rules from a data source may return a huge amount of data. In this case, the user may either browse the extracted rules looking for relevant information, or refine the mining query to reduce the amount of returned information. This second option seems more promising, because it allows the user to progressively restrict the scope of her/his request by specifying new selection criteria, that usually cannot be applied if rules are simply browsed.

In [2] we identified several classes of relevant association rules based on the adopted extraction criterion. The minimal specification for rule extraction requires the indication of the basic rule features, i.e., attribute(s) from which the rules are extracted and body and head cardinality, group(s) from which rules are extracted, and minimum thresholds for support and confidence. Furthermore, the following orthogonal extraction criteria (which correspond to optional clauses of the MINE RULE operator) may be specified:

- *Mining conditions,* which allow the specification of filtering conditions specifically on head and/or body of the rules to be extracted.
- *Clustering conditions,* which allow the partitioning of groups into subgroups (clusters) with common features, which are then coupled and on which further conditions may be specified.
- *Group filtering conditions,* which allow the selection of a subset of groups on which mining is performed.

The above criteria may guide the user in refining an initial mining query, by adding progressively more restrictive conditions. In the following sections, given a mining query $M_1$ and a refinement $M_2$ of it, we analyze the relationships that hold between $M_1$ and $M_2$. In particular, in Section 3.1 we discuss modifications of the basic features of association rules, while in the following sections we separately explore the effects of mining conditions and clustering conditions. For brevity, we do not consider group filtering conditions, because ([7]) the dominance relationship is not met.

## 3.1 Rule Features

In this section, we discuss the effect of modifying the basic characteristics of association rules, i.e., support and confidence thresholds, body and head cardinalities, and specification of rule attributes.

**Support and Confidence Thresholds.** The minimum thresholds for support and confidence determine the number (and relevance) of extracted rules. These parameters are usually calibrated by the user for each particular application. Indeed, excessively high minimum thresholds may significantly reduce the number of extracted rules, causing important information to be lost. In contrast, excessively low minimum thresholds yield a huge number of rules, most of which are not meaningful since not sufficiently frequent.

**Theorem 2:** Let $M_1$ and $M_2$ be two mining queries, identical apart from minimum support (resp. $s_1$ and $s_2$) and minimum confidence (resp. $c_1$ and $c_2$) thresholds. If $s_1 \leq s_2$ and $c_1 \leq c_2$, then $M_1 \supseteq M_2$. $\square$

**Body and Head Cardinalities.** The choice of the appropriate minimum and maximum cardinality for body and head may be the result of a refinement process. An inclusion relationship holds, as proved by the following theorem. An identical result holds for the cardinality of the head.

**Theorem 3:** Let $M_1$ and $M_2$ be two mining queries, identical apart from the cardinality of the body, whose minimum and maximum values are $b_1$ and $B_1$, and $b_2$ and $B_2$ resp.. If $b_1 \leq b_2$ and $B_1 \geq B_2$, then $M_1 \supseteq M_2$. $\square$

## 3.2 Mining Condition

The mining condition allows the user to impose filtering conditions either separately on the rule body and/or head, or correlating them. The absence of a mining condition is interpreted as an always true condition. Hence, both the case in which a mining condition is added, and the case in which a mining condition is refined, can be treated in the same way. The following theorem states that there is a dominance relationship between queries when implication holds between their respective mining conditions.

**Theorem 4:** Let $M_1$ and $M_2$ be two mining queries, identical apart from the respective mining conditions $m_1$ and $m_2$. If $m_2 \Rightarrow m_1$[1], then $M_1 \triangleright M_2$. $\square$

---

[1] We denote with $\Rightarrow$ predicate implication.

In the following particular case, the inclusion relationship holds.

**Corollary 1:** Let $M_1$ and $M_2$ be two mining queries, identical apart from the respective mining conditions, denoted as $m_1$ and $m_2$ respectively. Consider $m_2 = m_1 \wedge p$. If $p$ is a simple comparison predicate between a rule attribute and a constant or between two rule attributes, then $M_1 \supseteq M_2$. □

### 3.3 Clusters

Clusters are further partitions of groups based on the values of the clustering attribute(s). When a clustering attribute is specified, rules are extracted from couples of clusters inside the same group. Further conditions may be specified on the clustering attributes by means of the HAVING clause. The query FilteredSameDate in Section 1.1 is an example of clustering on the attribute date with a cluster filtering condition. In the following, we discuss the effect caused by the introduction of clustering.

**Adding Clusters.** Consider two mining queries $M_1$ and $M_2$, where $M_2$ differs from $M_1$ only by the addition of a clustering attribute. In $M_1$ only the trivial cluster, that coincides with the group itself, is considered and rules are extracted from pairs of groups. In $M_2$ instead, clusters introduce a further partitioning of groups. Rules are now extracted from the pairs of clusters identified in each group. Hence, given the same source data, the generated rule sets may be significantly different. Two opposite effects may be caused by the addition of a cluster. New rules can be generated: rules that are discarded as tautological for $M_1$ because body and head are not disjoint, are not tautological any more for $M_2$ if body and head are extracted from different clusters. In contrast, rules may disappear from the output rule set: since the size of clusters in a group is smaller than the group itself, the same rule $r$ extracted by $M_2$ may have lower values for support and confidence than that extracted by $M_1$. Then, if $r$ does not meet any more the support or confidence threshold, it is not extracted. Hence, we can conclude that the addition of a clustering atribute leads to a query $M_2$ which is uncomparable with $M_1$.

**Cluster Filtering Condition.** The cluster filtering condition selects cluster pairs inside groups from which rules are extracted. Its absence can be viewed as the *true* predicate. Consider two mining queries $M_1$ and $M_2$, with clustering conditions $h_1$ and $h_2$, respectively. The following theorem shows that $M_1$ dominates $M_2$ if $h_2$ is more restrictive than $h_1$.

**Theorem 5:** Let $M_1$ and $M_2$ be two clustered mining queries, identical apart from the respective clustering conditions, denoted as $h_1$ and $h_2$ respectively. If $h_2 \Rightarrow h_1$, then $M_1 \triangleright M_2$. □

## 4   Incremental Computation

The query refinement process may cause repeated extractions of association rules with slightly different features. Since, as shown in several works [1], the rule

*Input:* a source relation r, the rule set $I$.
*Output:* the dominated rule set $R$.
**begin**
  **for each** rule $r$ in $I$ **do**
    $r$.rule_groups := 0; $r$.body_groups := 0; insert $r$ into $R$;
  **end**
  **for each** valid group $g$ in r **do**
    compute the set $C_g$ of clusters $c_j$ in $g$;
    compute the set $P_g$ of valid cluster pairs $p_k$ in $g$;
    **for each** rule $r$ in $R$ **do**
      **if** $r$ is in some $p_k \in P_g$ **then** $r$.rule_groups := $r$.rule_groups + 1;
      **if** $r$ is in some $c_j \in C_g$ **then** $r$.body_groups := $r$.body_groups + 1;
    **end**
  **end**
  **for each** rule $r$ in $R$ **do**   *// Rule Selection Phase*
    $r$.support := $r$.rule_groups / AllGroups;
    $r$.confidence := $r$.rule_groups / $r$.body_groups;
    **if** $r$.support < min_support or $r$.confidence < min_confidence **then**
      discard $r$ from $R$;
  **end**
  **return** $R$;
**end.**

**Fig. 3.** Algorithm for incremental computation in case of dominance.

extraction process is typically a computationally expensive task that requires strongly optimized extraction techniques, when a query is refined, it becomes important to perform this task incrementally from a given rule set.

In the general case, incremental recomputation of a new rule set is not possible, but detecting the properties of inclusion and dominance allows us to significantly simplify the extraction process. In particular

*Inclusion:* given two mining queries such that $M_1 \supseteq M_2$, the second rule set can be obtained from the first rule set without scanning again the source data;
*Dominance:* given two mining queries such that $M_1 \triangleright M_2$, the second rule set can be obtained from the first one by means of a single, simple pass over the source data, with a very low complexity in space.

**Algorithm.** The dominance relationship $M_1 \triangleright M_2$ is characterized by the fact that rules appearinxg in both output rule sets have lower support and confidence in the second rule set than in the first. Consequently, it is necessary to recompute support and confidence, but only for the rules contained in the first rule set.

As a consequence, it is not necessary to perform again the complete rule extraction process: a single pass over the source data is sufficient, and can be performed by a program implementing the algorithm of Figure 3.

The complexity in space of the algorithm can be computed as follows: the first rule set contains $m$ rules, and body or head of each rule contains at most

$n$ elements. In order to store all rules, memory for $(n + n) \times m$ elements is required. Thus, the complexity in space is $O(n \times m)$. Observe that this result improves substantially with respect to the exponential complexity of the general extraction algorithms.

## 5  Conclusions and Future Work

This paper addresses the problem of incrementally refining association rules mining. Since several complex languages for the specification of mining queries are becoming now available, it is very important to allow the user to progressively refine the initial mining query with growingly complex criteria.

We initially define the relationships of equivalence, inclusion and dominance between two mining queries $M_1$ and $M_2$. An extensive analysis of the application of these comparison relationships to mining query pairs $M_1$ and $M_2$ allows us to identify several cases of query refinement in which some of the above relationships hold. Furthermore, we show that the rule set $\mathcal{R}_2$ output by $M_2$ can be obtained by means of an incremental recomputation technique based on the knowledge of rule set $\mathcal{R}_1$ output by $M_1$.

We finally observe that, although our mining queries are expressed by means of the MINE RULE operator [5], the proposed techniques can be applied to any language providing the same expressive power. Furthermore, we believe that incremental recomputation algorithms can exploit some intermediate results of the extraction process. We are currently exploring the benefits of this knowledge in the specific context of the MINE RULE prototype.

## References

1. R. Agrawal and R. Srikant. Fast algorithms for mining association rules in large databases. In *Proceedings of the 20th VLDB Conference*, Santiago, Chile, 1994.
2. E. Baralis and G. Psaila. Designing templates for mining association rules. *JIIS Journal of Intelligent Information Systems*, 9:7 – 32, 1997.
3. T. Imielinski, A. Virmani, and A. Abdoulghani. Datamine: Application programming interface and query language for database mining. *KDD-96*, 1996.
4. W. Klementtinen, H. Mannila, P. Romkainen, H. Toivonen, and A. I. Verkamo. Finding interesting rules from large sets of discovered association rules. *Third International Conference on Information and Knowledge Management*, 1994.
5. R. Meo, G. Psaila, and S. Ceri. A new SQL-like operator for mining association rules. In *Proceedings of the 22st VLDB Conference*, Bombay, India, 1996.
6. R. Ng, L. Lackshmanan, J. Han, and A. Pang. Exploratory mining and pruning optimizations of constrained associations rules. In *Proceedings of the ACM-SIGMOD 98*, Seattle, Washington, USA., June 1998.
7. G. Psaila. *Integrating Data Mining Techniques and relational Databases*. Ph.D. Thesis, Politecnico di Torino, 1998.

# The Item-Set Tree: A Data Structure for Data Mining[*]

## Alaaeldin Hafez[1], Jitender Deogun[2], and Vijay V. Raghavan[1]

**Abstract.** Enhancements in data capturing technology have lead to exponential growth in amounts of data being stored in information systems. This growth in turn has motivated researchers to seek new techniques for extraction of knowledge implicit or hidden in the data. In this paper, we motivate the need for an incremental data mining approach based on data structure called the item-set tree. The motivated approach is shown to be effective for solving problems related to efficiency of handling data updates, accuracy of data mining results, processing input transactions, and answering user queries. We present efficient algorithms to insert transactions into the item-set tree and to count frequencies of itemsets for queries about strength of association among items. We prove that the expected complexity of inserting a transaction is $\approx O(1)$, and that of frequency counting is $O(n)$, where n is the cardinality of the domain of items.

## 1  Introduction

Association mining that discovers dependencies among values of an attribute was introduced by Agrawal et al.[1] and has emerged as a prominent research area. The association mining problem also referred to as the *market basket* problem can be formally defined as follows. Let $I = \{i_1, i_2, \ldots, i_n\}$ be a set of items as $S = \{s_1, s_2, \ldots, s_m\}$ be a set of transactions, where each transaction $s_i \in S$ is a set of items that is $s_i \subseteq I$. An *association rule* denoted by $X \Rightarrow Y$, where $X, Y \subset I$ and $X \cap Y = \Phi$, describes the existence of a relationship between the two itemsets $X$ and $Y$.

Several measures have been introduced to define the *strength* of the relationship between itemsets X and Y such as support, confidence, and interest. The definitions of these measures, from a probabilistic model are given below.

**I.** *Support* $(X \Rightarrow Y) = P(X, Y)$, or the percentage of transactions in the database that contain both $X$ and $Y$.

**II.** *Confidence* $(X \Rightarrow Y) = P(X, Y) / P(X)$, or the percentage of transactions containing $Y$ in transactions those contain $X$.

**III.** *Interest*$(X \Rightarrow Y) = P(X, Y) / P(X)P(Y)$ represents a test of statistical independence.

---

[*] This research was supported in part by the U.S. Department of Energy, Grant No. DE-FG02-97ER1220, and by the Army Research Office, Grant No. DAAH04-96-1-0325, under DEPSCoR program of Advanced Research Projects Agency, Department of Defense.

[1] ahafez(raghavan)@cacs.usl.edu, The Center for Advanced Computer Studies, University of SW Louisiana, Lafayette, LA 70504, USA.

[2] Deogun@cse.unl.edu, The Department of Computer Science, University of Nebraska, Lincoln, NE 68588, USA.

Many algorithms [1,2,3,4,5,6,7,8], have been proposed to generate association rules that satisfy certain measures. A close examination of those algorithms reveals that the spectrum of techniques that generate association rules, has two extremes:

- A transaction data file is repeatedly scanned to generate large itemsets. The scanning process stops when there are no more itemsets to be generated.
- A transaction data file is scanned only once to build a complete transaction lattice. Each node on the lattice represents a possible large itemset. A count is attached to each node to reflect the frequency of itemsets represented by nodes.

In the first case, since the transaction data file is traversed many times, the cost of generating large itemsets is high. In the later case, while the transaction data file is traversed only once, the maximum number of nodes in the transaction lattice is $2^n$, n is the cardinality of $I$, the set of items. Maintaining such a structure is expensive.

Many knowledge discovery applications, such as on-line services and world wide web, require accurate mining information from data that changes on a regular basis. In world wide web, every day hundreds of remote sites are created and removed. In such an environment, frequent or occasional updates may change the status of some rules discovered earlier. Also, many data mining applications deal with itemsets that may not satisfy data mining rules. Users could be interested in finding correlation between itemsets, not necessarily satisfying the measures of the data mining rules.

Discovering knowledge is an expensive operation. It requires extensive access of secondary storage that can become a bottleneck for efficient processing. Running data mining algorithms from scratch, each time there is a change in data, is obviously not an efficient strategy. Building a structure to maintain knowledge discovered could solve many problems, that have faced data mining techniques for years, that is *database updates, accuracy of data mining results, performance,* and *ad-hoc queries.*

In this paper, we propose a new approach, that represents a compromise between the two extremes of the association mining spectrum. In the context of the proposed approach two algorithms are introduced. The first algorithm builds an item-set tree by traversing the data file once, that is used to produce mining rules. While the second algorithm allows users to apply on-line ad hoc queries on the item-set tree.

The item-set tree approach is introduced in section 2. In section 3, counting frequencies of itemsets is given. The item-set tree approach is evaluated and the paper is concluded in section 4.

## 2   The Item-Set Tree

The item-set tree $T$ is a graphical representation of the transaction data file $F$. Each node $s \in T$ represents a transaction group $s$. All transactions that are having the same itemset, belong to the same transaction group. Let $I=\{i_1, i_2,...,i_n\}$ be an ordered set of items. For two transactions $s_i=\{a_1, a_2,...,a_l\}$ and $s_j=\{b_1, b_2,...,b_k\}$, let $s_i \leq s_j$ iff $a_p \leq b_p$ for all $1 \leq p \leq min(l,k)$. We call $l$ and $k$, the lengths of $s_i$ and $s_j$, respectively.

Each node in tree $T$ represents either an encountered transaction, i.e., a transaction in the transaction file, or a subset of an encountered transaction. Node $s_i$ is ancestor node of node $s_j$, if $s_i \subset^e s_j$ that is $s_i=\{a_1, a_2,...,a_l\}$ and $s_j=\{a_1, a_2,...,a_k\}$, for some $l<k$. Moreover a node $s_i$ direct ancestor of node $s_j$ if $s_i$ is an ancestor of $s_j$ and

there is no other node $s_k$ such that $s_i \subset^e s_k \subset^e s_j$. Frequency of a node s is denoted by $f(s)$ representing the count of transactions that have the same transaction group s. The item-set tree is constructed by transactions inserting process: *The root node r represents the null itemset {}. A transaction s is inserted by examining (in order) the children of the root node r. Each time a node is inserted, f(r) is incremented by 1.* The insertion process successfully ends with one of the following cases.

**Case 1:** All nodes $s_j$ (children of r) are such that these do share no leading elements in s. When a leaf node s is inserted as a son of r, $f(s)$ is initiated to 1.

**Case 2:** $s=s_j$, the node already exists. $f(s_j)$ is incremented by 1.

**Case 3:** $s \subset^e s_j$, s is an ordered subset of node $s_j$. A node s, representing s, is inserted as a child of r and as a parent of $s_j$. $f(s) = f(s_j) +1$.

**Case 4:** $s_j \subset^e s$, node $s_j$ is an ordered subset of s. The subtree, that has $s_j$ as a root, is examined and the procedure starts over again

**Case 5:** $s \cap^e s_j \neq \phi$, there exists an ordered intersection between s and $s_j$. Two nodes are inserted. A node $s_i$, $s_i = s \cap^e s_j$, is inserted between r and $s_j$, and a node s is inserted as a child of $s_i$. $f(s_i) = f(s_j)+1$, and $f(s)$ is initiated to 1.

**Algorithm Construct (s,T)**
**s is an input itemset**
**T is the itemset tree**
**begin**
    *r=root*(T)
    increase *f(r)*
    **if** s = *items (r)* **then exit**
    choose T$_s$=*subtree*(r) such that s and *items(root*(T$_s$)) are comparable
    **if** T$_s$ does not exist **then**
        create a new son x for r, *items(x)* =s and *f(x)* =1
    **else if** *root*(T$_s$) $\subset^e$ s **then** call **Construct (s, T$_s$)**
        **else if** s $\subset^e$ *root*(T$_s$) **then**
            create a new node x, as a son of r and a father of *root*(T$_s$),
            *items(x)* =s and *f(x)* = f(*root*(T$_s$))+1
            **else** create two nodes x and y, x as the father of *root*(T$_s$),s.t.*items(x)* = s $\cap^e$
                *root*(T$_s$), *f(x)* = f(*root*(T$_s$))+1, and y as a son of x, s.t., *items(y)* = s ,
                *f(y)* = 1
**end**

**Figure 1: Algorithm Construct**

**Example 1:** Let $I=\{1,2,3,4\}$ and $F=\{\{1,2,3,4\}, \{1,2\}, \{1,3\}, \{2,3\}\}$ be a transaction file that has 4 transactions. In this example, we assume that all transaction in the transaction file F have occurred only once. The item-set tree T is fully constructed in 4 steps (for the 4 transactions). Various steps of the solution are shown in Figures 2.

Inserting all transaction of the transaction data file F, using algorithm Construct(s,T), requires scanning file F only once. An important characteristic of the Construct(s,T) algorithm, is that, no matter what the sequence of the inserted transactions is, the item-set tree T is always the same.

In sections 4.1 and 4.2, we study the performance of algorithm Construct(S,T).

186

**Step1:** $s=\{1,2,3,4\}$, $s$ is added as a child of $\{\}$ (case 1).

**Step2:** $s=\{1,2\}$, $s$ is added as a child of $\{\}$ and as a father of $\{1,2,3,4\}$ (case 3).

**Step3:** $s=\{1,3\}$, $s_1=\{1\}$ ($s_1=\{1,2\}\cap^e\{1,3\}$) is added as a child of $\{\}$ and as a father of $\{1,2\}$, $s$ is added as a child of $s_1$ (case 5).

**Step4:** $s=\{2,3\}$, $s$ is added as a child of $\{\}$ (case 1).

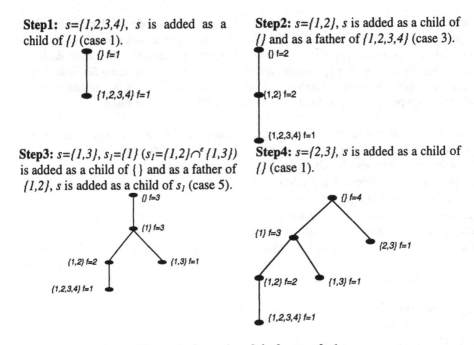

**Figure 2: Steps 1 and 4 of example 1.**

# 3 Frequency Counting

In order to answer ad hoc queries, we introduce algorithm Count. Algorithm Count calculates the frequency of an itemset $s$ by adding up frequencies of those encountered itemsets, that contain $s$. In the example 2, we demonstrate how to count frequencies of itemsets. Algorithm Count is given in Figure 3.

```
Algorithm Count(s,T)
input:    An item set s, and an item-set tree T.
Output: Frequency f of item set s.
begin
          r=root(T)
          if s⊆r then f(s)=f(s)+f(r) ; end
          while r<s and last-item(r)<last-item(s) do
                    traverse subtrees; T ,of r
                    call Count(s,T)
          enddo
end
```

**Figure 3: Algorithm Count**

**Example 2:** Let $T$ be the item-set tree constructed in example 1, and $s=\{2,3\}$ be the itemset to be counted. To count the frequency of itemset $s$, the item-set tree $T$ is traversed in order as shown in the following steps,

• Start from the smallest subtree with root node $\{1\}$. In this case, $s>\{1\}$ & $s\not\subset\{1\}$.

- The subtree of $\{1\}$ is orderly traversed; starting with node $\{1,2\}$. $s > \{1,2\}$ &s $\not\subset \{1,2\}$
- The subtree of $\{1,2\}$ is orderly traversed; starting with node $\{1,2,3,4\}$. $s \subset \{1,2,3,4\}$, $f=1$.
- Go back to next-subtree of $\{1\}$, node $\{1,3\}$. $s \not\subset \{1,3\}$, and the last element in $\{1,2,4\}$ equals the last element in $s$. No further traversing through this subtree.
- Go back to next-subtree of $\{\ \}$, node $\{2,3\}$. $s$ equals $\{2,3\}$. $f=1+1$, and no further traversing through this subtree. The procedure ends with $f(\{2,3\}) = 2$.

# 4 Performance Results

In this section, we study the performance of algorithms Construct and Count. We assume that, items are uniformly distributed over all transactions. In section 4.1, we give the expected number of nodes in the item-set tree T after inserting N transactions. In sections 4.2 and 4.3, the expected number of iterations to insert a transaction, and the expected number of iterations to count the frequency of an itemset, respectively, are given. In section 4.4, we discuss the results of our analytical study.

## 4.1 Number of Nodes in The Item-set tree

**Lemma 1.** *Given an ordered set $I=\{i_1, i_2, \ldots, i_n\}$, of n items, and a set of transaction nodes $V_k \in T$, $1 \le k \le K$, $1 \le K \le 2^n-1$, $V_k = \{a_1, a_2, \ldots, a_l\}$, $a_1 < a_2 < \ldots < a_l$, and items $a_i \in I$, $1 \le i \le l$, $1 \le l \le n$ which are uniformly distributed over itemset domain I, and an itemset $s_j = \{b_1, b_2, \ldots, b_r\}$ with items $b_1 < b_2 < \ldots < b_r$, $b_i \in I$, $1 \le i \le r$, $1 \le r \le n$ which are uniformly distributed over itemset domain I Algorithm* **Construct,** *produces an item-set tree T, with expected number of nodes K such that*

$$K \le N(1 + \tfrac{1}{48}) - \tfrac{N}{16}((n-1)(\tfrac{1}{2})^n + \tfrac{1}{3}(\tfrac{1}{2})^{2n-2})$$

*where N is number of inserted transaction.*

**Proof.** Before proving lemma 1, we first state and prove the following lemma. The following lemma makes the proof easier to describe.

**Lemma 2.** *Given an ordered set $I=\{i_1, i_2, \ldots, i_n\}$, of n items, and a set of transaction nodes $V_k \in T$, $1 \le k \le K$, $1 \le K \le 2^n-1$, $V_k = \{a_1, a_2, \ldots, a_l\}$, $a_1 < a_2 < \ldots < a_l$, and items $a_i \in I$, $1 \le i \le l$, $1 \le l \le n$ are uniformly distributed over itemset domain I. Let $s_j = \{b_1, b_2, \ldots, b_r\}$ be an itemset with items $b_1 < b_2 < \ldots < b_r$, $b_i \in I$, $1 \le i \le r$, $1 \le r \le n$ which are uniformly distributed over items domain I. Given that $s_j$ is not an empty itemset, the probability that there exist a node $V_k \in T$ such that the order intersection of $s_j$ and $V_k$ equals an item set Z, where $Z \ne \Phi$, $Z \ne s_j$, and $Z \ne V_k$, is*

$$P(S_j \cap^e V_k = Z,\ Z \ne V_k, Z \notin T) = (\frac{\frac{1}{3}-(n-1)(\frac{1}{2})^n - \frac{1}{3}(\frac{1}{2})^{2n-2}}{((1-(\frac{1}{2})^n)^2}) * (1 - \frac{K}{2^n-1}) * (\frac{K}{2^n-1})$$

**Proof.** First we state the assumptions:

- A transaction group (node) $V_k$ is in $T$ with probability $P(V_k \in T) = \frac{K}{2^n-1}$, where $K$ is the number of nodes in $T$.

- A transaction $s_j$ and a transaction group $V_k$ are each represented as a set of 1's and 0's, where 0 in position i means item $a_i \in I$ does not exist, and 1 in position i means item $a_i \in I$ does exist.
- Both $V_k$ and $s_j$ are not empty itemsets, i.e., the probability is conditioned, the probability of both $V_k$ and $s_j$ are not empty itemsets, is

$$P(V_k \neq \Phi \ \text{ and } \ S_j \neq \Phi) = P(V_k \neq \Phi) * P(S_j \neq \Phi) = (1 - (\tfrac{1}{2})^n)^2$$

- The item-set tree $T$ has already $K$ nodes, and each node either represents a transactions group or an ordered intersection of two transactions groups.
- All $K$ nodes in $T$ are distinct, i.e., $V_k \neq V_l$ for all nodes $k, l$ in $T$.
- both $V_k$ and $s_j$ are not empty itemsets,

We use the following table to demonstrate all the requirements needed ,

| Shared items | | X | | OR | | |
|---|---|---|---|---|---|---|
| $s_j$ | At least 1 | 1 | 0's or 1's | | 0 | At least 1 |
| $V_k$ | At least 1 | 0 | At least 1 | | 1 | 0's or 1's |

The following formula gives the required probability,

$$\sum_{x=2}^{x=n-1} ((\tfrac{1}{2}*\tfrac{1}{2} + \tfrac{1}{2}*\tfrac{1}{2})^{(x-1)} - (\tfrac{1}{2}*\tfrac{1}{2})^{(x-1)}) * (\tfrac{1}{2}*\tfrac{1}{2} + \tfrac{1}{2}*\tfrac{1}{2}) * (1 - (\tfrac{1}{2})^{(n-x)})$$

which could be written as

$$\tfrac{1}{3} - (n-1)*(\tfrac{1}{2})^n - \tfrac{1}{3}(\tfrac{1}{2})^{2n-2}$$

Since we assume that both $V_k$ and $s_j$ are not empty itemsets, the above formula should be divided by the probability of both $V_k$ and $s_j$ are not empty itemsets. Also, it should multiplied by $P(V_k \in T) = \frac{K}{2^n-1}$ & $P(Z \notin T) = 1 - \frac{K}{2^n-1}$. Now, the complete formula could be written as

$$\left(\frac{\tfrac{1}{3}-(n-1)(\tfrac{1}{2})^n - \tfrac{1}{3}(\tfrac{1}{2})^{2n-2}}{((1-(\tfrac{1}{2})^n)^2}\right) * (1 - \frac{K}{2^n-1}) * (\frac{K}{2^n-1})$$

**Proof of Lemma 1.** We use the same assumptions given in the proof of Lemma 2. For each new encountered transaction group, algorithm **Construct** inserts either 1 node or 2 nodes. So, the cost function should equal to $\sum_{s_j=s_1}^{s_j=s_N}[1+P(s_j \ \text{inserts 2 nodes})]$.

To insert two nodes in T, the following conditions must be satisfied; $\exists$ node $V_k \in T$ such that, $S_j \cap^e V_k = Z$, $Z \neq \Phi$, $Z \neq V_k$, $Z \neq S_j$, $V_k \in T$, and $Z \notin T$.
By using Lemma 2,

$$P(s_j \ \text{inserts 2 nodes}) = P(S_j \cap^e V_k = Z \ \text{ and } \ Z \neq \Phi, Z \neq S_j, Z \neq V_k, Z \notin T)$$

Or

$$Expected \ \ number \ \ of \ \ nodes = \sum_{K=1}^{k=N}[1 + (\frac{\tfrac{1}{3}-(n-1)(\tfrac{1}{2})^n - \tfrac{1}{3}(\tfrac{1}{2})^{2n-2}}{((1-(\tfrac{1}{2})^n)^2}) * (1 - \frac{k}{2^n-1}) * (\frac{k}{2^n-1})]$$

In the above formula, the following inequality, is always true for $n \geq 1$,

$$(1 - (\tfrac{1}{2})^n)^2 \geq \tfrac{1}{4}$$

Also, since values of $k$ could have any number between 1 and $2^n$-1, which means the following inequality always hold

$$(1 - \tfrac{k}{2^n-1}) * (\tfrac{k}{2^n-1}) \leq \tfrac{1}{4}$$

Using the above two inequalities, the upper bound of the expected number of nodes $K$ in an item-set tree with N transactions is

$$K \leq N(1+\tfrac{1}{48}) - \tfrac{N}{16}((n-1)(\tfrac{1}{2})^n + \tfrac{1}{3}(\tfrac{1}{2})^{2n-2})$$

## 4.2 Number of Iterations to Insert a Transaction

**Lemma 3:** *Given an ordered set $I=\{i_1,i_2, \ldots , i_n\}$, of n items, and a set of transaction nodes $V_k \in T$, $1 \leq k \leq K$, $1 \leq K \leq 2^n$-1, $V_k =\{a_1,a_2, \ldots , a_l\}$, $a_1 < a_2 < \ldots < a_l$, and items $a_i \in I$, $1 \leq i \leq l$, $1 \leq l \leq n$ are uniformly distributed over itemset domain I. Let $s_j=\{b_1,b_2, \ldots , b_r\}$ be an itemset with items $b_1 < b_2 < \ldots < b_r$, $b_i \in I$, $1 \leq i \leq r$, $1 \leq r \leq n$ which are uniformly distributed over items domain I. Given that all $V_k \in T$ and $s_j$ are not empty itemsets, the expected number of iterations algorithm Construct takes to enter a transaction into the item-set tree T is less than*

$$1 + n((n - 2) * 2^{n-1} + 1) * \frac{K}{(2^n-1)^3}$$

where $K$ is the number of nodes in $T$.

**Proof.** In order to insert a transaction $s_j$, with length $l$, in exactly one iteration, i.e., first level in the item-set tree $T$, there are two cases. First case, there exits a node $V_k \in T$ in first level of $T$, such that $V_k = S_j$, while the second case, where neither $s_j$ nor all ordered subset nodes of $s_j$ are in $T$. In other words, $V_k \notin T$ for all $V_k \subseteq^e S_j$. Let $P_\Phi = P(V_k \notin T, V_k \subseteq^e S_j)$, and $P_e = P(V_k \in T, S_j = V_k)$. The cost of inserting such transaction is less than

$$1 * (P_e + P_\Phi)$$

Now to insert a transaction $s_j$, with length $l$, in exactly two iterations, i.e., second level in the item-set tree $T$, there are two cases. First case, exactly one order subset of $s_j$ does exist in $T$, and there exits a node $V_k \in T$ in second level of $T$, such that $V_k = S_j$, while the second case, there exists exactly one order subset of $s_j$ and neither $s_j$ nor all other ordered subset nodes of $s_j$ are in $T$. Let $P_s = P(V_k \in T, V_k \subset^e S_j)$. The cost of inserting such transaction is less than

$$2 * (C_1^{l-1}(P_s P_e + P_s P_\Phi))$$

Since the maximum number of iterations is $l$, the expected cost of inserting transaction $s_j$ is $(P_e + P_\Phi) \sum_{i=1}^{l} i * (C_{i-1}^{l-1} P_s^{i-1})$         (1)

By following the same assumptions given in the proof of lemma 2, the

expected value of $P_s$ is $(\dfrac{(n-2)(\frac{1}{2})^{n+1}+(\frac{1}{2})^{2n}}{((1-(\frac{1}{2})^n)^2})*(\dfrac{K}{2^n-1})$

and, the expected value of $(P_\Phi+P_e)$ is $1-P_s$. Formula (1) could be written as

$$(1-P_s)*(P_s*l*(1+P_s)^{l-1}+(1+P_s)^l) \qquad (2)$$

Since $(1+P_s)^l=1+lP_s+l(l-1)P_s^2+....$,

Formula (2) could be written as

$$(1-P_s)*(lP_s+l(l-1)P_s^2+l(l-1)(l-2)P_s^3+...+1+lP_s+l(l-1)P_s^2+l(l-1)(l-2)P_s^3+...$$

By ignoring higher terms, the above formula could be

$$1+(2l-1)P_s$$

Since $l$ could go take any value between $1$ and $n$, then the expected number of

iterations is $\dfrac{1}{n}\sum\limits_{l=1}^{l=n}(1+(2l-1)*(\dfrac{(n-2)(\frac{1}{2})^{n+1}+(\frac{1}{2})^{2n}}{(1-(\frac{1}{2})^n)^2})*(\dfrac{K}{2^n-1}))$

Which could be written as $1+n((n-2)*2^{n-1}+1)*\dfrac{K}{(2^n-1)^3}$

### 4.3 Number of iterations to Count The Frequency of an Itemset

**Lemma 4.** *Given an ordered set $I=\{i_1,i_2,\ldots,i_n\}$, of $n$ items, and a set of transaction nodes $V_k \in T$, $1\le k \le K$, $1\le K \le 2^n-1$, $V_k=\{a_1,a_2,\ldots,a_l\}$, $a_1<a_2<\ldots<a_l$, and items $a_i\in I$, $1\le i \le l$, $1\le l \le n$ are uniformly distributed over itemset domain I. Let $s_j=\{b_1,b_2,\ldots,b_r\}$ be an itemset with items $b_1<b_2<\ldots<b_r$, $b_i\in I$, $1\le i \le r$, $1\le r \le n$ which are uniformly distributed over items domain I. Given that all $V_k\in T$ and $s_j$ are not empty itemsets, the expected number of iterations algorithm Count takes to count an itemset frequency in the item-set tree T, with K nodes is*

$$\dfrac{n-1}{2}+\left(\dfrac{1}{n}\right)*\left(\dfrac{\frac{4}{3}-(n+\frac{7}{3})(\frac{1}{2})^{n+1}-(\frac{1}{2})^{2n-2}-\frac{n(n-1)}{2}(\frac{1}{2})^{2n-1}}{(1-(\frac{1}{2})^n)^2}\right)*\left(\dfrac{K}{2^n-1}\right)$$

**Proof.** In order to count the frequency of an itemset $s_j$ with length $l$, where $O_1$ and $O_l$ are orders of first element and last elements in $s_j$, $i_1$, $i_l \in s_j$, respectively, all itemsets $S_j^P$ with first element has order $O_1$, and last element has order $O_k$, which could have $s_j$ as part of them should be checked. The number of such checks (or iterations) is $2^{O_l-O_1}$. The count stops when we reach the full set of $s_j$, we will call it $S_j^f$.

So, to count the frequency of itemset $s_j$ in exactly one iteration, there should be a node $V_k\in T$ such that $S_j^f \subseteq^e V_k$, or, with unsuccessful count, when the first visited node $V_k\in T$ such that $S_j^f \not\subseteq^e V_k$ and $V_k \not\subseteq^e S_j^P$. Let $\bar{P}_e=P(V_k \in T, V_k \subseteq^e S_j^f)$ and $\bar{P}_\Phi=P(V_k \notin T, V_k \subset^e S_j^P)$. The cost of counting such transaction is $1*(\bar{P}_e+\bar{P}_\Phi)$

Generally speaking, to count the frequency of an itemset $s_j$ with length $l$, where $O_l$ and $O_l$ are orders of first element and last elements in $s_{j,}$ $i_1,$ $i_l \in s_{j,}$, respectively in exactly $i$ iteration, The cost of counting is

$$i * (C_{i-1}^{2^{O_l-O_1}} \tilde{P}_e \tilde{P}_s^{i-1} + C_{i-1}^{2^{O_l-O_1}} \tilde{P}_s^{i-1} \tilde{P}_\Phi)$$

Since the maximum number of iterations is $2^{O_l-O_1}$, the expected cost of counting frequency of itemset $s_j$ is

$$(\tilde{P}_e + \tilde{P}_\Phi) \sum_{i=1}^{2^{O_l-O_1}} i * (C_{i-1}^{2^{O_l-O_1}} \tilde{P}_s^{i-1}) \tag{1}$$

The expected value of $\tilde{P}_s$ is

$$\left(\frac{(n-2)(\frac{1}{2})^{n+1} + (\frac{1}{2})^{2n}}{((1-(\frac{1}{2})^n)^2}\right) * \left(\frac{K}{2^n-1}\right)$$

since, $\tilde{P}_\Phi + \tilde{P}_e = 1 - \tilde{P}_s$, formula (1) could be written as follows

$$(1 - \tilde{P}_s) \sum_{i=1}^{2^{O_l-O_1}} i * (C_{i-1}^{2^{O_l-O_1}} \tilde{P}_s^{i-1})$$

which equals

$$(1 - \tilde{P}_s) * (\tilde{P}_s(2^{O_l-O_1})(1+\tilde{P}_s)^{2^{q-q_1}-1} + (1+\tilde{P}_s)^{2^{q-q_1}}) \tag{2}$$

Since, $(1+P)^x = 1 + xP + x(x-1)P^2 + .....$

$\tilde{P}_s(2^{q-q_1})(1+\tilde{P}_s)^{2^{q-q_1}-1} + (1+\tilde{P}_s)^{2^{q-q_1}}$ could be written as

$$1 + (\frac{(\frac{1}{2})^{2n-O_l+O_1-1}}{(1-(\frac{1}{2})^n)^2}) * (\frac{K}{2^n-1}) + (\frac{(\frac{1}{2})^{4n-2O_l+2O_1-1}}{(1-(\frac{1}{2})^n)^2}) * (\frac{K}{2^n-1})^2 - (\frac{(\frac{1}{2})^{4n-O_l+O_1-1}}{(1-(\frac{1}{2})^n)^2}) * (\frac{K}{2^n-1})^2 + ....$$

Algorithm Count, applies the search for all other itemsets, start with lower order items, i.e., items with order less than $O_l$, one at a time. Number of such itemsets, including $s_j$, is $O_l$. By neglecting higher terms, and sum over all possible itemsets, our formula could be written as

$$O_1 + O_1 \left(\frac{(\frac{1}{2})^{2n-O_l+O_1-1}}{(1-(\frac{1}{2})^n)^2}\right) * \left(\frac{K}{2^n-1}\right)$$

Taking an average over $O_l$, which ranges from $O_1$ to $n$, the above formula is converted to

$$O_1 + \left(\frac{O_1}{n-O_1+1}\right) * \left(\frac{(\frac{1}{2})^{n+O_1-2} - (\frac{1}{2})^{2n-1}}{(1-(\frac{1}{2})^n)^2}\right) * \left(\frac{K}{2^n-1}\right)$$

For simplification reason, since the minimum number of $O_1$ is 1, we will divide the second term by 1. Average value over $O_1$, which ranges from $l$ to $n$, the above formula, will be

$$\frac{n-1}{2} + \left(\frac{1}{n}\right) * \left(\frac{\frac{4}{3} - (n+\frac{7}{3})(\frac{1}{2})^{n+1} - (\frac{1}{2})^{2n-2} - \frac{n(n-1)}{2}(\frac{1}{2})^{2n-1}}{(1-(\frac{1}{2})^n)^2}\right) * \left(\frac{K}{2^n-1}\right)$$

## 4.4 Conclusions and Discussion

In this paper, we have introduced a new approach for association mining, called the item-set tree approach. The new approach solves some of the problems inherent in traditional data mining techniques, such as, data updates, accuracy of data mining results, performance, and user queries. The spectrum of techniques that generate association rules, has been studied, and two extreme cases have been analyzed. The main assumption in our study is that all items are equally likely to appear in an itemset. Although this assumption does not reflect the real life, but it gives a good indication about the performance of the item-set tree approach.

We have discussed the item-set tree approach in details. In our approach, the transaction file is read only once. The item-set tree approach maintains a structure to handle frequency counting of transaction data, that allows future updates. Two algorithms; first, to insert transactions into the item-set tree, and second, to count frequencies of itemsets are investigated. Our investigations of the two algorithms show that the costs of insertion and counting do not depend on the number of transactions. The expected cost of inserting a transaction is $\approx O(1)$, and the expected cost of counting the frequency of an itemset is $O(n)$, where n is the cardinality of the domain of items. We conclude that those items that are queried most by users should have low order values, while those items which rarely queried by users should have high order values. This can be accomplished by using prior knowledge of the pattern of user queries.

## References

[1] R. Agrawal, T. Imilienski, and A. Swami, "Mining Association Rules between Sets of Items in Large Databases," Proc. of the ACM SIGMOD Int'l Conf. On Management of data, May 1993.

[2] R. Agrawal, and R. Srikant, "Fast Algorithms for Mining Association Rules," Proc. Of the 20$^{th}$ VLDB Conference, Santiago, Chile, 1994.

[3] R. Agrawal, J. Shafer, "Parallel Mining of Association Rules," IEEE Transactions on Knowledge and Data Engineering, Vol. 8, No. 6, Dec. 1996.

[4] C. Agrawal, and P. Yu, "Mining Large Itemsets for Association Rules," Bulletin of the IEEE Computer Society Technical Committee on Data Engineering, 1997.

[5] S. Brin, R. Motwani, J. Ullman, and S. Tsur, "Dynamic Itemset Counting and Implication Rules for Market Basket Data," SIGMOD Record (SCM Special Interset Group on Management of Data), 26,2, 1997.

[6] S. Chaudhuri, "Data Mining and Database Systems: Where is the Intersection," Bulletin of the IEEE Computer Society Technical Committee on Data Engineering, 1997.

[7] H. Mannila, H. Toivonen, and A. Verkamo, "Efficient Algorithms for Discovering Association Rules," AAAI Workshop on Knowledge Discovery in databases (KDD-94), July 1994.

[8] M. Zaki, S. Parthasarathy, M. Ogihara, and W. Li, " New Algorithms for Fast Discovery of Association Rules," Proc. Of the 3$^{rd}$ Int'l Conf. On Knowledge Discovery and data Mining (KDD-97), AAAI Press, 1997.

# A New Approach for the Discovery of Frequent Itemsets

Rosa Meo

Politecnico di Torino
Dip. Automatica e Informatica, c.so Duca degli Abruzzi 24 - 10129 Torino, Italy
rosimeo@polito.it

**Abstract.** The discovery of the most recurrent association rules, in a large database of sales transactions requires that the sets of items bought together by a sufficiently large population of customers are identified. This is a critical task, since the number of generated itemsets grows exponentially with the total number of items. Most of the algorithms start identifying the sets with the lowest cardinality, and subsequently, increase it progressively. Our approach is different, since the sets to be considered at a time are determined by the items in the sets. The main advantage is a significant reduction of the CPU time required to update data structures in main memory. This paper presents an algorithm that requires only one pass on the database, presents linear scale-up property with the dimensions of the database and, as shown by the experiments, performs better than other classical algorithms.

## 1 Introduction

Association rules are a powerful and intuitive conceptual tool to represent the phenomena that are recurrent in data. The discovery of association rules has several applications in the analysis of business data, such as the basket data of supermarkets, failures in telecommunications networks, medical test results, health insurance, and many others.

In a database of transactions, an association rule $\mathcal{X} \Rightarrow \mathcal{Y}$ associates two sets of data (also called sets of items) which are found together in a transaction. Its utility is to show which kind of items are frequently correlated in customers' purchases. The statistical frequency of an association rule (or more generally of a set of items) is called *support* and is the percentage of transactions of the database in which all the items in the association rule are present.

The number of association rules that may be extracted from a very large database is exponentially large with the number of the items. The feasibility of the problem requires a threshold for the support is provided by the analyst in order to discover only the most frequent association rules. Nevertheless, even if the problem is stated like this, it still may be critical. The most important step of the algorithms that extract association rules is to identify all the sets of items $S$ whose support is higher than the threshold (called *large* itemsets). The computation of the effective support of a set of items requires that in reading the database a counter is allocated in main memory to keep track of the number of transactions that contain the set. If the number of the examined sets is not kept low enough while the reading of the database is performed, the total number of counters may be too large to fit in main memory, or too much effort is wasted to keep the support of sets that eventually reveal to be lower then the threshold.

The algorithms that have already been proposed [1, 2, 3, 4, 5, 6] solve this problem iteratively. They keep only a subset of the collection of sets in main memory at a time. In particular, in each iteration, the cardinality of the sets whose support is being computed is fixed. After the support of each of them is known, the *pruning* phase is executed, to get rid of those sets whose support is lower than the threshold. In the next iteration the support of the sets with increased cardinality is determined. These sets (called the *candidate* sets) are identified from the large itemsets found in the previous iteration. These algorithms execute the pruning phase once for each iteration, and perform as many iterations as the cardinality of the longest itemsets with sufficient support. Notice, also, that some of these algorithms [1, 3, 4, 6] perform a reading pass on the database for each iteration. This reading pass determines the number of I/O operations performed in each iteration which are the most expensive from the viewpoint of the execution time.

In this paper we propose a new approach for the identification of all the large itemsets. This approach is based on the observation that the collection of the sets that is maintained in the main memory in each iteration can be arbitrarily chosen. The itemsets are ordered lexicographically. The first iteration keeps the itemsets that start with the last item in the lexicographical order, while the subsequent iterations keep the itemsets that start with the other items, in the decreasing order. The purpose is to improve the efficiency in the generation of the candidate itemsets and in the reduction of the number of accesses to main memory required to update their support.

A new algorithm based on this approach is proposed. The algorithm is called Seq for the fact that in the first step, instead of building itemsets, builds sequences of items. Seq reduces I/O execution times because it makes a single reading pass on the database. Moreover, we will show with our experiments that Seq is specifically oriented to databases of very large dimensions and searches of very high resolution, where the minimum support is defined at very low levels. Seq reduces also CPU execution times because it requires only two accesses to main memory in the generation of a candidate itemset and when updating its support counter, regardless of the itemset length; moreover it executes the pruning phase once for each item, instead of once for each value of itemset cardinality (thousands times more in real databases!).

The paper is organized as follows. Section 2 introduces some preliminary definitions and presents the algorithm. Section 3 provides an evaluation of its properties. Finally, Section 4 shows the results of some experiments, while Section 5 will draw the conclusions.

# 2 Algorithm Seq

## 2.1 Preliminary definitions

1. The database is organized in transactions. Each transaction is represented with the items lexicographically ordered. We indicate with T[i] the item of transaction T in the position i (i starts from 0).
2. We call the set of all the possible items in the database the *Alphabet*. We consider it lexicographically ordered and indicate with $<$ the ordering operator and with $>$ the operator of opposite ordering.
3. Given a transaction T of length L, the sequence of all items extracted from T starting at position j is denoted as $\text{Seq}_T^j$ ($0 \leq j <$ L) and defined as follows:
$\text{Seq}_T^j = \langle T[j]\ T[j+1]\ T[j+2]\cdots T[L-1] \rangle$
T[j], the starting item in the sequence $\text{Seq}_T^j$, is called the *leader* of the sequence, whereas T[L-1], the last one, is called the *terminal* item.
The number of sequences in a transaction T is equal to the length of T. For example, the transaction T=$\langle ABCD \rangle$ has four sequences:
$\text{Seq}_T^0 = \langle ABCD \rangle$, $\text{Seq}_T^1 = \langle BCD \rangle$, $\text{Seq}_T^2 = \langle CD \rangle$ and $\text{Seq}_T^3 = \langle D \rangle$.
4. An ordered set, and thus also a sequence $S = \text{Seq}_T^j$, is stored in the main memory in a tree. The first item in the sequence ($\text{Leader}\{S\} = T[j]$) is saved on the root node of the tree; the second one (T[j+1]) on a son node of the first one, and so on. For example, the sequence $\langle ABCD \rangle$ would be saved on a tree with A on the root node, B on a son node of A and so on. A given tree is used to store all the sequences, having the same starting item. Figure 1 shows the tree with the two sequences $\langle ABCD \rangle$ and $\langle ABD \rangle$. The tree in the above example, is denoted as $\mathcal{T}_A^<$ since A is the item in the root node and $<$ is the operator of ordering of the items. Viceversa, we denote with $\mathcal{T}^>$ a

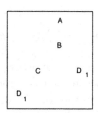

**Fig. 1.** $\mathcal{T}_A^<$ tree with the two sequences $\langle ABCD \rangle$ and $\langle ABD \rangle$.

tree in which $>$ is used as operator of ordering to store the items in the tree.
5. A counter is associated to the terminal node of each sequence. It keeps the number of transactions in which the sequence (composed of the items stored from the root node to the terminal node) occurs in. Observe also that the counter of a sequence not necessarily is stored in a leaf node of the tree: this is the case of the sequence $\langle ABC \rangle$, substring of the sequence $\langle ABCD \rangle$.

## 2.2 Description of the Algorithm Seq

Algorithm Seq works in two steps.

**First Step.** The database is read. For each transaction it finds all the sequences and stores them in the main memory in $\mathcal{T}^<$ trees. For example, the transaction $T_1 = \langle ABCD \rangle$ generates four sequences $\langle ABCD \rangle$, $\langle BCD \rangle$, $\langle CD \rangle$ and $\langle D \rangle$ that are stored in the four trees $\mathcal{T}_A^<$, $\mathcal{T}_B^<$, $\mathcal{T}_C^<$ and $\mathcal{T}_D^<$. If a sequence is found for the first time, the counter associated to the terminal node is set to 1; otherwise, it is incremented by 1. Figure 2 shows the trees $\mathcal{T}^<$ for a very simple database.

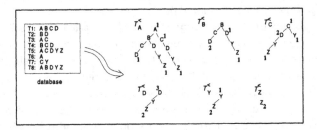

**Fig. 2.** The trees after the first step is completed.

At the end of the first step only the support of the sequences is known. However, the support of the itemsets can be determined from the support of the sequences as stated by the following theorem whose proof will be omitted.

*Theorem.* The support of an itemset $\mathcal{I}$, with item X as its first item, can be obtained as the sum of the counters of all the sequences of $\mathcal{T}_X^<$ containing $\mathcal{I}$. □

**Second Step.** It has the purpose to determine the support of the itemsets from the support of the sequences according to the previous theorem. The trees generated in the first step ($\mathcal{T}^<$) are used in order to produce a second set of trees ($\mathcal{T}^>$) in which the itemsets with the relative support counters are represented. Each tree $\mathcal{T}^<$ is read, starting from the tree $\mathcal{T}^<$ of the last item in the Alphabet and proceeding with the trees $\mathcal{T}^<$ of the other items in the decreasing order. The sequences of each tree $\mathcal{T}^<$ are taken with their counters, and from each of them *the subsets containing the Leader of the sequences* are determined and stored in a $\mathcal{T}^>$ tree (the other subsets, not containing the Leader, are determined while reading the other trees). These subsets are the itemsets. The counter associated to the terminal node of the itemset is incremented by the value of the counter of the sequence originating it. In this way, at the end of the reading of a generic tree $\mathcal{T}^<$, the counters of the itemsets originated from the sequences of that tree contain the correct value necessary to determine their support. If the support of an itemset is not sufficient, the itemset is deleted from its $\mathcal{T}^>$ tree.

*Sequence Subset Determination* In order to understand the technique used to produce the itemsets from the sequences, consider the reading of the tree $\mathcal{T}_D^<$ of Figure 2, and in particular the sequence $\langle DYZ \rangle$ (see Figure 3).

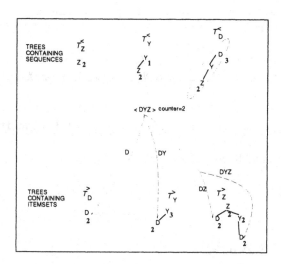

**Fig. 3.** The creation of the itemsets from the sequence $\langle DYZ \rangle$.

At this time, the trees $\mathcal{T}_Y^<$ and $\mathcal{T}_Z^<$ have been already read; in main memory there are the itemsets originated from the sequences that start with Y and Z. The generation of the itemsets of the sequence $\langle DYZ \rangle$ consists in the addition of the item D, Leader of the sequence, to all the subsets of the remaining portion of the sequence ($\langle YZ \rangle$). These latter subsets are the empty set and {Z},{Y}, {YZ}. The empty set corresponds to the determination of the itemset {D}: the root node of $\mathcal{T}_D^>$ is created only if the reading of the database in the first step has proved that item D has a sufficient support. As regards the other subsets, if their support is not sufficient, they are not found in $\mathcal{T}_Z^>$ and $\mathcal{T}_Y^>$ trees respectively, and no work is wasted considering their supersets. In the positive case, a leaf node containing the Leader D is added to the subset in the appropriate tree $\mathcal{T}^>$. The algorithm that creates the sequence subsets is reported.

```
procedure create_subsets (sequence S, counter c, list prune_list)
        X=Leader{S};
        list current_sets, previous_sets;
        for all items I ∈ S from last one to first one (I≠ X) do
            if exists T_I^> then
                leaf = add_leaf(T_I^>.root_node, X, c, prune_list);
                add T_I^>.root_node to current_sets;
            end if
            for all nodes P in previous_sets do
```

```
                    if exists a child node N of P with item I then
                        leaf = add_leaf(N, X, c, prune_list);
                        add N to current_sets;
                    end if
                end for
                swap current_sets into previous_sets;
            end for
end procedure
procedure add_leaf (node F, item X, counter c, list prune_list)
            if exists a child node N of F with item X then
                N.count = N.count + c;
            else
                allocate a new node N child of F with item X;
                N.count = c;
                add N to prune_list;
            end if
end procedure
```

## 2.3 Sequences Advantages

Seq receives several benefits with the representation in terms of sequences:

1. During the reading of the database, when not enough information is known to eliminate many itemsets, only the sequences are maintained in the main memory: the support of the sequences is a sort of "summary" of the support of the itemsets and enables the saving of many counters in main memory.

2. Seq saves CPU execution time because this latter one is not determined only by the total number of candidate itemsets kept in main memory but also by the number of accesses in main memory that each of them requires. Seq needs two accesses in main memory when it generates a new itemset and when it updates its support (see the code in Section 2.2), independently of the itemset length. On the contrary, for the generation of an itemset of length k, Apriori requires k accesses. Then, Apriori checks for the presence of k subsets of length (k-1) that requires k(k-1) accesses. Finally, when it updates the support of an itemset of length k it performs k accesses.

3. Seq executes the pruning phase very frequently (once for each item with sufficient support). Instead, traditionally, the pruning phase is run once for each level of itemset cardinality, that is about three orders of magnitude less.

## 2.4 Implementation of Seq

When very large databases are used, the number of sequences represented in the trees $\mathcal{T}^<$ might be too large to fit in the main memory. We had to change the algorithm to allow the buffer management. The algorithm swaps the content of the trees to disk in the first step and read it in the second one. Each tree is swapped to a separate file: $\mathcal{T}_A^<$ is swapped to file $\mathcal{F}_A$, $\mathcal{T}_B^<$ to $\mathcal{F}_B$, and so on. The sequences are written to disk in a compressed form. For example: once that the first sequence of $\mathcal{T}_A^<$, $\langle ABCD \rangle$ is written, the second one, $\langle ABDYZ \rangle$ can be represented substituting the prefix items common to the two consecutive sequences ($\langle AB \rangle$) with the prefix length (2). Especially if the transactions have many common sequences this technique saves a great amount of information.

# 3  Evaluation of Algorithm Seq

Three basic parameters characterize a given data mining problem: the total number N of the transactions, the average length L of the transactions and the number I of different items. Let us analyze their influence on the computational work of the presented algorithm and the access times to mass storage.

**Computational work** Computational work involved in step 1, i.e. in the construction of the trees containing sequences, is relatively small and is proportional to the product $L * N$, that is to the size of database. The evaluation of the computational work in step 2, that is in the generation of the trees of the subsets of items, grows exponentially with L and linearly N. However, L is limited and is characteristic of a specific application. Besides, computational time needed to construct the trees of the itemsets is relatively small with respect to the times necessary to read the database and to store and retrieve the trees from disk.

The execution time of Seq is nearly independent of the value of the minimum support. This point is rather important. Indeed, the concept of minimum support has been introduced to reduce the computational time, but it reduces the statistical significance of the search. Above all, if a certain value of the minimum support is reasonable for the itemsets of length equal to 1, it might be enormous for itemsets of length 2 or more. So, the new algorithm might be adopted in searches characterized by very small values of resolution.

**Access time to mass storage** Let $T_R$ be the time spent to read the database, that is the lower bound of any algorithm. However, $T_R$ must be increased by the time $T_F$ spent to save and retrieve $\mathcal{T}^<$ trees. Thus the upper bound of the total volume of data transferred with the mass storage amounts to the size of the database plus two times the sizes of the files of sequences. For very long databases this upper bound is slightly larger than the database size.

Two contrasting factors influence $T_F$ with respect to $T_R$. Indeed, the volume of data in the $\mathcal{T}^<$ trees would be larger than the whole database (because to any transaction correspond more sequences) for those databases in which transactions have very few common items. This is the case of synthetic databases of the experiments of Section 4. On the other side, repeated transactions require the same information amount of a single transaction: therefore $T_F < T_R$ in case transactions are frequently repeated or have many common items. $T_F$ can be considerably reduced if information represented by the trees of sequences is compressed. In our implementation we have adopted a very simple technique of compression but it would be possible to reduce $T_F$ with more sophisticated compression techniques even in the case of no repeated transactions.

# 4 Experiments

We have run our implementation of algorithm Seq using a PC Pentium II, with a 233 Mhz clock, 128 MB RAM and Debian Linux as operating system. We have worked on the same class of synthetic databases [1] that has been taken as benchmark by most of previous algorithms. Broadly, each transaction of these databases has been generated by addition of some items, extracted in a casually fashion, to a large itemset. For this "semi-casual" content, we believe that this database is not very suitable for an efficient execution of Seq: in most of the cases the total dimension of the files containing sequences gets comparable with the database dimension and execution time spent in I/O is not mainly determined by the database reading pass. The results of the experiments are shown in Figure 4.

In the left column of Figure 4 we compare the execution times of Seq with Apriori, one of the best algorithms. The three experiments analyzed refer to the three classes of databases characterized by increasing transaction length (5, 10, 15). For each database class, we show the execution times for different databases in which the average length of the large itemsets gets the values 2, 4, 6, 8, 12. Seq works better than Apriori in all the experiments, but the best gains occur when the average itemsets length is comparable with the transaction length. Observe also how Seq execution time is almost constant with respect to the average itemsets length, whereas Apriori increases the execution times because of the increasing number of reading passes on the database. Notice that, as the value of the minimum support decreases, Seq gets much better. This behavior is due to the fact that a certain number of itemsets with higher cardinality values result with sufficient support. In these conditions, Apriori must increase the number of reading passes on the database whereas the number of I/O operations performed by Seq remains almost constant. Furthermore, even when the number of I/O operations performed by Seq is comparable with Apriori, the execution times of Seq are still lower. Therefore, we have compared the number of candidate itemsets in main memory in order to ascertain whether this one was a favorable factor to Seq that could determine a lower CPU processing time. We have noticed that there is not a significant difference between the two algorithms. So, we have concluded that the computational work performed by Seq is lower than Apriori because of the lower number of accesses to main memory required in the generation and update of candidate itemsets, as already stated in Section 2.3.

The experiments on the scale-up properties with respect to the dimension of the database are shown in the first experiment of the second column. In this experiment the minimum support is fixed to 0.5, but analogous results are given with lower values. We adopted databases with 100, 200, 300 and 400 thousands of transactions. The linear behavior is still verified by both Seq and Apriori but with very different slopes! These different increases are due again to the number of I/O operations. Seq reads once the database, writes once the files with the sequences and then reads a certain number of them. However, the size of the files increase of a little fraction of the database size as this latter one increases. On the contrary, the number of I/O operations performed by Apriori are still determined by the repeated reading passes on the database.

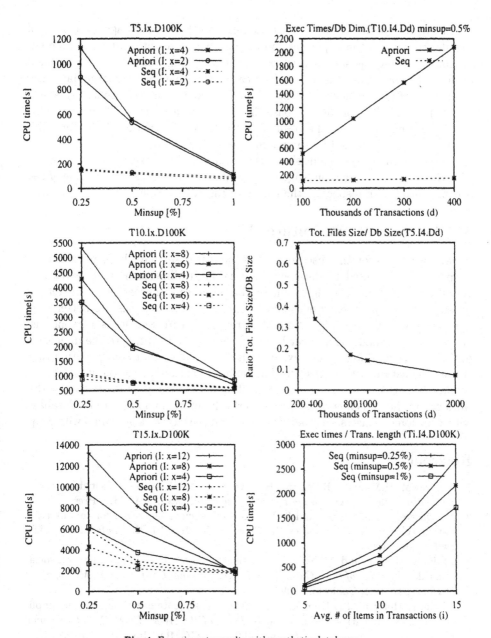

**Fig. 4.** Experiments results with synthetic databases.

The next experiment shows the ratio between the total storage occupation of the files containing the sequences and the database size with respect to different databases having the same statistics but different dimensions. This experiment confirms our previous evaluations. You can notice that for very large databases (2 millions of transactions) the size of the files containing the sequences is only a little fraction (7%) of the database size. In these cases, the I/O operations on the files do not influence the total time spent in performing I/O because this one is mainly determined by the reading pass of the database.

The remaining experiment shows the variation of the execution times of Seq with the average transaction length that confirms that the execution time of Seq is exponential with respect to the length of the transaction.

## 5 Conclusions and Future Work

A new technique for the discovery of frequent itemset have been presented. It is specifically oriented to databases of very large dimensions and searches of very high resolution. The algorithm Seq based on this approach is characterized by an increased processing efficiency, since its execution times are better than Apriori, one of the best algorithms of current literature. Seq needs only one pass on the database and has a linear behavior, almost constant, with the dimension of the database. Moreover our experiments have shown that Seq execution time is nearly constant with respect to the maximum cardinality of the itemsets.

Max-Miner [7] and Pincer-Search [6], new algorithms presented while this work was in the implementation phase, perform better than Apriori on databases with very long itemsets. Further work will compare these algorithms with Seq.

## References

1. R.Agrawal, H.Mannila, R.Srikant, H.Toivonen and A.I.Verkamo. Fast discovery of association rules. In *Knowledge Discovery in Databases*, AAAI/MIT Press, 1995.
2. A.Savasere, E.Omiecinski, and S.Navathe. An efficient algorithm for mining association rules in large databases. In *Proc. of the 21st VLDB Conference*, Zurich, Switzerland, 1995.
3. J.S.Park, M.Shen, and P.S.Yu. An effective hash based algorithm for mining association rules. In *Proc. of the ACM SIGMOD International Conference on Management of Data*, San Jose, California, 1995.
4. S.Brin, R.Motwani, J.D.Ullman, and S.Tsur. Dynamic itemsets counting and implication rules for market basket data. In *Proc. of the ACM SIGMOD International Conference on Management of Data*, vol.26,2 of SIGMOD Record, p.255-264, New York, 1997.
5. H.Toivonen. Sampling large databases for association rules. In *Proc. of the 22nd VLDB Conference*, Bombay, India, 1996.
6. D.I.Lim and Z.M.Kedem. Pincer-search: A new algorithm for discovering the maximum frequent set. In *Proc. of the EDBT'98 Conference*, Valencia, Spain, 1998.
7. R.J.Bayardo. Efficiently mining long patterns from databases. In *Proc. of the SIGMOD'98 Conference*, Seattle, WA, USA, 1998.

# K-means Clustering Algorithm for Categorical Attributes

S K Gupta[1] and K. Sambasiva Rao[2] and Vasudha Bhatnagar[3]

[1] Deptt. of Computer Science and Engineering, Indian Institute of Technology, Hauz Khas, New Delhi 110 016. INDIA. email: skg@cse.iitd.ernet.in
[2] Deptt. of Computer Science and Engineering, Indian Institute of Technology, Hauz Khas, New Delhi 110 016. INDIA .
[3] Deptt. of Computer Science., MotiLal Nehru College, Delhi University, Delhi, INDIA.

**Abstract.** Efficient partitioning of large data sets into homogeneous clusters is a fundamental problem in data mining. The hierarchical clustering methods are not adaptable because of their high computational complexity. The K-means based algorithms give promising results for their efficiency. However their use is often limited to numeric data. The quality of clusters produced depends on the initialization of clusters and the order in which data elements are processed in the iteration. We present a method which is based on the K-means philosophy but removes the numeric data limitation.

## 1 Introduction

Given a population of individuals described by a set of attribute values, clustering them into similar groups has many applications. The clustering problem is partitioning a population into clusters(see [1]). The population is a set of $n$ elements described by $m$ attributes. The goal is to construct a partition in which elements of a cluster are similar and elements of different clusters are dissimilar. It is generally not possible to define what it means to be similar. Also, comparing one clustering result with another is very difficult and judgement is generally subjective and application dependent. There are several ways of defining a measure of adequacy for a given partition, so that the defining measure can at least serve as an objective function to be optimized over all possible partitions. Many clustering algorithms are based on finding the partition that optimize such an objective function([2]).

Two such partitioning criteria are *Intraclass inertia criteria* [2] useful for numeric attributes and *New Condorcet criteria (NCC)* [2] useful for categorical attributes.

Clustering algorithms generally try to find a partition that optimizes the chosen partitioning criterion. Since the number of possible partitions is large, certain heuristics are used to find a nearly optimal solution. Clustering algorithms basically are of two types. Hierarchical clustering methods and K-means clustering methods. We consider the K-means approach in this paper.

These algorithms search for a nearly optimal partition with a fixed number of clusters. First an initial partition with a chosen number of clusters is built. Then, keeping the same number of clusters, the partition is improved iteratively. Each element is taken sequentially and reassigned to the cluster such that the partitioning criterion is most improved by the reassignment. Different solutions are obtained depending on which partitioning criterion is used. The most widely used criterion is the *Intraclass inertia* criteria.

The K-means [3] based algorithms give promising results. However their use is limited to numeric data only. Also there are some other problems associated with this algorithm and one can not guarantee efficient clustering if these problems are not solved. In the following sections, we describe these problems and their effect on convergence of algorithm and quality of output. The major handicap of the K-means based algorithms is that they are limited to numeric data. The reason is that these algorithms optimize an objective function defined on the euclidean distance measure between data points and means of clusters. Minimizing the objective function by calculating means limits their use to numeric data. Also the algorithm is dependent on the order in which data elements are processed in. A change in the order of input affects convergence of the algorithm and quality of the output.

Section 2 gives the proposed solution. Section 3 gives the performance study of the algorithm on different parameters based on synthetic data sets. In section 4 we summarize our work.

## 2 Proposed solution

In this section we present a clustering method to overcome the limitation of the K-means algorithm for numeric data only. We also present a new initialization method and input order which helps in faster convergence of the algorithm.

### 2.1 Extension to categorical data

Let $D = \{D_1, \ldots, D_n\}$ denote a set of n objects and $D_i = \{d_{i1}, \ldots, d_{im}\}$ be a data element represented by $m$ attribute values. Let $p$ be the number of clusters. The objective function that has to be minimized for K-means procedure is

$$F(p) = \sum_{k=1}^{p} \sum_{i=1}^{n_k} d(D_i, C_k) \tag{1}$$

where $D_i$ is data element $i$ and $C_k$ is centroid of cluster $k$. The term $d(D_i, C_k)$ is the total cost of assigning D to cluster k, i.e. the total dispersion of objects in cluster $k$ from its centroid $C_k$. In case of numeric attributes, this term is minimized if $c_{kj} = \frac{1}{n_k} \sum_{i=1}^{n_k} d_{ij}$ $j = 1, \ldots, m$ is minimized. Here $n_k$ is the number of elements in cluster $k$.

For categorical attributes, the similarity measure is defined as

$$d(D_i, C_k) = \sum_{j=1}^{N} (d_{ij}^{\Gamma} - C_{kj}^{\Gamma})^2 + wt \times \sum_{j=1}^{C} \delta(d_{ij}^c, c_{kj}^c) \qquad (2)$$

where $\delta(a, b) = 0$ for $a = b$ and $\delta(a, b) = 1$ for $a \neq b$. $d_{ij}^{\Gamma}$ and $C_{kj}^{\Gamma}$ are values of numeric attributes, and $d_{ij}^c$ and $c_{kj}^c$ are values of categorical attributes for the object $i$ and cluster $k$. $N$ and $C$ are the number of numeric attributes and categorical attributes respectively. $wt$ is the measure used to hold the categorical data from monopolizing the similarity measure and hence the clustering process. We can rewrite $F(p)$ as

$$F(p) = \sum_{k=1}^{p} \sum_{i=1}^{n_k} \left( \sum_{j=1}^{N} d_{ij}^{\Gamma} - c_{kj}^{\Gamma})^2 + wt \times \sum_{j=1}^{C} \delta(d_{ij}^c, c_{kj}^c) \right) = \sum_{k=1}^{p} (W_{nk} + W_{ck}) (3)$$

Let $C_j$ be the set containing all unique values in the categorical attribute $j$ and $p(c_j \epsilon C_j | k)$ the probability of value $c_j$ occurring in cluster $k$.

$$W_{ck} = wt \times \sum_{j=1}^{C} n_k (1 - p(c_{kj}^c \epsilon C_j | k)) \qquad (4)$$

where $n_k$ is number of objects in cluster $k$. $W_{ck}$ can be minimized if and only if $p(c_{kj}^c \epsilon C_j | k) \geq p(c_j \epsilon C_j | k)$ is minimized, for $c_{kj}^c \neq c_j$ for all categorical attributes.

The cost due to numeric attributes is minimized by calculating the numeric elements in centroid, while cost due to categorical attributes is minimized by selecting the categorical elements of centroid.

**Estimation of weight factor** The influence of $wt$ in clustering is significant. When $wt$ is zero, clustering depends only on numeric attributes. If $wt$ is greater than zero, an object may change cluster because it is closer to that cluster and its categorical attribute value is same as that of majority of objects in that cluster. This $wt$ depends on many factors like number of numeric and categorical attributes, number of possible values each categorical attribute can take and most importantly the distribution of numeric attributes. We propose a method which does not take the number of attributes into account. First we take a sample data from the original data. Apply the algorithm with various wt. For each $wt$, calculate the quality of clusters with respect to numeric attributes ($Q_N$) and categorical attributes ($Q_C$). Divide $Q_N$ and $Q_C$ with number of numeric and categorical attributes respectively. Then we find the $wt$ which minimizes $\frac{Q_N}{N} + \frac{Q_C}{C}$ When $wt$ is too high, clustering favours categorical attributes and this increases $Q_N$ and decreases $Q_C$. When $wt$ is too less, clustering favors numeric attributes, hence $Q_N$ decreases and $Q_C$ increases. There is a particular $wt$ for which the quality of clustering in numeric and categorical attributes will not favor either of them. The sum of fractions of qualities is minimized for this $wt$.

## 2.2  Initialization of clusters

The proposed initialization method (for details see[4])initializes each cluster with one record. For each subsequent record in data, find the cluster which is closest and assign the record to that cluster. This reduces the number of iterations while not effecting the quality of clustering. Thus we do clustering during initialization by making one pass on database.

In general, records which are close and are really members of same cluster will go to the same cluster in this initialization process. It is only the peripheral data elements of these clusters that move between the clusters during the iteration process, thereby decreasing the number of iterations. Problem comes when a cluster breaks and its data elements are distributed among many initialized clusters. However this kind of cluster breakage is very rare.

**Choosing initial k records**  One can choose these k records in any fashion, even randomly. But care should be taken that no two data records are identical. Other option is to divide range of each attribute into k segments and assign midpoint of each segment to attribute value of each initial record. For categorical attribute we find the first k frequent attribute values and assign each of them to one record. The detailed initialization procedure along with distance measure covering categorical attributes is presented in [4].

## 2.3  Order of input

There are n! possible ways of giving input. It is a known fact that the algorithm converges in oscillatory fashion. This kind of oscillation is due to the random distribution of data values when considered in the input order.

If we give input in uniform order i.e if the variation in data values is not drastic, the convergence may be faster. But there are many attributes involved and one can not identify such uniform ordering of data. For this we suggest to give the data in monotonic order of leading attribute. This is because, leading attribute is the one that is dominating the clustering process. In this way, the number of elements that are changing clusters very often due to the misplacement of some previous records will decrease.

## 2.4  New distance measurement for categorical data

Concept hierarchy plays an important role in KDD process as it specifies background and domain knowledge and helps in better mining of data. We propose a new distance measurement for attributes whose values can be put in a hierarchy. Consider the concept hierarchy given in Fig. 1. The 0-1 distance measurement treats the distance between red and blue as well as red and light red equal. According to our new distance measurement, we take a distance called primary distance. This primary distance will be the minimum possible distance between any two attribute values. We define distance between two data elements with respect to categorical attribute as d(i, j) = primary distance if attribute values have same parent in the hierarchy otherwise it is primary distance times the number of edges one has to move up to reach their common parent. So for Fig. 1, if primary distance is 1, distance between dark red and light red is taken as 1 while distance between light red and light green is 2. This kind of distance measurement is not only helpful for providing knowledge about categorical attributes but it can also be used for numeric attributes. For numeric data (Fig. 2) if the primary distance is one, distance between attribute values 20, 36 is one while distance between 20, 70 is two.

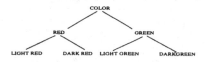 

**Fig. 1.** Concept hierarchy for Categorical attributes

**Fig. 2.** Concept hierarchy for Numerical attributes

To analyze the effect of this new distance measure on clustering, one needs a well organized database to extract hierarchy. The resulting clustering can be only be analyzed by applying it to a particular domain.

## 3 Performance Study

Results obtained are shown graphically in Fig.3 to Fig. 10. For details see [4]. In the graphs, 'Original' represents the values obtained when algorithm is applied on data without any modifications while 'Modified' represents the values obtained when algorithm is applied with the proposed modifications.

## 4 Conclusions

The proposed extension of K-means clustering method allows handling of both numeric and categorical attributes. A new distance measurement concept for categorical attributes is proposed. We proposed an initialization technique which helps in decreasing the number of iterations.

## References

1. F Murtagh: Multidimensional Clustering Algorithms. Physica-Verlag, Vienna., 1985.
2. P. Michaud: Clustering techniques. Future Generation Computer Systems, (13), 1997.
3. J. A. Hartigan: Clustering Algorithms. 1975.
4. K. Sambasiva Rao: K-means Clustering for Categorical Attributes. M. Tech. Thesis, Dec 1998, Indian Institute of Technology, New Delhi, India.

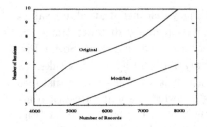

**Fig. 3.** Number of Iterations vs. Number of Records(Biased Data)

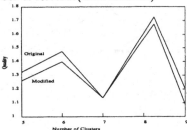

**Fig. 4.** Clustering Quality vs. Number of Records(Biassed Data)

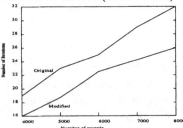

**Fig. 5.** Number of Iterations vs. Number of Clusters(Biased Data)

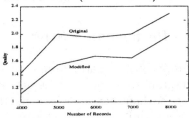

**Fig. 6.** Clustering Quality vs. Number of Clusters(Biassed Data)

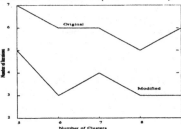

**Fig. 7.** Number of Iterations vs. Number of Records(Random Data)

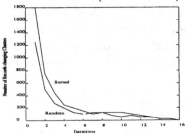

**Fig. 8.** Clustering Quality vs. Number of Records(Random Data)

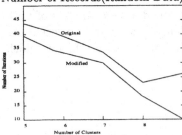

**Fig. 9.** Number of Iterations vs. Number of Clusters(Random Data)

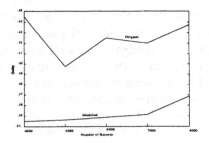

**Fig. 10.** Record Movement during Iterations

# Considering Main Memory in Mining Association Rules

Yongqiao Xiao, Margaret H. Dunham

Department of Computer Science and Engineering
Southern Methodist University
Dallas, Texas 75275-0122

**Abstract.** We propose a family of large itemset counting algorithms which adapt to the amount of main memory available. By using historical or sampling data, the potential large itemsets (candidates) and the false candidates are identified earlier. Redundant computation is reduced(thus overall CPU time reduced) by counting different sizes of candidates together and the use of a dynamic trie. By counting candidates earlier and counting more candidates in each scan, the algorithms reduce the overall number of scans required.

## 1   Introduction

Mining association rules has attracted a lot of interest in recent years[1, 4]. As introduced in [2], the association rule problem can be formally stated as: Let $I = \{i_1, i_2, \cdots, i_m\}$ be a set of literals called *items*. Let $D$ be a set of transactions, $T$, where $T \subseteq I$. Let $X \subset I$, $Y \subset I$, and $X \cap Y = \emptyset$ be called *itemsets*. An *association rule*, $X \Rightarrow Y$, holds in $D$ with *confidence c* if $c\%$ of the transactions in $D$ which contain $X$ also contain $Y$. The support of $X \Rightarrow Y$ is the percentage of transaction in $D$ which contain $Y \cup X$. Most algorithms to find association rules actually find *large itemsets*. A large itemset(or a frequent itemset) is an itemset which occurs in some minimum number (minimum support) of transactions. Finding association rules from large itemsets is relatively easy [2].

The well known approaches to finding large itemsets construct sets of candidate itemsets(or simply candidates), and then verify whether they are large itemsets by scanning the database. Most algorithms are based on the level-wise algorithm, Apriori[4, 8, 2]. It uses the property that an itemset is large only if all its subsets are also large, to generate the candidate $k$-itemsets, $C_k$, from the large $(k-1)$-itemsets, $L_{k-1}$. As each size of candidates requires one database scan, the number of database scans is the maximum size of candidates. With Apriori the number of candidates is low, however it also causes a lot of redundant computation. Here *redundant computation* means that extra CPU time (caused by unnecessary comparisons) is needed to count the itemsets. For example, candidates $A$, $AB$, $ABC$ are counted in scans 1, 2, 3 respectively. $A$ is counted in scan 1, but still needs to be compared(though not counted) in scans 2 and 3 to count $AB$, $ABC$. $AB$ is counted in scan 2, and still needs to be compared to count $ABC$ in scan 3.

PARTITION[9] reduces the database scans to two. It divides the database into small partitions such that each partition can be handled in main memory. Sampling[11] reduces the number of database scans to one in the best case and two in the worst by using sampling techniques. AS-CPA(Anti-Skew Counting Partition Algorithm)[7] is a family of anti-skew algorithms that filter out false candidate itemsets at an earlier stage. DIC(Dynamic Itemset Counting)[5] partitions the database into fixed sized intervals and counts the candidate itemsets earlier, i.e., all 1-itemsets are counted in the first interval, and in the second interval, both 2-itemsets and 1-itemsets are counted.

As seen in [4] and shown in the performance study below, limited main memory can be a problem when determining large itemsets. However, this issue has been surprisingly ignored in most of the literature. The objective of this paper is to address this issue. Section 2 describes main memory issues and provides further motivation for this research. In section 3, the two dynamic candidate partition algorithms which adapt to available main memory are briefly described as is the dynamic trie data structure which they use. Section 4 reports on preliminary performance results, and Section 5 concludes the paper.

## 2  Main Memory Issues

Let $m$ be the main memory size, $n$ the maximum size of candidates, $C_k$ the set of candidate $k$-itemsets, and $mem(C_k)$ the main memory requirement for $C_k$. There are two insufficient main memory cases:

1. $mem(\sum_{k=1}^{n} C_k) > m$ and $mem(C_k) \leq m$ for all $k$. There will be insufficient main memory for the database scan reduction algorithms [9,11,7,5]. However, the level-wise [4,8,2] algorithms still work in this situation.
2. $\sum_k mem(C_k) > m$ and $mem(C_k) > m$ for some $k$. There will be insufficient main memory for all the sequential algorithms. Only some parallel algorithms[3,6,10] have considered this case.

We observe that the main memory requirement for each scan (in Apriori) is different. In the middle scans there are more candidates and thus more main memory requirement, and in the beginning or ending scans there are less potential candidates and thus less main memory requirement.

The Apriori algorithm can be adapted to main memory limitations by two simple changes [4]:

1. If during scan $k$, all candidates of size $k$ do not fit into main memory, then divide the candidates into groups based on the available memory size and count each group separately.
2. Since the number of candidates found during the last scans of the database may be few, later scans may be combined to reduce the number of scans of the database. Thus different size candidate sets will be counted at the same time.

We refer to this improved version of Apriori as *AprioriMem*. This approach will result in multiple database scans for a pass with insufficient memory. Here the term *pass* indicates examining all candidates of one size. A *scan* is one complete reading of the database. With Apriori, scans and passes are identical. With AprioriMem, the total number of scans is:

$$\sum_{k=1}^{n} \lceil \frac{mem(C_k)}{m} \rceil, \tag{1}$$

The objective of our approach is to obtain a more even distribution of candidates across all the scans. Thus the number of database scans will be:

$$\lceil \frac{mem(\sum_{k=1}^{n} C_k)}{m} \rceil. \tag{2}$$

By distributing the candidates across all scans, main memory is fully utilized in each scan(the last scan may be underfull), and the number of scans can be reduced.

A simple approach, we call *Static Candidate Partition Algorithm (SCPA)*, is a generalization of AprioriMem and Sampling [12]. As with AprioriMem, when there is insufficient main memory, it partitions the candidates and counts each partition of candidates separately. The highlights of this algorithm include:

1. We assume the existence of results from prior sampling as input to the algorithm. This gives a set of potential large itemsets, *PL*.
2. All large itemsets can be found in two steps as in Sampling[11]. The first step is to determine the true large itemsets in the approximate set *PL*. The second step is to find the remaining large itemsets by counting the missing candidates (not counted in the first step, but may be true large itemsets).
3. Itemsets of different sizes may be counted during any database scan. So if during scan $k$, memory can hold more candidates than are in $C_k$, then candidates of size $k + 1$ and larger will be added to the scan until memory is full.
4. All missing candidates are generated in the second step at one time. This creates an exponential effect (too many missing candidates may be generated as shown in Lemma 1).

**Lemma 1.** *Let $n$ be the number of missing large 1-itemsets, and $m$ be the number of true large itemsets(i.e., $|TL|$) found in the first step of SCPA. There are at least $2^n \times (m + 1) - (m + n + 1)$ missing candidate itemsets generated.*
**Proof:** *see [12].*

## 3 Our Approach: Dynamic Candidate Partition Algorithms

We propose two algorithms based on the simple idea of the Static Partition Algorithm. The algorithms which we propose attack both of the insufficient memory problems discussed in the last section. As with SCPA, we assume that an approximate set of large itemsets, $PL$, is given. $PL$ may have been obtained from a sampling step or may be the actual set of large itemsets from an earlier database step. A more thorough discussion of these algorithms and their performance can be found elsewhere [12]

Unlike Sampling and SCPA, there is only one step, i.e., the missing candidates are generated dynamically and iteratively as needed. Compared to the static partition approach, the dynamic partition algorithms have the following features:

1. There is no separate step for the missing candidates. Instead the missing candidates are generated dynamically and counted in different database scans.
2. The exponential effect is avoided by the iterative generation of missing candidates.
3. They adapt to the available main memory, thus making maximum usage of main memory and reducing the number of database scans required.
4. A dynamic trie data structure is used to count the candidates so that there is less redundant computation between different scans.
5. Some false candidates can be identified and pruned away by employing the large itemsets from the previous scans.

We use a trie data structure, which is similar to that in [5] with some changes. We assume that all itemsets are listed in lexicographic order so that each item has a unique position in any path. For convenience, we view all the candidates generated from the $PL$ (i.e. $PL \cup BD^-(PL)$, where $BD^-(PL)$ is the negative border function in [11], which includes the itemsets all whose property subset itemsets are in $PL$) as existing in a *virtual trie*. In actuality this trie does not exist. Having this trie in mind, however, will help to understand how our proposed algorithms function. In effect, the algorithms dynamically choose a subset of the nodes in the trie to count (materialize) during each database scan. The algorithms differ in how these nodes are chosen. Both, however, ensure that the set of candidates chosen during each scan will fit into the available main memory. At any time, the (materialized) trie contains the maximum number of nodes needed for the itemsets being counted. Initially the trie contains the set of candidates been considered in the first database scan. At the end of each scan the trie is traversed, nodes are removed, and new nodes are added. When the algorithms terminate, only large itemsets remain. The difference between the trie data structure and the hash tree which has been previously used [4], lies in the fact that all nodes in the trie represent an itemset, while in the hash tree only leaf nodes contain the itemsets.

**Example 1:** *Figure 1 a) shows a sample trie for items $\{A, B, C, D, E, F, G, H, I, J\}$. Suppose that through historical information it is determined that the approximate set of large itemsets: $PL = \{A, B, C, E, AB, AC, AE, BC, BE, ABC, ABE\}$. The candidates for the first pass of SCPA, then, are: $PL \cup BD^-(PL)$ $(BD^-(PL) = \{D, F, G, H, I, J, CE\})$. Figure 1a) shows the trie which is used during the first step of SCPA. After the first step, suppose we find the large itemsets: $\{A, B, C, D, AB, AC, BC, ABC\}$, among which $A, B, C, AB, AC, BC, ABC$*

*are true large itemsets, and D is a missing large itemsets. The candidates for the second step are then: {AD, BD, CD, ABD, ACD, BCD, ABCD}, which are generated from the missing large itemset D. The trie for the second step is shown in Figure 1b). After the second step, we find the remaining large itemset: AD.*

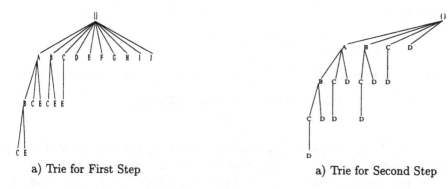

a) Trie for First Step          a) Trie for Second Step

**Fig. 1.** The Trie Data Structure Used in SCPA

To facilitate the dynamic algorithms, status information is kept for each node:

- ALL_COUNTED: The node and all its descendent nodes have been counted.
- ALL_UNCOUNTED: Neither the the node nor any of its descendents have been counted.
- DESCENDENT_UNCOUNTED: The node itself has been counted but at least one of its descendent nodes hasn't been counted.

During processing a transaction, a depth-first traversal over part of the trie is used to increment the counts of the itemsets in the trie.

The *Breadth-First Partition Algorithm (BFPA)* selects the candidates for each scan through a breadth-first traversal over the virtual trie until main memory is full, i.e., first candidate 1-itemsets, then candidate 2-itemsets and so on. When generating candidates, we assume that all immediate children of a node are generated together and counted in one scan. This reduces redundant computation as well as simplifying candidate generation,

**Example 2:** *Figure 2 shows the tries which are used to implement BFPA for Example 1 assuming there is enough memory for 15 nodes in the trie. The total number of database scans is two. In the first scan, all candidate 1-itemsets and some of the candidate 2-itemsets are counted. In Figure 2, we don't generate AE in the first scan, although the memory can still hold one more node, as AB, AC can not be held together with AE. At the end of this first scan, small itemsets are removed and new nodes are added using the negative border. The materialized trie for the second scan is shown in Figure 2b).*

The memory requirement for the dynamic algorithms, can be reduced by writing large itemsets to hard disk whose counting status is ALL_COUNTED.

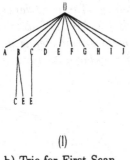

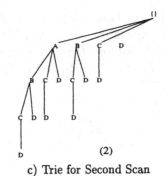

(1)

(2)

b) Trie for First Scan

c) Trie for Second Scan

**Fig. 2.** Breadth-First Partition Example

In Figure 2, $D$ has been written to the hard disk as $D$ has been counted, used for generating candidates, so no line is shown to that node in the figure.

One disadvantage of the breadth-first partition is that there is still redundant computation between different database scans, as the counting status value of a counted node may be DESCENDENT_UNCOUNTED. However, its redundant computation will be less than that of Apriori, as candidates of different sizes can be counted in one scan.

The Breadth-First Partition Algorithm is shown in Algorithm 1.

**Algorithm 1**
**Input:**
   $PL$: $PL_1 \cup PL_2 \cdots \cup PL_n$. //Probable large itemsets
   $I,D,s$ // items, database of transactions, minimum support
   $m$ // memory size(maximum number of candidates in memory)
**Output:**
   $L : L_1 \cup L_2 \cdots \cup L_n$ //Large Itemsets
**BFPA Algorithm:**
   *1)* $TRIE = I$ //initially 1-itemsets
   *2)* $k = 1$
   *3)* **while** $mem(TRIE \cup BD^-(PL_k)) < m$ **do begin**
   *4)*      $TRIE = TRIE \cup BD^-(PL_k)$; //expand the trie by one level
   *5)*      $k++$; **end**
   *6)* **repeat** //the negative border of $PL_k$ will span different scans
   *7)*      Find maximal $SS \subseteq PL_k$, where $mem(TRIE \cup BD^-(SS)) \leq m$.
   *8)*      $TRIE = TRIE \cup SS$;
   *9)*      $PL_k = PL_k - SS$;
   *10)*     $TL =$ {the true large itemsets in $TRIE$ found in $D$}
   *11)*     $ML =$ {the missing large itemsets in $TRIE$ found in $D$}
   *12)*     $TRIE = TL \cup ML$ //other small itemsets are removed from the trie
            //$BD^{-*}$ only generates the negative border that has NOT been
            //generated in previous scans.
   *13)*     $TRIE = TRIE \cup BD^{-*}(TRIE)$

*14)*    **while** $mem(BD^{-*}(ML \cup TL \cup PL_k)) \leq m$ **do begin**
*15)*      $TRIE = TRIE \cup (BD^{-*}(ML \cup TL \cup PL_k));$
*16)*      $k++;$ **end**
*17)*until $TRIE$ *does not change*
*18)*return $L = ML \cup TL;$

By processing the trie in a depth-first, rather than breadth first manner, a *Depth-First Partition Algorithm (DFPA)* is created. DFPA selects the candidates for each scan through a depth-first traversal over the virtual trie until main memory is full. The details of the DFPA algorithm are found in [12].

# 4   Performance Results

In this section we discuss the performance results comparing five different algorithms: DFPA, BFPA, SCPA, Apriori, and AprioriMem. The first four algorithms were actually implemented in C. The performance of AprioriMem was estimated based on the results of Apriori without any memory constraints.

We report on experiments performed using one synthetic data set from [4] D100K.T10.I4: transaction number of 100K, average transaction size of 10 and average size of large itemsets of 4. The number of items and large itemsets are set to 1000 and 2000 respectively as in [4]. Two minimum supports 0.5% and 0.1% were used, and for each minimum support we ran the algorithms with two memory sizes (number of nodes in trie) 500k and 50k.

Before running our algorithms for each minimum support, an approximate set of large itemsets is obtained by sampling with the same minimum support. In order to show how our algorithms perform when the approximate set is not accurate (very possible if obtained from historical data), we use a small sample size(25K) and the same minimum support (instead of reduced as was proposed for the Sampling algorithm) to find the approximate set.

We examined three metrics: the number of scans, candidates and comparisons. We report on the results of experiments for each metric in the subsequent three subsections.

## 4.1   Number of Scans

Table 1 shows the number of database scans of the algorithms for all four cases. The Apriori ran out of memory when the minimum support was 0.1%. We reran it on another machine with a larger memory to get the results. The numbers in the column Apriori are the pass numbers for Apriori with no memory constraints(so each pass can be put in the memory) as for the dynamic algorithms. The number of scans for AprioriMem in Table 1 was estimated by formula 1 based on the number of candidates for each pass of Apriori and the memory constraint.

Our dynamic algorithms (Depth-first and Breadth-first) have the fewest scans in all cases with memory constraints, because they employ the historical or sampling information to identify candidates earlier and fully utilize memory in each

| min_sup | max_mem | Depth-first | Breadth-first | Static | AprioriMem (Estimated) | Apriori (No Mem Cnstrnts) |
|---------|---------|-------------|---------------|--------|------------------------|---------------------------|
| 0.5% | 500k | 2 | 2 | 7 | $4^-$ | 4 |
| | 50k | 8 | 8 | 28 | $11^-$ | |
| 0.1% | 500k | 2 | 2 | 3 | $11^-$ | 11 |
| | 50k | 11 | 11 | 12 | $20^-$ | |

**Table 1.** Number of scans for D100K.T10.I4

scan. It is interesting to note that the static algorithm suffered from the exponential effect(too many candidates shown in Table 2 in the second step and thus too many scans), as the approximate set was not accurate enough due to high minimum support(0.5%) and small sample size(25K). By our dynamic iterative way of generating of the missing candidates, both the dynamic algorithms avoided the exponential effect.

## 4.2   Number of Candidates

Table 2 shows the total number of candidates examined by each algorithm. Not surprisingly, Apriori has the fewest number of candidates, as its candidate generation is level-wise. As AprioriMem has the same candidate numbers as Apriori, we only show its numbers in the column Apriori. Note that our dynamic algorithms employ the historical or sampling information to identify candidates earlier, but due to the inaccuracy of the approximate set some candidates may turn out to be false(not candidates of Apriori), thus we may have more candidates generated.

| min_sup | max_mem | Depth-first | Breadth-first | Static | Apriori (No Memory Constraints) |
|---------|---------|-------------|---------------|--------|--------------------------------|
| 0.5% | 500k | 433816 | 433816 | 1561579* | 370414 |
| | 50k | 431117 | 428251 | | |
| 0.1% | 500k | 530820 | 530531 | 532671 | 528586 |
| | 50k | 529017 | 528992 | | |

**Table 2.** Number of candidates for D100K.T10.I4

Compared to the static algorithm, both dynamic algorithms have fewer candidates. When the minimum support is high(the accuracy of the sampling is low), both Depth-first and Breadth-first do not suffer the exponential effect, as they use the dynamic iterative way to generate the missing candidates. With the minimum support decreasing thus increasing the accuracy of the sampling, both dynamic algorithms have candidate numbers closer to that of Apriori.

## 4.3 Redundant Computation Reduction

In order to measure the reduction of redundant computation by our dynamic algorithms, which directly impacts the CPU time, we use the number of comparisons for the algorithms. The comparisons reported only include those directly involved in counting. For our dynamic trie data structure, whenever item associated with a node is compared(even when not incrementing the counter), the number of comparisons is increased by one. With the hash tree data structure (in Apriori), for each $k$-itemset in the leaf node, $k$ comparisons is required to find out whether it is in the transaction.

| min_sup | max_mem | Depth-first | Breadth-first | Apriori (No Memory Constraints) |
|---------|---------|-------------|---------------|---------------------------------|
| 0.5%    | 500k    | 7.36e6      | 7.36e6        | 1.63e7                          |
|         | 50k     | 1.50e7      | 1.55e7        |                                 |
| 0.1%    | 500k    | 2.89e7      | 3.97e7        | 8.87e7                          |
|         | 50k     | 3.95e7      | 4.62e7        |                                 |

Table 3. Number of Comparisons for D100K.T10.I4

As shown in Table 3, both the dynamic algorithms have reduced the number of computations from that in Apriori. The major redundant computation reduction comes from the dynamic trie data structure and counting candidates of different sizes together in one scan. A depth-first traversal over part of the trie for counting reduces the number of comparisons required, as the common prefixes of the itemsets are counted only once for a transaction. By contrast, in the hash tree every candidate $k$-itemset requires at least $k$ comparisons regardless of their common prefixes. Also the itemsets which are counted in the previous scans are compared in later passes, as Apriori is level-wise.

As expected, Depth-first reduced more redundant computation than Breadth-first. This results from its depth-first nature. Depth-first counts a node and all its descendent nodes (which have been generated as potential candidates) in one scan, thus it does not need to compare these nodes again in later scans. Breadth-first needs to keep the nodes counted in the previous scans in the trie in order to count their descendent nodes in the later scans.

## 5 Conclusion and Future Work

We have proposed two dynamic algorithms for mining large itemsets. They are adaptive to the amount of memory available. By dynamic pruning and dynamic iterative generation of the missing candidates, they result in fewer database scans without increasing many candidates. Both the algorithms employ historical or sampling data to identify candidates earlier.

In the future we will perform experiments using more realistic datasets and compare to more algorithms. The Depth-first algorithm and the Breadth-first algorithm have complementary advantages and disadvantages. We are developing a hybrid approach of the Depth-first and the Breadth-first combining the best features of each.

# References

1. Rakesh Agrawal, Tomasz Imielinski, and Arun N. Swami. Mining association rules between sets of items in large databases. In Peter Buneman and Sushil Jajodia, editors, *Proceedings of the 1993 ACM SIGMOD International Conference on Management of Data*, pages 207–216, Washington, D.C., 26–28 May 1993.
2. Rakesh Agrawal, Heikki Mannila, Ramakrishnan Srikant, Hannu Toivonen, and A. Inkeri Verkamo. Fast discovery of association rules. In Usama M. Fayyad, Gregory Piatetsky-Shapiro, Padhraic Smyth, and Ramasamy Uthurusamy, editors, *Advances in Knowledge Discovery and Data Mining*, pages 307–328, Menlo Park, CA, 1996. AAAI Press.
3. Rakesh Agrawal and John C. Shafer. Parallel mining of association rules. *IEEE Transactions on Knowledge and Data Engineering*, 8(6):962–969, December 1996.
4. Rakesh Agrawal and Ramakrishnan Srikant. Fast Algorithms for Mining Association Rules in Large Databases. In *Proceedings of the Twentieth International Conference on Very Large Databases*, pages 487–499, Santiago, Chile, 1994.
5. Sergey Brin, Rajeev Motwanik, Jeffrey D. Ullman, and Shalom Tsur. Dynamic itemset counting and implication rules for market basket data. In *Proceedings of the ACM SIGMOD Conference*, pages 255–264, 1997.
6. Eui-Hong Han, George Karypis, and Vipin Kumar. Scalable parallel data mining for association rules. In *Proceedings of the ACM SIGMOD Conference*, pages 277–288, 1997.
7. Jun-Lin Lin and M. H. Dunham. Mining association rules: Anti-skew algorithms. In *Proceedings of the 14th International Conference on Data Engineering*, Olando, Florida, February 1998. IEEE Computer Society Press.
8. Heikki Mannila, Hannu Toivonen, and A. Inkeri Verkamo. Efficient algorithms for discovering association rules. In Usama M. Fayyad and Ramasamy Uthurusamy, editors, *AAAI Workshop on Knowledge Discovery in Databases (KDD-94)*, pages 181–192, July 1994.
9. Ashoka Savasere, Edward Omiecinski, and Shamkant B. Navathe. An efficient algorithm for mining association rules in large databases. In *Proceedings of the 21nd International Conference on Very Large Databases*, pages 432–444, Zurich, Swizerland, 1995.
10. Takahiko Shintani and Masaru Kitsuregawa. Hash based parallel algorithms for mining association rules. In *Proceedings of PDIS*, 1996.
11. Hannu Toivonen. Sampling large databases for association rules. In *Proceedings of the 22nd International Conference on Very Large Databases*, pages 134–145, Mumbai, India, 1996.
12. Yongqiao Xiao and Margaret H Dunham. Considering main memory in mining association rules. In *Technical Report-99-CSE-4, Department of Computer Science, Southern Methodist University*, 1999.

# Discovery of Association Rule Meta-Patterns

Giuseppe Psaila

Dipartimento di Elettronica e Informazione, Politecnico di Milano
P.za Leonardo da Vinci 32 - 20133 Milano, Italy
psaila@elet.polimi.it

**Abstract.** The user interested in mining a data set by means of the extraction of association rules has to formulate mining queries or *meta-patterns* for association rule mining, which specify the features of the particular data mining problem.

In this paper, we propose an exploration technique for the discovery of association rule meta-patterns able to extract *quality rule sets*, i.e. association rule sets which are meaningful and useful for the user. The proposed method is based on simple heuristic analysis techniques, suitable for an efficient preliminary analysis performed before applying the computationally expensive techniques for mining association rules.

## 1 Introduction

The research area named *Data Mining*, also known as *Knowledge Discovery in Databases*, knew an impressive growth in the last years. In the literature, a large number of papers appeared, with interesting and promising results, concerning a large variety of topics. In the early years the attention was primarily focused on the development of efficient techniques able to analyze and discover patterns from large and very large data sets. Several techniques were considered, from classification [7] to the discovery of similarities in time series [1], but the most investigated technique is the extraction of association rules [2, 3].

In a second moment, the researchers moved their attention to other topics, such as the development of specification languages [5, 8], that allow the user to specify a generic problem based on the extraction of association rules, and the integration of data mining techniques with relational databases [6], in order to develop systems [9] that exploit the presence of a relational database as repository for the analyzed data.

The developed techniques are powerful, but practical experiences show that their use is not easy and immediate. Thus, a methodological support should be provided. An attempt to give an answer to this problem is the *Knowledge Discovery Process* (KDP) proposed in [4]. The KDP starts with the comprehension of the context, followed by the selection of a significant data set. Then, after data are preprocessed and simplified, the KDP requires the user to identify a data mining task, choose the data mining method or technique and apply it. Finally, results are evaluated, in order to formalize the discovered knowledge.

The *Data Mining* phase of the KDP requires the choice and the application of a data mining technique; chosen the technique, the user is asked to drive the process, typically by selecting the features of the data that must be investigated. If the user chooses the extraction of association rules, such features are, e.g. the attribute whose values are associated by rules, etc.. The features relevant for the extraction of association rules constitute a *meta-pattern*.

However, it may be difficult to specify significant meta-patterns, when the data set to analyze is unknown, or has a large number of attributes.

In this paper, we propose a method to explore the data and identify meta-patterns for the extraction of association rules that, applied to the data set to analyze, cause the extraction of quality association rule sets. Such an exploration method is meant to be *preliminary*, in the sense that it must precede the actual extraction of association rules; hence, it must require light preliminary analysis of the data. Since exact techniques would require complex and expensive analysis of the data, we base the method on simple heuristic techniques.

The paper is organized as follows. Section 2 introduces the semantic framework and formalizes the concept of association rule meta-pattern. Section 3 provides an introductory overview of our method. Section 4 and 5 discuss in details the analysis phases required by the method. Section 6 draws the conclusions.

## 2 Meta-Patterns for Association Rules

The problem of mining association rules has been defined and mostly studied in the case of transaction data sets, where rules associate items sold in commercial transactions. However, the technique is general, and can be applied to any data set, whose structure might be complex. It is necessary to properly define what kind of information we like to mine from the analyzed data set. For this purpose, we introduce the concept of *meta-pattern for association rules*.

A *meta-pattern* for association rules is a tuple $p : \langle T, g, m, s, c \rangle$, where $T$, $g$, $m$, $s$ and $c$ are the parameters of the pattern. Their meaning is the following.

$T$: this parameter denotes the source data set. We assume that the data set is a relational table.[1] The notation $Schema(T)$ denotes the set of attributes (columns) of the table.

$m$: this parameter denotes the *rule attribute* (also named the *mined attribute*), i.e. the attribute on which rules are mined; if we denote the set of $m$'s values as $V_m$, an association rule associates values of $V_m$. More precisely, for a rule $r : B \Rightarrow H$, it is $B \subset V_m$, $H \subset V_m$, $|H| = 1$[2], $B \cap H = \emptyset$. The *size* of a rule $r : B \Rightarrow H$ is the number of values in the body and in the head, i.e. $size(r) = |B| + |H|$.

$g$: this parameter denotes the *grouping attribute*, w.r.t. which rules express regularities. The source data set is logically partitioned in groups having the same value for the grouping attribute[3]. Rules associate rule attribute's values that

---

[1] This assumption is motivated by the fact that data sets to analyze usually come from relational operational databases or ROLAP data warehouse servers.

[2] This constraint is motivated by the need for clarity in examples. In effect, the technique proposed in the paper is not affected by the cardinality of heads.

[3] For the sake of clarity, parameter $g$ (resp. $m$) of meta-patterns defines one single attribute. We can generalize assuming that $g$ (resp. $m$) defines a list of attributes.

(a)

| id | customer | product | day | month | id | customer | product | day | month |
|----|----------|---------|-----|-------|----|----------|---------|-----|-------|
| 1  | $c_1$ | A | 26 | 1 | 14 | $c_6$ | B | 26 | 1 |
| 2  | $c_1$ | B | 26 | 1 | 16 | $c_6$ | A | 26 | 1 |
| 3  | $c_1$ | C | 31 | 1 | 16 | $c_7$ | E | 32 | 2 |
| 4  | $c_2$ | C | 28 | 1 | 17 | $c_8$ | F | 32 | 2 |
| 5  | $c_2$ | D | 29 | 1 | 18 | $c_8$ | E | 32 | 2 |
| 6  | $c_2$ | E | 29 | 1 | 19 | $c_9$ | E | 33 | 2 |
| 7  | $c_3$ | F | 28 | 1 | 20 | $c_9$ | A | 33 | 2 |
| 8  | $c_3$ | A | 29 | 1 | 21 | $c_9$ | B | 34 | 2 |
| 9  | $c_4$ | B | 30 | 1 | 22 | $c_9$ | C | 34 | 2 |
| 10 | $c_4$ | D | 30 | 1 | 23 | $c_{10}$ | B | 35 | 2 |
| 11 | $c_4$ | E | 30 | 1 | 24 | $c_{10}$ | A | 35 | 2 |
| 12 | $c_5$ | F | 26 | 1 | 25 | $c_{11}$ | B | 36 | 2 |
| 13 | $c_5$ | A | 32 | 2 |    |       |   |    |   |

(b)

| | | |
|---|---|---|
| $A \Rightarrow B$ $s_r = 0.364$ $c_r = 0.667$ | $D \Rightarrow E$ $s_r = 0.182$ $c_r = 1$ |
| $A\,B \Rightarrow C$ $s_r = 0.182$ $c_r = 0.5$ | $F \Rightarrow A$ $s_r = 0.182$ $c_r = 0.667$ |
| $A\,C \Rightarrow B$ $s_r = 0.182$ $c_r = 1$ | $C \Rightarrow A$ $s_r = 0.182$ $c_r = 0.667$ |
| $B\,C \Rightarrow A$ $s_r = 0.182$ $c_r = 1$ | $C \Rightarrow B$ $s_r = 0.182$ $c_r = 0.667$ |
| $C \Rightarrow E$ $s_r = 0.182$ $c_r = 0.667$ | |

**Fig. 1.** (a) Table Transactions. (b) A rule set extracted from the table.

appear together in the same groups. In the following, the total number of groups is denoted as $G$.

$s$: this parameter specifies the *minimum support*. The support $s_r$ of a rule $r$ is defined as $s_r = G_r/G$, where $G_r$ is the number of groups that contain $r$. The support denotes the frequency with which the rule appears in groups. In order to select only relevant rules, a *minimum threshold $s$* for support is defined, so that only rules with $s_r \geq s$ are mined.

$c$: this parameter specifies the *minimum confidence*. The confidence $c_r$ of a rule $r$ is defined as $c_r = G_r/G_B$ where $G_B$ is the number of groups that contain at least the body $B$ of the rule. The confidence denotes the conditional probability of finding the entire rule in a group in which the rule's body is found. In order to select only rules with significant confidence, a *minimum threshold $c$* for confidence is defined, so that only rules with $c_r \geq c$ are mined.

The application of a meta-pattern $p$ to an instance of the source table $T$ produces a set of association rules, denoted as $R$.

**Example 1:** Consider table Transactions depicted in Figure 1.a. It reports data about commercial transactions. Each transaction has an identifier (attribute id), the customer that performed the transaction (attribute customer), the product object of the transaction (attribute product), the day in which the transaction is performed (attribute day), specified by means of the progressive number from the beginning of the year, the month of the transaction (attribute month), where 1 stands for January and 2 for February.

Consider $p : \langle$Transactions, customer, product, $0.15, 0.5\rangle$. It extracts rules from the table Transactions, such that rules associate products (mined attribute **product**) frequently purchased together by a single customer (grouping attribute **customer**); rules are considered relevant if they hold for at least 18% of customers (minimum support $s = 0.18$), and their conditional probability is at least 50% (minimum confidence $c = 0.5$). The meta-pattern produces the rule set shown in Figure 1.b. □

We now introduce some properties concerning association rule sets.[4]

**Proposition 1:** Consider an association rule meta-pattern $p : \langle T, g, m, s, c \rangle$ applied to a data set $T$. Let $g_i$ be a group in the data set $T$ partitioned by the grouping attribute $g$, and $R$ be the association rule set extracted by $p$. The upper bound for the size of rules in $R$ is the cardinality of the largest group in $T$, i.e. $max_{r \in R}(size(r)) \leq max(|g_i|)$. □

**Theorem 1:** Consider a meta-pattern $p$ and a table $T$. If there exists in $T$ a functional dependency $g \rightarrow m$ between the grouping attribute $g$ and the rule attribute $m$, $p$ applied to an instance of $T$ produces an empty rule set $R$. □

**Theorem 2:** Consider a meta-pattern $p$ and a table $T$. If there exists in $T$ a functional dependency $m \rightarrow g$ between $p.g$ and $p.m$, the highest minimum support to obtain a non-empty rule set $R$ is $s = 1/G$. □

## 3   Our Approach

Consider now a user having to analyze a data set. The user has to formulate a meta-pattern, but it is not easy to formulate a meta-pattern that produces a satisfactory rule set, i.e. a *quality rule set*, that can be effectively exploited, e.g. for decision making. In general, it is not possible to give an exact definition of *quality rule set*, because it depends on the applicative case and the user's expectations; however, several *quality factors* for rule sets can be identified.

- **Suitable number of rules.** The first factor perceived by the user is the number of mined rules. If they are too few, the rule set may be useless because it does not provide information. If they are too many, the rule set may be useless too, because it provides too much information.
- **Easy comprehension of rules.** An easily comprehensible rule is appreciated by the user. Typically, the size of a rule heavily affects the comprehension of the rule: small sized rules are preferable, because easily read and interpreted; large sized rules are difficult to read and to interpret.
- **Adequate synthesis level.** Association rules provide a synthetic view of the data set. An adequate synthesis level depends on the applicative case, but, to be significant, the rule set $R$ must synthesize a significant portion of the data.
- **Significance.** The significance of a rule set can be intended as the degree of useful information provided to the user. Rule sets with a significant number of unexpected rules are preferred by the user to rule sets which contain a large number of expected and obvious (depending on the applicative context) rules.

---

[4] For brevity, we do not report proofs. They can be found in [10].

Without any exploration method, the user can obtain a quality rule set only by performing several extraction trials. Unfortunately, when the data set is unknown, this approach can result in a large number of failures and waste of time, because the extraction of association rules from within a large data set is expensive in terms of execution time.

Consequently, the user need an exploration method to define suitable association rule meta-patterns, possibly based on a simple and fast preliminary analysis of the data.

## 4 Choosing the Attributes

The first issue to deal with while defining an association rule pattern is the definition of grouping and rule attributes. In this section, we discuss the phases of the proposed exploration method which concern the choice of attributes.

### 4.1 Grouping Attribute

The first parameter of a meta-pattern to identify is the grouping attribute $g$. To begin our discussion, we need the following definition.

**Definition 1:** Let $T$ be a table, whose schema $(a_1, \ldots, a_n)$ is denoted as $Schema(T)$. Let $a$ be an attribute of $T$ ($a \in Schema(T)$), and $V_a$ be the set of $a$'s values appearing in $T$. If the table is grouped by attribute $a$, the *average number of tuples in a group*, denoted as $\bar{n}_a$, is defined as $\bar{n}_a = |T| / |V_a|$. $\square$

High values of $\bar{n}_a$ denote that groups contain a large number of tuples. Consequently, it is possible to extract a large number of rules, with relevant size (Prop. 1). Low values of $\bar{n}_a$ denote that groups contain a small number of tuples. Consequently, it is possible to extract rules whose size is small (Prop. 1).

*Attribute Selection.* Evaluated $\bar{n}_a$, the user selects the attributes considered more interesting, based on the quality criteria introduced in Section 3. Attributes are ranked by increasing values of $\bar{n}_a$: those with the lowest values of $\bar{n}_a$ are preferable, because the size of rules is limited by small size of groups (Proposition 1). Attributes with value of $\bar{n}_a$ equal to 1 must be discarded, as illustrated by the following theorem. In our experience, we found that value of $\bar{n}_a$ greater than 1 but less than 5 or 6 give the best results in terms of comprehension of the resulting rule set.

**Theorem 3:** Consider a table $T$ and an attribute $a$ of $T$ ($a \in Schema(T)$). If $\bar{n}_a = 1$, every association rule pattern $p$ with parameter $g = a$ produces an empty set of rules. $\square$

**Example 2:** Consider the table Transactions of Figure 1.a. The ranked attributes with associated the cardinality of their set of values and the corresponding value for $\bar{n}_a$ are reported in the following table.

| Attribute | $|V_a|$ | $\bar{n}_a$ | | Attribute | $|V_a|$ | $\bar{n}_a$ | |
|-----------|---------|-------------|--|-----------|---------|-------------|--|
| id | 25 | 1 | *discarded* | product | 6 | 4.17 | *selected* |
| customer | 11 | 2.27 | *selected* | month | 2 | 12.5 | *not selected* |
| day | 9 | 2.78 | *selected* | | | | $\square$ |

## 4.2 Rule Attribute

The second parameter to specify in an association rule meta-pattern is the rule attribute $m$. To lead on our discussion, we need the following definition.

**Definition 2:** Let $T$ be a table, whose schema $(a_1, \ldots, a_n)$ is denoted as $Schema(T)$. Let $a$ and $b$ be two attributes of the table $(a, b \in Schema(T))$, and $V_a$ and $V_b$ be the sets of $a$'s and $b$'s values, respectively, appearing in $T$. The *density of $b$'s values w.r.t. $a$'s values* $\overline{d}_{a,b}$ is defined as $\overline{d}_{a,b} = |V_b| / |V_a|$. $\square$

In other words, given two attributes $a$ and $b$, $\overline{d}_{a,b}$ gives an idea of the distribution of values of the (possible) rule attribute $b$ w.r.t. the (possible) grouping attribute $a$. Two situations illustrate the importance of the density of mined values w.r.t. groups. High values of $\overline{d}_{a,b}$ denote that items in $V_b$ may appear in a large number of groups. Consequently, the meta-pattern would extract a large number of rules, possibly of relevant size, and with high support. This is in contrast with the quality criteria discussed in Section 3. Low values of $\overline{d}_{a,b}$ denote that the rule attribute has too few values w.r.t. the grouping attribute. Consequently, most of groups may contain the entire set $V_b$, causing the extraction of all possible permutations of values in $V_b$ with very high support.

We now introduce two indexes that can provide useful indications about the choice of the rule attribute.

**Definition 3:** Let $T$ be a table, whose schema $(a_1, \ldots, a_n)$ is denoted as $Schema(T)$. Let $a$ and $b$ be two attributes of the table $(a, b \in Schema(T))$. Suppose that $T$ is grouped by attribute $a$; for each group $g_i$, we denote with $z_i$ the number of distinct values of $b$ that appear in the group $g_i$. The *average number of distinct values of attribute $b$ in a group*, denoted as $\overline{a}_{a,b}$, and the *maximum number of distinct values of attribute $b$ in a group*, denoted as $\overline{u}_a, b$, are defined as $\overline{a}_{a,b} = (\sum_{g_i} z_i) / |V_a|$, $\overline{u}_{a,b} = max_{g_i}(z_i)$. $\square$

**Definition 4:** Let $T$ be a table, whose schema $(a_1, \ldots, a_n)$ is denoted as $Schema(T)$. Let $a$ and $b$ be two attributes of the table $(a, b \in Schema(T))$, and $V_b$ be the set of $b$'s values appearing in $T$. Suppose that $T$ is grouped by attribute $a$; $\overline{a}_{a,b}$ is the average number of distinct values of $b$ in a group. The *average fraction of the set of $b$'s values in each group*, denoted as $\overline{f}_{a,b}$, is defined as $\overline{f}_{a,b} = \overline{a}_{a,b} / |V_b|$. $\square$

In other words, by means of $\overline{a}_{a,b}$ it is possible to see if the pair of attributes is suitable for small sized rules, which are preferable based on the quality criteria. Furthermore, by means of $\overline{f}_{a,b}$ it is possible to estimate how many values of the rule attribute appear together in the same group: if they are too many ($\overline{f}_{a,b}$ close to 1), it may happen that almost all the permutations of $b$'s values have a very high support and would be extracted by the meta-pattern; this is in contrast with the quality criteria.

Finally, some useful properties can be proved by means of the indexes.

**Theorem 4:** Consider a table $T$ and a pair of attributes $(a, b)$ of $T$ $(a, b \in Schema(T))$. If the functional dependency $a \rightarrow b$ holds, it is $\overline{a}_{a,b} = 1$. $\square$

| Pair $(a,b)$ | $\overline{d}_{a,b}$ | | Pair $(a,b)$ | $\overline{d}_{a,b}$ $\overline{a}_{a,b}$ $f_{a,b}$ | |
|---|---|---|---|---|---|
| (product, id) | 4.16 | discarded | (customer, day) | 0.82 1.45 0.15 | selected |
| (day, id) | 2.78 | discarded | (day, product) | 0.67 2.2 0.37 | selected |
| (customer, id) | 2.27 | discarded | (customer, product) | 0.55 2.27 0.36 | selected |
| (product, customer) | 1.83 | discarded | (product, month) | 0.33 1.83 0.92 | not selected |
| (product, day) | 1.5 | discarded | (day, month) | 0.22 1 0.50 | not selected |
| (day, customer) | 1.22 | discarded | (customer, month) | 0.18 1.09 0.55 | not selected |

**Fig. 2.** The ranked list of attribute pairs.

**Theorem 5:** Consider an association rule meta-pattern $p$ applied to a table $T$, where $g$ and $m$ are the grouping and rule attributes, respectively. The upper bound for the size of rules in $R$ is $\overline{u}_{g,m}$, i.e. $max_{r \in R}(size(r)) \leq \overline{u}_{g,m}$. □

*Attribute Selection.* Evaluated $\overline{d}_{a,b}$, the user selects those pairs considered more promising, based on the quality criteria introduced in Section 3. Pairs of attributes are ranked by decreasing values of $\overline{d}_{a,b}$: those with low values of $\overline{d}_{a,b}$ are preferable, provided that this value is not too small. In our experience on practical cases, we observed that the range of values for $\overline{d}_{a,b}$ that gives the best results in terms of quality of the extracted rule set is between 0.01 and 0.1.

A significant help can be obtained by $\overline{a}_{a,b}$ and $\overline{f}_{a,b}$. As far as the former is concerned, small groups are preferable (e.g. from 2 to 5), to concentrate on meta-patterns that possibly extract small sized rules. As far as the latter is concerned, low values are preferable, because values of $\overline{f}_{a,b}$ close to 1 denotes that almost all the set of mined values is frequently present in groups.

Moreover, a pair $(a, b)$ should not be selected whether there exists a functional dependency between $a$ and $b$. In fact, by Theorem 1, the dependency $a \rightarrow b$ causes the generation of an empty rule set $R$. By Theorem 2, the dependency $b \rightarrow a$ causes the extraction of rules only if the minimum support is $s = 1/G$; thus, rules does not represent regularities (they appear in one single group) and are useless. Observe that the existence of a functional dependency $a \rightarrow b$ is putted in evidence when $\overline{a}_{a,b} = 1$, as shown by Theorem 4.

Finally observe that pairs of attributes with $\overline{d}_{a,b}$ greater than 1 should not be considered: in fact, the extracted rules would be of relevant size, with a very high support and consequently very numerous, so that none of the quality criteria would be met. For such pairs, $\overline{a}_{a,b}$ and $\overline{f}_{a,b}$ should not be considered.

**Example 3:** Consider table Transactions of Figure 1.a, and the attributes selected as grouping attribute in Example 2. We consider all the pairs between one of the selected grouping attributes and the remaining attributes, and compute $\overline{d}_{a,b}$ for each of them. We obtain the list reported in Figure 2.

We obtain a relevant number (6) of pairs that are discarded because the value of $\overline{d}_{a,b}$ is greater than 1. On the opposite side, three pairs are not selected because the value is too low. This is not surprising: in the case of the pair (product, month) almost all the products appear in both the two considered months; this situation is confirmed by the very high value (0.92) of $\overline{f}_{a,b}$. The same is for the pair (customer, month), for which we also notice a very small value of $\overline{a}_{a,b}$ (1.09) and a significant value of $\overline{f}_{a,b}$ (greater than 0.5). Finally, the pair (day, month) does not give rise to any association, since each day belongs to one single month (a functional dependency, as pointed out by $\overline{f}_{a,b} = 1$).

To conclude, observe that in this example the values of $\overline{d}_{a,b}$ for the three selected attribute pairs range from 0.55 to 0.82. This seems to be in contrast with our previous assertion that good values are from 1% to 10%. However, this is a toy example, with a very small number of rows. The range 1% to 10% demonstrated to be fine for real large data sets. Furthermore, the example also shows the importance of $\overline{a}_{a,b}$ and $\overline{f}_{a,b}$ to better comprehend the situation. □

## 5 Minimum Support and Confidence

Once a set of pairs $(g, m)$ has been selected, the third phase of the exploration method completes the meta-patterns identifying suitable minimum thresholds for support and confidence.

Here, the user is asked to indicate a measure of the number of rules he/she considers interesting. Then, by means of a heuristic technique that performs simple analysis of the data, minimum threshold values that approximately respect the interest measure are identified.

**Number of Distinct Rule Attribute Values.** The user defines the number $n_v$ of distinct values for the rule attribute $m$ associated by rules in the set $R$.
**Coverage of Rule Attribute Values.** The user defines the coverage ratio $r_c$, i.e. the percentage of distinct values of the rule attribute $m$ appearing in the extracted rules w.r.t. the entire set $V_m$.[5]

We now introduce the heuristic technique for the minimum support.

*Pre-analysis of the data.* The goal of this step is the extraction from the data set of the subset of values $\overline{V}_m \subseteq V_m$, with $|\overline{V}_m| = n_v$, having the highest support values. Each value in $\overline{V}_m$ is ordered w.r.t. its frequency: denoting a value as $v_i$, with $1 \leq i \leq |\overline{V_m}|$, and its frequency as $pr(v_i)$, it holds $pr(v_i) \geq pr(v_{i+1})$, for each $1 \leq i < |V_m|$

$\overline{V}_m$ contains the values with the highest support because, in absence of any kind of knowledge about the real data distribution, these are those with the highest probability of composing rules with the highest supports.

*Evaluation of Minimum Support and Confidence.* Computed the set $\overline{V}_m = \{v_i | 1 \leq i \leq n_v\}$ of $n_v$ most frequent values of $m$, consider the set of pairs $K = \{(v_{j,1}, v_{j,2}) | 1 \leq j \leq l, v_{j,1} = v_j, v_{j,2} = v_{j+l}\}$, where $l$ is the ceil of the quotient $n_v/2$. For each pair $k_j \in K$, compute the actual frequency $pr(k_j)$ with which the pair appears in groups. At this point, choose the pair $\overline{k}$ which is immediately over the third quartile, and take $pr(\overline{p})$. The value $s = pr(\overline{p})$ is then used in the meta-pattern as minimum support.

Let us determine the minimum confidence: for each pair of values $k_j = (v_{j,1}, v_{j,2})$ having sufficient support, compute the two conditional probabilities $pr(v_{j,1}|v_{j,2})$ and $pr(v_{j,2}|v_{j,1})$, and compute the average $\overline{pr}$ of all the computed conditional probabilities. The value $c = \overline{pr}$ is then used as minimum confidence.

---

[5] Observe that $n_v = |V| \times r_c/100$.

**Example 4:** Consider the pair (`customer`,`product`) selected in Example 3. We now identify the minimum support and confidence values. The three tables below reports the result of the analysis performed on the source data set. In particular, the left table reports the support of each product, listed in decreasing support order. Then, we choose to consider all the products ($n_v = 6$), as a consequence of the fact that the number of distinct products is very small; the middle table reports the support of the three considered pairs of products, listed in decreasing support order. Finally, the right table shows the conditional probabilities of each pair of products with support greater than zero. We establish a minimum support $s = 0.18$ and a minimum confidence $c = 0.59$, getting the rule set in Ex. 2.

| prod. | gr. | supp. | prod. | gr. | supp. | pair | gr. | supp. | cond. | prob. | cond. | prob. |
|-------|-----|-------|-------|-----|-------|------|-----|-------|-------|-------|-------|-------|
| A | 6 | 0.55 | C | 3 | 0.28 | (A,C) | 2 | 0.18 | C\|A | 0.33 | D\|E | 0.4 |
| B | 6 | 0.55 | F | 3 | 0.28 | (E,D) | 2 | 0.18 | A\|C | 0.66 | E\|D | 1 |
| E | 5 | 0.45 | D | 2 | 0.18 | (B,F) | 0 | 0 | | | | □ |

**Discussion 1:** It is known from statistics that given the frequencies (probabilities) $pr(e_1)$ and $pr(e_2)$ of two events $e_1$ and $e_2$, if they are independent the joint frequency is $pr(e_1) \times pr(e_2)$. However, we are analyzing data that in general do not meet the independence hypothesis; consequently, the joint frequency is $pr(e_1) \times pr(e_2|e_1)$, where $pr(e_2|e_1)$ is the conditional probability of $e_2$ given $e_1$. Hence, we have to compute the actual joint probability of each pair of values.

In order to reduce the complexity of this computation, we limit the search to a sample composed of $n_v/2$ pairs. The sample is chosen in such a way it is composed of a limited number of heterogeneous pairs, that involves all the $n_v$ considered values. Obtained that the frequencies of the sample pairs, we take the frequency of the pair immediately over the third quartile. This is consequence of the fact that the support of some pair in the sample may be too low; the third quartile avoids the suggested minimum support to be affected by such pairs. □

## 6 Conclusions and Future Work

In this paper, we addressed the problem of defining meta-patterns for the extraction of association rules. A meta-pattern defines the features of data mining problems based on the known techniques for extracting association rules. These features are the source data set, the grouping attribute, the mined attribute, the minimum thresholds for support and confidence.

This work is motivated by the observation that the definition of a meta-pattern that produces a quality association rule set, i.e. a rule set which is comprehensible, meaningful and informative for the user, is not a trivial task, because the data to analyze are totally or partially unknown.

We propose an exploration heuristic technique that, by means of simple queries over the data, at first drives the user in the choice of the grouping and mined attributes, then, based on a suitable interest measure provided by the user, suggests the minimum thresholds for support and confidence.

*Experiences.* We experienced the proposed exploration method in practical cases. In particular, a pool of users engaged in the analysis of data describing enrollment of students to courses of a university adopted the proposed method. They were not familiar with data mining techniques and at the beginning of their work they found difficult to understand what kind of information to extract from the database and formulate meta-patterns.

By means of the exploration method proposed in this paper, they were able to quickly address the problem, focusing their attention to a limited number of promising meta-patterns. Finally, with a limited effort, they were able to identify suitable values for minimum support and confidence, obtaining rule sets with the desired synthesis level. The users considered very informative the generated rules, and were satisfied by the fastness with which they obtained such results.

*Future work.* In our opinion, there is a significant amount of work to do in the direction addressed by this paper. In fact, there is need for a methodological framework that covers the different activities concerning the *data mining* phase of the knowledge discovery process: these activities range from the definition of mining meta-patterns, to the evaluation of extracted rule sets.

As far as the definition of meta-pattern is concerned, we are now studying a method that exploits the typical star data schema of data warehouses, to discover complex meta-patterns based on the mining operator introduced in [8], which is defined on a more complex semantic model than that considered in this paper, and takes advantage by the structure of the data warehouse.

# References

1. R. Agrawal, K. I. Lin, H. S. Sawhney, and K. Shim. Fast similarity search in the presence of noise, scaling, and translation in time-series databases. In *Proceedings of the 21st VLDB Conference*, Zurich, Switzerland, September 1995.
2. R. Agrawal and R. Srikant. Fast algorithms for mining association rules in large databases. In *Proceedings of the 20th VLDB Conference*, Santiago, Chile, 1994.
3. R. Bayardo. Efficiently mining long patterns from databases. In *Proceedings of the ACM-SIGMOD International Conference on the Management of Data*, Seattle, Washington, USA., June 1998.
4. U. M. Fayyad, G. Piatetsky-Shapiro, P. Smyth, and R. Uthurusamy. *Advances in Knowledge Discovery and Data Mining.* AAAI Press / The MIT Press, 1996.
5. J. Han, Y. Fu, W. Wang, K. Koperski, and O. Zaiane. DMQL: A data mining query language for relational databases. *In Proceedings of SIGMOD-96 Workshop on Research Issues on Data Mining and knowledge Discovery*, 1996.
6. T. Imielinski. From file mining to database mining. *In Proceedings of SIGMOD-96 Workshop on Research Issues on DM and KD*, pages 35–39, May 1996.
7. M. Mehta, R. Agrawal, and J. Rissanen. Sliq: A fast scalable classifier for data mining. In *Proceedings of EDBT'96, 6th International Conference on Extending Database Technology*, Avignon, France, March 1996.
8. R. Meo, G. Psaila, and S. Ceri. A new SQL-like operator for mining association rules. In *Proceedings of the 22st VLDB Conference*, Bombay, India, 1996.
9. R. Meo, G. Psaila, and S. Ceri. A tightly coupled architecture for data mining. In *IEEE Intl. Conference on Data Engineering*, Orlando, Florida, Febrary 1998.
10. G. Psaila. Discovery of association rule meta-patterns. Technical Report 99.33, Politecnico di Milano, Dip. Elettronica e Informazione, Milano, Italy, June 1999.

# Fuzzy Functional Dependencies and Fuzzy Association Rules

Yuping Yang[1], Mukesh Singhal[2]

[1] Department of Computer and Information Science,
The Ohio State University Columbus, OH 43210, USA
yangy@cis.ohio-state.edu
[2] Div. of Computer-Communications Research, National Science Foundation,
4201 Wilson Blvd., Room 1145, Arlington, VA 22230, USA
msinghal@nsf.gov

**Abstract.** This paper proposes fuzzy association rule which is a more generalized concept than boolean, quantitative, and interval association rules. Fuzzy association rule is a spectrum of definitions. Each particular fuzzy association rule can be defined by adding restrictions on the fuzziness depending on the needs of practical situations. The definition of fuzzy association rule also fills in the gap between fuzzy functional dependencies and clusters and results in a whole spectrum of concepts which is called data association spectrum. Such a unified view has practical implications. For example, various data mining problems can be converted to clustering problems and take advantage of the availability of a large number of good clustering algorithms.

*Key Words:* Fuzzy association rule, fuzzy functional dependency, measurement.

## 1 Introduction

One of the main subjects in the data mining research is association rule mining [1, 3]. Let $R = \{a_1, a_2, ..., a_m\}$ be a relation schema, which is a set of attributes (column titles) defining the format of relations. Let $r$ be an instance of $R$, i.e., $r$ is a relation with the attributes of $R$. This means that $r$ is composed of many tuples, each tuple has exactly $m$ entries and each entry is under one of the $m$ attributes $a_i$, $i = 1, 2, ..., m$. An association rule [1, 2] is an implication written as $a \Rightarrow b$ where $a$ is a value or vector in an attribute set $X(\subset R)$ and $b$ is a value or vector in an attribute set $Y(\subset R)$. An association rule has support and confidence. The support of the rule $a \Rightarrow b$ is $s$ if $s$ tuples in $r$ contain both $a$ and $b$ in attribute sets $X$ and $Y$. The confidence of the rule is $c$ ($c \leq 1$, a percentage) if $c$ of all tuples that contain $a$ also contain $b$. This is called a boolean association rule problem [8]. Usually, minimal threshold of support and confidence are given before the mining operation starts and only those rules whose supports and confidences are higher than the minimal threshold are selected as useful rules.

A more general form of association rule, the quantitative association rule [8], or interval association rule [9], is defined as an implication $A \Rightarrow B$, $A$ is a vector of intervals each of which is in one of the attributes in $X$. $B$ is defined similarly with respect to $Y$. The support of the rule is $s$ if $s$ tuples fall in intervals of $A$ when projected to $X$ and also fall in intervals of $B$ when projected to $Y$. The confidence of the rule is $c$ ($c \leq 1$, a percentage) if $c$ of all the tuples that fall in intervals in $A$ also fall in intervals in $B$.

## 1.1 A Motivating Example

A large corporation schedules and implements hundreds of projects each year to improve its productivity and quality of its products. An association rule mining is done to help company management to better understand how the company's business is benefiting from these projects.

To keep discussion simple, assume the relational table to be mined has only four attributes: budget, time, productivity, and quality. Each row in the table represents a project. The budget entry of the row contains the amount of funds spent on the project. The time entry contains the length of time to complete the project. The productivity entry contains measurable relative productivity improvement in some parts of company's business due to the completion of the project. The quality entry contains measurable relative quality improvements in some of the company's products and services.

For each row in the table, budget and time entries represent a point (budget,time) in a two dimensional space and productivity and quality entries also represent a point (productivity,quality) in another two dimensional space.

A mined quantitative association has the form $A \Rightarrow B$, where $A$ is a set of points in the budget-time space and $B$ is a set of points in the productivity-quality space. Under the definition of quantitative association rule, $A$ and $B$ have to be in rectangles [8]. However, this example clearly shows that the restriction to rectangles is not necessary.

## 1.2 Contributions of This Paper

The initial motivation of this paper is that this "cubic" shape restriction of the antecedent and consequent of the quantitative association rule should be removed. This is necessary because in the real world, the actual shape of the antecedent and consequent may not be in "cubic" shape. By removing this restriction, a spectrum of association rules are defined in this paper. The most general form, i.e., the generic form of the the association rule definition is free of any "shape" restriction and this type of rules are shown to be useful by the above example. The shape concept is introduced into the association rule only after some kind of measurement is used. Different measurements can be used to define different forms of (fuzzy) association rules, from the most generic rule to the simplest rule, i.e., boolean association rule.

This paper also explores the similarity between boolean association rule and the classical functional dependency. For a relation schema $R$ and an instance $r$

(a dataset) of $R$, let attribute set $X \subseteq R$, and $Y \subseteq R$. If $Y$ depends on $X$ in the sense of classical functional dependency, written as $X \to Y$, then this classical functional dependency may contain a set of boolean association rules. It is easy to compute these rules: if a value $a$ appears in the attribute set $X$ of a sufficient number (above a threshold) of tuples, and $b$ is the value in $Y$ corresponds (on the same tuple as) to $a$, then $a \Rightarrow b$ is a boolean association rule. The support of this rule is sufficient and the confidence of this rule is 100%.

Still another interesting discovery is that this relationship between functional dependency and association rule exists parallelly between fuzzy functional dependency and fuzzy association rules.

Graphically, a boolean association rule can be represented by two points in a two dimensional space (details will be discussed later in this paper). This graphical representation can be extended to quantitative and the more general fuzzy association rules by using clusters of points on a two dimensional space.

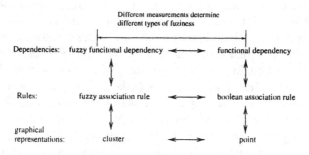

**Fig. 1.** Sketch of Relationships Discussed in the Paper

As sketched in Fig.1, a number of relationships are discussed in this paper. These concepts and their relationships form a symmetric grid, which we called data association spectrum. The details of this spectrum will be discussed in the following sections.

The significance of such a spectrum is that it provides some insight into the relationship among these concepts. For example, it is known that association rules can be mined by using some scanning algorithm such as Apriori algorithm, and it is also known that some spatial clustering algorithms can be used to find clusters. From this spectrum, it is clear that fuzzy association rules can be mined by using some spatial clustering algorithms. So, one practical implication of the establishment of the data association spectrum is that it can help to solve some practical mining problems such as to find·appropriate mining algorithms to some particular rule mining problems.

Compared to other extensions such as H-rule [10] which extends the association rule concept to data associations across multiple relations, the focus of the current paper is that it extends the set-to-set (which includes the point-to-point boolean association rule [1] as a special case) association rule within a single relational (or transactional) dataset to the most generalized form: the generic form, as defined in Section 2.

Section 2 defines the generic form of the fuzzy association rule. Section 3 discusses some measurements that will be used in further specifying fuzzy association rules. Section 4 defines some more specific fuzzy association rules using measurements. Section 5 explores the relationship between fuzzy functional dependencies and fuzzy association rules. Section 6 explores the relationship between fuzzy association rules and clusters. Section 7 concludes the paper with some insight to the nature of the association rule mining problem.

# 2 Fuzzy Association Rule (Generic Form)

## 2.1 A Geometric View of the Association Rule

Supermarket basket data are frequently used in the discussions of the association rule mining. A basket dataset is composed of a large number of shopping records. Assume the support threshold is set to 800 for a boolean association rule mining problem, and the confidence threshold is set to 50%. Suppose there are total of 1,200 customers bought cake mix and total of 1,000 customers bought both cake mix and cake icing. (cake mix) $\Rightarrow$ (cake icing) is a boolean association rule with support 1,000, and confidence $1,000/1,200 = 83.3\%$. This rule has a geometric interpretation in a XY space. For X, 1 is used to denote a shopping record containing cake mix. For Y, 1 is used to denote "buy cake icing" and 0 to denote "not buy cake icing". This rule can be viewed as involving two points, (1,1) and (1,0). The support 1,000, interpreted geometrically, means that there are 1,000 overlapped dots (1,1) in XY space. The confidence 83.3%, interpreted geometrically, means that 83.3% of all dots, whose projection on subspace X is 1, are at (1,1).

More generally, a data set $r$ (such as the basket dataset) can be viewed as a set of dots in a $m$-dimensional space $R = \{X_1, X_2, ..., X_m\}$. In the case of basket data, $m$ is the number of different type of goods in the supermarket. An attribute, or a set of attributes can be viewed as a subspace of $R$. Let $A \Rightarrow B$ be an association rule, where $A$ and $B$ are individual values or vectors in some subspaces of $R$. Also suppose $A$ is in subspace $X(\subseteq R$, $X$ represents a subset of goods in the market) and $B$ is in subspace $Y(\subseteq R)$. Conceptually, there are two sets of axes, one for X and one for Y. A boolean association rule only involves two points in space $R$. A quantitative association rule [8] or an interval association rule [9] involves high dimensional cubes, one on the axes of $X$ with dimension $|X|$ (the number of attributes in $X$) and the other on the axes of $Y$ with dimension $|Y|$.

With this geometric interpretation, one can see that in association rules such as the quantitative association rule, the "cubic" shape of the antecedent and the consequent is subjective. This observation motivates a more generalized definition of association rule.

## 2.2 The Generic Form of Association Rules

Support and confidence are two basic conditions in the definition of association rules. These two conditions should exist in the more generalized association rule definition. In the following discussion, $P_1[X]$ denotes the projection of $P_1$, which is in space $R$, into subspace $X$.

**Definition 1: Fuzzy Association Rule (Generic Form)**
$R$ is a relation schema with $m$ attributes. $X \subset R; Y \subset R$. $f_x$ is a strength function on $X$ and $f_y$ is a strength function on $Y$. $\alpha_x$ and $\alpha_y$ are support thresholds. $\beta$ is a confidence threshold. Also, let $P_1$ and $P_2$ be two sets of ($m - dimensional$) points in $R$, $P_1[X] \subseteq P_2[X]$.
A fuzzy association rule $P_2[X] \Rightarrow P_1[Y]$ holds if the following two conditions are satisfied:

1. (support condition) If $f_x(P_1[X]) \geq \alpha_x$, $f_y(P_1[Y]) \geq \alpha_y$.
2. (confidence condition) If $f_x(P_1[X])/f_y(P_1[Y]) \geq \beta$.

This generic form of association rule is free of any "shape" restrictions on the antecedent or consequent of the rule. If the antecedent and consequent are restricted to cubes, this generic form of association rule can be reduced to the quantitative association rule [8] and interval association rule [9]. In practice, the kind of restrictions applied to this generic form can be tailored to the needs of particular applications.

The restriction can be achieved by providing measurement (distance) in the $m$ dimensional space $R$. Intuitively, by varying the type of measurement used, one can "carve" different shapes of the antecedent and consequent. For example, in a two dimensional space, a distance $D_1(p_1, p_2) = \mid x_1 - x_2 \mid + \mid y_1 - y_2 \mid$ defined between two points $p_1 = (x_1, y_1)$ and $p_2 = (x_2, y_2)$ carves out a rectangular shaped fuzzy association rule. A distance $D_2(p_1, p_2) = \sqrt{(x_1 - x_2)^2 + (y_1 - y_2)^2}$ carves out a circular shaped fuzzy association rule.

As this paper focuses on establishing the concept frame work for a spectrum of fuzzy association rules, a particular shaped fuzzy association rule and its usefulness in practical applications is not elaborated here. One of the shapes, the rectangular shape, corresponds to quantitative association rule [8] and is recognized as a useful type of rule.

## 3 Combining Measurements

Before discussing the fuzzy association rules defined by using measurements and even before the discussion of various measurements, the combination of measurements is discussed first. A combining operation defines a measurement in the high dimensional space by combining measurements in the lower dimensional spaces. A well defined combining operation is needed because the number of dimensions should not affect the definition of a fuzzy rule. In other words, a fuzzy rule defined using a particular type of measurement in a low dimensional space should use the same type of measurement, after combination, in the high dimensional space. The following definition is adopted and modified from the fuzzy EQ relation in [4]:

**Definition 2: Measurement**
*Let R be a relation schema, r be a relation over R, and $X \subseteq R$. Then, D is a measurement in X if*
1. $D(a,a) = 0, \forall a \in X.$ *a could be $\perp$ (undefined).*
2. $D(a,b) > 0, \forall a,b \in X, a \neq b.$
3. $D(a,b) = D(b,a), \forall a,b \in X.$

The second condition is needed to ensure that decompositions over fuzzy functional dependency have the lossless join property, as proved in [4].

There are many ways to combine measurements defined in lower dimensional subspaces into measurement in higher dimensional space. We define the most general form of combining operation as:

**Definition 3: Combination Measurement (Generic Form)**
*Let $R(A_1, A_2, ..., A_n)$ be a relation schema, r be a relation over R, and tuples $t_1, t_2 \in r$. Let measurements $D_1, D_2, ..., D_k$ be defined on mutually non-intersecting subschemas (subspaces) of R: $S_1, S_2, ..., S_k$, respectively. Then, the combination measurement D is defined as*

$$D(t_1, t_2) = f(D_1(t_1[S_1], t_2[S_1]), ..., D_k(t_1[S_k], t_2[S_k])). \qquad (1)$$

*where f is a function of k positive variables and satisfies the following conditions:*
1. $f = 0,$ *if all the variables are equal to zero.*
2. $f > 0,$ *if at least one of the variables is nonzero.*
3. $f(a_1, a_2, ..., a_k) \geq f(0, ..., 0, a_i, 0, ..., 0),$ *i = 1, 2, ..., k.*

Depending upon how $f$ is defined, there can be many different variations of the combining operation for measurements. For example, if $f$ is a function using maximum, i.e., $f = max(*, *, ..., *)$, then the combining operation is the same as in [4–6]. We define two particular combining operations as presented below:

**Definition 4: Combination Measurement (MAX)**
*Let $R(A_1, A_2, ..., A_n)$ be a relation schema. Let measurements $D_1, D_2, ..., D_k$ be defined on mutually non-intersecting subschemas (subspaces) of R: $S_1, S_2, ..., S_k$, respectively. Then, a combination measurement D can be defined as*

$$D(t_1, t_2) = max\{D_1(t_1[S_1], t_2[S_1]), ..., D_k(t_1[S_k], t_2[S_k])\}. \qquad (2)$$

**Definition 5: Combination Measurement (MUL)**
*Let $R(A_1, A_2, ..., A_n)$ be a relation schema. Let measurements $D_1, D_2, ..., D_k$ be defined on mutually non-intersecting subschemas (subspaces) of R: $S_1, S_2, ..., S_k$, respectively. Then, a combination measurement D can be defined as*

$$D(t_1, t_2) = \sqrt{(D_1(t_1[S_1], t_2[S_1])^2 + ... + D_k(t_1[S_k], t_2[S_k])^2)} \qquad (3)$$

The following definition is also adopted from [4]. It is nothing more than a formal and short way of saying that the tuple is meaningful in subspace X. This definition is needed for the convenience of subsequent rule definitions.

**Definition 6: X–defined**
*Let $R = (X_1, X_2, ..., X_n)$, and each $X_i$ has data domain $dom(A_i)$, $i = 1, 2, ... , n$. Also, $X \subseteq R$. A tuple $t = (a_1, a_2, ..., a_n)$ is X-defined, if for each attribute $X_i \in X$, $t[X_i] \neq \perp$ (undefined).*

Also, for convenience of reference, we call a volume which contains a data point $p$ a *neighborhood* of $p$ and denote it by $\delta(p)$. This notion is needed in the subsequent definition for defining a cluster (a dense set of points) centered around a central point.

A particular neighborhood can be defined by using a particular form of measurement. Let $R$ be a relation schema, subschema (subspace) $X \subseteq R$, $r$ be an instance (a dataset) of $R$, a tuple $t_0 \in r$, and $D$ be a measurement defined on subspace $X$. Let $c > 0$ be a constant, then $t_0[X]$ can have a neighborhood defined as

$$\{t[X] \mid \quad D(t[X], t_0[X]) < c\} \tag{4}$$

## 4 Some Specific Fuzzy Association Rules

This section discusses several measurement definitions and the resulting measurement based definitions of fuzzy association rules. Each measurement based definition of fuzzy association rule is a particular case of the generic form of fuzzy association rule defined in the last section.

**Definition 7: Fuzzy Association Rule (Neighborhood)**
*Let $r$ be a relation over schema $R$, and subschemas (subspaces) $X, Y \subset R$. Given an XY-defined tuple $t_0 \in r$, a neighborhood $NX(t_0[X])$ of $t_0[X]$ in subspace $X$ and a neighborhood $NY(t_0[Y])$ of $t_0[Y]$ in subspace $Y$, a density function $f$ defined on both $X$ and $Y$, $\delta_X > 0$, $\delta_Y > 0$, $\alpha > 0$, $\beta > 0$. A fuzzy association rule $t_0[X] \Rightarrow t_0[Y]$ holds in $r$ if all of the following four conditions are satisfied:*

1. *(cluster condition in X)$f(S_1[X]) \geq \delta_X$, where $S_1 = \{t \mid t[X] \in NX(t_0[X])\}$.*
2. *(cluster condition in Y) $f(S_2[Y]) \geq \delta_Y$, where $S_2 = \{t \mid t[Y] \in NX(t_0[Y])\}$.*
3. *(support condition) $n_1 = \mid \{t \mid t$ is XY-defined, $t[X] \in NX(t_0[X]), t[Y] \in NY(t_0[Y])\} \mid \geq \alpha$.*
4. *(confidence condition) $n_1/n_2 \geq \beta$, where $n_2 = \mid \{t \mid t$ is X-defined, $t[X] \in NX(t_0[X])\} \mid$.*

Compared to Definition 1, the first two are extra conditions intended to make the antecedent and consequent "dense" enough so that the rule is useful in practical situations. The last two conditions are just the same support and confidence condition being defined more specifically in terms of neighborhoods. The set $S_1$ is called the rule base, $NX(t_0[X])$ is the body of the rule base, the set $S_2$ is the rule target, $NY(t_0[Y])$ is the body of the rule target, $\{t \mid t$ is XY–defined, $t[X] \in NX(t_0[X]), t[Y] \in NY(t_0[Y])\}$ the rule support set, and the combined neighborhood $NX(t_0[X]) \times NY(t_0[Y])$ in subspace XY is the body of the rule support set. The body concept is the generalization of the high dimensional cube concept used in the quantitative association rule [8].

If the shape of a neighborhood is a cube in a high dimensional subspace, the restricted rule is exactly the quantitative association rule [8] or interval association rule [9]. Also, a single rule definition may use more than one measurement as the next example shows.

### Definition 8: Fuzzy Association Rule (Measurement)
*Let $r$ be a relation over schema $R$ and subschemas (subspaces) $X, Y \subset R$. Let $D_1$ be a measurement on $X$ and $D_2$ be a measurement on $Y$. $c > 0$, $\alpha > 0$, $\beta > 0$, $\delta > 0$ are given. Let tuple $t_0$ be $XY$–defined. A fuzzy association rule $t_0[X] \Rightarrow t_0[Y]$ holds in $r$ if:*

- *(support condition) $s \geq \alpha$, where*
  *$s = |\ \{\ t \mid t$ is $XY$–defined and $D_1(t[X], t_0[X]) \geq c * D_2(t[Y], t_0[Y])$, $D_1(t[X], t_0[X]) \leq \delta\}\ |$.*
- *(confidence condition) $s/b \geq \beta$, where $s$ is defined above, and*
  *$b = |\ \{t \mid D_1(t[X], t_0[X]) \leq \delta\}\ |$.*

The support and the confidence conditions can be changed by varying $\delta$ (support threshold) and $\beta$ (confidence threshold), and also by varying $c$ (strength of the implication).

## 5    Fuzzy Dependencies and Fuzzy Rules

The Definition 8 for the fuzzy association rule is very similar to that of the fuzzy functional dependency defined in [4–6], except that the inequality may not hold for all data points in XY.

In Definition 8, if the minimum support condition is dropped and the inequality holds for all data points in XY, the result is an exact definition of fuzzy functional dependency:

### Definition 9: Fuzzy Functional Dependency (Generic Form)
*Let $r$ be a relation over $R$. $X, Y \subset R$. A fuzzy functional dependency (ffd) $X \hookrightarrow Y$ holds in $r$ if for all tuples $t_1, t_2 \in r$, $t_1[X] \in NX(t_2[X])$, or $t_2[X] \in NX(t_1[X])$ implies that either both $t_1[Y]$ and $t_2[Y]$ are undefined or there is a subspace $Y'$ of $Y$, $t_1[Y'] \in NY'(t_2[Y])$ or $t_2[Y'] \in NY'(t_1[Y])$.*

Definition 9 is more general than previously defined fuzzy functional dependencies in [4–6] because the more general concept of neighborhood is used.

**Definition 10: Fuzzy Functional Dependency (Measurement)**
*Let r be a relation over schema R, and $X, Y \subset R$, $D_1$ is a measurement on X and $D_2$ is a measurement on Y. $c > 0$ is a constant. A fuzzy functional dependency (ffd) $X \hookrightarrow Y$ holds in r if for all X–defined tuples $t_1, t_2 \in r$,*

$$D_1(t_1[X], t_2[X]) \geq c * D_2(t_1[Y], t_2[Y]) \tag{5}$$

The above definition includes both cases in the definition of fuzzy functional dependency in [4]. To be specific, in [4], for defining fuzzy functional dependency, the conditions that $t_1$ and $t_2$ should be satisfied are one of the following:

1. If there exists a nonempty set $Y' \subseteq Y$, such that $t_1[Y''] \neq \bot$, $t_2[Y''] \neq \bot$, for each $Y'' \in Y'$, and $t_1[Y\text{-}Y'] = t_2[Y\text{-}Y'] = \bot$, then, $t_1$ and $t_2$ should satisfy:

$$D_1(t_1[X], t_2[X]) \geq D_2(t_1[Y'], t_2[Y']) \tag{6}$$

This case is included in our definition.
2. If $t_1[Y] = t_2[Y] = \bot$.
   In this case, we have $D_2(t_1[Y], t_2[Y]) = 0$ according to our measurement definition. So, $D_1(t_1[X], t_2[X]) \geq c * D_2(t_1[Y], t_2[Y])$ will hold.

Definition 10 not only includes previous definition of fuzzy functional dependency, with the use of threshold c, definition 10 is also more generalized.

If the underlying relation is not a fuzzy one, but a classical relation, fuzzy functional dependency will reduce to the classical functional dependency. Therefore, our definition of the fuzzy functional dependency, being a more general one than that in [4], is indeed a generalization of the classical functional dependency.

Comparing definitions 8 and 10, we can see that the fuzzy association rule and the fuzzy functional dependency are so closely related, that the essential difference is just that the fuzzy functional dependency is an assertion over all data points of the subspace.

## 6 Fuzzy Association Rules and Clusters

We can also define clusters using measurement. The following is one of the cluster definitions:

**Definition 11: Cluster (Measurement)**
Let X be a subspace of R, i.e., $X \subseteq R$. Let D be a measurement defined on X, $\alpha > 0$ and $\delta > 0$ are given. A cluster in X is a set of points $p_1, p_2, ..., p_k$ such that $D(p_i, p_j) \leq \delta$, $\forall$ i, j = 1, 2, ..., k, and $k \geq \alpha$.

As shown in Fig.2, a fuzzy association rule can be viewed as a special cluster which crosses two different subspaces. Assume $r$ is an instance of schema $R$, and $X, Y \subset R$. Let $D_x$ and $D_y$ be measurements on $X$ and $Y$, respectively. Suppose Definition 8 is used as the definition of the fuzzy association rule, and $D_x$, $D_y$ as measurements in $X$ and $Y$, strength of implication is $c > 0$, rule base quality is $\delta > 0$, support threshold is $\alpha$, and confidence threshold is $\beta$.

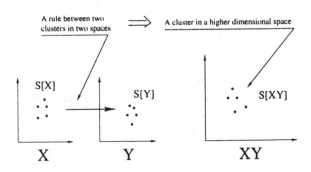

**Fig. 2.** Rules and Clusters

Let $S$ be a set of tuples in $r$ satisfying a fuzzy association rule $S[X] \Rightarrow S[Y]$ under definition 8, i.e., $\forall p_i, p_j \in S$, $p_i$ and $p_j$ satisfy: $D_x(p_i[X], p_j[X]) < \delta$, $c * D_y(p_i[Y], p_j[Y]) < D_x(p_i[X], p_j[X])$, and $\mid S[XY] \mid = s > \alpha$. If we take $delta_{cluster} = \max\{delta, delta/c\}$ and $\alpha_{cluster} = \mid S[XY] \mid$, then, $S[XY]$ is also a cluster under definition 11 with parameters $delta_{cluster}$ and $\alpha_{cluster}$.

This kind of association between fuzzy association rules and clusters is useful in computation. Let's return to the motivating example at the beginning of this paper. The distribution of the data points in space X = (budget, time) are uneven. It is dense in some areas and sparse in others and similar situation exists for space Y = (productivity, quality). It is computationally efficient to first find all clusters in X and Y, respectively. Then, only for those acceptable clusters (which are dense enough and the count of data points are large enough) we try to match them into fuzzy association rules. In this particular example, a fast clustering algorithm, with some modification, can be used as a fuzzy association rule mining algorithm.

## 7   Conclusion and Future Work

This paper proposed the concept of the fuzzy association rule, which is the most generalized form of the set-to-set association rule within a single relational dataset (this can be easily translated into transactional dataset and vice versa), explored the essential commonalities as well as differences between functional dependencies and association rules, and the relationship between fuzzy association rules and clusters.

| Topological | Measurement based | single point |
|---|---|---|
| fuzzy funcitonal depdendency (Generic) | fuzzy functional dependency (measurement) | functional depdendency |
| fuzzy association rule (Generic) | fuzzy association rule (measurement) | association rule |
| cluster (Generic) | cluster (measurement) | point |
| | clustering algorithms | exhaustive scan algorithms (Apriori, etc.) |

**Fig. 3.** Data Association Spectrum

For very large databases, the concept of fuzzy association rule is very useful in two ways. First, the fuzziness allows data miners to concentrate on clusters instead of individual data points. Second, sometimes the fuzziness reflects more faithfully to the real world complexity because in many cases, the relationship between data are fuzzy by nature, and we would lose insight to the nature of the problem if we only concentrate on small details.

The concept of functional dependency can take various forms. By using various definitions of measurements (distance measure), various forms of functional dependencies can be obtained. All these different forms of functional dependency constitute a spectrum of concepts, from the most abstract concept of fuzzy functional dependency to the simplest concept of classical functional dependency commonly used in the relational database theory. This concept spectrum may be called fuzzy functional dependency spectrum and is represented by the second row in Fig.3.

Similarly, the association rules can take various forms. By using different definitions of measurements, different forms of association rules can be obtained. The most abstract concept among them is the generic form of fuzzy association rule defined in Section 2 and the simplest one is the boolean association rule [1]. The quantitative [8] and the interval association rules [9] are two of the concepts somewhere in the middle of this spectrum of concepts. We call this spectrum the fuzzy association rule spectrum and is represented by the third row in Fig.3.

The concept of the most abstract form of fuzzy functional dependency is closely related to the most abstract form of fuzzy association rule. The various forms of fuzzy functional dependencies defined by using various kinds of measurement are closely related to the fuzzy association rules defined by using the same kind of measurement. This parallelism suggests that these two concept spectra can be put into a common data association spectrum, as shown in Fig.3.

Also, by varying the definition of measurement, various clusters can be obtained. There is also a similar spectrum exist in the definition of clusters from the most general one, i.e., the topological one, to the singlest one, i.e., a point. We call this a cluster spectrum and is represented by the fourth row in Fig.3.

Together, all three concept spectra constitute a bigger spectrum, which we call data association spectrum. What is achieved here is a deeper understanding to the nature of a series of problems such as association rule mining and clustering and their relationships. For example, between the concept of fuzzy functional dependency and cluster, there is a concept of fuzzy association rule (because functional dependency is data value association on the whole dataset and association rule is data value association on partial dataset). So, if a clustering algorithm cannot even be used in mining any fuzzy association rules, it cannot be used to find any fuzzy functional dependencies.

There is a whole spectrum of practical problems that can be regarded as fuzzy association rule mining problems. Because of the complexity of fuzzy association rule mining problem, there is still a lot to be explored such as the different types of the fuzzy association rules, the interestingness issues in fuzzy association rule mining, and new data mining algorithms for discovering fuzzy association rules.

# References

1. Agrawal, R., Imielinski, T., Swami, A.: Mining Association Rules Between Sets of Items in Large Databases. In Proc. (ACM SIGMOD) Int'l Conference on Management of Data, (1993), 207-216.
2. Agrawal, R., Srikant, R.: Fast Algorithm for Mining Association Rules. In Proc. 20th VLDB (1994), 478-499.
3. Han, J., Cai, Y., Cercone, N.: Data-Driven Discovery of Quantitative Rules in Relational Databases. In IEEE Translations on Knowledge and Data Engineering, (1993), 5(1): 29-40.
4. Saxena, P.C., Tyagi, B.K.: Fuzzy Functional Dependencies and Independencies in Extended Fuzzy Relational Database Models. In Fuzzy Sets and Systems 69 (1995), 65-89.
5. Liu, W.-Y.: Extending the Relational Model to Deal with Fuzzy Values. In Fuzzy Sets and Systems 60 (1993), 207-212.
6. Raju, K., Majumdar, A.: Fuzzy Functional Dependencies and Lossless Join Decomposition of Fuzzy Relational Database Systems. In ACM Transactions on Database Systems, Vol. 13, No.2, 1988.
7. Piatetsky-Shapiro, G.: Discovery, Analysis, and Presentation of Strong Rules. In Knowledge Discovery in Databases. Editors G. P.-Shapiro and W. J. Frawley, AAAI Press/MIT Press, (1991) 229-248.
8. Srikant, R., Agrawal, R.: Mining Quantitative Association Rules in Large Relational Tables. In Proc. (ACM SIGMOD) Int'l Conference on Management of Data, (1996), 1-12.
9. Miller, R.J., Yang, Y: Association Rules over Interval Data. In Proc. (ACM SIGMOD) Int'l Conference on Management of Data, (1997).
10. Yang, Y., Singhal, M: H-Rule Mining in Heterogeneous Databases. In Proc. of The Third Pacific-Asia Conference on Knowledge Discovery and Data Mining, published in Lecture Notes in Artificial Intelligence 1574, Methodologies for Knowledge Discovery and Data Mining, by Springer-Verlag, (1999), 99-103.

# Performance Evaluation and Optimization of Join Queries for Association Rule Mining*

Shiby Thomas**          Sharma Chakravarthy

Database Systems Research and Development Center
Computer and Information Science and Engineering Department
University of Florida, Gainesville FL 32611
email: {sthomas, sharma}@cise.ufl.edu

**Abstract.** The explosive growth in data collection in business organizations introduces the problem of turning these rapidly expanding data stores into nuggets of actionable knowledge. The state-of-the-art data mining tools available for this integrate loosely with data stored in DBMSs, typically through a cursor interface. In this paper, we consider several formulations of association rule mining (a typical data mining problem) using SQL-92 queries and study the performance of different join orders and join methods for executing them. We analyze the cost of the different execution plans which provides a basis to incorporate the semantics of association rule mining into future query optimizers. Based on them we identify certain optimizations and develop the Set-oriented Apriori approach. This work is an initial step towards developing "SQL-aware" mining algorithms and exploring the enhancements to current relational DBMSs to make them "mining-aware" thereby bridging the gap between the two.

## 1 Introduction

A large number of business organizations are installing data warehouses based on relational database technology and it is extremely important to be able to mine nuggets of useful and understandable information from these data warehouses. The initial efforts in data mining research were to cull together techniques from machine learning and statistics to define new mining operations and develop algorithms for them. A majority of the mining algorithms were built for data stored in file systems and coupling with DBMSs was provided through ODBC or SQL cursor interface. However, integrating mining with relational databases is becoming increasingly important with the growth in relational data warehousing technology.

There have been several research efforts recently aimed at tighter integration of mining with database systems. On the one hand, there have been several language proposals to extend SQL with specialized mining operators. A few examples are DMQL [4], M-SQL [6] and the *Mine rule* operator [7]. However, these proposals do not address the processing techniques for these operators inside a database engine. On the other hand, researchers have addressed the issue

* This work was supported in part by the Office of Naval Research and the SPAWAR System Center – San Diego, by the Rome Laboratory, DARPA, and the NSF Grant IRI-9528390
** Current affiliation: Oracle Corporation, New England Development Center, One Oracle Drive, Nashua, NH 03062, USA. Email: shthomas@us.oracle.com

of exploiting the capabilities of conventional relational systems and their object-relational extensions to execute mining operations. This entails transforming the mining operations into database queries and in some cases developing newer techniques that are more appropriate in the database context. The UDF-based (user defined function) approach in [2], the SETM algorithm [5], the formulation of association rule mining as "query flocks" [10] and SQL queries for mining [9] all belong to this category.

Two categories of SQL implementations for association rule mining – one based purely on SQL-92 and the other using the object-relational extensions to SQL (SQL-OR) – are presented in [9]. The experimental results show that SQL-OR outperforms SQL-92 for most of the datasets. However, the object-relational extensions like table functions and user-defined functions (UDFs) used in the SQL-OR approaches are not yet standardized across the major DBMS vendors and hence portability could suffer. Moreover, optimization and parallelization of the object-relational extensions could be harder.

In this paper, we analyze the performance of the various SQL-92 approaches and study the implications of different join orders and join methods. The motivation for this study is to understand how best can we do with SQL-92. We derive cost formulae for the different approaches in terms of the relational operators and the input data parameters. These cost expressions can be used in any cost based optimizer. Based on the performance experiments and the cost formulae, we identify certain optimizations and develop the Set-oriented Apriori approach that performs better than the best SQL-92 approach in [9]. We also study the scale-up properties of Set-oriented Apriori.

The rest of the paper is organized as follows: We review association rule mining and a few SQL formulations of it in Section 2. In Section 3, we present a cost based analysis of the SQL approaches. Section 4 presents the performance optimizations and their impact on the execution cost and discusses the Set-oriented Apriori approach. We report the results of some of our performance experiments in Section 5 and conclude in Section 6.

## 2 Association Rules

Association rules capture recurring patterns in large databases of transactions, each of which is a set of items. The intuitive meaning of a typical association rule $X \rightarrow Y$, where $X$ and $Y$ are sets of items, is that the items in $X$ and $Y$ tend to co-occur in the transactions. An example of such a rule might be that "60% of transactions that contain beer also contain diapers; 5% of all transactions contain both these items". Here 60% is called the *confidence* of the rule and 5% the *support* of the rule. The problem of mining association rules is to find *all* rules that satisfy a user-specified minimum support and confidence threshold. This problem can be decomposed into two subproblems of finding the *frequent* itemsets (item combinations with minimum support) and generating the rules from them [1].

### 2.1 Apriori Algorithm

The basic Apriori algorithm [3] for discovering frequent itemsets makes multiple passes over the data. In the $k$th pass it finds all itemsets having $k$ items called the $k$-itemsets. Each pass consists of two phases – the candidate generation phase and the support counting phase. In the candidate generation phase, the set of frequent $(k - 1)$-itemsets, $F_{k-1}$ is used to generate the set of potentially frequent candidate $k$-itemsets, $C_k$. The support counting phase counts the support of all the itemsets in $C_k$ by examining the transactions and retains the itemsets having the minimum support. The algorithm terminates when $C_{k+1}$ becomes empty.

## 2.2 Apriori candidate generation using SQL

We briefly outline the SQL-based candidate generation process in [9] here. $C_k$ is obtained by joining two copies of $F_{k-1}$ as:

insert into $C_k$ select $I_1.item_1, \ldots, I_1.item_{k-1}, I_2.item_{k-1}$
from      $F_{k-1}\ I_1, F_{k-1}\ I_2$
where     $I_1.item_1 = I_2.item_1$ and $\ldots$ and $I_1.item_{k-2} = I_2.item_{k-2}$ and
             $I_1.item_{k-1} < I_2.item_{k-1}$

The join result which is a set of $k$-itemsets is further pruned using the subset pruning strategy that all subsets of a frequent itemset should be frequent. The subset pruning can be accomplished in SQL by additional joins with $(k-2)$ more copies of $F_{k-1}$.

## 2.3 Support counting by K-Way joins

In this approach, the support counting is formulated as a join query. The transaction data is stored in a relational table $T$ with the schema *(tid, item)*. For a given tid, there are as many rows in $T$ as the number of items in that transaction. For real-life datasets, the maximum and minimum number of items per transaction differ a lot and the maximum number of items could even be more than the number of columns allowed for a table. Hence, this schema is more convenient than alternate representations. In the $k^{th}$ pass, $k$ copies of the transaction table T are joined with the candidate table $C_k$ and is followed up with a group by on the itemsets as shown in Figure 1. Note that the plan tree generated by the query processor could look quite different from the tree diagram shown below.

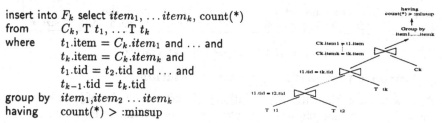

insert into $F_k$ select $item_1, \ldots item_k$, count(*)
from      $C_k$, T $t_1, \ldots$ T $t_k$
where    $t_1.item = C_k.item_1$ and $\ldots$ and
            $t_k.item = C_k.item_k$ and
            $t_1.tid = t_2.tid$ and $\ldots$ and
            $t_{k-1}.tid = t_k.tid$
group by   $item_1, item_2 \ldots item_k$
having    count(*) > :minsup

**Fig. 1.** Support Counting by K-way join

**Subquery optimization.** The basic KwayJoin approach can be optimized to make use of common prefixes between the itemsets in $C_k$ by splitting the support counting phase into a sequence of $k$ nested subqueries [9].

## 3 Analysis of execution plans

We experimented with a number of alternative execution plans for this query. We could force the query processor to choose different plans by creating different indices on $T$ and $C_k$, and in some cases by disabling certain join methods. We analyze two different execution plans below.

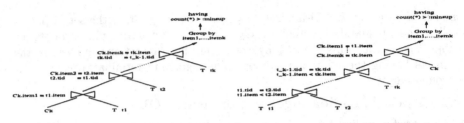

**Fig. 2.** K-way join plan with $C_k$ as outer relation

**Fig. 3.** K-way join plan with $C_k$ as inner relation

In the cost analysis, we use the mining-specific data parameters and knowledge about association rule mining (Apriori algorithm [3] in this case) to estimate the cost of joins and the size of join results. Even though current relational optimizers do not use this mining-specific semantic information, the analysis provides a basis for developing "mining-aware" optimizers. The cost formulae are presented in terms of operator costs in order to make them general; for instance join$(p, q, r)$ denotes the cost of joining two relations of size $p$ and $q$ to get a result of size $r$. The data parameters and operators used in the analysis are summarized in Table 1.

| $R$ | number of records in the input transaction table |
|---|---|
| $T$ | number of transactions |
| $N$ | average number of items per transaction $= \frac{R}{T}$ |
| $F_1$ | number of frequent items |
| $S(C)$ | sum of support of each itemset in set $C$ |
| $s_k$ | average support of a frequent $k$-itemset $= \frac{S(F_k)}{|F_k|}$ |
| $R_f$ | number of records out of $R$ involving frequent items $= S(F_1)$ |
| $N_f$ | average number of frequent items per transaction $= \frac{R_f}{T}$ |
| $C_k$ | number of candidate k-itemsets |
| $C(n, k)$ | number of $k$-combinations possible out of a set of size $n$: $= \frac{n!}{k!(n-k)!}$ |
| group$(n, m)$ | cost of grouping $n$ records out of which $m$ are distinct |
| join$(p, q, r)$ | cost of joining two relations of size $p$ and $q$ to get a result of size $r$ |

**Table 1.** Notations used in cost analysis

### 3.1 KwayJoin plan with $C_k$ as outer relation

Start with $C_k$ as the outermost relation and perform a series of joins with the $k$ copies of $T$. The final join result is grouped on the $k$ items to find the support counts (see Figure 2). The choice of join methods for each of the intermediate joins depends on the availability of indices, the size of intermediate results, amount of available memory etc. For instance, the efficient execution of nested loops joins require an index (*item, tid*) on $T$. If the intermediate join result is large, it could be advantageous to materialize it and perform sort-merge join.

For each candidate itemset in $C_k$, the join with $T$ produces as many records as the support of its first item. Similarly, the relation obtained after joining $C_k$ with $l$ copies of $T$ contain as many records as the sum of the support counts of the $l$-item prefixes of $C_k$. Hence the cost of the $l^{th}$ join is join$(C_k * s_{l-1}, R, C_k * s_l)$ where $s_0 = 1$. Note that values of the $s_i$'s can be computed from statistics collected in the previous passes. The last join (with $T_k$) produces $S(C_k)$ records

– there will be as many records for each candidate as its support. $S(C_k)$ can be estimated by adding the support estimates of all the itemsets in $C_k$. A good estimate for the support of a candidate itemset is the minimum of the support counts of all its subsets. The overall cost of this plan expressed in terms of operator costs is:

$$\{\sum_{l=1}^{k-1} \text{join}(C_k * s_{l-1}, R, C_k * s_l)\} + \text{join}(C_k * s_{k-1}, R, S(C_k)) + \text{group}(S(C_k), C_k)$$

## 3.2 KwayJoin plan with $C_k$ as inner relation

In this plan, we join the $k$ copies of $T$ and the resulting $k$-item combinations are joined with $C_k$ to filter out non-candidate item combinations. The final join result is grouped on the $k$-items (see Figure 3). The result of joining $l$ copies of $T$ is the set of all possible $l$-item combinations of transactions. We know that the items in the candidate itemset are lexicographically ordered and hence we can add extra join predicates as shown in Figure 3 to limit the join result to $l$-item combinations (without these extra predicates the join will result in $l$-item permutations). When $C_k$ is the outermost relation these predicates are not required. A mining-aware optimizer should be able to rewrite the query appropriately. The last join produces $S(C_k)$ records. The overall cost is:

$$\{\sum_{l=1}^{k-1} \text{join}(C(N,l) * T, R, C(N,l+1) * T)\} + \text{join}(C(N,k) * T, C_k, S(C_k)) +$$
$$\text{group}(S(C_k), C_k), \text{where} C(N,1) * T = R$$

## 3.3 Effect of subquery optimization

The subquery optimization (see [9] for the details) makes use of common prefixes among candidate itemsets. Unfolding all the subqueries will result in a query tree which structurally resembles the KwayJoin plan tree shown in Figure 2. Subquery $Q_l$ produces $d_k^l * s_l$ records where $d_k^j$ denotes the number of distinct $j$ item prefixes of $C_k$. In contrast, the $l^{th}$ join in the KwayJoin plan results in $C_k * s_l$ records. The total cost of this approach can be estimated as below where trijoin($p, q, r, s$) denotes the cost of joining three relations of size $p, q, r$ respectively producing a result of size $s$.

$$\{\sum_{l=1}^{k} \text{trijoin}(R, s_{l-1} * d_k^{l-1}, d_k^l, s_l * d_k^l)\} + \text{group}(S(C_k), C_k)$$

We observed tremendous performance improvements because of this optimization. The number of distinct $l$-item prefixes is much less compared to the total number of candidate itemsets. This results in correspondingly smaller intermediate tables as shown in the analysis above, which is the key to the performance gain.

**Experimental datasets.** We used synthetic data generated according to the procedure explained in [3] for our experiments. The results reported in this paper are for the datasets – T5.I2.D100K and T10.I4.D100K. (for scale-up experiments we used other datasets also). For example, the first dataset consists of 100 thousand transactions, each containing an average of 5 items. The average size of the maximal potentially frequent itemsets (denoted as $I$) is 2. The transaction table corresponding to this dataset had approximately 550 thousand records.

Both datasets had a total of 1000 items. The second dataset has 100 thousand transactions, each containing an average of 10 items (total of about 1.1 million records) and the average size of maximal potentially frequent itemsets is 4.

All the experiments were performed on PostgreSQL Version 6.3 [8], a public domain DBMS, installed on a 8 processor Sun Ultra Enterprise 4000/5000 with 248 MHz CPUs and 256 MB main memory per processor, running Solaris 2.6. Note that PostgreSQL is not parallelized. It supports nested loops, hash-based and sort-merge join methods and provides finer control of the optimizer to disable any of the join methods. We have found it to be a useful platform for studying the performance of different join methods and execution plans.

## 4 Performance optimizations

The cost analysis presented above provides some insight into the different components of the execution time in the different passes and what can be optimized to achieve better performance. In this section, we present three optimizations to the KwayJoin approach (other than the subquery optimization) and discuss how they impact the cost.

### 4.1 Pruning non-frequent items

The size of the transaction table is a major factor in the cost of joins involving $T$. It can be reduced by pruning the non-frequent items from the transactions after the first pass. We store the transaction data as (tid, item) tuples in a relational table and hence this pruning can be achieved simply by dropping the tuples corresponding to non-frequent items by joining $T$ and $F_1$. The pruned transactions are stored in table $T_f$ which has the same schema as that of $T$.

For some of the synthetic datasets we used in our experiments, this pruning reduced the size of the transaction table to about half its original size. This could be even more useful for real-life datasets which typically contains lots of non-frequent items. For example, some of the real-life datasets used for the experiments reported in [9] contained of the order of 100 thousand items out of which only a few hundred were frequent. Figure 4 shows the reduction in transaction table size due to this optimization for our experimental datasets. The initial size ($R$) and the size after pruning ($R_f$) for different support values are shown.

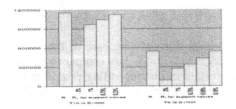 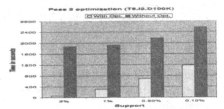

**Fig. 4.** Reduction in transaction table size by non-frequent item pruning   **Fig. 5.** Benefit of second pass optimization

### 4.2 Eliminating candidate generation in second pass

In the second pass, $C_2$ is almost a cartesian product of the two $F_1$s used to generate it and hence materializing it and joining with the $T$'s (or $T_f$'s)

could be expensive. The generation of $C_2$ can be completely eliminated by formulating the join query to find $F_2$ as below. The cost of second pass with this optimization is join($R_f$, $R_f$, $C(N_f, 2)$) + group($C(N_f, 2), C(F_1, 2)$). Even though the grouping cost remains the same, there is a big reduction from the basic KwayJoin approach in the join costs.

> insert into $F_2$ select p.item, q.item, count(*) from $T_f$ p, $T_f$ q
> where      p.tid = q.tid and p.item < q.item
> group by   p.item, q.item having count(*) > :minsup

Figure 5 compares the running time of the second pass with this optimization to the basic KwayJoin approach for the T5.I2.D100K dataset (similar trends were observed for other datasets also). For the KwayJoin approach, the best execution plan was the one which generates all 2-item combinations, joins them with the candidate set and groups the join result.

## 4.3 Set-oriented Apriori

The SQL formulations of association rule mining is based on generating item combinations in various ways and similar work is performed in all the different passes. Therefore, storing the item combinations and reusing them in subsequent passes will improve the performance especially in the higher passes. In the $k^{th}$ pass of the support counting phase, we generate a table $T_k$ which contains all $k$-item combinations that are candidates. $T_k$ has the schema $(tid, item_1, \ldots, item_k)$. We join $T_{k-1}$, $T_f$ and $C_k$ as shown below to generate $T_k$. The frequent itemsets $F_k$ is obtained by grouping the tuples of $T_k$ on the $k$ items and applying the minimum support filtering.

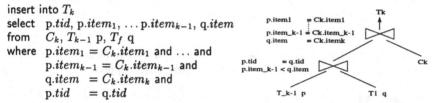

```
insert into Tk
select  p.tid, p.item₁, ... p.itemₖ₋₁, q.item
from    Cₖ, Tₖ₋₁ p, T_f q
where   p.item₁ = Cₖ.item₁ and ... and
        p.itemₖ₋₁ = Cₖ.itemₖ₋₁ and
        q.item  = Cₖ.itemₖ and
        p.tid   = q.tid
```

**Fig. 6.** Generation of $T_k$

We can further prune $T_k$ by filtering out item combinations that turned out to be non-frequent. However, this is not essential since we join it with the candidate set $C_{k+1}$ in the next pass to generate $T_{k+1}$. The only advantage of pruning $T_k$ is that we will have a smaller table to join in the next pass; but at the expense of joining $T_k$ with $F_k$. We use the optimization discussed above for the second pass and hence do not materialize and store $T_2$. Therefore, we generate $T_3$ directly by joining $T_f$ with $C_3$ as:

```
insert into T₃ select p.tid, p.item, q.item, r.item
from       T_f p, T_f q, T_f r, Cₖ
where      p.item = C₃.item₁ and q.item = C₃.item₂ and r.item = C₃.item₃
           and p.tid = q.tid and q.tid = r.tid
```

We can also use the Subquery approach to generate $T_3$ if that is less expensive. $T_3$ will contain exactly the same tuples produced by subquery $Q_3$.

The Set-oriented Apriori algorithm bears some resemblance with the three-way join approach in [9], the SETM algorithm in [5] and the AprioriTid algorithm in [3]. In the three-way join approach, the temporary table $T_k$ stores for each transaction, the identifiers of the candidates it supported. $T_k$ is generated by joining two copies of $T_{k-1}$ with $C_k$. The generation of $F_k$ requires a further join of $T_k$ with $C_k$. The candidate generation in SETM is different and hence the support counting queries are also different. The size of the intermediate tables $T_k$ generated by Set-oriented Apriori is much smaller compared to the corresponding ones of SETM. AprioriTid makes use of special data structures which are difficult to maintain in the SQL formulation.

**Cost comparison.** The $k^{th}$ pass of Set-oriented Apriori requires only a single 3-way join[3] due to the materialization and reuse of item combinations and the cost is $\text{trijoin}(R_f, T_{k-1}, C_k, S(C_k)) + \text{group}(S(C_k), C_k)$. The table $T_{k-1}$ contains exactly the same tuples as that of subquery $Q_{k-1}$ and hence has a size of $s_{l-1} * d_k^{l-1}$. Also, $d_k^k$ is the same as $C_k$. Therefore, the $k^{th}$ pass cost of Set-oriented Apriori is the same as the $k^{th}$ term in the join cost summation of the subquery approach.

Figure 7 compares the running times of the subquery and Set-oriented Apriori approaches for the dataset T10.I4.D100K for 0.33% support. We show only the times for passes 3 and higher since both the approaches are the same in the first two passes.

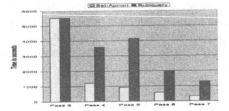
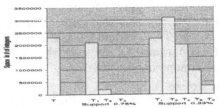

**Fig. 7.** Benefit of reusing item combinations

**Fig. 8.** Space requirements of the set-oriented apriori approach

**Space overhead.** Storing the item combinations requires additional space. The size of the table $T_k$ is the same as $S(C_k)$, which is the total support of all the $k$-item candidates. Assuming that the *tid* and *item* attributes are integers, each tuple in $T_k$ consists of $k + 1$ integer attributes. Therefore, the space requirement of $T_k$ is $|T_k| * (k+1)$. Figure 8 shows the size of $T_k$ in terms of number of integers, for the dataset T10.I4.D100K for two different support values. The space needed for the input data table $T$ is also shown for comparison. $T_2$ is not shown in the graph since we do not materialize and store it in the Set-oriented Apriori approach. Note that once $T_k$ is materialized $T_{k-1}$ can be deleted unless it needs to be retained for some other purposes.

## 5 Performance experiments

We compared the performance of Set-oriented Apriori with the Subquery approach (the best SQL-92 approach in [9]) for a wide range of data parameters and support values. We report the results on two of the datasets – T5.I2.D100K and T10.I4.D100K – described in Section 3.3.

---

[3] Note that this may be executed as two 2-way joins since 3-way joins are not generally supported in current relational systems.

Figure 9 shows the total time taken for each of the different passes of the Subquery and Set-oriented Apriori approaches. We ran the SETM algorithm [5] also for a few support values and found it to be an order of magnitude slower. Set-oriented Apriori performs better than Subquery for all the support values. The first two passes of both the approaches are similar and they take approximately equal amount of time. The difference widens for higher numbered passes as explained in Section 4.3. For T5.I2.D100K, $F_2$ was empty for support values higher than 0.3% and therefore we chose lower support values to study the relative performance in higher numbered passes.

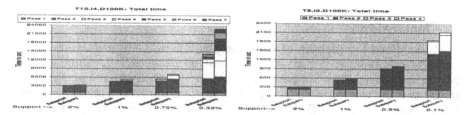

**Fig. 9.** Comparison of Subquery and Set-oriented Apriori approaches

In some cases, the optimizer did not choose the best plan. For example, for joins with $T$ ($T_f$ for Set-oriented Apriori), the optimizer chose nested loops plan using (item, tid) index on $T$ in many cases where the corresponding sort-merge plan was faster – an order of magnitude faster in some cases. We were able to experiment with different plans by disabling certain join methods (disabling nested loops join for the above case). We also broke down the multi-way joins into simpler two-way joins to study the performance implications. The reported times correspond to the best join order and join methods.

In all the experiments, we measured the CPU and I/O times separately. An interesting observation is that the I/O time is less than one third of the CPU time. This shows that there is a need to revisit the traditional optimization and parallelization strategies designed to optimize for I/O time, in order to handle the newer decision support and mining queries efficiently.

## 5.1 Scale-up Experiment

Figure 10 shows how Set-oriented Apriori scales up as the number of transactions is increased from 10,000 to 1 million. We used the datasets T5.I2 and T10.I4 for the average sizes of transactions and itemsets respectively. The minimum support level was kept at 1%. The first graph shows the absolute execution times and the second one shows the times normalized with respect to the times for the 10,000 transaction datasets. It can be seen that the scale-up is linear.

The scale-up with increasing transaction size is shown in Figure 11. In these experiments we kept the physical size of the database roughly constant by keeping the product of the average transaction size and the number of transactions constant. We fixed the minimum support level in terms of the number of transactions, since fixing it as a percentage would have led to large increases in the number of frequent itemsets as the transaction size increased. The numbers in the legend (e.g. 1000) refer to this minimum support. The execution times increase with the transaction size, but only gradually. The main reason for this increase was that the number of item combinations present in a transaction increases with the transaction size.

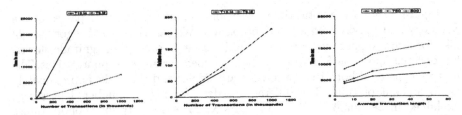

**Fig. 10.** Number of transactions scale-up

**Fig. 11.** Transaction size scale-up

## 6 Conclusion

We explored the problem of developing SQL-aware implementations of association rule mining. We analyzed the best available SQL-92 formulation – KwayJoin approach with Subquery optimization – primarily from a performance perspective and conducted detailed performance experiments to understand how well current relational DBMSs handle such queries. Based on the cost evaluation and the performance study we identify certain optimizations and develop a set-oriented version of the apriori algorithm. For the higher numbered passes, Set-oriented Apriori performs significantly better than the Subquery approach. The cost analysis presented in this paper points to useful enhancements to current optimizers to make them more "mining-aware". We also studied the scale-up behavior of Set-oriented Apriori with respect to increase in the number of transactions and average transaction size.

## References

1. R. Agrawal, T. Imielinski, and A. Swami. Mining association rules between sets of items in large databases. In *Proc. of the ACM SIGMOD Conference*, pages 207–216, Washington, D.C., May 1993.
2. R. Agrawal and K. Shim. Developing tightly-coupled data mining applications on a RDBMS. In *Proc. of the KDD Conference*, Portland, Oregon, August 1996.
3. R. Agrawal and R. Srikant. Fast Algorithms for Mining Association Rules. In *Proc. of the VLDB Conference*, Santiago, Chile, September 1994.
4. J. Han, Y. Fu, K. Koperski, W. Wang, and O. Zaiane. DMQL: A data mining query language for relational datbases. In *Proc. of the 1996 SIGMOD DMKD workshop, Montreal, Canada*, May 1996.
5. M. Houtsma and A. Swami. Set-oriented mining of association rules. In *Int'l Conference on Data Engineering*, Taipei, Taiwan, March 1995.
6. T. Imielinski, A. Virmani, and A. Abdulghani. Discovery Board Application Programming Interface and Query Language for Database Mining. In *Proc. of the KDD Conference*, Portland, Oregon, August 1996.
7. R. Meo, G. Psaila, and S. Ceri. A new SQL like operator for mining association rules. In *Proc. of the VLDB Conference*, Bombay, India, Sep 1996.
8. PostgreSQL Organization. *PostgreSQL 6.3 User Manual*, February 1998. http://www.postgresql.org.
9. S. Sarawagi, S. Thomas, and R. Agrawal. Integrating Association Rule Mining with Relational Database Systems: Alternatives and Implications. In *Proc. of the ACM SIGMOD Conference*, Seattle, Washington, June 1998.
10. S. Tsur, et al. Query Flocks: A Generalization of Association Rule Mining. In *Proc. of the ACM SIGMOD Conference*, Seattle, Washington, June 1998.

# Efficient Bulk Loading
# of Large High-Dimensional Indexes

Christian Böhm and Hans-Peter Kriegel

University of Munich, Oettingenstr. 67, D-80538 Munich, Germany
{boehm,kriegel}@informatik.uni-muenchen.de

**Abstract.** Efficient index construction in multidimensional data spaces is important for many knowledge discovery algorithms, because construction times typically must be amortized by performance gains in query processing. In this paper, we propose a generic bulk loading method which allows the application of user-defined split strategies in the index construction. This approach allows the adaptation of the index properties to the requirements of a specific knowledge discovery algorithm. As our algorithm takes into account that large data sets do not fit in main memory, our algorithm is based on external sorting. Decisions of the split strategy can be made according to a sample of the data set which is selected automatically. The sort algorithm is a variant of the well-known Quicksort algorithm, enhanced to work on secondary storage. The index construction has a runtime complexity of $O(n \log n)$. We show both analytically and experimentally that the algorithm outperforms traditional index construction methods by large factors.

## 1. Introduction

Efficient index construction in multidimensional data spaces is important for many knowledge discovery tasks. Many algorithms for knowledge discovery [JD 88, KR 90, NH 94, EKSX 96, BBBK 99], especially clustering algorithms, rely on efficient processing of similarity queries. In such a setting, multidimensional indexes are often created in a preprocessing step to knowledge discovery. If the index is not needed for general purpose query processing, it is not permanently maintained, but discarded after the KDD algorithm is completed. Therefore, the time spent in the index construction must be amortized by runtime improvements during knowledge discovery. Usually, indexes are constructed using repeated insert operations. This *'dynamic index construction'*, however, causes a serious performance degeneration. We show later in this paper that in a typical setting, every insert operation leads to at least one access to a data page of the index. Therefore, there is an increasing interest in fast bulk-loading operations for multidimensional index structures which cause substantially fewer page accesses for the index construction.

A second problem is that indexes must be carefully optimized in order to achieve a satisfactory performance (cf. [Böh 98, BK 99, BBJ+ 99]). The optimization objectives [BBKK 97] depend on the properties of the data set (dimension, distribution, number of objects, etc.) and on the types of queries which are performed by the KDD algorithm (range queries [EKSX 96], nearest neighbor queries [KR 90, NH 94], similarity joins [BBBK 99], etc.). On the other hand, we may draw some advantage from the fact that we do not only know a single data item at each point of time (as in the dynamic index construction) but a large amount of data items. It is a common knowledge that a higher fanout and storage utilization of the index pages can be achieved by applying bulk-load operations. A higher fanout yields a better search performance. Knowing all data *a priori* allows us to choose an alternative data space partitioning. As we have shown in [BBK 98a], a strategy of splitting the data space into two equally-sized portions causes, under certain circumstances, a poor search performance in contrast to an unbalanced split. Therefore, it is an important property of a bulk-loading algorithm that it allows to exchange the splitting strategy according to the requirements specific to the application.

The currently proposed bulk-loading methods either suffer from poor performance in the index construction or in the query evaluation, or are not suitable for indexes which do not fit into main memory. In contrast to previous bulk-loading methods, we present in this paper an algorithm for fast index construction on secondary storage which provides efficient query processing and is generic in the sense that the split strategy can be easily exchanged. It is based on an extension of the Quicksort algorithm which facilitates sorting on secondary storage (cf. section 3.3 and 3.4). The split strategy (section 3.2) is a user-defined function. For the split decisions, a sample of the data set is exploited which is automatically generated by the bulk-loading algorithm.

## 2. Related Work

Several methods for bulk-loading multidimensional index structures have been proposed. Space-filling curves provide a means to order the points such that spatial neighborhoods are maintained. In the Hilbert R-tree construction method [KF 94], the points are sorted according to their Hilbert value. The obtained sequence of points is decomposed into contiguous subsequences which are stored in the data pages. The page region, however, is not described by the interval of Hilbert values but by the minimum bounding rectangle of the points. The directory is built bottom up. The disadvantage of Hilbert R-trees is the high overlap among page regions.

VAM-Split trees [JW 96], in contrast, use a concept of hierarchical space partitioning for bulk-loading R-trees or KDB-trees. Sort algorithms are used for this purpose. This approach does not exploit *a priori* knowledge of the data set and is not adaptable.

Buffer trees [BSW 97] are a generalized technique to improve the construction performance for dynamic insert algorithms. The general idea is to collect insert operations to certain branches of the tree in buffers. These operations are propagated to the next deeper level whenever such a buffer overflows. This technique preserves the properties of the underlying index structure.

## 3. Our New Technique

During the bulk-load operation, the complete data set is held on secondary storage. Although only a small cache in the main memory is required, cost intensive disk operations such as random seeks are minimized. In our algorithms, we strictly separate the split strategy from the core of the construction algorithm. Therefore, we can easily replace the split strategy and thus, create an arbitrary overlap-free partition for the given storage utilization. Various criteria for the choice of direction and position of split hyperplanes can be applied. The index construction is a recursive algorithm consisting of the following subtasks:
- determining the tree topology (height, fanout of the directory nodes, etc.)
- choice of the split strategy
- external bisection of the data set according to tree topology and split strategy
- construction of the index directory.

### 3.1 Determination of the Tree Topology

The first step of our algorithm is to determine the topology of the tree resulting from our bulk-load operation. The height of the tree can be determined as follows [Böh 98]:

$$h = \left\lceil \log_{C_{\text{eff,dir}}} \left( \frac{n}{C_{\text{eff,data}}} \right) \right\rceil + 1$$

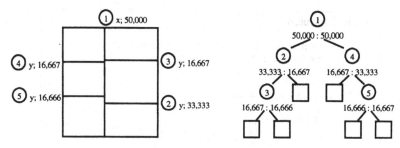

**Figure 1:** The Split Tree.

The fanout is given by the following formula:

$$\text{fanout}(h, n) = \min\left(\left\lceil \frac{n}{C_{\text{eff,data}} \cdot C_{\text{eff,dir}}^{h-2}} \right\rceil, C_{\text{max,dir}}\right)$$

### 3.2 The Split Strategy

In order to determine the split dimension, we have to consider two cases: If the data subset fits into main memory, the split dimension and the subset size can be obtained by computing selectivities or variances from the complete data subset. Otherwise, decisions are based on a sample of the subset which fits into main memory and can be loaded without causing too many random seek operations. We use a simple heuristic to sample the data subset which loads subsequent blocks from three different places in the data set.

### 3.3 Recursive Top-Down Partitioning

Now, we are able to define a recursive algorithm for partitioning the data set. The algorithm consists of two procedures which are nested recursively (both procedures call each other). The first procedure, *partition()*, that is called once for each directory page has the following duties:

- call the topology module to determine the fanout of the current directory page
- call the split-strategy module to determine a split tree for the current directory page
- call the second procedure, *partition_acc_to_split_tree()*

The second procedure partitions the data set according to the split dimensions and the proportions given in the split tree. However, the proportions are not regarded as fixed values. Instead, we will determine lower and upper bounds for the number of objects on each side of the split hyperplane. This will help us to improve the performance of the next step, the external bipartitioning. Let us assume that the ratio of the number of leaf nodes on each side of the current node in the split tree is $l : r$, and that we are currently dealing with $N$ data objects. An exact split hyperplane would exploit the proportions:

$$N_{\text{left}} = N \cdot \frac{l}{l+r} \quad \text{and} \quad N_{\text{right}} = N \cdot \frac{r}{l+r} = N - N_{\text{left}}.$$

Instead of using the exact values, we compute an upper bound for $N_{\text{left}}$ such that $N_{\text{left}}$ is not too large to be placed in $l$ subtrees with height $h-1$ and a lower bound for $N_{\text{left}}$ such that $N_{\text{right}}$ is not too large for $r$ subtrees:

$$N_{\text{max,left}} = l \cdot C_{\text{max,tree}}(h-1) \qquad N_{\text{min,left}} = N - r \cdot C_{\text{max,tree}}(h-1)$$

An overview of the algorithm is depicted in C-like pseudocode in figure 2. For the presentation of the algorithm, we assume that the data vectors are stored in an array on secondary

```
index_construction (int n)
{
            int h = (int)(log (n/Ceffdata) / log (Ceffdir) + 1) ;
            partition (0, n, h) ;
}

partition (int start, int n, int height)
{
            if (height == 0) {
                        ... // write data page, propagate info to parent
                        return ;
            }
            int f = fanout (height, n) ;
            SplitTree st = split_strategy (start, n, f) ;
            partition_acc_to_splittree (start, n, height, st) ;
            ... // write directory page, propagate info to parent
}

partition_acc_to_splittree (int start, int n, int height, SplitTree st)
{
            if (is_leaf (st)) {
                        partition (start, n, height - 1) ;
                        return ;
            }
            int mtc = max_tree_capacity (height - 1) ;
            n_maxleft = st->l_leaves * mtc ;
            n_minleft = N - st->r_leaves * mtc ;
            n_real = external_bipartition (start, n, st->splitdim,
                                n_minleft, n_maxleft) ;
            partition_acc_to_splittree (start, n_real,
                        st->leftchild, height) ;
            partition_acc_to_splittree (start + n_real, n - n_real,
                        st->rightchild, height) ;
}
```

**Figure 2:** Recursive Top-Down Data Set Partitioning.

storage and that the current data subset is referred to by the parameters *start* and *n*, where *n* is the number of data objects and *start* represents the address of the first object.

The procedure *index_construction(n)* determines the height of the tree and calls *partition()* which is responsible for the generation of a complete data or directory page. The function *partition()* first determines the fanout of the current page and calls *split_strategy()* to construct an adequate split tree. Then *partition_acc_to_splittree()* is called to partition the data set according to the split tree. After partitioning the data, *partition_acc_to_splittree()* calls *partition()* in order to create the next deeper index level. The height of the current subtree is decremented in this indirect recursive call. Therefore, the data set is partitioned in a top-down manner, i.e. the data set is first partitioned with respect to the highest directory level below the root node.

## 3.4 External Bipartitioning of the Data Set

Our bipartitioning algorithm is comparable to the well-known Quicksort algorithm [Hoa 62, Sed 78]. Bipartitioning means to split the data set or a subset into two portions according to the value of one specific dimension, the split dimension. After the bipartitioning step, the "lower" part of the data set contains values in the split dimension which are lower than a threshold value, the *split value*. The values in the "higher" part will be higher than the split value. The split value is initially unknown and is determined during the run of the bipartitioning algorithm.

Bipartitioning is closely related to sorting the data set according to the split dimension. In fact, if the data is sorted, bipartitioning of any proportion can easily be achieved by cutting the sorted data set into two subsets. However, sorting has a complexity of $o(n \log n)$, and a complete sort-order is not required for our purpose. Instead, we will present a bipartitioning algorithm with an average-case complexity of $O(n)$. The basic idea of our algorithm is to adapt Quicksort as follows: Quicksort makes a bisection of the data according to a heuristically chosen pivot value and then recursively calls Quicksort for both subsets. Our first modification is to make only one recursive call for the subset which contains the split interval. We are able to do that because the objects in the other subsets are on the correct side of the split interval anyway and need no further sorting. The second modification is to stop the recursion if the position of the pivot value is inside the split interval. The third modification is to choose the pivot values according to the proportion rather than to reach the middle.

Our bipartitioning algorithm works on secondary storage. It is well-known that the Mergesort algorithm is better suited for external sorting than Quicksort. However, Mergesort does not facilitate our modifications leading to an $O(n)$ complexity and was not further investigated for this reason. In our implementation, we use a sophisticated scheme reducing disk I/O and especially reducing random seek operations much more than a normal caching algorithm would be able to.

The algorithm can run in two modes, *internal* or *external*, depending on the question whether the processed data set fits into main memory or not. The internal mode is quite similar to Quicksort: The middle of three split attribute values in the database is taken as pivot value. The first object on the left side having a split attribute value larger than the pivot value is exchanged with the last element on the right side smaller than the pivot value until left and right object pointers meet at the bisection point. The algorithm stops if the bisection point is inside the goal interval. Otherwise, the algorithm continues recursively with the data subset containing the goal interval.

The external mode is more sophisticated: First, the pivot value is determined from the sample which is taken in the same way as described in section 3.2 and can often be reused. A complete internal bipartition runs on the sample data set to determine a suitable pivot value. In the following external bisection (cf. figure 3), transfers from and to the cache are always processed with a blocksize half of the cache size. Figure 3a shows the initialization of the cache from the first and last block in the disk file. Then, the data in the cache is processed by internal bisection with respect to the pivot value. If the bisection point is in the lower part of the cache (figure 3c), the right side contains more objects than fit into one block. One block, starting from the bisection point, is written back to the file and the next block is read and internally bisected again. Usually, objects remain in the lower and higher ends of the cache. These objects are used later to fill up transfer blocks completely. All remaining data is written back in the very last step into the middle of the file where additionally a fraction of a block has to be processed. Finally, we test if the bisection point of the external bisection is in the split interval. If the point is outside, another recursion is required.

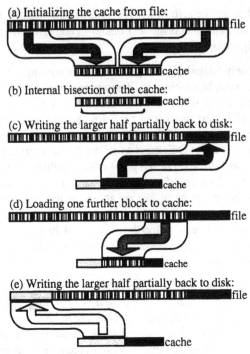

(a) Initializing the cache from file:

(b) Internal bisection of the cache:

(c) Writing the larger half partially back to disk:

(d) Loading one further block to cache:

(e) Writing the larger half partially back to disk:

**Figure 3:** External Bisection.

### 3.5  Constructing the Index Directory

As data partitioning is done by a recursive algorithm, the structure of the index is represented by the recursion tree. Therefore, we are able to create a directory node after the completion of the recursive calls for the child nodes. These recursive calls return the bounding boxes and the corresponding secondary storage addresses to the caller, where the information is collected. There, the directory node is written, the bounding boxes are combined to a single bounding box comprising of all boxes of child nodes, and the result is again propagated to the next higher level. A depth-first post-order sequentialization of the index is written to the disk.

### 3.6  Analytical Evaluation of the Construction Algorithm

In this section, we will show that our bottom-up construction algorithm has an average case time complexity of $O(n \log n)$. Moreover, we will consider disk accesses in a more exact way, and thus provide an analytically derived improvement factor over the dynamic index construction. For the file I/O, we determine two parameters: The number of random seek operations and the amount of data read or written from or to the disk. Unless no further caching is performed (which is true for our application, but cannot be guaranteed for the operating system) and provided that seeks are uniformly distributed variables, the I/O processing time can be determined as

$$t_{i/o} = t_{seek} \cdot \text{seek\_ops} + t_{transfer} \cdot \text{amount} .$$

In the following, we denote by the cache capacity $C_{cache}$ the number of objects fitting into the cache:

$$C_{cache} = \frac{\text{cachesize}}{\text{sizeof (object)}}$$

**Lemma 1.** Complexity of *bisection*

The bisection algorithm has the complexity O($n$).

**Proof (Lemma 1)**

We assume that the pivot element is randomly chosen from the data set. After the first run of the algorithm, the pivot element is located with uniform probability at one of the $n$ positions in the file. Therefore, the next run of the algorithm will have the length $k$ with a probability $1/n$ for each $1 < k < n$. Thus, the cost function $C(n)$ encompasses the cost for the algorithm, $n + 1$ comparison operations plus a probability weighted sum of the cost for processing the algorithm with length $k - 1$, $C(k)$. We obtain the following recursive equation:

$$C(n) = n + 1 + \sum_{k=1}^{n} \frac{C(k-1)}{n}$$

which can be solved by multiplying with $n$ and subtracting the same equation for $n - 1$. This can be simplified to $C(n) = 2 + C(n-1)$, and, $C(n) = 2 \cdot n = O(n)$.

❏

**Lemma 2.** Cost Bounds of Recursion

(1) The amount of data read or written during one recursion of our technique does not exceed four times the file-size.

(2) The number of seek operations required is bounded by

$$\text{seek\_ops}(n) \le \frac{8 \cdot n}{C_{\text{cache}}} + 2 \cdot \log_2(n)$$

**Proof (Lemma 2)**

(1) follows directly from Lemma 1 because every compared element has to be transferred at most once from disk to main memory and at most once back to disk.

(2) In each run of the external bisection algorithm, file I/O is processed with a blocksize of cachesize/2. The number of blocks read in each run is therefore

$$\text{blocks\_read}_{\text{bisection}}(n) = \frac{n}{C_{\text{cache}}/2} + 1$$

because one extra read is required in the final step. The number of write operations is the same and thus

$$\text{seek\_ops}(n) = 2 \cdot \sum_{i=0}^{r_{\text{interval}}} \text{blocks\_read}_{\text{run}}(i) \le \frac{8 \cdot n}{C_{\text{cache}}} + 2 \cdot \log_2(n).$$

❏

**Lemma 3.** Average Case Complexity of Our Technique

Our technique has an average case complexity of O($n \log n$) unless the split strategy has a complexity worse than O($n$).

**Proof (Lemma 3)**

For each level of the tree, the complete data set has to be bisectioned as often as the height of the split tree indicates. As the height of the split tree is determined by the directory page capacity, there are at most

$$h(n) \cdot C_{\text{max,dir}} = O(\log n)$$

bisection runs necessary. Therefore, our technique has the complexity O($n \log n$).

❏

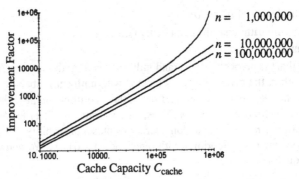

**Figure 4:** Improvement Factor for the Index Construction According to Lemmata 1-5.

**Lemma 4.** Cost of Symmetric Partitioning

For symmetric splitting, the procedure *partition()* handles an amount of file I/O data of

$$\left( \log_2(\frac{n}{C_{cache}}) + \log_{C_{max,dir}}(\frac{n}{C_{cache}}) \right) \cdot 4 \cdot filesize$$

and requires

$$\left( \log_2(\frac{n}{C_{cache}}) + \log_{C_{max,dir}}(\frac{n}{C_{cache}}) \right) \cdot \left( \frac{8 \cdot n}{C_{cache}} + 2 \cdot \log_2(n) \right)$$

random seek operations.

**Proof (Lemma 4)**

Left out due to space limitations, cf. [Böh 98].

**Lemma 5.** Cost of Dynamic Index Construction

Dynamic X-tree construction requires $2\,n$ seek operations. The transferred amount of data is $2 \cdot n \cdot pagesize$ .

**Proof (Lemma 5)**

For the X-tree, it is generally assumed that the directory is completely held in main memory. Data pages are not cached at all. For each insert, the corresponding data page has to be loaded and written back after completing the operation.

❑

Moreover, no better caching strategy for data pages can be applied, since without preprocessing of the input data set, no locality can be exploited to establish a working set of pages. From the results of lemmata 4 and 5 we can derive an estimate for the improvement factor of the bottom-up construction over dynamic index construction. The improvement factor for the number of seek operations is approximately:

$$Improvement \approx \frac{C_{cache}}{4 \cdot \left( \log_2(\frac{n}{C_{cache}}) + \log_{C_{max,dir}}(\frac{n}{C_{cache}}) \right)}$$

It is almost (up to the logarithmic factor in the denominator) linear in the cache capacity. Figure 4 depicts the improvement factor (number of random seek operations) for varying cache sizes and varying database sizes.

# 4. Experimental Evaluation

To show the practical relevance of our bottom-up construction algorithm, we have performed an extensive experimental evaluation by comparing the following index construction techniques: Dynamic index construction (repeated insert operations), Hilbert R-tree construction and our new method. All experiments have been computed on HP9000/780 workstations with several GBytes of secondary storage. Although our technique is applicable to most R-tree-like index structures, we decided to use the X-tree as an underlying index structure because according to [BKK 96], the X-tree outperforms other high-dimensional index structures. All programs have been implemented in C++.

In our experiments, we compare the construction times for various indexes. The external sorting procedure of our construction method was allowed to use only a relatively small cache (32 kBytes). Note that, although our implementation does not provide any further disk I/O caching, this cannot be guaranteed for the operating system. In contrast, the Hilbert construction method was implemented with internal sorting for simplicity. The construction time of the Hilbert method is therefore underestimated by far and would worsen in combination with external sorting when the cache size is strictly limited. All Hilbert-constructed indexes have a storage utilization near 100%.

Figure 5 shows the construction time of dynamic index construction and of the bottom-up methods. In the left diagram, we fix the dimension to 16, and vary the database size from 100,000 to 2,000,000 objects of synthetic data. The resulting speed-up of the bulk-loading techniques over the dynamic construction was so enormous that a logarithmic scale must be used in figure 5. In contrast, the bottom-up methods differ only slightly in their performance. The Hilbert technique was the best method, having a construction time between 17 and 429 sec. The construction time of symmetric splitting ranges from 26 to 668 sec., whereas unbalanced splitting required between 21 and 744 sec. in the moderate case and between 23 and 858 sec. for the 9:1 split. In contrast, the dynamic construction time ranged from 965 to 393,310 sec. (4 days, 13 hours). The improvement factor of our methods constantly increases with growing index size, starting from 37 to 45 for 100,000 objects and reaching 458 to 588 for 2,000,000 objects. The Hilbert construction is up to 915 times faster than the dynamic index construction. This enormous factor is not only due to internal sorting but also due to reduced overhead in changing the ordering attribute. In contrast to Hilbert construction, our technique changes the sorting criterion during the sort process according to the split tree. The more often the sorting criterion is changed, the more unbalanced the split becomes because the height of the

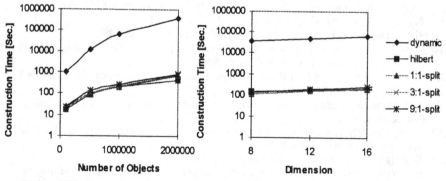

**Figure 5:** Performance of Index Construction Against Database Size and Dimension.

split tree increases. Therefore, the 9:1-split has the worst improvement factor. The right diagram in figure 5 shows the construction time for varying index dimensions. Here, the database size was fixed to 1,000,000 objects. It can be seen that the improvement factors of the construction methods (between 240 and 320) are rather independent from the dimension of the data space.

Our further experiments, which are not presented due to space limitations [Böh 98], show that the Hilbert construction method yields a bad performance in query processing. The reason is the high overlap among the page regions. Due to improved space partitioning resulting from knowing the data set *a priori*, the indexes constructed by our new method outperform even the dynamically constructed indexes by factors up to 16.8.

## 5. Conclusion

In this paper, we have proposed a fast algorithm for constructing indexes for high-dimensional data spaces on secondary storage. A user-defined split-strategy allows the adaptation of the index properties to the requirements of a specific knowledge discovery algorithm. We have shown both analytically and experimentally that our construction method outperforms the dynamic index construction by large factors. Our experiments further show that these indexes are also superior with respect to the search performance. Future work includes the investigation of various split strategies and their impact on different query types and access patterns.

## 6. References

[BBBK 99] Böhm, Braunmüller, Breunig, Kriegel: '*Fast Clustering Using High-Dimensional Similarity Joins*', submitted for publication, 1999.

[BBJ+ 99] Berchtold, Böhm, Jagadish, Kriegel, Sander: '*Independent Quantization: An Index Compression Technique for High-Dimensional Data Spaces*', submitted for publication, 1999.

[BBK 98a] Berchtold, Böhm, Kriegel: '*Improving the Query Performance of High-Dimensional Index Structures Using Bulk-Load Operations*', Int. Conf. on Extending Database Techn., EDBT, 1998.

[BBKK 97] Berchtold, Böhm, Keim, Kriegel: '*A Cost Model For Nearest Neighbor Search in High-Dimensional Data Space*', ACM PODS Symp. Principles of Database Systems, 1997.

[BK 99] Böhm, Kriegel: '*Dynamically Optimizing High-Dimensional Index Structures*', subm., 1999.

[BKK 96] Berchtold, Keim, Kriegel: '*The X-Tree: An Index Structure for High-Dimensional Data*', Int. Conf. on Very Large Data Bases, VLDB, 1996.

[BSW 97] van den Bercken, Seeger, Widmayer: '*A General Approach to Bulk Loading Multidimensional Index Structures*', Int. Conf. on Very Large Databases, VLDB, 1997.

[Böh 98] Böhm: '*Efficiently Indexing High-Dimensional Data Spaces*', PhD Thesis, University of Munich, Herbert Utz Verlag, 1998.

[EKSX 96] Ester, Kriegel, Sander, Xu: '*A Density-Based Algorithm for Discovering Clusters in Large Spatial Databases with Noise*', Int. Conf. Knowl. Disc. and Data Mining, KDD, 1996.

[Hoa 62] Hoare: '*Quicksort*', Computer Journal, Vol. 5, No. 1, 1962.

[JD 88] Jain, Dubes: '*Algorithms for Clustering Data*', Prentice-Hall, Inc., 1988.

[JW 96] Jain, White: '*Similarity Indexing: Algorithms and Performance*', SPIE Storage and Retrieval for Image and Video Databases IV, Vol. 2670, 1996.

[KF 94] Kamel, Faloutsos: '*Hilbert R-tree: An Improved R-tree using Fractals*'. Int. Conf. on Very Large Data Bases, VLDB, 1994.

[KR 90] Kaufman, Rousseeuw: '*Finding Groups in Data: An Introduction to Cluster Analysis*', John Wiley & Sons, 1990.

[NH 94] Ng, Han: '*Efficient and Effective Clustering Methods for Spatial Data Mining*', Int. Conf. on Very Large Data Bases, VLDB, 1994.

[Sed 78] Sedgewick: '*Quicksort*', Garland, New York, 1978.

[WSB 98] Weber, Schek, Blott: '*A Quantitative Analysis and Performance Study for Similarity-Search Methods in High-Dimensional Spaces*', Int. Conf. on Very Large Databases, VLDB, 1998.

# Implementation of Multidimensional Index Structures for Knowledge Discovery in Relational Databases

Stefan Berchtold[1] Christian Böhm[1,2], Hans-Peter Kriegel[2] and Urs Michel[2]

[1] stb gmbh, Ulrichsplatz 6, 86150 Augsburg, Germany
[2] University of Munich, Oettingenstr. 67, D-80538 Munich, Germany
Stefan.Berchtold@stb-gmbh.de
{boehm,kriegel,michel}@informatik.uni-muenchen.de

**Abstract.** Efficient query processing is one of the basic needs for data mining algorithms. Clustering algorithms, association rule mining algorithms and OLAP tools all rely on efficient query processors being able to deal with high-dimensional data. Inside such a query processor, multidimensional index structures are used as a basic technique. As the implementation of such an index structures is a difficult and time-consuming task, we propose a new approach to implement an index structure on top of a commercial relational database system. In particular, we map the index structure to a relational database design and simulate the behavior of the index structure using triggers and stored procedures. This can easily be done for a very large class of multidimensional index structures. To demonstrate the feasibility and efficiency, we implemented an X-tree on top of Oracle 8. We ran several experiments on large databases and recorded a performance improvement of up to a factor of 11.5 compared to a sequential scan of the database.

## 1. Introduction

Efficient query processing in high-dimensional data spaces is an important requirement for many data analysis tools. Algorithms for knowledge discovery tasks such as clustering [EKSX 98], association rule mining [AS 94], or OLAP [HAMS 97], are often based on range search or nearest neighbor search in multidimensional feature spaces. Since these applications deal with large amounts of usually high-dimensional point data, multidimensional index structures must be applied for the data management in order to achieve a satisfactory performance.

Multidimensional index structures have been intensively investigated during the last decade. Most of the approaches [Gut 84, LS 89] were designed in the context of geographical information systems where two-dimensional data spaces are prevalent. The performance of query processing often deteriorates when the dimensionality increases. To overcome this problem, several specialized index structures for high-dimensional query processing have been proposed that fall into two general categories: One can either solve the $d$-dimensional problem by designing a $d$-dimensional index. Examples are the TV-tree [LJF 95], the SS-tree [WJ 96], the SR-tree [KS 97] or the X-tree [BKK 96]. We refer to this class of indexing techniques as multidimensional indexes. Alternatively, one can map the $d$-dimensional problem to an equivalent 1-dimensional problem and then make use of an existing 1-dimensional index such as a B$^+$-tree. Thus, we provide a mapping that maps each $d$-dimensional data point into a 1-dimensional value (key). We refer to this class of indexing techniques as mapping techniques. Examples for this category are the Z-order [FB 74], the Hilbert-curve [FR 89, Jag 90], Gray-

Codes [Fal 85], or the Pyramid-tree [BBK 98]. We refer to [Böh 98] for a comprehensive survey on the relevant techniques.

Recently, there is an increasing interest in integrating high-dimensional point data into commercial database management systems. Data to be analyzed often stem from productive environments which are already based on relational database management systems. These systems provide efficient data management for standard transactions such as billing and accounting as well as powerful and adequate tools for reports, spreadsheets, charts and other simple visualization and presentation tools. Relational databases, however, fail to manage high-dimensional point data efficiently for advanced knowledge discovery algorithms. Therefore, it is common to store productive data in a relational database system and to replicate the data for analysis purposes outside the database in file-based multidimensional index structures. We call this approach the *hybrid solution*.

The hybrid solution bears various disadvantages. Especially the integrity of data stored in two ways, inside and outside the database system, is difficult to maintain. If an update operation involving both, multidimensional and productive data fails in the relational database (e.g. due to concurrency conflicts), the corresponding update in the multidimensional index must be undone to guarantee consistency. Vice versa, if the multidimensional update fails, the corresponding update to the relational database must be aborted. For this purpose, a two-phase commit protocol for heterogeneous database systems must be implemented, a time-consuming task which requires a deep knowledge of the participating systems. The hybrid solution involves further problems. File systems and database systems usually have different concepts for data security, backup and concurrent access. File-based storage does not guarantee physical and logical data independence. Thus, schema evolution in "running" applications is difficult.

A promising approach to overcome these disadvantages is based on object-relational database systems. Object-relational database systems are relational database systems which can be extended by application-specific data types (called *data cartridges* or *data blades*). The general idea is to define data cartridges for multidimensional attributes and to manage them in the database. For data-intensive applications it is necessary to implement multidimensional index structures in the database. This requires the access to the block-manager of the database system, which is not granted by most commercial database systems. The current universal server by ORACLE, for instance, does not provide any documentation of a block-oriented interface to the database. Data cartridges are only allowed to access relations via the SQL interface. Current object-relational database systems are thus not very helpful for our integration problem.

We can summarize that using current object-relational database systems or pure relational database systems, the only possible way to store multidimensional attributes inside the database is to map them into the relational model.

In this paper, we propose a technique which allows a direct mapping of the concepts of specialized index structures for high-dimensional data spaces into the relational model. For concreteness, we concentrate here on a relational implementation of the X-tree on top of Oracle-8. The X-tree, an R-tree variant for high-dimensional data spaces, is described in detail in section 4.1. The presented techniques, however, can also be applied to other indexing approaches such as the TV-Tree [LJF 95] or the SS-Tree

[WJ 96]. Similarly, the underlying database system can be exchanged using the same concept we suggest. The general idea is to model the structure of the relevant components of the index (such as data pages, data items, directory pages etc.) in the relational model and to simulate the query processing algorithms defined on these structures using corresponding SQL statements.

The simulation of mapping techniques is pretty straightforward and is therefore not explained in depth in this paper. One just stores the 1-dimensional value in an additional column of the data table and then searches this column. Obviously, a database index is used to support the search. Thus, the whole query process is done in three steps:

1. compute a set of candidates based on the 1-dimensional key
2. refine this set of candidates based on the $d$-dimensional feature vectors
3. refine this set of candidates by looking up the actual data items

## 2. Simulation of Hierarchical Index Structures

The implementation of hierarchical index structures is much more complex than the implementation of mapping techniques. This applies to any implementation strategy. The reason for this is that hierarchical index structures have a complex structure that dynamically changes when inserting new data items. Thus, algorithms do not run on a previously given structure and have to be implemented recursively. To demonstrate that even in this complex scenario, an implementation of an index structure on top of a commercial database system can be done relatively easy and is preferable compared to a legacy implementation, we implemented the X-tree, a high-dimensional index structure, based on R-trees.

### 2.1 Simulation

The basic idea of our technique is to simulate the X-tree within the relational schema. Thus, we keep a separate table for each level of the tree. One of those tables stores the data points (simulating the data pages) the other tables store minimum bounding boxes and pointers (simulating the directory pages). Figure 1 depicts this scenario. In order to insert a data item, we first determine the data page in which the item has to be inserted. Then, we check whether the data page overflows and if it does, we split the page according to the X-tree split strategy. Note that a split might also cause the parent page in the directory to overflow. If we have to split the root node of the tree which causes the tree to grow in height, we have to introduce an additional table[1] and thus change the schema. A practical alternative is to pre-define tables for a three or four level directory. As only in case of very large databases, an X-tree grows beyond height four, by doing so we can handle a split of the root node as an exception that has to be handled separately. Thus, the schema of the tree becomes static. All these actions are implemented in stored procedures.

In order to search the tree, we have to join all tables and generate a single SQL statement that queries the entire tree. This statement has to be created dynamically whenever

---

1. A technical problem arises here when dealing with commercial database systems: Oracle 8, for instance, ends a transaction whenever a DDL command is executed. This means that if we use Oracle 8, an insert operation on a tree that caused the root node to be split cannot be undone by simply aborting the current transaction.

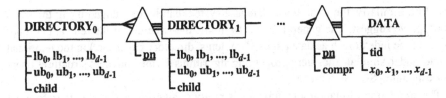

**Figure 1:** Relational Schema (Including B$^+$-Tree Indexes) of the X-Tree.

the schema of the X-tree changes due to tree growth. If we process range queries, the SQL statement is rather simple. The details are provided in section 2.3.

### Relational Schema

All information usually held in the data pages of the X-tree is modeled in a relation called DATA. A tuple in DATA contains a $d$-dimensional data vector, which is held in a set of $d$ numerical attributes $x_0, x_1, ..., x_{d-1}$, a unique tuple identifier (*tid*), and the page number (*pn*) of the data page. Thus, DATA has the schema "DATA ($x_0$ FLOAT, $x_1$ FLOAT, ..., $x_{d-1}$ FLOAT, *tid* NUMBER NOT NULL, *pn* NUMBER NOT NULL)". Intuitively, all data items located in the same data page of the X-Tree share the same value *pn*.

The $k$ levels of the X-tree directory are modeled using $k$ relations DIRECTORY$_0$, ..., DIRECTORY$_{k-1}$. Each tuple in a relation DIRECTORY$_i$ belongs to one entry of a directory node in level $i$ consisting of a bounding box and a pointer to a child node. Therefore, DIRECTORY$_i$ is of the scheme "DIRECTORY$_i$ ($lb_0$ FLOAT, $ub_0$ FLOAT, ...., $lb_{d-1}$ FLOAT, $ub_{d-1}$ FLOAT, *child* NUMBER NOT NULL, *pn* NUMBER NOT NULL)". The additional attribute *child* represents the pointer to the child node which, in case of DIRECTORY$_{k-1}$, references a data page and *pn* identifies the directory node the entry belongs to. Thus, the two relations DIRECTORY$_{k-1}$ and DATA can be joined via the attributes *child* and *pn* which actually form a 1:$n$-relationship between DIRECTORY$_{k-1}$ and DATA. The same relationship exists for two subsequent directory levels DIRECTORY$_i$ and DIRECTORY$_{i+1}$. Obviously, it is important to make the join between two subsequent levels of the directory efficient. To facilitate index-based join methods, we create indexes using the *pn* attribute as the ordering criterion. The same observation holds for the join between DIRECTORY$_{k-1}$ and DATA. To save table accesses, we also added the quantized version of the feature vectors to the index. The resulting relational schema of the X-Tree enhanced by the required indexes (triangles) is depicted in Figure 1.

### Compressed Attributes

If we assume a high-dimensional data space, the location of a point in this space is defined in terms of $d$ floating point values. If $d$ increases, the amount of information, we are keeping, also increases linearly. Intuitively however, it should be possible to keep the amount of information stored for a single data item almost constant for any dimension. An obvious way to achieve this is to reduce the number of bits used for storing a single coordinate linearly if the number of coordinates increases. In other words, as in a high-dimensional space we have so much information about the location of a point, it should be sufficient to use a coarser resolution to represent the data space. This technique successfully has been applied in the VA-file [WSB 98] to compute nearest neighbors. In the VA-file, a compressed version of the data points is stored in one file and the exact data is stored in another file. Both files are unsorted, however, the ordering of the points in the two files is identical. Query processing is equivalent to a sequential scan of the compressed file with some look-ups to the second file whenever this is necessary. In particular a look-up occurs, if a point cannot be pruned from the nearest neighbor search only based on the compressed representation.

In our implementation of the X-tree, we suggest the similar technique of *compressed attributes*. A compressed attribute summarizes the $d$-dimensional information of an entry in the DATA table in a single-value representation. Thus, the resolution of the data space is reduced to 1 byte per coordinate. Then, the 1-byte coordinates are concatenated and stored in a single attribute called *comp*. Thus the scheme of DATA changes to DATA (REAL $x_0$, REAL $x_1$, REAL $x_{d-1}$, RAW[$d$] *comp,* INT *tid,* INT *pn*). To guarantee an efficient access to the compressed attributes, we store *comp* in the index assigned to DATA. Thus, in order to exclude a data item from the search, we first can use compressed representation of the data item stored in the index and only if this is not sufficient, we have to make a look-up to the actual DATA table. This further reduces the number of accesses to the DATA table because most accesses are only to the index.

## 2.2 Index Creation

There are two situations when one intends to insert new data into an index structure: Inserting a single data item, and building an index from scratch given a large amount of data (bulk-load). We are supposed to handle these two situations separately, due to efficiency considerations. The reason for this is that a dynamic insert of a single data item is usually relatively slow, however, knowing all the data items to be inserted in advance, we are able to preprocess the data (e.g. sort) such that an index can be built very efficiently. This applies to almost all multidimensional index structures and their implementations.

The dynamic insertion of a single data item involves two steps: determining an insertion path and, when necessary, a local restructuring of the tree. There are basically two alternatives for the implementation: An implementation of the whole insert algorithm (e.g. using embedded SQL), or directly inserting the data point into the DATA relation and then to raise triggers which perform the restructuring operation.

In any implementation, we first have to determine an appropriate data page to insert the data item. Therefore, we recursively look-up the directory tables as we would handle it in a legacy implementation. Using a stored procedure, we load all affected node entries into main memory and process them as described above. Then, we insert the data item into the page. In case of an overflow, we recursively update the directory, according to [BKK 96].

If an X-Tree has to be created from scratch for a large data set, it is more efficient to provide a bulk-load operation, such as proposed in [BBK 98a]. This technique can also be implemented in embedded SQL or stored procedures.

## 2.3 Processing Range Queries

Processing a range query using our X-Tree implementation with a $k$-level-directory involves $(k + 2)$ steps. The first step reads the root level of the directory (DIRECTORY$_0$) and determines all pages of the next deeper level (DIRECTORY$_1$) which are intersected by the query window. These pages are loaded in the second step

```
SELECT data.*
FROM directory_0 dir_0, directory_1 dir_1, data
WHERE
        /* JOIN */
                        dir_0.child = dir_1.pn
            AND     dir_1.child = data.pn
        /* 1st step*/
            AND     dir_0.lb_0 ≤ qub_0 AND qlb_0 ≤ dir_0.ub_0
            AND     ...
            AND     dir_0.lb_{d-1} ≤ qub_{d-1} AND qlb_{d-1} ≤ dir_0.ub_{d-1}
        /* 2nd step */
            AND     dir_1.lb_0 ≤ qub_0 AND qlb_0 ≤ dir_1.ub_0
            AND     ...
            AND     dir_1.lb_{d-1} ≤ qub_{d-1} AND qlb_{d-1} ≤ dir_1.ub_{d-1}
        /* 3rd step */
            AND     ASCII(SUBSTR(data.comp,1,1)) BETWEEN qclb_0 and qcub_0
            AND     ...
            AND     ASCII(SUBSTR(data.comp,1,1)) BETWEEN qclb_{d-1} and qcub_{d-1}
        /* 4th step */
            AND     data.x_0 BETWEEN qlb_0 AND qub_0
            AND     ...
            AND     data.x_{d-1} BETWEEN qlb_{d-1} AND qub_{d-1}
```

**Figure 2:** An Example for an SQL Statement Processing a Range Query.

and used for determining the qualifying pages in the subsequent level. The following steps read all $k$ levels of the directory in the same way, thus filtering between pages which are affected or not. Once the bottom level of the directory has been processed, the page numbers of all qualifying data pages are known. The data pages in our implementation contain the compressed (i.e. quantized) versions of the data vectors. Step number $(k + 1)$, the last filter step, loads these data pages and determines candidates (a candidate is a point whose quantized approximation is intersected by the query window). In the refinement step $(k + 2)$, the candidates are directly accessed (the position in the data file is known) and tested for containment in the query window.

In our relational implementation, all these steps are comprised in a single SQL statement (c.f. Figure 2 for a 2-level directory). It forms an equi-join between each pair of subsequent directory levels (DIRECTORY$_j$ and DIRECTORY$_{j + 1}$, $0 \leq j \leq k - 2$) and an additional equi-join between the last directory level DIRECTORY$_i$ and the DATA relation. It consists of $(k + 2)$ AND-connected blocks in the WHERE-clause. The blocks refer to the steps of range query processing as described above. For example, the first block filters all page numbers of the second directory level qualifying for the query. Block number $(k + 1)$ contains various substring-operations. The reason is that we had to pack the compressed attributes into a string due to restrictions on the number of attributes which can be stored in an index. The last block forms the refinement step. Note that it is important to translate the query into a single SQL statement, because client-/server communication involving costly context switches or round-trip delays can be clearly reduced.

The particularity of our approach is that processing of joins between $(k + 1)$ tables is more efficient than a single scan of the data relation provided that the SQL statement is transformed into a suitable query evaluation plan $(QEP)$. This can be guaranteed by hints to the query optimizer. Query processing starts with a table scan of the root table. The page regions intersecting the query window are selected and the result is projected to the foreign key attribute *child*. The value of this result is used in the index join to efficiently search for the entries in DIRECTORY$_1$ which are contained in the corresponding page region. For this purpose, an index range scan is performed. The corresponding directory entries are retrieved by internal-key-accesses on the corresponding base table DIRECTORY$_1$. The qualifying data page numbers are again determined by selection and projection to the *child*-attribute. An index range scan similar to the index scan above is performed on the index of the DATA-table containing the page number, and the quantized version of the data points. Before accessing the exact representation of the data points, a selection based on the compressed attribute is performed to determine a suitable candidate set. The last step is the selection based on the exact geometry of the data points.

## 3. Experimental Evaluation

In order to verify our claims that the suggested implementation of multidimensional index structures does not only provide advantages from a software engineering point of view but also in terms of performance, we actually implemented the X-tree on top of Oracle 8 and performed a comprehensive experimental evaluation on both, synthetic and real data. Therefore, we compared various query processing techniques for high-dimensional range queries in relational databases:

1.  sequential scan on the data relation,

2.  sequential scan on the data relation using the COMPRESSED attributes technique

3.  standard index (B-tree) on the first attribute

4.  standard index on all attributes concatenated in a single index

5.  standard indexes on each attribute (inverted-list approach)

6.  X-tree-simulation with and without COMPRESSED attributes technique

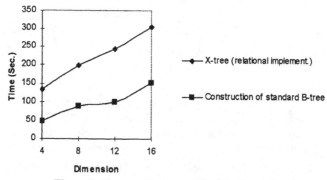

**Figure 3:** Times to Create an X-tree in Oracle 8.

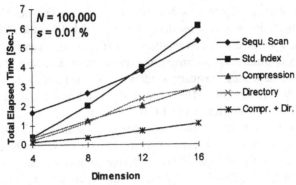

**Figure 4:** Performance for Range Queries (Synthetic Data) for Varying Dimensions.

As first experimental results show, the variants 4 and 5 demonstrate a performance much worse than all other variants. We will therefore not show detailed results for these techniques.

In our first experiment, we determine the times for creating an X-tree on a large database. Therefore, we bulk-load the index using different techniques. The results of this experiment are shown in figure 3. The relational implementation requires, depending on the dimensionality of the data set, between one and five minutes to build an index on a 100,000 record 16-dimensional database. For this experiment, we use the algorithms described in [BBK 98a] for bulk-loading the X-tree caching intermediate results in a operating system file. The times for the standard B-tree approach and the X-tree approach show that a standard B-tree can be built about 2.5 times faster. However, both techniques yield a good overall performance.

In the next experiment, we compare the query performance of the different implementations on synthetic data. The result of an experiment on 100,000 data items of varying dimensionality is presented in figure 4. The performance of the inverted lists approach and the standard index on a single attribute is not presented due to bad performance. It can be seen that both, the compressed attributes technique and the X-tree simulation yield high performance gains over all experiments. Moreover, the combination of both these techniques outperforms the sequential scan and the standard index for

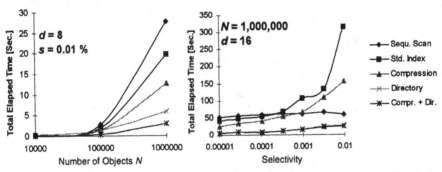

**Figure 5:** Performance for Range Queries (Synthetic Data) for Varying Database Size (a) and for Varying Selectivity (b).

all types of data over all dimensions. It can also be seen that the combination of the directory and the compressed attributes technique yields a much better improvement factor than each single technique. The factor even improves for higher dimensions, the best observed improvement factor in our experiments was 11.5.

In the experiment depicted in figure 5a, we investigate the performance of the implementations when varying the size of the database. Again, the relational implementation of the X-tree with compressed attributes outperforms all other techniques by far. The acceleration even improves with growing database size.

In the last experiment on real data, we investigate the performance for varying selectivities. The results of this experiment on 1,000,000 16-dimensional feature vectors are shown in figure 5b. The data comes from a similarity search system of a car manufacturer and each feature vector describes the shape of a part. As we can observe from the chart, our technique outperforms all other techniques. The effect of the compressed attributes, however, was almost negligible. Thus, the performance of the X-tree with and without compressed attributes is almost identical. This confirms our claim that implementing index structures on top of a commercial relational database system shows very good performance for both, synthetic and real data.

## 4. Conclusions

In this paper, we proposed a new approach to implement an index structure on top of a commercial relational database system. We map the particular index structure to a relational database design and simulate the behavior of the index structure using triggers and stored procedures. We showed that this can be done easily for a very large class of multidimensional index structures. To demonstrate the feasibility and efficiency we implemented an X-tree on top of Oracle 8. We ran several experiments on large databases and recorded a performance improvement of up to a factor of 11.5 compared to a sequential scan of the database.

In addition to the performance gain, our approach has all the advantages of using a fully-fledged database system including recovery, multi-user support and transactions. Furthermore, the development times are significantly shorter than in a legacy implementation of an index.

## References

[ALSS 95] Agrawal R., Lin K., Sawhney H., Shim K.: *'Fast Similarity Search in the Presence of Noise, Scaling, and Translation in Time-Series Databases'*, Proc. of the 21st Conf. on Very Large Databases, 1995, pp. 490-501.

[AS 94] Agrawal R., Srikant R.: *'Fast Algorithms for Mining Association Rules'*, Proc. of the 20st Conf. on Very Large Databases, Chile, 1995, pp. 487-499.

[BBB+ 97] Berchtold S., Böhm C., Braunmueller B., Keim D. A., Kriegel H.-P.: *'Fast Similarity Search in Multimedia Databases'*, Proc. ACM SIGMOD Int. Conf. on Management of Data, 1997, Tucson, Arizona.

[BBK 98] Berchtold S., Böhm C., Kriegel H.-P.: *'The Pyramid-Technique: Towards indexing beyond the Curse of Dimensionality'*, Proc. ACM SIGMOD Int. Conf. on Management of Data, Seattle, pp. 142-153,1998.

[BBK 98a] Berchtold S., Böhm C., Kriegel H.-P.: *'Improving the Query Performance of High-Dimensional Index Structures Using Bulk-Load Operations'*, 6th. Int. Conf. on Extending Database Technology, Valencia, 1998.

[BBKK 97]Berchtold S., Böhm C., Keim D., Kriegel H.-P.: 'A Cost Model For Nearest Neighbor Search in High-Dimensional Data Space', ACM PODS Symposium on Principles of Database Systems, 1997, Tucson, Arizona.

[Ben 75] Bentley J.L.: 'Multidimensional Search Trees Used for Associative Searching', Communications of the ACM, Vol. 18, No. 9, pp. 509-517, 1975.

[Ben 79] Bentley J. L.: 'Multidimensiuonal Binary Search in Database Applications', IEEE Trans. Software Eng. 4(5), 1979, pp. 397-409.

[BKK 96] Berchtold S., Keim D., Kriegel H.-P.: 'The X-tree: An Index Structure for High-Dimensional Data', 22nd Conf. on Very Large Databases, 1996.

[BKSS 90] Beckmann N., Kriegel H.-P., Schneider R., Seeger B.: 'The $R^*$-tree: An Efficient and Robust Access Method for Points and Rectangles', Proc. ACM SIGMOD Int. Conf. on Management of Data, Atlantic City, NJ, 1990.

[Böh 98] Böhm C.: 'Efficiently Indexing High-Dimensional Data Spaces', Ph.D. Thesis, Faculty for Mathematics and Computer Science, University of Munich, 1998.

[EKSX 98] Ester M., Kriegel H.-P., Sander J., Xu X.: 'Incremental Clustering for Mining in a Data Warehousing Environment', Proc. 24th Int. Conf. on Very Large Databases (VLDB '98), NY, 1998, pp. 323-333.

[Fal 85] Faloutsos C.: 'Multiattribute Hashing Using Gray Codes', Proc. ACM SIGMOD Int. Conf. on Management of Data, 1985, pp. 227-238.

[FB 74] Finkel R, Bentley J.L. 'Quad Trees: A Data Structure for Retrieval of Composite Keys', Acta Informatica 4(1), 1974, pp. 1-9.

[FR 89] Faloutsos C., Roseman S.: 'Fractals for Secondary Key Retrieval', Proc. 8th ACM SIGACT/SIGMOD Symp. on Principles of Database Systems, 1989, pp. 247-252.

[Gut 84] Guttman A.: 'R-trees: A Dynamic Index Structure for Spatial Searching', Proc. ACM SIGMOD Int. Conf. on Management of Data, 1984.

[HAMS 97]Ho C.T., Agrawal R., Megiddo N., Srikant R.: Range Queries in OLAP Data Cubes. SIGMOD Conference 1997: 73-88

[HS 95] Hjaltason G. R., Samet H.: 'Ranking in Spatial Databases', Proc. 4th Int. Symp. on Large Spatial Databases, Portland, ME, 1995, pp. 83-95.

[Jag 90] Jagadish H. V.: 'Linear Clustering of Objects with Multiple Attributes', Proc. ACM SIGMOD Int. Conf. on Management of Data, Atlantic City, NJ, 1990, pp. 332-342.

[JW 96] Jain R, White D.A.: 'Similarity Indexing: Algorithms and Performance', Proc. SPIE Storage and Retrieval for Image and Video Databases IV, Vol. 2670, San Jose, CA, 1996, pp. 62-75.

[KS 97] Katayama N., Satoh S.: 'The SR-tree: An Index Structure for High-Dimensional Nearest Neighbor Queries', Proc. ACM SIGMOD Int. Conf. on Management of Data, 1997, pp. 369-380.

[LJF 95] Lin K., Jagadish H. V., Faloutsos C.: 'The TV-Tree: An Index Structure for High-Dimensional Data', VLDB Journal, Vol. 3, pp. 517-542, 1995.

[LS 89] Lomet D., Salzberg B.: 'The hB-tree: A Robust Multiattribute Search Structure', Proc. 5th IEEE Int. Conf. on Data Eng., 1989, pp. 296-304.

[MG 93] Mehrotra R., Gary J.: 'Feature-Based Retrieval of Similar Shapes', Proc. 9th Int. Conf. on Data Engeneering, 1993.

[NHS 84] Nievergelt J., Hinterberger H., Sevcik K. C.: 'The Grid File: An Adaptable, Symmetric Multikey File Structure', ACM Trans. on Database Systems, Vol. 9, No. 1, 1984, pp. 38-71.

[WJ 96] White D.A., Jain R.: 'Similarity indexing with the SS-tree', Proc. 12th Int. Conf on Data Engineering, New Orleans, LA, 1996.

[WSB 98] Weber R., Scheck H.-J., Blott S.: 'A Quantitative Analysis and Performance Study for Similarity-Search Methods in High-Dimensional Spaces', Proc. Int. Conf. on Very Large Databases, New York, 1998.

[WW 80] Wallace T., Wintz P.: 'An Efficient Three-Dimensional Aircraft Recognition Algorithm Using Normalized Fourier Descriptors', Computer Graphics and Image Processing, Vol. 13, pp. 99-126, 1980.

# Similarity between Event Types in Sequences

Heikki Mannila[1] and Pirjo Moen[2]

[1] Microsoft Research,
One Microsoft Way, Redmond, WA 98052-6399, USA
mannila@microsoft.com
[2] University of Helsinki, Department of Computer Science,
P.O. Box 26, FIN-00014 Helsinki, FINLAND
pirjo.moen@cs.helsinki.fi

**Abstract.** *Similarity* or distance between objects is one of the central concepts in data mining. In this paper we consider the following problem: given a set of event sequences, define a useful notion of similarity between the different types of events occurring in the sequences. We approach the problem by considering two event types to be similar if they occur in similar contexts. The context of an occurrence of an event type is defined as the set of types of the events happening within a certain time limit before the occurrence. Then two event types are similar if their sets of contexts are similar. We quantify this by using a simple approach of computing centroids of sets of contexts and using the $L_1$ distance. We present empirical results on telecommunications alarm sequences and student enrollment data, showing that the method produces intuitively appealing results.

## 1 Introduction

Most data mining research has concentrated on set-oriented tabular data. There are, however, important types of data that do not fit within this framework. One such form of data are *event sequences* that occur in many application areas. An event sequence is an ordered collection of events from a finite set of *event types*, with each event of the sequence having an occurrence time. See Fig. 1 for an example of an event sequence.

A real-life example of an event sequence is the event or error log from a process such as telecommunications network management. Here the event types are the possible error messages, and the events are actual occurrences of errors at certain times. Also a web access log from a single session of a user can be viewed as an event sequence. Now the event types are the web pages, and an individual event is a request for a particular page at a particular time. Other examples of application areas in which event sequences occur are user interface design (event types are different user actions), criminology (types of crime), biostatistics (different symptoms), etc. In each of these applications, the data consists of one or several event sequences. Note that an event sequence is different from a time series in that a time series describes a variable with a continuous value over time, whereas an event sequence consists of discrete events.

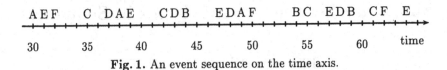

**Fig. 1.** An event sequence on the time axis.

There has been some research on data mining methods for sequences of events: see, e.g., [10, 12–16]. In this paper we consider a problem related to exploratory data analysis of event sequences. Suppose we are given a set of event sequences from an application domain about which only little domain knowledge is available. Then one interesting aspect is to gain understanding about the *similarity between event types*: which types of events are similar in some useful sense?

Consider, for example, an application of studying web browsing behavior. In such an application we might be willing to determine two web pages to be similar if they provide the users with the same type of information. Finding this type of similarity in this application is probably quite easy. What is, however, more interesting is that would it be possible to find a same type of similarity information from the data alone?

Recently, there has been considerable interest in defining intuitive and easily computable measures of similarity between complex objects and in using abstract similarity notions in querying databases [1–7, 11, 17, 19]. In this paper we describe a method for finding similarities between event types from large sets of event sequences. Such similarity information is useful in itself, as it provides insight into the data. Moreover, similarities between event types can be used in various ways to make querying the data set more useful.

Our approach to defining similarity between different event types is based on the following simple idea: two event types are similar, if they occur in similar *contexts*. That is, two event types $A$ and $B$ are similar, if the situations in which they occur in the sequences in some way resemble each other. Abstractly, we define the similarity between event types $A$ and $B$ by taking the sets of all contexts of $A$ and $B$, and then computing the similarity between these sets of contexts.

To formalize this intuitive idea, we need to answer several questions: (1) What is a context of an occurrence of an event type? (2) What does it mean that two sets of contexts are similar? An answer to the second question typically requires answering a simpler question: (3) Given two contexts, what is their distance? There are several ways of answering these questions, and the most suitable definition often depends on the application domain. In this paper we discuss different alternative answers for these questions and show that even simple answers can yield experimental results that are interesting from the practical point of view.

The rest of this paper is organized as follows. In Sect. 2 we define the basic concepts: event types, events, and event sequences. Then in Sect. 3 we discuss ways of defining the context of an occurrence of an event type, and in Sect. 4 we present notions for computing similarity between sets of contexts. Experimental results are presented in Sect. 5. Section 6 discusses alternative methods and presents some conclusions.

## 2 Basic Concepts

A realistic way of modeling events is to consider a set $R = \{A_1, \ldots, A_k\}$ of *event attributes* with domains $Dom(A_1), \ldots, Dom(A_k)$. An *event* is a $(k + 1)$-tuple $(a_1, \ldots, a_k, t)$, where $a_i \in Dom(A_i)$ and $t$ is a real number, the *occurrence time* of the event. Then an *event sequence* is a collection of events over $R \cup \{T\}$, where the domain of the attribute $T$ is the set of real numbers $\mathbb{R}$. The events in the event sequence are ordered by ascending occurrence times $t$.

*Example 1.* In the telecommunications domain events have attributes such as *alarm type*, *module*, and *severity*, indicating the type of alarm, the module that sent the alarm, and the severity of the alarm, respectively.

*Example 2.* In a web log events have attributes like *page* (the requested page), *host* (the accessing host), and the occurrence time of the request.

Often it is enough to study a simplified model of events where the only event properties considered are the type and the occurrence time of the event. Let a set $\mathcal{E}$ be the set of event types. Given this set $\mathcal{E}$, an event is a pair $(e, t)$ where $e \in \mathcal{E}$ is the type of the event and $t \in \mathbb{R}$ is the occurrence time of the event. Then an *event sequence* $S$ is an ordered collection of events, i.e., $S = \langle (e_1, t_1), (e_2, t_2), \ldots, (e_n, t_n) \rangle$, where $e_i \in \mathcal{E}$, and $t_i \leq t_{i+1}$ for all $i = 1, \ldots, n-1$. The length of the sequence $S$ is, therefore, $|S| = n$. We can also consider even more simplified sequences that consist only of event types in temporal order. Such a sequence $S = \langle e_1, e_2, \ldots, e_n \rangle$, where each $e_i \in \mathcal{E}$, is called an *event type sequence*.

*Example 3.* Consider the event sequence in Fig. 1. A sequence

$$S = \langle (A, 30), (E, 31), (F, 32), \ldots, (E, 64) \rangle.$$

is this same sequence presented as a sequence of (event type, time) -pairs.

## 3 Contexts of Events

Our basic idea is that the similarity or distance between two event types is determined by the similarity between contexts of occurrences of these event types. To make this intuition precise, we have to define what a context is and what it means that two sets of contexts are similar. In this section we address the first of the questions.

We start with a simple definition. Consider an event sequence $S = \langle (e_1, t_1), (e_2, t_2), \ldots, (e_n, t_n) \rangle$, and let $i \in \{1, \ldots, n\}$ and $W$ be a time parameter. Then a context of the event $(e_i, t_i)$ in $S$ is the set of all the types of the events that occur within $W$ time units before $t_i$. That is,

$$\mathrm{con}((e_i, t_i), S, W) = \{ e_j \mid (e_j, t_j) \in S \text{ and } t_i - W \leq t_j < t_i \}.$$

Given an event type $A$, the set of all the contexts of occurrences of $A$ in $S$ is defined as

$$\text{contexts}(A, S, W) = \{ \text{con}((e_i, t_i), S, W) \mid (e_i, t_i) \in S \text{ and } e_i = A \}.$$

That is, $\text{contexts}(A, S, W)$ is a collection of sets $\text{con}((e_i, t_i), S, W)$ where $e_i = A$. If there is no risk for confusion, we use an abbreviation $\text{contexts}(A)$ for the set of contexts of the event type $A$. The size of the set of contexts is denoted by $|\text{contexts}(A)|$.

*Example 4.* Consider the event type set $\mathcal{E} = \{A, B, C, D, E, F\}$ and the event sequence $S$ in Fig. 1. If we look at what happens within 3 time units before occurrences of an event type $A$, we get the following set of contexts

$$\text{contexts}(A, S, 3) = \{\emptyset, \{C, D\}, \{D, E\}\}.$$

When looking at the sequence using the same time window of 3 time units, we can notice that the set of contexts of an event type $B$ is exactly the same as the set of contexts of the event type $A$, i.e., $\text{contexts}(A, S, 3) = \text{contexts}(B, S, 3)$.

The definition of contexts above is by no means the only possible one. First, we could use sequences instead of sets in the definition of $\text{con}((e_i, t_i), S, W)$, i.e., we could define the context of an occurrence of an event type to be a sequence, not a set. This approach would be more in line with the idea of analyzing sequences; however, it would lead to severe computational problems.

The second choice made in the above definition of contexts is that we consider only a one-sided context. An alternative would be to define $\text{con}((e_i, t_i), S, W)$ to be the set of those event types which have an occurrence at a time between $t_i - W$ and $t_i + W$. This modified definition would be useful, for example, for genome or protein data, where both directions of the sequence are equally meaningful. Our main applications, however, are in sequences where there is a natural direction, that of advancing time, and hence, we use one-sided contexts.

There seldom is a single natural notion of similarity. For example, by varying the set of event types which is considered when computing contexts, or by changing the time window, we can obtain very different similarity notions.

## 4 Similarity between Sets of Contexts

The previous section showed how we define the set of contexts of an event type. What is left is defining the similarity between two sets of contexts. This turns out not to be trivial.

Each context of an occurrence of an event type is a subset of the set of all event types $\mathcal{E}$. We can, hence, identify each context with an $m$-dimensional vector of 0's and 1's, supposing that the number of the event types in $\mathcal{E}$ is $m$. For two such vectors, the similarity or distance between them can be naturally defined as the *Hamming distance*, i.e., the number of positions in which the vectors differ. This corresponds to using a symmetric difference between the sets of events. Given two event types of $A$ and $B$, their sets of contexts $\text{contexts}(A)$

and contexts($B$) are, however, two sets of vectors in an $m$-dimensional space. Thus, instead of defining similarity between two context vectors we have to define how similar or different two sets of vectors are.

A statistical approach is to view contexts($A$) and contexts($B$) as samples from two distributions $f_A$ and $f_B$ of the $m$-dimensional hypercube and define the similarity between the event types $A$ and $B$ as the similarity between $f_A$ and $f_B$. This can, in turn, be defined for example by using the Kullbach-Leibler distance [8, 9]:

$$d(f_A \parallel f_B) = \sum f_A(x) \cdot \log \frac{f_B(x)}{f_A(x)}$$

or the symmetrized version of it: $d(f_A \parallel f_B) + d(f_B \parallel f_A)$. Here the summation variable $x$ varies over all of the $2^m$ points of the hypercube, and hence, direct application of the formula is not feasible.

Another related alternative is to view the set contexts($A$) as a sample from a multivariate normal distribution and compute the likelihood of obtaining the set contexts($B$) as a sample from that distribution. That is, for an event type $C \in \mathcal{E}$, let $\mu_C^A$ and $\sigma_C^A$ be the mean and the variance of coordinate $C$ in the vectors in the set contexts($A$). Given a vector $(\delta_C)_{C \in \mathcal{E}} \in$ contexts($B$), the likelihood of this vector, given the set contexts($A$), is proportional to

$$\prod_{C \in \mathcal{E}} \exp(-((\delta_C - \mu_C^A)^2 / \sigma_C^A)) = \exp(-\sum_{C \in \mathcal{E}} ((\delta_C - \mu_C^A)^2 / \sigma_C^A)).$$

The logarithmic likelihood $g(B|A)$ of the whole set contexts($B$) = $\{(\delta_{iC}) \mid i = 1, \ldots, |\text{contexts}(B)|\}$ is then

$$g(B|A) = -\sum_i \sum_{C \in \mathcal{E}} ((\delta_C - \mu_C^A)^2 / \sigma_C^A).$$

This formula can be used as a distance function. To make it symmetric, we can use the form $g(B|A) + g(A|B)$.

A problem with this approach is that it can impose a high value of dissimilarity on the basis of a single event type. If for some $C \in \mathcal{E}$ we have that the set contexts($A$) contains no set with $C$ in it, then $\mu_C^A = 0$ and $\sigma_C^A = 0$. If now at least one context of $B$ contains $C$, then $g(B|A) = -\infty$, indicating that $B$ is infinitely far from $A$. In a way this conclusion is justified: no context of $A$ included $C$, but at least one context of $B$ did. However, in most cases we would not like to draw such an extreme conclusion on the basis of difference in one event type.

A way of alleviating this problem would be to use priors on the presence of an event type in a context. Intuitively, one way of doing this corresponds to adding to each set of contexts an empty context and a context containing all the event types in $\mathcal{E}$. Then the variance $\sigma_C^A$ cannot be zero for any $C$.

We use, however, mainly an even simpler alternative. We identify each set contexts($A$) with its centroid vector cev($A$), i.e., the vector cev($A$) = $(\mu_C^A)_{C \in \mathcal{E}}$, and define the distance between the sets contexts($A$) and contexts($B$) as the $L_1$-distance between the vectors cev($A$) and cev($B$):

$$d(\text{contexts}(A), \text{contexts}(B)) = |\text{cev}(A) - \text{cev}(B)| = \sum_{C \in \mathcal{E}} |\mu_C^A - \mu_C^B|.$$

It is well-known that this distance measure is a metric.

This approach has the advantage of being robust in the sense that a single event type cannot have an unbounded effect on the distance. The measure is also very fast to compute. A drawback is that the sizes of the sets contexts($A$) and contexts($B$) are not taken into account. In the application domains we consider, all the sets of contexts have more or less the same cardinality, so this problem is not severe.

## 5 Experimental Results

We have evaluated our method using both synthetic and real-life data. For reasons of brevity, we present in the following only some results on two real-life data sets, not on synthetic data.

Evaluating the success or failure of an automatic way of defining similarity between event types is not as straightforward as evaluating algorithms for prediction. For prediction tasks, there normally is a simple baseline (predicting the majority class) and for attribute-based data we can use, for example, C4.5 as a well-understood reference method. For assigning similarity to event types, however, no comparable reference points exist.

### 5.1 Course Enrollment Data

From the course enrollment data of the Department of Computer Science at the University of Helsinki we selected 18 often occurring courses and used them as the event types. Each sequence consisted of enrollments of one student; the lengths of the sequences varied from 1 to 18 depending on how many of the 18 courses the student had enrolled to. Totally, the data set contained enrollments of 5 519 students. Because the enrollments to courses had not occurrence times, we selected to a context of an occurrence of a course at most 5 courses that the student had enrolled to before he enrolled to the course considered.

The intuitive expectation is that two courses in this data set will be similar if they are located approximately at the same stage of the curriculum. Each course has a recommended term in which the department suggests it should be taken. Thus, to investigate how well our similarity measure satisfies the intuition, we compared the distances produced by our method with the background distances between the courses. The background distance between two courses is defined as the difference (as the number of terms) of the ordinal numbers of the recommended terms. The background distance takes values from 0 to 7. The results of this comparison are shown in Fig. 2. There is a clear correlation between the background distance and the distance produced by our method. The correlation coefficient between these variables is 0.4666.

There are some interesting pairs of courses which have a low distance according to our method. For example, the most similar pair of courses is formed by the courses *Social Role of ADP* and *Computer Graphics*. These are both courses that are typically taken during the 3rd or 4th study year, so their sets of contexts are rather similar. On the other hand, the distances between the course *Social Role of ADP* and the first year courses are rather high, indicating very different sets of contexts, as is natural.

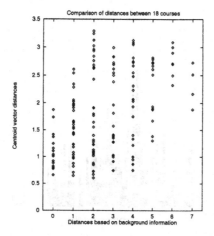

**Fig. 2.** A plot of distances based on the background information and $L_1$ distances of centroid vectors computed from the student enrollment data.

Also the courses *Fundamentals of ADP* and *Programming Pascal* are found to be very similar. This is understandable because they are the first two courses recommended to be taken. Therefore, the contexts of their occurrences are very often empty sets, or only contain the other course of them, and thus, the sets of contexts are nearly the same.

On the other hand, there are pairs of courses which are given a high distance by our method. For example, the courses *Information Systems* and *Data Structures Project* have the highest distance between all pairs of the 18 courses. These courses are compulsory courses to every student and they are usually both taken somewhere in the middle of the studies. Still, their sets of contexts vary a lot, indicating that not all the students follow the recommended study plan.

The student enrollment data set contained only the selected 18 courses. If all the other courses provided by the department were taken into account, the distances between the courses would give an even more realistic view of the relationships between them. Also taking into account the exact terms when the students enrolled to the different courses would change the values of the distance measure. In our experiments the context of an occurrence of a course gives us only the information that these courses were taken before this course, not how many terms ago this was done. If, however, the exact times were considered, the sets of contexts could be very different, at least for those courses which are recommended to be taken later during the studies.

## 5.2 Telecommunication Alarm Data

In our telecommunication data set there were 287 different alarm types and a total of 73 679 alarms. The data was collected during 50 days. The number of occurrences of alarm types differed a lot: from one occurrence to 12 186 occurrences. The mean number of occurrences of alarm types was 257.

First we experimented with 23 alarm types that occurred from 100 to 200 times in the whole alarm sequence and computed with our method the distances

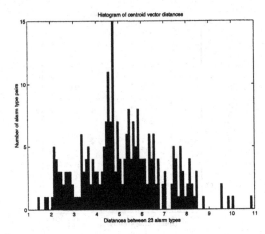

**Fig. 3.** Distribution of distances between 23 alarm types occurring 100 to 200 times in the whole alarm sequence.

between them with a time window of 60 seconds. Figure 3 presents the distribution of these distances. The distribution resembles the normal distribution. The high absolute values of the distances indicate, however, that these alarm types in general are not very similar. The most similar pair of the alarm types are alarm types 2583 and 2733. In the whole alarm sequence they occur 181 and 102 times, respectively. The most dissimilar pair is the pair of alarm types 1564 and 7172 which occur 167 and 101 times in the whole alarm sequence. The number of occurrences seems not to explain why the first two alarm types are determined similar and the other two very dissimilar. A more probable explanation is that the alarm types 2583 and 2733 belong to the same group of alarm types whereas alarm types 1564 and 7172 describe very different kind of failures in the telecommunication network. When looking more throughly at the distances, we noticed that the alarm type 7172 is pretty dissimilar with all the other alarm types, the smallest distance with value over 5 it has with the alarm type 7010.

From these 23 alarm types we chose some types for the second experiment. We considered one of the chosen alarm types at a time. We modified the sequence so that every occurrence of the chosen alarm type $A$ was indepedently changed to an event of the type $A'$ with the probability of 0.5. Then we computed the contexts for each of the now 24 alarm types and the distances between these sets of contexts. The assumption was the same as with the synthetic data: the alarm types $A$ and $A'$ should be the most similar alarm type pair. This was, however, not the case with none of the chosen alarms. The reason was that the sets of contexts of the original alarm types were not very homogeneous. Therefore, the sets of the contexts of alarm types $A$ and $A'$ could not be that, either.

For the third experiment with the telecommunication alarm data, we chose eight alarm types that occurred from 10 to 1 000 times in the whole alarm sequence. By looking at these alarm types, we wanted to find out how the distances change when the size of the time window $W$ varies. The values of $W$ used were

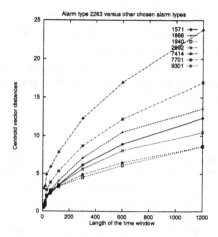

**Fig. 4.** Comparison of distances between alarm type 2263 and seven other alarm types with different sizes of time window $W$.

10, 20, 30, 60, 120, 300, 600, and 1200 seconds. Figure 4 describes how the distances between alarm type 2263 and seven other chosen alarm types vary with the size of the time window $W$. The number of occurrences of alarm type 2263 was about 1000. Already with contexts of window size 60 seconds, the order of the distances is rather stable: those alarm types that have very dissimilar sets of contexts have larger distance than those that have more similar sets of contexts. The values of the distances also indicate the difference in the number of occurrences of the chosen alarm types. For example, alarm type 7414 occurs only 10 times in the whole alarm sequence whereas alarm type 2263 occurs about 1000 times. Therefore, it is rather obvious that, especially with longer time windows, the sets of contexts of these alarm types are very different and the distance between them becomes very large. Similar observations can also be made when looking at any of the other chosen alarm types.

## 6 Conclusions

We have described a method for defining similarity between event types on the basis of contexts in which the event types occur in sequences. We have evaluated the method using both synthetic and real-life data and shown that it works well.

Several extensions of the method are possible. As mentioned in Sect. 3, instead of using sets as contexts, we could also use sequences. Then, to define the similarity between sets of contexts we could not, however, use the straightforward centroid approach of this paper. The distance between two event sequences can be computed reasonably fast using edit distance type of approaches (see, e.g, [11,18]), but combining these distances to an overall similarity measure for sets of context sequences remains an open problem.

We mentioned in passing in Sect. 3 that one can vary the set of event types that are considered when forming the contexts. This gives possibilities for tailoring the resulting similarity metric to various needs. Semiautomatic ways of finding which event types to consider would, however, be needed.

The empirical behavior of our method on other application domains is also an interesting area for future work. For example, sequences rising from web browsing activity and electronic commerce as well as protein sequences are good candidates for successful applications.

# References

1. R. Agrawal, C. Faloutsos, and A. Swami. Efficiency similarity search in sequence databases. In *FODO'93*, pages 69 – 84. Springer-Verlag, Oct. 1993.
2. R. Agrawal, K.-I. Lin, H. S. Sawhney, and K. Shim. Fast similarity search in the presence of noise, scaling, and translation in time-series databases. In *VLDB'95*, pages 490 – 501. Morgan Kaufmann, Sept. 1995.
3. G. Das, H. Mannila, and P. Ronkainen. Similarity of attributes by external probes. In *KDD'98*, pages 23 – 29. AAAI, Aug. 1998.
4. D. Q. Goldin and P. C. Kanellakis. On similarity queries for time-series data: Constraint specification and implementation. In *CP'95*, pages 137 – 153. Springer-Verlag, Sept. 1995.
5. H. Jagadish, A. O. Mendelzon, and T. Milo. Similarity-based queries. In *PODS'95*, pages 36 – 45. ACM, May 1995.
6. Y. Karov and S. Edelman. Similarity-based word sense disambiguation. *Computational Linguistics*, 24(1):41 – 59, Mar. 1998.
7. A. J. Knobbe and P. W. Adriaans. Analysing binary associations. In *KDD'96*, pages 311 – 314. AAAI, Aug. 1996.
8. S. Kullbach. *Information Theory and Statistics*. John Wiley Inc., NY, USA, 1959.
9. S. Kullbach and R. A. Leibler. On information theory and sufficiency. *Annals of Mathematical Statistics*, 22:79 – 86, 1951.
10. P. Laird. Identifying and using patterns in sequential data. In *ALT'93*, pages 1 – 18. Springer-Verlag, Nov. 1993.
11. H. Mannila and P. Ronkainen. Similarity of event sequences. In *TIME'97*, pages 136 – 139. IEEE, May 1997.
12. H. Mannila and H. Toivonen. Discovering generalized episodes using minimal occurrences. In *KDD'96*, pages 146 – 151. AAAI, Aug. 1996.
13. H. Mannila, H. Toivonen, and A. I. Verkamo. Discovering frequent episodes in sequences. In *KDD'95*, pages 210 – 215. AAAI, Aug. 1995.
14. H. Mannila, H. Toivonen, and A. I. Verkamo. Discovery of frequent episodes in event sequences. *Data Mining and Knowledge Discovery*, 1(3):259 – 289, 1997.
15. R. A. Morris, L. Khatib, and G. Ligozat. Generating scenarios from specifications of repeating events. In *TIME'95*. IEEE, Apr. 1995.
16. T. Oates and P. R. Cohen. Searching for structure in multiple streams of data. In *ICML'96*, pages 346 – 354. Morgan Kaufmann, July 1996.
17. D. Rafiei and A. Mendelzon. Similarity-based queries for time series data. *SIGMOD Record*, 26(2):13–25, May 1997.
18. P. Ronkainen. Attribute similarity and event sequence similarity in data mining. PhLic thesis, Report C-1998-42, University of Helsinki, Department of Computer Science, Helsinki, Finland, Oct. 1998.
19. D. A. White and R. Jain. Algorithms and strategies for similarity retrieval. Technical Report VCL-96-101, Visual Computing Laboratory, University of California, San Diego, USA, July 1996.

# Mining Generalized Association Rule Using Parallel RDB Engine on PC Cluster

Iko Pramudiono, Takahiko Shintani,
Takayuki Tamura*, Masaru Kitsuregawa

Institute of Industrial Science, The University of Tokyo
7-22-1 Roppongi, Minato-ku, Tokyo 106, Japan
{iko,shintani,tamura,kitsure}@tkl.iis.u-tokyo.ac.jp

**Abstract.** Data mining has been widely recognized as a powerful tool to explore added value from large-scale databases. One of data mining techniques, generalized association rule mining with taxonomy, is potential to discover more useful knowledge than ordinary flat association mining by taking application specific information into account. We proposed SQL queries, named TTR-SQL and TH-SQL to perform this kind of mining and evaluated them on PC cluster. Those queries can be more than 30% faster than Apriori based SQL query reported previously. Although RDBMS has powerful query processing ability through SQL, most data mining systems use specialized implementations to achieve better performance. There is a tradeoff between performance and portability. Performance is not necessarily sufficiently high but seamless integration with existing RDBMS would be considerably advantageous. Since RDB is already very popular, the feasibility of generalized association rule mining can be explored using the proposed SQL query instead of purchasing expensive mining software. In addition, parallel RDB is now also widely accepted. We showed that paralleling the SQL execution can offer the same performance with those native programs with 10 to 15 nodes. Since most organizations have a lot of PCs, which are not fully utilized. We are able to exploit such resources to explore the performance significantly.
Keywords: data mining, parallel RDBMS, query optimization, PC cluster

## 1 Introduction

Data mining has attracted lots of attention to solve decision support problems such as that faced by large retail organizations. Those organizations have accumulated large amount of transaction data by mean of data collection tools such as POS and they want to extract value added information such as unknown buying patterns from that large databases. One method of data mining to deal with this kind of problem is association rule mining.[1] This mining that is also known as "basket data analysis" retrieves information like "90% of the customers who buy A and B also buy C" from transaction data.

---

* Currently at Information & Communication System Development Center, Mitsubishi Electric, Ohfuna 5-1-1 Kamakura-shi Kanagawa-ken 247-8501, Japan

Currently, database systems are dominated by relational database system (RDBMS). However most of data mining systems employ special mining engines and do not use the query processing capability of SQL in RDBMS. Although integration of data mining system with RDBMS provides many benefits, among others: easier system maintenance, flexibility and portability, [5] has reported that in case of association rule mining this approach has a drawback in performance. Association rule mining has to handle very large amounts of transaction data, which requires incredibly long computation time.

We proposed large-scale PC cluster as cost effective platform for data intensive applications such as data mining using parallel RDBMS, which offers the advantages of the integration without sacrificing the performance. [8]

SQL approach can be easily enhanced with non-trivial expansion to handle complex mining tasks. Recently, [6] has proposed SQL query to mine generalized association rule with taxonomy based on Apriori algorithm[3] that we will refer as "Sarawagi Thomas"-SQL or ST-SQL from now on. In generalized association rules, application-specific knowledge in the form of taxonomies (is-a hierarchies) over items are used to discover more interesting rules.

We propose two new queries to mine generalized association rule, TTR-SQL and TH-SQL, and examine their effectiveness through real implementation on the PC cluster. We also compare the performance with directly coded C program.

## 2 Mining Generalized Association Rule with Taxonomy

### 2.1 Association Rule Mining

A typical example of association rule is "if a customer buys $A$ and $B$ then 90% of this kind of customers buy also $C$". Here 90% is called the *confidence* of the rule. Another measure of a rule is called the *support* of the rule.

Transactions in a retail database usually consist of an identifier and a set of items or itemset. $\{A, B, C\}$ in above example is an itemset. An association rule is an implication of the form $X \implies Y$ where $X$ and $Y$ are itemsets. An itemset $X$ has support $s$ if $s\%$ of transactions contain that itemset, here we denote $s = support(X)$. The support of the rule $X \implies Y$ is $support(X \cup Y)$. The *confidence* of that rule can be written as the ratio $support(X \cup Y)/support(X)$.

The problem of mining association rules is to find all the rules that satisfy a user-specified minimum support and minimum confidence, which can be decomposed into two subproblems:

1. Find all combinations of items, called large itemsets, whose support is greater than minimum support.
2. Use the large itemsets to generate the rules.

Since the first step consumes most of processing time, development of mining algorithms has been concentrated on this step.

## 2.2 Generalized Association Rule with Taxonomy

In most cases, items can be classified according to some kind of "is a" hierarchies. [7] For example "Sushi is a Japanese Food" and also "Sushi is a Food" can be expressed as taxonomy as showed in figure 1. Here we categorize sushi as descendant and Japanese food and food are its ancestors. This tree can be implemented as a taxonomy table such as shown in the same figure. By including taxonomy as application specific knowledge more interesting rules can be discovered.

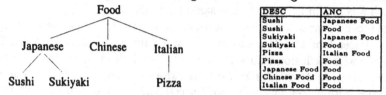

| DESC | ANC |
| --- | --- |
| Sushi | Japanese Food |
| Sushi | Food |
| Sukiyaki | Japanese Food |
| Sukiyaki | Food |
| Pizza | Italian Food |
| Pizza | Food |
| Japanese Food | Food |
| Chinese Food | Food |
| Italian Food | Food |

**Fig.1.** Taxonomy example and its table

Since support counting for each itemset must also includes the combinations of all ancestors for each item, generally this kind of mining requires significantly more time.

# 3 Mining Algorithms on SQL

Most of the algorithms developed to mine association rule was intended to pursuit effectiveness so somehow they neglect integration with existing system. Some exception such as SETM[4] reported SQL expression of association rule mining. Recently pure SQL implementation of the well known Apriori algorithm has been reported but the performance is far behind its object oriented SQL extensions or other more loosely integrated approachs [5]. [6] extended the query to mine generalized association rule with taxonomy. In this paper we name this SQL query as ST-SQL in connection to the names of its authors. In addition [6] also extended the query further to handle sequential pattern as well.

In our experiment we employ ordinary standard SQL since it is widely used. We propose a new query to mine generalized association rule that we call TTR-SQL and compare it with the ST-SQL. We also examine a variant of TTR-SQL named TH-SQL. TH-SQL incorporates candidate pruning feature of Apriori.

## 3.1 ST-SQL

The SQL query of ST-SQL that we used for comparison is described in figure 3. This query is based on Cumulate algorithm proposed in [7]. Cumulate algorithm itself is based on Apriori algorithm for mining boolean or flat association rule, and it is extended with optimizations that make use of the characteristics of generalized association rule such as pruning itemsets containing an item and its ancestors and pre-computing the ancestors of each item. However since we have TAXONOMY table in form (*descendant, ancestor*), the latter optimization for pre-computing the ancestors is implicitly incorporated. The transaction data is normalized into the first normal form $(transactionID, item)$.

In the first pass, we count the support of the items in the extended transaction data to determine the large itemsets for pass 1 (F_1). Here extended transaction data is the data that also takes form $(transactionID, item)$. It contains not only items in transactions but also all their ancestors. It is created by a subquery SXTD that employs a union operation. The clause SELECT DISTINCT in the subquery is to ensure that there are no duplicate records due to extension of items with a common ancestor in the same transaction.

In the second pass we apply the optimization to prune item pairs that contain both the descendant and the ancestor from second pass' large itemsets F_2. This is done with exclusion clause NOT IN that excludes item pairs that match $(ancestor, descendant)$ or $(descendant, ancestor)$ in taxonomy table. The rule that contains both descendant and ancestor is trivially true and hence redundant. [7] proved that this optimization is only needed at second pass since candidate itemset pruning of Apriori algorithm guarantees the later passes will not contain such kind of itemsets. The query also employs the second pass optimization described in [5] that uses F_1 directly instead of materializing C_2 first.

The query for third pass or later is the same with the query for flat association rule described in [5]. We use the so called Subquery method for support counting since it is reported to have the best time. Figure 2 gives illustration how it is executed. AGGR is a symbol to denote support counting process such as GROUP BY and COUNT.

First we generate the candidate itemsets for $k$-th pass C_k by a cascade of $k-1$ joins. The first join generates a superset of the candidate itemsets by self-joining previous pass' large itemsets F_k-1. We assume that the items are lexicographically ordered. The subsequent joins prune that superset by checking the membership in F_k-1 of all its $(k-1)$-length subsets. This is done by skipping one item after another from the $k$-length itemsets in the superset at each join. [3] suggested that this pruning can drastically reduce the number of candidate itemsets.

The support counting involves second stage and third stage of figure 2. A cascade of $k$ times subquery Q_l is required. Subquery Q_l generates all distinct transactions whose $l$ items match the first $l$ items of C_k. This subquery is cascaded $k$ times to obtain all $k$-length itemsets in the transaction data or $k$-itemsets. Those $k$-itemsets are summed up to determine the large itemsets of pass $k$ F_k. Inside each subquery Q_l, subquery SXTD is executed again to include the $l$-th item into the result.

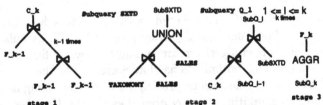

**Fig. 2.** Execution tree for $k$-th pass of ST-SQL ($k \geq 3$)

CREATE TABLE SALES (id int, item int);
CREATE TABLE TAXONOMY (desc int, anc int);

- PASS 1

CREATE TABLE F_1 (item_1 int, cnt int);

INSERT INTO F_1
    SELECT    item AS item_1, COUNT(*)
    FROM     (SUBQUERY SXTD)
    GROUP BY item
    HAVING COUNT(*) >= :min_support;

SUBQUERY SXTD
    SELECT    id, item FROM    SALES UNION
    SELECT DISTINCT p.id, p.anc
    FROM     SALES p, TAXONOMY t
    WHERE    p.item = t.desc;

- PASS 2

CREATE TABLE F_2 (item1 int, item2 int, cnt int);

INSERT INTO F_2
    SELECT i1.item1, i2.item1, COUNT(*)
    FROM F_1 i1, F_1 i2, (SUBQUERY SXTD) t1, t2
    WHERE t1.id = t2.id
    AND t1.item = i1.item1
    AND t2.item = i2.item1
    AND i1.item1 < i2.item1
    AND (i1.item1, i2.item1)
        NOT IN ( SELECT anc, desc FROM TAXON-
OMY
        UNION SELECT desc, anc FROM TAXON-
OMY)
    GROUP BY i1.item1, i2.item2
    HAVING COUNT(*) >= :min_support;

- PASS k (k > 2)
CREATE TABLE C_k (item1 int, item2 int,
    ... item_k int);
CREATE TABLE F_k (item1 int, item2 int,
    ... item_k int, cnt int);

INSERT INTO C_k   -candidate itemsets
    SELECT i1.item1, i1.item2,
        ... , i1.item_k-1, i2.item_k-1
    FROM F_k-1 i1, F_k-1 i2, F_k-1 i3,
        ... F_k-1 i_k
    WHERE i1.item1 = i2.item1
    AND i1.item2 = i2.item2
        .
        .
    AND i1.item_k-2 = i2.item_k-2
    AND i1.item_k-1 < i2.item_k-1
-pruning by checking memberships in (k-1) subsets
    AND i1.item2 = i3.item1    -skip item1
    AND i1.item3 = i3.item2
        .
        .
    AND i1.item_k-1 = i3.item_k-2
    AND i2.item_k-1 = i3.item_k-1
        .
        .
    AND i1.item1 = i_k.item1    -skip item_k-2
        .
        .
    AND i1.item_k-3 = i_k.item_k-3
    AND i1.item_k-1 = i_k.item_k-2
    AND i2.item_k-1 = i_k.item_k-1

INSERT INTO F_k   -large itemsets
    SELECT t.item1, t.item2, ...,
        t.item_k, COUNT(*)
    FROM (SUBQUERY Q_k) t
    GROUP BY t.item1, t.item2, ..., t.item_k
    HAVING COUNT(*) >= :min_support;

- for any l between 1 and k
SUBQUERY Q_l
    SELECT d_l.item1, d_l.item2, ... , d_l.item_l, t_l.id
    FROM (SUBQUERY SXTD) t_l,
        (SUBQUERY Q_l-1) r_l-1,
        (SELECT DISTINCT item1, ...
        item_l FROM C_k) d_l
    WHERE r_l-1.item1 = d_l.item1
    AND r_l-1.item2 = d_l.item2
        .
        .
    AND r_l-1.item_l-1 = d_l.item_l-1
    AND r_l-1.tid = t_l.tid
    AND    t_l.item = d_l.item_l

**Fig. 3.** SQL query of ST-SQL

---

CREATE TABLE SALES (id int, item int);
CREATE TABLE RXTD (id int, item int);
CREATE TABLE TAXONOMY (desc int, anc int);

- PASS 1

CREATE TABLE F_1 (item_1 int, cnt int);
CREATE TABLE R_1 (id int, item_1 int);

CREATE TABLE TAX_H (desc int, anc int);

INSERT INTO R_1
    SELECT    id, item AS item_1
FROM    SALES UNION
    SELECT DISTINCT p.id, p.anc
    FROM     SALES p, TAXONOMY t
    WHERE    p.item = t.desc;

INSERT INTO F_1
    SELECT    item AS item_1, COUNT(*)
    FROM     R_1
    GROUP BY item_1
    HAVING COUNT(*) >= :min_support;

INSERT INTO TAX_H   -taxonomies pruning
    SELECT    t.desc, t.anc
    FROM     F_1 c, TAXONOMY t
    WHERE    t.desc = c.item_1

- PASS k
CREATE TABLE RTMP_k    (id int, item_1 int,
    item_2 int, ... , item_k-1 int)
CREATE TABLE R_k (id int, item_1 int,
    item_2 int, ... , item_k int)
CREATE TABLE F_k    (item_1 int,
    item_2 int, ... , item_k int, cnt int);

-(k-1)-length temporary transaction data
INSERT INTO RTMP_k
    SELECT    p.id, p.item_1, p.item_2, ...,
        p.item_k-1
    FROM     R_k-1 p, F_k-1 c
    WHERE    p.item_1 = c.item_1
    AND      p.item_2 = c.item_2
        .
        .
    AND      p.item_k-1 = c.item_k-1;

INSERT INTO R_k   -k-length itemsets
    SELECT    p.id, p.item_1, p.item_2,
        ... , p.item_k-1, q.item_k-1
    FROM     RTMP_k p, RTMP_k q
    WHERE    p.id    = q.id
    AND      p.item_1 = q.item_1
    AND      p.item_2 = q.item_2
        .
        .
    AND      p.item_k-2 = q.item_k-2
    AND      p.item_k-1 < q.item_k-1
    AND      (p.item_k-1, q.item_k-1)
        NOT IN ( SELECT anc, desc FROM TAX_H
        UNION SELECT desc, anc FROM TAX_H)

INSERT INTO F_k   -large itemsets
    SELECT    item_1, item_2, ..., item_k,
        COUNT(*)
    FROM     R_k
    GROUP BY item_1, item_2, ..., item_k
    HAVING COUNT(*) >= :min_support;

DROP TABLE RTMP_k;
DROP TABLE R_k-1;

**Fig. 4.** SQL query of TTR-SQL

INSERT INTO R_k
    SELECT    p.id, p.item_1, p.item_2,
        ... , p.item_k-1, q.item_k-1
    FROM     RTMP_k p, RTMP_k q, C_k c
    WHERE    p.id    = q.id
    AND      p.item_1 = q.item_1
        .
        .
    AND      p.item_k-2 = q.item_k-2
    AND      p.item_k-1 < q.item_k-1
        .
    AND      p.item_1 = c.item_1
        .
        .
    AND      p.item_k-1 = c.item_k-1
    AND      q.item_k-1 = c.item_k

**Fig. 5.** SQL query modification of TH-SQL

## 3.2 TTR-SQL

TTR-SQL query is described in figure 4. We named this query TTR-SQL from "mining Taxonomy using Temporary Relations" since it utilizes temporary relations to preserve transaction data between passes in the similar fashion as SETM algorithm.[4] However SETM is intended for flat association rule mining and it is inefficient to handle generalized association rule mining since we have to add all ancestors for each item included in transaction. We employ following optimizations to this query:

1. Prune taxonomies whose descendant is not included in the large itemsets of first pass.
   This is obvious since we do not need them in later processing. For example with taxonomy in figure 1, suppose that item "Pizza" has too little support so that it is excluded from large itemsets of first pass in F_1. Then we can remove {Pizza, Italian Food}, {Pizza, Food} and {Italian Food, Food} from the taxonomy table. Some of our experiments show the size of taxonomy table can be reduced up to 100 times smaller. Mining with many passes will receive most benefit from this optimization.
2. Pruning candidate itemsets containing an item and its ancestor.
   As mentioned before rule, such as "Sushi → Japanese Food", that contains both descendant and ancestor is trivially true and we can neglect it. TTR-SQL implements this optimization in every pass except first pass.

In the first pass we include all ancestors of each item from taxonomy table that matches the descendant. We use taxonomy table again to prune candidate itemsets later but since most of items in transaction data do not meet minimum support we can eliminate them from taxonomy table as explained in the first optimization. Thus we use the subset of taxonomy table TAX_H instead in second optimization's pruning. Table TAX_H only consists of entries whose descendants are included in large itemsets of first pass. The first pass of TTR-SQL differs from that of ST-SQL in the way that we generate the extended transaction data as a table named R_1. We can replace the generation of R_1 with a subquery to avoid materialization cost.

In other passes we employ second optimization while generating $k$-itemsets into R_k. The execution tree is shown in figure 7. First, we include $k-1$-itemsets, that match large itemsets from previous pass F_k-1, into the $k-1$-length temporary transaction data RTMP_k along with their transaction IDs. Then this RTMP_k is used to generate lexicographically ordered $k$-itemsets by self-join. During this generation process, we exclude $k$-itemsets that contains both descendant and ancestor using taxonomy table subset TAX_H. This second optimization also uses exclusion clause NOT IN, the same way as the second pass of ST-SQL. We only need to check the $k-1$-th item pairs since the items in the itemsets are lexicographically ordered so that previous items are already checked in the previous passes. The generated $k$-itemsets are included in R_k that also

287

contains transaction IDs. Lastly, large itemsets in F_k are determined from those k-itemsets whose support are larger than minimum support.

Temporary transaction data RTMP_k need not always be materialized. We could avoid the materialization cost of RTMP_k by replacing RTMP_k with a subquery and include the subquery into R_k generation query.

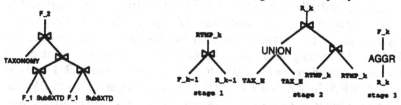

**Fig.6.** Execution tree for second pass of ST-SQL

**Fig.7.** Execution tree for $k$-th pass of TTR-SQL ($k \geq 2$)

## 3.3 TH-SQL

We can incorporate the candidate pruning feature of Apriori algorithm into the TTR-SQL to avoid pruning with taxonomy table in every pass which could be expensive. By doing this, we do not need second optimization of TTR-SQL in the first pass anymore since one pruning with taxonomy table in second pass alone is sufficient. Since this query combines best features from TTR-SQL and ST-SQL, we call it TH-SQL which stands for "Taxonomy Hybrid".

TH-SQL's modification to the TTR-SQL query for pass $k \geq 3$ is depicted in figure 5 where we replace the exclusion clause with a selection join with candidate itemsets C_k. C_k is generated at the beginning of each pass using the same query as ST-SQL. However the second pass remains the same with TTR-SQL except we use TAXONOMY instead of TAX_H for the ancestor pruning. We show execution tree at pass $k \geq 3$ of TH-SQL in figure 8.

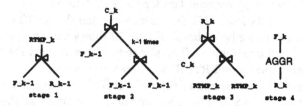

**Fig. 8.** Execution tree for $k$-th pass of TH-SQL ($k \geq 3$)

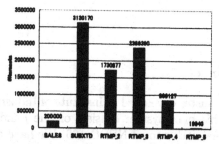

**Fig.9.** Cardinality of RTMP_k (1% min. support)

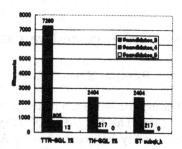

**Fig.10.** Effect of candidate pruning (1% min. support)

## 3.4 Comparison of Three Approaches

ST-SQL completes its first and second passes faster than two other queries. [3] has reported that SETM produces very large R_2 compared with Apriori which leads to performance degradation. However we found that the executions of these passes are basically using the same execution tree for all queries. The most efficient execution tree of second pass ST-SQL is shown in figure 6. It allows early filtering of transactions based on the first pass large itemsets F_1 instead of larger C_2. It only does not materialize the intermediate result of the joins. Hence the time difference is limited to the materialization of R_1 and the generation of RTMP_2. In addition TTR-SQL also requires generation of TAX_H. Our performance evaluation shows that those costs differences are relatively very small.

The time required by ST-SQL is dominated by support counting (stage 2 and 3). We can derive from figure 2 that at pass $k$ larger than three, ST-SQL uses the result of subquery SXTD each time it executes subquery Q_l. This means it has to read the entire transactions from disk $k$ times each pass. Thus the execution time of ST-SQL at pass $k \geq 3$ is proportional with the $k$ multiplied by the size of extended transaction data in addition to the cost for joins in subquery Q_l. Even if the cost for joins decreases as the number of candidate itemsets becomes smaller for large $k$, this cost of subquery SXTD makes ST-SQL inefficient for data mining with many passes.

On the other hand, the dominan factors in execution of TTR-SQL dan TH-SQL are the generation of RTMP_k and R_k. However the size of RTMP_k of both TTR-SQL and TH-SQL generally shrinks as the $k$ increases. This general behaviour is shown in figure 9. The figure also shows that the size of extended transaction data can be one magnitude larger than the original transaction data. R_k is also becoming smaller as well. We can expect that our proposed queries will perform better at passes over two for most of datasets.

The size of R_k relation of TH-SQL is smaller than that of TTR-SQL because of the candidate pruning beforehand. Figure 10 shows how this pruning reduces the number of candidate itemsets. This size reduction will affect the time required for the support counting and RTMP_k generation stages.

Thus we expect that execution time of TH-SQL < execution time of TTR-SQL < execution of ST-SQL which we are going to examine at the next section by real implementation.

# 4 Performance Evaluation

## 4.1 Parallel Execution Environment

The experiment is conducted on a PC cluster developed at Institute of Industrial Science, The University of Tokyo. This pilot system consists of one hundred commodity PCs connected by ATM network named NEDO-100. We have also developed DBKernel database server for query processing on this system. Each

PC has Intel Pentium Pro 200MHz CPU, 4.3GB SCSI hard disk and 64 MB RAM.

The performance evaluation using TPC-D benchmark on 100 nodes cluster is reported[8]. The results showed it can achieve significantly higher performance especially for join intensive query such as query 9 compared to the current commercially available high end systems.

### 4.2 Dataset

Synthetic transaction data generator developed at IBM Almaden is used for this experiment with parameters described in table 1. [3] Transaction data is distributed uniformly corresponds to transaction ID among processing nodes' local hard disk while the taxonomy table is replicated to each node.

### 4.3 Performance Evaluation of ST-SQL, TTR-SQL, and TH-SQL

In this section, we compared the three SQL queries proposed in the previous section. The performance evaluation is done on five nodes. The experiments over varied number of nodes will be given at the next subsection.

Figure 11 shows a typical execution time of the three queries. The minimum support is set to 2.5%. The mining is four passes long. We can see that although ST-SQL is superior to the other queries up to second pass, it spends too much time in the third pass and later. In overall, TTR-SQL and TH-SQL are 30 % faster than ST-SQL for this minimum support. Since the required time for ST-SQL proportional to the number of required passes $k$, ST-SQL will suffer when $k$ is larger, such as when the minimum support is smaller. This is a major drawback since usually we want smaller minimum support with higher confidence to generate more interesting rules.

But contrary to our expectation, even that tuples in R_k of TH-SQL is reduced up to 50% than that of TTR-SQL as shown in figure 12, we do not see any remarkable performance improvement with TH-SQL when compared to TTR-SQL. Since the dataset itself is small, the gain achieved might be relatively small. Thus we are planning to perform larger scale experiments to examine it.

Candidate generation of SETM at second pass generally produces extremely large R_2. However current pruning method is useless at this pass. An effective pruning of R_2 will considerably improve the performance of SETM as well as TTR-SQL and TH-SQL, which is also left for further investigation.

The speedup ratio, that is the gain achieved by parallelization, of our algorithms shown in figure 13 indicates that they can be parallelized well. The execution is 9 times faster with 10 nodes. This result supports the feasibility of data mining with parallel RDB engine, we will give report on comparison with specialized data mining program in the next subsection.

However the smaller size of data at each node degrades the speedup ratio when we increase the number of nodes over 20. At this point the parallelization overhead, such as communication cost, corrupts the gain.

**Table.1.** Dataset paremeters

| Sise of transaction data | 12.8MB |
|---|---|
| Number of transactions | 200000 |
| Average transaction length | 5 |
| Sise of taxonomy | 182KB |
| Number of items | 20000 |
| Number of roots | 50 |
| Number of levels | 3 |
| Average fanout | 20 |

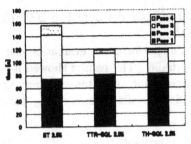

**Fig.11.**Execution time and pass contribution(1 node)

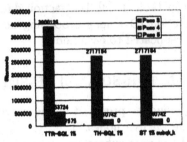

**Fig.12.** Cardinality of R_k

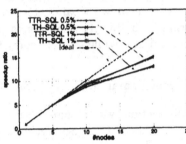

**Fig.13.** Speedup ratio

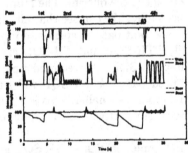

**Fig.14.** Execution trace for ST-SQL (5 nodes, 2.5% min. support)

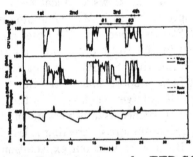

**Fig.15.** Execution trace for TTR-SQL (5 nodes, 2.5% min. support)

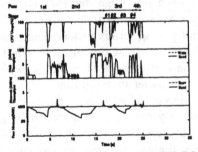

**Fig.16.** Execution trace for TH-SQL (5 nodes, 2.5% minimum support)

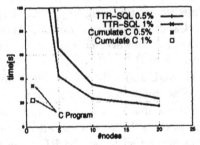

**Fig.17.** Execution time comparison with directly coded program

We have recorded the execution traces of ST-SQL, TTR-SQL and TH-SQL as shown in figure 14 to 16 respectively. Note that most of the time the query execution is CPU bound process. Significant network activities are observed only during the aggregation process when nodes exchange data to obtain overall support count.

When we look further into the execution trace of ST-SQL query, during the second stage of third pass we will recognize three bursts of disk read indicating the execution of subquery SXTD. Between those burst we see drops in the free memory that indicates that the intermediate result of each subquery $Q\_l$ consumes considerable amount of memory. Another observation to the fourth pass will reveals four similar patterns of disk activities dominate the execution time of this pass. The trace gives us the evidence for our analysis that this kind of disk read will dominate the pass with small candidate itemsets $C\_k$ thus ST-SQL is not suitable for mining with many passes.

Execution trace of TTR-SQL in figure 15 shows similar pattern repeated every pass at passes more than two. It also reveals that CPU becomes idle when it materializes the relation into disk. However in contrast to ST-SQL, it utilizes memory better that allows TTR-SQL to handle larger transaction data. We also observe that the introduction of candidate itemset pruning in TH-SQL does not affect the execution trace in figure 16 much because the size of TAX_H, $F\_k$ and $C\_k$ are very small.

## 4.4 Performance comparison of parallelized TTR-SQL with sequential C-code

In this section, we would like to compare the performance of directly coded C program with the parallelized SQL. It is true that C code is much faster than the SQL but by employing SQL we are able to integrate mining mechanism into the database system seamlessly. Recently so many PCs are used in any organizations and all of them are not necessarily fully utilized at all. In addition, most of the relational middleware at present have the capability of parallel extension. We could exploits such potential of parallelization by utilizing abundant resources. Here we use the SQL engine which we developed over PC cluster [8]. The performance evaluation results are shown at figure 17. The results for two different minimum supports are given. On average, we can achieve the same level of execution time by employing 10 - 15 nodes. Due to the space limit, we are not able to show the detail trace information of parallel execution but still there remains some room for optimization to reduce synchronization. We exemplified that we could archive reasonable performance by activating around 10 nodes. This might look expensive. But recent reduction of hardware price suggests that SQL implementation on PC cluster would be one of the alternatives.

## 5 Summary and Conclusion

The ability to perform data mining using standard SQL queries will benefit data warehouses with the better integration with RDBMS. It also allows easier porting codes among different systems, a task that require a lot of efforts with specialized "black box" programs.

Generalized association rule mining with taxonomy is one of the complicated mining task that used to depend on specialized programs. As far as authors know only one pure SQL-92 query available to perform data mining on generalized association rule, namely ST-SQL that is proposed in [6].

We presented two new SQL queries, TTR-SQL that utilizes temporary relations and TH-SQL that combines the best features from two queries mentioned earlier such as candidate pruning. We have evaluated the three queries and showed that our proposed queries can achieve better performance up to 30% for data mining with four passes. We can expect more improvement with more passes. Our analysis indicated that the execution time at pass $k$ of ST-SQL is at least proportional with $k$ times the size of transaction data. This results in poor performance for pass larger than three.

PC cluster is a prospective platform for parallel RDBMS with its high cost-performance. We also have made performance comparison with data mining program written natively in C. We found that 10 to 15 nodes are enough to match the specialized program.

# References

1. R. Agrawal, T. Imielinski, A. Swami. Mining Association Rules between Sets of Items in Large Databases. In Proc. of the ACM SIGMOD Conference on Management of Data, 1993.
2. R. Agrawal, J.C. Shafer. Parallel Mining of Association Rules: Design, Implementation and Experience. IBM Research Report RJ 10004, 1996.
3. R. Agrawal, R. Srikant. Fast Algorithms for Mining Association Rules. In Proc. of the VLDB Conference, 1994.
4. M. Houtsma, A. Swami. Set- oriented Mining of Association Rules. In Proc. of International Conference on Data Engineering, 1995.
5. S. Sarawagi, S. Thomas, R. Agrawal. Integrating Association Rule Mining with Relational Database Systems: Alternatives and Implications. In Proc. of the ACM SIGMOD Conference on Management of Data, 1998.
6. S. Sarawagi, S. Thomas. Mining Generalized Association Rules and Sequential Patterns Using SQL Queries. In Proc. of KDD, 1998.
7. R. Srikant, R. Agrawal. Mining Generalized Association Rules. In Proc. of VLDB, 1995.
8. T. Tamura, M. Oguchi, M. Kitsuregawa. Parallel Database Processing on a 100 Node PC Cluster: Cases for Decision Support Query Processing and Data Mining. In Proc. of SC97: High Performance Networking and Computing, 1997.

# Modeling KDD Processes within the Inductive Database Framework

Jean-François Boulicaut*, Mika Klemettinen†, and Heikki Mannila‡ *

* INSA de Lyon, LISI Bâtiment 501, F–69621 Villeurbanne cedex, France
† University of Helsinki, Department of Computer Science
P.O. Box 26, FIN–00014 University of Helsinki, Finland
‡ Microsoft Research, One Microsoft Way, Redmond, WA 98052-6399, USA

**Abstract.** One of the most challenging problems in data manipulation in the future is to be able to efficiently handle very large databases but also multiple induced properties or generalizations in that data. Popular examples of useful properties are association rules, and inclusion and functional dependencies. Our view of a possible approach for this task is to specify and query inductive databases, which are databases that in addition to data also contain intensionally defined generalizations about the data. We formalize this concept and show how it can be used throughout the whole process of data mining due to the closure property of the framework. We show that simple query languages can be defined using normal database terminology. We demonstrate the use of this framework to model typical data mining processes. It is then possible to perform various tasks on these descriptions like, e.g., optimizing the selection of interesting properties or comparing two processes.

## 1  Introduction

Data mining, or knowledge discovery in databases (KDD), sets new challenges to database technology: new concepts and methods are needed for general purpose query languages [8]. A possible approach is to formulate a data mining task as locating interesting sentences from a given logic that are true in the database. Then the task of the user/analyst can be viewed as querying this set, the so-called *theory* of the database [12].

Discovering knowledge from data, the so-called KDD process, contains several steps: understanding the domain, preparing the data set, discovering patterns, postprocessing of discovered patterns, and putting the results into use. This is a complex interactive and iterative process for which many related theories have to be computed: different selection predicates but also different classes of patterns must be used.

For KDD, we need a query language that enables the user to select subsets of the data, but also to specify data mining tasks and select patterns from the corresponding theories. Our special interest is in the combined pattern discovery and postprocessing steps via a querying approach. For this purpose, a closure

---

* Email: jfboulic@lisi.insa-lyon.fr, mklemett@cs.helsinki.fi, mannila@microsoft.com.

property of the query language is desirable: the result of a KDD query should be an object of a similar type than its arguments. Furthermore, the user must also be able to cross the boundary between data and patterns, e.g., when exceptions to a pattern are to be analysed. This gives rise to the concept of *inductive databases*, i.e., databases that contain inductive generalizations about the data, in addition to the usual data. The KDD process can then be described as a sequence of queries on an inductive database. The inductive database concept has been suggested in [8, 11]. In this paper, we use the simple formalization we introduced in [4]. However, the topic is different. In [4], we considered the **MINE RULE** operator as a possible querying language on association rule inductive databases. Here we emphasize the genericity of the framework and its use for KDD process modeling. It leads us to propose a research agenda to design general purpose query languages for KDD applications. Our basic message is very simple: (1) An inductive database consists of a normal database associated to a subset of patterns from a class of patterns, and an evaluation function that tells how the patterns occur in the data. (2) An inductive database can be queried (in principle) just by using normal relational algebra or SQL, with the added property of being able to refer to the values of the evaluation function on the patterns. (3) Modeling KDD processes as a sequence of queries on an inductive database gives rise to chances for reasoning and optimizing these processes.

The paper is organized as follows. In Section 2 we define the inductive database framework and introduce KDD queries by means of examples. Section 3 considers the description of KDD processes and the add-value of the framework for their understanding and their optimization. Section 4 is a short conclusion with open problems concerning the research in progress.

## 2   Inductive Databases

The *schema of an inductive database* is a pair $\mathcal{R} = (\mathbf{R}, (\mathcal{Q}_\mathbf{R}, e, \mathcal{V}))$, where $\mathbf{R}$ is a database schema, $\mathcal{Q}_\mathbf{R}$ is a collection of patterns, $\mathcal{V}$ is a set of *result values*, and $e$ is the *evaluation function* that defines pattern semantics. This function maps each pair $(\mathbf{r}, \theta_i)$ to an element of $\mathcal{V}$, where $\mathbf{r}$ is a database over $\mathbf{R}$ and $\theta_i \in \mathcal{Q}_\mathbf{R}$ is a pattern. An instance of the schema, an inductive database $(\mathbf{r}, s)$ over the schema $\mathcal{R}$ consists of a database $\mathbf{r}$ over the schema $\mathbf{R}$ and a subset $s \subseteq \mathcal{Q}_\mathbf{R}$.

**Example 1** *If the patterns are boolean formulae about the database, $\mathcal{V}$ is {true, false}, and the evaluation function $e(\mathbf{r}, \theta)$ has value true iff the formula $\theta$ is true about $\mathbf{r}$. In practice, a user might select the true or the false formulas from the intensionally defined collection of all boolean formulas.*   □

At each stage of manipulating the inductive database $(\mathbf{r}, s)$, the user can think that the value of $e(\mathbf{r}, \theta)$ is available for each pattern $\theta$ which is present in the set $s$. Obviously, if the pattern class is large (as it is the case for boolean formulas), an implementation can not compute all the values of the evaluation function beforehand; rather, only those values $e(\mathbf{r}, \theta)$ that user's queries require to be computed should be computed.

A typical KDD process operates on both of the components of an inductive database. The user can select a subset of the rows or more generally select data from the database or the data warehouse. In that case, the pattern component remains the same. The user can also select subsets of the patterns, and in the answer the data component is the same as before.

The situation can be compared with deductive databases where some form of deduction is used to augment fact databases with a potentially infinite set of derived facts. However, within the inductive database framework, the intensional facts denote generalizations that have to be learned from the data. So far, the discovery of the patterns we are interested in can not be described using available deductive database mechanisms.

Using the above definition for inductive databases it is easy to formulate query languages for them. For example, we can write relational algebra queries, where in addition to the normal operations we can also refer to the patterns and the value of the evaluation function on the patterns. To refer to the values of $e(r, \theta)$ for any $\theta \in s$, we can think in terms of object-oriented databases: the evaluation function $e$ is a method that encodes the semantics of the patterns.

In the following, we first illustrate the framework on association (Section 2.1), and then we generalize the approach and point out key issues for query evaluation in general (Section 2.2).

## 2.1 Association Rules

The association rule mining problem has received much attention since its introduction in [1]. Given a schema $R = \{A_1, \ldots, A_n\}$ of attributes with domain $\{0, 1\}$, and a relation $r$ over $R$, an *association rule* about $r$ is an expression of the form $X \Rightarrow B$, where $X \subseteq R$ and $B \in R \setminus X$. The intuitive meaning of the rule is that if a row of the matrix $r$ has a 1 in each column of $X$, then the row tends to have a 1 also in column $B$. This semantics is captured by *frequency* and *confidence* values. Given $W \subseteq \mathbf{R}$, $support(W, r)$ denotes the fraction of rows of $\mathbf{r}$ that have a 1 in each column of $W$. The frequency of $X \Rightarrow B$ in $\mathbf{r}$ is defined to be $support(X \cup \{B\}, \mathbf{r})$ while its confidence is $support(X \cup \{B\}, \mathbf{r})/support(X, \mathbf{r})$. Typically, we are interested in association rules for which the frequency and the confidence are greater than given thresholds. Though an exponential search space is concerned, association rules can be computed thanks to these thresholds on one hand and a safe pruning criteria that drastically reduce the search space on the other hand (the so-called apriori trick [2]).

However, the corresponding inductive database schema defines intensionally all the potential association rules. In this case, $\mathcal{V}$ is the set $[0, 1]^2$, and $e(r, \theta) = (f(\mathbf{r}, \theta), c(\mathbf{r}, \theta))$, where $f(\mathbf{r}, \theta)$ and $c(\mathbf{r}, \theta)$ are the frequency and the confidence of the rule $\theta$ in the database $\mathbf{r}$. Notice that many other objective interestingness measures have been introduced for that kind of patterns (e.g., the J-measure [15] or the conviction [5]). All these measures could be taken into account by a new evaluation function.

We now describe the querying approach by using self-explanatory notations

| $s_0$ | $e(r_0).f$ | $e(r_0).c$ |
|---|---|---|
| $A \Rightarrow B$ | 0.25 | 0.33 |
| $A \Rightarrow C$ | 0.50 | 0.66 |
| $B \Rightarrow A$ | 0.25 | 0.50 |
| $B \Rightarrow C$ | 0.50 | 1.00 |
| $C \Rightarrow A$ | 0.50 | 0.66 |
| $C \Rightarrow B$ | 0.50 | 0.66 |
| $AB \Rightarrow C$ | 0.25 | 1.00 |
| $AC \Rightarrow B$ | 0.25 | 0.50 |
| $BC \Rightarrow A$ | 0.25 | 0.50 |

| $s_1$ | $e(r_1).f$ | $e(r_1).c$ |
|---|---|---|
| $A \Rightarrow B$ | 0.33 | 0.33 |
| $A \Rightarrow C$ | 0.66 | 0.66 |
| $B \Rightarrow A$ | 0.33 | 1.00 |
| $B \Rightarrow C$ | 0.33 | 1.00 |
| $C \Rightarrow A$ | 0.66 | 1.00 |
| $C \Rightarrow B$ | 0.33 | 0.50 |
| $AB \Rightarrow C$ | 0.33 | 1.00 |
| $AC \Rightarrow B$ | 0.33 | 0.50 |
| $BC \Rightarrow A$ | 0.33 | 1.00 |

| $s_2$ | $e(r_2).f$ | $e(r_2).c$ |
|---|---|---|
| $B \Rightarrow C$ | 0.50 | 1.00 |

Instance $r_0$

| A | B | C |
|---|---|---|
| 1 | 0 | 0 |
| 1 | 1 | 1 |
| 1 | 0 | 1 |
| 0 | 1 | 1 |

**Table 1.** Patterns in three instances of an inductive database.

for the simple extension of the relational algebra that fits to our need [2].

**Example 2** *Mining association rules is now considered as querying inductive database instances of schema $(R, (\mathcal{Q}_R, e, [0, 1]^2))$. Let us consider the data set is the instance $r_0$ in Table 1 of the relational schema $R = \{A, B, C\}$.*

*The inductive database $idb = (r_0, s_0)$ associates to $r_0$ the association rules on the leftmost table of Table 1. Indeed, in such an example, the intensionally defined collection of all the association rules can be presented. We illustrate (1) the selection on tuples, and (2) the selection on patterns in the typical situation where the user defines some thresholds for frequency and confidence.*

1. *$\sigma_{A \neq 0}(idb) = (r_1, s_1)$ where $r_1 = \sigma_{A \neq 0}(r_0)$ and $s_1$ contains the association rules in the middle table of Table 1.*
2. *$\tau_{e(r_0).f \geq 0.5 \wedge e(r_0).c \geq 0.7}(idb) = (r_2, s_2)$ where $r_2 = r_0$ and $s_2$ contains the association rules from the rightmost table (on the top) of Table 1.*

*To simplify the presentation, we have denoted by $e(\mathbf{r}).f$ and $e(\mathbf{r}).c$ the values for frequency and confidence.* □

An important feature is that operations can be composed due to the closure property.

**Example 3** *Consider that the two operations given in Example 2 are composed and applied to the instance $idb = (r_0, s_0)$. Now, $\tau_{e(r_0).f \geq 0.5 \wedge e(r_0).c \geq 0.7} (\sigma_{A \neq 0}(idb)) = (r_3, s_3)$ where $r_3 = \sigma_{A \neq 0}(r_0)$ and $s_3$ is reduced to the association rule $C \Rightarrow A$ with frequency 0.66 and confidence 1.* □

The selection of association rules given in that example is rather classical. Of course, a language to express selection criteria has to be defined. It is out of the scope of this paper to provide such a definition. However, let us just emphasize that less conventional association rule mining can also be easily specified.

**Example 4** *Consider an instance $idb = (r_0, s_0)$. It can be interesting to look for rules that have a high confidence and whose right-hand side does not belong to a set of very frequent attributes $F$: $\tau_{e(r_0).c \geq 0.9 \wedge e(r_0).rhs \notin F}(idb)) = (r_0, s_1)$. The intuition is that rhs denotes the righ-hand side of an association rule. The*

---

[2] Selection of tuples and patterns are respectively denoted by $\sigma$ and $\tau$. As it is always clear from the context, the operation can also be applied on inductive database instances while formally, we should introduce new notations for them.

*rules in $s_1$ are not all frequent (no frequency constraint) but have a rather high confidence while their right-hand sides are not very frequent. Indeed, computing unfrequent rules will be in practice untractable except if other constraints can help to reduce the search space (and are used for that during the mining process).* □

The concept of exceptional data w.r.t. a pattern or a set of patterns is interesting in practice. So, in addition to the normal algebraic operations, let us introduce the so-called *apply operation*, denoted by $\alpha$, that enables to cross the boundary between data and patterns by removing the tuples in the data set such that all the patterns are true in the new collection of tuples.

In the case of association rules, assume the following definition: a pattern $\theta$ is false in the tuple $t$ if its left-hand side holds while its right-hand side does not hold; in the other cases a pattern is true. In other terms, an association rule $\theta$ is true in a tuple $t \in r$ iff $e(\{t\}, \theta).f = e(\{t\}, \theta).c = 1$. Let us define $\alpha((r, s)) = (r', s)$ where $r'$ is the greatest subset of $r$ such that $\forall \theta \in s$, $e(r', \theta).c = 1$. Note that $r' \setminus r$ is the collection of tuples that are exceptions w.r.t. the patterns in $s$.

**Example 5** *Continuing Example 2, assume the instance $(r_0, s_4)$ where $s_4$ contains the rule $AC \Rightarrow B$ with frequency 0.25 and confidence 0.5. Let $\alpha((r_0, s_4)) = (r_4, s_4)$. Only the tuple $\langle 1, 0, 1 \rangle$ is removed from $r_0$ since the rule $AC \Rightarrow B$ is true in the other ones. The pattern $AC \Rightarrow B$ remains the unique pattern ($s_4$ is unchanged) though its frequency and confidence in $r_4$ are now 0.33 and 1, respectively.* □

## 2.2 Generalization to Other Pattern Types

The formal definition we gave is very general. In this section, we first consider an other example of data mining task where inductive database concepts can be illustrated. We also point out crucial issues for query evaluation.

One typical KDD process we studied is the discovery of approximate inclusion and functional dependencies in a relational database. It can be useful either for debugging purposes, semantic query optimization or even reverse engineering [3]. We suppose that the reader is familiar with data dependencies in relational databases.

**Example 6** *Assume $R = \{A, B, C, D\}$ and $S = \{E, F, G\}$ with the two following instances in which, among others, $S[\langle G \rangle] \subseteq R[\langle A \rangle]$ is an inclusion dependency and $AB \to C$ a functional dependency (see Table 2(a–b)).* □

Dependencies that almost hold are interesting: it is possible to define natural error measures for inclusion dependencies and functional dependencies. For instance, let us consider an error measure for an inclusion dependency $R[X] \subseteq S[Y]$ in **r** that gives the proportion of tuples that must be removed from $r$, the instance of $R$, to get a true dependency. With the same idea, let us consider an error measure for functional dependencies that gives the minimum number of rows that need to be removed from the instance $r$ of $R$ for a dependency $R : X \to B$ to hold.

**Example 7** *Continuing Example 6, a few approximate inclusion and functional dependencies are given (see Table 2(c)).* □

| A | B | C | D | | E | F | G | | Inclusion dependencies | Error | Functional dependencies | Error |
|---|---|---|---|---|---|---|---|---|---|---|---|---|
| 1 | 2 | 4 | 5 | | 1 | 2 | 3 | | $R[\langle B \rangle] \subseteq S[\langle E \rangle]$ | 0 | $B \to A$ | 0.5 |
| 2 | 2 | 2 | 3 | | 2 | 3 | 4 | | $R[\langle D \rangle] \subseteq S[\langle E \rangle]$ | 0.25 | $C \to A$ | 0.25 |
| 3 | 1 | 1 | 2 | | 3 | 2 | 2 | | $S[\langle E \rangle] \subseteq R[\langle B \rangle]$ | 0.33 | $BC \to A$ | 0.25 |
| 4 | 2 | 2 | 3 | | | | | | $R[\langle C, D \rangle] \subseteq S[\langle E, F \rangle]$ | 0.25 | $BCD \to A$ | 0.25 |
| (a) | | | | (b) | | | | | (c) | | | |

**Table 2.** Tables for Examples 6 and 7.

It is now possible to consider the two inductive databases that associate to a database all the inclusion dependencies and functional dependencies that can be built from its schema. Evaluation functions return the respective error measures. When the error is null, it means that the dependency holds. Indeed, here again it is not realistic to consider that querying can be carried out by means of queries over some materializations of all the dependencies that almost hold.

**Example 8** *Continuing again Example 6, a user might be interested in "selecting" only inclusion dependencies between instances r and s that do not involve attribute R.A in their left-hand side and have an error measure lower than 0.3. One expects that a sentence like $R[\langle C, D \rangle] \subseteq S[\langle E, F \rangle]$ belongs to the answer. The "apply" operation can be used to get the tuples that are involved in the dependency violation. One can now search for functional dependencies in s whose left-hand sides are a right-hand side of a previously discovered inclusion dependency. For instance, we expect that a sentence like $EF \to G$ belongs to the answer. Evaluating this kind of query provides information about potential foreign keys between $R = \{A, B, C, D\}$ and $S = \{E, F, G\}$.* □

*Query evaluation* We already noticed that object-relational query languages can be used as a basis for inductive database query languages. However, non-classical optimization schemes are needed since selections of properties lead to complex data mining phases. Indeed, implementing such query languages is difficult because selections of properties are not performed over previously materialized collections. First one must know efficient algorithms to compute collection of patterns and evaluate the evaluation function on very large data sets. But the most challenging issue is the formal study of selection language properties for general classes of patterns: given a data set and a potentially infinite collection of patterns, how can we exploit an active use of a selection criteria to optimize the generation/evaluation of the relevant patterns.

**Example 9** *When mining association rules that do not involve a given attribute, instead of computing all the association rules and then eliminate those which contain that attribute, one can directly eliminate that attribute during the candidate generation phase for frequent sets discovery. Notice that such a simple trick can not be used if the given attribute must be avoided in the left-hand side only.* □

The complexity of mining frequent association rules mainly consist of finding frequent sets. Provided boolean constraints over attributes, [16] show how to optimize the generation of frequent sets using this kind of constraints during the generation/evaluation process. This approach has been considerably extended in [14]. Other interesting ideas come from the generalization of the `apriori` trick, and it can be found in different approach like [6] or [17]. [6] propose an algorithm that generalize the `apriori` trick to the context of frequent atomsets. This typical inductive logic programming tool enable to mine association rules from multiple relations. [17] consider query flocks that are parametrized Datalog queries for which a selection criteria on the result of the queries must hold. When the filter condition is related to the frequency of answers and queries are conjunctive queries augmented with arithmetic and union, they can propose an optimizing scheme. In the general framework, three important questions arise:

1. *How to evaluate a class of similar patterns faster than by looking at each of them individually?* An explicit evaluation of all the patterns of the schema against the database (and all databases resulting from it by queries) is not feasible for large data sets. Safe pruning criteria have to be found.

2. *How to evaluate patterns without looking at the whole data set?* This is an important issue to reduce dimensionality of the mining task, e.g., via sampling. In somes cases, it might be also possible not to use the data set and perform a simple selection over a previously materialized collection of patterns or more or less condensed representation [11].

3. *How to evaluate operation sequences, e.g., in replays, more efficiently?* Compiling schemes can be defined for this purpose. For instance, crucial issues are the study of pattern selection commutativity for useful classes of patterns. The formal study of selection criteria for pattern classes that are more complex than frequent sets is to be done.

A framework for object-oriented query optimization when using expensive methods [7] can also serve as a basis for optimization strategies.

## 3   Inductive Databases and KDD Processes

Already in the case of a unique class of patterns, real-life mining processes are complex. This is due to the dynamic nature of knowledge acquisition, where gathered knowledge often affects the search process, giving rise to new goals in addition to the original ones.

In the following, we introduce a scenario about telecommunication networks fault analysis using association rules. It is a simplified problem of knowledge discovery to support off-line network surveillance, where a network manager tries to identify and correct faults based on sent alarms. A comprehensive discussion on this application is available in [10].

Assume that the schema for the data part is $R = $ *(alarm type, alarming element, element type, date, time, week, alarm severity, alarm text)*. We consider items as equalities between attributes and values, while rule left-hand and right-hand sides are sets of items. Notice also that we use in the selection conditions expressions that concern subcomponents of the rules. Typically, one wants to select rules with a given attribute on the left-hand side (LHS) or on its right-hand

| alarm type | alarming element | element type | date | time | week | alarm severity | alarm text |
|---|---|---|---|---|---|---|---|
| 1111 | E1.1 | ABC | 980119 | 233605 | 4 | 1 | LINK FAILURE |
| 2222 | E2 | CDE | 980119 | 233611 | 4 | 3 | HIGH ERROR RATE |
| 3333 | A | EFG | 980119 | 233627 | 4 | 1 | CONNECTION NOT ESTABLISHED |
| 4444 | B2.1 | GHI | 980119 | 233628 | 4 | 2 | LINK FAILURE |

| $s_0$ | $e(r_0).f$ | $e(r_0).c$ |
|---|---|---|
| alarm_type=1111 $\Rightarrow$ element_type=ABC | 0.25 | 1.00 |
| alarm_type=222 $\Rightarrow$ alarming_element=E2, element_type=CDE | 0.25 | 1.00 |
| alarm_type=1111, element_type=ABC $\Rightarrow$ alarm_text=LINK_FAILURE | 0.25 | 1.00 |
| alarm_type=5555 $\Rightarrow$ alarm_severity=1 | 0.00 | 0.00 |

**Table 3.** Part of an inductive database consisting of data part $r_0$ (upper table) and rule part $s_0$ (lower table).

side (RHS), or give bounds to the number of occurring items. Self-explanatory notations are used for this purpose. A sample of an instance of this schema is given in Table 3.

*Scenario* The network manager decides to look at association rules derived from $r_0$, the data set for the current month. Therefore, he/she "tunes" parameters for the search by pruning out all rules that have confidence under 5% or frequency under 0.05% or more than 10 items (phase 1 in Table 4). The network manager then considers that attributes "alarm text" and "time" are not interesting, and projects them away (phase 2). The number of rules in the resulting rule set, $s_2$, is still quite large. The user decides to focus on the rules from week 30 and to restrict to 5 the maximum amount of items in the rule (phase 3). While browsing the collection of rules $s_3$, the network manager sees that a lot of rules concern the network element $E$. That reminds him/her of maintenance operation and he/she decides to remove all rules that contain "alarming element = $E$ or its subcomponent" (phase 4). We omit the explanation of dealing with the taxonomy of components. The resulting set of rules seems not to show anything special. So, the network manager decides to compare the behavior of the network to the preceding similar period (week 29) and find out possible differences (phases 5–6). The network manager then picks up one rule, $s_8$, that looks interesting and is very strong (confidence is close to 1), and he wants to find all exceptions to this rule; i.e. rows, where the rule does not hold (phases 7–8).

Except for the last phases, the operations are quite straightforward. In the comparison operation, however, we must first replay the phases 3–4. This is because we have to remove the field "week" from the schema we used in creating rules for week 30, so that we can compare these rules with the rules from week 29. Then we create for week 29 the same query (except for the week information), take the intersection from these two rulesets, and calculate the frequencies and confidences of the rules in the intersection. The search for exceptions is performed using the *apply operation* introduced in Section 2.

This simple scenario illustrates a typical real-life data mining task. Due to the closure property, KDD processes can be described by sequences of operations, i.e., queries over relevant inductive databases. In fact, such sequences of queries are abstract and concise descriptions of data mining processes. An inter-

| Phase | Operation | Query and conditions |
|---|---|---|
| 1 | *Selection* | $\tau_{F_1}((r_0, s_0)) = (r_0, s_1)$<br>$F_1 = e(r_0).f \geq 0.005 \wedge e(r_0).c \geq 0.05 \wedge |LHS| \leq 10$ |
| 2 | *Projection* | $\pi_T((r_0, s_1)) = (r_1, s_2)$<br>$T = R \setminus \{alarm\ text, time\}$ |
| 3 | *Selection* | $\tau_{F_2}(\sigma_{C_1}((r_1, s_2)))) = (r_2, s_3)$<br>$C_1 = (week = 30)$ and $F_2 = |LHS \cup RHS| \leq 5$ |
| 4 | *Selection* | $\tau_{F_3}((r_2, s_3)) = (r_2, s_4)$<br>$F_3 = (alarming\ element = E*) \notin \{LHS \cup RHS\}$ |
| 5 | *Replay 3–4 (week 30)* | $\tau_{F_3}(\tau_{F_2}(\pi_U(\sigma_{C_1}((r_1, s_2)))))) = (r_3, s_5)$<br>$U = T \setminus \{week\}$, other conditions as in 3–4 |
| 6 | *Replay 3–4 (week 29)* | $\tau_{F_3}(\tau_{F_2}(\pi_U(\sigma_{C_2}((r_1, s_2)))))) = (r_4, s_6)$<br>$C_2 = (week = 29)$, other conditions as in 5 |
| 7 | *Intersection* | $\cap((r_3, s_5), (\emptyset, s_6)) = (r_3, s_7)$ |
| 8 | *Apply* | $\alpha((r_3, s_8)) = (r_5, s_9)$ |

**Table 4.** *Summary of the phases of the experiment.*

esting point here is that these descriptions can even be annotated by statistical information about the size of selected dataset, the size of intermediate collection of patterns etc., providing knowledge for further use of these sequences.

# 4  Conclusions and Future Work

We presented a framework for inductive databases considering that the whole process of data mining can be viewed as a querying activity. Our simple formalization of operations enables the definition of mining processes as sequence of queries, thanks to a closure property. The description of a non-trivial mining process using these operations has been given and even if no concrete query language or query evaluation strategy is available yet, it is a mandatory step towards general purpose query languages for KDD applications.

Query languages like M-SQL [9] or MINE RULE [13] are good candidates for inductive database querying though they are dedicated to boolean and association rule mining, respectively. A simple Pattern Discovery Algebra has been proposed in [18]. It supports pattern generation, pattern filtering and pattern combining operations. This algebra allows the user to specify discovery strategies, e.g., using different criteria of interestingness but at a macroscopic level; implementation issues or add-value for supporting the mining step are not considered.

We introduced, as an example, an inductive database for association rules, and gave a realistic scenario using simple operations. It appears that without introducing any additional concepts, standard database terminology enable to carry out inductive database querying and that recent contributions to query optimization techniques can be used for inductive database implementation. A significant question is whether the inductive database framework is interesting for a reasonable collection of data mining problems. We currently study KDD processes that need different classes of patterns.

# References

1. R. Agrawal, T. Imielinski, and A. Swami. Mining association rules between sets of items in large databases. In *SIGMOD'93*, pages 207 – 216, May 1993. ACM.

2. R. Agrawal, H. Mannila, R. Srikant, H. Toivonen, and A. I. Verkamo. Fast discovery of association rules. In *Advances in Knowledge Discovery and Data Mining*, pages 307 – 328. AAAI Press, 1996.

3. J.-F. Boulicaut. A KDD framework to support database audit. In *WITS'98*, volume TR 19, pages 257 – 266, December 1998. University of Jyväskylä.

4. J.-F. Boulicaut, M. Klemettinen, and H. Mannila. Querying inductive databases: A case study on the MINE RULE operator. In *PKDD'98*, volume 1510 of *LNAI*, pages 194 – 202, September 1998. Springer-Verlag.

5. S. Brin, R. Motwani, J. D. Ullman, and S. Tsur. Dynamic itemset counting and implication rules for market basket data. In *SIGMOD'97*, pages 255 – 264, 1997. ACM Press.

6. L. Dehaspe and L. De Raedt. Mining association rules in multiple relations. In *Proceedings 7th Int'l Workshop on Inductive Logic Programming*, volume 1297 of *LNAI*, pages 125–132. Springer-Verlag, 1997.

7. J. M. Hellerstein. Optimization techniques for queries with expensive methods. *ACM Transaction on Database Systems*, 1998. Available at http://www.cs.berkeley.edu/~jmh/miscpapers/todsxfunc.ps.

8. T. Imielinski and H. Mannila. A database perspective on knowledge discovery. *Communications of the ACM*, 39(11):58 – 64, November 1996.

9. T. Imielinski, A. Virmani, and A. Abdulghani. DataMine: Application programming interface and query language for database mining. In *KDD'96*, pages 256 – 261, August 1996. AAAI Press.

10. M. Klemettinen, H. Mannila, and H. Toivonen. Rule discovery in telecommunication alarm data. *Journal of Network and Systems Management*, 1999. To appear.

11. H. Mannila. Inductive databases and condensed representations for data mining. In *Proceedings of the International Logic Programming Symposium (ILPS'97)*, pages 21 – 30, October 1997. MIT Press.

12. H. Mannila. Methods and problems in data mining. In *ICDT'97*, volume 1186 of *LNCS*, pages 41–55. Springer-Verlag, 1997.

13. R. Meo, G. Psaila, and S. Ceri. A new SQL-like operator for mining association rules. In *VLDB'96*, pages 122 – 133, September 1996. Morgan Kaufmann.

14. R. Ng, L. Lakshmanan, J. Han, and A. Pang. Exploratory mining and pruning optimizations of constrained associations rules. In *SIGMOD'98*, pages 13 – 24, 1998. ACM Press.

15. P. Smyth and R. M. Goodman. An information theoretic approach to rule induction from databases. *IEEE Transactions on Knowledge and Data Engineering*, 4(4):301 – 316, August 1992.

16. R. Srikant, Q. Vu, and R. Agrawal. Mining association rules with item constraints. In *KDD'97*, pages 67 – 73, 1997. AAAI Press.

17. D. Tsur, J. D. Ullman, S. Abiteboul, C. Clifton, R. Motwani, S. Nestorov, and A. Rosenthal. Query flocks: A generalization of association-rule mining. In *SIGMOD'98*, pages 1 – 12, 1998. ACM Press.

18. A. Tuzhilin. A pattern discovery algebra. In *SIGMOD Workshop on Research Issues on Data Mining and Knowledge Discovery, Technical Report 97-07 University of British Columbia*, pages 71 – 76, 1997.

# Research Issues in Web Data Mining

Sanjay Kumar Madria, Sourav S Bhowmick, W. -K Ng, E. P. Lim

Department of Computer Science, Purdue University
West Lafayette, IN – 47907, USA
skm@cs.purdue.edu

Center for Advanced Information Systems, School of Applied Science
Nanyang Technological University, Singapore 639798
{p517026, awkng, aseplim}@ntu.edu.sg

**Abstract.** In this paper, we discuss mining with respect to web data referred here as web data mining. In particular, our focus is on web data mining research in context of our web warehousing project called WHOWEDA (*Warehouse of Web Data*). We have categorized web data mining into threes areas; web content mining, web structure mining and web usage mining. We have highlighted and discussed various research issues involved in each of these web data mining category. We believe that web data mining will be the topic of exploratory research in near future.

## 1 Introduction

Most users obtain WWW information using a combination of search engines and browsers, however, these two types of retrieval mechanisms do not necessarily address all of a user's information needs. Recent studies provide a comprehensive and comparative evaluation of the most popular search engines [1] and WWW database [15]. The resulting growth in on-line information combined with the almost unstructured web data necessitates the development of powerful yet computationally efficient web data mining tools. Web data mining can be defined as the discovery and analysis of useful information from the WWW data. Web involves three types of data; data on the WWW, the web log data regarding the users who browsed the web pages and the web structure data. Thus, the WWW data mining should focus on three issues; *web structure mining, web content mining* [6] and *web usage mining* [2,8,10]. Web structure mining involves mining the web document's structures and links. In [16], some insight is given on mining structural information on the web. Our initial study [3] has shown that web structure mining is very useful in generating information such visible web documents, luminous web documents and luminous paths; a path common to most of the results returned. In this paper, we have discussed some applications in web data mining and E-commerce where we can use these types of knowledge. Web content mining describes the automatic search of information resources available on-line. Web usage mining includes the data from server access logs, user registration or profiles, user sessions or transactions etc. A survey of some of the emerging tools and techniques for web usage mining is given in [2]. In our discussion here, we focus on the research issues in web data mining with respect to WHOWEDA [5,7].

## 2 WHOWEDA

In WHOWEDA (warehouse of web data), we introduced our web data model. It consists of a hierarchy of web objects. The fundamental objects are Nodes and Links, where nodes correspond to HTML text documents and links correspond to hyper-links interconnecting the documents in the WWW. These objects consist of a set of attributes as follows: Nodes = [url, title, format, size, date, text] and link = [source-url, target-url, label, link-type]. We materialize web data as web tuples representing directed connecting graphs, comprised of web objects (Nodes and Links). We associate with each web table a web schema that binds a set of web tuples in a web table using meta-data in the form of connectivities and predicates defined on node and link variables. Connectivities represent structural properties of web tuples by describing possible paths between node variables. Predicates on the other hand specify the additional conditions that must be satisfied by each tuple to be included in the web table. In Web Information Coupling System (WICS) [7], a user expresses a web query in the form of a query graph consisting of some nodes and links representing web documents and hyperlinks in those documents, respectively. Each of these nodes and links can have some keywords imposed on them to represent those web documents that contain the given keywords in the documents and/or hyperlinks. When the query graph is posted over the WWW, a set of web tuples each satisfying the query graph are harnessed from the WWW. Thus, the web schema of a table resembles the query graph used to derive the web tuples stored in web table. Some nodes and links in the query graph may not have keywords imposed, and are called unbound nodes and links.

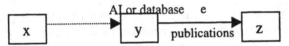

http://www.cs.stanford.edu/people/faculty.html          data mining

Consider a query to find all data mining related publications by the CS faculty starting with the web page http://www.cs.stanford.edu/people/faculty.html. The query above may be expressed as shown above. The above query graph is assigned as schema to the web table generated in response the query. The schema corresponding to the above query graph can be formally expressed as $<X_n, X_l, C, P>$ where $X_n$ is the set node variables; x,y,z in the example above, $X_l$ is the set of link variables; - (unbound link) and e in the example, C is set of connectivities ; $k_1 \wedge k_2$ where $k_1 = x<->y$, $k_2 = y<e>z$ and P is a set of predicates as follows : $p_1 \wedge p_2 \wedge p_3 \wedge p_4$ such that $p_1$ (x) = [x.url EQUALS http://www.cs.standford.edu/people/faculty.html], $p_2$ (e) = [e.label CONTAINS "publications"], $p_3$ (y) = [y.text contains "AI or database"], $p_4$ (z) = [z.text CONTAINS "data mining"]. The query returns all web tuples satisfying the web schema given above. These web tuples contain the faculty page, the faculty member's page that should contain the word such "AI or database" and the respective publications page if it contains the word "data mining". Thus, many instances of the query graph shown above will be returned as web tuples. We show one of the instance of the above query graph below.

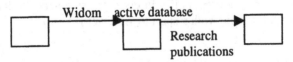

http://www.cs.stanford.edu/people/faculty.html          web data mining

# 3 Web Structure Mining

Web structure mining aims to generate structural summary about web sites and web pages. The focus of structure mining is therefore on link information, which is an important aspect of web data. Given a collection of interconnected web documents, interesting and informative facts describing their connectivity in the web subset can be discovered. We are interested in generating the following structural information from the web tuples stored in the web tables.

- Measuring the frequency of the local links in the web tuples in a web table. Local links connect the different web documents residing in the same server. This informs about the web tuples (connected documents) in the web table that have more information about inter-related documents existing at the same server. This also measures the completeness of the web sites in a sense that most of the closely related information are available at the same site. For example, an airline's home page will have more local links connecting the "routing information with air-fares and schedules" than external links.

- Measuring the frequency of web tuples in a web table containing links which are interior; links which are within the same document. This measures a web document's ability to cross-reference other related web pages within the same document.

- Measuring the frequency of web tuples in a web table that contains links that are global; links which span different web sites. This measures the visibility of the web documents and ability to relate similar or related documents across different sites. For example, research documents related to "semi-structured data" will be available at many sites and such sites should be visible to other related sites by providing cross references by the popular phrases such as "more related links".

- Measuring the frequency of identical web tuples that appear in a web table or among the web tables. This measures the replication of web documents across the web warehouse and may help in identifying, for example, the mirrored sites.

- On average, we may need to find how many web tuples are returned in response to a query on some popular phrases such as "Bio-science" with respect to queries containing keywords like "earth-science". This can give an estimation of the results returned in response to some popular queries.

- Another interesting issue is to discover the nature of the hierarchy or network of hyperlinks in the web sites of a particular domain. For example, with respect URLs with domains like .edu, one would like to know how most of the web sites are designed with respect to information flow in educational institutes. What is the flow of the information they provide and how are they related conceptually. Is it possible to extract a conceptual hierarchical information for designing web sites of a particular domain. This will help for example in building a common web schema or wrappers for educational institutes. Thus it can make query processing easier.

- What is the in-degree and out-degree of each node (web document)? What is the meaning of high and low in- and out-degrees? For example, a high in-degree may be a sign of a very popular web site or document. Similarly, a high out-degree may be a sign of luminous web site. Out-degree also measures a site's connectivity.

- If a web page is directly linked to another web page or are near to each other then we would like to discover the relationships among those web pages. The two web pages might be related by synonyms or ontology or having similar topics, both the web pages are in the same server and in that case both the pages may be authored by the same person.

While the above information is discovered at the inter-document level, web structure mining can also have another direction - discovering the structure of web documents themselves. Web document structure mining can be used to reveal the structure (schema) of web pages. While this would be useful for navigational purpose and several other operations such comparing and integrating web page schemes can be made possible. This type of structure mining would facilitate web document classification and clustering on the basis of structure. It will also contribute towards introducing database techniques for accessing information in web pages by providing a reference schema. Related work on schema discovery of semi-structured documents includes [11,12]) and is similar to approach of using representative objects in [14]. Another work [13] derives a type hierarchy using measures similar to support and confidence encountered earlier, to represent the inherent structure of large collections of semi-structured data.

### 3.1 Web Bags

Most of the search engines fail to handle the following knowledge discovery goals:

- From the query's result returned by search engines, a user may wish to locate the most visible web sites [3,4] or documents for reference. That is, many paths (high fan in) can reach that sites or documents.

- Reversing the concept of visibility, a user may wish to locate the most luminous web sites [3,4] or documents for reference. That is, web sites or documents which have the most number of outgoing links.

- Furthermore, a user may wish to find out the most traversed path for a particular query result. This is important since it helps the user to identify the set of most popular interlinked web documents that have been traversed frequently to obtain the query result.

We have defined a concept of a web bag in [3] and used web bags for the types of the knowledge discovery discussed above. Informally, a web bag is a web table containing multiple occurrences of identical web tuples. Note that a web tuple is a set of inter-linked documents retrieved from the WWW that satisfies a query graph. A web bag may only be created by projecting some of the nodes from web tuples of a web table using the web project operator. A web project operator is used to isolate the data of interest, allowing subsequent queries to run over a smaller, perhaps more structured web data. Unlike its relational counterpart, a web project operator does not eliminate identical web tuples autonomously. Thus, the projected web table may contain identical web tuples (i.e., a web bag).

Using web bags, we discover visible web documents, luminous web documents and luminous paths [3]. Below we define the three types of knowledge. Then we discuss the applications of three types of knowledge, which we are currently working.

**Visibility of Web Documents :** Visibility of web documents D in a web table W measures the number of different web documents in W that have links to D. We call such documents visible since they are visible in the web table as they are linked by large number of distinct nodes. The significance of a visible node D is that the document D is relatively more important compared to other documents or nodes in W for the given query. In a web table, each node variable may have a set of visible nodes. All of these may not be useful to the user. Thus, we explicitly specify a threshold value to control the search for visible nodes. The visibility threshold indicates that there should exist at least some reasonably substantial evidence of the visibility of instances of the specified node variable in the web table to warrant the presentation of visible nodes. As an application, consider a query graph involving some keywords such as " types of restaurants" and "items" given below, where dotted lines implies unbound node and link. We assume that such a site is there on WWW which provides a list of types of restaurants (i.e., Italian, Asian, etc.) which further have names of those restaurants. We also assume that there is a web site which provides list of items for all types of restaurants.

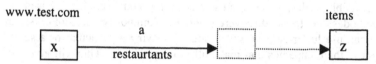

The results returned in response to the query graph imposing such predicates in our web warehouse system will return the instances of restaurants selling different items. For example, the three web tuples corresponding to the query graph are as given below.

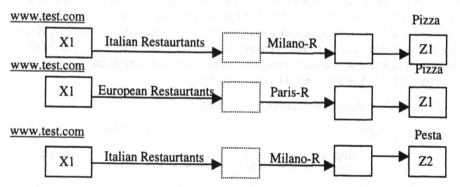

From the results returned, we can find the most visible web pages by providing very high visibility threshold [see [3] for further details]. Assume that this gives Z1 as the most visible web page (having more incoming links from different URLs) which has details about pizza. This can give an estimate about the different restaurants which sell pizzas. By lowering the visibility-threshold, we can get another set of visible web pages, and assume that this time we get the set as {Z1, Z2} where Z2 is an instance of a web-page which provides details of Pasta. Note that it is possible that some restaurants can sell both pizza and pasta. By comparing the set of different URLs corresponding to the restaurants, we can derive the association rules such "out of 80% of restaurants which offer pizza to their customers, 40% also provide pasta. Further, we can cluster (group) these restaurants according to type and can generate rules like out of 80% of restaurants which sell pizza, 40% which sell pasta also are of Italian types.

Consider another example where a new business venture wants to do some analysis of their web sites which display products for buying. By finding the visibility of its web site with respect to other web sites selling such (or related) products, the company can find ways to redesign (including changes in product's price etc.) its web site to improve visibility. For example, if a web site sells PC monitors, they must be providing links to web sites which sell CPU. Thus, if a web site finds that its visibility is lower in comparison to other web sites selling CPUs then the web site needs to improve in terms of design, products, etc.

**Luminosity of Web Documents** : Reversing the concepts of visibility , luminosity of a web document D in a web table W measures the number of outgoing links, i..e, the number of other distinct web documents in W that are linked from D. Similar to the determination of visible nodes, we explicitly specify the node variable y based on which luminous nodes are to be discovered and the luminosity threshold. As an application, one can use luminosity of a web site, displaying a particular or a set of products, to identify the companies that make all those products. This will given an estimate of the type that a company whenever it makes a product "A" also makes a set of products "B and C". Note that a company can make a product B and/or C only with out necessarily making a product A or it may be possible that a certain percentage of companies demonstrate such rules. We want to generate association rules such as X% of all the electric companies which makes a product "A", Y% of them also makes a set of other products "B and C" (support). Also, we can generate a rule like whenever a company makes a product, it also makes certain other products, for example, X% of companies which make a product A may also make a product B and C (confidence). Such rules help a new electric company in taking a decision such as the set of products the company should start manufacturing together.

Consider the following web tuples in a web table.

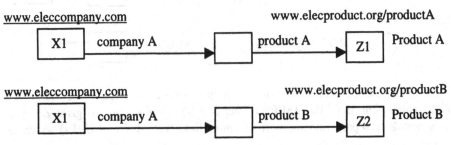

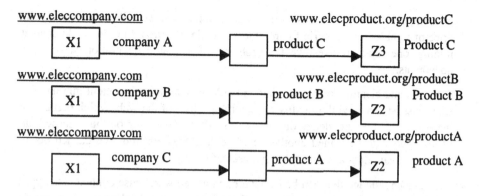

Note that in above example, certain companies (20%) if they make a product A also make products B and C. However, the company C makes only the product A. That is, 40% of companies which make a product A , 20% of them also make products B and C.

**Luminous Paths**: Luminous paths in a web table is set of inter-linked nodes (paths) which occurs some number of times across tuples in the web table. That is, occurrences of this set of inter-linked nodes is high compared to the total number of web tuples in the web table. An implication is that in order to couple the query results from the WWW, most of the web tuples in the web table has to traverse the luminous paths. As an application, luminous paths can be used to optimize the visualization of query results. Once the results are returned, one needs to browse the nodes (web pages) in the set of luminous paths only once. For example, it may be possible that between two web pages there may exists two paths such that one is a subset of another. In that case, common paths (web pages) need to browse only once.

Another interesting application is to find whether two given queries are similar. Consider that two web tables $T_1$ and $T_2$ corresponding to two query graphs $Q_1$ and $Q_2$. If we find that sets of luminious paths in the two web tables have common sets of luminous paths or sub-paths then we can infer that the corresponding query graphs are similar. We would also like to find the similar relationships; that is, whether, they are conceptually related or the keywords present in two web pages are synonyms to each other, or they are topically related.

## 4 Web Content Mining

Web content mining involves mining web data contents. In effect web content mining is the analog of data mining techniques for relational databases since we can expect to find similar types of knowledge from unstructured data residing in web documents. The unstructured nature of web data forces a different approach towards web content mining. In WHOWEDA, currently we primarily focus on mining useful information from the web hypertext data. In particular, we consider the following issues of web content mining in the web warehouse context:

- Similarity and difference between web content mining in web warehouse context and conventional data mining. In case of web data, documents are totally unstructured and different attributes in documents may have semantically similar meaning across WWW or vice versa. For example, one web site could display the price of same car in numeric figure others may do in words. In order to do content mining, one must first resolve the problems of semantic integration across web documents.

- Selection and cleaning of type of data in the WWW to do web content mining. The user must be provided the facility to identify a subset of the web, which pertains to the domain of the knowledge discovery task. Then, depending on the specific kind of knowledge to be mined another level of data selection must be carried out to extract relevant data into a suitable representative model.

- Types of knowledge that can be discovered in a web warehouse context. The types of knowledge to be discovered are as follows: generalized relation, characteristic rule, discriminate rule, classification rule, association rule, and deviation rule [9].

- Discovery of types of information hidden in a web warehouse which are useful for decision making. Web data sources being heterogeneous, diverse and unstructured, are difficult to categorize. In many cases, the user would be even more unsure about the knowledge hidden beneath the contents of a document than that in a database. An interactive and iterative process is therefore necessary to enable exploratory data mining. A suitable data mining query language is one of the means to materliaze such a user-mediated process.

- To perform interactive web content mining. A graphical user interface is helpful for interactive mining of multiple-level rules because it facilitates interactive modification of the threshold values, warehouse concept mart (discussed later), concept levels, output styles and formats.

## 5 Web Usage Mining

Web usage mining [2] is the discovery of user access patterns from web server logs, which maintain an account of each user browsing activities. Web servers automatically generate large data stored in sever referred as logs containing information about the user profile, access pattern for pages, etc. This can provide information that can be used for efficient and effective web site management and the user behavior. Apart from finding paths traversed frequently by users as a series of URLs, associations indicate which sites are likely to be visited together can also be derived.

In WHOWEDA, the user initiates a coupling framework to collect related information. For example, a user may be interested in coupling a query graph "to find the hotel information" with the query graph "to find the places of interest". From this query graph, we can generate some user access pattern of coupling framework. We can generate a rule like "50% of users who query "hotel" also couple their query with "places of interest". This information can be used in the warehouse in local coupling; coupling of materialized web tables containing information on hotels with places of interests. Another information that can be of interest is to find coupled concepts from the coupling framework. This can be used in organizing web sites. For example, web documents that provide information on "hotels" should also have hyperlinks to web pages providing information on "places of interest". These coupled concepts can also be used to design the Warehousing Concept Mart (WCM), discussed in next section.

# 6 Warehouse Concept Mart

Knowledge discovery in web data becomes more and more complex due to the large number of data on WWW. We are building the concept hierarchies involving web data to use them in knowledge discovery. We call such collection of concept hierarchies a Warehouse Concept Mart (WCM). The concept mart is build by extracting and generalizing terms from web documents to represent classification knowledge of a given class hierarchy. For unclassified words, they can be clustered based on their common properties. Once the clusters are decided, the keywords can be labeled with their corresponding clusters, and common features of the terms are summarized to form the concept description. We can associate a weight at each level of concept marts to evaluate the importance of a term with respect to the concept level in the concept hierarchy. The concept marts can be used for the following:

## Web Data Mining and Concept Mart

Warehouse Concept Mart (WCM) can be used for web data or content mining. In web content mining, we make use of the warehouse concept mart in generating some of the useful knowledge. We are mining association rules techniques to mine the association between words appearing in the concept mart at various levels and in the web tuples returned as the result of a query. Mining knowledge at multiple levels may help WWW users to find some interesting rules that are difficult to be discovered otherwise. A knowledge discovery process may climb up and step down to different concepts in the warehouse concept mart's level with user's interactions and instructions including different threshold values.

# 7 Conclusions

In this paper, we have discussed some web data mining research issues in context of the web warehousing project called WHOWEDA (*Warehouse of Web Data*). We have defined three types of web data mining. In particular, we discussed web data mining with respect to web structure, web content and web usage. An important part of our warehousing project is to design the tools and techniques for web data mining to generate some useful knowledge from the WWW data. Currently we are exploring the ideas discussed in this paper.

## References

1. H. Vernon Leighton and J. Srivastava. Precision Among WWW Search Services (Search Engines): Alta Vista, Excite, Hotbot, Infoseek, Lycos. http://www.winona.msus.edu/is-f/library-f/webind2/webind2.htm, 1997.
2. R. Cooley, B. Mobasher and J. Srivsatava. Web Mining: Information and Pattern Discovery on the Word Wide Web. In Proceedings of the 9th IEEE International Conference on Tools with AI (ICTAI,97), Nov. 1997.
3. Sourav S. Bhowmick, S. K. Madria, W.-K. Ng, E.-P. Lim, Web Bags : Are They Useful in Web Warehouse? In proceedings for 5th International Conference on Foundation of Data Organization, Japan, Nov. 1998.

4. T. Bray. Measuring the Web. In Proceedings of the 5$^{th}$ Intl. WWW Conference, Paris, France, 1996.

5. Wee-Keong Ng, Ee-Peng Lim, Chee-Thong Huang, Sourav Bhowmick, Fengqiong Qin. Web Warehousing : An Algebra for Web Information. In Proceedings of the IEEE Advances in Digital Libraries Conference, Santa Barbara, U.S.A., April 1998.

6. Shian-Hua Lin, Chi-Sheng Shih, Meng Chang Chen, et al. Extracting Classification Knowledge of Internet Documents with Mining Term Associations: A Semantic Approach. In Proceedings of 21st Annual International ACM SIGIR Conference on Research and Development in Information Retrieval, Melbourne, Australia, 1998.

7. Sourav S. Bhowmick, W.-K. Ng, E.-P. Lim. Information Coupling in Web Databases. In Proceedings of the 17th International Conference on Conceptual Modelling(ER'98), Singapore, November 16-19, 1998.

8 D. Backman and J. Rubbin, Web Log Analysis: Finding a Recipe for Success. http://techweb.comp. com/nc/811/811cn2.html, 1997.

9. M.S. Chen, J. Han and P.S. Yu. Data Mining: An Overview from a Database Perspective. IEEE Transaction on Knowledge and Data Engineering, 8:866-833, 1996.

10. J. Pitkow, In Search of Reliable Usage Data on the WWW. In Proceedings of the 6$^{th}$ International World Wide Web Conference, Santa Clara, California, April, 1997.

11. K. Wang, H. Liu. Discovering Typical Structures of Documents : A Road Map Approach, ACM SIGIR, August 1998.

12. K. Wang, H. Liu. Schema Discovery for Semistructured Data. In Proceedings of International Conference on Knowledge Discovery and Data Mining, Newport Beach, AAAI, Aug. 1997.

13. S. Nestorov, S. Abiteboul, R. Motwani. Inferring Structure in Semistructured Data. In Proceedings of International Workshop on Management of Semistructured Data, 1997.

14. S. Nestorov , J. Ullman, J. Widom, S. Chawathe. Representative Objects: Concise Representations of Semistructured, Hierarchical Data. In proceedings of IEEE International Conference on Data Engineering, pp. 79-90, Birmingham, U.K., 1997.

15. D. Florescu, A. Levy, A. Mendelzon. Database Techniques for the World Wide Web, A Survey, SIGMOD Record, 1998.

16. Ellen, Spertus. ParaSite : Mining Structural Information on the Web. In proceedings of 6$^{th}$ International WWW Conference, April 1997.

# DAMISYS: An Overview

M.C.Fernández, O.Delgado, J.I.López, M.A.Luna, J.F.Martínez, J.F.B.Pardo,
and J.M.Peña

Department of Computer Science, Universidad Politécnica de Madrid,
Boadilla del Monte, 28660 Madrid, Spain
`cfbaizan@fi.upm.es`, `rsdm-group@nova.ls.fi.upm.es`

**Abstract.** Since KDD first appeared the research has been mainly focused on the development of efficient algorithms to extract hidden knowledge. As a result, a lot of systems have been implemented during the last
decade. A common feature of these systems is that they either implement
a specific algorithm or they are specific for a certain domain. As new algorithms are designed, existing systems have to be adapted, which means
both redesigning and recompiling. Consequently, there is an urgent need
to design and implement systems in which adding new algorithms or en-
hancing existing ones does not require recompiling and/or redesigning
the whole system. In this paper we present the design and implementation of DAMISYS (*DAta MIning SYStem*). The innovative factor of
DAMISYS is that it is an engine of KDD algorithms which means that it
is able to run different algorithms that are loaded dynamicly during runtime. Another important feature of the system is that it makes possible
to interact with any Data Warehouse, due to the connection subsytem
that has been added.

## 1 DAMISYS

The lack of easibily extendible systems integrated with *Data Warehouses* motivated out research in which the main goal was to design a system that had the
features of **Extensibility, Code reusability, GUI independence, DBMS
independence, Data base integration** and **Optimization support.**

In this context, the term **extensibility** means the capability to add, delete
and/or update the set of algorithms the system can execute. DAMISYS is a
system in which adding new algorithms does not involve either redesigning or
compilating the system.

Studying in detail data mining algorithms [4] it is straightforward to see that
they share some functions. Division of algorithms in basic operations makes it
possible to interchange operations among different algorithms. This allows us to
provide **code reusability.** Another goal DAMISYS achieves is **GUI independence.** This means that functions like user query requests, administrative tasks
and system monitorization are controled by different applications using the same
communication protocol.

**DBMS independence** allows DAMISYS to use multiple data repository
architectures. rom now on the term data repository will be used to name the

element that holds and manages (data storage, recovery, update and query) the data we want to analyze.

Data repository services give DAMISYS the capability to use these systems to store final/intermediate results permanently/temporally. There is also other useful information, like different preprocessing results from the same original data, that can be stored to reduce system response time and to rise system performance. We have called this use of data repositories **data base integration**. DAMISYS also implements a series of mechanisms to support future optimization policies. Some of these mechanisms are: algorithm division in basic operations, intermediate result management, parallel algorithm execution, to name a few. [2].

## 2 Architecture

DAMISYS architecture has two levels of division. The first level defines a number of *subsystems*. Each of these subsystems is subdivided, in a second level, into different *modules*. We call *subsystem* to each of the components of our design that is executed in parallel with other subsystems and performs some general system functions. Any of these subsystems could be run concurrently in multiple processors in a parallel shared-memory computer.

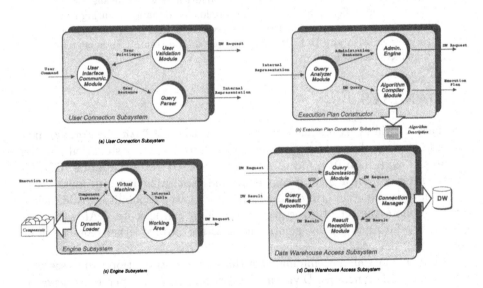

**Fig. 1.** *User Connection Subsystem*

On the other hand, *modules* achieve specific operations. The aim of this group of specific operations is to perform the general functions provided by the subsystem to others subsystems or to any external program. The differences between subsystem and module concept is that the former must be executed in parallel with other subsystems and performs general features; the modules are not necessary concurrent components and they deal with specific operations. Each of the modules belongs to a unique subsystem and provides specific mechanisms to achieve final subsystem tasks. The architecture proposed divides DAMISYS system in four different subsystems: *User Connection Subsystem*, *Execution Plan Constructor*, *Engine Subsystem*, *Data Warehouse Access Subsystem* As a new user query is received by the *User Connection Subsystem* it is translated into an internal DAMISYS format (*Internal Representation*). The *Execution Plan Constructor* processes the query and defines how to solve it by means of a structure called *Execution Plan*. *Esecution Plans* describe which algorithms will be used to solve the query and the values of algorithm parameters. The *Engine Subsystem* takes an *Execution Plan* and executes it. The tasks described in an *Execution Plan* are divided into a series of specific transformations and functions that are called *Basic Operations*. Finally, any of the subsystems may require data from the Data Warehouse supporting the system (in order to execute algorithms) This service is provided by the *Data Warehouse Access Subsystem* that makes it possible to connect DAMISYS to any Data Warehouse system.

## 2.1  User Connection Subsystem

It provides communication services to GUI external applications and it transforms messages sent by these applications into an *Internal Representation* This subsystem also provides user validation and role checking each time a user connection is established. User interfaces do not need to be executed on the same machine where the DAMISYS is running, as its communication interface is able to provide remote request submission, as well as concurrent user interfaces connection. *User Connection Subsystem* has been divided into three modules (see Figure 1(a)):

*User Interface Communication Module* controls the information exchanged between DAMISYS and remote GUIs. It provides abstract interface functions that hides protocol-dependent implementations. On the other hand, *Query Parser* analyses and checks lexical and syntax sentence construction and translates it into a DAMISYS format. Semantical checking is performed by another module.

## 2.2  Execution Plan Constructor

This subsystem creates *Execution Plans* from the *Internal Representation* of user sentences using a high description of the algorithm. The *Execution Plan Constructor* has been structured in three modules (see Figure 1(b)):

The service offered by this subsystem starts when an *Internal Representation* from *User Connection Subsystem* is submitted to *Query Analyzer Module*: In case of an administration command, it is sent to the *Administration Engine*, otherwise it is compiled by the *Algorithm Compiler Module* that uses a high level description of the appropriate algorithm, sets the values of the algorithm parameters, and finally, this module submits an *Execution Plan* to the *Engine Subsystem* and requests its execution service[1].

## 2.3  Engine Subsystem

This is the most important component of DAMISYS architecture because this subsystem deals with the resolution of *Execution Plans*. This function is achieved by translating them into a chain of transformations that are implemented in *components* that are loaded dynamicly. These component executions are called *instances*. This subsystem is composed by the following modules: **Virtual Machine, Dynamic Loader** and **Working Area**.

Once the *Execution Plan* is obtained, the engine performs a series of steps in order to get a chain of *Basic Operations* ready to be started to run inside *Virtual Machine* module the engine. Thus, in this module, *Execution Plans* are read and interpreted, to obtain the group of *Basic Operation* which are needed to execute the algorithm. All this process requires the next steps: *Execution Plan* interpretation; Construction of *Basic Operations* chain; Execution of the chain; and Result returning. The *Working Area* contains the *internal data components* and their manager as well as different system resources. In order to be able to manage the amounts of data used and created into *Engine Subsystem* some structures are required. These structures are called *Internal Tables*, and represent data base tables, which are read and written by the *Basic Operations* chains. The *Internal Tables* are stored in the *Working Area*. The main feature of *Internal Tables*, from the point of view of memory usage, is the pages division. *Dynamic Loader* module offers *instances* of *Basic Operations* of algorithms. The load of basic components of an algorithm is done when system needs its execution. Loader module disposes of a Basic Components Cache where it sets those components loaded at that moment into system.

## 2.4  Data Warehouse Access Subsystem

This module provides a common communication method between DAMISYS and any Data Warehouse system. This subsystem is divided into four main modules: **Query Submission Module, Query Result Receiver, Query Result Repository** and **Connection Manager**. *Query Submission Module* receives the requests and processes them before sending commands to the Data Warehouse system. Queries are temporally stored in the *Query Result Repository* *Query Submission Module* runs without interruption and it does not wait for query results. As a consequence, multiples queries could be solved in parallel.

When an answer is received from the Data Warehouse *Query Result Reception Module* matchs this answer with the request stored in *Query Result Repository* and submits the message to the requester subsystem.

---

[1] In order to apply a specific algorithm this module has to compile its high level description. This algorithm description is defined using *DAMISYS/ALG* language. *DAMISYS/ALG* grammar has a C++-like syntax with some simplifications. Detailed syntax of this language is a broad topic to be completely described in this paper.

Finally, *Connection Manager* provides a series of functionalities that allow to the other modules to access the Data Warehouse services. This module implements the abstract interface between DAMISYS system and the data source. This function avoids direct interaction among the rest of the modules of this subsystem and the specific protocol required for a particular Data Warehouse architecture in a concrete configuration[2].

## 3 Conclusions and Future Work

All the objectives proposed in the section 1 has been completely achieved.

Although optimization mechanisms are implemented, there are only some naive optimization policies developed. Our research is now focused on provide more complex and useful policies that may enhance DAMISYS system performance. The addition of new policies does not require a new design of any of the subsystems, because new policies only need subsystem mechanisms to perform their action, and these mechanisms are already available.

TCP/IP protocol may be translated into CORBA communication. This change could be performed to interconnect DAMISYS system with GUI applications and Data Warehousing system, as well as, to distribute DAMISYS subsystems among different computers.

## References

1. Fayyad, U.M.; Djorgovski, S.G.: Automating the Analysis and Cataloging of Sky Surveys. Advances in Knowledge Discovery and Data Mining, AAAI/MIT Press, 1.996: 471–493
2. Graefe, G.: Volcano, an Extensible and Parallel Dataflow Query Processing System. IEEE Trans. on Knowledge and Data Eng., 1.994: 120–135
3. Holsheimer, M.; Kersten, M.L.: Architectural Support for Data Mining. Technical Report, CWI, Number CS-R9429, 1.994
4. Menasalvas, E.: Integrating Relational Databases and KDD Process: Mathematical Modelization of the Data Mining Step of the Process. Phd Thesis, disserted Politachnical University (UPM), Spain, 1.998
5. Matheus, C.J.; Piatesky-Shaphiro, G.: Selecting and Reporting What is Interesting: The KEFIR Application to Heatlhcare Data. Advances in Knowledge discovery and Data Mining, AAAI/MIT Press, 1.996: 399–421

---

[2] The basic protocol calls are implemented by specific Data Warehouse Drivers (DWD).

# Mining Interval Time Series

Roy Villafane[1], Kien A. Hua[1], Duc Tran[1], Basab Maulik[2]

[1]University of Central Florida, School of Computer Science
{villafan, kienhua, dtran}@cs.ucf.edu
[2]Oracle Corporation
bmaulik@us.oracle.com

**Abstract.** Data mining can be used to extensively automate the data analysis process. Techniques for mining interval time series, however, have not been considered. Such time series are common in many applications. In this paper, we investigate mining techniques for such time series. Specifically, we propose a technique to discover temporal containment relationships. An item $A$ is said to *contain* an item $B$ if an event of type $B$ occurs during the time span of an event of type $A$, and this is a frequent relationship in the data set. Mining such relationships allows the user to gain insight on the temporal relationships among various items. We implement the technique and analyze trace data collected from a real database application. Experimental results indicate that the proposed mining technique can discover interesting results. We also introduce a quantization technique as a preprocessing step to generalize the method to all time series.

## 1 Introduction

Numerous data mining techniques have been developed for conventional time series (e.g., [1], [13], [3], [10], [14].) In general, a time series is a sequence of values of a given variable ordered by time. Existing mining techniques treat these values as discrete events. That is, events are considered to happen instantaneously at one point in time, e.g., the speed is 15 miles/hour at time $t$. In this paper, we consider an event as being "active" for a period of time. For many applications, events are better treated as intervals rather than time points [5]. As an example, let us consider a database application, in which a data item is locked and then unlocked sometime later. Instead of treating the lock and unlock operations as two discrete events, it can be advantageous to interpret them together as a single interval event that better captures the nature of the lock. When there are several such events, an interval time series is formed. An example is given in Figure 1; interval event $B$ begins and ends during the time that interval event $A$ is occurring. Furthermore, interval event $E$ happens during the time that interval event $B$ happens (is active). The relationship is described as $A$ *contains* $B$ and $B$ *contains* $E$. Formally, let *BeginTime(X)* and *EndTime(X)* denote the start time and end time of an event $X$, respectively. Event $X$ is said to contain event $Y$ if *BeginTime(X)* < *BeginTime(Y)* and *EndTime(X)* > *EndTime(Y)*. We note that the containment relationship is transitive. Thus, $A$ also contains $E$ in this example (but this and several edges are not shown to avoid clutter).

The problems of data mining association rules, sequential patterns and time series have received much attention lately as Data Warehousing and OLAP (On-line Analytical Processing) techniques mature. Data mining techniques facilitate a more automated search of knowledge from large data stores which exist and are being built by many organizations. Association rule mining [2] is perhaps the most researched problem of the three. Extensions to the problem include the inclusion of the effect of time on association rules [6][11] and the use of continuous numeric and categorical attributes [12]. Mining sequential patterns is explored in [4]. Therein, a pattern is a sequence of events attributed to an entity, such as items purchased by a customer. Like association rule mining, [4] reduces the search space by using knowledge from size $k$ patterns when looking for size $k+1$ patterns. However, as will be explained later, this optimization cannot be used for mining interval time series. In [9], there is no subgrouping of items in a sequence; a sequence is simply a long list of events. To limit the size of mined events and the algorithm runtime, a time window width is specified so that only events that occur within time w of each other are detected. Unlike [4], the fact that sub-events of a given-event are frequent cannot be used for optimization purposes.

The name *interval event sequence* does not imply that the interval events happen sequentially, as we have seen that intervals may overlap. A partial order can be imposed on the events to transform the sequence into a graph. Let this relation be called the containment relation. Applying this relation to the above example yields the graph in Figure 2. This graph represents the containment relationship between the events. A directed edge from event $A$ to event $B$ denotes the fact that $A$ *contains* $B$. We note that a longer event sequence would normally consist of several directed graphs as illustrated in Figure 2. Furthermore, events can repeat in a sequence. For instance, events of type A occur twice in Figure 2. Each event is a unique instance, but the nodes are labeled according to the type of event.

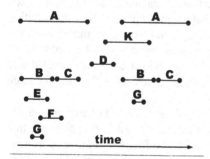

**Fig. 1.** Interval Events

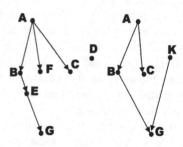

**Fig. 2.** Containment Graph

Data mining can be performed on the interval sequence by gathering information about how frequently such containments happen. Given two event types $S$ and $D$, all edges $S{\rightarrow}D$ in the containment graph represent instances of the same containment relationship. Therefore, associated with each containment relationship is a count of its instances. For example, the count for $A$ *contains* $B$ is 2 in Figure 2. Given a threshold, a mining algorithm will search for all containments, including the transitive ones, with a count that meets or exceeds that threshold. These mined containments can shed light on the behavior of the entity represented by the interval time series. The proposed technique can have many applications. We will discuss some in section 2.

A related work was presented in [7]. Therein, a rule discovery technique for time series was introduced. This scheme finds rules relating patterns in a time series to other patterns in that same or another series. As an example, the algorithm can uncover a rule such as "a period of low telephone call activity is usually followed by a sharp rise in call volume." In general, the rule format is as follows:

If $A1$ and $A2$ and ... and $Ah$ occur within $V$ units of time, then $B$ occurs within time $T$.

This rule format is different from the containment relationship defined in the current paper. The mining strategies are also different. The technique in [7] uses a sliding window to limit the comparisons to only the patterns within the window at any one time. This approach significantly reduces the complexity. However, choosing an appropriate size for the window can be a difficult task. As we will discuss later, our technique does not have this problem.

The remainder of this paper is organized as follows. Section 2 covers some applications where this technique is useful. Algorithms, functions, measures and other items related to the mining process are discussed in section 3. Experimental studies are covered in section 4. Finally, we provide our concluding remarks in section 5.

## 2 Applications

Several applications exist where mining containment relationships can provide insight about the operation of the system in question. A database log file can be used as input to the mining algorithm to discover what events happen within the duration of other events; resource, record, and other locking behavior can be mined from the log file. Some of this behavior is probably obvious since it can be deduced by looking at query and program source code. Other behavior may be unexpected and difficult to detect or find because it cannot be deduced easily, as is the case for large distributed and/or concurrent database systems.

Another application area is mining system performance data. For example, a file open / file close event can contain several operations performed during the time that the file is open. Some of these operations may affect the file, while other operations are not directly associated with the file but can be shown to occur only during those times which the file is open. Other interesting facts relating performance of the CPU to disk performance, for example, can be studied. Although performance data is not usually in interval event format, it can be converted to that format by using quantization methods.

In the medical field, containment relationship data can be mined from medical records to study what symptoms surround the duration of a disease, what diseases surround the duration of other diseases, and what symptoms arise during the time of a disease. For example, one may find that during a FLU infection, a certain strain of bacteria is found on the patient, and that this relationship arises often. Another discovery might be that during the presence of those bacteria, the patient's fever briefly surpasses 107 degrees Fahrenheit.

Factory behavior can also be mined by looking at sensor and similar data. The time during which a sensor is active (or above a certain threshold) can be considered an interval event. Any other sensors active during/within that time window are then considered to have a containment relationship with the first sensor. For example, it is possible to detect that the time interval during which a pressure relief valve is activated always happens within the time interval in which a new part is being moved by a specific conveyor belt.

# 3 Mining Interval Time Series

## 3.1 From Series of Interval Events to Containment Graph

Both of the containment graphs shown in the introduction are minimally connected for simplicity of illustration. However, the algorithms and measures described in this paper use a transitively closed version of a containment graph. A straightforward algorithm converts an interval event series into this kind of graph. It takes a list of event endpoints, sorted by time stamp, of the form

<time_stamp, event_id, end_point in {begin,end}, event_type}

where each interval event has two such tuples: one for the beginning time and one for the ending time. By having the input in this format, the entire graph can be loaded and build with one pass through the input data, and searching the graph for the location of a containment (as each new containment is added to it) becomes uncecessary. The output is a directed containment graph $G=(V,E)$, where each node in $V$ corresponds to an individual interval event and is of the form

<event_id, event_type, begin_time_stamp, end_time_stamp>

and each directed edge in $E$ from a node $Vi$ to a node $Vk$ exists because interval event $Vi$ contains interval event $Vk$. The constructed graph is transitively closed in order to reduce the complexity of the mining algorithms.

## 3.2 Quantization

It might be desirable to apply interval event mining to a dataset that is not in interval event form. Continuously varying data is not fit for mining because of the potentially infinite number of different values that a parameter can assume. In such cases, there might not be any repetition of containments, rendering the mining algorithm useless. By setting thresholds and/or discretizing, quantitative performance data can be classified into bins, and these bins can be considered intervals (that is, an interval event occurs during the time that the given parameter is within the specified bin value range).

Suppose we have a day's worth of log data for CPU, disk and network interface usage. By carefully selecting predicates, such as *C1:0<=CPU.busy<30%*, *C2:30%<=CPU.busy<70%*, *C3:CPU.busy>=70%*, *D1:disk.busy<40%*, *D2:disk.busy>=40%*, *N1:network.busy<75%*, and *N2:network.busy>=75%*, continuously varying performance data can be transformed into these discrete bin values according to which predicate is satisfied by a measurement point. Furthermore, whenever two or more of these predicates occur contiguously, the time during which this happens can be interpreted as an interval of type *X*, where *X* is in *{C1, C2, C3, D1, D2, N1, N2}*. Using these "bin-events", containments such as "when network usage is at or above 55%, disk usage is at or above 40%, and when such disk usage is observed, CPU usage during that time dips below 30%, and this behavior was observed with P% support" can be discovered.

Quantization can be done in several ways, and many methods have been researched in various areas both within and outside computer science. Some important considerations include determining how many discrete values the data should be pigeonholed into, the number of observations that should fall into each discrete value, and the range of continuous values that each discrete value should represent. To achieve some kind of grouping, clustering methods can be used along a parameter's range of observations, thereby coalescing similar values. This, of course, assumes that such groups exist in the data. The output of the regression tree methods in [8] can be used to segment continuous values into meaningful subgroups. The numeric ranges chosen for attributes in output from using [12] can also be utilized for segmentation. In the absence of such patterns, another method is to statistically separate the continuous data by using standard deviation and average metrics. This is the approach used in this paper for transforming the Oracle performance data. Another method is to select equally sized ranges, without guaranteeing that each range will have an equal number of or a significant number of observations. In contrast, the observations could be sorted and then divided up into bins of equal size, without regard to the significance of the numeric attribute. The choice of which quantization method to use is heavily dependent on the domain that the data is coming from.

### 3.3 Containment Frequency and Support

In the field of data mining, a recurrent theme is that of constraint measures that the user specifies, which any piece of knowledge extracted must satisfy. Support, confidence, and interestingness are some of the most common. In interval time series mining, several functions can be used for selecting useful knowledge. Each of these measures will be referred to as a counting predicate. The usefulness and interestingness of the mined containments depend on which counting predicate is chosen. A factor driving the selection is the domain of data being mined, and consequently the form that the interval event data takes.

Some of the most straightforward counting predicates involve measures of items in the containment graph. The most obvious counting predicate is the number of times that a given containment appears. For this measure, the containment frequency measures the number of times a containment appears in the graph, where each containment counted does not share any nodes (interval events) with any other instance of that containment. Multipath containment frequency relaxes this requirement, and thus counts the number of times a containment exists, given all possible paths that exist in the graph. Node frequency is the number of distinct nodes which comprises the set of all combined nodes from all the paths for a given containment. Similarly, edge frequency is number of distinct edges (size-two containments) which comprises the set of all combined edges from all the paths for a given containment. Multipath node frequency and multipath edge frequency relax the distinctness requirement in a fashion similar to the difference between containment frequency and multipath containment frequency, so a node/edge can be counted multiple times. Examples of these counting predicates follow.

### 3.3.1 Counting Predicates and Containments Enumeration

Define a containment (or path) as a tuple of the form $CC = <n1, n2, ..., nk>$, where each $n(i)$ is an interval event, and is labeled by its interval event type ID. Each $n(i+1)$ is contained by $n(i)$ for all $1<=i<=k-1$ and there exists a directed edge $E(n(i), n(i+1))$ in the containment graph for all such $i$. As discussed, containment frequency can be measured in different ways. In addition, because the graph is a lattice, an internal node can have several parent nodes. This property translates into entire subpaths that can be shared by several nodes. When counting the frequency of a path, should nodes be allowed to appear in more than one path? For example, in the containment graph in Figure 3, how often does containment $<A, B, X, Y, Z>$ occur? If nodes can appear on more than one path, then the counting predicate is called *multipath containment frequency* and the frequency of containment $<A, B, X, Y, Z>$ is 2. If the nodes on a path cannot appear on more than one path, then the counting predicate is called *containment frequency* and the result is 1. The *edge frequency* in this example is 6 and *node frequency* is 7. The relationships between containment frequency, edge frequency, node frequency, and the multipath variations of these counting predicates will vary according to the shape of the containment graph, which in turn is determined by how interval events contain each other. Table 1 shows the counting predicates and values corresponding to each predicate.

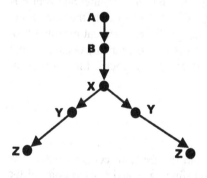

**Fig. 3.** Shared subcontainments

**Table 1.** Counting predicates for Figure 3

| Counting Predicate | Value |
|---|---|
| containment frequency | 1 |
| multipath containment frequency | 2 |
| edge frequency | 6 |
| multipath edge frequency | 8 |
| node frequency | 7 |
| multipath node frequency | 10 |

In determining the support of a containment, to maintain consistency with other data mining methods, support is defined as a percentage indicating how much the frequency measurement relates to the maximum frequency possible for the problem instance. Table 2 shows the percentage of what number, for each counting predicate, corresponds to the support percentage of that counting predicate for a given frequency of that counting predicate.

**Table 2.** Support measures

| Counting Predicate | Support |
|---|---|
| Containment frequency | percentage of the maximum number of containments of that size that can exist |
| Multipath containment frequency | percentage of the maximum number of containments of that size that can exist, for all possible root-to-leaf paths in the graph |
| Edge frequency | percentage of the total number of edges in the graph |
| Multipath edge frequency | percentage of the total number of edges in all possible root-to-leaf paths of the graph |
| Node frequency | percentage of the total number of nodes in the graph |
| Multipath node frequency | percentage of the total number of nodes in all possible root-to-leaf paths of the graph |

### 3.3.2 Multipath Counting Predicates

When would a multipath counting predicate be favored over its non-shared counterpart? A non-shared counting predicate only indicates what percentage of the containment graph supports a given containment. It does not readily differentiate where there is overlap among instances of a given containment and where there is not. For example, in Figure 4, the containment frequency for $<B, A, F>$ is 2 because there are at most 2 unique occurrences of this containment given the restrictions of that counting predicate. In contrast, the multipath containment frequency is 24 (3*4*2). Likewise, the node frequency is 9, and in contrast the multipath node frequency is 72 (3*24). In certain problem domains, the fact that there is overlap between several instances of the same containment is useful information. Suppose that interval event $B$ is a disk failure, interval event $A$ is a network adapter failure, and interval event $F$ is a network failure. The fact that these events happen at approximately the same time, thus causing the amount of overlap seen in the example, has a different meaning than if these containments happened at different times. The events probably occur together because of a malicious program virus attack that is set off at a specific time of day, for example.

### 3.4 Mining algorithms

There are several ways to mine the data to find the frequent containments. The naive approach is to traverse the lattice on a depth-first basis and at each point of the traversal enumerate and count all paths. Another way is to search for containments incrementally by path size; this is the approach used in this paper. A path is described by the sequence of node types in the path. Because there is a one-to-many mapping from the node types to the transaction ID's, a path can exist multiple times in the entire graph. This graph can be traversed using lattice traversal algorithms, or it can be stored in relational database tables and mined using SQL statements.

### 3.4.1 Naive Algorithm for Mining Containments

Perform a depth-first traversal of the lattice whereby all the possible paths throught the lattice are explored. At each node visit of the traversal, there exists a traversal path $TP$ by which this node was reached. This corresponds to the recursive calls that the program is following. Path $TP$ is $<tp1, tp2, tp3, ..., tpn>$, where $tp1$ is the topmost node in the path and $tpn$ is the current node (can be internal or leaf node) being visited by the traversal algorithm. By definition, $tp1$ has no parent and hence, there is no interval event which contains $tp1$. For each subpath (containment) of $TP$ of the form $TPS$ in $\{<tp(n-1), tpn>, <tp(n-2), tp(n-1), tp>, ..., <tp1, tp2, ..., tp(n-1), tpn>\}$, increment this subpath's counter in the path list $PL$ which indicates the number of times that this path (containment) appears. When the entire lattice has been traversed, the paths in $PL$ that satisfy the counting predicates (such as *containment frequency* >= *minimum mining containment frequency*) are presented to the user. This exhaustive counting method will find all possible containments. Herein lies the disadvantage: the number of frequent containments will typically be a small (or very small) subset of all the possible containments, so this algorithm might not have a chance to run to completion because of the large amount of storage required to store all the paths. We discuss this algorithm because it helps to illustrate the mining technique.

### 3.4.2 Growing Snake Traversal, Shared Node Multiple Containments

Unlike several other data mining methods, when finding frequent containments it is not always possible to prune the search space by using mining results of previous iterations. A corresponding statement, if it held, would be the fact that if a containment $CSUB$ has frequency $CSUB.FREQ$ for a given counting predicate, then any containments $CSUPER$ of which $CSUB$ is a subcontainment possess the following property: $CSUPER.FREQ <= CSUB.FREQ$. Unfortunately, this property can not be exploited by mining in stages for incrementally larger containments, because several of these larger containments can potentially share a smaller containment. Sharing leads to violation of this property. Containment $<A, B, X, Y, Z>$ shown in Figure 3 illustrates this: the containment frequency for $<A, B, X>$ is 1, but the containment frequency for $<A, B, X, Y, Z>$ is 2, a higher value. Results are similar for the other counting predicates.

To reduce the amount of storage required for intermediate results, the Growing Snake Traversal, as the name implies, starts by mining all size 2 containments. A traversal is done as in the naive algorithm, except that only paths of the form $<tp(n-1), tpn>$ are enumerated. When all such containments have been found, only those that satisfy the selected counting predicates are retained. Multiple counting predicates can be mixed in a boolean expression, forming a *counting predicate function* to be satisfied by each mined containment. Allowing this freedom for the user broadens the applications of the mining method because the user can decide what counting predicates or counting predicate function(s) must be met by a mined containment in order for it to be considered useful knowledge. Next, containments of size 3 (having form $<tp(n-2), tp(n-1), tpn>$) are enumerated and the same counting predicate function is applied to select useful containments. This is repeated until the maximum containment size is reached. Algorithm 1 contains the details.

*Algorithm 1.*

```
Input: Containment graph CG, containment predicate
function CPF
Output: Set FINAL_CONT of mined containments
containment_bucket array CA[] (each element containing
CASIZE containments)
containment_bucket FINAL_CONT
int k = 0
- for containment size CS = 2 to CG.max_containment_size
    - for each containment CCL in CG of size CS
    -      put CCL in current bucket CA[k]
    - if CA[k] is full
        - sort CA[k]
        - allocate a new bucket CA[k+1]
        - k=k+1
    - endif
- endfor
- merge all CCL's in all CA buckets into the FINAL_CONT
  bucket, putting in only those that meet the
  criteria of sufficient frequency, sufficient node
  frequency, sufficient edge frequency, and/or other
  counting predicate(s) (an n-way merge is used to merge
  the buckets, or an iteration of 2-way merges could also
  be used)
- delete all containments in CA
- endfor
```

For each containment size *CS*, the step of containment enumeration is followed by a merge-count because the enumeration has to happen in stages in order to effectively use the limited amount of RAM (Random Access Memory) in today's computers. For example, given about 7 hours worth of interval data from discretized performance data from a system running an Oracle database application, the memory usage for the algorithm can at times exceed 300MB. Randomly accessing such a structure on a computer with sufficient disk space to store it but not enough RAM for it all to be on-line at once will cause thrashing, rendering the algorithm ineffective. A merge-count allows the use of very large datasets. The *CASIZE* parameter is chosen such that the size of each *CA[k]* is small enough to fit in physical RAM. Although it is not shown, our implementation of the algorithm ensures that a containment is not counted twice by pruning paths which exist entirely within subsections of the graph which have already been visited. For edge frequency and node frequency counting predicates, the small number of duplicate edges and nodes that arise during the merge step (as a result of paths which are partially in an explored region of the graph) are eliminated during the merge phase of the algorithm.

In our experiments, the entire containment graph was kept on-line. The graph does not need to be stored completely on-line, however. A modification to the algorithm will permit mining datasets where the containment graph is larger than available RAM space by only keeping events in memory that are active during the current timestamp. Consequently, the section of the containment graph being mined is built dynamically as access to it is required. Our algorithm already resorts to merging for generating the mined containments, so a combination of these two techniques yields an algorithm that is limited only by available secondary storage. Furthermore, the data access and generation pattern (if using multiple 2-way merges) is sequential, so a group of devices that support sequential access, such as tape drives, could also be used by the algorithm.

## 4  Experimental Results

Experiments were run on a Dell PowerEdge 6300 server with 1GB RAM and dual 400Mhz Pentium processors for the synthetic data, and on a Dell Pentium Pro 200Mhz workstation with 64MB RAM. The first experiment consisted of mining containment relations from an artificially generated event list. A Zipf distribution was used in selecting the event types and a Poisson arrival rate was used for the inter-event times. This smaller list is beneficial in testing the correctness of the programmed algorithm because the output can be readily checked for correctness.

In the second experiment, disk performance data from an Oracle database application was converted from quantitative measurements to interval events by quantizing the continuous values into discrete values. The disk performance data consists of various parameters for several disks, measured at 5-minute time intervals. Discrete values were chosen based on an assumed normal distribution for each parameter and using that parameter's statistical z-score. "Low", "average" and "high" were assigned to a value by assigning a z-score range to each discrete value. Values used were "low", corresponding to $z\text{-}score<-0.5$, "average" corresponding to a $z\text{-}score$ in $[-0.5, 0.5]$, and "high" corresponding to a $z\text{-}score>0.5$. The resulting quantized versions of the parameters were close to uniformly distributed in terms of the number of occurrences of each range, so this quantization method provided good results in this case.

Some containment results gathered from looking at the output of the sar utility of the Sun machine the database was running on are shown in Table 3. Additionally, several containments were the average service time parameter of disk id's 40, 18, 20 and 25 were near their mean value, contained several other quantized values of parameters of other disks, revealing interesting interactions among several disk performance metrics which were obtained by running the mining algorithm. Table 4 shows the CPU run times for mining the Oracle dataset. Figure 5 shows the relationship between varying Zipf, Poisson arrival times and number of mined interval events for the synthetic data set, which consists of 500 events and 8 event types.

**Table 3.** Some Oracle dataset results

| Param 1 | Param 2 | Description |
|---|---|---|
| Page faults 'high' | namei 'high' | During the time that the number of page faults is above average, the number of namei function requests is also high. This is probably an indication that files are being opened and accessed, thus increasing the RAM file cache size and reducing the amount of RAM available to execute code |
| 'average' CPU usage by system | vflt 'low' | During average usage of the CPU by the system code, the number of address translation page faults was below average. This might be an indication that much system code is non-pageable, so very little page faults are generated |
| 'average' CPU usage by system | slock 'average' | During average usage of the CPU by the system, there is an average number of lock requests requiring physical I/O. |

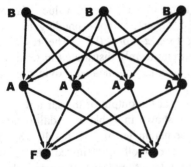

**Fig. 4.** Multiple shared subcontainments

**Table 4.** CPU time for execution of mining algorithm vs. number of containments mined for Oracle data

| cpu time (sec) | # of events |
|---|---|
| 40 | 178 |
| 104 | 286 |
| 367 | 335 |
| 543 | 387 |

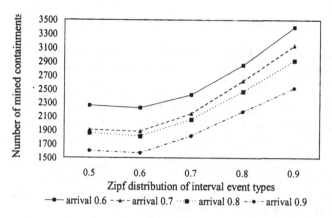

**Fig. 5.** Synthetic data results

# 5 Concluding Remarks

Numerous data mining techniques have been developed for conventional time series. In this paper, we investigated techniques for interval time series. We consider an event to be "active" for a period of time, and an interval time series is a sequence of such interval events. We pointed out that existing techniques for conventional time series and sequential patterns cannot be used. Basically, interval time series are mined differently than event series because an event has both a starting and ending point, and therefore the containment relationship has different semantics than simply happens-before or happens-after. To address this difference, we proposed a new mining algorithm for interval time series.

To assess the effectiveness of our technique, we ran the mining algorithm on system performance trace data acquired from an application running on an Oracle database. Traditionally, spreadsheet and OLAP (On-line analytical processing) tools have been used to visualize performance data. This approach requires the user to be an expert and have some knowledge of what to explore. Unsuspected interactions, behavior, and anomalies would run undetected. The data mining tools we implemented for this study address this problem. Our experimental study indicates that it can automatically uncover many interesting results.

To make the techniques more universal, we proposed a quantization technique which transforms conventional time series data into an interval event time series, which can then be mined using the proposed method. To illustrate this strategy, we discussed its use in a number of applications.

# References

1. Agrawal, R., Faloutsos, C. and Swami, A.  Efficiency Similarity Search in Sequence Databases. Proceedings of the Conference of Foundations of Data Organization, 22. 1993.
2. Agrawal, R., Imielinski, T. and Swami, A. Mining Association Rules Between Sets of Items in Large Databases. ACM SIGMOD, 1993.

3. Agrawal, R., Psaila, G., Wimmers, E.L. and Zait, M. Querying Shapes of Histories. Proceedings of VLDB, 1995.

4. Agrawal, R. and Srikant, R. Mining Sequential Patterns. IEEE Data Engineering, 1995.

5. Bohlen, M.H., Busatto, R. and Jensen, C.S. Point- Versus Interval-based Temporal Data Models. IEEE Data Engineering, 1998.

6. Chakrabarti, S., Sarawagi, S. and Dom, B. Mining Surprising Patterns Using Temporal Description Length. Proceedings of the 24th VLDB Conference, 1998.

7. Das, G., Lin, K., Mannila, H., Renganathan, G. and Smyth, P. Rule Discovery From Time Series. The Fourth International Conference on Knowledge Discovery & Data Mining, 1998.

8. Morimoto, Y., Ishii, H. and Morishita, S. Efficient Construction of Regression Trees with Range and Region Splitting. Proceedings of the 23rd VLDB Conference, 1997.

9. Mannila, H., Toivonen, H. and Verkamo, A.I. Discovery of Frequent Episodes in Event Sequences. Data Mining and Knowledge Discovery 1, 259-289, 1997.

10. Rafiei, D. and Mendelzon, A. Similarity-Based Queries for Time Series Data. SIGMOD Record, 1997.

11. Ramaswamy, S., Mahajan, S. and Silberschatz, A. On the Discovery of Interesting Patterns in Association Rules. Proceedings of the 24th VLDB Conference, 1998.

12. Rastogi, R. and Shim, K. Mining Optimized Association Rules with Categorical and Numeric Attributes. IEEE Data Engineering, 1998.

13. Shatkay, H. and Zdonik, S.B. Approximate Queries and Representations for Large Data Sequences. Proceedings of the 12th International Conference on Data Engineering, 1996.

14. Yazdani, N. and Ozsoyoglu, Z.M. Sequence Matching of Images. Proceedings of the 8th International Conference on Scientific and Statistical Database Management, 1996.

# A New Modeling Technique Based on Markov Chains to Mine Behavioral Patterns in Event Based Time Series

S. Massa, M. Paolucci, P.P. Puliafito

DIST - Department of Communication, Computer and System Sciences
University of Genoa
Via Opera Pia, 13 - 16145 Genova – ITALY
{silviam, paolucci, ppp} @dist.unige.it

**Abstract.** A new modeling technique to mine information from data that are expressed in the form of events associated to entities is presented. In particular such a technique aims at extracting non-evident behavioral patterns from data in order to identify different classes of entities in the considered population. To represent the behavior of the entities a Markov chain model is adopted and the transition probabilities for such a model are computed. The information extracted by means of the proposed technique can be used as decisional support in a large range of problems, such as marketing or social behavioral questions. A case study concerning the university dropout problem is presented together with further development of Markov chain modeling technique in order to improve the prediction and/or interpretation power.

## 1 Introduction

This paper presents an approach to the problem of mining information from large data sets based on the application of Markov chains.

Data mining represents the core activity of the so-called Knowledge Discovery in Databases (KDD) process, which aims at extracting hidden information from large collections of data. Data mining techniques can be divided into five classes of methods according to their different goals that is the different kind of knowledge they aim to extract [1]. These methods include predictive modeling (i.e. decision trees [2]), clustering [3], data summarization (i.e. association rules [4]), dependency modeling (i.e. causal modeling [5], [6]) and finally change and deviation detection [7].

When the time represents an important attribute characterizing the available information, the data can usually be associated with a time-ordered sequence of events. The analysis of such a sequence could then provide knowledge about the behavior of the system that, at least ideally, has generated the data. The mined knowledge in such cases could successively be used to predict, with a sort of „black box" pattern matching approach, the evolution of the considered system from the observation of its past behavior. To this end, the approach that has been studied in this work tries to exploit a model based on the theory of Markov chains in order to provide a statistical representation of the properties of the observed system. The data organized into a temporal sequence are mined in order to extract the probability of transition among the possible states in which the system could evolve. The specific framework for which such probabilities should be identified has to be a priori defined, taking into account the general characteristics of the considered context of application. In other words, when using the proposed approach, the identification of the system states should be considered a modeling parameter that clearly can influence the effectiveness of the whole mining process.

The work presented in this paper has been developed with reference to a particular case study that is about the problem of university dropouts. A modeling technique based on Markov chains to deal with the data about the university students has been developed in order to obtain the population at risk. The paper is organized as follows. The paper begins with a short introduction to Markov chains. Then the proposed modeling technique is explained step by step also through an example database. Finally the dropout case study is presented with possible improvements to the proposed model.

## 2    Markov chains

### 2.1    Introduction to Markov chains

The theory of Markov chains ([8], [9], [10]) is often used to describe the system asymptotic behavior by means of relevant simulation algorithms (Gibbs sampling [11], Metropolis, Metropolis-Hastings [12]). The use of Markov chains simplifies the modeling of a complex, multi-variant population by focusing on the information associated with the system state.

This basic property of Markov chains allows to describe easily the behavior of systems whose evolution can be modeled by a sequence of stochastic transitions from one state to another in a discrete set of possible states, which occur in correspondence of time or events.

### 2.2    Definitions and basic properties

Let $X^{(k)}$ be a set of possible states of a system, at the k-th step or value of time, for any entity of a considered population. If the state of an entity at a generic k-th step can be expressed through a vector of variables, then $X^{(k)}$ can be written as follows:

$$X^{(k)} = \left\{ \underline{x}_1^{(k)}, \underline{x}_2^{(k)}, \ldots, \underline{x}_w^{(k)} \right\} \tag{1}$$

where w is the number of possible states, for the considered entity, at k-th step.

Then, such a system could be modeled through Markov chains only if the probability distribution of a generic state $\underline{x}_{j_{k+1}}^{(k+1)} \in X^{(k+1)}$ depends entirely on the value of the state vector assumed at the k-th step, i.e., $\underline{x}_{j_k}^{(k)} \in X^{(k)}$.

Formally:

$$p(\underline{x}_j^{(k+1)} \mid \underline{x}_i^{(k)}, \underline{x}_v^{(k-1)}, ..., \underline{x}_w^{(0)}) = p(\underline{x}_j^{(k+1)} \mid \underline{x}_i^{(k)}) \qquad \forall\, i, v, ..., w \qquad (2)$$

of course, equation (2) is verified for any step k.

To define the Markov chain we need to know the initial probability of a generic state $\underline{x}_j^{(0)}$, $p_{\underline{x}_j}^{(0)}$, $\forall j$ and the transition probability for any possible state $\underline{x}_j^{(k+1)}$ to follow the state $\underline{x}_i^{(k)}$ that is denoted by matrix $T_{\underline{x}_i, \underline{x}_j}^{(k)}$. If the transition probability does not depend on the step k (e.g. for stationary systems), the Markov chain is said homogeneous and the transition probability could be written as $T_{\underline{x}_i, \underline{x}_j}$. Using the transition probabilities, the probability for the state $\underline{x}_j^{(k+1)}$ at time k+1, denoted by $p_{\underline{x}_j}^{(k+1)}$ can be easily computed from the correspondent probabilities at time k as follows:

$$p_{\underline{x}_j}^{(k+1)} = \sum_i p_{\underline{x}_i}^{(k)} T_{\underline{x}_i \underline{x}_j}^{(k)} \qquad (3)$$

Given the vector of initial probabilities, $\underline{p}^{(0)}$, equation (3) determines the behavior of the chain for all the time instants. The probabilities at step k can be viewed as a row vector, $\underline{p}^{(k)}$, and the transition probabilities at step k as a matrix, $T^{(k)}$, or simply T if the chain is homogeneous. Equation (3) can be expressed as:

$$\underline{p}^{(k+1)} = \underline{p}^{(k)} T^{(k)} \qquad (4)$$

For a homogeneous chain, $T^k$, that is the k-th power of the matrix T, gives the transition probabilities at k step to obtain:

$$\underline{p}^{(k+1)} = \underline{p}^{(0)} T^k \qquad (5)$$

# 3 Application of Markov chains to the mining of time series

## 3.1 Mining information by means of Markov chains

The class of addressed problems takes the form of time series analysis to extract non-evident behavioral pattern from data. In the next sections a modeling technique aiming at applying Markov chain theory to data mining problems, which can be modeled with time-series, is presented. The application of such a modeling approach to a case study represented by the analysis of university dropouts will follow.

## 3.2  Definition of the problem

In general, given a population made of a finite number of entities, each entity can be associated with a series of successive events that characterize its behavior.

Let e be a generic entity from the considered population and $<s_1\ s_2\ s_3...s_n>$ a sequence of successive events. Then the association between the entity e and its relevant series of events can be written as follows:

$$e \leftrightarrow <s_1\ s_2\ s_3...s_n> \tag{6}$$

where $n = n(e)$ is the number of events of the series.

Let us consider a database of customer transactions where the various entities are represented by the customers and the events by their economic transactions (Table 1).

Table 1. An example of customer transactions.

| Cust_id | Transaction_time | Item_id_bought | Amount Paid (£) |
|---------|------------------|----------------|-----------------|
| 1 | 20/1/98 | 10 | 5 |
| 1 | 20/1/98 | 12 | 2 |
| 2 | 21/1/98 | 2 | 3 |
| 3 | 22/1/98 | 22 | 6 |
| ... | ... | ... | ... |

The various items are classified in three market classes, as stated by the following Table 2.

Table 2. An example of market classes for the items.

| Item_id | Class |
|---------|-------|
| 1-10 | A |
| 11-20 | B |
| 21-30 | C |

To present a probabilistic approach to analyze the sequence of states that characterizes each component of the considered population, as a first modeling step, the state of an entity in the time must be defined by specifying a state vector. The elements of such a vector are the various variables characterizing the events. These variables are provided, in general, as the result of grouping operations on the events.

Formally the state of an entity, at a time t, is expressed by a state vector that is a function of the same entity and of t, that is:

$$\forall t,\ t \in \Re^+,\ \exists \underline{x} \in X^{(t)} : f(e, t) \rightarrow \underline{x} \tag{7}$$

where $X^{(t)}$ is the state space of f.

Such a grouping step could correspond, in the above example, to the definition of a set of values for the state variables computed for each customer as the total expense of the last month (e.g. 30 days) and the corresponding percentage distribution for the different market classes grouped by transaction period.

Grouping by transaction period requires the time to be sampled in an appropriate way. The sampling should be performed in order to identify time reference points that should result significant for the considered case, and allows expressing the state function as:

$$f(e_j, t_i) \rightarrow \underline{x}, \quad e_j \in P \qquad \text{entity set}$$

$$\underline{x} \in X^{(t_i)} \qquad \text{state space for f;}$$

$$t_i \in T \qquad \text{set of sampling times.}$$

(8)

In the considered transaction example, the 30th of each month has been chosen as reference day, and the time horizon is 12 months.

**Table 3.** A possible definition of a state vector for the customers.

| $e_j$ | $t_i$ | m | a | b | c |
|-------|-------|---|---|---|---|
| 1 | 30/1/98 | 7 | 80 | 20 | 0 |
| 2 | 30/1/98 | 3 | 42 | 0 | 58 |
| ... | ... | ... | ... | ... | ... |
| 1 | 30/2/98 | 5 | 30 | 20 | 50 |

In this case, the state vector of the customer entity is made of four variables:

$$f(e_j, t_i) = (m, a, b, c) \qquad i=1,\dots,30; \ j=1,\dots,n$$

(9)

where m represents the total monthly expense, and a, b and c represent the percentage distribution of the total monthly expense on the three market classes defined in Table 2. The values of a, b, c and m are intended to be within suitable admission range. In order to be able to represent the problem through a Markov chain model, the admission ranges should be specified through a finite number of possible states for each $t_i$. In general, this means to identify a discrete space for the state and a mapping function that associates an actual state space point with a point in the discrete space.

In the case of the considered example such a discrete state space could be represented by a set of four qualitative levels related to the total monthly expense variable. Then the needed mapping could be obtained by specifying the interval of values of the actual state variables corresponding to such qualitative values. In terms of the state function this could be expressed as:

$$f(e_j, t_i) \rightarrow \underline{x}_q, \quad e_j \in P \qquad \text{entity set;}$$

$$\underline{x}_q \in X_q^{(t_i)} \qquad \text{discrete state space for f}$$

$$X_q^{(t_i)} = [x_1, \dots, x_{n(t_i)}]$$

(10)

$t_i \in T$ set of sampling times.

In the proposed example, the total expense and the percentage for market classes could be approximated by using, for instance, the value mapping specified in Tables 4 and 5.

**Table 4 and 5.** The value range for the state variables.

| Month_expense | Value | | Expense_distribution | Value |
|---|---|---|---|---|
| Expense ≤ 5 | Very low | | 0 < Distrib. < 20 | Poor |
| 5< Expense ≤ 10 | Low | | 20 ≤ Distrib. < 40 | Medium low |
| 10<Expense≤100 | Average | | 40 ≤ Distrib. < 60 | Medium high |
| Expense > 100 | High | | 60 ≤ Distrib. < 80 | Rich |

At the end of these modeling steps, each customer and each sampling time are associated with a record containing the aggregated sampled and discrete values. The resulting table is in general composed by records in the form: [Entity_id, Sampling_Time, Discrete component 1... Discrete component n] and represents, for each entity, its time evolution in the state space.

Let us define $n_i^{(k)}$ as the number of entities that are in the state $\underline{x}_i$ at sampling time k. Considering a pair of states that are contiguous in time, i.e. which are associated with two successive sampling times, the transition probability (1) can be expressed as:

$$p_{i,j}^{(k,k+1)} = \frac{n_{i,j}^{(k,k+1)}}{n_i^{(k)}} \qquad \sum_j p_{i,j} = 1 \qquad (11)$$

Let $I_w=\{w_1,w_2,...,w_r\}$ the set of the states at stage w. Through equation (11) the matrix $T^{(k)} = \left\{p_{i,j}^{k,k+1}\right\}$ is obtained, where $i \in I_k$ represents the set of indexes relevant to the starting states and $j \in I_{k+1}$ the set of indexes of the arriving states. In general $T^{(k)}$ is not a square matrix because the number of starting states, that is the number of rows of the matrix, is generally different from the number of the arriving states, that is represented by the number of its columns.

In general the probability $p_{i,j}^{(k,h)}$ to reach a state $\underline{x}_j$ at a stage h from a state $\underline{x}_i$ at a stage k (k and h not contiguous) can be expressed, extending equation (4), as:

$$p_{i,j}^{(k,h)} = \underline{e}_i^T \cdot \prod_{z=k}^{h-1} T^{(z)} \cdot \underline{e}_j \qquad (12)$$

where $\underline{e}_i^T$ is a row (transposed) vector having 1 in the i-th component and 0 in any other position and $\underline{e}_j$ is a column vector with 1 in the j-th component and 0 anywhere else.

**Table 6.** The transition probability computed for the customer transactions example

| $t_0$ | $Tot_0$ | $t_1$ | $Tot_1$ | Prob. |
|---------|-----------|---------|-----------|-------|
| 30/1/98 | Very low | 30/2/98 | Very low | 0,75 |
| 30/1/98 | Very low | 30/2/98 | Average | 0,25 |
| 30/1/98 | low | 30/2/98 | Very high | 0,2 |
| 30/1/98 | low | 30/2/98 | Average | 0,4 |
| 30/1/98 | low | 30/2/98 | High | 0,4 |
| 30/1/98 | High | 30/2/98 | High | 1 |
| ... | ... | ... | ... | ... |

Considering the example of the customer transactions, where only one state variable is analyzed, let us denote with $t_0$ and $t_1$ two successive sampling instants, with $[Tot_0]$ the state vector at sampling instant $t_0$ and with $[Tot_1]$ the same at $t_1$. Then, the probability values that characterize the Markov chains can be computed according to (11) as represented in Table 6.

Now, to give a measure of the statistic importance of the information resulting from this kind of analysis, the concept of support has to be introduced. The support is frequently used in data mining to evaluate the reliability of the association rules [13] [14].

Let us now develop a suitable definition to apply the concept of support to the Markov chain modeling technique here presented. The statistic importance of the transactions leaving from a state $x_i$ at time k is expressed by the support of the considered state that can be defined as follows:

$$\sigma(\underline{x}_i^k) = \frac{n_i^k}{\sum_i n_i^k} \tag{13}$$

In the following section a more detailed example of the proposed method is provided.

# 3    Case study: The analysis of university dropouts

The case study that will be presented concerns an approach to the more general problem of the university dropouts. The data mining method previously described, is used to show implicit correlation between the different elements of a student state (the number of passed exams, the average mark, changes of residence and so on) and the decision to give up studying.

In our case the goal consists in the extraction of typical patterns from data ending with drop out or degree, through data mining.

The analysis of such patterns leads to identify the set of students who run the risk of dropping-out and therefore to determine high-risk situations in the students' careers.

## 3.1 Description of the problem

In the above-described context the "entities" are simply university students observed for a period of twenty years (from 1978 to 1998). Therefore the data set includes either students who have already left the university or students who are still attending in 1998.

Table 7. An example of the students' personal data

| ID_code | Matriculation_date | Degree_date | Dropout date |
|---------|--------------------|-------------|--------------|
| 1 | 1/11/88 | 20/4/94 | |
| 2 | 1/11/89 | | 1/5/95 |
| ... | ... | ... | ... |

The students' personal data are inserted in a table that reports, for each student, the matriculation date, the date of degree or the date of the first "non-enrollment" that can be considered as the dropout date.

The exams passed by the students are considered as the "events" that characterize their curriculum; therefore a student's state is given by a three aggregated variables vector: the number of passed exams, the average mark and the student's condition (attending/graduate/dropped-out) as coded in Table 9.

Time here represents the distance from the matriculation date and it is sampled non-homogeneously to reflect only specific moments that are particularly significant during an academic year.

Table 8. The state variable values for the students' data

| ID_code | Sampling time | Number of passed exams | Average mark | Condition code |
|---------|---------------|------------------------|--------------|----------------|
| 1 | 5 | 1 | 25 | A |
| ... | ... | ... | ... | ... |
| 1 | 72 | 28 | 26 | D |
| 2 | 5 | 2 | 20 | A |
| ... | ... | ... | ... | ... |
| 2 | 24 | 3 | 22 | G |
| 3 | 5 | 1 | 21 | A |
| ... | ... | ... | ... | ... |

Table 9. The condition codes

| Description | Condition code |
|-------------|----------------|
| Attending | A |
| Graduate | G |
| Drop-out | D |

The expression (6) for the drop-out case study and a given time horizon turns to be:

$$f(e_{j}, t_{i}) = \underline{x}, \quad j = (1,\dots,n), \; n = \text{number of observed students};$$
$$t_{i} \in T, \qquad T = <5, 12,\dots, 240> \text{ time instants vector};$$
$$\underline{x} \in X, \qquad X = <\text{passed exams, average mark, attending/graduate/drop out}> \tag{14}$$

The discretization step described by (10) is here achieved by considering suitable ranges for the average mark values to avoid an excessive state scatter and to maintain a sufficient support level.

Table 10. Classes for the average mark

| Average mark | Code |
|---|---|
| 27-30 | High |
| 23-26 | Medium |
| 18-22 | Low |

Let k and k+1 be two generic successive stages; then, let N, F and S represent the components of the state, respectively the number of passed exams, the average mark range and the condition code. Each state component obviously has values depending on the stage. The computation of the transition probabilities, performed through (11), is summarised in Fig.1.

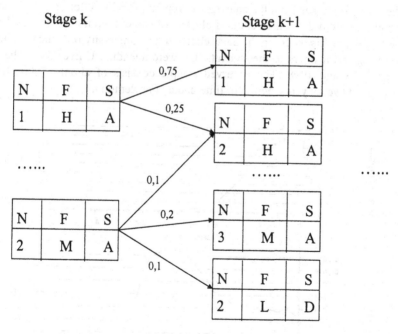

Fig. 1. The computed transition probabilities

The final result of the computing transition probabilities process is a sequence of matrices $T^{(k)}$, corresponding to the transition from states in the k-th stage to states in the (k+1)-th one. For each stage there are two absorbing states, one associated with degree (G) and the other with drop-out (D).

For students still attending in a generic state $\underline{x}_i^{(k)}$ it is possible to calculate the possibility to reach each of the absorbing states, $p_{i,D}^{(k)}$ and $p_{i,G}^{(k)}$. The way to get the two probabilities is similar. Taking for example $p_{i,D}^{(k)}$:

$$p_{i,D}^{(k)} = \sum_{w=k+1}^{h_f} \underline{e}_i^T \cdot \prod_{z=k}^{w-1} T^{(z)} \cdot \underline{e}_D \tag{15}$$

where $\underline{e}_D$ has 1 in correspondence to the absorbing state D and $h_f$ is the final stage of the time horizon considered.

Obviously the following relation holds:

$$p_{i,D}^{(k)} + p_{i,G}^{(k)} = 1 \tag{16}$$

The result of the application of Markov chains can be used, in the present context, to discover the sets of students with different risk degree of dropout, but it can also constitute the basis for further more accurate analysis of individual behavior.

The first goal comes from the analysis of dropout probability for each intermediate state and then from the construction of clusters of students combined by the dropout risk level. Figure 2 is based on the data relative to the University of Genoa, Faculty of Engineering and it refers to the students that were attending University in the years between 1978 and 1998. The observed sample consists of about 15000 students relative to the twenty years' period of time under consideration.

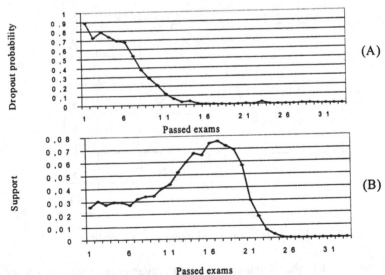

**Fig. 2.** (A) Dropout probability and (B) number of attending students versus passed exams for the considered sample and relative to the 4th year at University.

The computation of the transition probabilities for each state (Figure 1) could be used to associate a probability value to the possible behavioral patterns that is the possible sequence of states that characterize the behavior of a subset of students. The evaluation of the most likely behavioral patterns starting from a state can be used to forecast the behavior of a single student that belongs to that state.

Figure 2 represents in (A) the trend of the dropout probability corresponding to the number of passed exams while (B) gives a measure of the support, based on (13), of the probabilistic information provided above.

A more complete representation of the experimental results is currently under development. One of such possible representations consists in the construction of dropout risk clusters. Such clusters can be useful to identify appropriate actions to try to influence the behavior of the dropout risk students and, as a consequence, the evolution of their careers. Being $T^{(k)}$ dependent on that actions, the fact that the transition probabilities $T^{(k)}$ could significantly change in the long range, can be inferred. In this case the model based on Markov chains could be used for planning and control.

Another use of the proposed Markov chain based modeling technique is to improve the knowledge about possible future behavior of a single student. A better description of the dynamic behavior or of the structural characteristics of the student, in terms of state dimension, is in general useful to this aim.

In the following section further improvements of the model will be presented in order to minimize the effects of the above mentioned problems.

## 3.2 Entropy driven state space expansion

Results deriving from the use of Markov chain based modeling technique may imply local phenomena of uncertainty in terms of lack of discrimination power, particularly in the post-evaluation analysis of single cases. This means that in some „critical points" the scattering degree of probability may be particularly high. For these cases the value of entropy function associated to a particular state $\underline{x}_i^{(k)}$

$$E(\underline{x}_i^{(k)}) = -\sum_j p_{i,j}^{(k,k+1)} * \log_2 p_{i,j}^{(k,k+1)} \qquad (17)$$

can be used as a measure of uncertainty.

Post-evaluation analysis generally implies some advisory activities and, when the value of entropy for a state exceeds an a-priori fixed threshold $\mu$, it could be even more convenient for such an advisory function to apply some techniques that allow the refinement of knowledge and the reduction of the uncertainty.

Such techniques may include, for example, a drill down procedure like the extension of the dimension of the state space (number of credits gained by the student, age of the student, current increment in the number of passed exams...) or the introduction of „memory" in terms of personal patterns associated to a given state.

## 4. Conclusions

The behavior and the choices of an individual can often be referred to the behavior of the groups of people that statistically represent them. This paper defines an approach based on Markov chains to define clusters of people with a homogeneous behavior and to identify individual pattern that represent the behavior of the single component of the cluster. Such behaviors can be described through Markov chains as a series of transitions characterized by time.

The proposed method has been applied to a case study concerning the problem of university dropouts. In such a context the proposed modeling technique can be used in order to define clusters of students associated with different dropout risk degree.

Another use of the method concerns the analysis of the individual patterns in order to identify possible policies aimed at lowering the dropout risk levels. Then, in this sense, the proposed method can be used for planning and control activities.

## References

[1] Geman S., Geman D. (1984) "Stochastic relaxation, Gibbs distributions and the Bayesian restoration of images", IEEE Transactions on Pattern Analysis and Machine Intelligence, vol.6, pp. 721-741

[2] Gelfand A.E., Smith A.F.M. (1990) "Sampling based approaches to calculating marginal densities", Journal of the American Statistical Association, vol.85 pp.398-409

[3] Metropolis N., Rosenbluth A.W., Rosenbluth M.N., Teller E. (1953) "Equation of state calculations by fast computing machines", Journal of Chemical Physics, vol.21 pp.1087-1092

[4] Hastings W.K. (1970) "Monte Carlo sampling method using Markov chains and their applications", Biometrika, vol.57 pp. 97-109

[5] Agrawal R., Srikant R. (1994) "Fast algorithms for mining association rules in large databases" in Proc. of VLDB Conference, Santiago, Chile.

[6] Mannila H., Toivonen H., Verkamo I. (1994) "Efficient Algorithms for discovering association rules". In KDD-94: AAAI Workshop on Knowledge Discovery in Databases.

[7] Agrawal R., Srikant R. (1995) "Mining Sequential Patterns". IBM Research Report.

[8] Howard R.A. (1960) „Dynamic programming and Markov processes". John Wiley.

[9] Neal, R. (1993) Probabilistic Inference using Markov Chain Monte Carlo Methods. Dept. of Computer Science, University of Toronto.

[10] Diaconis, P., Stroock, D. (1991) Geometric Bounds for eigenvalues of Markov Chains. Annals of Applied Probability, 1, 36-61.

[11] Arnold S. F. (1993) Gibbs Sampling. In Handbook of Statistics, 9, 599-626.

[12] Chib S., Greenberg E. (1995) Understanding the Metropolis-Hastings Algorithm. The American Statistician. 49, #4, 329-335.

[13] R.Agrawal, T.Imielinski, A. Swami (1993) Mining Association Rules between Sets of Items in Large Databases, Proceeding of the 1993 ACM SIGMOD Conference.

[14] M.Klemettinen, H.Mannila, P.Ronkainen, H.Toivonen, I.Verkamo (1994) Finding Interesting Rules from Large Sets of Discovered Association Rules, Third International Conference on Information and Knowledge Management, Gaithersburg, Maryland.

# SQL/LPP+: A Cascading Query Language for Temporal Correlation Verification

Chang-Shing Perng and D. Stott Parker

Dept. of Computer Science, University of California, Los Angeles
{perng,stott}@cs.ucla.edu

**Abstract.** In this paper, we present SQL/LPP+, a temporal correlation verification language for time series databases. SQL/LPP+ is an extension of SQL/LPP[6] and inherits its ability to define time series patterns. SQL/LPP+ enables users to cascade multiple patterns using one or more of Allen's temporal relationships, and obtain the desired aggregates or meta-aggregates of the composition. The issues of pattern composition control are also discussed.

## 1 Introduction

### 1.1 Motivation

Discovering temporal correlation among events is a fundamental method for finding causality of events. The study of causality is considered to be one of the most important tasks for most natural and social scientists. Although there are many different approaches to identify cause and effect among events, the simplest and the most intuitive way is to observe historical data and check the likelihood that a set of events occurs in a particular temporal order. Since the occurrence of events is not predictable, continuous observation or measurement of the subject phenomenon is a common way to track events. For example, the Richter reading and stock indices need to to be continuously recorded in order to catch important seismic and economic events respectively. The result of these observation and measurement is time series data[1]. Hence time series data is often the only scientific ground on which to build theories. Events, in this representation, are **time series patterns** which possess some special features.

We define **temporal correlation** as the likelihood that a given set of events occurs in a particular time period. To extract knowledge from data, domain experts first propose hypotheses about the temporal correlation of events, then develop a specialized program to verify their hypotheses. **Temporal correlation verification(TCV)** is the task of finding temporal correlation among events.

For example, we would like to know how likely DJIA will decline after a period of high interest rates, and how likely the total seasonal rainfall in Los

---

[1] If the observation is done at regular time steps, then the result is **regular** time series. Otherwise, it is **irregular**.

Angeles will increase after a 3-month period of high sea water temperature. While establishing the real cause and effect relations among these events requires profound domain knowledge, we believe temporal correlation verification is a necessary part of the theory construction and researchers can benefit from utilizing temporal correlation verification languages.

## 1.2 Motivating Examples

*Example 1.* This example is a typical case in technical analysis of stocks[4]. A **Double Bottom** formation is commonly seen as a pattern that signals a market bottoms. A short-term stock trader might be interested to know what are the winning rate, average profit, maximal loss and total number of trades if he/she had simply bought a stock when he/she saw the pattern forms and held it for a fixed number of trading days.

*Example 2.* Everyone in the stock market may be interested to know, based on financial history, how likely a downtrend of the DJIA lasts for more than 6 months during periods that the 30-year T-bond yield was below 5.0%.

By examining these example, it is easy to see that these problems have common features. In each case, the events of interest are not individual records. Instead, they are represented by a group of records in continuous time intervals. The temporal correlation among the events can be verified by counting the occurrences of the corresponding time series patterns. By current available technology, solving each problem requires tedious procedural program coding. Consider the fact these hypothesis tests are usually run only once or need frequent modification, the cost of this kind of knowledge extraction is fairly high. If there is a formal language that can express all these patterns, then domain experts no longer need to spend their valuable time in coding/debugging and can concentrate more on perfecting their theory. Computer scientists can also focus on improving the language and the execution efficiency instead of helping domain experts in a case-by-case manner. The need for a declarative language which permits fast formulation and execution of queries is obvious.

## 1.3 The Problems

In the aspect of data granularity, knowledge discovery in databases (KDD) and data mining[2] in time series differ from those in set-oriented data. As stated by Shatkay[7],

> Individual values are usually not important but the relationships between them are.

It is continuous time series segments, instead of individual records, that represent events. Any attempt to design a time series data mining language must provide a way to define patterns that represent events.

From the view point of KDD and data mining, Shatkay's statement can be further improved to:

Individual time series segments are usually not important, but the *correlationships* between them are.

While occurrences of patterns represent events, it is very hard for a human mind to learn anything from a large number of events. Another level of abstraction is required. For each of the motivating examples, the answer should consist of only one or a few numerical values instead of a listing of all related events. *The purpose of TCV query languages is to provide that extra level of abstraction.*

### 1.4 The Basic Idea

Recognizing the importance of TCV problems, in this paper we attempt to generalize the problem and to design a formal language that is expressive enough to address TCV problems in an unambiguous manner. The language we propose, SQL/LPP+, serves as a problem definition language for TCV problems as VHDL serves for hardware description and XML for documentation. Although the LPP model[5] provides a fairly efficient execution model, we do not exclude the possibility that future research can perform with greater efficiency.

We believe that a temporal correlation verification language should provide users a way to specify:

1. The (one or more) patterns of interest.
2. The temporal coupling relationship(s) among them.
3. The aggregates (statistics) of interest, which might be simple aggregates or meta-aggregates (Section 3.2).
4. The control of pattern occurrence counting, that is, whether an occurrence of a (syntactically) preceding pattern should couple with only one or multiple occurrences of the following pattern.

Our idea is to cascade pattern queries. Each pattern, with associated aggregates, is specified in a syntactic order and is connected by a combination of temporal relationships. Then the system follows the syntactic order to find occurrences of each pattern and update aggregates associated with them. The final value of the aggregates is the output of the verification.

## 2 Defining SQL/LPP+ Patterns

In this section, we briefly review the pattern defining capability that SQL/LPP+ has inherited from SQL/LPP. For more details, please see [5, 6].

SQL/LPP+ patterns, like procedures, functions and triggers, are first-class objects in time series databases. A simple SQL/LPP+ pattern describes the properties of a single segment. In contrast, a composite SQL/LPP+ pattern is formed from multiple already defined patterns.

### Simple SQL/LPP Pattern Declaration

```
CREATE ROW TYPE quote( date datetime, price  real, volume int )
CREATE TABLE daily_stocks(symbol lvarchar, quotes TimeSeries(quote))
```

The main body of a simple SQL/LPP pattern is a segment of a certain element type. A number of public attributes can be defined by the ATTRIBUTE···IS clause. Pattern sentences and search directives are placed in WHERE and WHICH_IS clauses respectively.

The following example demonstrates basic pattern declaration.

*Example 3.* Consider an **uptrend** pattern in a daily stock price database to be a continuous period which satisfies the following two conditions:

1. The closing price of each day, except the first day, is higher than the one of the previous day.
2. The length of the period is at least 5 days.

The pattern *uptrend* can be expressed as:

```
CREATE PATTERN uptrend AS
  SEGMENT s OF quote  WHICH_IS FIRST MAXIMAL, NON-OVERLAPPING
  ATTRIBUTE date IS last(s,1).date
  ATTRIBUTE low  IS first(s,1).price
  ATTRIBUTE high IS last(s,1).price
  WHERE [ALL e IN s]( e.price > prev(e,1).price)
        AND length(s) >= 5
```

This pattern has three publicly accessible attributes, *date, low* and *high*. The attributes define the only part that other statements can access. The search directive FIRST MAXIMAL tells the search engine to report only the longest segment once a group of *adjacent* answers are found. Another search directive NON-OVERLAPPING states that reported answers must not overlap with each other. The rest of the statement should be clear without explanation.

### Composite Pattern Definition

A composite pattern is declared as a concatenation of multiple non-overlapping patterns. The search directives of subpatterns can be overridden by specifying new search directives. The following example demonstrates the use of composite patterns.

*Example 4.* Assume pattern **downtrend** is defined symmetrically to pattern *uptrend* in Example 3. The pattern *double_bottom* consists of 4 trends as shown in Figure 1. The pattern has the following properties:

1. The starting point is 20% higher than the local maximum.
2. The difference of the two bottoms is less than 5% of the first bottom.
3. The ending point is higher than the local maximum.

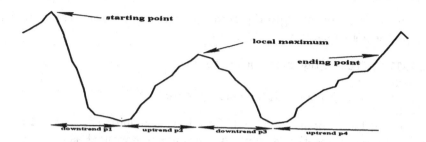

**Fig. 1.** Double-bottom pattern

```
CREATE PATTERN double_bottom AS
   {downtrend p1; uptrend p2; downtrend p3;
    uptrend   p4 WHICH_IS ALL, NON-OVERLAPPING}
   WHICH_IS NON-OVERLAPPING
   ATTRIBUTE date IS last(p4).date
   ATTRIBUTE price IS last(p4).high
   WHERE (p1.high > p2.high*1.2)
         AND (abs(p1.low-p3.low) < 0.05*p1.low)
         AND (p4.high > p2.high)
```

# 3   Temporal Correlation Verification in SQL/LPP+

## 3.1   Relative Relationships of Segments

As indicated in [1], given 2 time series segments, there are 13 basic temporal relationships if we include all symmetric cases. SQL/LPP+ adopts them as the basic relationships in TCV problem. To transform these relationships to the form that cascading querying can apply, we define shadow functions.

**Definition 1.** *Given a time series segment $ts[x, y]$ and a temporal relationship $R$, the* **shadow function** *$\Gamma$ is defined as $\Gamma(ts[x, y], R) = \{ts[x', y']| R(ts[x, y], ts[x', y'])\}$.*

The shadow functions of the basic temporal relationships are shown in Table 1.
   These relationships are used directly in SQL/LPP+ to specify the temporal coupling of two patterns. SQL/LPP+ allows users to combine two or more relationships by logical connectives **AND** and **OR**. The interpretation of composite relationships is: given a segment $s$ and relationships $R_1$ and $R_2$,
$\Gamma(s, (R_1 \; AND \; R_2)) = \Gamma(s, R_1) \cap \Gamma(s, R_2)$ and
$\Gamma(s, (R_1 \; OR \; R_2)) = \Gamma(s, R_1) \cup \Gamma(s, R_2)$.
Users must be aware that some combinations can result in an empty shadow and should be avoided.
   Allen's 13 interval relationships and their combinations can represent any relative temporal relationships. However, an interesting question is how to represent the relationship: *pattern A is, at most 10 days and at least 3 days, before*

*pattern B.* We introduce **glue**[2] patterns to solve this problem. For example, we can define a glue pattern **glue_3_10** as:

```
CREATE PATTERN glue_3_10 on quote as
  SEGMENT s
  WHERE count(s) >= 3 AND count(s) <=10;
```

Then we define a composite pattern $C$ as the concatenation of $A$ and **glue_3_10**. The relationship mentioned above can be simply represented as **C meets B**. By using glue patterns, users can also specify the length range of the overlapping part of two segments.

| # | Relationship(R) | Shadow Function $\Gamma(ts[x,y], R)$ |
|---|---|---|
| (1) | before | $\{ts[x',y'] \| y < x'\}$ |
| (2) | meets | $\{ts[x',y'] \| y = x'\}$ |
| (3) | left_overlaps | $\{ts[x',y'] \| x < x', x' < y < y'\}$ |
| (4) | left_covers | $\{ts[x',y'] \| x < x', y = y'\}$ |
| (5) | covers | $\{ts[x',y'] \| x < x', y > y'\}$ |
| (6) | right_covered | $\{ts[x',y'] \| x = x', y < y'\}$ |
| (7) | equal | $\{ts[x',y'] \| x = x', y = y'\}$ |
| (8) | right_covers | $\{ts[x',y'] \| x = x', y > y'\}$ |
| (9) | covered | $\{ts[x',y'] \| x > x', y < y'\}$ |
| (10) | left_covered | $\{ts[x',y'] \| x > x', y = y'\}$ |
| (11) | right_overlaps | $\{ts[x',y'] \| x' < x < y', y > y'\}$ |
| (12) | met | $\{ts[x',y'] \| x = y'\}$ |
| (13) | after | $\{ts[x',y'] \| x > y'\}$ |

**Table 1.** The shadow functions of Allen's 13 Interval Relationships. By default, every relationship has $x \le y$ and $x' \le y'$

## 3.2 Aggregation and Meta-Aggregation

A key design goal of SQL/LPP+ is to support summearization of occurrences of interesting pattern coupling. Aggregation on pattern occurrences serves the purpose of summarization. We introduce the syntax and semantics of SQL/LPP+ aggregates in this subsection.

The traditional definition of aggregation is just to find the final result of the aggregates. However, by observing the computation process, we can see that for any aggregate function $f$ and time series $t$ of length $n$, $f_1(t), \cdots, f_n(t)$ is again a sequence and is itself valuable information. So we can apply aggregate functions on this sequence again and construct an aggregate of aggregates. We call it **meta-aggregate**.

---

[2] The term *Glue* is borrowed from TeX[3].

Take $max(sum(t))$ for an example. We have:

$$max_1(sum_1(t)) = sum_1(t) = t_1$$

$$max_{i+1}(sum_{i+1}(t)) = \begin{cases} max_i(sum_i(t)) \text{ if } max_i(sum_i(t)) > sum_{i+i}(t), \ i+1 \le n \\ sum_{i+1}(t) \qquad \text{otherwise} \end{cases}$$

$$max(sum(t)) = max_n(sum_n(t)) = MAX_{i=1}^{n}\left(\sum_{j=1}^{i} t_j\right)$$

Figure 2 shows an example of $max(sum(t))$ calculation.

| $i$ | 1 | 2 | 3 | 4 | 5 | 6 | 7 | 8 | 9 | 10 |
|---|---|---|---|---|---|---|---|---|---|---|
| $t_i$ | 3 | -2 | 1 | 7 | -4 | -2 | 1 | 8 | -4 | -3 |
| $sum_i(t)$ | 3 | 1 | 2 | 9 | 5 | 3 | 4 | 12 | 8 | 5 |
| $max_i(sum_i(t))$ | 3 | 3 | 3 | 9 | 9 | 9 | 9 | 12 | 12 | 12 |

**Fig. 2.** An example of meta-aggregates $max(sum(t))$ calculation. Given the sequence $t$ shown above. The result of $max(sum(t)) = 12$.

Meta-aggregates cannot be constructed arbitrarily. For example, $max(t) + t$ is not a valid aggregate expression. To define meta-aggregates, we start from simple expressions. **Simple expressions** are formed by constants and pattern attributes, and complete under arithmetic operations. For example, assume $p$ is a pattern alias and $c_1$ and $c_2$ are attributes of $p$, then $p.c_1$, $p.c_1 * p.c_2 + 3$ and $(p.c_1 - p.c_2)/p.c_1$ are simple expressions.

In this paper, we only discuss 5 aggregate functions: *count*, *sum*, *avg*, *min* and *max*. Other aggregates can also be defined in the similar way. Assume $exp$ is a simple expression, $f$ is an aggregate function, **aggregate expressions** are defined as:

1. Constants and $f(exp)$ are aggregate expressions.
2. If $E$ is an aggregate expression, then $f(E)$ is also an aggregate expression.
3. If $E_1$ and $E_2$ are aggregate expressions, then $E_1 \odot E_2$ is also an aggregate expression where $\odot$ is an arithmetic operation.

For example, $min(avg(p.c_1))$, $max(p.c_1) - min(p.c_1)$ and $avg(max(p.c_1) - min(p.c_2) + 4) - 2$ are aggregate expressions but $p.c_1$ and $avg(p.c_1) + p.c_2$ are not.

## 3.3 Single-segment SQL/LPP+ Test Cases

In rest of this section, we present the SQL/LPP+ language by a few examples. First, we demonstrate the aggregation and meta-aggregation of SQL/LPP+.

*Example 5.* Assume a user has constructed a time series view which contains **price**(the daily closing stock price), **ma5**(the 5-day moving average) and **ma20**(the

20-day moving average). The user wants to test a trading strategy called **moving average crossover**: Whenever he/she sees **ma5** cross over **ma20**, he/she buys 100 shares the next day, holds it till he/she sees **ma20** cross over **ma5** then sells all the holding the next day. He/She would like to test the strategy and see how well would have the strategy worked on IBM stock. First, we have to create the pattern which represents the period of interest and find the entry and exit price of every trade.

```
CREATE PATTERN crossover ON quote_and_ma AS
  SEGMENT crsovr WHICH_IS MINIMAL, NON_OVERLAPPING
  ATTRIBUTE entry       IS first(crsovr,2).price
  ATTRIBUTE exit        IS last(crsovr,1).price
  WHERE first(crsovr,1).ma5 > first(crsovr,1).ma20
    AND last(crsovr,2).ma5 < last(crsovr,2).ma20
```

The following SQL/LPP+ code creates a **test** that summarizes the performance of this trading strategy. The aggregates we are interested in are the number of trades, the average profit of each trade, the maximal loss in a single trade and the maximal drawdown (the accumulated loss).

```
CREATE TEST crsovr_profit ON quote_and_ma AS
  { PATTERN    crossover crsovr
    ATTRIBUTE trades           IS count()
    ATTRIBUTE avg_profit       IS avg(crsovr.exit-crsovr.entry)
    ATTRIBUTE max_single_loss  IS max(crsovr.entry-crsovr.exit)
    ATTRIBUTE max_drawdown     IS max(sum(crsovr.entry-crsovr.exit)))
  }
  REPORT *;
```

Note that **max_drawdown** is defined by the meta-aggregate $max(sum(.))$. This test is a single-segment verification. So no temporal relationship is involved. The **REPORT** clause specifies which attributes should be reported. $*$ is a shorthand for all attributes.

The last part of the code specifies the tuple-level SELECT operation which extends SQL by adding a clause

```
BY TESTING test_name test_alias IN time_series_field
```

The main purpose of the following code is to specify what stocks to test and what attributes to report.

```
SELECT  qm.symbol, cp.trades, cp.avg_profit,
          cp.max_single_loss, cp.max_drawdown
BY TESTING crsovr_profit cp IN qm.quotes
FROM quote_and_ma qm
WHERE  qm.symbol = "IBM"
```

When the SELECT statement is issued to a SQL/LPP+ system, the system will first find the record that contains IBM stock price data, then search the occurrences of **crossover** and calculate the value of attributes for output.

Suppose there is a daily stock price database which contains quote data spanning 20 years. There are roughly 5000 records and $12,502,500$ segments for each stock. This example is a demonstration in which only 4 quantities, the only things matter to a trader, are extracted from all the information.

## 3.4 Multi-segment SQL/LPP+ Test Cases

In this subsection, we discuss how to define multi-segment tests in SQL/LPP+ and the use of temporal relationships.

*Example 6.* The following code defines a test to verify whether the famous Double Bottom pattern is really a profitable signal in stock trading.

```
CREATE TEST db_profit ON quote AS
  {PATTERN    double_bottoms db
   ATTRIBUTE db_count       IS count()
   ATTRIBUTE max_entry_price IS max(db.price)
  }
  MEETS
  {SINGLE     PATTERN uptrend ut
   ATTRIBUTE ut_count        IS count()
   ATTRIBUTE avg_profit      IS avg(ut.high-ut.low)
   ATTRIBUTE winning_rate    IS up_count/db_count }
  REPORT winning_rate,max_entry,avg_profit;
```

This segment of SQL/LPP+ defines a test case named **db_profit** on a time series of **quote** type. In the **BY TESTING** clause, each pattern is described in a block delimited by { and }. The first pattern to be searched for is the **double_bottom** pattern. It is given an alias ''db''. The **ATTRIBUTE** line describes the aggregates to calculate. **count()** keeps the total number of occurrences of this pattern found by the system. **avg(db.price)** calculates the average of the value in the **price** field of every found occurrence. Between the pattern blocks, **MEETS** is the temporal relationship of the patterns to be verified. In the next pattern block, the keyword **SINGLE** denotes that for each occurrence of the preceding pattern, **double_bottoms**, the system is to find at most one **uptrend**. (If **MULTIPLE** were placed here, then for each occurrence of **double_bottoms**, the system would find as many **uptrends** as possible while subject to the restart search directives specified in **uptrend**.) The first pattern does not need the **SINGLE/MULTIPLE** directive and is always controlled by its own search directives. Each time an occurrence of a pattern is found, only the attributes in the block of that pattern are updated. The **REPORT** clause lists the attributes to report.

The tuple-level **SELECT** sentence is omitted because it is very similar to the one in the previous example.

The execution control is intuitive. Pattern searching follows the syntactic order in which patterns are specified. When the search engine finds an occurrence of the $i$-th pattern, it computes the shadow of the segment according to the temporal relationship specified between the $i$-th and the $(i+1)$-th patterns and attempts to find the occurrence of the $(i+1)$-th pattern. If it can not find one, it tries to find next occurrence of the $i$-th pattern only if MULTIPLE is specified for the $i$-th pattern.

## 4 Conclusion

In this paper, we have presented SQL/LPP+. The language provides an intuitive temporal coupling notation to specify combinations of Allen's 13 temporal relationships. We have also extended the concept of aggregation and introduced meta-aggregation. With meta-aggregation, SQL/LPP+ users can obtain not only the aggregate value of the time series but also the aggregates of aggregates. We believe meta-aggregation is essential in time series data mining.

Currently, temporal correlation verification is a rarely touched area in KDD and data mining. Previous work is isolated in each application domain. In this paper, we have shown that many problems, in domains from natural science and social science to stock trading, all have the same problem structure. The contribution of this paper is to provide a level of abstraction on these problems by proposing a language that can formulate the problems of interest. With a TCV language like SQL/LPP+, it becomes possible to simultaneously benefit researchers in numerous fields by improving the language and the efficiency of test case evaluation.

## References

1. Allen, J.F. *Maintaining knowledge about temporal intervals.* Communications of the ACM, vol.26, (no.11), Nov. 1983. p.832-43.
2. Usama M. Fayyad, Gregory Piatetsky-Shapiro, Padhraic Smyth, and Ramasamy Uthurusamy, *Advances in Knowledge Discovery and Data Mining*, ISBN 0-262-56097-6, MIT Press, 1996.
3. D.E. Knuth . *The Texbook : A Complete Guide to Computer Typesetting With Tex.* Addison-Wesley Pub Co; ISBN: 0201134489 , April 1988.
4. R. D. Edwards, J. Magee. *Technical Analysis of Stock Trends.* 7th Edition, AMACOM, May 1, 1997.
5. C.S. Perng, D.S.Parker SQL/LPP:a Time Series Extension of SQL based on Limited Patience Patterns, Technical Report 980034 UCLA, Computer Science.
6. C.S. Perng, D.S.Parker SQL/LPP:a Time Series Extension of SQL based on Limited Patience Patterns, DEXA 1999.
7. Hagit Shatkay, Stanley B. Zdonik. *Approximate Queries and Representations for Large Data Sequences.* ICDE 1996: 536-545

# Temporal Structures in Data Warehousing

Peter Chamoni, Steffen Stock

FG Wirtschaftsinformatik und Operations Research
Gerhard-Mercator-Universitt GH Duisburg
Lotharstr. 63 LF 221
47048 Duisburg
Germany

chamoni@uni-duisburg.de, stock@uni-duisburg.de

**Abstract.** Following the paradigm of on-line analytical processing (OLAP) every representation of business objects in management support systems is multidimensional. Dynamic changes of business structures like consolidations have to be modeled in the data warehouse framework. For reasons of consistency in analytical applications it is necessary to add temporal components to the data model. Objects and relations between objects will be provided with time stamps corresponding to known methods of temporal data storage. This enhancement of the OLAP-approach allows even after changes of structural data (dimensions) an appropriate comparative analysis between arbitrary periods. But any access to multidimensional cubes make it necessary to evaluate a meta cube.

**Keywords.**
Multidimensional databases, data warehouse, management support systems, temporal data, OLAP

## 1 Introduction

The development of management support systems is characterized by the cyclic up and down of buzz words. Model based decision support and executive information systems were always restricted by the lack of consistent data. Nowadays data warehouses try to cover this gap by providing actual and decision relevant information to allow the control of critical success factors. This is not only a snapshot of operational performance but also a view on the time series of relevant variables and parameters. Therefore the use of time stamps is crucial for data warehouse application. This paper provides concepts of temporal databases for management support systems that will lead to approaches of data warehouse architectures.

## 2 Temporal data

In "temporal databases" we store versions of objects which are tracking the evolution of these objects over a period of time. The attributes of time of these versions are called time stamps. They mark a special point or interval on the time axis. In this context we only consider time as a series of discrete time units. The granularity of time measurement depends on the application area. We call a chronon the smallest relevant time unit which is atomic [JDBC98, 376] so that the time axis could be interpreted as a series of chroni. As most objects do not alter their attributes in every chronon we prefer to stamp these objects with time intervals.

Temporal information systems distinguish between valid time and transaction time. A valid time of a fact (instance of an object) gives the interval of time in which the observed object keeps a constant state. The transaction time (point in time) of a database is the time when a fact is current and retrievable in the database [JDBC98, 371]. Databases with either valid times or transaction times are called temporal databases [JDBC98, 375].

There are two temporal enhancements of RDBMS: time stamps of attributes or time stamps of tuple. Within the attribute stamping every time-dependent attribute gets a time stamp for the beginning and the end of the period of validity. This violates the 1NF because we insert many versions of one attribute in a tuple, whereas the tuple stamping avoids this effect by providing two special attributes "beginning of period" and "end of period" in every tuple. Nevertheless we have to copy every tuple even when there is only a change in one attribute which gives a high redundancy in the database. Otherwise we use a temporal normalization to avoid these redundancies. In general we have to consider valid times and transaction times in temporal databases. The use of the one or the other dependens on the application case.

## 3  Models of temporal data warehouses

Almost all implementations of temporal databases are OLTP oriented. Little is known about the handling of evolutionary structures [RoCR94, 138] in analytical information systems like executive information systems or OLAP applications. Here we do not manipulate atomic data items in a transaction system but analyse complex dynamic data structures as to find in corporative consolidation trees.

### 3.1  Fundamentals of data warehousing

A data warehouse is a concept for a corporative data storage where a common business semantic meets consistent information that is of potential relevance for decisions. Its application field is the management task of planning, analysing and controlling the companies key processes. Inmon [Inmo96, 33] defines a data warehouse as "... a subject oriented, integrated, non-volatile, and time variant collection of data in support of management's decisions."

The special challenge in building a data warehouse is to deliver decision relevant information in time from internal and external sources, to store multi-dimensional business objects in an efficient way and to present the information for an intuitive use with a high performance [ChGl98]. Periodic updates pump cleaned, compressed and enriched data from OLTP systems into a data warehouse where in respect to a conceptual data model the multidimensional objects are redundantly stored. All data items in a data warehouse are time dependent. This results from the permanent shift of states in the operational database and the periodical transfer of historical data into the archives. Another aspect lies in the scheduling of the data import into the warehouse. But this fact only determines the limit for values of a chronon. A chronon has to be smaller than the update cycle.

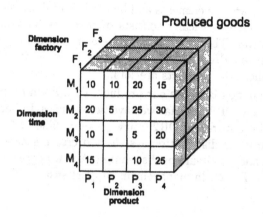

**Fig. 1.** OLAP cube

Multidimensional database design needs approaches for modeling dimensions (sets of logically connected elements) with aggregation and disaggregation operators to build structures within the dimensions. Each business object will be described by these structures (dimensions) and by quantities (facts). The basic attribute of a business object is the dimension of time (periods) as in all business contexts the time dependency is obvious.

In Fig.1 we see a multidimensional cube that is opened up by sets of dimensions (factory, time, product). The quantities will be imported with reference to the mapping and the synchronization from the OLTP databases. One can notice that each component of a data warehouse (structure and facts) is temporal. Therefore it is necessary to establish the time relation on every level of data modeling.

## 3.2 Multidimensional modeling

While modeling a multidimensional data cube the inherent dimension of time has to be fixed in its granularity. This granularity of time in most cases is dependent on the chroni of the underlying operational information systems. OLAP modeling and temporal databases have the definition of granularity of time in common.

We will explain the temporal extension of multidimensional databases by the above mentioned example shown as OLAP cube in Fig.1.

The chosen granularity of time in this example is MONTH. That means that the valid time for the version of an object is explicitly expressed by the dimension TIME. The transaction time is irrelevant since the attributes of any object stored in the data warehouse must not be altered by definition. This means that we only store historical facts in the OLAP cube which are periodically inserted and stamped by the dimension TIME.

It is much more relevant to consider the change of structures relating to time. Structural data are the elements and hierarchies of dimensions which span the cube. Each hierarchy basically consists of relations between father-nodes and son-nodes in a tree. There can be multiple hierarchies on every dimension. Consider the dimension PRODUCTS with a tree built by distribution regions DR0, DR1, DR2 where the products are sold.

Now, assume that we distribute our products P1,..,P4 in period M1 and M2 in the regions DR1 and DR2 but that we have two changes. In period M2 we will produce and distribute in region DR2 a new product called P5. After a month in M3 we restructure our distribution system and create a new region DR3 in which products P4 and P5 should be distributed. A new aggregation tree will be valid for period M3 (Fig.2). In management support systems there is an urgent

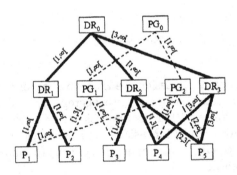

**Fig. 2.** Multiple time stamped consolidation trees

need for exception reporting and comparison of historical and actual data. The evolution of structures in business organizations must therefore be kept in data warehouses. A straight forward idea to store the valid times of structures is to give every component in a hierarchy (tree) an attribute time stamp. This can be done by stamping all historical relations in a consolidation tree (Fig.2). Then we can read the tree for every period of its life span. The time intervals give the validity of every consolidation-relation with a left closed and right open time interval (n short for Mn). So we see the emerging of product P5 in month M2 distributed in DR2 and the shift of P4 and P5 to region DR3 in month M3.

As the elements of a dimension are used to describe different OLAP cubes we can not give these elements a global time stamp. This is also true for the nodes of the different trees. But when we provide only time stamps on the edges of a graph we have to analyse every consolidation path before an OLAP access. Another way of storing different structures is the tuple time stamping. Concerning the example we decompose the tree in time relations (node1; node2; [beginning of valid time, end of valid time[). Actually in this special case of consolidation trees we see no difference between attribute and tuple time stamps.

The implementation of either attribute or tuple time stamps should be done by matrices of valid times as is shown in Fig.3.

| $[1,\infty[$ | $DR_0$ | $DR_1$ | $DR_2$ | $DR_3$ | $P_1$ | $P_2$ | $P_3$ | $P_4$ | $P_5$ |
|---|---|---|---|---|---|---|---|---|---|
| $DR_0$ | | $[1,\infty[$ | $[1,\infty[$ | $[3,\infty[$ | | | | | |
| $DR_1$ | | | | | $[1,\infty[$ | $[1,\infty[$ | | | |
| $DR_2$ | | | | | | | $[1,\infty$ | $[1,\infty[$ | $[2,\infty[$ |
| $DR_3$ | | | | | | | | $[3,\infty[$ | $[3,\infty[$ |
| $P_1$ | | | | | $[1,\infty[$ | | | | |
| $P_2$ | | | | | | $[1,\infty[$ | | | |
| $P_3$ | | | | | | | $[1,\infty[$ | | |
| $P_4$ | | | | | | | | $[1,\infty[$ | |
| $P_5$ | | | | | | | | | $[2,\infty[$ |

**Fig. 3.** Matrix of valid time stamps

Each row and every column of the quadratic matrix is described by the nodes of the consolidation tree. Every existing father-son-relation obtains a time stamp as entry in the table. In the shaded cells we see the derived valid times of the leaves and the root of the considered tree. The arrows in Fig.4 stand for the union of all contributing time intervals. An inspection of the table gives the structure of a dimension and the changes of this structure relating to time.

For all structural information in form of consolidation trees we need a matrix representation. This technique is necessary not only for diverse trees in one or more dimensions of a special cube but also for different cubes (neglecting the hypercube approach). This fact leads to the idea of multidimensional meta cubes where the structure of a complete OLAP system is stored. Beside all used dimensions except the dimension TIME (time itself is not time valid) a meta dimension cubes is introduced so that every single dimension structure in every cube can be stored with its time stamps in the meta cube.

Any access to a temporal multidimensional database (see Fig.4) by OLAP-queries must use the information of the meta cube. Following a drill down into a cube for an individual time period each related consolidation tree has to be taken in account. The advantage of this concept is an easy support of all data analysis which are time related. So we can compare historical data (facts) or actual data on a basis of time different consolidation structures. The option of valid time stamping should be added to classical OLAP architectures to provide

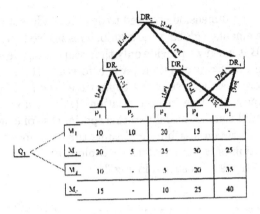

**Fig. 4.** Consolidation tree and fact table

not only time-dependent facts but also the access to evolutionary changes of business structures.

## 4 Conclusion

It is shown that a data warehouse generally needs temporal components to model structural data. The special architecture of data warehouses has a strong impact on the use of temporal extensions in databases. Only few concepts of temporal relational databases are transferable. To store time dependent structural data we suggest the use of meta cubes wherein global time information about every relation is available. In summary you can say that every data warehouse supports valid times for facts but seldom for stored business structures or rules. This paper offers the extension of concept models and implementations of a data warehouse towards a temporal database has been shown in this paper.

## References

[ChGl98a] Chamoni, Peter; Gluchowski, Peter: Analytische Informationssysteme - Einordnung und Ueberblick. In: Chamoni, Peter; Gluchowski, Peter (ed.): Analytische Informationssysteme. Data Warehouse, On-Line Analytical Processing, Data Mining. Berlin 1998, pp. 3 - 25.

[Inmo96] Inmon, William H.: Building the Data Warehouse. 2. ed., New York 1996.

[JDBC98] Jensen, Christian et al.: A consensus glossary of temporal database concepts - February 1998 Version. In: Etzion, Opher et al. (ed.): Temporal databases: research and practice. Berlin, Heidelberg 1998., p. 367 - 405.

[RoCR94] Roddick, John et al.: A taxonomy for schema versioning based on the relational and entity relationship models. In: Elmasri, Ramez et al. (ed.): Proceedings of the 12th international conference on the entity-relationship approach, Arlington, 1993-12-15 - 1993-12-17. Berlin et al. 1994., p. 137 - 148.

# Target Group Selection in Retail Banking through Neuro-Fuzzy Data Mining and Extensive Pre- and Postprocessing

Thomas Wittmann, Johannes Ruhland

Lehrstuhl für Wirtschaftsinformatik, Friedrich-Schiller-Universität Jena
Carl-Zeiß-Str. 3, 07743 Jena, Germany
Tel.: +49 - 3641 - 943313, Fax: +49 - 3641 - 943312
email: t.wittmann@wiwi.uni-jena.de, j.ruhland@wiwi.uni-jena.de

**Abstract.** Based on a real-life problem, the target group selection for a bank's database marketing campaign, we will examine the capacity of Neuro-Fuzzy Systems (NFS) for Data Mining. NFS promise to combine the benefits of both fuzzy systems and neural networks, and are thus able to learn IF-THEN-rules, which are easy to interpret, from data. However, they often need extensive preprocessing efforts, especially concerning the imputation of missing values and the selection of relevant attributes and cases. In this paper we will demonstrate innovative solutions for various pre- and postprocessing tasks as well as the results from the NEFCLASS Neuro-Fuzzy software package.

**Keywords.** Database Marketing, Data Mining, Missing values, Neuro-Fuzzy Systems, Preprocessing

## 1    Introduction

Companies doing database marketing experience target group selection as a core problem. At the same time they are often confronted with a huge amount of data stored in their data banks. These could be a rich source of knowldege, if only properly used. The new field of research, called Knowledge Discovery in Databases (KDD) aims at closing this gap by developing and integrating Data Mining Algorithms, which are capable of 'pressing the crude data coal into diamonds of knowledge'. In this case study we describe how to support a bank's new direct mailing campaign based on data about their customers and their reactions on a past campaign. The database consists of 186.162 cases (656 of them being respondents and the rest non-respondents) and 43 attributes, e.g. date of birth, sum of transactions etc., as well as the responding behaviour. We will describe how Neuro-Fuzzy Systems can be used as Data Mining tools to extract descriptions of interesting target groups for this bank. We will also show which preprocessing and postprocessing steps are indispensable to make this Neuro-Fuzzy Data Mining kernel work.

# 2 Neuro-Fuzzy Systems as Data Mining Tools

Neuro-Fuzzy Systems (NFS) represent a new development in the field of Data Mining tools. They promise to combine the benefits of both fuzzy systems and neural networks, because the hybrid NFS-architecture can be adapted and also interpreted during learning as well as afterwards. There is a wide variety of approaches summed up under the term 'Neuro-Fuzzy Systems' [1]. Here we focus on a specific approach called NEFCLASS (NEuro Fuzzy CLASSification), which is available as freeware from the Institute of Information and Communication Systems at the University of Magdeburg, Germany (http://fuzzy.cs.uni-magdeburg.de/welcome.html). NEFCLASS is an interactive tool for data analysis and determines the correct class or category of a given input pattern. A fuzzy system is mapped on a neural network, a feed-forward three-layered Multilayer Perceptron. The (crisp) input pattern is presented to the neurons of the first layer. The fuzzification takes place when the input signals are propagated to the hidden layer, because the weights of the connections are modelled as membership functions of linguistic terms. The neurons of the hidden layer represent the rules. They are fully connected to the input layer with connection weights being interpretable as fuzzy sets. A hidden neuron's response is connected to one output neuron only. With output neurons being associated with an output class on a 1:1 basis, each hidden neuron serves as a classification detector for exactly one output class. Connections from hidden to output layer do not carry connection weights reflecting the lack of rule confidences in the approach. The learning phase is divided into two steps. In the first step, the system learns the number of rule units and their connections, i.e. the rules and their antecedents, and in the second step, it learns the optimal fuzzy sets, that is their membership functions [2].

In recent years various authors have stressed the benefits of using these NFS for Data Mining [2]. The effectiveness of these algorithms is empirically proven for small files like the iris data (see e.g. [3] or [4]). But when it comes to analyzing real-life problems, their main advantages, the ease of understandability and the capability to process automatically large data bases remains a much acclaimed desire rather than a proven fact, though. Regarding classification quality, in a previous study based on a real-life data file and criteria [5], we have found Neuro-Fuzzy Systems as good as other algorithms tested. Their advantages are ease of interpretation (fuzzy IF–THEN rules ) and their ability to easily integrate a priori knowledge to enhance performance and/or classification quality. However, two severe problems may jeopardize Neuro-Fuzzy Data Mining, especially for large databases:

- Inability to handle missing values, which is especially true for the NEFCLASS product considered. All cases with missing values have to be excluded. In datasets where missing values are common, this brute force approach bears a high risk of altogether deleting relevant learning patterns.
- Run time behavior can be most annoying when working on large databases. Moreover the interpretability of the resulting rule set decreases with many input

variables and thus many rules, because a lot of NFS, e.g. NEFCLASS, are not able to pick the relevant attributes.

It has turned out that pre- and postprocessing efforts are indispensible for Neuro-Fuzzy Systems (like most Data Mining algorithms). The Knowledge Discovery in Databases paradigm as described by [6] offers a conceptual framework for the design of a knowledge extracting system that consists of preprocessing steps (data selection; imputation of missing values; dimensionality reduction), a Data Mining kernel and postprocessing measures. For each step we have to develop tools to solve the problems mentioned in an integrated fashion, which means that they should guarantee an uninterrupted data flow and allow to use experts' background knowledge.

Next, we will show, how we have implemented the different units of the KDD process by resorting to existing approaches and developing own solutions. We will demonstrate the efficiency of this system by a target group selection case study.

## 3 Data Selection

To promote a new product, one of Germany´s leading retail banks had conducted a locally confined but otherwise large mailing campaign. To efficiently extend this action to the whole of the country, a forecast of reaction probablilty based on demographic and customer history data is required. Eliminating data items that are low on reliability and/or widespread and consistent availability, we end up with 28 independent variables. Next, cases with extreme value constellations were identified as outliers using standard descriptive procedures and eliminated.

## 4 Imputation of Missing Values

Missing values often occur in real life databases and can cause severe problems for Data Mining. This applies to Data Warehouses in particular, where data are collected from many different, often heterogeneous sources. Different solutions have been developed in the past to solve this problem. First, one can delete all cases with at least one missing value (listwise deletion). But this leads to a great loss of information [7]. Secondly, one can use different methods of parameter estimation, especially by means of maximum likelihood functions [8]. These algorithms are very time consuming because of exhaustive estimations and thus are running against the Data Mining philosophy. The most promising approach, however, is to explicitly impute the missing data. Here, we can distinguish two prime directions according to the way the redundancies in the data base are used:

- Approaches that try to impute the missing valus by setting up relationships between the attributes. These relationships (regressions or simple ratios), computed over the complete cases, and the known values of an incomplete case are used to calculate an appropriate imputation value. The most famous algorithm here is the regression based imputation by [9].

- Algorithms that use the corresponding value of the most similar complete case for imputation. As this nearest-neighbour-approach proves to be computationally inefficient, one often clusters cases into groups and uses cluster centers in place of cases to carry out similarity and distance calculations.

Although this last approach seems to be very attractive, it is still very time consuming in the clustering step. Another way we have tried, is to use the infomation of a decision tree for imputation. This decision tree is developed by the C5.0 algorithm [10], which is by far more efficient than any clustering algorithm. The basic idea is as follows: C5.0 analyses a discrete dependent variable and builds a decision tree from the influence set, using variables with strongest discriminating power for the top splits. In the leaves of the tree the number of cases belonging to each class may be recorded. Theses numbers should ideally be close to 0 or 100% For an example see figure 1 with 22 cases described by two attributes found relevant, s.l. profession and age group. We interpret the leaves of the tree as homgeneous groups of cases. To put widespread experience in a nutshell, this method can efficiently and robustly model data dependencies. When building the tree the algorithm can also utilize cases with missing values by making assumptions about the distribution of the variable affected which leads to the fractional numbers in the leaves, as shown in Figure 1 [10].

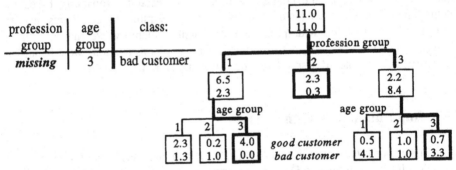

**Fig. 1.** C5.0-decision-tree based imputation.

To use this tree for imputation we first have to compute a quality score for each eligible imputation value (or imputation value constellation in case more than one attribute is missing) which will be based on the similarity between the case with the missing data and each path down the tree to a leaf. This is done by an Approximate nearest neighbour approach (ANN): The ANN method computes similarity as the weighted sum of the distance at every knot (top knots receive a higher weight) including a proxy-knot for the class variable to generate absolutely homogeneous end leaves. Finally, this score is multiplied by a „significance value", too.

Secondly, we have to identify the best imputation value (constellation) by the quality scores of all possible imputation values. To visualize this problem one can draw a (n+1)-dimensional plot for a case with n missing values (see Figure 2 a displaying our score as a function of value constellations). To find a suitable imputation value set different methods are possible, which we have borrowed from the defuzzification strategies in fuzzy set theory.

*Center of Gravity approach*: Here, the imputation value(s) correspond to the attributes' values for the center of the quality plot (In Figure 2 a) this is (2,3) for attribute 1 and 2 respectively). But this approach does not seem suitable for reasons already discussed in fuzzy set theory [11].

*Maximum approach*: This method uses the constellation with the maximum quality score for imputation. This will not always yield unique results, because the decision tree does not have to be developed completely. Hence, some variables might not be defined. In Figure 2 a) for example, attribute 2 will not enter the tree if attribute 1 equals 3. There are several solutions. We can use the best constellation that is completely defined (*Single Max*) ((1,4) in Figure 2 a) or do an unrestricted search for the maximum and in case this constellation is not unique, use a surrogate procedure on the not-yet-defined attribute(s). The surrogate value can be the attribute's global mean (*Global Max Mean*) (leading to (3,2) for the example in Figure 2 a) or the value with the highest average quality, the average being computed over the defined variables (*Global Max Dice*) ((3,4) in Figure 2 a). Applied to the case of Fig. 2a) this means averaging over variable 1 to get the (marginal) quality distribution displayed in Figure 2 b). Based on this „plot II" we calculate the surrogate value, shown in figure 2 c), as follows:

$$q_n^{subst} = q_v^{orig} * \left\{ 1 - \tau \left[ \frac{q_{max}^{plot\ II} - q_n^{plot\ II}}{q_{max}^{plot\ II} - q_{min}^{plot\ II}} \right] \right\}. \tag{1}$$

$q_n^{subst} =$    surrogate quality score of imputation value (constellation) n,

$q_v^{orig} =$    original quality score of v; this not completely defined constellation covers constellation n,

$q_n^{plot\ II} =$    quality score of imputation value (constellation) n in plot II,

$q_{max}^{plot\ II}, q_{min}^{plot\ II} =$    maximum/ minimum quality score in plot II,

$\tau =$    factor determining how much the optimal imputation value (constellation) found by Global Max dominantes other imputation values (constellations) $(0 \leq \tau \leq 1)$:

$\tau = 0 \rightarrow \quad q_n^{subst} = q_v^{orig}$

$0 < \tau \leq 1 \rightarrow \quad q_n^{subst} \in [q_v^{orig} * (1-\tau); q_v^{orig}]$ according to $q_n^{plot\ II}$.

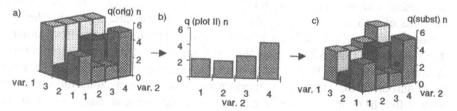

**Fig. 2.** Quality plot and defuzzification by Global Max Dice.

In essence, this amounts to using the marginal score distribution of variable 2 to modulate branches where the decision tree is not fully developed. This definition of a surrogate value is not so essential, because the fact, that the decision tree algorithm did not take into consideration that attribute shows its small discriminating power. But the maximum approach has a distinctive benefit, because it allows some kind of multiple imputation [12] without really imputing different values for one missing data by a simple extension of the method. For each missing value constellation, the n best value tuples are stored together with their quality scores (n can be chosen freely, n=1 corresponds to single imputation) and choose one of them randomly according to its quality score. In doing so we avoid the often criticized reduction of variance inherent to ordinary, deterministic imputation methods [12]. In SPSS for example, this problem is solved by artificially adding variance enlarging noise, whereas the method explained above seems much more elegant and appropriate.

In our case we had 4 attributes with missing data in 0.3%, 27.5% , 50.7% and 86.4% of all cases. Therefore, we would have lost 95% of all cases if using the listwise deletion technique. This would lead to a very high loss of information, especially because all but nine (=1.4%) of all respondents would have to be dropped. The traditional imputation algorithms build their models only on the complete cases. But only 5% of all cases are complete; thus we can hardly trust the regression parameters or clusters. The C5.0-algorithm also uses cases with missing data, although this is done in a very brute force way. This is why we have chosen this method. We have used *Global Max Dice* for defuzzification with n=3, i.e. multiple imputation.

## 5 Dimensionality Reduction

Neuro-Fuzzy Systems like NEFCLASS, which are not able to identify the most relevant attributes for the rules, suffer from a combinatorical explosion in both run time and in breadth and depth of the rule base. Therefore a *selection of the relevant attributes* is inevitable [13]. For this purpose, we have different methods at hand. On the one hand, by the search algorithm employed, we can distinguish heuristic (e.g. forward or backward selection [13], Relief algorithm [14]), complete (e.g. FOCUS [15]) and stochastic methods (e.g. by genetic algorithms [16]) [17]. On the other hand, different approaches use different evaluation functions. In the wrapper approaches each subset of attributes is evaluated based on the classification quality of the target Data Mining algorithm [18]. One common feature of these approaches is that they are very time consuming and not appropriate for Data Mining, whose idea is to process large amounts of data in a short time. Another method is the filter approach. Here, the quality of the selected attributes is evaluated by some form of heuristics different from the target Data Mining algorithm with the hope of capturing discriminating quality in a function that is much easier to evaluate. Examples are the Relief algorithm or FOCUS [15]. Their shortcoming is that the evaluation function's bias may differ from the classifier's bias. To sum up, we can state an efficiency-effectiveness-dilemma, proving none of the single solutions to be optimal.

To overcome this dilemma, we have developed a model combining different approaches in a stepwise procedure [19]. In each step we eliminate cases with methods that are more sophisticated, but also less efficient than the method in the predecessor step. The choice of methods in each step depends to a large extend on the data situation. In our first prototype application example we have used the following methods to study the feasability of our general approach. The first step follows the filter idea. In three substeps we have stepwise eliminated attributes by different methods.

— First of all, to eliminate irrelevant variables. we have looked at variables' entropies and the interrelationship of each independent attribute and the output variable. The entropy as a measure for the information conveyed by a discrete-value attribute is (in the case of binary data) computed according to the well-known formula:

$$\text{entropy}_i = -(p_{i0} * ld(p_{i0}) + p_{i1} * ld(p_{i1})). \tag{2}$$

$p_{i0}, p_{i1}$ = probability of 0 / 1 in variable i.

Based on the entropy we have computed a so-called e-value as e = 1 - entropy. The idea is to eliminate attributes with a high e-value, i.e. attributes with low information. Rules based on these variables might be correct, but their support is too small. In addition we performed a $\chi^2$-test for independence of the output variable from each potential influence (considered in isolation). A so-called attribute's u-value is computed as the 2-sided p-value for this test. The idea is to rule out attributes, which have a u-value higher than a specific significance level, i.e. which have no significant correlation with the output variable. However, this does not raise a claim on statistical profoundness, but serves as a heuristic clue. Moreover, as univariate analyses will not take supression and related interaction effects into account, this procedure is heuristic rather than rigid. Based on both values we have calculated a so-called del-value as a measure of how reliably a variable can be deleted and which allows for compensation between u- and e-value by defining del= u*e and use a threshold for this (here 0.19=0.02*0.95). By doing so we have managed to delete 6 irrelevant attributes.

— In the second substep, we have clustered the remaining attributes via a complete linkage clustering (with correlation serving as a proximity measure) and eliminated 3 redundant variables. Doing a factor analysis instead will result in even lower information loss at the price of interpretability.

— In the third substep, we have used a C5.0 decision tree to identify the attributes with the highest information power. They are located in the first layers of the tree. Here, we have used the first five layers und could eliminate 6 variables not appearing in this layers and thus being just weakly relevant. Again this is a very heuristic but very fast procedure.

Neuro-Fuzzy methods may now start. The second data compression step now consists of a backward elimination with wrapper evaluation. We have eliminated attributes in a stepwise way until the classification quality of the target Neuro-Fuzzy System derived has decreased significantly. This is, of course, a very time consuming method. But it is inevitable for the final selection of the attributes. Due to the preceeding heuristic selection and thinning out steps this wrapper approach has been feasible in this stage now.

To reduce the run time we do not only have to select the relevant attributes but also *select the relevant cases.* A small sample should be drawn containing all prototypes necessary to cover the input space. Previous studies have also shown that NEFCLASS needs a balanced sample with respect to classes. Therefore we have drawn a training sample by pure random sampling consisting of about 300 respondents and 300 non-respondents. Unfortunately, this file was very small due to the small amount of respondents. This might lead to a high degree of randomness in the sample quality. But sensitivity analyses have shown that this was not the case. We have also tried more intelligent sampling methods, such as stratified sampling or jack-knifing. But this did not lead to better results.

## 6 Data Mining with NEFCLASS

NEFCLASS learns the number of rule units and their connections, i.e. the rules. If the user restricts the maximum number of rules, the best rules are selected according to an optimisation criterion [1]. This maximum rule number and the number of fuzzy sets per input variable are the most important user defined parameters. The optimal number of rules heavily depends on the attribute subset used, which obviously complicates the wrapper step. Therefore, we have optimized this parameter after every fifth iteration of the variable backward elimination process. The classification quality depends on the number of rules in an almost step-like fashion. Thus it makes sense to redefine the number of rules in a rather heuristic approach at the left edge of a step.

The number of fuzzy sets per input variable was generally set to two. For the binary variables this is an obvious choice, and for continuous attributes we also identified two fuzzy sets as being sufficient. Using more fuzzy sets will enhance classification quality just marginally, but exponentially increases the number of rules. After having identified the optimal parameters and the optimal attribute subset, we have finally trained NEFCLASS coming up with a rule base with 4 influencing attributes and 10 rules. The classification quality was quite good with 72.7% of correctly classified cases in the independent validation set (respondents: 68.7%; non-respondents: 77,7%). The rules (for the sake of simplification in a matrix notation) and the membership functions are shown in figure 3 a).

## 7 Rule postprocessing

For all our efforts in attribute reduction, the resulting rule base still bears room for improvement. In figure 3 for example, we have aggregated the rules based on a C5.0 decision tree. One can identify relevant variables, as decision trees locate them at the root and the first knots of the tree. The rules are sorted by these attributes. In such a sorted tableau one can simply identify and eliminate redundant variables and rules (e.g. if the total number of transactions is large then it is an respondent disregarding the values of the other three attributes). There is, of course, no guarantee that the classification quality will not deteriorate significantly when the pruned rule base is applied to data from outside the calibration sample. In close analogy to overfitting problems in neural networks, checking out validation samples is highly recommended.

In this study we have aggregated the rule base manually, but a tool is being developed, that will not only aggregate rules automatically, but also represent them to the user in an adequate and interactive way.

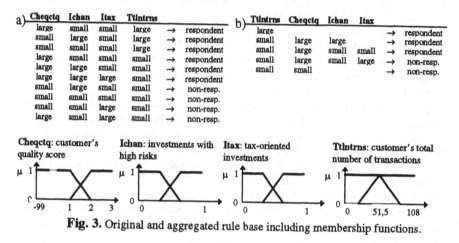

**Fig. 3.** Original and aggregated rule base including membership functions.

# 8 Conclusion

This study has shown the great prospects of Neuro-Fuzzy Data Mining. The results affirmed the previous experience that Neuro-Fuzzy Systems are not able to outperform alternative approaches, e.g. neural nets and discriminant analysis, with respect to classification quality. But they provide a rule base that is very compact and well understandable. Extensive preprocessing activities have been necessary, especially concerning the imputation of missing values and selection of relevant attributes and cases. Besides, we believe that these tools are also of general relevance. Intelligent postprocessing can further enhance the resulting rule base's power of expression. In this paper, we have shown some promising approaches for these steps as well as their effectiveness and efficiency. Of course, we are still far away from an integrated data flow. But our experience with the single modules described above is very promising. However, these first results have to be further validated for different Neuro-Fuzzy Systems and different data situations. Our final goal is to integrate these modular solutions into a comprehensive KDD tool box.

Funding for this project was provided by of the Thuringian Ministry for Science, Research and Culture. Responsibility for content is entirely with the authors.

# References

1. Nauck, D., Klawonn, F., Kruse, R. (1996), Neuronale Netze und Fuzzy-Systeme. 2. Aufl., Braunschweig Wiesbaden 1996.
2. Nauck, D. (1995), Beyond Neuro-Fuzzy: Perspectives and Directions, In: Proceedings of the third European Congress on Intelligent Techniques and Soft Computing (EUFIT'95), Aachen, August 28-31 1995, p. 1159-1164.
3. Halgamuge, S. K., Mari, A., Glesner, M. (1994), Fast Perceptron learning by Fuzzy Controlled Dynamic Adaption of Network Parameters, In: Kruse, R., Gebhardt, J., Palm, R. (Hrsg.), Fuzzy Systems in Computer Science, Wiesbaden 1994, p. 129-139.
4. Nauck, D., Nauck, U., Kruse, R. (1996), Generating Classification Rules with the Neuro-Fuzzy System NEFCLASS, In: Proceedings Biennial Conference of the North American Fuzzy Information Processing Society (NAFIPS'96), Berkley, June 19-22, 1996.
5. Ruhland, J., Wittmann, T. (1997), Neurofuzzy Systems In Large Databases - A comparison of Alternative Algorithms for a real-life Classification Problem, In: Proceedings EUFIT'97, Aachen, Germany, September 8-11 1997, Aachen 1997, p. 1517-1521.
6. Fayyad, U., Piatetsky-Shapiro, G., Smyth, P. (1996b), Knowledge Discovery and Data Mining: Towards a Unifying Framework, In: Simoudis, E., Han, J. (Hrsg.), Proceedings of Second International Conference on Knowledge Discovery and Data Mining (KDD-96), Portland, Oregon, August 2-4, 1996, Menlo Park 1996, p. 82-88.
7. Gupta, A., Lam, M. S. (1996), Estimating missing values using neural networks, In: Journal of the Operational Research Society 2/96, p. 229-238.
8. Little, R. J. A., Rubin, D. B. (1987), Statistical analysis with missing data, New York u.a. 1987.
9. Buck, S. F. (1960), A method of estimation of missing values in multivariate data suitable for use with an electronic computer, In: Journal of the Royal Statistical Society, Series B 1960, p. 302-306.
10. Quinlan, J. R. (1996), C4.5. Programs for Machine Learning, San Mateo, 1993.
11. Geyer-Schulz, A. (1995), Fuzzy Rule-Based Expert Systems and Genetic Machine Learning, Heidelberg 1995.
12. Rubin, D. B. (1987), Multiple Imputation for Nonresponse in Surveys, New York 1987.
13. Caruana, R., Freitag, A. A. (1994), Greedy Attribute Selection, in: Machine Learning: Proceedings of the Eleventh International Conference (San Francisco, CA), New Brunswick, NJ 1994, p. 28-36.
14. Kira, K., Rendell, L. A., A practical approach to feature selection, in: Sleeman, D., Edwards, P., Proceedings of the Ninth International Workshop on Machine Learning (ML92), San Mateo 1992, p. 249-256.
15. Almuallim, H., Dietterich, T.G. (1992), Efficient algorithms for identifying relevant features, in: Proceedings of the Ninth Canadian Conference on Artificial Intelligence, Vancouver 1992, p. 38-45.
16. Bala, J., De Jong, K., Huang, J. (1996), Using learning to facilitate the evolution of features for recognizing visual concepts, in: Evolutionary Computation 1996 4 (3), p. 297-311.
17. Dash, M., Liu, H. (1997), Feature selection for classifcation, In: Intelligent Data Analysis 3/97.
18. Freitas, A. A. (1997), The Principle of Transformation between Efficiency and Effectiveness: Towards a Fair Evaluation of the Cos-Effectiveness of KDD Techniques, in: Principles of Data Mining and knowledge discovery; first European Symposium; proceedings/ PKDD '97, Trondheim, Norway, June 24-27, 1997, p. 299-306.
19. Wittmann, T., Ruhland, J. (1998), Untersuchung der Zusammenhänge zwischen Fahrzeugmerkmalen und Störungsanfälligkeiten mittels Neuro Fuzzy Systemen, in: Kuhl, J., Nissen, V., Tietze, M., Soft Computing in Produktion und Materialwirtschaft, Göttingen 1998, p. 71-85.

# Using Data Mining Techniques in Fiscal Fraud Detection

F. Bonchi[±,*], F. Giannotti[*], G. Mainetto[*], D. Pedreschi[±]

[*] CNUCE–CNR, Via S. Maria 36, 56126 Pisa
{F.Giannotti,G.Mainetto}@cnuce.cnr.it

[±] Dipartimento di Informatica, Università di Pisa, C.so Italia 40, 56125 Pisa
{bonchi,pedre}@di.unipi.it

**Abstract.** Planning adequate audit strategies is a key success factor in "a posteriori" fraud detection, e.g., in the fiscal and insurance domains, where audits are intended to detect tax evasion and fraudulent claims. A case study is presented in this paper, which illustrates how techniques based on classification can be used to support the task of planning audit strategies. The proposed approach is sensible to some conflicting issues of audit planning, e.g., the trade-off between maximizing audit benefits vs. minimizing audit costs.

## 1    Introduction

Fraud detection is becoming a central application area for knowledge discovery in databases, as it poses challenging technical and methodological problems, many of which are still open [1, 2]. A major task in fraud detection is that of constructing *models*, or *profiles*, of fraudulent behavior, which may serve in decision support systems for:

- preventing frauds (*a priori* fraud detection), or
- planning audit strategies (*a posteriori* fraud detection).

The first case is typical of domains such as credit cards and mobile telephony [3, 4]. The second case concerns a whole class of applications, namely whenever we are faced with the problem of constructing models by analyzing historical audit data, to the purpose of planning effectively future audits. This is the case, e.g., in the fiscal and insurance domain, where an adequately targeted audit strategy is a key success factor for goverments and insurance companies. In fact, huge amounts of resources may be recovered in principle from well-targeted audits: for instance, the form of tax evasion consisting in filing fraudulent tax declarations in Italy is estimated between 3% and 10% of GNP [5]. This explains the increasing interest and investments of governments and insurance companies in intelligent systems for audit planning.

This short paper presents a case study for planning audits in the fiscal fraud detection domain. Audit planning is usually a difficult task, in that it has to take into account constraints on the available human and financial resources to carry out the audits themselves. This complexity is present in our case study, too. Therefore, the proposed planning has to face two conflicting issues:

- *maximizing audit benefits*, i.e., define subjects to be selected for audit in such a way that the recovery of evaded tax is maximized, and
- *minimizing audit costs*, i.e., define subjects to be selected for audit in such a way that the resources needed to carry out the audits are minimized.

The case study has been developed within a project aimed at investigating the adequacy and sustainability of KDD in the detection of tax evasion.

## 2. Planning Audit Strategies in the Fiscal Domain

In this section, a methodology for constructing profiles of fraudulent behavior is presented, aimed at supporting audit planning. The reference paradigm is that of the KDD process, in the version of *direct knowledge extraction* [6]. The reference technique is that of classification, using *decision trees* [7].

### 2.1 Identification of Available Data Sources

The dataset used in the case study consists of information from tax declarations, integrated with data from other sources, such as social benefits paid by taxpayers to employees, official budget documents, and electricity and telephone bills. Each tuple in the dataset corresponds to a (large or medium) company that filed a tax declaration in a certain period of time: we shall use the word *subject* to refer to such companies. The initial dataset consists of 80643 tuples, with 175 numeric attributes (or features), where only a few are categorical. From this dataset, 4103 tuples correspond to *audited* subjects: the outcome of the audit is recorded in a separate dataset with 4103 tuples and 7 attributes, one of which represents the *amount of evaded tax ascertained by the audit*. Such feature is named *recovery*. The recovery attribute has value zero if no fraud is detected.

### 2.2 Identification of a Cost Model

Together with domain experts, a *cost model* has been defined, to be included in the predictive model. In fact, audits are very expensive in both human and financial resources, and therefore it is important to focus audits on subjects that presumably return a high recovery. The challenging goal is therefore to build a classifier, which selects those interesting subjects.

The cost model in our case study has been developed as follows. First, a new attribute *audit_cost* is defined, as a derived attribute, i.e., a function of other attributes. *audit_cost* represents an estimation, provided by the domain expert, of the cost of an audit which grows with the square of the sum of employees number and of sales volume of the subject to be audited. Next, we define another derived attribute *actual_recovery*, as the recovery of an audit without the audit costs. Therefore, for each tuple *i*, we define:

$$actual\_recovery(i) = recovery(i) - audit\_costs(i)$$

The attribute *actual_recovery* is used to discriminate between subjects with a positive or negative value for such attribute. The key point is in using the cost model *within* the learning process itself, and not only in the evaluation phase.

The target variable of our analysis is constructed from *actual_recovery*, by defining the *class of actual recovery – car* in short – in such a way that, for each tuple *I*:

car(i) =        *negative*      *if actual_recovery(i) <= 0*
              *positive*      *if actual_recovery (i) > 0*

The goal is a predictive model able to characterize the positive subjects, which are eligible to be audited.

## 2.3 Preparation of Data for Analysis

**Data transformation.** This phase was extremely time consuming, due to the presence of legacy systems, huge operational databases (hierarchical and relational), inconsistent measure units and data scales.

**Data cleaning (row removal).** Noisy tuples, i.e., those with excessively deviating attribute values, have been removed, as well as those tuples with too many null attribute values. After data cleaning, the initial audited subjects became 3880: 3183 tuples in negative *car* (82%), and 697 in positive *car* (18%).

**Attribute selection (column removal).** The selection of relevant attributes is a crucial step, which was taken together with domain experts. The available 175 attributes were reduced 20, by removing irrelevant, derived ones.

**Choice of training-set and test-set.** The correct size of the training set is an important parameter in a classification experiment. While the size of the training set increases, the complexity of the induced model also increases, as the training error (i.e., the misclassification rate on training-set tuples) decreases. This does not imply that large training-sets are necessarily better: a complex model, with a low training error, may behave poorly on new tuples. This phenomenon is named *overfitting*: the classifier is excessively specialized on the training tuples, and has a high misclassification rate on new (test) tuples. The classical remedies to overfitting include downsizing the training-set, and increasing the pruning level.

Our case study adopts an incremental samples approach to sizing the training-set [8], consisting in training a sequence of classifiers over increasingly larger, randomly generated subsets of the dataset – 10%, 20%, 33%, 50%, 66%, 90% of the total dataset. We discovered that the resulting classifiers improve with increasing training-sets, independently from the pruning level. In other words, and not unsurprisingly, there is no risk of overfitting, since the size of the dataset is relatively small with respect to the complexity of the knowledge to be extracted.

As a consequence, the 3880 tuples in the dataset were partitioned as follows:
– training set: 3514 tuples            – test set: 366 tuples.

## 2.4 Model Construction

We remind that our goal is a binary classifier with the attribute *car* (class of actual recovery) as target variable. The decision trees are trained to distinguish between positive *car* (fruitful audits) and negative *car* (unfruitful audits). Once the training phase is over, the test-set is fed to the classifier, to check whether it is effective in selecting on the new tuples. In our case, it is relevant not only the misclassification rate of the classifier on the test-set, but also the *actual_recovery* (= ascertained evaded tax − audit cost) obtained from the audits of the subjects from the test-set which are classified as positive. This value can be matched against the real case, where all (366) tuples of the test-set are audited. This case, which we call *Real*, is characterized by the following:

- audit#(Real) = #(test-set) = 366
- actual_recovery(Real) = $\sum_{i \in \text{test-set}}$ actual_recovery(i) = 159.6 M Euro
- audit_costs(Real) = $\sum_{i \in \text{test-set}}$ audit_costs(i) = 24.9 M Euro

where recovery and costs are expressed in million euros. As the test-set consists of audited subjects, by comparing the values of the *Real* case with those of the subjects classified as positive by the various classifiers, it is possible to evaluate the potential improvement of using data mining techniques to the purpose of planning the audits.

Therefore, the classifiers resulting from our experiments are evaluated according to the following metrics, which represent domain-independent (1 and 2) and domain-dependent (3 through 6) indicators of the quality of a classifier $X$:

1. confusion_matrix(X)
2. misclassification_rate(X)
3. actual_recovery(X)
4. audit_costs(X)
5. profitability(X)
6. relevance(X)

where:

1. The *confusion matrix*, which summarizes the prediction of classifier X over the test-set tuples, is a table of the form:

| classified **negative** | classified **positive** | |
|---|---|---|
| *#TN* | *#FP* | really **negative** |
| *#FN* | *#TP* | really **positive** |

where the sets *TN*, *TP*, *FN*, *FP* are defined as follows, using the notation $pred_X(i)$ to denote the *car* (either positive or negative) of a tuple $i$ predicted by classifier $X$:

- $TN = \{i \mid pred_X(i) = car(i) = \text{negative}\}$
  is the set of tuples with negative class of actual recovery which are classified as such by classifier $X$ (*true negative* subjects);
- $FP = \{i \mid pred_X(i) = \text{positive } AND \ car(i) = \text{negative}\}$
  is the set of tuples with negative class of actual recovery which are misclassified as positive by classifier $X$ (*false positive* subjects); these are non fraudulent subjects which will be audited, according to $X$, with a negative actual recovery ;
- $FN = \{i \mid pred_X(i) = \text{negative } AND \ car(i) = \text{positive}\}$
  is the set of tuples with positive class of actual recovery which are misclassified as negative by classifier $X$ (*false negative* subjects); these are fraudulent subjects

373

which will not be audited, according to $X$, although the audit would have a positive actual recovery (a loss for missing a fruitful audit);

- $TP = \{i \mid pred_X(i) = car(i) = positive\}$
  is the set of tuples with positive class of actual recovery which are classified as such by classifier $X$ (*true positive* subjects).

2. The *misclassification rate* of $X$ is the percentage of misclassified test-set tuples. More precisely, it is the ratio between the cardinality of (*FP UNION FN*) and the cardinality of the test-set:

- $misclassification\_rate(X) = \#(FP\ UNION\ FN) * 100 / \#(test\text{-}set)$

3. The *actual recovery* of $X$ is the total amount of actual recovery for all tuples classified as positive by $X$:

- $actual\_recovery(X) = \sum_{i \in P} actual\_recovery(i)$, where $P = TP\ UNION\ FP$

4. The *audit costs* of $X$ is the total amount of audit costs for all tuples classified as positive by $X$:

- $audit\_cost(X) = \sum_{i \in P} audit\_cost(i)$

5. The *profitability* of $X$ is the average actual recovery per audit, i.e., the ratio between the total actual recovery and the number of audits suggested by $X$:

- $profitability(X) = actual\_recovery(X) / \#P$

6. The *relevance* of $X$ relates profitability (a domain-dependent metric) and misclassification rate (a domain-independent metric):

- $relevance(X) = 10 * profitability(X) / misclassification\_rate(X)$

**Classifier Construction.** We considered two distinct approaches to classifier construction, each driven by two different policies in audit planning: on one hand, we can aim at keeping *FP* as small as possible, in order to minimize wasteful costs. On the other hand, we can aim at keeping *FN* as small as possible, in order to maximize evasion recovery. The two policies are clearly conflicting: as *FP* shrinks, *TP* shrinks accordingly, while *FN* (and *TN*) inevitably grows; the situation is dual when *FN* shrinks. The first policy is preferable when resources for audits are limited, the second when resources are in principle infinite. In practice, it is needed to find an acceptable trade-off between the two conflicting policies, by balancing the level of actual recovery with the resources needed to achieve it. The classifier construction method is therefore presented highlighting the parameters that may adequately tuned to reach the desired trade-off.

**Parameter tuning.** The following is the list of main tuning methods used in our case study, which we perceive as most relevant for the whole class of applications.

- The *pruning level*: the absence of overfitting enabled us to use a low pruning level (less than 10%) in all experiments: the resulting trees are therefore as large as at least 90% of the corresponding trees obtained without pruning.
- The *misclassification weights*: these are constants that can be attached to the misclassification errors – *FP* and *FN* in our case. The tree construction algorithm uses the weights to minimize errors associated with greater weights, by modifying the probability of misclassification rate. Misclassification weights are the main tool to bias the tree to minimize either *FP* or *FN* errors.

- The *replication of minority class* in the training-set: typically, a classifier is biased towards the majority class in the training-set. In our case study the majority class is that with *car = negative*. Thus, another approach to minimize *FN* is to artificially replicate the positive tuples, up to achieving a balance between the two *car*'s.
- The *adaptive boosting*: the idea is to build a sequence of classifiers, where classifier *k* is built starting from the errors of classifier *k*-1 [9]. The majority of votes casted by the different classifiers establishes the classification of a new tuple. Votes are weighted with respect to the accuracy of the classifiers. This technique yields a sensible reduction of misclassification rate.

## 2.5 Model evaluation

We now present two classifiers, as an illustration of the above construction techniques, and assess their quality and adequacy to the objectives. The former classifier follows the "minimize *FP*" policy, whereas the latter classifier follows the "minimize *FN*" policy.

**Classifier A.** Experiment *A* simply uses the original training-set, and therefore we obtain a classifier construction biased towards on the majority class of training-set, i.e., the negative car. As a consequence, we enforce the "minimize *FP*" policy without using misclassification weights. To reduce errors, we employ 10-trees adaptive boosting. The confusion matrix of the obtained classifier is the following:

| classified **negative** | classified **positive** | |
|---|---|---|
| 237 | 11 | really **negative** |
| 70 | 48 | really **positive** |

Classifier *A* prescribes 59 audits (11 of which wasteful), and exhibits the following quality indicators:
- misclassification_rate(A) = 22% (81 errors)
- actual_recovery(A) = 141.7 M Euro  — profitability(A) = 2.401
- audit_costs(A) = 4 M Euro  — relevance(A) = 1.09

Profitability of model *A* is remarkable: 141.7 Meuro are recovered with only 59 audits, which implies an average of 4,649 Meuro per audit. In comparison with *Real* case, *A* allows to recover 88% of the actual recovery of *Real* with 16% of audits.

**Classifier B.** Experiment *B* adopts the "minimize *FN*" policy, and tries to bias the classification towards the positive *car*. A training-set with replicated positive tuples is prepared, with a balanced proportion of the two classes, in conjunction with misclassification weights that make *FN* errors count three times as much as *FP* errors (i.e., weight of *FP* = 1 and weight of *FN* = 3). Adaptive boosting (3-trees) is also adopted. The confusion matrix of the obtained model *B* is the following:

| classified **negative** | classified **positive** | |
|:---:|:---:|:---|
| *150* | *98* | really **negative** |
| *28* | *90* | really **positive** |

Classifier *B* prescribes 188 audits (more than 50% of which wasteful), and exhibits the following quality indicators:

– *misclassification_rate(B)* = 34% (126 errors)
– *actual_recovery(B)* = 165.2 M Euro     – *profitability(B)* = 0.878
– *audit_costs(B)* = 12.9 M Euro          – *relevance(B)* = 0.25

**Combined classifiers.** More sophisticated models can be constructed by suitably combining diverse classifiers together. For instance, predictions of two classifiers can be put in *conjunction*, by considering fraudulent the subjects classified as positive by both classifiers. Conversely, predictions can be put in *disjunction*, by considering fraudulent the subjects classified as positive by either classifiers. The following are the indicators for the model *A and B*, which prescribes 58 audits:

– actual_recovery(*A and B*) = 141.7 M Euro
– audit_costs(*A and B*) = 3.9 M Euro
– profitability(*A and B*) = 2.44

and the indicators for the model *A or B*, which prescribes 189 audits:

– actual_recovery(*A or B*) = 165.1 M Euro
– audit_costs(*A or B*) = 13.0 M Euro
– profitability(*A or B*) = 0.87

Clearly, conjunction is another means to pursue the "minimize *FP*" policy, and conversely disjunction for the "minimize *FN*" policy. The first policy usually yields more profitable models, as the examples show. This form of combination may be iterated, e.g. combining the classifier *A and B* with another classifier *C* (a trade-off between *A* and *B*), obtaining a model *A and B and C* which prescribes 43 audits:

– actual_recovery(*A and B and C*) = 56.0 M Euro
– audit_costs(*A and B and C*) = 3.2 M Euro
– profitability(*A and B and C*) = 1.3

and a model ((*A and B*) *or C*) which prescribes 80 audits:

– actual_recovery((*A and B*) *or C*) = 144.0 M Euro
– audit_costs((*A and B*) *or C*) = 5.2 M Euro
– profitability((*A and B*) *or C*) = 1.8

Classifiers can be combined also by voting, and we have built classifiers where at least n classifiers out of a set of n+m decide the number of audits to plan.

# 3. Concluding Remarks

The first consideration coming from the experience sketched in this paper is about the complexity of the KDD process. While the objectives of the various phases of the KDD process are clear, little support is provided to reach such objectives. Two main issues are, and will remain in the near future, the hot topics of KDD community research agenda:

- the first point is methodology: it is crucial to devise methods tailored to relevant classes of similar applications;
- the second point is the need to identify the basic features of an integrated development environment, able to support the KDD process in all its phases.

Our experience indicates that a suitable integration of deductive reasoning, such as that supported by logic database languages, and inductive reasoning, such as that supported by decision trees, provides a viable solution to many high-level problems in the selected class of applications. In particular, we found such integration useful in the phase of model evaluation, where the uniform representation in the same logic formalism of data for the analysis and the results of the analysis itself allows a high degree of expressiveness. In another paper [10], we show how the entire KDD process here identified can be conveniently formalized and realized by using a query language that integrates the capabilities of deductive rules with the inductive capabilities of classification.

We conclude by mentioning that in our experiments we used C5.0 [11], the most recent available version of the decision tree algorithm that Quinlan has been evolving and refining for many years.

# References

1. Fawcett, T, Provost, F., "Adaptive Fraud Detection", *Data Mining and Knowledge Discovery, Vol. 1, No. 1*, pp. 291-316, (1997).
2. Uthurusamy, R., "From Data Mining to Knowledge Discovery: Current Challenges and Future Directions", in *Knowledge Discovery in Databases*, Piatesky-Shapiro and Frawley (eds.), AAAI Press, Menlo Park, CA, (1991).
3. Fawcett, T, Provost, F., "Robust Classification Systems for Imprecise Environment", *Proc of the 15th Int. Conf. AAAI-98*, (1998).
4. Stolfo, S., Fan, D., Lee, W., Prodromidis, A., Chan, P., "Credit Card Fraud detection using Metalearning: Issues and Initial Results", Working Notes AAAI-97, (1997).
5. Tanzi, V., Shome, P., "A Primer on Tax Evasion", in *IMF Staff Papers, No 4*, (1993).
6. Berry, M., Linoff, G., *Data Mining Techniques for Marketing, Sales and Customer Support*, Wiley Computer Publishing, New York, USA (1997).
7. Breiman, L., Friedman, J. H., Olshen, R. A., Stone, P. J., *Classification and regression trees*, Belmont, CA, Wadsworth (1984).
8. Indurkhya, N., Weiss, S. M., *Predictive Datamining: a pratical guide*, Morgan Kaufman, San francisco, CA, (1998).
9. Freund, Y., "Boosting a Weak Learning Algorithm by Majority", *Information and Computation, 121(2)*, pp. 256-285, (1995).
10. Bonchi, F., Giannotti, F., Mainetto, G., Pedreschi, D., "A classification-based methodology for planning auditing strategies in fraud detection", accepted at *KDD'99*.
11. http://www.rulequest.com/

# Analysis of Accuracy of Data Reduction Techniques

Pedro Furtado and H. Madeira

University of Coimbra
Portugal
pnf@dei.uc.pt

**Abstract.** There is a growing interest in the analysis of data in warehouses. Data warehouses can be extremely large and typical queries frequently take too long to answer. Manageable and portable summaries return interactive response times in exploratory data analysis. Obtaining the best estimates for smaller response times and storage needs is the objective of simple data reduction techniques that usually produce coarse approximations. But because the user is exposed to the approximation returned, it is important to determine which queries would not be approximated satisfactorily, in which case either the base data is accessed (if available) or the user is warned. In this paper the accuracy of approximations is determined experimentally for simple data reduction algorithms and several data sets. We show that data cube density and distribution skew are important parameters and large range queries are approximated much more accurately then point or small range queries. We quantify this and other results that should be taken into consideration when incorporating the data reduction techniques into the design.

## 1. Introduction

Data warehouses integrate information from operational databases, legacy systems, worksheets or any external source, to be used for decision support. The data warehouse must have efficient exploration tools, which, regardless of data size, may give fast reasonably approximate answers to users exploring the data interactively and multidimensional models are usual for the interactive exploration of the data in Online Analytical Processing (OLAP). To build the data cube, facts and dimensions must be identified as well as the data granularity. The dimensions can be products, stores and time with granularity of days. The space needed is calculated as in:

*time span = three years*
*# products = 100.000 products (of which only 20% are sold daily)*
*# stores = 100*
*n° of records in the fact table = 3 × 365 × 20.000 × 100 = 2.19Gbytes*
*average record size = 8 attributes × 4 bytes = 32 bytes*

These figures do not include indexes, materialized views and other fact tables. A complete data warehouse such as this one could have 70 GBytes of size. Data reduction techniques can be applied to any data cube derived from the facts or materialized views to reduce parts of the multidimensional space and obtain fast response times for approximate answers. This in turn is very important for exploring the data. There are several alternative data reduction techniques, such as sampling [2, 7, 8], singular values decomposition (SVD) [6], wavelets [10], histogram-based techniques such as MHIST [5], clustering algorithms such as BIRCH [14] and index trees. These techniques are summarized in [9]. Data analysis needs for approximate answers directly expose the user to the estimates obtained. Although the reduced data is frequently associated with a very coarse initial approximation of the data, accuracy is very important. Even the simplest histogram-based reduction techniques return very small errors for large range queries encompassing whole summary regions. But queries may not encompass whole regions and answers to smaller range queries are also important. Furthermore, the possible absence or slow access of base data stored in tertiary memory or the reduction of summary tables in which points represent aggregated values require higher accuracy. In any case the exploration tool must be able to determine which queries are inaccurate and either access the base data or warn the user. Typical estimation errors are determined experimentally in this paper. The input data set is reduced using alternative techniques and several classes of queries are issued to determine the average estimation error. The experiment involves different data distributions and characteristics such as skew, density and sparseness. The results obtained in these experiments are used to conclude the accuracy that can be expected from data reduction algorithms. The paper is organized as follows. In section 2 alternative generic reduction strategies are discussed. Section 3 presents the data reduction strategies and section 4 the data sets used in the experiments. Section 5 shows the point and range error results that were obtained from the experiments and the conclusions that can be drawn from such results. Section 6 concludes the paper.

## 2. Alternative Reduction Strategies

In this section we address the strategies for histogram-based data reduction and the impact on storage of choosing a given strategy.

Multidimensional data points are represented in relational OLAP (ROLAP) as tuple$(a_1,...,a_n,v_1,...,v_m)$. The multidimensional view can be obtained from the tuples by using the dimension attributes $a_i$ as axis and the values $v_i$ as the data cube contents. The task of the reduction algorithm is to derive approximate values for sets of value attributes $v_i$ in the data cube regions, reducing the data set size (for simplicity we will consider only one value attribute). The reduced data can be stored as a summary, loaded or maintained in memory for fast answers to queries from tools exploring the data.

### 2.1 Classification of Reduction Techniques

The types of data reduction techniques we evaluate divide the multidimensional space into regions and approximate each region by a summarized description. Fast querying and searching is obtained by accessing the summarized descriptions. A generic summary is a set of regions $R([a_{1s},a_{1e}],...,[a_{ns},a_{ne}],coeff_1,...,coeff_x)$ forming a histogram where a region is usually called bucket or cell. We define some important properties of data reduction techniques regarding the resulting histograms:

- *Reduction strategy* - distinguishes algorithms producing fixed grids (*fixed grid strategy* - FG) or variable sized buckets (*variable grid strategy* - VG).

- *Variable grid strategy adaptability* - measures the degree to which the space partitioning strategy is able to adapt to the data distribution.

- *Approximation'function* - used to determine the coefficients that approximate the data in each bucket. Those coefficients will be kept in the bucket.

- *Approximation function adaptability* - measures the degree to which the approximation function is able to adapt to the data distribution.

The *fixed grid strategy* (FG) imposes a fixed grid upon a multidimensional space view of the input data and approximates each grid cell by the approximation function coefficients. The *variable grid partitioning strategies* (VG) determines the best bucket partitioning of the same multidimensional space. A generic bucket produced by the VG strategy is represented by the structure bucket(MBR(ll_point,ur_point), data), where MBR denotes the region minimum bounding rectangle. Buckets produced by the fixed grid strategy can be represented more compactly by either the structure bucket(bucket_ID, data), where bucket_ID is determined by a computation on the indices, or stored as multidimensional array cells as cell(data) where the cell position is also determined by computation on the indices. Variable grid strategies use alternative algorithms to partition the space into buckets dynamically. There are recent proposals for both fixed grid and variable grid algorithms. Regression is used in [1] and wavelets in [11]. These are fixed grid techniques that use the approximation function and occasionally outliers to obtain a higher adaptability. Mhist [5] is a variable grid technique. In this paper we consider mainly fixed grid techniques because, by storing only the reduced values (molap organization), a lot of space is saved in comparison with adaptable techniques (which must store the buckets as explained before) and reduced values are accessed by simple computation of an offset. The extra space can be traded for lower reduction rates to improve approximations.

Data with smooth variations is usually easier to approximate by most algorithms and large peaks often disturb the approximation. For this reason the use of outliers is important in histogram-based techniques whenever there are strong "thin" peaks such as a point completely divergent from the normal trend. Nevertheless, outliers are very expensive in terms of storage space: they require the storage of both the point coordinates and the value and do not provide associative access (must be searched). An outlier is stored as Outlier(point, value).

Summary tables (or materialized views) are frequently computed to speed-up query answering in data warehouses: group-by queries are issued to compute partial sums on alternative combinations of dimension attributes, building the summary or materialized view. It is possible to recover range values from partial sums using the independence assumption or linear regularization [3]. This way, aggregation can be used as a data reduction technique.

## 2.2 Storage Cost Analysis of Fixed and Variable Grid Strategies

Variable grid strategies must store bucket boundaries, while fixed grid strategies store only the approximation coefficients. This subsection compares the storage space for the two alternative strategies to quantify the overhead incurred by the VG strategy. The storage space occupied by both strategies is simply,

$$ss(fixed\_grid) = sizeofcoeffs \qquad \text{(molap organization)} \qquad (1)$$

$$ss(variable\ grid) = 2 \times PRSZ + sizeofcoeffs \qquad \text{(bucket tuples)}$$

Given the following quantities,

$$Point\ reduction\ factor\ PRF = \frac{\#\ buckets}{\#\ points} \qquad (2)$$

$$Storage\ reduction\ factor\ SSR = \frac{space\ occupied\ by\ summary}{initial\ space} \qquad (3)$$

$$Points\ representation\ size\ PRSZ = size\ of\ coordinates \times n° \text{ of dimensions} \qquad (4)$$

Figure 1 compares SSR against PRF for VG and FG strategies considering 2 to 10 dimensions and coordinates with 2 to 4 bytes (PRSZ between 4 and 40). The data values size considered was 4 bytes.

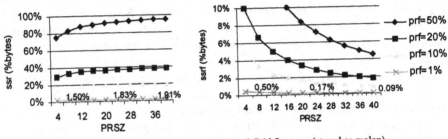

(a) Variable Grid Strategy    (b) Fixed Grid Strategy (stored as molap)

**Fig. 1.** Storage Reduction Factors for Fixed grid and Adaptable Strategies

This figure quantifies the space overhead required to represent the buckets in adaptable strategies and, conversely, the space gains when fixed grid strategies are used. For instance, for a point reduction to 10% of an original five dimensional space (with each dimension represented by 2 bytes: PRSZ = 10), the reduced data occupies 17% of the original data size for the adaptable strategies and 3% for the fixed grid approach. This shows that adaptable partitioning strategies incur in high storage space overhead in comparison to fixed grid strategies, which also offer faster computation. These are strong motivations for the choice of these algorithms instead of variable grid ones, although the lack of partitioning adaptability must be compensated by approximation function adaptability, requiring more coefficients in each cell (e.g. Wavelets) (bucket partitioning vs. coefficients storage overhead).

# 3. Data Reduction Techniques

The data reduction techniques work on a multidimensional view of the input data, which must be cubed by parts (by loading arrays from tables such as in [12] – in production systems - or issuing queries against the database that retrieve the regions successively) to be fed as input to the reduction algorithm. It is preferable to apply the reduction only to non-empty points (those appearing in the rolap table) because the approximation error will be much larger if zeroes are also approximated. Empty positions are indicated by heavily compressed zero bitmap cuboids. The data reduction algorithms used in the experiments are:

- *Average* (g) – this gold experiment simply returns the average value. If the error is large, the data set will be difficult to approximate.

- *Outliers* (ol) – This algorithm simply extracts extremes, storing them as outliers. It can be used with any other technique, smoothing peak data variations. Outliers are stored as outlier(point, value) pair in table tuples.

- *Mhist* (mhist) – This VG technique was proposed in [5] for selectivity estimation. It implements space partitioning by analyzing marginal frequencies. Buckets are stored in table tuples as bucket(bucket_ll,bucket_ur, avg).

- *Fixed Grid* (fgrid) – This FG technique divides the space into equal-sized regions and computes the average for each one. It is stored as a multidimensional array as cell[avg].

- *Regression* (regr) – We used the implementation of linear regression described in Quasi-Cubes [1]. This FG technique approximates the values in a column or row bucket by a line described by the parameters $m$ and $b$ in $y = m \times x + b$ and stores (m,b) in the bucket cell in a multidimensional array: cell[(m,b)].

- Wavelets (wav) – The wavelets technique (FG) was proposed for selectivity estimation in [11] and for data cube reduction in [10]. Wavelets represent a function in terms of a coarse overall shape, plus details that range from coarse to fine. Wavelet coefficients had to be stored together with a location identifier because smaller coefficients were stripped from the array of coefficients: cell[set(locator,coeff)].

In Figure 2 we further characterize the techniques.

| technique | Partition strategy | Adapt algorithm | Approx. function | Approx. adaptability | Storage cost |
|---|---|---|---|---|---|
| outliers | FG | - | extract extremes | choice of extremes | very high |
| fgrid | FG | - | average | - | low |
| regr | FG | - | linear regression | choice of line | low |
| wav | FG | - | wavelet | keep larger coeffs | medium |
| mhist | VG | marg. freq | average | - | high |
| clustering | VG | clusters | average | - | high |
| aggregate | - | - | average(sum,..) | - | medium |

**Fig. 2.** Characterization of Techniques

## 4. Datasets

We have tested synthetic and typical warehouse data sets. The synthetic data sets were random (completely random values), zipf [13], and clustered (n clusters following the normal distribution). Figure 3 shows typical shapes for those distributions. The zipf distribution (figure 3(a) and (b)) is said to be typical of many real data distributions in databases [13]. The skewed zipf distributions (figure 3(b)) contains high thin peaks which are often difficult to approximate by fixed grid techniques but can be extracted as outliers. Skewed clustered distributions (figure 3(c)) also show some peaks, but those peaks are thick and therefore cannot be handled efficiently by outliers. Adaptable techniques handle these skews much better than fixed grid techniques because they adapt the bucket boundaries to the topography.

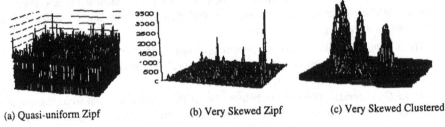

| (a) Quasi-uniform Zipf | (b) Very Skewed Zipf | (c) Very Skewed Clustered |

**Fig. 3.** Typical Synthetic Data Sets

Typical warehouse data sets were taken from several data warehouses in [4], including the sales dataset (product×days×stores = revenue: 60 ×184×20) and summaries resulting from roll-up operations (e.g days to weeks) (figure 4).

| Data Set | Distribution | Data Set | Distribution |
|----------|--------------|----------|--------------|
| Zipf | Skewed Zipf | Sales | Sales Data Cube (97% sparse) |
| Cluster | Normal Cluster | Sales-agreg | Week Roll-Up Sales Data Cube |
| Cluster-Skew | Skewed Cluster | | |

**Fig. 4.** Typical Data Sets

## 5. Experiments

Two error measures were used: the point query error and the range query error.

$$perror_{estimation} = \cdot \frac{\sum |v_{estimated} - v_{exact}|}{\sum all\_points \; v_{exact}} \qquad (5)$$

$$Rerror_{estimation} = \frac{|\sum range \; v_{estimated} - \sum range \; v_{exact}|}{\sum range \; v_{exact}} \qquad (6)$$

These error measures are plotted against storage space reduction. Query experiments were held for *small ranges* with areas ranging from 1 to 10.000 points and *large ranges*. For each sub-category we made 10,000 queries of the type range-sum query. We first discuss the results for clustered and zipf synthetic data sets which reveal important characteristics. Then we show the results for the SALES data set.

## 5.1 Clustered Distributions

We use four clustered data sets to show how skew and sparseness influence the results,

| Data set | stdev | %cluster centers | Sparseness | Characterization |
|---|---|---|---|---|
| Random | --------- | | 10% | Uniform |
| Cl_Skew | σ=0.02 | 0.25% | 10% | Skewed |
| Cl_Lskew | σ=0.02 | 0.025% | 10% | Very Skewed |
| Cl_Skew_LSp | σ=0.02 | 0.25% | 80% | Skewed, Sparse |

Figure 5 shows the point error for these data sets. The x-axis represents the storage space reduction factor (the output data size as a percentage of the input data size) when the input data is represented either as a data cube (%DC) or using a rolap organization (the data cube is the most compressed representation for non-sparse data sets - dimension attributes are implicit -, while rolap is the most compressed organization for sparse data sets - data cubes must represent empty points as zeroes). From the reduced data, only *fgrid* and *regr* are stored in small data cube representations, while wavelets must store a large number of coefficients in each cell, *ol* must store the points in tuples and *mhist* must store the buckets in tuples as well. Figures 5(a) ,(b) and (c) refer to dense data sets and 5(d) to a sparse version of 5(b).

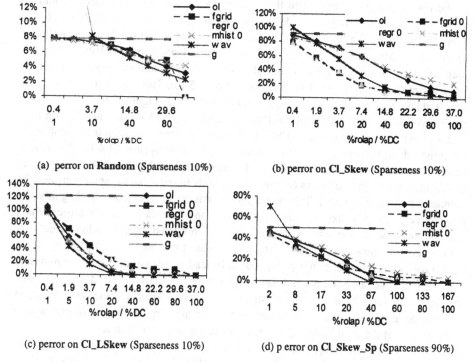

(a) perror on **Random** (Sparseness 10%)

(b) perror on **Cl_Skew** (Sparseness 10%)

(c) perror on **Cl_LSkew** (Sparseness 10%)

(d) p error on **Cl_Skew_Sp** (Sparseness 90%)

**Fig. 5.** Perror for Clustered Data Sets

**Discussion of Results:** Figure 5(a) shows a point error of 8% for the gold experiment and a random distribution. Summaries occupying less than 10% of the data cube do not achieve any significant reduction of estimation error. The techniques progressively become more effective as more storage space is allocated for the reduced histogram. With about 80% of the data cube (30% of the rolap input) the error is halved to 4%. Figure 5(b) shows an estimation error of 90% for the gold experiment on skewed cluster distributions. With about 20% of the data cube size (7% of rolap input size) *fgrid* and *regr* techniques reduce the error to 20%, *waveletes* to 30% and *mhist* or *outliers* to 60%. With 80% of the data cube (30% of rolap) both *wavelets* and *regression* techniques reduce the average point error to 4%. These results suggest that very large reduction rates produce high estimation errors. Comparing (a), (b) and (c) we can see that skew is a source of approximation difficulty for very large reduction rates. The gold experiment (g) gives a clue to quantify the degree of this difficulty. The skew increases from the Random distribution to Cl_Skew and to Cl_Lskew and the point error for the gold experiment was 10%, 95% and 125% respectively. *Wavelets* are particularly well succeeded for skewed distributions, but have difficulty approximating low skew distributions for very large reduction rates, because wavelet coefficients occupy a significant space and important coefficients should not be dropped (higher reduction rates are obtained by dropping more coefficients, starting by the least significant ones). The three techniques - *wav*, *ol* and *mhist* - would be superior to *fgrid* and *regr* considering the point reduction factor (PRF) but that superiority is often lost by considering the storage space reduction factor (SSRF) (see figure 5(b)). Still, for very skewed distributions the adaptability (coefficient or point adaptability in the case of wavelets or outliers respectively) allows these techniques to yield better results than *fgrid* or *regr* (see figure 5(c)). Even *regr* achieves better results than *fgrid* because it is slightly more adaptable. Figure 5(b) and (d) were generated similarly but with totally different sparseness (10% on (b) and 80% on (d)). In this case the same reduction to 40% of the data cube size corresponds to completely different reduction if rolap input is considered (15% in (b) against 67% in (d)). This is because the non-reduced data cube can become considerably larger than the rolap representation due to sparseness (non-existent points in the rolap organization must be represented in the data cube). The estimation error is small when compared against the non-reduced data cube size (because a large fraction of the data cube are zeroes which are not included in the approximation) but, if compared against rolap size, it is comparable to those in Figure 5(b). This has two major implications: it is advantageous to compute reduced data cubes instead of normal data cubes when data sets are sparse because the normal data cube wastes a large space with zeroes, while the reduced version is much more compact with a small error. On the other hand, in order to be accurate, these reduced data cubes occupy a space that corresponds to a large portion of the initial rolap space, both for dense or sparse data sets.

Figure 6 shows the range query estimation errors vs query size for clustered data sets using a reduced data cube to (3.7% rolap / 10% DC ) in (a), (b) and (c), and a reduction to (14.8% rolap / 40% DC ) in (d). The query size is the query range volume.

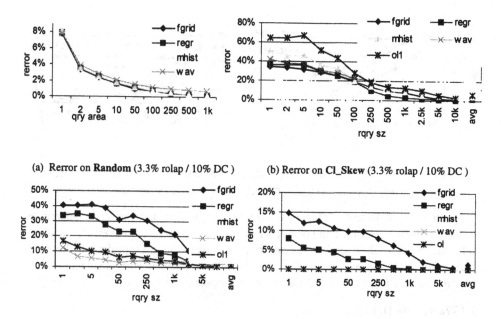

(a) Rerror on **Random** (3.3% rolap / 10% DC )        (b) Rerror on **Cl_Skew** (3.3% rolap / 10% DC )

(c) Rerror on **Cl_LSkew** (3.7% rolap / 10% DC )   (d) Rerror on **Cl_Lskew_Sp** (14.8% rolap / 40% DC )

**Fig. 6.** Range Query Errors for Clustered Datasets and Reductions as Indicated

Results in figure 6 show that large range queries return reasonably accurate results. This result is logical. For instance, *fgrid* buckets lying completely within the query range contribute with error 0 to the result because the bucket average value is used. For the random data set, ranges with areas above 500 points had an error below 0.4%. The results are not so good for skewed distributions (b) and for very skewed distributions (c). Figure 6(c) and (d) show that more adaptable techniques (*mhist, ol, wav*) are able to approximate very skewed distributions much more accurately than simpler techniques such as *regr, fgrid* or aggregation (these should use outliers to adapt to large skews). When a large portion of the data cube is kept (Figure 6(d)) and adaptable techniques are used the approximation is more accurate. Very sparse data sets have a very small number of non-empty points per unit area. To achieve real reduction of the rolap input in this case buckets must be very large and large range queries frequently select only a small number of non-empty points, giving significant estimation errors.

## 5.2 Zipf Distribution

Next we show the point and range error results for very skewed zipf data set.

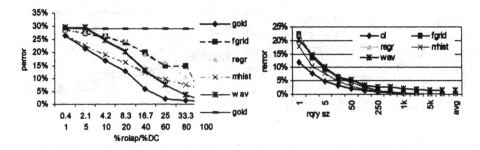

(a) Point Error for Zipf Skewed Data Set    (b) Range Error for Zipf Skewed Data Set (20%DC)

**Fig. 7.** Point and Range Errors for Zipf Skewed Distribution

**Discussion of Results:** This is a skewed distribution and the most adaptable techniques (wavelets, mhist and outliers) held the best results for point errors. Outliers held the best result overall because they eliminate the thin peaks of the zipf distribution. This means that outliers should be used together with other techniques for isolated points that are very distant from the approximation.

### 5.3 Warehouse Data Sets

We have chosen a normal (**Sales**) and an aggregated (**Sales-aggreg**) warehouse data set. Figure 8 shows results for **Sales-aggreg**, a very dense data set summarizing sales.

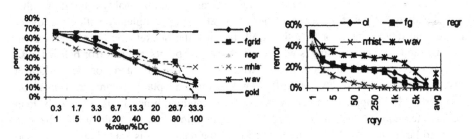

(a) Point Error on **Sales-aggreg**    (b) Range Error an **Sales-aggreg** (20%DC)

**Fig. 8.** Point and Range Errors for Sales-aggreg Data Set

The dense Sales roll-up data set was difficult to approximate. Point errors are always large. *regr* was the best technique for large reduction rates and *wav* or *outl* for smaller reduction rates. This is because *regr* is more space efficient and *wav* or *outl* are more adaptable to the data distribution but less space efficient. *mhist* and *regr* achieved better results than the other techniques for range queries.

The multidimensional view of rolap data is frequently very sparse. Most data sets presented before were dense but the Sales data set of Figure 9 is very sparse (97%).

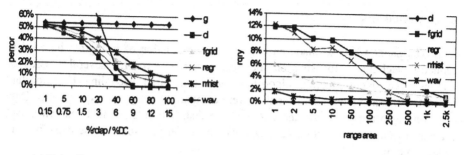

(a) Point Error     (b) Range Query Error (80% rolap/ 12%DC)

**Fig. 9.** Point and Range Errors for the Sales Data set

In Figure 9(a) the estimation error is reduced to very small values with only 9% to 15% of the data cube (*wav* or *outl* are able to reduce the error to an insignificant amount with just 9% of the data cube). But the remarks made concerning sparse data sets apply here as well. 15% of the data cube corresponds to 100% of the rolap input size! The estimation error is so small simply because no storage space reduction was achieved (comparing to the rolap input). If the rolap data occupied 20 GB, the reduced data cube would occupy 20 GB as well. When compared against rolap size, the estimation error is comparable to the dense data set case. The range query results were also obtained for a small reduction rate considering the rolap data size (to 80%). For this size the range query errors are small using the *wav* or *outl* adaptable techniques.

### 5.4 Experiment Conclusions

The estimation error varies a lot with different data sets and distribution skews. Even the simplest techniques can obtain small estimation errors for range queries with large size (with a large number of non-empty points). But when querying typical sparse data sets, small ranges or points, the estimation error is frequently large. Even when a significant fraction of the input data size is allocated to the reduced summary, the error is still significant. For several data sets the estimation error does not decay exponentially as more space is allocated to the approximation. In the case of sparse data cubes, although they can be highly reduced, such reduction does not correspond to a large compression of the base (rolap) data. The tool doing analysis on the reduced summaries should rely on a minimum number of non-zero values to determine if a query can be answered with sufficient accuracy. This threshold could be for instance 1000 non-empty values, but the actual value depends on the data reduction rate.

None of the techniques seems to be substantially better than the other ones for all data sets. Although more sophisticated techniques such as *mhist* or *wavelets* obtain a lower point reduction factor (prf), they incur in higher storage overhead (for storing the buckets and coefficients), such that the approximation is not much better than the one obtained using compact molap reduced data sets from simpler algorithms. Still, adaptability is important to approximate irregular and skewed data sets. It is possible to conclude that the best results can be achieved by using a fixed grid strategy with some adaptability that can be obtained by either using strongly adaptable approximating functions such as wavelets or outliers.

# 6. Conclusions

In this paper we have made an experimental evaluation of histogram-based data reduction techniques focusing on the approximation error for several classes of queries. The data reduction algorithms were classified according to important characteristics and those characteristics were compared through the experiments. Data sets were also analyzed to determine how the distribution, skew and sparseness are relevant to the approximation accuracy. We have derived some guidelines for data reduction tools.

# References

[1] D. Barbara and M. Sullivan, "Quasi-Cubes: A space-efficient way to support approximate multidimensional databases," Technical Report, ISE Dept., September 1997.

[2] W. G. Cochran. Sampling Techniques. Wiley, New York, third edition, 1977.

[3] C. Faloutsos, H. V. Jagadish, Nikolaos Sidiropoulos: Recovering Information from Summary Data. In VLDB'97, Proceedings of 23rd International Conference on Very Large Data Bases, August 25-29, 1997, Athens, Greece.

[4] R. Kimball. The Datawarehouse Toolkit. John Wiley & Sons, 1996 ISBN 0-471-15337-0.

[5] V. Poosala, Y. Ioannidis. Selectivity Estimation Without the Attribute Value Independence Assumption. Proceedings of the $23^{rd}$ VLDB Conference, Athens, Greece, 1997.

[6] W.H. Press, S.A. Teukolsky, W.T. Vetterling, and B.P. Flannery. Numerical Recipes in C, The Art of Scienti_c Computing. Cambridge University Press, Cambridge, MA, 1996.

[7] C.-E. Sarndal, B. Swensson, and J. Wretman. Model Assisted Survey Sampling. Springer-Verlag, New York, 1992.

[8] S. Sudman. Applied Sampling. Academic Press, New York, 1976.

[9] Special issue on data reduction techniques od the bulletin of the Technical Committee on Data Engineering of the IEEE Computer Society, December 1997, Vol. 20, n 4.

[10] Jeffrey Scott Vitter, Min Wang, B. Iyer, "Data Cube Approximation and Histograms via Wavelets". $7^{th}$ International Conference on Information and Knowledge Management, Bethesda, Maryland, November 1998.

[11] Yossi Matias, J. S. Vitter, Min Wang, "Wavelet-Based Histograms for Selectivity Estimation" in In Proceedings of the 1998 International Conference on the Management of Data, Seattle, Washington, June 1-4 1998.

[12] Y. Zhao, P. M. Deshpande, J. F. Naughton, " An Array-Based Algorithm for Simultaneous Multidimensional Aggregates" in Sigmod ' 97, AZ, USA.

[13] G. K. Zipf. Human Behaviour and the principle of least effort. Addison-Wesley, Reading, MA, 1949.

[14] T. Zhang, R. Ramakrishnan and M. Livny. (1996) BIRCH: an Efficient Data Clustering Method for Very Large Databases, Proc. 1996 SIGMOD, pp. 103-114.

# Data Swapping: Balancing Privacy against Precision in Mining for Logic Rules

Vladimir Estivill-Castro and Ljiljana Brankovic

Department of Computer Science & Software Engineering,
The University of Newcastle, Callaghan, NSW 2308, Australia.

**Abstract.** The recent proliferation of data mining tools for the analysis of large volumes of data has paid little attention to individual privacy issues. Here, we introduce methods aimed at finding a balance between the individuals' right to privacy and the data-miners' need to find general patterns in huge volumes of detailed records. In particular, we focus on the data-mining task of classification with decision trees. We base our security-control mechanism on noise-addition techniques used in statistical databases because (1) the multidimensional matrix model of statistical databases and the multidimensional cubes of On-Line Analytical Processing (OLAP) are essentially the same, and (2) noise-addition techniques are very robust. The main drawback of noise addition techniques in the context of statistical databases is low statistical quality of released statistics. We argue that in data mining the major requirement of security control mechanism (in addition to protect privacy) is not to ensure precise and bias-free statistics, but rather to preserve the high-level descriptions of knowledge constructed by artificial data mining tools.

## 1 Introduction

New data collection technologies automatically capture millions of transactions. Every phone-call, purchase at a super-market, visit to a Web page, use of a credit card, etc., can now be easily logged together with its associated attribute information. Knowledge discovery and data mining (KDDM) has emerged as the technology to overcome the information overload and facilitate analysis and understanding of massive volumes of data [2,3]. While KDDM technology is maturing rapidly into commercial products that incorporate advances from the fields of statistics, machine learning and databases, little emphasis has been placed on privacy issues [14–17]. The predominant applications of KDDM are marketing applications which have regarded identification of individual profiles and attributes as a central goal of the process. Meaningful patterns that lead to understanding generic behaviours constitute an invaluable resource for corporations that need to know their customers, not only to preserve them in an increasingly competitive market, but also to extend their commercial relationship in even more saturated markets.

Naturally, the application of KDDM technology is extending to other domains where the issues of individual privacy are certainly very delicate [10]. Examples of such domains are the analysis of bank transactions for money laundering detection, income tax returns or insurance claims for fraud detection, medical records for the discovery of groups at risk, etc. All these domains demand the development of technology that provides a balance between the data miners' need to find generic patterns and the individuals' right to privacy. We introduce methods aimed at finding this balance. However, to achieve this objective involves a trade-off in the context of statistical databases as well as in KDDM applications [6, 7]. We argue that, in KDDM, the major requirement of security control mechanisms (in addition to protect privacy) is not to ensure precise and bias-free statistics, but rather to preserve the high-level descriptions of knowledge constructed by KDDM tools. In particular, we focus on the data-mining task of induction with decision trees.

We base our security-control mechanism on noise-addition techniques used in statistical databases. Section 2 presents a justification for such a choice. In Section 3, we concentrate on the use of the decision tree as inductive tools for building classifiers for knowledge discovery. In Section 4, we propose an extension of a method presented in Section 2 and apply it to privacy protection in the context of KDDM. In Section 5, we support this proposal by empirical results in a case study, namely, the Wisconsin Breast Cancer Database [12] (or simply the WBC data) [1]. In Section 6, we provide concluding remarks regarding the effectiveness of the proposed security mechanism.

## 2 Balancing disclosure

There are three main reason why the notions from statistical databases are relevant to our task.

First, the tabular data model of statistical databases and the multidimensional cubes of OLAP are very similar [21]. It is not hard to show that the abstract model of statistical databases [8] is equivalent to multidimensional matrix model, which is in turn essentially the same as the multidimensional cube in OLAP. A statistical database can be equivalently modelled by *d-dimensional matrix* (table, cube) in the following way. Denote attributes in the database by $A_1, A_2, \ldots, A_d$ (the number of attributes $d$ is often refereed to as the *degree* of the database). For each attribute, order the values that actually exist in the database. If the attribute is numerical, this can simply be increasing order; for categorical attributes, find some natural order. Let $a_1^j, a_2^j, \ldots, a_{|A_j|}^j$ be the sequence of values of the attribute $A_j$. Construct a $d$-dimensional matrix $S$ of the size $|A_1| \times |A_2| \times \ldots \times |A_d|$, so that its element $s_{r_1, r_2, \ldots, r_d}$ ($r_j \in \{a_1^j, a_2^j, \ldots, a_{|A_j|}^j\}$, $j \in \{1, \ldots, d\}$), represents the result of the following query:

$$\text{COUNT } (A_1 = a_{r_1}^1 \wedge A_2 = a_{r_2}^2 \wedge \ldots \wedge A_d = a_{r_d}^d).$$

The multidimensional matrix model and the abstract model of statistical databases are equivalent in the sense that it is possible to transform one form into another

---

[1] Data set retrieved from the University of California at Irvine.

without loss of information. This is not true for tabular model, whose entries contain summary statistics, as it has suffered information loss during the process of aggregation [1].

Second, statistical databases have made progress in protecting individual values while allowing general statistics and patterns to be produced. In a statistical database some attributes are of confidential nature (eg., HIV diagnosis). Ideally, it should be impossible for a statistical user to deduce any significant information about individual values of these attributes. However, it should be said that any statistic involving the confidential attribute reveals 'some' information about its individuals values. It is the matter of a security policy to define what it is to be understood by 'significant' information. For example, the statistic SUM(City=Sydney; Blood_count)=11.8 reveals that no patient from Sydney has blood count over 11.8; this information is clearly insignificant.

If disclosure of a confidential value occurs, the database is said to be *compromised*. A *positive compromise* occurs if a user discloses the exact value of a confidential attribute, and a *partial compromise* occurs if a user is able to obtain substantial information about a confidential value, without disclosing it exactly [1]. Partial compromise includes: *negative compromise*, that is, disclosing the fact that, for a particular individual, an attribute does not have a certain value, or its value does not lie within a certain range; *approximate compromise*, ie., revealing that a confidential value lies in the given range; *probabilistic compromise*, where a confidential value is disclosed with a certain probability; *relative compromise* [13], where the relative order of magnitude of two or more confidential values is revealed. Security-control mechanisms in a statistical database can not (1) provide statistical users with sufficient amount of high quality statistics (statistical quality is measured by the consistency, bias and precision), and *at the same time*, (2) prevent exact and partial disclosure of confidential individual information. Thus, various techniques have been proposed for balancing these objectives, but none of them is both effective and efficient. The techniques can be classified into *query restriction* and *noise addition*. Query restriction includes Query size control, Query set overlap control, Maximum order control, Partitioning, Cell suppression, and On the other hand, noise addition includes Output perturbation, Random sample techniques, Data Perturbation, Probability Distribution Data Perturbation.

The third reason why we refer to statistical databases is that recent suggestions to privacy protection for the context of KDDM [6, 7, 17] map directly to the framework of methods in statistical databases.

We concentrate on *Probability distribution data perturbation* methods [1, 11]. These replace the original database with a new one that has the same probability distribution. We shall describe so-called *data swapping* technique, which is particularly suitable for privacy protection in knowledge discovery. Data swapping interchanges the values in the records of the database in such a way that low-order statistics are preserved [8]. We recall that $k$-order statistics are those that employ exactly $k$ attributes. A database $D$ is said to be $\kappa$-transformable if there exists a database $D'$ that has no records in common with $D$, but has the same $k$-order COUNTs as $D$, for $k \in \{0, \ldots, \kappa\}$. However, finding a general data swap is an intractable problem [8]. *Approximate data swapping* [20] replaces the original database (or a portion of it) with randomly generated records, so that the new database has similar $\kappa$-order statistics as the original one. In the context of statistical databases, the drawbacks of this method are high implementation cost, unsuitability for on-line dynamic databases and low precision. We shall apply *Data Swapping* in Section 4 for privacy in a KDDM context.

## 3 Inducing Classifiers

One of the most common KDDM tasks consists of *building classifiers* [2]. This task takes as input a set of classes and a training set consisting of pre-classified cases, and builds a model of some kind that can be applied to unclassified data in order to assign it a class. More precisely, we can think of a classifier as a function $f : A_1 \times \ldots A_d \to C$, and of an $n$-record training set as a collection of $n$ points $f(x^i) = c_i$, $i = 1, \ldots, n$ for the function $f$. The training set is typically presented as cases in attribute-vector format; that is, each case is a row in a table and the $i$-th cases is a vector $x^i = (id, x_1^i, \ldots, x_d^i, c_i)$. The first entry $id$ is an identifier that uniquely identifies this case. The $j$-th attribute of the $i$-th case has value $x_j^i \in A_j$, $i = 1, \ldots, n$ and $j = 1, \ldots, d$. Finally, $c_i \in C$ is the class for the $i$-th case. The goal of the model is not only to have high-predicting power on unseen (future) cases, but also, specially for knowledge discovery, to describe how the class depends on the attributes. That is, for knowledge discovery, the computer tools should provide some understanding of the data.

We shall consider decision trees where an internal node, labelled with the categorical attribute $A_t$, has $|A_t|$ edges connecting the node to its $|A_t|$ children, each edge labelled with one of the values in the set $A_t$. The label $a_j^t$ of the edge indicates that this child (usually the $j$-th for categorical attributes) is to be tried next when classifying a record, if and only if the record has the value $a_j^t$ as its $t$-th attribute (that is, $x_t = a_j^t$). If the $t$-th attribute is numerical (also referred as continuos), then typically, the internal node has only two outgoing edges (and thus only two children), associated with the intervals $x_t < b$ and $x_t \geq b$, for some bound $b$. The edge labelled $x_t < b$ is selected if and only if the $t$-th attribute of the record is less than the bound $b$.

Fig. 1 shows the decision tree built by the latest version of Quinlan's famous decision tree builder, now named C5 (the earlier versions are C4.5 [19] and ID3 [18]). The training set are the first 200 cases of the WBC Data. The tree indicates that the first attribute to be tested is attribute $A_2$ and if this is greater than 1 then attribute $A_3$ should be inspected next. If the case exhibits a value greater than 2, the case is to be classified as malignant. A total of 88 would end up at this leaf, but although the leaf classifies them as malignant, 7 training cases arriving here are benign.

There are many variants of decision trees in the statistical [4] and the machine learning literature [19,22]. Decision trees are interesting because the classifiers can be associated with logic rules. That is, decision trees give an insight into

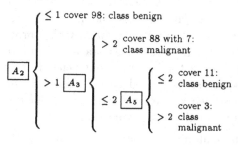

| | Rule | Cover |
|---|---|---|
| 1 | Uniformity of Cell Size $\leq 1$ $\Rightarrow$ benign | 98 [0.990] |
| 2 | Uniformity of Cell Shape $\leq 2$ $\wedge$ Single Epithelial Cell Size $\leq 2$ $\Rightarrow$ benign | 96 [0.990] |
| 3 | Uniformity of Cell Size $> 1$ $\wedge$ Single Epithelial Cell Size $> 2$ $\Rightarrow$ malignant | 78 [0.938] |
| 4 | Uniformity of Cell Size $> 1$ $\wedge$ Uniformity of Cell Shape $> 2$ $\Rightarrow$ malignant | 88 [0.911] |
| | DEFAULT $\Rightarrow$ benign | |

**Fig. 1.** Decision tree and rules constructed by C5 with 200 cases. Attribute $A_2$ is 'Uniformity of Cell Size', $A_3$ is 'Uniformity of Cell Shape' and $A_5$ is 'Single Epithelial Cell Size'.

dependencies between attribute values and classes and allow the production of explicit knowledge in a form amendable to human understanding; they also facilitate construction of SQL expressions for efficient record retrieval from large databases. This is harder for statistical techniques like linear discriminants or connectionist approaches like neural networks that encode the model in learned real valued coefficients and numerical forms. For example, for the tree in Fig. 1, C5 produces the rules presented in Fig. 1. In order to classify a case, all [2] rules whose antecedent matches the case are selected and a vote is taken according to the confidence factors. If no rule applies the default rule is used. The rules also indicate the number of cases in the training set that match their antecedent.

Decision trees and their logic rules help understand the data. First, they indicate which are the attributes that have most influence in determining the class. In Fig. 1, not all 9 attributes are used but only 3. Also, the rules express patterns. In this example, large values in the uniformity of cell size indicate malignant diagnosis while small values in the uniformity of cell size are strong indication of benign diagnosis.

## 4 Our Proposal

We now propose algorithms to ensure confidentiality, up to partial disclosure, via noise addition. We use noise addition to construct a new training set which is released to the miner. The new training set is a perturbed version of the original training set so that the data miner may have access to individual records but will have uncertainty that the given class is accurate. We release original values, but the original assignment of cases to classes is never made public. However, the miner should be able to obtain general patterns in the new training set that are a reflection of patterns in the original training set. Note that we take the

---

[2] Note that in general there may be more than one applicable rule (for example, because the case is missing the value for some tested attribute).

approach that KDDM is an exploratory, rather than confirmatory, approach to data understanding. As opposed to statistical data analysis, the miner does not aim at obtaining a definite, unbiased statistical test that answers with a probabilistic degree of confidence if the data fits a preconceived statistical model. More simply, KDDM is not about hypothesis testing but about generation of plausible hypothesis. Of course the hypothesis generated by the miner will require formal statistical analysis to ensure their validity and significance. KDDM should provide an efficient filter in the vast universe of hypotheses.

We constructs a new training set by building decision trees. Intuitively, the process of building a tree expands a node by the most informative attribute that splits its cases maximising homogeneity of the class labels in the children. This greedy approach tends to overfit the data; and thus, typically, the process is halted although leaves may not be homogeneous. We first observe that if we randomly permute the class labels within the cases of each heterogeneous leaf, the new tree would classify training cases and new cases as the original tree. For example, in the tree of Fig. 1, the second leaf is heterogeneous with 7 cases with the label benign and 81 cases with the label malignant. So if we strip the label from the attribute vectors, randomly permute the 88 class labels and reattach them to the cases, we still have a node with a majority of malignant cases. All training cases will follow the same path and will be classified the same as in the original tree. At this stage the tree has not changed.

A few things would be different. The tree built on the 200 training cases (with the original class labels) makes 7 mistakes out of 200 (they are false positives, that is, the tree labels 7 cases as malignant while they are in fact benign) This is an error rate of 3.5% in the training set. However, the same decision tree (with the labels permuted as suggested) will exhibit an error rate between 3.5% and 7% in the new training set. Thus, if the miner ever builds the tree of Fig. 1, the miner will potentially observe a larger error rate.

However, our proposal is that we need to trade-off accuracy in classification for confidentiality. Namely, the only way we can guarantee that the snooper never finds a case $x$ where the class $f(x)$ is known with certainty (total disclosure) is if the models built from the data have less predictive accuracy in classification. Note that we expect miners not to use the models they built for classification, but for data understanding and for discovering trends and patterns. Thus, the real question is, how different are the rules generated and the patterns observed if different induction algorithms are used in the new training set? For example, what does C5 build when it only sees the new training set of 200 cases for the WBC data? Note that, at least 186 are the same original cases (at most 7 labels get swapped creating at most 14 attribute vectors where the new label is different from the original one). But because we do not release the tree of Fig. 1, the miner does not know which cases have swapped label and can not have 100% certainty that any case in the new training set has its original class attached to it. Since, at least 186 cases are the same, and potentially on average even more, the cases in the new training set have a high probability of having their original class label. Here again the trade-off is apparent.

# 5  Case study

Our experiment is aimed at identifying if the induction of rules by C5 or others on the perturbed training set can still find the general patterns in the original data. We use the full WBC Database that holds 699 records. The miner does not see the original tree. Because the swapping is random, we repeat the generation of the new training set 10 times. For reasons that we explain later, we originally expected that trees built out of the perturbed training sets would be larger than the original tree, and also that there would be more specific rules. However, this effect is very much corrected when the data sets are larger. While the tree built by C5 with the original 699 cases has 16 leaves and produces a rule set of 8 rules and a default rule, the average tree size produced from the ten perturbed training sets is 13 ( ±2.3 with a 95% ). Thus, it is reasonable to expect that tree size is preserved by our methods as the data sets get larger. The rule set was slightly larger, the average was 9 ( ±1.2 with a 95% confidence). We should point out that 7 out of 16 leaves in the original tree have cases from both classes and the maximum data swap is 22 cases.

For important knowledge discovery aspects, like most relevant attributes, we note that 9 out of 10 trees built from the independent perturbed training sets used 'Uniformity of Cell Size' at the root, and thus, ranking it as the most informative attribute for classification. Typically, nodes one level deep preserved the attribute selected, however, 'Uniformity of Cell Shape' was pushed further down or not used in 30% of the new trees.

We say that an attribute is identified as relevant if it appears in the tree, and thus, in the rules. With respect to identification of relevant attributes, the original tree used 7 of the 10 possible attributes. Six of these 7 attributes were identified as relevant most of the time. In fact, in all of the 10 new decision trees, 4 of these seven attributes were identified as relevant. One attribute, was identified 9 times an only in one new tree it was not used. We already mentioned that the attribute 'Uniformity of Cell Shape' was dropped 3 out of 10 times. One attribute, 'Single Epithelial Cell Size', was used in only 2 of the ten new trees. However, in the original tree, this attribute is only used once and at depth 4. Also the attribute that was dropped 3 times was used only once in the tree (note that numerical attributes can be used more than once by further divisions of the domain). Thus, all attributes that were used twice or more in the original tree and thus, they are even more relevant, are preserved by our swapping approach.

Now we analyse the rules. Table 1 shows the 4 rules that appeared exactly or in very similar format in the rule sets generated from the 10 perturbed data sets. A rule was classified as very similar if the same attributes were tested and the bounds tested were no more than 1 away or if the negated rule was generated and was similar. The other 4 original rules were also generated, but not out of each of the 10 perturbed training sets. Perhaps indicating less general patterns. Table 1 also shows rules that emerged in at least 70% of the new sets of rules.

Thus, even in this smaller sets, C5 was able to recuperate the pattern that small values in the 'Uniformity of Cell Size' and the 'Single Epithelial of the Cell Size' are strong indication of benign diagnosis while large values of this attributes

| Fully preserved rules | |
|---|---|
| Uniformity of Cell Size $\leq$ 2 <br> $\wedge$ Clump Thickness $\leq$ 3 $\Rightarrow$ benign | (cover 271) <br> [0.996] |
| Uniformity of Cell Size $\leq$ 4 <br> $\wedge$ Marginal Adhesion $\leq$ 3 $\wedge$ Bare Nuclei $\leq$ 2 $\Rightarrow$ benign | (cover 406) <br> [0.990] |
| Clump Thickness > 3 $\wedge$ Bare Nuclei > 3 <br> $\wedge$ Bland Chromatin > 2 $\Rightarrow$ malignant | (cover 186) <br> [0.952] |
| Clump Thickness > 5 <br> $\wedge$ Uniformity of Cell Size > 2 $\Rightarrow$ malignant | (cover 165) <br> [0.946] |
| Preserved rules in 70% of perturbations | |
| Uniformity of Cell Size > 2 $\wedge$ Uniformity of Cell Shape > 2 <br> $\wedge$ Bare Nuclei > 2 $\Rightarrow$ malignant | (cover 211) <br> [0.948] |

Table 1. List of rules preserved by learning from perturbed training sets.

indicate malignant diagnosis. We consider this results remarkable given the fact that decision tree induction is know to be very brittle [18]. That is, slightly perturbed training sets, or noise in the data, produces very different decision tress and sets of rules.

The second question we investigated is what happens if the miner does not use C5 to analyse the published data set, but some other method to induce logic rules. First, we used CN2 [5] to induce logic rules form the original West Cancer dataset and our 10 perturbed data sets. Space is insufficient to present the detailed comparison. Nevertheless, we are very pleased to observe that mining from both (perturbed data sets as well as the original dataset) resulted in the identification of 'Clump Thickness' and 'Uniformity of Cell Size' as very relevant attributes (always tested first or second). Also mining form the original or from perturbed datasets resulted in 'Single Epithelial Cell Size', 'Large Bare Nuclei' and 'Marginal Adhesion' as relevant. There was also coincidence in the cut-off values where these attributes split the benign and malignant classes. We were impressed that CN2 labelled 'Clump Thickness' as very relevant above 'Uniformity of Cell Size' while C5 never placed this attribute at the root of its trees. Thus, we see these results as a virtue of our security mechanism. It does not obscure what are the preferences (biases) of particular inductive methods. What CN2 finds most relevant is preserved in the perturbed training sets.

However, CN2 is more brittle to noise and while the number of rules generated in the original data was 19, the average number of rules among the 10 perturbed datasets was 31 (with a 95% confidence interval of $\pm$2. We see this as a problem of CN2 and that decision trees are affected by noise [14].

Next, we used EVOPROL [9], a genetic programming tolls for inducing classification rules. Again, the rules and pattern discovered in the perturbed sets were analogous and parallel to those obtained in the original set. Once again, this method considered 'Clump Thickness' more relevant than 'Uniform Cell Size' in both (original and perturbed datasets), using it more often and earlier in the rules. The impact of noise in the length of classifiers was much less evident. Thus, we see that the miner is free to use the induction mechanism and obtains very similar results as if it had been provided the original data set.

# 6 Discussion

Our experiment shows the merits of our proposed method for ensuring partial disclosure while allowing a miner to explore detailed data. Baring in mind that data miners are primarily interested in general patterns, and not so much in obtaining unbiased statistical indicators, we have proposed a low-cost security control mechanism. Our data swapping consists of finding a $\kappa$-transformation of a given database $D$, but we relax the condition that $D$ and the new $D'$ have no records in common. The swapping is performed over the confidential attribute only (in this article, the confidential attribute is the class label $C$), as a random shuffling within heterogeneous leaves of the decision tree. Clearly, all the statistics which do not involve this attribute will be preserved. Similarly, the statistics that involve the confidential attribute and whose query sets are defined by internal nodes or homogeneous leaves of a decision tree will also be preserved. Since the heterogeneous leaves have a vast majority of records belonging to a single class and no straightforward way for further splitting, we can argue that the most seriously disturbed statistics will be those that involve a small number of records, and have no obvious impact on the function $f$ that is to be learned. Furthermore, we can balance the statistical precision against the security level by choosing to perform the swapping in the internal nodes, rather than in the leaves of the decision tree: the closer to the root, the higher the security but lower the precision.

Finally we would like to comment that data size also plays a role. For example, if we use the first 200 cases of the breast-cancer database, our methods leads to new training sets that ensure partial disclosure, but the decision trees built by the miner are larger (8 leaves and 7 rules seems to be the expected values). This seems to be due to several aspects. First, C5 is trying to minimise expected accuracy in new cases inducing from a perturbed training set. So, in learning from the new training set, it overfits such small new training set and needs to produce larger trees and more rules. For example, a prototypic malignant case that would land on the second leaf of the tree in Fig. 1 may have its label changed to benign by our noise addition. So, if this case (with swapped label) appears in the new training set, C5 will require a very specific additional rule or a deeper path in the tree to carve it out when surrounded from many similar malignant cases. In fact, some rules generated by C5 from the new training set have a very small cover, indicating to the miner (snooper) that this are potentially outliers whose label our method has swapped. However, the miner would still have no absolute certainty.

# References

1. N. R. Adam and J. C. Wortmann. Security-control methods for statistical databases: A comparative study. *ACM Computing Surveys*, 21(4):515–556, 1989.
2. M.J.A. Berry and G. Linoff. *Data Mining Techniques — for Marketing, Sales and Customer Support*. John Wiley & Sons, NY, USA, 1997.

3. A. Berson and S.J. Smith. *Data Warehousing, Data Mining, & OLAP.* Series on Data Warehousing and Data Management. McGraw-Hill, NY, USA, 1998.

4. L. Breiman, J.H. Friedman, R.A. Olshen, and C.J. Stone. *Classification and Regression Trees.* Wadsworth and Brooks, Monterrey, CA, 1984.

5. P. Clark and T. Niblett. The CN2 induction algorithm. *Machine Learning,* 3(4):261–283, 1989.

6. C. Clifton. Protecting against data mining through samples. In *Thirteenth Annual IFIP WG 11.3 Working Conference on Database Security,* Seatle, WA, July 1999.

7. C. Clifton and D. Marks. Security and privacy implications of data mining. In *SIGMOD Workshop on Data Mining and Knowledge Discovery,* Montreal, Canada, June 1996. ACM.

8. D. E. R. Denning. *Cryptography and Data Security.* Addison-Wesley, 1982.

9. V. Estivill-Castro. Collaborative knowledge acquisition with a genetic algorithm. In *Proceedings of the IEEE International Conference on Tools with Artificial Intelligence (ICTAI-97),* pages 270–277. IEEE Press, 1997.

10. K. C. Laudon. Markets and privacy. *Communications of the ACM,* 39(9):92–104, 1996.

11. C. K. Liew, U. J. Choi, and C.J. Liew. Inference control mechanism for statistical database: Frequency-imposed data distortions. *Journal of the American Society for Information Science,* 36(6):322–329, 1985.

12. O.L. Mangasarian and W.H. Wolberg. Cancer diagnosis via linear programming. *SIAM News,* 23(5):1–18, September 1990.

13. M. Miller and J. Seberry. Relative compromise of statistical databases. *The Australian Computer Journal,* 21(2):56–61, 1989.

14. D.E. O'Leary. Knowledge discovery as a threat to database security. In G. Piatetsky-Shapiro and W.J. Frawley, editors, *Knowledge Discovery in Databases,* pages 507–516, Menlo Park, CA, 1991. AAAI Press.

15. D.E. O'Leary. Some privacy issues in knowledge discovery: the OECD personal privacy guidelines. *IEEE Expert,* 10(2):48–52, April 1995.

16. P. R. Peacock. Data mining in marketing: Part 2. *Marketing Management,* 7(1):15–25, 1998.

17. G. Piatetsky-Shapiro. Knowledge discovery in personal data vs privacy: a mini-symposium. *IEEE Expert,* 10(2):46–47, April 1995.

18. J.R. Quinlan. Induction of decision trees. *Machine Learning Journal,* 1:81–106, 1986.

19. J.R. Quinlan. *C4.5: Programs for Machine Learning.* Morgan Kaufmann Publishers, San Mateo, CA, 1993.

20. S. Reiss. Practical data-swapping: The first step. *ACM Transaction on Database Systems,* 9(1):20–37, 1984.

21. A. Shoshani. OLAP and statistical databases: similarities and differences. In *Proceedings of the Sixteenth ACM SIGACT SIGMOD SIGART Symposium of Principles of Database Systems,* pages 185–196, Tucsom, AZ, US, 1997. PODS, ACM.

22. C.S. Wallace and J.D. Patrick. Coding decision trees. *Machine Learning,* 11:7–22, 1993.

# Author Index

# Lecture Notes in Computer Science

For information about Vols. 1–1606
please contact your bookseller or Springer-Verlag